Priest, Parish, and People

Priest, Parish, and People

Saving the Faith in Philadelphia's "Little Italy"

RICHARD N. JULIANI

University of Notre Dame Press

Notre Dame, Indiana

Manufactured in the United States of America

Library of Congress Cataloging-in-Publication Data

Juliani, Richard N.
Priest, parish, and people : saving the faith in Philadelphia's "little Italy" /
Richard N. Juliani.
p.   cm.
Includes bibliographical references and index.
ISBN-13: 978-0-268-03265-4 (pbk. : alk. paper)
ISBN-10: 0-268-03265-3 (pbk. : alk. paper)
1. Church work with immigrants—Catholic Church.   2. Italian Americans—History.
3. Philadelphia (Pa.)—Church history.   I. Title.
BX2347.8.I46J85   2007
282'.7481108951—dc22
2006032467

CONTENTS

PREFACE

My interest in the religious life of Italian Americans owes much to the late Monsignor Bartholomew Fair, beginning from the time when he was a pastor in the Archdiocese of Philadelphia. I am greatly indebted to him for many acts of kindness, but especially for bringing me to St. Mary Magdalen dePazzi Church in South Philadelphia to meet Monsignor Vito Mazzone, who was then its pastor, one afternoon in the late 1960s. It was with some trepidation that I went, because I had been warned that Father Mazzone was a difficult man who would probably be unwilling to make parish records available to me. I still recall standing in the entrance of the rectory and hearing Father Fair's voice as he said, "Vito, this is my friend, Richard." Mazzone not only granted me immediate and extensive access to his sacramental ledgers but also invited me to use his desk and office while I studied this historic parish. It was, however, only the beginning of a long and productive experience.

Subsequently, Father John DeMayo, the first archdiocesan archivist, introduced me to the Consultors' Minutes, the record of deliberations between bishops and their priestly advisers on Church matters. And I soon became almost a lodger at the Philadelphia Archdiocesan Historical Research Center (PAHRC), an inexhaustible repository of materials bearing on Church history. The PAHRC staff represents a group of professional archivists and historians whose enthusiasm, intelligence, and congeniality have enormously contributed to my efforts. This group includes its director, Joseph J. Casino, Archivist Christine Friend, Archivist Brent Stauffer, and Office Manager Lois Wilson. In particular, Shawn Weldon, PAHRC Archivist and Records Manager, embodies the highest professional standards as an archivist, historian, and humanist. His indefatigable pursuit of materials as well as his cogent criticisms and original ideas contributed far more to my work than I can adequately thank him for. I wish to applaud the entire PAHRC staff not merely for aiding my research but also for making the time spent so pleasant. They exemplify what an outstanding research facility is all about.

I am also indebted to Father John J. Sheridan, O.S.A., Archivist of the St. Thomas of Villanova Province, and Father Fernando Rojo Martinez, O.S.A., Postulatore Generale of the Augustinian General Archives in Rome, for enabling me to use records related to Our Lady of Good Counsel parish and school. I thank Sister Francis Marie, Archivist of the Franciscan Missionary Sisters of the Sacred Heart, who supplied published and unpublished material on the orphanage and school at St. Mary Magdalen dePazzi as well as the vintage photograph of its sisters and students that appears in this book. Similarly, Sister Elizabeth Chambers, Sister Paola Canziani, and Sister Louise Giugni of the Daughters of Charity provided consultation that stretched from Albuquerque, New Mexico, to their mother house in Rome. I also owe my gratitude to Father Donato P. Silveri, the last pastor of St. Mary Magdalen dePazzi parish, before it was closed by the Archdiocese of Philadelphia, for his constant faith in this project. I must mention the late Dr. Sofia A. Janelli, who, as interim custodian, long held the personal papers of Monsignor Antonio Isoleri. And I especially would have wanted to thank Father Gianfausto Rosoli of the Missionary Society of St. Charles, and formerly the director of the Centro Studi Emigrazione in Rome, who unfortunately died while this work was in a preliminary stage, for his encouragement.

Another person, however, became uniquely essential to my endeavor. I first met Father Alfred M. Natali, O.S.A., sometime in the 1980s, when he resided at the rectory of St. Mary Magdalen dePazzi. Like many of the founding members of this parish, as well as other residents of the early Italian community in Philadelphia, he was a native of Genoa. As we prowled the attic above the main church one afternoon, seeking materials that might relate to its early years, he pointed to a small crate that held the papers of Isoleri and asked me if I would like to have them. At that moment, Natali became responsible for what I would be able to accomplish. Along with other guardians, Natali had preserved much of the record of the religious experience of Philadelphia's Italians. I carried the fragile wooden box to the trunk of my car, not sure at all what use I would make of the invaluable, but daunting, collection that it contained.

For several years, I occasionally looked at the contents of the crate that I had brought home, upwards of 20,000 pages of sermons, letters, and notes, mainly in Italian, sometimes in English, in Isoleri's careful, cursive script. But the longer that I examined these materials, the more compelling they became. I grew increasingly aware that these papers, illuminating a priestly life in a distant time, represented a unique collection, perhaps analogous to the diary of a slave or the letters of a soldier from the battlefields of the Civil War. As I began to read and translate them, I separated spiritual tracts from more worldly items. They depicted Isoleri's struggle to build his parish and to defend it and himself from various threats and adversaries.

Isoleri's papers are not without their limitations. While their pages mainly reflected his side of disputes with ministers of other faiths or with the sisters who instructed at the parish school or even with his ecclesiastical superiors, the absence of their own records, largely lost with the passage of time, makes opposing views far less available. When I later sought to use the archives of one religious order, I learned that my "one-sided" materials were actually filling gaps in its history. And when I sought to balance Isoleri's account of his encounters with Philadelphia prelates from Bishop James Wood to Cardinal Dennis Dougherty, I discovered that many of their personal papers had been destroyed.

The rich and concrete details of Isoleri's papers, nonetheless, enabled me to document and interpret not only the religious activities of his congregation but what was transpiring in the secular life of immigrants as well. What began as a biography of a priest gradually became the history of his parish and then a study of the encounter of Italians with their religion, along with its implications for the growth of their community in one American city. Consequently, I remain immensely grateful to Father Natali, whose name and generosity appropriately made him so close to being "Father Christmas," who granted me the extraordinary gift of access to these rare papers.

Along with those who have already been identified, I must acknowledge a few more persons who facilitated my work. Louise Green, Jacqueline Mirabile, Bente Polites, and other reference librarians and Thérèse Dougherty of the Interlibrary Loan Department at Falvey Library of Villanova University answered many queries and requests. Similarly, Rachel Schaller of the Office of University Information Technologies has been indispensable in guiding me through the preparation of this manuscript. Charlotte Vent, secretary of the Sociology Department, carried out innumerable tasks that not only ensured the completion of my work but alleviated much anguish as well. My good friend Professor Robert Melzi, an invaluable resource, rescued me by clarifying obsolete forms of the Italian language or other intricacies of translation that had stymied my efforts. Umberto LaPaglia turned over to me his extensive collection of materials, assembled over many years, on the history of Our Lady of Good Counsel Church and the Italian Augustinians who served it. Among my faculty colleagues at Villanova University, Father Joseph Ryan, O.S.A., provided invaluable critical comments as my work progressed. Similarly, Professor Adele Maiello of the Faculty of Political Science at the University of Genoa has offered thoughtful suggestions and support for several years. I owe a special note of gratitude to Barbara Hanrahan, director of the University of Notre Dame Press, who recognized the significance of my manuscript and guided it through many months by her kind and invaluable advice. Similarly, I wish to express my appreciation to editors Rebecca DeBoer and Ann Aydelotte for their meticulous care and labor on my text, and to Margaret A. Gloster, art director, for her care and creativity on its exterior cover.

I also thank Alexandra and Rick, who grew up much too fast and left home to pursue their lives before their father could finish his own work. I especially hope that what I have studied and written about will serve them as immigrants and pilgrims of another age to find what they seek. My wife and best friend,

Sandra Juliani, once again, stands out as my critic and guide through the re-search, analysis, and writing. She honors the memory of her Amendola, Costan-tino, Marcantonio, and Spiro ancestors by the intelligence and energy that she has devoted to my work, and by which she has made it our work. Without her, it would have been impossible for me to carry it out. And without her to share my life, it would not have been worth doing.

Finally, as a scholar who spent many years engaged in research and as a writer who labored to express its subject clearly, I must beg one indulgence. Whatever level of achievement my work has reached, it pales beside the type of accomplishment reflected by the life of Antonio Isoleri. If it appears at times that the author is paying homage to Isoleri, then so be it, and it is done without apology. For Isoleri was an extraordinary man.

Priest, Parish, and People

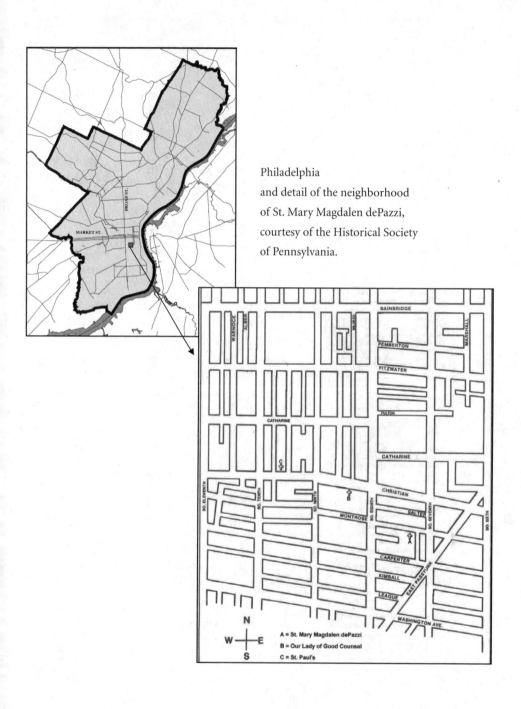

Philadelphia
and detail of the neighborhood
of St. Mary Magdalen dePazzi,
courtesy of the Historical Society
of Pennsylvania.

Introduction

To know the history of Italians in America, we must study their religious life. For Italian immigrants, once beyond the family, seeking the meaning of new experiences, securing a place in a new society, and finding solace when faced by new tribulations often meant turning to persons and institutions that told them what to think and how to live. For many of them, religion not only offered solutions to these problems but also provided a device through which the larger society was refracted and by which their own community was built.[1]

Sociologists and anthropologists have identified the basic elements of communal life—producing the material things by which we survive, reproducing the next generation, transmitting the old culture to young people, protecting ourselves from external threats and establishing order within our group, defining ultimate beliefs and objectives, and finding time for leisure through which we restore our energies. They have also identified basic institutions—the economy, family, education, politics, religion, and recreation—that carry out these tasks in modern societies. Recognizing the importance of "institutional completeness," that is, a complete array of these arrangements to satisfy the needs of individuals as well as to sustain group survival, religion takes on an indispensable function for any type of human community, but it serves an especially important role for immigrant communities.[2]

Previous studies on immigration in general and on ethnic communities in particular have examined how religion affected adjustment to America. They have described its role in the struggle of immigrants to preserve their ethnic identity and culture, the part of the church in the assimilation of the foreign born, and the tensions between the piety of immigrants and the efforts of eccle-siastical leaders who seek to control them. But the place of religion remains a problem for anyone who attempts to understand immigrant life in America. And while studies of religion also recognize the importance of "institutional completeness," they have failed, with some notable exceptions, to adequately describe its role in the building of an immigrant colony and in the ethnic com-munity that succeeds it.[3]

Although attention has been paid to ethnic diversity in American reli-gious history, it has often been selective, and the experience of some groups, such as the Italians, despite being a large part of the population, remains to be adequately examined. Even an exemplary study of conflict within American Catholicism, defining the great issue of the late nineteenth century as the need to reconcile the whole with its parts, focused only on the Irish and Germans.[4] And a more recent effort, praised for giving "due notice to ethnic diversity" and being sensitive to the calls for justice expressed by various groups, almost en-tirely omits Italians.[5] As one critic succinctly observed, this neglect represents "a flagrant case of ecclesiastical colonialism that has distorted the interpretation of American Catholicism."[6] Despite work by recent scholars, the Italian chapter in American Catholic history remains far from fully explored.

In view of the magnitude of immigration from Italy as well as its presence as a component of the Catholic population, Italians remain a neglected aspect of American religious history. Conversely, the religious experience of Italians represents a dimension of their adjustment to America that deserves more at-tention than it has previously been accorded as an issue of immigration history. For despite the political conflict of nationalists with the Holy See in their home-land, together with the rejection of religion by nonbelievers among them, im-migrant Italians, largely at least nominally Catholic, found the Catholic Church a highly visible aspect of the social landscape of urban America. Italian Catholics in America, however, encountered their traditional faith in a setting that was dif-ferent not only geographically but also socially and politically. Unlike in much of Europe, it was a minority religion, beset by Protestants and proselytizers in a plu-ralistic society. For Catholicism, the neighborhood parish eventually became a fortress that defended the fidelity of its members by services, sermons, and popu-lar piety. From older roots, it developed newer functions that made it a center for spiritual life, education, social services, and recreation. By doing so, the parish be-came a source of group cohesion, personal identity, and adjustment to urban life. But with the transformation of religious institutions in America, the parish also mediated assimilation as its members became Americans, and thus it reflected a much larger reality of immigrant life. Thus, to know the history of Catholicism or immigrant life in America, we must understand the role of the parish.[7]

The experience of Philadelphia's Italians allows us to see the parish in the con-text of religious and immigrant history. In November 1852, Bishop John Neumann founded the Italian Mission of St. Mary Magdalen dePazzi, the first church specifically for Italians in America. It was located on Marriott (now Montrose) Street, between Seventh and Eighth Streets, in the district of Moyamensing but later was incorporated by redrawn boundaries into the southeast quadrant of the city. Although a small cluster of immigrants from Italy had already settled in that area, as their number subsequently increased, Philadelphia eventually had one of the largest Italian populations in the nation. While it spawned other immigrant communities in the city as well as in outlying areas, South Philadelphia long remained the hub of Italian settlement. And if South Philadelphia arguably remained synonymous with "Little Italy," then St. Mary Magdalen dePazzi was its principal institution in the late nineteenth century.[8]

Scholars have too often offered erroneous comments or paid meager attention to St. Mary Magdalen dePazzi. For example, after mentioning Bishop Neumann's founding of an Italian church in Philadelphia, a nineteenth-century historian found little else of importance about it.[9] Although once stationed at nearby Our Lady of Good Counsel, an Augustinian observer inexcusably, perhaps deliberately, identified St. Anthony's in New York City as the first Italian church in America.[10] A later writer thoroughly confused St. Mary Magdalen dePazzi with a church in Hoboken, New Jersey, thus filling its history with misinformation.[11] Although recognizing the primacy of St. Mary Magdalen dePazzi, a sociologist turned exclusively to parish life in New York City.[12] But local historians have also neglected it. A priest who wrote an early history of Philadelphia Catholicism identified St. Mary Magdalen dePazzi in his index as the city's first Italian church but ignored both its local and national implications in his text.[13] And even a recent history of the archdiocese failed to find the life and extraordinarily long tenure of its most celebrated pastor to be worth noting.[14] If we are to correct these deficiencies, we need to become better acquainted with the history of this parish along with the experience of Italians as Catholics in Philadelphia.

St. Mary Magdalen dePazzi, however, was not a disembodied institution but one of human drama and performers. Its history reflects the aspirations of immigrants who held a secular faith in the city of Philadelphia and who believed that its opportunities, along with their own hard work, could provide the material rewards that had been denied them in their places of origin. But these Italians also carried a more traditional faith, whose renewal gave them spiritual comfort during life's disappointments, trials, and tragedies. The priests who led this church and congregation were its principal players, while its parishioners made up the supporting cast. The story of St. Mary Magdalen dePazzi is ultimately about immigrants and their priests who together sought, believed in, and built on both kinds of faith in Philadelphia.

Although several priests nurtured the growth of parish life at St. Mary Magdalen dePazzi—and this work is about all of them—one stands above all others as the city's Little Italy evolved into a large, visible, and stable ethnic community.

Antonio Isoleri was not quite twenty-five years old and had been ordained only ten months when he arrived in Philadelphia on January 5, 1870. Before his death sixty-two years later in 1932, he served fifty-six years as pastor of St. Mary Magdalen dePazzi. During that time he became prominent in the Italian colony as well as respected throughout Philadelphia. By his personal character and accomplishments, Isoleri made a unique mark on local history and in the larger experience of Italians in America. But he is remembered today only by a handful of older residents as a powerful and dynamic figure who left an indelible imprint on them and their community.[15]

Great statesmen are more likely than the foot soldiers who serve under them to leave extensive collections of personal documents and memoirs. We know more about the lives of prime ministers and kings than we do about the common people. And within the world of religious institutions, we know more about princes of the Church than about lesser members of the clergy. Yet the priest who ministered in the front lines of spiritual experience often held a position of strategic significance for the parish church and the secular community. Antonio Isoleri was such a figure. His life, although unusual in many ways, contained much of the ordinary. For him, a religious vocation was not simply a matter of personal piety in pursuit of salvation but was also a matter of confronting the mundane and material struggles found in a temporal world. At the same time, his story discloses that no person takes the journey through his days alone. Every biography is also a history. By his efforts at creative writing, his struggle to interpret the painful politics of his land of origin, his devotion to religious faith, his service as pastor to his flock, and his vigorous leadership of the Italian colony, Isoleri's life reflects his personal odyssey as an immigrant as well as the history of his community.

The reader who seeks only to know the life of the priest who is the main figure of these pages may become confused as the subject shifts to what may appear to be a different book. But behind this narrative and analysis, the "sociological imagination" that links history and biography, while reducing the dichotomy between "the public and the private," provides its guiding premise.[16] And whatever it is called, it places human interaction within a context that occasionally requires us to momentarily set aside the priest's tale before returning to it with a better understanding.

The life of Isoleri, therefore, should neither be presented, nor can it be properly understood, apart from the broader situation in which it unfolded. The period from his arrival in America in 1869 until his death in 1932 was a significant chapter in immigrant, religious, and political history. And it embraced an enormously important stage, or more accurately several stages, of the Italian experience in America. When Isoleri disembarked in New York City in late 1869, he was one of only 2,891 Italians recorded as entering the United States in that year. The entire population of the nation in 1870 included only 17,157 persons born in Italy. The Federal Census for that year reported only 516 Italians for the city of Philadelphia, with 301 of them living in South Philadelphia.[17] Among a Catholic population in the Diocese of Philadelphia of about 220,000, the only church for Italians had a congregation of about 400 members.[18] And the next September following Isoleri's departure from the land of his birth, Italian troops entered the Porta Pia, captured Rome, and unified Italy. The loss of Rome ended the temporal power of the Catholic Church and brought the papacy to the lowest point of its modern history.

During Isoleri's years in Philadelphia, Italian immigration to America underwent a vast transformation. Increasing to nearly 56,000 in the first decade after his arrival, immigration from Italy grew steadily until it reached its peak just before World War I. From 1871 to 1930, Italy sent 4,625,677 immigrants to America.[19] Although they often returned to their homeland, many others settled permanently. From an army of young male laborers when mass immigration began, women and children increasingly joined them by the early twentieth century. From the northern regions of previous years, their origins shifted overwhelmingly to villages and towns of the Mezzogiorno and Sicily. The passage of the National Origins Quota Acts all but ended immigration from Italy in the 1920s.

By 1930 the U.S. population included 1,790,429 persons born in Italy, the highest figure ever reached, and 2,756,453 others who were American born but fully or partly of Italian parentage, for a total of 4,546,882 Italian Americans. In Philadelphia some 68,156 residents were natives of Italy, with 43,383 of them, or about 50 percent of all foreign-born whites, living in South Philadelphia.[20] By that year the Catholic population in the Archdiocese of Philadelphia reached about 812,550 members.[21] The archdiocese eventually established twenty-three nationality parishes for Italians in the city and its surrounding area, with about 89,000 members in their congregations.[22] But other churches became de facto Italian parishes as newcomers crowded into neighborhoods, thus making them a part of the Catholic population who could not be easily counted. In February 1929 the Lateran Treaty and the Concordat resolved the "Roman question," thus ending nearly sixty years of tension between Italy and the Vatican. Through these agreements with Fascist Italy, the Church reached a promising moment that was widely celebrated in Italian churches in Philadelphia.

Within this framework, the story of St. Mary Magdalen dePazzi, along with its pastors and people, could be seen as a self-contained, uneventful tale of a single parish and as only a minor episode of local history. But this remarkable era spans from well before the start of mass immigration from Italy through the initial development of immigrant ghettos in American cities to a time when Italians had become so well assimilated in the United States as to be no longer regarded as a serious problem. The recounting of this saga transcends mere parish history or Isoleri's part as pastor and constitutes an important chapter in the rediscovery of the Italian American past.

While some scholars have favorably portrayed the nationality parish as a decisive, but often overlooked, institution in the adjustment of Italian Catholics in America, other writers have viewed it as a deterrent to assimilation.[23] Its role was actually much more complicated. Isoleri sought to make his parish a device that enabled its members to retain their *italianità* while at the same time permitting them to become Americans. He sought to help them to remain what they had previously been while he facilitated what they inevitably were becoming. And this story engages some central issues of religious and immigrant history in general—it recognizes the role of the priest in immigrant life, the tensions of popular piety with ecclesiastical bureaucracy, and the influence of religious experience on assimilation. And unlike an earlier perspective depicting immigrants as being uprooted, isolated, and alienated, it allows us to see their parish life as a bridge between old and new cultures that eased adjustment and encouraged assimilation while also building their own community.[24]

It is important to distinguish what the present study is about from what some readers may want it to be about. It is a study in the historical sociology of an immigrant community and its institutions. While it enters into religious history, there are many questions that it raises but does not answer. Without comparing the religious life of Italians in Philadelphia with that found in other cities, or their religious experience with more recent immigrant groups, or the complex relationships of pastors and sisters who served in parishes, it provides material for subsequent scholars who wish to pursue these topics. The story of Isoleri, his parish, and its relationship to the community deserves to be told first and by itself. Yet that particular focus has implications beyond itself.

The nationality parish, set aside for the exclusive use of a single immigrant group, did not begin with the Italians, nor did it end with them. But from its earliest days, it has often been part of a troubled legacy of Catholicism in America. German Catholics in Philadelphia, in seeking to separate themselves from the congregation of St. Mary's, initiated plans for their own church in 1787. When they opened Holy Trinity two years later, against the wishes of the Reverend John Carroll, superior of the Catholic mission in America, a highly contentious era of Church history began. More than two centuries later, Catholicism in America seeks to accommodate newcomers from Africa and Asia by a policy of enculturation that provides continuity, particularly in liturgical forms, with their traditional cultural heritage. Between the historical boundaries of earlier Germans and the current migration, the encounter of Italian immigrants with American Catholicism offers a benchmark by which to evaluate its efforts to deal with cultural diversity. The recent decisions by Church authorities in Philadelphia, Boston, Chicago, St. Louis, and elsewhere to close nationality parishes that once housed immigrant congregations, as well as the current need to serve new immigrants, make the case of St. Mary Magdalen dePazzi both timely and timeless. This situation of Italian Catholics in Philadelphia was not and is not an entirely unique case. In many respects, it could be also found wherever Italians formed immigrant colonies and faced the difficult task of adjusting both in a secular and in a religious sense to life in America. While differing in details, their more general dimensions were quite similar. Consequently, the Philadelphia case resonates with familiarity throughout the history of urban America. It is an encounter that Church leaders today would be well advised to reexamine as they face the immigrant groups of more recent years, if they wish to avoid the mistakes of the past.

CHAPTER ONE

The Italian Church in Philadelphia

The first European settlers in the Delaware Valley were Swedish and Dutch farmers who arrived in the early seventeenth century. Under the leadership of William Penn, a colony with Philadelphia as its center was later established mainly by Quakers from Great Britain on the western shore of the Delaware River in 1682. Almost immediately afterward, Dutch Quakers and Mennonites, and then German Pietists, founded Germantown in an area northwest of the original city. The first Catholics, new arrivals of English, French, German, and Irish origin, further diversified the population of colonial Philadelphia. The later presence of Italian Catholics developed as a part of this long history of ethnic and religious experience in Philadelphia.[1]

Early Catholicism in Philadelphia

As early as 1708, not quite thirty years after the founding of Penn's colony, Catholics reportedly celebrated mass for the first time in Philadelphia. In 1729, Father Joseph Greaton, a London-born Jesuit and the founder of Catholicism in the city, purchased property on Chestnut Street, where he said mass in a small chapel. Although a previous law had forbade the saying of mass anywhere in the British empire, a 1701 provision permitted its celebration in a chapel within a private residence. Catholics were the only Christian denomination at the time not permitted to hold their own public services. Father Greaton, however, planned to remedy the situation.

Greaton's intentions precipitated the first serious test of Penn's objective of religious toleration in the colony. In 1733, Greaton bought property on Walnut Street, between Third and Fourth Streets, where he established St. Joseph's, the first public site for the observance of the Catholic liturgy in the following year. As a result of the opening of the chapel, the lieutenant governor convened the ruling council of the colony to seek its judgment as to whether British law permitted Roman Catholicism. After long deliberation, the council adjourned without reaching a decision. A few days later, when the governor implored the council to reach an opinion, it concluded that Penn's Law of the Liberty of Conscience superseded any prior laws restricting Catholics. With this decision, rendered on the feast day of Saint Ignatius Loyola, the founder of the Jesuit order, the immediate problem was resolved, and Catholicism was formally established in Philadelphia.

Despite the Reformation and the brutal civil war in England in this period, predominantly Protestant Pennsylvania accepted the Catholic presence, and other priests joined Greaton in promoting it. Father Henry Neale, another Jesuit, reported in 1741 to his provincial: "We have at present all liberty imaginable in the exercise of our business, and are not only esteemed, but reverenced, as I may say, by the better sort of people."[2] But Catholicism soon faced other challenges.

While early Catholics, as most other residents of the colony, were mainly of English origin, their population soon became much more diverse. By the 1740s, with the influx of German Catholics, the Jesuits had sent missionaries to rural communities on the western borders of Pennsylvania. With the outbreak of the French and Indian War in 1755, when the British expelled Catholics from French Canada, most of them relocated to Louisiana, but some Acadians found their way to Philadelphia. In November 1755, three ships arrived at the port, carrying 454 French Canadian refugees. Germans and French Canadians thus were in the vanguard of immigration that eventually produced a heterogeneous Catholic population.[3]

Although the founding of St. Joseph's marked the establishment of Catholicism in the city, the growth of the urban population required more churches. In 1763, St. Mary's was founded on South Fourth Street, only a short distance from St. Joseph's, by another Jesuit, Father Robert Harding. Although the proximity of the two churches was partly a result of economic expediency, another factor may have been important. After an arson attempt on a Catholic church in Lancaster, Pennsylvania, fear of similar acts also brought newer and older churches closer together in Philadelphia and encouraged an early clustering of Catholic facilities.

When the climate for Catholics became more favorable (despite the incident in Lancaster), thus allowing further construction of churches, the matter of ethnic diversity still had to be addressed. Holy Trinity (1789) at Sixth and

Spruce Streets and St. Augustine's (1796) on Fourth Street, below Vine, were soon opened, but no church was designated as a parish before 1844, when that term was first applied with a canonical (or territorial) reference. St. Joseph's, St. Mary's, and St. Augustine's had substantially English-origin congregations. Holy Trinity was intended mainly, but not exclusively, for the spiritual needs of Germans. Some French Catholics—refugees from Acadia, and others fleeing the slave insurrection of Toussaint L'Ouverture in Haiti or the revolution in France—had also been absorbed by Holy Trinity, as evidenced in tombstone inscriptions in its cemetery behind the church. With the opening of Holy Trinity, ethnic diversity had become a more salient aspect of Philadelphia Catholicism.

Throughout these years, however, Philadelphia Catholics had been threatened not only by anti-Catholic sentiment but also by internal dissension. When Henry Conwell became their second bishop in 1820, he inherited a turbulent situation resulting from three decades of lingering conflict over the rights of lay trustees to control property and nominate pastors at Holy Trinity and St. Mary's, which was about to enter a new phase. Only two days after his arrival, Conwell heard Father William Hogan, St. Mary's rector, deliver a sermon attacking the former administrator of the diocese. Responding to the sermon and to charges of immorality, Conwell sought to mildly rebuke him, but Hogan replied by criticizing Conwell in his sermon on the next Sunday. When Conwell suspended Hogan, the bishop antagonized the trustees, who supported the priest. Despite efforts to resolve their differences, the conflict accelerated until Conwell closed the church "against clergy and people" and then excommunicated Hogan. While Hogan defended himself in pamphlets assailing Conwell, the schism was widened by disputed elections of trustees, bitter polemics, and physical violence until it reached the state courts and legislature. Before the dispute among clergy, lay trustees, and their bishop was resolved in 1831, it offered the stage for a dramatic performance by an Italian priest at St. Mary's. But "Hoganism," as it would become known, sustained hierarchical concerns about separate churches for immigrants as well as about popular pastors for many years to come in Philadelphia.[4]

The First Italian Catholics in Philadelphia

During these early years, the presence and participation of Italians in the Catholic Church in Philadelphia were only scant and episodic. From the 1760s to the 1790s such family names as Mignati, Cancemi, Cangemy, Mignio, Orlandy, Amico, Botello, Cuneo, and Ghirardini are scattered through baptismal records, with Polumbo and Morelli among the participants in marriage ceremonies at St. Joseph's Church. Similarly, at Holy Trinity in the late 1790s, baptisms are recorded for members of the Lammetta and Molinari families. But identifying surnames as Italian, without further evidence, is risky. The baptismal entry, however, for Anna Maria Orlandino at St. Joseph's in 1780 describes her as the child of "Paul Orlandino, Genoese." This case strengthens the argument that other baptisms involved Italians. But while wills and other documents support this conclusion, even if these entries were for Italians, their total number remained relatively small.[5] Moreover, it may be argued that "few colonial Italians had the opportunity or the desire to observe Catholic practices and that distance and poor means of communication prevented their attending church, except on very special occasions."[6] But despite this persuasive conjecture, available sources of data render Italians as only a small part of the total population of the city.

While little is known about early Italians in Philadelphia, there is one extraordinary exception. Giovanni Battista Sartori, born in Rome in 1765, was the son of the papal jeweler and a close associate of Pius VI. In 1797 the younger Sartori reportedly wrote to Robert Morris, the Philadelphia financier, proposing the establishment of diplomatic ties between the United States and the Papal States. Shortly afterward, President John Adams nominated and the Senate confirmed Sartori as the first of eleven American consuls who would serve before the fall of the Papal States in 1870. But diplomatic records also show that Sartori served from 1829 to 1841 (and perhaps even longer) as the consul general of the Papal States to the United States. His dual service as consul for both governments gives Sartori a unique position in diplomatic history. Although his family's estate was located in present-day Trenton, New Jersey, much of his business and social life unfolded in Philadelphia, where he remained connected to St. Augustine's Church. After the death of his second wife in 1828, Sartori and his daughters took up residence in Leghorn, and he remained in Italy until his own death in 1853. Sartori's sons, however, found success in America, where their families remained socially prominent well into the twentieth century.[7]

In the nineteenth century, both the size and diversity of the Catholic population in Philadelphia greatly expanded. From the 1830s onward, Irish immigrants in particular increased the number of Catholics in the city. Largely as a result of arrivals from Ireland, the number of Catholic churches also grew rapidly, with nine new ones in a thirteen-year period, with all but one of them beyond the original city limits.[8] One church, St. Paul's, although in Moyamensing rather than in Philadelphia proper, and with a predominantly Irish congregation at its founding in 1843 on the north side of Christian Street, between Ninth and Tenth Streets, would be almost at the center of Little Italy by the end of the century. But in contrast to the Irish population, the number of Italians rose slowly in the early years of the century.

During this period, names of apparently Italian origin continued to appear in the sacramental records of local churches. Baptisms at St. Joseph's included members of families such as Franchi, Sartori, Fagioli, and Carlino (or Carbino). Marriages at the same church involved the names Bellini (or Bettini), Genari,

Trabalice, Ambrosi, DeAngeli, Viti, Battesta, Logno (or Togno), diPisola, Oliveri, and Pizzini either as spouses or witnesses. From 1804 onward, St. Augustine's Church also had a growing number of Italians, with such families as Sartori, Fagioli, Zepero, Balordo, Foli, Lametti, Filippi, Luciani, Pittaluga, DeAngeli, Rebolla, Diaccheri, and Peichetti found among its marriages and baptisms. The actual number of Italians in St. Augustine's congregation, however, was lower than that suggested by the sacramental ledgers. A parish census, which reported slightly more than three thousand members, listed only eight natives of Italy and Switzerland counted together in 1838. The Italians in the congregation may have represented no more than one family, but the absence of reliable records leaves the question unanswered. Unlike other churches, however, Italian priests served at St. Augustine's. Although the church had been initially staffed by Irish Augustinians from Dublin, their order, founded in Rome, always had had a strong presence in Italy, which helps to explain the presence of Italian priests at St. Augustine's before other churches in the city. Early clergy included two secular priests, Father Balthassar Torelli (1806–1807) and Father P. Rosetti (1819–1821), who briefly served at the Augustinian church.

A special event occasionally amplified the Italian presence in Philadelphia, as when Bishop Conwell presided at the marriage of Vincent Cavaradossi deThoel, the Sardinian consul to the United States, to Marie Antoinette D'Aurainville at St. Joseph's in January 1828. One witness to the ceremony, identified as N. Garibaldi, the vice consul of Sardinia at this time, actually was Angelo Garibaldi, who later served as the Sardinian consul in Philadelphia until his death in 1855. Angelo was the brother of Giuseppe Garibaldi, the famed military leader of the Risorgimento.

The Italian presence in religious affairs took on greater drama when Angelo Inglesi, a native of Rome, briefly appeared at the height of the Hoganism controversy. Soon after his arrival in autumn 1823, Inglesi, having obtained the right to officiate as a priest from Father William V. Harold, the acting vicar general, offered mass at St. Joseph's. With local Catholicism paralyzed by Conwell's conflict with the trustees at St. Mary's, Inglesi proposed himself as pastor if Hogan would only resign. When Harold opposed the proposal, Inglesi then withdrew his offer. As Conwell sought answers to charges that Inglesi had not only been married but had also defrauded the bishop of New Orleans and others, information from Quebec began to cast doubt on his credentials. With a possible scandal emerging, it was rumored that Gaspar DeAbbate, the Sardinian consul, had not only encouraged Inglesi to assume his priestly duties without Conwell's consent, but he was also about to sue the bishop. As the argument over Inglesi raged within the larger tempest over trusteeism, he suddenly left Philadelphia, never to return, before reportedly dying in Santo Domingo in June 1825.[9]

But if Inglesi provided a provocative moment for Catholicism in Philadelphia, an ex-priest and a bishop from Italy would incite even greater disruptions across Canada and the United States about two decades later. Alessandro Gavazzi, a former member of the Barnabite order, had participated in the 1848–49 revolution in Rome before becoming a Protestant and staunch critic of the papacy. After fleeing Italy to join other foes of the papacy in London, he arrived in New York City in March 1853. In June, Archbishop Gaetano Bedini also reached New York with the twofold mission of exploring the possibility of regularizing diplomatic relations with the government of the United States and of meeting with priests and bishops to discuss problems facing the Church in North America. Gavazzi, meanwhile, began a lecture tour in which he sought to deliver his indictment of the papal opposition to Italian independence, but also to follow Bedini and foment dissent against the prelate. In particular, Gavazzi charged that Bedini had not only supported Austria against Italian nationalists in Bologna, but was singularly responsible for the execution of Ugo Bassi, another ex-priest and patriot. Despite Gavazzi's efforts, Bedini was warmly received by clergy and laity in Boston, Detroit, Chicago, Milwaukee, and even Indian country of the upper Great Lakes region without any unpleasant incident in the early months of his visit.[10]

In July, however, when Bedini came to Philadelphia, he encountered his first failure. He had sought to persuade the trustees at Holy Trinity, who had renewed their sporadic defiance of diocesan authorities, to cede control of parish property. But when Bedini arrived at their church, the parishioners blocked his entrance. Then by refusing an offer of lodging from Bishop Neumann, ostensibly because it might discredit his efforts in the negotiations with the trustees at Holy Trinity, Bedini not only offended the local prelate but aggravated his own predicament. Beneath what he had given as his reason for refusing the invitation, the urbane Bedini was somewhat uncomfortable with Neumann's lack of sophistication. After only three days, finding himself in an untenable situation, Bedini fled from Philadelphia.

Bedini's failure in Philadelphia, however, would be mild compared to what awaited him in other cities. By the end of 1853, Gavazzi had succeeded in convincing some listeners that Bedini had truly been the "bloody butcher of Bologna." The newspapers of major cities vigorously debated the allegations against Bedini. Violence burst open in December, when perhaps as many as 1,000 protestors marched on the archbishop's residence in Cincinnati, Ohio, where the Italian prelate was staying. Some sixty of them were arrested, nine others were shot by police, and one demonstrator was killed. In January 1854, as residents of Wheeling, West Virginia, awaited a visit from Bedini, his critics distributed handbills reiterating Gavazzi's charges. When Bedini arrived in that city, a hostile mob smashed window panes at the Catholic cathedral. These actions made clear what Bedini faced in other cities.

By January of 1854, the hostility against Bedini continued to mount. He was burned in effigy in several cities in the Midwest. A crowd rioted in opposition to him in Baltimore. By mid-January, public opinion had turned decidedly against him. In late January, Senator Lewis Cass of Michigan, father of the U.S. Ambassador to Italy, introduced a resolution to the Senate, seeking to clarify Bedini's status as a diplomat and to ensure the protection of the government for him. After a spirited debate, the resolution failed, but it had served to bring the Bedini affair before the entire nation.

By the end of January, Bedini's visit was drawing to its climax. In New York City, Italian and German exiles planned a mass meeting that included a mock trial, which would present the case against him. Seventy prominent critics signed an affidavit that contained the charges that Gavazzi had first brought against Bedini. Among the signers, Giovanni Francesco Secchi deCasali, the editor and publisher, argued that neither Gavazzi's lectures nor his own editorials in *L'Eco d'Italia* but rather Bedini's actions in Italy were responsible for the opposition.

As an angry public sought him, Bedini seemed to have disappeared. But from wherever he was hiding, Bedini had written twice to Neumann to inquire if it would be safe to return to Philadelphia. In his reply, Neumann assured Bedini that after consultation with his priests he could not only offer his assurance that it would be safe to come, but he hoped it would be a long visit. Neumann, however, would never hear again from Bedini, who had decided that he had seen enough of the United States. Meanwhile, in early February, another mass meeting in Philadelphia condemned the members of the U.S. Senate who had supported Bedini. It was the last public protest against him. Despite a hostile mob waiting for him on a nearby dock, Bedini had left Staten Island on a ship bound for England about a week earlier.

Because of its subsequent implications, the Bedini affair, as it came to be known, cannot be ignored. But as Giovanni Pizzorusso and Matteo Sanfilippo, two Italian scholars of Church history, have persuasively pointed out, it was what Bedini later wrote about his visit that is important. After returning to Italy, he prepared a detailed report that not only offered a wide-ranging assessment of the condition of Catholics in the United States, but also included the earliest attempt to address their problems as immigrants in foreign lands. His claim that two-thirds of them would lose their faith in America because of the lack of their own clergy would become a recurrent lament among Church officials in Rome. But Bedini also became the first person to pose the dilemma of the ethnic parish, that is, one served by priests who came from the same country as the immigrants themselves, which would dominate the reports of ecclesiastical officials for the next fifty years. In particular, Bedini argued that although the ethnic parish might be the means of saving the faith of immigrant Catholics, it might interfere with the unity of the Church in North America, while it also relegated its members to a perpetual position of lower status alongside a population of Anglo-Saxon origins.[11]

Bedini's report provided a seminal reflection on the spiritual problems of foreign-born Catholics that would reverberate in the discussion and efforts by ecclesiastical authorities to find ways of saving the faith of immigrants over the next half century. But while he may have even been first to perceive the need for immigrant parishes, his conclusion for at least one case came after the fact. For when Bedini arrived on his visit to the United States in the early summer of 1853, the Italian Mission that came to be known as St. Mary Magdalen dePazzi had already been established in Philadelphia. And despite the temptation to see him as anticipating an "Italian problem," the founding of this church owed more to local circumstances than to the ideas of a visiting prelate from Rome.

Mariani and a "Church for the Italians"

Through the 1840s, Italians played only a limited part in Philadelphia Catholicism, but change was on the horizon. Sacramental ledgers for St. Joseph's (1848–1853), St. Mary's (1838–1852), and Holy Trinity (1848–1852) record about thirty baptisms and five marriages involving Italians, yet their small but increasing population sought religious services and instruction in their own language. Two priests, Cosimo Antonio Della Nave and Peter Folchi, organized a meeting at Old St. Joseph's Church on Fourth Street and Willing's Alley, where Italians gathered in a schoolroom in March 1852 to discuss a plan for a church of their own. When the number of Italians attending mass on Sundays reportedly reached about six hundred, John Neumann, installed as bishop of Philadelphia only few months earlier, allowed them the use of the chapel at the cathedral for their services in August. At the same time, religious instruction was initiated for their children on Sunday afternoons at St. Paul's Church on Christian Street.[12]

Bishop Neumann soon took a decisive step on behalf of the Italians in Philadelphia. As their population gradually increased in the city, the Church, both in Italy and in America, opposed their nationalistic aspirations in the native land. But beyond the political issues in their homeland and the strains of adjustment in a new location, the defection of Italians from Catholicism, later to be defined as a part of the "Italian problem," had also become a source of concern. But whether motivated by politics or pastoral considerations, the need for a church for Italians was apparent. In September, Neumann purchased a small chapel and adjacent cemetery, previously owned by African American Methodists, on Marriott (later renamed Montrose) Street, between Seventh and Eighth Streets in Moyamensing, beyond the southern boundary of the city. On this site the church of St. Mary Magdalen dePazzi, named in honor of a sixteenth-century Florentine Carmelite nun, was established. In October 1852 the *Catholic Herald* announced the purchase, albeit with an erroneously simplified name:

> "Church for the Italians"—On last Sunday a small chapel, intended for
> the use of the Italians of this city, was blessed by the Rev. Mr. Mariani, (by

16 Priest, Parish, and People*

the authority of the Bishop) under the invocation of St. Mary Magdalen. The edifice is situated near Eighth and Christian. It was built and formerly used for Protestant worship, but it has lately been purchased and refitted for its present purpose. It is small, but will, no doubt, answer for some time to come. This congregation formerly worshiped in the Cathedral chapel.[13]

In June 1853 the organization of a congregation for Italian Catholics, under the Reverend Gaetano Mariani, was announced again, with the laying of a cornerstone, now wrongly reported as in the district of Southwark—a building of 50 feet with wings at its front corners and stairs that led to galleries, increasing in its width to 66½ feet to accommodate about five hundred worshipers. The plan called for a brick front covered with mastic in imitation of brownstone in an Italian style, and three entrance doors, each facing an aisle, and crowned by bell towers on its wings, with a doorway in the base of each tower. A figure of the patron saint in bas-relief was to be placed above the main door, under the words "Laudate Dominum." No rental of pews would be made, and the entire church would be free to all Catholics. But while some renovation of the old Methodist chapel had begun, this ambitious plan for a new building had to be postponed for another year.[14]

Born in Florence on February 3, 1800, Mariani had been ordained as a Franciscan priest in his native city at the age of twenty-four.[15] Beyond his religious training, he had also acquired some medical skills; before leaving Italy, he had been made a knight of the Order of St. Joseph in Tuscany for his work during cholera epidemics in Leghorn and Pisa. Emigrating from his native country, he arrived in New York City in 1851, where he remained nine months, waiting for an opportunity to minister among Italians in America. During this time, Mariani resided at the Church of the Transfiguration in Manhattan, where he began to learn the language of his new country. On October 7, 1851, Bishop Francis Patrick Kenrick's reply to a letter from Mariani, in regard to a possible post in Philadelphia, instead mentioned his own imminent appointment as the bishop of Baltimore. For Mariani, however, the eventual connection to St. Mary Magdalen dePazzi had been set in motion, although it was to be carried out by Neumann, Kenrick's successor.[16]

In late 1851, Mariani assumed a position as professor of music at St. Charles Borromeo Seminary in Philadelphia, which he held for only a brief period.[17] Nearly from the moment of his arrival, Mariani was an interested observer of the efforts of the Italians to secure their own church. He was soon chosen by Neumann as the first rector of the new mission of St. Mary Magdalen dePazzi. Fathers John Tornatore and Andrew Rossi from the seminary, Cosimo Della Nave of St. Joseph's, and Felix Villanis, a New York priest, as well as laymen John Raggio, Vito Viti, and Ambrose Monachesi (probably Nicolà Monachesi, the well-known artist) also participated in the effort.[18] After the blessing of the chapel in October 1852, it appears that religious services were not held for another year. On the first page of the sacramental ledger, Mariani's brief note (translated here) not only attested to his own feelings but also to the actual beginning of the new church: "The 23rd of the month of October 1853 was the beginning of the little Italian chapel dedicated to St. Mary Magdalen de Pazzi, established in the city of Philadelphia between 8th and 7th Streets through the kindness of the Most Reverend Monsignor Neumann, worthy Apostolic Roman Bishop of the city and diocese of Philadelphia. The Rev. Gaetano Mariani was designated its pastor and authorized to bless the chapel on the same day of its beginning."[19]

Mariani's mission almost immediately enjoyed modest success, as a donation of $11 to St. John's Orphan Asylum was reported for "St. Magdelane dePaza" in December 1853. Similarly, when the diocese announced the schedule for the newly introduced Forty Hours Devotion, St. Mary Magdalen dePazzi was listed as a site for May 1854. In the same month, with the need for a larger building to accommodate the congregation, Neumann laid the cornerstone for a church and rectory. Although dedicated in October 1854, the project was not completed for another three years, at a reported cost of $18,500. But the real meaning of what had been initiated was provided by Mariani himself, when he described St. Mary Magdalen dePazzi as the first church to be established for Italians anywhere in the United States.[20]

The small, but steady, growth of the congregation under Mariani's leadership was reflected in baptisms recorded for the next twelve years. From the first entry in December 1853,[21] then after six more in the next year, the number rose to twenty-six, ranging from eighteen to thirty each year until Mariani's death in early 1866. The names of "irlandesi" occasionally appeared in the registers. But the baptisms also revealed the presence of families who were beginning to normalize the population of an incipient community.

TABLE 1.1   Baptisms at St. Mary Magdalen dePazzi
(December 1853–January 1866)[22]

Year	Number	Year	Number
1853	1	1860	30
1854	6	1861	21
1855	26	1862	23
1856	19	1863	23
1857	19	1864	18
1858	19	1865	19
1859	28	1866	1

Total 253

Among the distinctive aspects of the congregation was that many members were Ligurian in origin, particularly from the area near the city of Chiavari, south of Genoa. Of baptisms involving Italians in the first twelve years, the origins of at least one parent were provided in 202 cases; of this number, some 121 gave Chiavari or a place nearby far more often than anywhere else. But whether it participated in these rites or not, the neighborhood could be seen as Genoese, or even more precisely as Chiavarese.[23] However, congregation and neighborhood actually were more complicated in pattern, with other ethnic groups, particularly the Irish, taking part in activities. Between 1854 and 1857, when the original church was being constructed, the names of its nine-member building committee—John Raggio, John Kerns, Thomas Timmins, Patrick Cain, James Questa, Patrick McAuliffe, John Cassidy, Philip Kelly, and N. J. Costello—reflect its mixed character.[24] While Raggio and Questa were Italian, other members of the committee were Irish. And sacramental records confirmed the lingering presence of the Irish.[25]

For his part, Mariani provided not only spiritual comfort but also material aid to his congregation. Despite the limited resources of his flock, he oversaw its financial affairs with some success. His 1859 report of receipts and expenses revealed either the meager resources of the congregation or its unwillingness to contribute to the support of the church. He listed only $471 in receipts from regular collections for the previous year but, somewhat surprisingly, another $234 from special collections. The church fair in November 1858, after deducting expenses, generated an additional $1,361 in income, while another $14 came from uncertain sources.[26] The trustees who had served in 1858—William Loughlin, Patrick Reilly, and John Rogers—would be retained for another year. Their names reaffirm the necessity or desirability of Irish involvement in financial affairs at the church. (But John Rogers was almost certainly the same person as John Raggio.)

Mariani was also gaining a reputation for his medical knowledge. With many people alleged to owe their renewed health and vigor to him, "he was called upon daily by numbers of patients who had the greatest confidence in his skill, and he effected many cures, some of which were and are considered to be wonderful."[27] Even the secular press reported that Mariani had earned renown: "the sick flocked to the parsonage from all parts of the city, the rich and poor alike seeking his aid."[28] He did not demand fees but accepted whatever donation his patients could afford. Although he treated anyone who came to him, his healing abilities held special significance for his own congregation and neighborhood.

Beyond his spiritual, material, and medical roles, Mariani carried out other tasks that contributed to the cohesion of his fragile community. On the day after Maria Lagomarsino Pejano, wife of Agostino Pejano, died in early September 1861, Mariani wrote a letter noting that the deceased had lived in Philadelphia for about five years, had been ill for about two years, had received the last rites, and had been buried in St. Mary's Cemetery, and that Angela Cuneo had paid two dollars for two masses and the funeral at the Italian church. The letter, with the signed endorsement of Victor A. Sartori, the Italian consul in Philadelphia, eventually reached the parish of Santa Maria Assunta in the town of Certenoli, the birthplace of the dead woman, in the province of Genoa. Mariani's correspondence, presumably routine, did more than simply convey news to Italy of another death in Philadelphia, for it also affirmed the ties between places of origin and destination. The Italians, even as they were building a new community, remained a part of their older, now faraway one.[29]

Mariani's tenure as first rector of St. Mary Magdalen dePazzi lasted twelve years. Near the end of 1865 he was severely injured in an accidental fall in the church. As Mariani's health declined, Father Gaetano Sorrentini was appointed as coadjutor in late February 1866 in order to meet the spiritual needs of the congregation. Shortly afterward, Mariani died at the parish rectory at 3:30 A.M. on March 8, 1866, precisely forty-two years to the day of his ordination as a priest. By the time of his death, his reputation had transcended his temporal accomplishments. In the distinctive idiom of the faith that Mariani had served, it was later noted that he had died "in the odor of sanctity." His own church was far too small to accommodate the many mourners who attended his funeral. At St. Paul's, nearby at Tenth and Christian Streets, the Solemn Requiem Mass was celebrated by its pastor with most of the prominent clergy of the archdiocese in attendance; the people filled the pews and crowded the streets outside. Ironically, the final rites for the founding rector of the first Italian church had to be held at a site that would eventually develop a reputation, or perhaps already had, as one that did not welcome Italians among its members.[30]

Mariani bequeathed his small church and residence without any debt, a material legacy that had modestly prospered and grown under his stewardship, and left his other belongings to Bishop James Wood in trust for his pastoral successors and their congregations. Mindful of his own spiritual needs, Mariani willed $600 to a Franciscan convent in Allegheny, New York, for 1,200 masses for the repose of his soul, and the remainder, slightly in excess of $600, to religious institutions in Philadelphia. But his main bequest—church property that already belonged to the diocese—was a prelude to unpleasant complications. Property ownership, parish control, and lay trustees had long been troublesome issues and brought great turmoil from the time of Mariani's death until Antonio Isoleri's arrival four years later. They would not only close the Italian Mission temporarily but would also nearly extinguish it permanently.[31]

Sorrentini:
Priest and Pamphleteer

Mariani was succeeded as a pastor by Sorrentini, whose prior experience made
· him appear to be a good choice for the Italian church. But before long, his appointment brought it to the brink of disaster. Although Sorrentini already had
an impressive record as a priest, his sometimes controversial past, intertwined
with broader aspects of Church history in America, suggested that his leadership would augur a less favorable future for St. Mary Magdalen dePazzi.

Almost immediately after becoming bishop of Philadelphia in 1852, Neumann encountered several issues that seriously challenged his administration
of the diocese. Among these problems, the Vincentian order, which had staffed
the faculty of the diocesan seminary of St. Charles Borromeo since 1841 but
which now recognized a lack of priests for their other labors, concluded that it
was necessary to relinquish this responsibility. At about the same time, Father
Thaddeus Amat, the rector of the seminary, was appointed as the new bishop of
Monterey, California. As the Vincentians departed from the seminary, another
member of the order, Father John Tornatore, consented to serve one year as pro-
rector to facilitate its transfer to the control of diocesan clergy.[32]

When he assumed his new position in California, Bishop Amat appointed Sorrentini as the secretary of the Diocese of Monterey. Born in Rome on
August 1815, and receiving his early education in Naples, he had returned to the
city of his birth to attend the Collegio Romano before being ordained there in
1839. For a few years, Sorrentini taught Scripture and Theology at a seminary
at Amalfi, near Naples. The Congregation of Propaganda Fide then sent him
for about three years to the patriarchate of Jerusalem, where he was involved
in the establishment of St. John's Hospital, before health problems forced him
to return to Rome. In the autumn of 1854, Sorrentini appeared to have joined
other missionaries in their westward trek in America as Amat's secretary and
as a pastor in Monterey. But Sorrentini surfaced in Philadelphia in the ensuing
year. At age thirty-six and as a subject of the Papal States, he filed a declaration of intention to become an American citizen. In another five years, in 1860,
specifically renouncing his political allegiance to Pope Pius IX, Sorrentini completed his naturalization proceedings in Philadelphia. But it was at this time
that he was also reported to be the vicar general in Monterey and a pastor in
Santa Barbara.[33]

During these years, Sorrentini manifested ability and ambition, requesting
an honorary title of Apostolic Missionary in 1855. Propaganda Fide responded
by rejecting his request as inappropriate on account of his actual position as a
missionary but named him as Missionary of the Diocese of Monterey. But old
scores continued to haunt Sorrentini. In 1856, Propaganda Fide informed Amat
of a claim by another priest in Jerusalem that a sum of sixteen *scudi* was still

owed to him by Sorrentini from their earlier days in the Holy Land. But these matters were mere trifles beside other problems that lay ahead for him.[34]

As vicar general, Sorrentini soon found himself at the center of a conflict between Bishop Amat and Franciscan missionaries in California. By early 1858 a spirited exchange of letters debated the Franciscans' role in California before higher authorities at Propaganda Fide in Rome. Amat appeared to be ready to recommend, and perhaps already had proposed, that the Franciscans be removed, or else he and his own priests would depart from the diocese. In January 1858 the superior general of the Franciscan order responded that Amat's prejudice against the friars resulted from the influence of his advisers and in particular of Sorrentini, whose animosity against them went back to his days in the Holy Land.[35]

Amat sent Sorrentini to Rome in March, ostensibly to recruit priests for the Monterey diocese, but also to report on the dispute with the Franciscans and to defend himself before Propaganda Fide. In a letter to Propaganda Fide supporting the Franciscans, Archbishop J. S. Alemany of San Francisco conveyed their fear that Sorrentini had been sent to deliver complaints about them to Rome. But while Sorrentini remained the subject of correspondence, Propaganda Fide not only acknowledged his primary task as finding priests for his diocese, it also announced that a student from the Vincentian seminary of Brignole Sale in Genoa would be assigned to Monterey.[36]

By the autumn of 1858 the focus in the dispute between Amat and the Franciscans had shifted to Sorrentini. Although Amat still defended Sorrentini against the charges brought by the Franciscans, the situation eventually forced Sorrentini to leave Monterey. He described his unhappy condition and state of mind in a letter to a friend. Released from his obligations to the Diocese of Monterey, Sorrentini would serve briefly in a parish in Louisiana.[37]

Sorrentini had returned by this time to Philadelphia, as his naturalization in 1860 indicates, where he became preoccupied with revolutionary politics in Italy. His brief tract, *New Lights and True Light on the Revolution in Italy,* carried the approbation of the bishop of Philadelphia (presumably the site of its publication) on its title page and identified its author as a Roman citizen, despite Sorrentini's naturalization in that year. As its author, Sorrentini condemned the struggle for independence and unification in Italy, which, rather than being seen as the wish of its people, was the work of secret societies "begotten of hatred to the Catholic religion, of the Piedmontese thirst for aggrandizement, of English bigotry and French ambition." The final act of "this deplorable tragedy" would present "Cavour, Garibaldi, Mazzini, the personifications of Machiavellianism, piracy, and communism, enthroning a libertine monarch on the ruins of religion, that in the loss of his temporal dominion the Pope may be a slave, and the Church, the creature of the State."[38]

In the next year, Sorrentini produced a similar tract, dedicated to Bishop Wood, with Philadelphia as the location of the author, and a local newspaper, the

Catholic Herald and Visitor, as its publisher. In introductory remarks addressed
to Wood, the author described a recent occasion at a private home, apparently
in the same city, in which men and women of different faiths had joined him in
a discussion of Italian politics. After attempting to clarify their understanding
of the situation, he had decided that the long and complicated answer required
him to write a pamphlet that would prove that "the present war in Italy is a war
directed against the Church, intended for its destruction; and that the Italian
hierarchy has never demeaned itself by association with the atheistical tyrants
for the elevation of a false liberty; and that it has, on that account, been subjected to cruel and arbitrary persecution."[39]

Sorrentini's pamphlet was a more scholarly and astute analysis of the Italian situation than his previous one. He cleverly placed the voice of Wood into
his argument by quoting from a letter that the bishop had sent to Pius IX, while
pointing out that the diocese had recently contributed nearly $30,000 in sup-
port of the Holy See. Sorrentini had not only presented a vigorous defense of
the papacy for the public in Philadelphia but had also conspicuously positioned
its bishop in the document by his ingratiating remarks. Having left California,
shrouded in controversy, he was now securing his position in a new location. In
the aftermath of his scuffle with the Franciscans, however, Sorrentini was not
only establishing his reputation with the bishop of Philadelphia but resolving
matters with Rome as well.

Despite his erudite support for the papacy, authorities in Rome remained
uncertain about Sorrentini. He wrote to Propaganda Fide from St. Peter's Church
in New Castle, Delaware, after being appointed its pastor in March 1865.[40] In
reply to a request for an explanation of his whereabouts, Sorrentini sent his
tracts on Italian politics and twenty *scudi* to the pope as Peter's Pence along with
a letter in which he attempted to defend himself.[41] His efforts soon produced
the results that he sought.

Wood found Sorrentini to have appropriate credentials for the appointment as Mariani's successor as rector of the Italian church. Reputed to be "a
ripe scholar, and an accomplished linguist, having mastered nine languages, an
accomplishment that aided him in parochial work of mixed nationalities,"
Sorrentini, with his penchant for music and painting and his energy at phi-
lanthropy, all together supposedly made him widely popular. He was also an
experienced administrator, a protégé of Amat, and a fiercely supportive and articulate defender of the papacy.[42] By his lavish praise in his writings, Sorrentini
had already not only demonstrated his loyalty to Wood but had also earned the
confidence of the bishop. And whatever problems he may have had with the
disgruntled friars in California, these matters of the past deserved to be forgotten. In March 1866, Wood appointed Sorrentini to the post of rector of St. Mary
Magdalen dePazzi.[43]

"A Period of Trouble"

Despite a promising beginning, instead of the long and fruitful period that might have been anticipated at this point, Sorrentini's tenure was a brief and trouble-plagued time for St. Mary Magdalen dePazzi. And it culminated in a serious threat to the mission that would be masked by discreet silence in subsequent years. Sorrentini's pastorate lasted less than one year, from March 1866 to February 1867. In later years it would be recalled that he "remained in charge only a few months, on account of some misunderstanding between him and the people [before] the church was closed for a time."[44] In a few more years, it was even more tersely remembered: "A period of trouble and Church closed." By all accounts, it was a time that many people preferred to forget.[45]

The circumstances of the closing can now be reconstructed. Although sacramental records show an almost entirely Italian population, other sources reveal a more diverse congregation as well as a new identity for the church. Even before Mariani's death, a newspaper describing the Forty Hours Devotion in late January 1866 identified it as "the little Italian Church of St. Marie Madeleine dePazzi" and noted that the preaching was done both in Italian and English, "as a large part of the congregation speak the latter tongue."[46] The new version of the name cannot be dismissed as an error, but rather hinted at a French element that would grow more visible in the near future.

After becoming rector, Sorrentini made physical improvements to the church for which, while placing him in financial debt to Bishop Wood, he received compliments from the public. A new altar, with a fine fresco painting above it, was erected. A marble statue of the Blessed Virgin had been given to the church, and one of Saint Joseph was being sculpted by another artist. In April 1866, Sorrentini signed a note indicating a debt of $1,000 to Wood for repairs.[47] Although incorrectly spelling his name as "Father Sarrantino," a newspaper noted that the Italian Catholic Church on Marriott Street, below Eighth, "has been much improved since the institution of the present Pastor."[48] But as later improvements were reported, with more compliments for its rector (with his name properly spelled), St. Mary Magdalen dePazzi had become the Church of the Immaculate Conception.[49]

When the diocesan press reported in 1866 that May devotions to the Blessed Virgin were being celebrated for the first time in the Church of the Immaculate Conception, what was occurring was clear. In effect, St. Mary Magdalen dePazzi was being treated as a new church. With Wood attending and Sorrentini preaching in French and Italian, a certain Miss McCaffrey delighted the congregation with her fine singing, but her choice of language was not reported. During the same month, devotions were conducted in English and Italian in the morning and in French in the evening. On the final Sunday of May, a procession of French girls and other Catholics closed the ceremonies. Commending Sorrentini for his zeal, another newspaper account declared that if it could be enlarged, Immaculate Conception would rank among the leading churches of the city.[50]

During the summer of 1866, the presence of the French in the congregation continued to be noted. When the Feast of the Assumption was celebrated, with what was described as an immense crowd attending, the church was far too small, and influential residents of the neighborhood were being urged to have it enlarged. Again it was identified as the Church of the Immaculate Conception when it was reported that "the French element is largely represented in this church; there were some 400 of that nationality present during the services on Sunday. As to the Irish, *ça va sans dire.*"[51] While the French still were a novelty, the Irish could be taken for granted. In subsequent weeks an Irish Augustinian from Dublin, seeking donations from American Catholics, preached at one mass while Sorrentini gave sermons in Italian and French. The Church of the Immaculate Conception offered something for each of its constituent groups.[52]

In the autumn of 1866 the Church of the Immaculate Conception, as it had come to be known, while still also called "the Italian church," projected a healthy condition and promising future. In November its annual fair made a substantial profit, while its rector was commended for his energy and devotion. In December, on the feast day of its new patron saint, an elaborate agenda reflected the complexity of the congregation. At the first High Mass in the morning, Sorrentini preached in Italian. At a later mass on the same day, with "a special choir" providing "splendid music," Father P. A. Stanton, an Augustinian priest, gave the homily in English to the Irish congregants. At evening vespers and Benediction, Sorrentini spoke in French.[53]

The transition from Mariani to Sorrentini had been a critical one for the church. The change of its name (and patron saint) from St. Mary Magdalen dePazzi to the Immaculate Conception of the Blessed Virgin, along with the diversity of its congregation, reflected an effort to transform it. How this sequence of events unfolded remains less obvious. Founded as the Italian Mission with an Irish presence, the French had apparently entered it. The offering of services in their language reflected another ethnic population in the neighborhood, but the diocese was now also designating the Church of the Immaculate Conception as the site of worship for French Catholics throughout the city.

One aspect of the situation was easily anticipated and understood—the reaction of the Italians as they watched what was once theirs becoming something else. While the Irish had always had a place in the congregation, they took only a limited part in the activities. But the increasing French presence represented a more serious threat. And the new name and patron saint were portents of further loss and change, at least for the Italians. The volatile experiment that was taking place in the parochial laboratory on Marriott Street was heading toward an explosion.

At the center of the situation, Sorrentini, despite his success in some matters, had been provoking resentment even from the altar by harshly criticizing the Italian members of his congregation. He did not wish to see women who were poorly dressed in the church and was even ready to have them escorted out of the building. By claiming that the Italians were all "organ grinders," he offended them further. He made a cryptic allusion to the carrying of pistols and knives. And he announced that a monthly charge of ten *soldi* (about fifty cents) would be assessed on anyone who wanted to attend services. In response, his critics spread the rumor that he would prefer to set fire to the church than have it run by the Italians. If these charges were true, it would seem that Sorrentini was more suited to discussing his ideas and writings in the parlors of affluent Philadelphians than in serving the Italians of the parish.[54]

The tumultuous events of the year and one-half following Sorrentini's appointment brought about the most precarious period in the early history of St. Mary Magdalen dePazzi. Controversy and crisis would not only close the church but would also eventually restore its original character. In January 1867 a group of discontented Italians met to elect nine trustees. Although the trustees believed that they were acting in conformity with legislation by the state assembly, an article in the Catholic press expressed some concern: "This church is commonly known as the 'Italian church.' . . . Though so called, the ever faithful Irish comprise the great mass of the congregation, and consequently are, almost the only support of the church." It maintained that the Irish members were more in number, better Catholics, and more generous in financial support than the Italians. It also questioned the election of the trustees on the grounds that the church had never been incorporated; thus, "we are at a loss to understand by what right these Italians are thus acting." But the Italians had already executed the first maneuver in their battle to regain control of the church that had once been theirs alone.[55]

The actual condition of the Italian Mission was partly revealed by the financial statement prepared by Sorrentini for the period from March 1866, when he became its rector, to his departure in February 1867. He reported $5,957 in expenses for the maintenance of the church and rectory along with $4,789 in credits. In addition to $1,584 from collections, Sorrentini listed $2,000 received from Bishop Wood; $130 from an excursion; $1,000 from the annual fair; and another $75 "from Italians." Under Sorrentini's management, the church was not prospering.[56] The modest amount "from Italians," listed separately from collections, not only confirmed the greater support of the Irish but also suggested that the Italians found themselves a separate congregation within their own church. But their meager financial support was less the cause of a problem than it was an effect of a broader conflict between them and their rector.

Within what had been founded as their own church, the Italians had witnessed the steady deterioration of their position until it reached a crucial point, when Bishop Wood, who recognized the seriousness of the situation, requested their newly elected trustees to meet with him in January 1867. In a report on the meeting, undoubtedly reflecting the official view of the diocese, the *Catholic Standard,* under the now-familiar heading of "The Church of the Immaculate Conception," stated that it had formerly been called St. Mary Magdalen dePazzi, and Catholics of the southern section of the city still knew it as "the Italian Church." But it continued: "For some time past a difficulty has existed between the present pastor, Rev. G. Sorrentini, and a few discontented Italians, whose efforts are directed towards obtaining control of the Church." After noting that the Italians had engaged an attorney, it reiterated the argument that since the church had not been legally incorporated under lay ownership but was held in the name of ecclesiastical authority, the trustees could not gain control or possession.[57]

Interdict

Bishop Wood had not been at all receptive to the plight of the Italians. Addressing them in Italian at their meeting in early 1867, he declared that he had not come to argue with them, but only to offer his views. Reminding them that they had received the benefits of religious instruction in their own language when Father Mariani was their rector, Wood maintained that they still enjoyed this privilege, despite recent troubling events. But in responding to the petition that stated their grievances and expressed the hope that he would approve of their actions, Wood delivered a blow. He told them that the petition was not only not pleasing but also offensive.

Wood's opposition was mainly based upon the persistent threat that trusteeism had represented for the Church in Philadelphia. With an implied reference to Hoganism, the bishop informed the Italians that the history of administration by trustees had been a sorrowful one. And now they had elected trustees who, if it were in their power, would take all authority away from their bishop. After insisting that ecclesiastical property must be held by the Church, Wood unfolded a thinly veiled threat to the Italians. If it were held by trustees, rather than by the Church, he warned them that such a state of affairs would mean that their church not only would be without an altar but also without the sacraments. Whatever the Italians understood at this point, what Wood had in mind would be made abundantly clear four months later.

The meeting ended with the bishop reasserting his authority over the dissidents. He insisted that they must not only cease any further wrongful actions but must also undo what they had already done. Stating that he would do all that was necessary for the welfare of the church, Wood added that as a general commands his army or a captain does his ship, so a bishop must command in ecclesiastical affairs. And he ordered the Italians henceforth to be examples of piety, faith, humility, and devotion.

One almost immediate result of the dispute between Wood and the Italian trustees was the removal of Sorrentini. Whether he resigned voluntarily or was dismissed by the bishop, its second rector left St. Mary Magdalen dePazzi in February 1867.[58] With his departure, however, the conflict was still not resolved; it had simply taken on another dimension. The appointment of a new priest, now added to the agenda of issues that separated the Italians and Church authorities, would further aggravate the contention between them.

Wishing to avoid a repetition of the Hoganism era, Wood had intervened quickly and directly, but his early efforts failed. While he had attempted to reason with the Italians, he had also threatened and intimidated them. Now, locked in conflict with adversaries whose people in their native country were at war with the Papal States, Wood had underestimated their willingness to accept submission to ecclesiastical authority or to give up their own struggle with the Church in this country as well. After their meeting in January, another letter to the bishop, signed by eight trustees, showed the precise concerns that the Italians placed before Wood in March 1867:

> The undersigned Trustees of the Italian Church of the Immaculata Concezione, formerly Santa Maria Madalena dePazzi, elected in conformity with the Acts of Assembly of the Commonwealth of Pennsylvania respectfully represent that the said Church and property thereto attached is not receiving the attention and care necessary for its preservation and protection—. That the person ostensibly in charge of said property is careless of his trust, and neglectfull [sic] of his duties as a Custodian—. That he is seldom to be seen or found upon the premises, and being engaged in another business, at a considerable distance from the place where his services are required, the said property is exposed to depredations, and in reality suffers for want of proper supervision.
>
> Your Trustees, very respectfully request that your Reverence will direct that the keys of said property shall be placed in their hands, and that they will become responsible for the security and good condition of the property and liquidate all expenses incurred therefore—. In calling your attention to this matter, we do so with the hope that the seriousness and importance of the Complaints made by the Italian Congregation will induce your Reverence to give us speedy information upon the points stated, accompanied by your authority to receive the Keys referred to—. Will your Reverence please oblige us with an immediate answer, that we may leave what other procedings [sic] it may be necessary for us to adopt—.[59]

The letter again indicated, as the *Catholic Standard* had noted two months earlier, that the object of discontent was Sorrentini himself and that the protesters included prominent members of the Italian community. But while the letter was carefully constructed and politely expressed, Wood's reaction remained unfavorable and would not become any better.

The Italians again pleaded their case in another letter, with the same return address (821 Carpenter Street), on May 20. With Sorrentini gone, the absence of a priest was a matter of great concern. The trustees, learning that Wood was about to leave for Rome, implored him to appoint a priest, whom they claimed had been promised, as rector. They also expressed their fear that they would be left without a priest.[60] Wood, however, had already decided on his next step. Less than one week later, on Sunday, May 26, he applied his strongest sanction against them:

> We make known by the present circular to all the faithful under our jurisdiction that the celebration of Mass, the administration and reception of the Sacraments, as well as all and any religious ceremonies, are forbidden in the church of St. Mary Magdalen diPazzi. And that it is forbidden to all the Faithful to be present at Mass, to receive the Sacraments or to assist at any religious ceremonies in the same church under penalty of incurring the usual ecclesiastical censures. This prohibition will remain in force until removed by Our Authority.[61]

In his letter, co-signed by Father August J. McConomy, diocesan secretary, Wood placed the church under interdict and closed it entirely. The letter referred to St. Mary Magdalen dePazzi rather than to the Church of the Immaculate Conception. The same message was also given in Italian "a tutti gli Italiani fedeli di questa Chiesa di Santa Maria Magdalena di Pazzi."[62] The use of Italian implied that the Irish and French members were not among the insurgents and therefore did not need to be addressed.

Realizing that they had no chance of success by appealing any further to local Church authorities, the trustees placed their case before Pius IX in Rome. On June 4, six trustees addressed a message offering their own interpretation of the situation to the Holy Father. On behalf of the Italian colony in Philadelphia, they expressed their dissatisfaction with the now-departed Sorrentini as well as with Bishop Wood. They focused on Wood's closing of the church, which had occurred on a day when it was "regurgitating with people expecting to assist at mass," and on his failure to appoint another priest, thus depriving its people of the comforts of religion. The Italians even proposed one "Rossi" as the priest whom they had in mind to replace Sorrentini. And on one matter they appeared especially adamant: they did not care where he came from, but their new priest must speak "the Italian language and dialect." Their petition pleaded the case of families ignorant of the language of their new country who could not otherwise express themselves, those adults who would die without the comforts of religion, and those children who were forced to attend Protestant schools where they found themselves "awash with perniciousness."[63]

The dissident trustees, having greatly underestimated Wood's power, appeared to have little chance of actually prevailing in any dispute with him. After converting from Protestantism, Wood had spent one year as a seminarian at the College of Propaganda Fide in Rome. As an alumnus and "insider" for any issue placed before Propaganda Fide, as this one would be, Wood had not merely a great advantage but an insurmountable one. And if personal relationships and past experiences were not enough to consolidate Wood's power in Rome, the Holy See had an obligation to the bishop of Philadelphia for financial support that was greater than that of any other American prelate. With extraordinarily bad timing, the Italians had placed their petition before the authorities in Rome in late June 1867, when Wood had personally presented to the pope a donation of about $60,000, the largest sum ever contributed by any diocese in the United States.[64]

The response from Rome in September, however, contained a surprise. In a brief letter, signed with "Carissimo Fratello" before his name, Cardinal Alessandro Barnabò, the prefect of Propaganda Fide, indicated that although the pope regarded the conduct of the parish trustees to be semi-schismatic, he advised Wood to name a worthy priest to the Italian church.[65] Perhaps Wood himself had become more conciliatory, but the decision from the pope and Propaganda Fide appeared to be a substantial victory for the Italian trustees. Sorrentini, the object of their complaints, had been deposed. Saint Mary Magdalen dePazzi had been restored as the patron. The parish would be reopened. And the leaders of the dissent would remain, as least for a little while, as trustees.

On his return from Rome the trustees presented another letter to Wood in September, which began with a diplomatic expression of obedience but ended with a clear indication of their intention to persist in defiance. In their native language, they politely informed him that they, as trustees of the Italian church of St. Mary Magdalen dePazzi, together with all other Italian residents of the city, rejoiced in hearing of his most pleasant trip to Rome as well as of his perfect health, and finally of his most happy return to the diocese. After this declaration of deference, however, the trustees turned to the issues that interested Wood even more. They expressed their confidence that his goodwill and clemency would soon bring an Italian priest to minister to the four hundred souls who had been deprived of the comforts of the religion in whose womb they were born and wished to die, but who at present were like a flock without a shepherd, scattered in the most remote corners of the earth. And so they hoped that his kind heart would no longer permit such disorder and disgrace. They also reaffirmed the readiness of the entire congregation to support the priest who might be sent to them as well as the Church and their religion.[66]

It was not a statement of any further resistance by the trustees or congregation, but one of almost complete submission, until its final paragraph, which presented a clear ultimatum to the bishop. The trustees declared that if he remained *ostinato* (stubborn or pigheaded) and unwilling to comply with their request for an Italian priest, they would not only ring out the news of his answer but also seek to exercise their right to an Italian priest in some other manner. Given Wood's character, it was neither a message that he could accept with equanimity nor a proposal that was likely to incur his support. But despite this challenge to his authority, the solution to the affair was not far away.

In the autumn of 1867, Wood gave his own version in a letter to Propaganda Fide of why he had found it necessary to place the Italian church under interdict and why he would not accept "Rossi" as its pastor. Recounting the background of the dispute, he expressed his great sorrow at having to take the action. But along with Sorrentini's lively manner, Wood cited the influence of certain malicious individuals in the congregation as the main source of the trouble. He characterized the trustees as being rash and presumptuous as well as ignorant and ill mannered. After noting that they had turned to civil law to pursue their aim of gaining control of the church, he was especially annoyed by their changing the locks on the doors of the property shortly after his action in May. But he also indicated his hope that an Italian-speaking priest would soon be appointed.[67] In December, Propaganda Fide again advised him on how to handle the problem of the Italian church.[68] After several months of silence, in a letter to Propaganda Fide in early April 1868, Wood reported "the happy news that our good Italians have made a full and most perfect submission."[69]

The Restoration of Order

With this resolution of the conflict between trustees and bishop, St. Mary Magdalen dePazzi was reopened and a period of healing began. In the end the parish was not only renewed, but it entered a period of steady growth and stability. In the same month that Wood informed Rome of the compliance of the Italians, he also named a Jesuit, Father Charles Cicaterri, as rector. Born in Rome in 1817, Cicaterri had entered the order in 1846 before teaching at the Jesuit novitiate in Frederick City, Maryland, in the 1850s and at Georgetown College in Washington, DC, in the 1860s.[70] Although Cicaterri, the first of several temporary rectors at St. Mary Magdalen dePazzi, was only intended to serve on loan from his order until the usual operations of the church could be restored, signs of rebirth began to appear during his five months from April to September 1868. In June 1868 the *Catholic Standard* carried an item under the heading of "Santa Maria Maddalena dePazzi," an emphatic gesture to the restoration of the church's Italian identity. In the same month, Wood assisted Cicaterri by preaching at a mass, probably his first participation in any function at the church since the interdict had been lifted. But even more important, it also meant that the Italian Mission was returning to favor with the bishop.[71]

After a few more months, Wood appointed Father James Rolando, a Vincentian, as the second of the temporary rectors at St. Mary Magdalen dePazzi. Born in Pieve di Teco in 1815, Rolando came to the United States in 1842, was ordained to the priesthood in New Orleans, and began a career in which he held almost every important position in his order. He served as Master of Novices at its seminary in Missouri, then as Visitor of the Congregation to the United States for six years. Rolando returned to Italy and became the director of the Vincentian seminary of Brignole Sale in Genoa in 1862. During this period, Rolando met a student, Antonio Isoleri, who made a highly favorable impression on him. When Rolando returned to America, sometime in late 1868 or early 1869, he succeeded Cicaterri at the Italian church in Philadelphia, where he served for about eight months before being sent to Paris by his order.[72]

After his departure from St. Mary Magdalen dePazzi, James Rolando was succeeded by Father Joseph Rolando, a native of the Piedmont assigned to the Diocese of Newark, New Jersey, who only remained at the Italian church in Philadelphia until October 1870. But during his eight months as its rector, St. Mary Magdalen dePazzi continued its recovery. In January 1869 the *Catholic Standard* reported that the Forty Hours Devotion had been held in the "neat little Italian church."[73] In the next month it conducted religious instruction and devotions on Tuesday evenings, with Stations of the Cross and Benediction on Friday evenings until the end of Lent.[74] On Ascension Thursday in May, Bishop Wood again visited St. Mary Magdalen dePazzi, offering mass and distributing First Communion to fifteen children, confirming thirty-one other persons, and addressing them in Italian, before a procession closed the ceremonies. In December, the celebration of Christmas at St. Mary Magdalen dePazzi, under Father Rolondo, was noted as having "met with the greatest success."[75] The church appeared also to have reached financial solvency and contributed $148 in a special collection for the pope at the same time.[76]

Another problem—the expedient, but undesirable, temporary appointment of priests at St. Mary Magdalen dePazzi—remained. And the recent debacle involving Sorrentini and the trustees made a better choice for its rector urgent if the church were to have a future at all. In May 1869, Bishop Wood wrote Cardinal Barnabò to request a graduate of the Collegio Brignole Sale for the Italian Mission in Philadelphia. Since returning from Genoa, James Rolando, remembering an outstanding seminarian there, had recommended Antonio Isoleri to Wood for the position. Propaganda Fide forwarded Wood's request to the rector of the seminary, who, in his reply to Propaganda Fide in June, proposed Isoleri. In the following month, Propaganda Fide notified Wood that Isoleri had been assigned to the Diocese of Philadelphia. As eager to assume his appointment as Wood had been to solve his problem, Isoleri did not have to wait long. On November 24, 1869, he sailed for America. In October 1870, when Joseph Rolando ended his brief term as rector, Isoleri began his tenure as the "second founder" of St. Mary Magdalen dePazzi.[77]

Although an Italian presence had long preceded Isoleri's arrival in Philadelphia, it was, along with its church, about to enter an important new phase.[78] Itinerant Italian musicians and artists had visited the city since the middle of the previous century. In the first decades of the nineteenth century, along with performers and teachers of art and music, an increasing number of other Italians had begun to settle permanently in the city—as tavern owners, entertainment impresarios, language teachers, food and tobacco shopkeepers, and importers. While the local economy remained preindustrial, Italians lived and worked in widely scattered locations throughout the city. Unlike larger immigrant groups, they had not yet gathered together in ways that announced a collective presence to other Philadelphians. With limited relations and cooperation among themselves, they had not yet formed a community in the early years of the nineteenth century.

By the 1850 Federal Census, however, Philadelphia's Italians, mainly from Liguria but also from Tuscany and with a handful from other regions, having grown noticeably in numbers, had begun to concentrate in areas along the southern boundary of the city. By this time, newcomers in shared lodgings also reflected the development of communal patterns in their living and work arrangements. But, in contrast to those in New York City, Philadelphia's Italians were conspicuously absent from local demonstrations supporting republicanism and independence for Italy. With more personal aspirations and lower political consciousness, they primarily sought work in the expanding economy of the city. And over the next two decades the Italians continued to evolve from a small, inchoate population to a larger community of residential clusters, voluntary associations, private property ownership, commercial enterprises, civic leadership, and social stratification. In this context the recent troubles at the Italian church had not only set the agenda for the immediate future but had also left a perception of the local bishop among its congregation that Isoleri would soon encounter as its new pastor. And if he ever believed that the political turmoil of his homeland had been entirely left behind, Isoleri would discover, as did other Italians, that it had not only preceded him but also remained an important part of his life in Philadelphia. If the dispute over the Italian chapel had created a tempest in the immigrant community, the politics of Italy was drawing Philadelphia's Catholics into a larger storm of controversy.

CHAPTER **TWO**

European Politics, American Catholicism, and Italian Immigration

In the climate of the 1860s, the politics of nation and world amplified the politics of parish and diocese, and St. Mary Magdalen dePazzi Church found itself in the middle of a grander stage. Italian Catholics, whether still living in their native land or as immigrants in foreign places, faced personal challenges that coincided with larger battles. For Philadelphia's Italians, the struggle for independence in Italy complicated their role in a new city and nation. Like their counterparts in their homeland, the conflict between the forces of a new nation and an old faith reflected the one between their identity as Italians and their fidelity as Catholics. To some extent, it was an experience shared by other Catholics in America, regardless of their ethnic origins.

American Catholicism and the Risorgimento

During these turbulent times, American Catholics were confronted with several issues in their efforts to support the papacy against republican and anticlerical nationalists in Italy. What they were asked to do, what they could do, and what they eventually did required debate among themselves as well as development in their identity as citizens of their nation and adherents to their faith. In their support for the papacy, American Catholics mobilized four principal resources: newspaper propaganda, military volunteers, financial contributions, and public demonstrations. The consequences not only eventually defined the relationship of American Catholics to the Italian struggle for nationhood but also set parameters for the subsequent experience of Italians in America.

In Philadelphia and other cities, support for the papacy, after a conspicuous silence, often followed a sequence that began with press exhortations and ended with public demonstrations. After the Nativist riots (street clashes between Catholics and Protestants that paralyzed the city) two decades earlier, Philadelphia Catholics by the 1860s had assumed a relatively quiet and passive stance, neither presenting themselves as a political bloc at the polling place nor appearing in public protests. An 1864 editorial in the diocesan newspaper, decrying the fact that "the Catholics of this city seem to despise all prominent representation," asked why no significant voice, conduct, or influence could be found among the 133,000 Catholics in the city, and it called on them to unite under the leaders who were being urged to come forward. But while seeking to avoid any repetition of the violence that had wracked the city in 1844, Catholics had not yet found a sufficient cause to resort to overt action. But before the decade ended, as their situation changed, Philadelphia's Catholics would emerge in a united, visible expression of their beliefs and interests. At the urging of their own hierarchy at home, the defense of their faith, or more precisely their support for the Church in Rome against the efforts of Italian nationalists, provided the cause.[1]

The Catholic Press and the Risorgimento

While American Catholic opinion in general toward the struggle for Italian independence and unification remains less clear, the views of the Catholic press were more visible. In Philadelphia, Catholic newspapers often reported events and expressed opinions on conditions in Italy.[2] An 1864 editorial, for example, in assessing one leader who would remain the object of sharp criticism throughout these years, stated its conviction that the temporal power and territorial integrity of the Church had more than human protection:

> Garibaldi's banner has inscribed on it, "Rome or Death." And Rome or death is the aim of his life. . . .
> But Rome belongs to the Popes. . . . It is plain that this is not a mere human fact. It evidently has a divine cause. Can such a creature as Garibaldi undo it? Impossible. The Church is the Church of God. Rome has always been the governmental seat of the Church. Would Heaven permit such a creature as Garibaldi to revert such a fact? Common sense answers, no![3]

Catholic journalism, however, was defined by more than religious affiliation; its staffs and political character were almost entirely Irish during these years. The Catholic press often carried more news about events in Ireland than in America. Some newspapers routinely published classified listings of births, marriages, and deaths in Ireland. This emphasis also contributed to the position taken toward the Italian situation. When it did not directly object to British politics in Ireland, the Catholic press opposed England's role in other countries, such as in Italy. When Giuseppe Garibaldi met the prince of Wales in London in 1864, a Philadelphia Catholic paper seized the opportunity to condemn England: "But is not the Prince a Guelph, and did not all Protestant England prostrate itself before Garibaldi, chiefly because he had 'Death to the Papacy!' inscribed on his lawless banner? . . . Princes are often punished by their own weapons. What country would weep if this should be the case in the present instance? None. The nations hate England for its wickedness."[4]

After the brief, ill-fated Roman Republic, when Garibaldi offered his followers only "hunger, thirst, forced marches, battles and death" in their retreat from Rome, he captured the minds and hearts not only of Italians but also of supporters of republicanism throughout the world. At the same time, he also gained the animosity and opposition of the Catholic Church. When he returned to the battlefields of his homeland in 1859–60, after his success against the forces of the Kingdom of Naples, Garibaldi sought to continue his campaign until he defeated papal troops and their French allies and took possession of Rome. But his plan was aborted by the fateful encounter of Garibaldi and his small army of guerrillas with King Victor Emmanuel and Piedmontese forces in October 1860. In 1862, when Garibaldi attempted to take Rome with another band of volunteers, his effort was abruptly halted with his defeat and wounding at Aspromonte. When his next attempt to reach Rome was thwarted by the French and papal forces at Mentana in 1867, Garibaldi had solidified his place as the object of Catholic vituperation.[5]

By their earlier success, nationalists had gained most of the territory of the former Papal States for the new Kingdom of Italy. After 1860, Garibaldi's objectives had shifted toward the remaining papal territory, but particularly the city of Rome. With the "Roman question," the Catholic press in America increased its defense of the Papal States, by now reduced to the Eternal City and its surrounding region.

In Philadelphia, Catholic newspapers sought to discredit Garibaldi by separating him from a revolution whose impending success could no longer be denied. Under the headline, "Garibaldi and Rome," an 1867 editorial argued: "This notorious brigand has again come to the surface, and has issued an address announcing that the time is at hand to overthrow the rule of the pope in Rome, and restore that city to the Kingdom of Italy." To the *Catholic Standard*, Garibaldi had no legitimacy as a revolutionary, being nothing more than a "notorious brigand," indeed a "red republican and guerilla." Its analysis of the Italian situation disconnected ordinary people from leaders who were dangerous to papal interests.

Declaring that "the majority of the Italian people are in favor of the pope retaining his temporal power, and are content to live under his authority," it also sought to distinguish Victor Emmanuel from other political figures, albeit by a tenuous margin. By the recent treaty with France, he had pledged to protect papal territory and proclaimed it a crime for Italians to join or aid any movement against Rome. The editorial concluded: "while we look upon Victor Emmanuel as little better than Garibaldi," Napoleon III was compelled to see that Italy respect the treaty, thus ensuring that the Holy Father would triumph over his enemies.[6]

During the autumn of 1867, the *Catholic Standard* expanded its argument. Workers and peace advocates at a conference in Geneva were described as "so ridiculous as to have brought down on them the laughter of all Europe." But while arguing that the Red Shirt republicans of European politics, beyond being enemies of the pope and Catholicism, opposed all forms of worship, it again made Garibaldi the target. When he appeared at the meeting in Geneva, clad in red shirt and Aspromonte wound, Garibaldi offered several proposals. While the first five were nothing more than "the usual platitudes and flummery," the next two, in which he called for the abolition of the papacy and the adoption of a religion of reason, truth, and God, enraged the Catholic press.[7]

The provocation came from more than Garibaldi's words at the conference in Switzerland. As an irate Philadelphia Catholic editor remarked, "God had not yet been sufficiently insulted by these miscreants, outcasts from every country in Europe." But the proposals had prompted a German delegate to declare that "Garibaldi is a second Jesus Christ; he will overthrow the counterfeiters of Christianity," and Garibaldi and his German supporter enthusiastically embraced each other. To the Catholic journalist, however, an act of blasphemy "belched forth, which we almost shrink from copying . . . we can scarcely bear to transfer it to the paper before us." Clearly, "he who admires Garibaldi, cannot be a friend of Christ, whose adorable Name that wretch allowed to be applied to himself." Describing the events at Geneva as the work of "worse than heathens" who had devised foolish things against God and Christ, the writer concluded: "he that dwelleth in Heaven hath *laughed* at them and the Lord hath *derided* them! So shall it ever be!"[8]

In late 1867 the *Catholic Standard,* continuing to depict Garibaldi as the greatest enemy of the temporal power of the papacy, contrasted him to Victor Emmanuel and to Giuseppe Mazzini, the republican revolutionary. While they also opposed the papacy and sought Rome as a political objective, Garibaldi's passion had made him "an enemy of religion and a foul-mouthed blasphemer." The newspaper even offered a back-handed compliment to Mazzini, describing him as "an infidel from the conviction of a perverted intellect." But in Garibaldi's case, it provided the astounding explanation, inconceivable to all but the most gullible Catholic readers, that his antipathy to Rome could only be understood as a result of diabolic possession.[9]

Catholic criticism included the possibility that Garibaldi had been used by others: "a fit instrument in the hands of the crafty men that are encompassing, for their own ends, the overthrow of the Temporal Power." This view ironically echoed the idealism of Garibaldi's own admirers by using the elegant metaphor that he had been "the falcon with which Italy went to hunt." But the final judgment remained an overwhelming condemnation: "We can understand the motives that impel statesmen, even when they are opposed to us, but for a maniac like Garibaldi we can have nothing but loathing."[10]

The Catholic press was not the only defender of the papacy or critic of Italian leaders. The messages of Bishop Wood and his priests, accompanied by the hint of a higher authority, served as another instrument of propaganda. Unlike Gaetano Sorrentini in his scholarly writings on Italian politics in the early 1860s, the clergy were more likely to address these issues in homilies. While most sermons and lectures have been lost to posterity, the few remaining fragments reveal a judgment similar to that of the Catholic press on political matters. But a priest sometimes surpassed the press in colorful language, such as when Father Patrick R. O'Brien, pastor of St. Peter's Church in Wilmington, Delaware, argued that "Victor Emmanuel and his followers might be well compared to so many vipers that suck the blood of the mother that gave them birth."[11]

Wood, however, was the most important Catholic voice in Philadelphia in the late 1860s. At a reception after his return from Rome in September 1867, his remarks, along with the reaction of his audience, expressed Catholic opinion on the Italian situation. When he asserted that "the Pope sits as firmly on his throne now as he did when all this agitation to overthrow him was first begun," his listeners applauded. When he mentioned "Poor Garibaldi," they laughed. When he informed them that Garibaldi, despite his promise to take Rome, had been wounded and taken prisoner at Aspromonte, they again interrupted with applause. And when he declared that Garibaldi's plans had been entirely frustrated, the audience cheered.[12]

American Volunteers for the Papal Army

While Philadelphia Catholics praised the pope and assailed the credibility and reputation of Italian nationalists by seeking to influence public opinion, other efforts to support the papacy were emerging in America and Italy. From the early stirrings of the movement for Italian independence, the papacy had recognized the inevitability of its involvement, the limitations of its resources, and the necessity for foreign support. In addition to alliances with France and Austria, the Holy See soon invited Catholics of other countries to enlist as volunteers in its defense. In 1860, when Italian forces first invaded the Papal States, it had recruited courageous adventurers for its ill-fated Irish Battalion. While their efforts had been unable to prevent the loss of papal territory in central Italy, they had set a precedent for the eventual defense of Rome itself.[13]

With the growing likelihood of an assault on Rome, a call for volunteers for the papal army was made in New York City in 1868. Early in May the *Freeman's Journal* reported that the papal government was seeking 1,000 volunteers for an American battalion of Zouaves under the command of their own officers.[14] After giving the terms for enlistment, the newspaper asked, "What say our Catholic friends?" Since the late 1840s the *Freeman's Journal* had served as Archbishop John Hughes's principal means of swaying public opinion in support of the papacy against Italian nationalism. The *Freeman's Journal* had once again picked up this cause.[15]

In Philadelphia the *Catholic Standard*, reacting cautiously to the news from New York, pointed out that an authorization for the recruitment of foreign volunteers for the pope's army could only come from the papal minister of war. Even more important, it also noted that any proposal for recruitment of Americans by a foreign government violated the Neutrality Act of 1818. The *Catholic Standard* refused to believe that Rome was so unaware of American federal law that it had authorized any plan of this sort.[16] But despite these doubts, the call for American volunteers indeed had originated in Rome. Church documents, dated May 1868, described the conditions essential for the formation of such a battalion of volunteers for the defense of the Holy See, along with a muster roll of papal infantry. At the same time, General Hermann Kanzler, pro-minister of the pontifical armed forces, had corresponded with Propaganda Fide in regard to the formation of the American battalion.[17] But as these developments transpired in Rome, an unanticipated response defeated the project.

Although willing to support the pope in other ways, several American bishops had quickly rejected the proposal. After learning that General Carlo Tevis had been authorized by the Holy See to raise a battalion of American volunteers, Bishop Martin J. Spalding of Baltimore expressed his disapproval in a letter to Propaganda Fide in May 1868. In the next month, after obtaining a recruitment circular, Spalding again indicated his opposition in another letter to Rome. Two weeks later, Spalding was joined by Archbishops John B. Purcell of Cincinnati, John McCloskey of New York, and Peter Kenrick of St. Louis in another letter that reasserted their loyalty to the Holy See, acknowledged the importance of the temporal dominion of the papacy, and recalled their prior financial support of the pope. After denouncing the intrigues of Tevis and James A. McMaster, the editor of the *Freeman's Journal*, Spalding and his colleagues argued that American Catholics could not be expected to bear the excessive expense of maintaining a volunteer battalion in the defense of Rome.[18]

The archbishops succeeded in their argument. In July 1868, Cardinal Alessandro Barnabò replied in a letter on behalf of Pius IX to Spalding, who was instructed to convey its contents to the other archbishops. Barnabò informed them that the Holy Father, after considering their contentions, had ordered that all steps in regard to the raising of an American battalion be abandoned.[19] While it had seemed implausible to the Catholic press in Philadelphia that the plan for American volunteers had originated in Rome, the correspondence of the archbishops with Propaganda Fide confirmed that it actually had. But with the pope's directive, American Catholics had to find other means of supporting the papacy.

Financial Support for the Papacy:
Peter's Pence and More

While four archbishops had opposed the recruitment of volunteers, the American hierarchy was willing to pursue other alternatives. In particular, it supported the revival of the Peter's Pence, the Anglo-Saxon tax that had been levied in the Middle Ages but had been abandoned since the Reformation. While sources differ on the details of its resumption in Europe, American participation in the revived collecting of a subsidy for the Holy See is well documented. When the Temporal Power was briefly threatened by the revolutionary movement in Rome in 1848–49, bishops in the United States solicited financial aid from their congregations. A pastoral letter, issued by the Seventh Provincial Council of Baltimore in 1849, referred to "the circumstances of peculiar difficulty in which the Chief Bishop is placed by the temporary privation of his temporal dominions and of the revenues annexed to them." It exhorted Catholics as children of the Church to demonstrate their sincere sympathy by contributing some of their worldly substance to enable the pope to meet the expenses of his government and to carry on the affairs of the Church.[20]

Although the results of the earlier effort are not clear, this initiative set a precedent for a more successful appeal twenty years later. Even before the final occupation of Rome by Italian forces, the renewed Peter's Pence had already become a principal means of income for the Holy See. Official figures are not available, but one report claimed that annual income from this collection had reached about £360,000 (or $1,850,000) by 1866. And after the occupation of Rome, the total contribution for one year reputedly approached £800,000 (or $4 million).[21]

The American hierarchy played an important part in supporting the papacy by the Peter's Pence. A pastoral letter, drafted at the Second Plenary Council in Baltimore in 1866, declared that it was essential for Catholics everywhere to aid the pope. The bishops argued that the wealth of the former Papal States in central Italy had been expropriated by the new Italian nation and that the position of the pope had become embarrassed and precarious. They directed that an annual collection be taken in all dioceses in America on the Sunday nearest the Feast of Saints Peter and Paul.

The response in Philadelphia to the bishops was generally favorable. The *Catholic Standard* emphatically supported monetary assistance to the papacy but limited its endorsement to only what had been authorized by the hierarchy.[22] In this position the newspaper still stood in opposition to its New York rival, McMaster's *Freeman's Journal*. Philadelphia pastors and their parishes answered the call of the bishops with special collections. Although Father John Kelly of St. Malachy's Church had added some criticism of Bishop Wood when he sent his contribution to Rome in June 1868, the Peter's Pence was an acceptable alternative to the military recruitment banned by federal law.[23]

The wealth of American Catholics, tapped by its hierarchy, became an important source of financial aid to Rome—a role that would not be relinquished but would grow even more significant in the years ahead. Philadelphia, moreover, had emerged as one of the principal benefactors to the papal treasury. Its churches donated $60,636 from their congregations in a special collection for the Holy Father on April 7, 1867. Even St. Mary Magdalen dePazzi, one of its poorer churches, contributed the respectable sum of $363 to this effort. As noted earlier, Wood himself had delivered about $60,000 to the pope, the largest amount from any American diocese, when he arrived in Rome in late June 1867. Two years later, Philadelphia Catholics donated another $33,950, with St. Mary Magdalen dePazzi contributing $148, in September 1869.[24]

When Wood wrote to Rome in 1872 about his Italian church in Philadelphia, he reminded Propaganda Fide of his magnanimity by including another check in support of the Peter's Pence. But while Propaganda Fide replied by expressing the gratitude of the Holy Father for the donation, it did not offer Wood much help in his problem with the Italians in Philadelphia.[25]

Public Protest:
The Cathedral Demonstration of 1870

When Napoléon III was deposed in September 1870, leaving Rome without its protector, Victor Emmanuel's forces took over the city and Pius IX retreated to the Vatican. Philadelphia's Catholics remained ready to support the papacy as well as to repudiate the criticism of not engaging in "prominent representation" that had been raised against them six years earlier. Bishop Wood soon provided them with the means. In a message read at all the churches of the diocese in November, he announced a plan for a mass meeting of the laity "to protest against the unlawful invasion and occupation of the States of the Church, and to make a public expression of our sincere veneration and affection for our Holy Father." Wood also directed that a special Pro Papa prayer be added to every mass as long as the occupation of Rome continued. On Sunday, December 4, demonstrations supporting the pope took place in several American cities with large Catholic populations as well as in London.[26]

In Philadelphia an estimated crowd of 30,000 protested not only the loss of Rome but also "the spoliation of the Holy Father." Assembling at their parishes, groups of men, behind musical bands with national flags and religious banners, marched to the Cathedral of Sts. Peter and Paul. Some 10,000 men were able to enter, while the rest crowded the streets outside. Various ethnic groups besides the Italians were represented among the marchers. Of 108 vice presidents and eight secretaries appointed to organize the demonstration, only two names appear— J. M. Olivier (probably Joseph Olivieri) and Joseph Uberti (a well-known artist)— that were recognizable as members of the Italian community. Moreover, the list of participating churches failed to include St. Mary Magdalen dePazzi.[27]

Inside the cathedral, prominent laymen denounced the new Italy while the crowd frequently interrupted with applause. Judge James Campbell proclaimed of its king that "history will endorse and consign him to infamy. The historian has unfortunately often portrayed and dissected the spoliator, but never so sacrilegious and mean a one as Victor Emmanuel." Joseph R. Chandler, a former congressman, minister to Naples, and editor of the *North American*, read the protest document, then castigated Italian unification as a sham. General William A. Stokes decried the "insolent hypocrisy" of anyone who professed himself to be a faithful Catholic and obedient son but would invade Rome and imprison the pope. Daniel Dougherty asked what freedom could the pope have under a monarch who broke his pledge to France, the country that made Italy a nation and him its king. He also indicted Victor Emmanuel for not restraining the ruffian rabble who cried out for the division of property and made heroes of assassins who sought to overthrow all government, banish all religion, ignore the name of God, and erect altars to the Goddess of Reason. John P. O'Neill defended the papacy and praised the personal character of Pius IX. Pierce Archer, speaking for younger Catholics, accused Victor Emmanuel of taking advantage of the embarrassments of the pope's allies and assailed the lack of fidelity among those who had turned traitor. J. Duross O'Bryan argued that recent events in Rome were "an instance of barbarity that even Atilla [*sic*] refrained from committing."[28]

After the speeches, Chandler called for a vote on the formal proposals of the protest. The men inside the cathedral shouted their thunderous assent, which was repeated a moment later by the throng of supporters outside. Wood closed the event with a benediction. Mark L. Vallette, a prominent Catholic journalist, wrote that the meeting had shown to the world that Philadelphia Catholics had joined their co-religionists in repudiating "the scheme of Italian unity" that was contrary to "the dictates of natural law, the teachings of Holy Scripture, and the law of nations."[29]

While a Catholic writer could be expected to praise the meeting, the secular press of Philadelphia similarly recognized its significance. One paper reported greater enthusiasm and interest than ever before seen in the city in regard to Catholic affairs.[30] Another described "one of the most remarkable meetings that ever occurred in Philadelphia," before adding: "Very few events, in the history of the Catholic Church, have created such a deep feeling of abhorrence and dismay among its believers, as the invasion of Rome by the Italian troops, and the destruction of the temporal power of the Pope, by the force of arms."[31] The *Evening Telegraph* noted other possible consequences of the demonstration: "If the Pope could find many such advocates, the duration of Victor Emmanuel's reign over Rome might well be questioned, and it would not be difficult to turn the tide of public sentiment on the Roman question against the advocates of Italian unity."[32]

The secular press, however, disagreed with some Catholic views expressed at the cathedral on the Italian situation. While describing the meeting as "eminently respectable," the *Evening Bulletin* rejected the contentions on the righteousness and blessedness of the pope's civil government. It was, instead, an undeniable fact that papal dominion had provided "a despotism the most cruel, trivial and pitiful of any in the world." Yet, the *Evening Bulletin* continued, American Catholics, who would not have tolerated this government even briefly, could profess their sentimental admiration for it from a safe distance. The Papal States had been defeated by pious Catholics whose actions were approved by others who lived within the shadow of the Vatican, whose faith could not be doubted, and whose knowledge of abuses had come from bitter experience. The *Evening Bulletin* concluded that destruction of the civil state might be beneficial for the Church, as the pope might find himself with more power as a spiritual leader; and it added that this opinion was probably shared by Catholics who had lived under the regime of the Papal States as well as by liberal Catholics who preferred their pope as the head of a great Church to the ruler of a petty despotism.[33]

The *Morning Post* took a similar position. While respecting their opinions and motives and without doubting their sincerity and piety, the *Morning Post* reminded the participants in the meeting in colorful, but penetrating, language of the contradiction between their religious interests as Catholics and the political values expected of Americans:

> Yet, it is impossible not to regret that American citizens should permit their fidelity to their religion to make them unfaithful to republican principles. Believe what you please, pray to Jove, have trust in Boodha, doubt with Voltaire, worship the sun as the visible form of Deity, but do not make a spiritual faith the servant of an earthly ambition. The highest, the purest religion cannot rule in worldly affairs without wronging itself. The vicar of God cannot collect taxes from wine and tobacco.[34]

The defeat of the Papal States should not be seen as a blow against Catholicism, the *Morning Post* contended. Rejecting the views of some Catholics, it pointed out that Victor Emmanuel was a Catholic, but not a hypocrite, and that the soldiers who entered Rome were also Catholics, but not traitors to their faith. It argued that even some Catholics who accepted the pope's infallibility considered his temporal power to be incompatible with his spiritual jurisdiction. The *Morning Post* concluded its editorial with an elegant observation:

> The right of the people to rule is the granite foundation of Republicanism. That the American citizens should deny to the people of Rome what they jealously claim for themselves is not a cheerful spectacle. It is an amazing inconsistency, which no religious fervor can explain. We read the record of the meeting yesterday with sadness; yet we cannot believe that all American Catholics will endorse it. Surely there must be many who do not believe that because the Holy Father is the head of the Church, he must also be the tyrant of a rebellious province, the bar to the union of a nation, and an obstacle to the march of freedom.[35]

Since the 1840s, Philadelphians—residing in the cradle of American liberty—had staged public demonstrations in enthusiastic support for the republican movements then sweeping Europe. Although Italy moved toward a monarchy rather than toward a republic, they still sympathized with the Italian cause. But regardless of what political views other citizens held or how the secular press saw their actions, the great majority of Philadelphia Catholics had now joined their co-religionists in New York, London, and elsewhere, pouring themselves into a massive demonstration of support for the papacy. In New York one newspaper had described it as a part of "the most profound, exciting and important religious topic of the day."[36]

The demonstration at the cathedral had provided Philadelphia Catholics with an opportunity to express their identity, cohesion, and ideology. Galvanized by the "Roman question," they had lifted themselves from the passivity that had prompted criticism by their own press only four years earlier, and they now found a new political environment, largely initiated by their own public action. Catholics had become a visible and united component of the civic community. At the same time, however, in Philadelphia and elsewhere, a few dissenting Catholics—exceptions to the generally shared position—shared republican values and favorable sentiments for the Italians. One pastor in New York City, more catholic than Catholic, objected to the wording of the protest, dissented from the idea that the pope should be above all civil power, and even declared that the Italians had as much right to Italy as the Irish believed that they had to Ireland.[37] But whatever sympathy Philadelphia Catholics had previously shown for Italian nationalism, once it crossed the Tiber, they could no longer easily endorse it, at least not in public.

A prominent Catholic, unable to attend the protest meeting at the cathedral, expressed his opinion in a letter to the bishop, which was published in the diocesan newspaper. Noting that the Holy Father had been driven from Rome at least twice before in the long history of the Church and that his persecutors had always reached ignominious ends, the writer predicted a similar fate for the present effort at Italian unity: "It will soon vanish and disappear as a drop of poison in the vast ocean."[38] What many, if not most, Italians saw as the most glorious moment of the modern era of their history, the writer condemned not only with certainty and arrogance but also with a faulty sense both of the history and the future of Italy. He argued that the Italians themselves had been unable to protect the pope and his temporal domain; and, even worse, they had perhaps betrayed the pope and their faith by the establishment of a secular state. But his sentiments, delivered so near to the beginning of mass migration from Italy, reflected a negative perception and hostile attitude toward Italians that would also darken their experience in America.

Patriotism and Faith

Those Italians who were already building their own community in Philadelphia faced a difficult situation in their relationship with the Church. With each success by nationalist forces in Italy, the fidelity of Italians as Catholics, even in an American city far away, was questioned by others. While Italians in Philadelphia must have felt some satisfaction, at least in private, with the outcome of the political situation in Italy, their sentiments could not contribute to their place as Catholics. But Church authorities could not afford to confront this issue too openly or too aggressively, for any further dispute, as had already occurred at St. Mary Magdalen dePazzi, could destroy their delicate bonds with the Italians. Nor could the Church allow itself to lose any influence over its members. It had been fortunate to have such an articulate polemicist as Sorrentini among the clergy who were more loyal to the Papal States than to the new Italy, although his case had had a nearly disastrous outcome. The events in Rome could only provide a new challenge for Catholicism as well as a new chapter of Italian history after September 1870.

The annexation of Rome and the unification of Italy marked the end of the struggle for independence and sovereignty that had begun nearly one half-century earlier. But instead of economic development and social stability, the new nation encountered stagnation and disruption. Unable to provide for a population that exceeded its capacity to meet basic needs, Italy failed to put into place the political system that might have reduced regional differences, stabilized living conditions, and created a harmonious social order. Within a short period of time it was increasingly apparent to many Italians that the only way to find any immediate relief or long-term well-being, for themselves and their families, was through emigration. Almost at the moment that modern Italy was born, much of its population discovered that their lives had to be pursued elsewhere.[39]

In Philadelphia at this time, the period of temporary rectors was coming to an end at St. Mary Magdalen dePazzi. But, in inheriting a congregation that had severely tested its bishop and had only recently been released from his interdict, its next rector had to resolve problems both within the parish and with the diocese. And, in assuming leadership of a people who had recently gained independence but who were about to leave their land of origin in unprecedented numbers, he would encounter issues of old homeland and new nation. In brief, he had to help his flock retain their religious faith while they took on a new secular identity and found a place in a new country.

When he arrived in Philadelphia in January 1870, therefore, Antonio Isoleri had inherited a difficult situation. It existed around him and within him. Bishop Wood had sought the best candidate, one faithful to Church and pope, as the rector for the recently reopened Italian Mission. After nearly a year in Philadelphia, Isoleri was formally named to the position, but the troubles of a new nation, a beleaguered Church, and a torn people accompanied it. Before leaving his native Liguria, Isoleri had praised the movement for a free Italy and extolled the House of Savoy in his poetry. Now, only a month after becoming the rector of St. Mary Magdalen dePazzi, the *Catholic Standard* noted "A. Izzoleri" in its list of participants at the cathedral who were supporting Pius IX. Almost immediately immersed in the turmoil that Italian politics inflicted on American Catholicism, he now shared the anguish and ambivalence of Italians caught between "patria e religione."[40]

CHAPTER **THREE**

Portrait of a Young Priest

The formation of Antonio Isoleri's personal and priestly character began in Villanova d'Albenga in Liguria, where he was born on February 16, 1845, the last of seven sons of Francesco and Gerolama Isoleri. On the day following his birth he was baptized in the local church as Antonio Angelo Giacinto Isoleri, taking the names of three uncles who were Capuchin priests. From this place of origin, near the ancient walled city of Albenga on the Tyrrhenian coast, he started down the path that eventually led to Philadelphia.[1]

The Making of a Missionary

In an autobiographical sketch written many years later, Isoleri claimed that his parents had taught him to read before he entered school. At a young age the precocious Isoleri had displayed aspirations for a religious vocation when he gathered other children in pretend events and processions before his own play altar, once even on the feast of Saint Luigi Gonzaga, when several adults participated and found edification in his preaching. Then, at the age of ten, Isoleri began his formal education as a day student at a state school in Albenga. He later recalled that he had been much like the children of other comfortable, but not wealthy, families who have to "catch fire" as students. When he eventually "ignited," Isoleri attained the status of *con corona* by winning the highest honors in grammar and rhetoric. In four years of elementary school and five more at the secondary level in Albenga, Savona, and Genoa, he continued to win honors not only for his academic work but also for good conduct. He strongly disliked mathematics but quickly acquired an interest in and talent for poetry.

At sixteen, Isoleri entered the diocesan seminary at Albenga to determine whether he had a call to a religious vocation. While completing his studies in philosophy with honors, his health became somewhat delicate, and the serious boy who he had been was being replaced by an even more serious young man. In his emotional life he alternated between an often melancholy character and a happier disposition. He sought companions for their qualities of mind and heart and preferred to be recognized on the basis of similar virtues in himself.

As an eighteen-year-old seminarian, Isoleri returned to Villanova d'Albenga, where he delivered a sermon on John the Baptist to the congregation of his parish church. At this time he began to write what he later described as a philosophical and hypochondriac work in an effort to overcome his tendency toward melancholy. He imitated the style of Alexander Young, a writer whom he did not simply read but also loudly declaimed in his seminary room, as he also did the tragedies of Vittorio Alfieri, the Catholic poet and dramatist of the eighteenth century.

Isoleri spent the year 1863–64 as a student prefect at the diocesan college at Rocca in Loano, where he began his studies in theology while also sharpening his skills as a lyric poet and playwright. In the next academic year he was assigned as a prefect to the Nobile College of the Missions in Savona. In October 1866, in the midst of a cholera epidemic, Isoleri entered the renowned Collegio Brignole Sale for foreign missions, which was operated by the Vincentians of the Lazarist order in Genoa.[2] Three years later, after completing his studies, he was ordained as a priest in Savona on March 13, 1869, but illness prevented him from celebrating his first mass for another two weeks until Easter Sunday, March 28. With his formal training concluded, Isoleri's future remained momentarily uncertain.

Inspired by the life of a missionary priest who had died in China, Isoleri anticipated an assignment to the Far East, but the decision about his future belonged to God and to his ecclesiastical superiors. Their eventual decision not only abruptly ended his days in Italy, but also brought him to another life in a new world. On June 21 he heard for the first time the name of an American city, Philadelphia, which was to be his destination as a missionary. A few days later, on the feast of Saints Peter and Paul, the first great missionaries of Christianity, he learned that Father James Rolando, a Vincentian recently at the seminary, had proposed to Bishop James Wood of Philadelphia that the Congregation of Propaganda Fide appoint Isoleri as the rector of the Italian Mission at St. Mary Magdalen dePazzi in that city. In late August, Isoleri left his office at the apostolic college and returned to Villanova d'Albenga for a two-month vacation. It was to be his final visit home.

Isoleri's imminent departure for a distant land was particularly difficult for his father, who pleaded with the bishop of Albenga to persuade the young missionary to change his mind. But his mother, a tender-hearted woman who had cried in earlier years when he returned from vacations to his school in Albenga, only three miles away, felt even greater sorrow. Isoleri long remembered with anguish the bitter moment of departure on Sunday, October 24, 1869 when his mother had to be separated from her youngest son in her final embrace. With this poignant parting from his parents, Isoleri returned to Genoa for his last days in Italy. On November 25, his superior at the college delivered a final message and placed a crucifix in the hands of the young priest, who exchanged farewells with friends and departed for his new mission in America. He followed a route through Savona, Nice, and Marseilles to a Lazarist residence in Paris. Isoleri had never traveled very far before, nor did he know much of the world. He would confess much later on that his shame of eating in public had allowed him to eat only twice during the two nights and nearly three days between Marseilles and Paris. Two weeks after arriving in Paris, he left for Le Havre, from where he sailed on the *Saint Laurent,* a French steamer bound for New York City, on December 17, 1869. But after embarking for America, he ate even less during his Atlantic voyage, having lost much of his appetite on a sometimes stormy sea.[3]

The Lyre of the Leronica:
"Patria e Religione"

Isoleri's prodigious writings from his seminary days to his final years comprise a comprehensive portrait of his life as well as a means of understanding the part that he eventually played as a pastoral and secular leader. Despite his modest origins, his diverse talents, facile mind, and receptive spirit allowed him to become a more urbane and sophisticated person in response to the challenges that awaited him in Philadelphia.

With his personal traits and aptitudes as a foundation, Isoleri's formal education at Brignole Sale in Genoa further contributed to his development. The college, founded in 1852, by the Marquis Antonio Brignole Sale and Artemisia Negrone, spouses and staunch supporters of the papacy, primarily trained French and Italian seminarians for the foreign missions. Its program, however, afforded students not only the orthodox teachings of Catholic doctrine but also exposure to the Enlightenment and Modernism in the mid-nineteenth century. Not long after his arrival as a student, Isoleri's notes reveal his own exploration of Auguste Comte's Positivism and the Religion of Humanity. From its founding to the midpoint of the next century, the Collegio Brignole Sale sent six hundred missionaries to the Near East, the South Pacific, and North America. (Besides James Rolondo, who served on the faculty after being at St. Mary Magdalen dePazzi in Philadelphia, Brignole Sale alumni included Giovanni A. Vassallo, Giuseppe Ascheri, and Winand Wigger, the third bishop of Newark, New Jersey. These men not only became Isoleri's friends at the seminary but also remained an important part of his life in Philadelphia.[4]) From his early days as a student through his later life as a pastor, Isoleri cultivated an impressive command of several languages. In addition to Latin (required for the priesthood), Italian, French, and eventually English, there was his native Ligurian dialect, which was another language in itself. And he would acquire some familiarity with other regional dialects of Italy amid the immigrants of Philadelphia.[5]

Isoleri would eventually earn a well-deserved reputation as a prolific writer and public speaker. He frequently tested the fragile ground of religious and political controversy as he sought to forge a community among Philadelphia's Italians while binding up the wounds that they had incurred as supporters of a newly independent and unified Italy. Isoleri also searched, as an enthusiastic writer of poetry, prose, and drama, for some source for his own comfort. An assertive thinker, he was nevertheless humble in his assessment of his own ideas. He was a devoted priest in his allegiance to pope and Church, as much an Italian as he was a Catholic. As priest, patriot, and poet, Isoleri embodied the elusive spirit of the Renaissance culture of his native land.

Three volumes of his writings, the *Lira Leronica*,[6] began with material that he had placed in a bookcase of his father's library in the family home in Villanova d'Albenga, before he left for America. Isoleri later admitted that he should have made more corrections to his early writing, sometimes composed on the banks of the Lerrone, the stream that swiftly passed under the walls of Villanova d'Albenga; but if "un po' di gloria" (a little glory) came from his work, then he insisted that it should reflect upon the aged parents who had sacrificed so much to put him on the road to the priesthood. He concluded his introduction by confessing that a little glory also comes "alla religione ed alla patria," two terms that he cherished as much as the names of his dearest relatives.[7] In the final volume of the *Lira Leronica,* he modestly declared that his writing was not to be recommended for its literary merit but for friendship and charity, as it was intended to be sold to benefit the parish orphanage at St. Mary Magdalen dePazzi. But modesty did not prevent Isoleri from seeing another possible value in his writing. With good humor, he aptly anticipated the precise use that his work now serves by giving the instruction that to read the book we would know him better than from his photograph, which was also to be found there.[8]

His poems embraced a wide range of subjects, but his attachment to his native land was evident when he focused on the difficulties inflicted by nature on the common people of his region. In what was perhaps his first poem, written when he was only sixteen years old, Isoleri pleaded with God, on behalf of the *contadini* (peasants), bathed in sweat, who were laboring in vain to end the drought of 1861. In later poems he dealt with pests, plagues, and famines as well as with saints, holidays, and celebrations. With great affection, Isoleri described such local customs as the shepherds who offered *un agnellino* (a young lamb), and were the first to kiss the new-born infant at midnight mass on Christmas Eve in his village. His poems not only reflected on political events, deaths of relatives, personal experiences, and friends but also on such gentle splendors of nature as the pine forests near Albenga or the first violets of spring, as well as the beauty that he found in the urban settings of Savona or Genoa.

Isoleri's most engaging theme, both for its relevance to the problem of Church-state relations in Italy in the 1860s and for its later implications for the Italian immigrant community in Philadelphia, was his linking of religion and patriotism. When first proclaimed in 1859–60, the new Italy threatened the future of the Papal States, the temporal power of the pope, and the role of the Church. Well aware of past difficulties and persisting tensions but convinced that religion and patriotism were compatible, Isoleri vigorously displayed his enthusiasm for Italian independence. As early as 1862, during his first year of secondary-level education at the *liceo*, in a birthday tribute to King Victor Emmanuel II, Isoleri's lyrics consoled Italy with the hope of a Redeemer. Behind the principal voices of Italia, Libertà, Felicità, and Valore, a chorus intoned:

> All of us fully aroused by noble ardors,
> The youth in the footsteps of his father,
> Will move with the Italian squadrons
> To drive tyranny from you.[9]

With impassioned verse, Isoleri expressed his ardent support for the monarchy as the instrument of Italian unification. These lines, urging a confederation of Italian states, with a garrison of their own troops rather than those of the French in Rome, reflected the sensibilities of a young man intoxicated by the long-awaited triumph of his mother country.

Although excused from military service by his clerical status, Isoleri became almost obsessed with the themes of patriotism and faith. His exemption, however, apparently disturbed him, and he addressed it in a poem dedicated to Raffaele Biale, the bishop of Albenga as well as the person responsible for the deferment, in November 1865. Bluntly titled "La mia leva," or "My Draft," Isoleri wove together his love of native country and religion. Having been released from his military obligation, he stated his intention to enlist in the apostolic service as a foreign missionary. Linking patriotism and faith in other poems written before he left Italy as well as in his sermons and speeches throughout his later years in Philadelphia, Isoleri sounded the principal note of his lyre.[10] And when different political factions debated the future of Italy, he gave his own answer in 1864:

> It is the trumpet of the King of Savoy
> That already echoes from the Po to the Scilla.[11]

In the next year, Isoleri again expressed his preference for a monarchy that would unite all of Italy:

> My sons, from Milan to Palermo,
> Let a cry rise, free and strong:
> Long live the pact that Italy has already signed
> With Victor Emmanuel as its King![12]

His patriotic sentiments were their most strident when he turned his attention to the liberation of the Veneto from Austrian control in an 1866 poem. After his customary praise for the king, Isoleri concluded:

> But war with the Germans! Let's charge with the bayonet!
> Until Venice of Italy will be—
> Let's go to the Mincio, let's run to the Po!
> Victor our King called us there.
> Savoy! Savoy! Let's charge with the bayonet
> Until Italy united will be.
> Farewell, father and mother. Our country has called me,
> I will join the squadron, I know not if I will return.
> I will fight as a brave man to live or to die!
> I will be worthy of praise, that's why I wish to go.
> If I die, grieve for me, and raise a tomb for me!
> If I return, happily, we will thank heaven.[13]

If these lines appeared bloodthirsty, especially from the pen of a seminarian, they nevertheless indicated the nationalistic fervor of his early years.

As his ordination neared, Isoleri's poetry abruptly shifted away from his preoccupation with patriotism. He had apparently grown aware of the impending collision between the emerging nation and the papacy as well as of the personal dilemma that it posed for Catholic Italians. After another poem on the liberation of the Veneto, written in the summer of 1866, he rarely returned to exclusively political themes until Italy entered World War I many years later. By October 1866, in a poem composed in Villanova d'Albenga, Isoleri was now prompted by his wish to join in the spiritual liberation of Italy. He declared:

Long live God! If he calls me, without care
I give up my country and my life:
To pour the baptismal waters
For those who were stained by sin.[14]

Then, Isoleri asked all his relatives—father, mother, brothers, nephews, uncles, cousins—not to cry but rather to pray that God be his protector. He had now enlisted in a different kind of army.

Mysticism and Final Farewell

Until 1868, Isoleri believed that he was preparing himself to be a missionary in Asia. In February at the Collegio Brignole Sale, he conceived the idea of writing a tragic drama on the martyrdom of four French priests in Korea in 1866. He finished the play, entitled "Religione e Patria o i Martiri Coreani," a little more than one week later in early March.[15] He hoped to put the finishing touches on his work if he had the good fortune to visit the places consecrated by the holy blood of these martyrs as well as to know the language and customs of the Korean people.[16] But he sensed his eventual destination when he bade farewell to Giovanni Vassallo, his recently ordained friend who had been appointed to the diocese of Newark, New Jersey, in June 1868. Commenting on the path that his own priestly career would soon take, Isoleri wrote:

If an Italian discovered it, let Italians
Consecrate American soil to God!
Have courage then, and faith, my friend.
Everything else is in vain.[17]

It was at this time that he experienced a brief mystical interlude. After a fall on a stairway at the seminary, he was confined for about five weeks from March to April 1869. In his opening words to a light-hearted poem addressed to the Greek god of healing, Isoleri exclaimed, "Aesculapius, I've broken my head!"[18] In the lines that followed, he expressed his chagrin over the medical treatment to which he was subjected. But while still recuperating, he was ordained, and Isoleri's attitude changed. He now offered a more deeply spiritual poem that described his reception of the holy viaticum, the Eucharist administered in the final rites to the dying, as a visit by Jesus. He had presented either a transient episode of religious ecstasy, reflecting his own state of mind after his ordination twelve days earlier, or merely the thoughts of an imaginative young priest with a profoundly religious sensibility.[19] The mysticism of his poetry recurred when Isoleri celebrated his first mass at Easter in 1869. In a footnote to a poem, probably added a few years later, he referred to a miracle in which the eyes of the Virgin Mary had moved, in an icon in the church of Sant' Agostino in Loano.[20] And he claimed to have witnessed the same miracle once before in March 1864.

Isoleri's life entered a new stage with his appointment as a missionary to Philadelphia's Italians in June 1869. Although he still did not know the exact nature of his ministry, he added two stanzas to another eucharistic hymn that he had written a few months earlier. With lines that began, "I am crossing the Alps and ocean . . . Filadelfia already awaits me," Isoleri acknowledged that his own odyssey had begun.[21]

Despite his firm commitment to his missionary vocation, Isoleri's separation from his native soil remained difficult for him. On the day of his departure from his beloved Villanova d'Albenga, he wrote another farewell. Unlike in his poem "L'Addio del giovane Missionario," of October 1866, he now expressed himself in prose. In his opening words, while noting that he never had had the opportunity to kiss the soil of Rome, the place where so many martyrs had spilled their blood, he bade farewell to the Eternal City. Then, addressing the pope himself, Isoleri restated his preference for an assignment to the Far East: "I aimed at China; and you directed me to the United States. You spoke; I am leaving." By these words, he was also making a gesture of submission to his superiors. Turning to his destination, Isoleri asked for the pope's blessing: "But bless me and Philadelphia. Bless above all that part of the vineyard that I must cultivate." Whatever disappointment he felt, Isoleri had accepted the call to his new location (now even using its American spelling). But he again shifted his message and added a political twist: "Oh, glorious and magnanimous family of Savoy, family of Saints and Heroes, Farewell! Oh! Wisely govern Italy that the Lord has placed under your scepter. Make it strong, glorious, happy, among all nations of the earth. But be sure that you make it so, that you lead it back repentant to the Vicar of Christ, so that he blesses it, and with it your flags and swords."[22]

Isoleri remained deeply concerned with the increasing tensions between the new kingdom and the Vatican. Loyal to the House of Savoy, he still linked the emergence of Italy as a nation to the will of God and sought to reconcile it with the papacy. As in his earlier writing, rather than choose between *religione* and *patria*, Isoleri again attempted to unite them, an effort that he would repeat throughout his years in Philadelphia.

Isoleri's farewell became more impassioned as he addressed Italy itself: "You are the garden of the world, the smile of God." No Romantic poet or opera composer expressed more deeply his affection for Italy than did this son of the Riviera di Ponente at this moment, in his parting salute: "Farewell, beloved country!" He continued in the militant patriotism of his earlier years: "If I was not called by heaven to be among the apostolic flock, I would be ready to spill my blood for you, as the bravest of your soldiers, my brothers;—my life would be neither of my parents nor of my own, so strongly do I love you! And therefore by thinking of you, my heart will always be touched, and is touched, by bidding you farewell, and tears wash my cheeks."[23] But he saved his greatest anguish for his separation from his parents: "Farewell then, dearest ones! Wipe your eyes . . . We will see one another again up there, where we will embrace one another never to be separated again. Farewell! Farewell! Father, Mother, Farewell!"

He then addressed his other relatives and friends, repeating what he had already said to his parents. With almost childlike innocence, he cited the places that he was leaving behind: "Farewell, paternal home! Dear places of my early years." Along with Villanova d'Albenga, "my native land, whose ten towers are reflected in the waters of the Arroscia and Lerone," he listed the sites of his formative years: Albenga, his second home; Loano, where he had seen a vision of the Virgin; Savona, where he had been ordained; and Genoa, where he had studied at the Collegio Brignole Sale. To this litany he added the names of Bishop Biale, who had been a "Father, more than a pastor"; then his superiors; and finally his own companions. Turning once again to his destination, "We leave then for Philadelphia. Bless me, oh Parents, and with you bless me, Lord! Holy Mary of Graces, protect me and assist me! My guardian angel, guide me! My protector saints, always intercede for me. Farewell, beloved country. Farewell, dear relatives and friends. We will see each other again in heaven!"[24] With these poignant words, Isoleri closed his life in Italy. His parting remarks embodied the sentiments of other emigrating Italians who left behind their cherished relatives and homeland. While many returned to their places of origin, many more, Isoleri among them, did not. With his articulate and eloquent voice, Isoleri had spoken for them all.

An assessment of the artistic merit of Isoleri's writings is beyond the scope of our study. His early poems, with their lyrical phrases, moving passages, and colorful images, although not distributed beyond the volumes that he himself privately published, held considerable promise. Two comedies were performed at the seminary college that he attended in 1866–67. His play on the Korean martyrs reportedly was staged later in Philadelphia. But Isoleri's writings remained almost entirely a personal matter.[25]

The significance of Isoleri's poetry, prose, and drama, however, is found in what they convey about him as a person. Each piece presents, as he himself had claimed in the introduction to the *Lira Leronica*, a revealing portrait. His lines reveal a deep love of his family and native land, an intense spirituality, a passion for language, and a keen intellect. While Isoleri frequently prefaced a poem with a quotation from Scripture, at other times he quoted Petrarch, Dante, or even an Italian revolutionary and writer such as Silvio Pellico. If Isoleri had remained in his homeland, he would eventually have been appointed as a seminary professor or to a position within the hierarchy of the Church. Instead, he accepted the call to serve as a missionary priest to the Italians in Philadelphia.

As the rector chosen to reopen the recently interdicted Italian church, however, Isoleri had been made not only the spiritual leader of Philadelphia's Italians but also the principal instrument of ecclesiastical control over a population
whose relationship to Roman Catholicism had been complicated by politics in
their homeland. Isoleri's early writings, moreover, enthusiastically celebrating
Italian nationalism and Savoyard patriotism, indicated his own potential to become an Italian version of William Hogan. If his superiors were aware of his
political views, it was with some risk that they appointed him. The sentiments
manifested in his *scritti* would not disappear in his new life; they would still define his character and lead him into controversy and jeopardy. But beneath his
formal and austere veneer was a tenderness for his people, his two nations, and
his religious faith, which would be further nourished by the challenges of the
American experience. At the same time, through his writings, Isoleri could escape from the rigors of parish management and the reality of the mean streets of
an American city far away from the Arcadian splendor of the Riviera di Ponente
or the cosmopolitan charms of Genoa.

CHAPTER FOUR

The Challenge of Leadership

In December 1869, Antonio Isoleri, twenty-four years of age, sailed to America. On the evening of December 29 he was met by Father Giovanni Vassallo, who had gone from the Collegio Brignole Sale in Genoa to the diocese of Newark, New Jersey, one year earlier, and now greeted fellow *Brignolini* on their arrival at New York harbor. After a week with Vassallo in Orange, New Jersey, Isoleri, accompanied by his friend, reached his final destination of Philadelphia on January 5, 1870. At St. Mary Magdalen dePazzi he met Father Joseph Rolando, its last temporary rector. Isoleri was about to begin a ministry to the Italian colony that would only end at his death fifty-six years later. While preoccupied by his own adjustment to a new society, he nevertheless would seek to cultivate the spiritual life of his people within a building adequate to serve as their church. Over the next half-century his personal life and efforts would be so closely intertwined with St. Mary Magdalen dePazzi that biography and parish history are inseparable. And he was also so deeply involved with the immigrant community that his own life was nearly indistinguishable from the history of Philadelphia's Little Italy.

Little Italy in 1870

Although the Civil War had sharply reduced immigration to America, the Italian community in Philadelphia had completed its first stage of development. By 1870, Italian-born residents, numbering about five hundred, showed a clear pattern of concentration in South Philadelphia. Although fewer in number than their fellow countrymen in New York City, Philadelphia's Italians comprised two-thirds of all Italians in Pennsylvania. Nearly three hundred children, born in Italy or elsewhere, lived with one or two parents who were natives of Italy. Italian-born males exceeded females by a 2:1 ratio; some 62 percent of the males and nearly 60 percent of the females were between fifteen and forty-four years old in a predominantly male and young population. Their households usually consisted of a core nuclear family extended by the presence of other relatives or boarders. These families lived not only in single family dwellings but also in buildings with as many as six other family units. Unlike New York City, Philadelphia offered relatively few large tenements.[1]

The occupations of Philadelphia's Italians in 1870 ranged from laborer and domestic servant to physician and manufacturer, from unskilled worker to apprentice and owner. Italians produced goods and provided services, toiled in factories, and sold items in neighborhood stores, but they rarely reached managerial positions in large firms or had professional careers. Most worked in skilled crafts and small commerce, often related to food, clothing, shoes, or construction, jobs that had increasingly replaced employment as street musicians and statue-peddlers during the past ten years. And while Italians generally remained impoverished or earned only meager wages, some of them had incomes that allowed property ownership.

In addition to their church, with the founding of their first beneficial society in 1867, Italians had embarked on a concerted presence in the city. Some were assuming positions of leadership and becoming *prominenti* in the immigrant community. During the decade ahead, the origins of newcomers would shift from the region of Liguria, from where the pioneers who had founded and nurtured the early community had come, to Southern Italy and Sicily. While Philadelphia's Little Italy reaffirmed earlier patterns of settlement, it also became a magnet for new arrivals who sought security by working and living with other Italians. Thus, a daunting pastoral challenge faced the newly appointed rector of the Italian Mission.

Finding a New Voice: Italian, American, and Catholic

Although recruited for the Italian church in Philadelphia, Isoleri did not immediately assume his post. In late January, three weeks after his arrival, he reflected on his situation in a letter to Vassallo, beginning with an unhappy observation on his living accommodations: "I write you a few lines from the room given me today in the Philadelphia seminary." From his room at St. Charles Borromeo at Eighteenth and Race Streets, Isoleri described his first encounters with the

Italian congregation. Having spent some time "with Rolando because he was a little sick," Isoleri himself was in good health. He had preached on Sundays and, with Brignole Sale alumni Giuseppe Alizeri and Winand Wigger (later the bishop of Newark), at Forty Hours Devotion, and he had been the principal celebrant at a Solemn High Mass where about thirty Italians received communion. In a postscript, Isoleri added that he stayed with Rolando until January 26 and directed Vassallo to address any reply to him to the Italian church.[2]

Isoleri's letter revealed his early expectations for his ministry: "the Italians, as usual, did not give us much work . . . and to speak sincerely I do not envy anything about the position of Rolando, although I have been destined primarily for it, but when the time comes, I will accept whatever office is given to me, saying: I do not excuse myself from labor." On the evening of March 21, 1870, Isoleri delivered a sermon that began a parish mission for the Italians led by Alizeri and other Vincentians from Germantown. From his opening words, "Children of the sinner Adam—we enter the world in sin; but the grace of Holy Baptism cancels it and makes us children of God," Isoleri delivered his message in the emphatic manner that he would use throughout his years as a priest. When the mission ended, a positive appraisal that its services had been well attended and that many people had received the sacraments was an auspicious assessment of Isoleri's future.[3]

While adjusting to his post, Isoleri was absorbed by the task of learning English. His letter to Vassallo, written in Italian and English versions, indicated that he found the new language both strange and formidable. After amending his English text, substituting "room" for "cell" in resignation to his vocation, he awkwardly wrote: "You know how difficult is the study of English . . . the study of english idiom is painful . . . you who know my antipathy against it . . . beseech often for me . . . that I can succeed shortly and without I lose the patience." But his postscript, written in Italian, showed that he still relied on his sense of humor: "I confess that it is a presumption to write in English without knowing an 'h' [that is, anything]; but I am certain that you will forgive me, or better than that you will overlook my ignorance, because my angel covers it with his wings. . . . Pray for me to all the saints, and especially the English saints, so that I can soon and easily learn this blessed language. . . . Then only, I believe and I hope that I will know something about my strength."

In a memoir written years later, Isoleri compared his attitude toward the English language to how he had once felt about mathematics: "although such study had pleased him as much, years earlier, as did the study of mathematics," that is, not at all. But as he mastered a new tongue, Isoleri was also finding a powerful new voice.[4]

Assigned first as a chaplain to the Sisters of the Good Shepherd at Holy Trinity parish at Twenty-second and Walnut Streets, where he remained for six months, Isoleri also said mass and preached at St. Mary Magdalen dePazzi.

Despite misgivings, he was adjusting to his surroundings and even beginning to overcome his difficulties with English. At an evening service during Passion Week, he delivered his first sermon in English at the Italian church. And as he later described it, "il ghiaccio fu rotto," he had broken the ice of English.

On the same occasion, Isoleri's linguistic success was surmounting ethnic boundaries. Addressing his mainly Irish audience, he delivered a sympathetic message:

> God be blessed, my dear brethren, that after three months since I did land in this country, He gave me to preach a little sermon in your beautiful but difficult language. In this short time I observed in silence your piety and the respect that you show to the priest: I was silent and praying. But now with a heart full of admiration and love for you, I cry aloud to call you my Brethren, to name you the supporters, the Apostles of the Catholic faith in this country. Oh yes: every evil if not so prejudicial we think the persecution of England in order to destroy the Catholic religion in Ireland, made it stronger here, and propagated here by means of every emigrant Irish.[5]

Although Isoleri's main subject was the sorrows of the Virgin Mary, his remarks had other implications. Far from the political turmoil and anticlericalism of Italy, he had found among the Irish in America an outlook that warmly embraced Catholicism. But his appreciation was also a response to their support for the Italian church in Philadelphia.

Isoleri's new language did not prevent him from returning to his original one, especially when dealing with the unresolved politics of Italy or the challenges facing Italians as immigrants in America. While he was unable to ignore the conflict between new state and old religion in the land that he had left behind, he also had to face a related issue as a priest in the immigrant colony. The annexation of Rome by the new Kingdom of Italy posed a dilemma for Italian Catholics; it forced them to choose between loyalty to their nation and fidelity to their Church. Those who remained faithful to Catholicism were deprived of their secular heroes. While Mazzini, Garibaldi, and Victor Emmanuel were acceptable to anticlerical Italians, Catholics and their priests had to find other persons who might be apotheosized. And, for Italians in America, a hero also had to be relevant to a new life in the New World.

Isoleri found a solution in the figure of Christopher Columbus. In April 1870, he reflected on "religione" and "patria" in a composition, possibly his first since coming to Philadelphia, written in Italian and probably intended as a sermon. By taking Columbus as its subject, Isoleri celebrated his own relocation from Genoa. He argued that the man who unites religion and politics is a saint, a hero, and a genius, and that Columbus had been such a man, whose discovery of America had extended the reign of God on earth through the Catholic

Church. Indeed, if Dante had written the *Divine Comedy* in the sixteenth century, it would have included a canto on Columbus in Paradise. Isoleri urged Italians to reclaim the explorer's ashes for reburial among other national heroes in the church of Santa Croce in Florence. He also defended early Italian contributions and later immigrants to America, with Columbus as the device with which to unite disparate origins and identities into a cohesive community. It was a choice that was flattering to Italians, acceptable to the Church, and pertinent to America.[6]

Defending the Faith

Isoleri had inherited a situation that was partly defined by politics in Italy. The demonstration at Philadelphia's cathedral had reaffirmed its relevance for America in 1870. Although sharing the sentiments expressed at the protest, Isoleri reconciled himself to the loss of the Temporal Power by the Holy See while still thinking positively of the future of the Church. But if Catholic protests were occasional reminders of the problem, the members of other denominations furnished even greater provocations. When the president of a Waldensian seminary in Italy spoke at the First Reformed Presbyterian Church in Philadelphia, identifying the pope as the anti-Christ, Isoleri saw this charge as "un diluvio di bestemmia," a flood of blasphemy. Although outraged, he was not yet ready to make a public response. In the next year, however, after becoming rector of St. Mary Magdalen dePazzi, he did not hesitate to reply more openly.[7]

A newspaper account of remarks made by the Reverend Dr. Mark Anthony DeWolfe Howe, bishop-elect of the Episcopal Diocese of Central Pennsylvania, and the Reverend Dr. John Saul Howson, a prominent Anglican visitor from England, at St. Luke's Church in Philadelphia gave Isoleri the opportunity to defend the Catholic Church in November 1871.[8] Provoked by Howe's comments on conditions in Rome, Isoleri's homilies—prepared in both Italian and English for the different constituencies of his church—offered an alternative assessment of the political situation in Italy.[9] Without stirring up more controversies, Isoleri intended to answer the Protestant observers by speaking for the cause of truth and for the honor of his country. In regard to Protestant efforts to gain converts and establish churches in Italy, he asked what encouragement could Episcopalians find where Catholicism was so deeply rooted: "Protestants of all denominations would do better to stay at home, than to go and try to convert the Italians." Taking up the Temporal Power, he accused Protestants in general, but particularly English Protestants, of making "a gross, a ridiculous mistake." Moreover, "that Church which destroyed paganism in its very residence will not die for want of two square feet of land. . . . The foundation of this Church is resting upon living stones . . . and thousands of angels form the crown of her summit."

In regard to fidelity, Isoleri stated that in Italy more Catholics than ever before were joining pilgrimages, praying for the pope's delivery, attending mass, and making confessions. He asserted: "they go every day to see their beloved Pio [Pius IX], to kneel down before him, to ask his blessing, and to assure him of their unshaken devotion." If their government was doing anything bad, the people would show themselves as Catholics by electing new representatives. Echoing the pro-unification political writer Vincenzo Gioberti, Isoleri suggested that the pope might become president of an Italian republic or that Victor Emmanuel might name a priest or friar as prime minister and go himself to St. Peter's to serve as an altar boy for the pope. To Howe's denial of any plan to convert Catholics or to create a schism but rather intending only to assist "Romish ecclesiastics" who sought to reform and purify their own Church, Isoleri answered: "no Italian priest or layman will ever make a good Episcopalian or Protestant . . . Italians have too much brains in their head . . . they are and will be Catholics or nothing." He was ingratiating himself with his Italian audience.

Directing his remarks against Howson the visiting Anglican, Isoleri charted the future of Italian politics. Objecting that Protestants had misconstrued papal authority, he asked, "Who ever said the pope was infallible in deciding political matters?" Isoleri anticipated no problems for European states in regard to the Church of Rome. He disagreed with Howson's appraisal that Roman Catholicism in England, despite the conversion of many prominent and educated persons, had been weakened by the Italian situation. Seeing the contradiction, Isoleri asked how Catholicism could be losing ground while gaining such churchmen as Cardinals Wiseman, Newman, and Manning and such laymen as the Marquis of Bath, along with well-known American converts. Isoleri added, "Yes, we got, and still we get a hundred for one we occasionally give to Protestants; we give the worst, and we get the best." Having vindicated Italians as Catholics, he was now defending Catholicism in England as well as in America. Disputing Howson on other matters as well, Isoleri pointed out that two Italians, Pope Gregory I and Saint Augustine of Canterbury, gave England the true faith: "It is Italy who converted England, but England will never convert Italy, never. They may send money and bibles through their many agents; Italy will never become Protestant." He predicted that the Episcopalian chapel in Rome would eventually become another Catholic church, before claiming that Howson had actually come to America to find a husband for his daughter.

With erudition and eloquence, Isoleri appraised the future of the papacy. Unlike speakers at the cathedral in the previous year, he did not defend the past but recognized the loss of the Temporal Power. Aware of the paradox facing the papacy, Isoleri realized that the pope, deprived of secular power in Italy, was gaining greater authority as a spiritual leader. By accepting an inevitable situation, Isoleri's progressive views offered a promising role for the papacy in the modern world.[10]

Isoleri did more than address Protestant efforts among Italians. By asserting an essential connection between being Italian and being Catholic, he had
extended to the members of his congregation a pastoral embrace that included
a collective identity. By an emphatic and persuasive manifesto of who and what
they were, which drew them toward a cohesive sense of self, he had joined secular leaders in laying a foundation for their community.

Devotions and Development

Isoleri emerged as the spiritual head of St. Mary Magdalen dePazzi, however,
primarily through his devotional agenda. On his arrival in Philadelphia, Bishop
Wood was in Rome for the Vatican Council of 1869–70. When Isoleri joined
Gaetano Sorrentini, Joseph Rolando, and other priests in a reception at the
cathedral to welcome Wood home in April 1870, their first meeting augured
well for the future.[11] In September, with the loss of Rome to nationalist forces,
the papacy began the task of restoring its relationship with Italians, whether
in Italy or in the immigrant colonies of American cities. Isoleri, only twenty-
five years old and a priest for less than two years, and finally named as rector of St. Mary Magdalen dePazzi on October 14, 1870, faced a similar task of
rebuilding the relationship between immigrant Italians and their Church in
America.

At the core of its development, St. Mary Magdalen dePazzi was participating in a devotional program, already begun in Gaetano Mariani's time, which
was to expand further and be widely shared by American Catholics. Along with
regularly scheduled masses and sacraments, the liturgical year included Forty
Hours Devotion in January, Stations of the Cross and Benediction of the Blessed
Sacrament during Lent, and a parish mission or retreat in the spring. The archbishop confirmed parishioners in April or May. The Feast Day of Saint Joseph,
Easter, All Saints, Christmas—but also Thanksgiving Day, in a concession to a
new society—and eventually Columbus Day were observed with special programs. Solemn ceremonies and a lively street procession made the patronal feast
day of Saint Mary Magdalen dePazzi, which at that time fell on May 27 but was
usually celebrated on the nearest Sunday, a unique occasion for the congregation and the community.[12]

In the 1870s ceremonies and celebrations unfolded at St. Mary Magdalen
dePazzi in a distinctive pattern. Baptisms, confirmations, and marriages increased in number. The annual parish mission, conducted by Italian Passionists
from Hoboken or Franciscans from Trenton, and by non-Italian clergy as well,
usually was bilingual, with sermons and confessions in Italian and English. Fathers Giuseppe Ascheri, Valentine Valentini, and Francis Pila regularly assisted.

For important occasions, special liturgies, with Vassallo and Rolando joining Isoleri at the altar and in the pulpit, and Solemn High Masses by Haydn, Mozart, or Mercadante, sung by a full choir, elegantly enriched the services.

Even before Isoleri's arrival, the volume of religious services had demonstrated the need for help in meeting the spiritual demands of the Italian Mission. After Bishop Wood requested another priest, the rector at the Collegio Brignole Sale designated Giuseppe Ascheri for assignment to Philadelphia in September 1871. Although Ascheri became a frequent participant at St. Mary Magdalen dePazzi, he did not join its regular clergy but served at other churches in Reading, then West Chester, Pennsylvania, and later at St. Stephen's in Philadelphia, before going to Missouri. And despite the acute need for assistance, Isoleri remained the only priest in residence for nearly twenty years.[13]

From his first year as rector, Isoleri's efforts attracted favorable attention. One observer noted: "The wants of the Church are many, its resources few, as it has no parochial aid." Isoleri, however, managed to make improvements. He obtained a painting of the Crucifixion, donated by himself and a parish family, that had been done by a "celebrated artist of Genoa"; and at about the same time a new roof was placed on the old church. Isoleri also intended to erect a new pastoral residence and school. In October 1871, the success of a sacred music concert at the church, before an audience that included the Italian consul, set a precedent for other public events to support the building fund.[14]

By the next year, lay organizations in the congregation joined into improvement efforts that reflected the growth of the church. The men of the San Giuseppe Society, with about one hundred fifty members, contributed their monthly dues to the gift of a new altar, while the women of the Mount Carmel Society provided another altar dedicated to the Blessed Virgin. Some two hundred young members of the Society of the Holy Child procured a banner for their group.[15]

In February 1872, Isoleri, particularly aware of the need of a school for Italian children, announced plans for the annual fair for the benefit of the church. He had obtained a reliquary and tabernacle—"the largest and most splendid . . . probably to be found in this country," which held many authenticated relics of distinguished saints—to be awarded by the highest bid to another parish. Other prizes included two vases donated by the Italian consul and a veil donated by his wife. As the event approached, Isoleri was praised for having "labored incessantly since his connection with this church to advance the interests of his Catholic countrymen in this city." In April, after a spirited competition between Irish and German Catholics, St. Peter's parish won the coveted prize, and the fair, with a reported $5,000 profit that was to be safely invested until construction began, was declared a "complete success." But this happy and profitable event was about to bring serious trouble to Isoleri and his congregation.[16]

Teaching the Italians a Lesson

Isoleri faced a complicated challenge if he were to meet all the needs of his flock. Along with erasing the debt left by previous rectors, compounded by the meager resources of the congregation, he had to convince his Italians that Catholicism remained their spiritual home, despite the unresolved conflict in their homeland and the Protestant efforts to teach them something else in the new country. As rector of St. Mary Magdalen dePazzi, Isoleri found himself in a unique position. His church provided a place where Italians might find a shared identity. And by pursuing objectives that went beyond religious matters, Isoleri was not only building his church but strengthening the surrounding community as well.

In the spring of 1872, Isoleri's efforts brought him into conflict with Bishop Wood. While Isoleri, of course, had taken no part in the events that had closed the church, the volatile situation that had preceded his arrival at St. Mary Magdalen dePazzi, fueled by the lingering displeasure of a bishop whose flock had defied him, was about to be reignited. When Isoleri attempted to initiate a building program, Wood's response would teach him whatever he still did not know about it. The bishop left no record of his side of their dispute, but Isoleri's detailed notes give the only existing version of the events of the ensuing weeks.[17]

At St. Mary Magdalen dePazzi the rectory, with its low beams and high humidity, was not only harmful to health but also in such poor condition that it was sometimes described as a log cabin or worse. Accustomed to comforts in Genoa, Isoleri was not pleased by what he found in Philadelphia, but the demand for religious instruction and general education for Italian children was even more urgent. By Christmas 1870, he had organized about fifty children into the Society of the Holy Child for catechetical instruction. He saw it as the mustard seed that "so small and scorned, but thrown into the soil germinates, grows and becomes a great tree, and the birds of the sky come and make their nests upon its branches." Having grown to about two hundred members by May 1872, the parish clearly needed its own school. Isoleri believed that upward of about two hundred Neapolitan child musicians, who were without parents, could be rescued from the streets by such a facility. Held by their masters as little slaves in rags, they were ashamed to appear with the better-dressed Genoese children at Sunday school. He argued that by saving their nationality and language, their faith would also be saved. But a parish school was also needed, because Philadelphia's public schools were really Protestant schools.[18]

About two weeks before his formal appointment as rector, in September 1870, Isoleri and a group of Italian laymen had submitted a plan for a new rectory and school to Wood. According to Isoleri, the bishop approved the project. Seeking to implement it with prudence and moderation, Isoleri formed a committee to ensure support and to allocate responsibility to his congregation. He obtained title to the street in front of the church and the plot of land on which he intended to erect the buildings. With Italians and Americans generously contributing to the project, they had organized a concert, then a fair. After accumulating about $1,800, Isoleri invested it toward the overall goal. With the bishop, priests, and other Catholics supporting it, he believed that his effort had been blessed, because the $5,000 from the fair, together with other income, reached the $6,000–$7,000 that was required to begin construction.

The priest soon encountered unexpected opposition from his bishop. In April 1872, when Isoleri reported his fund-raising success, Wood agreed that he might begin the project. But two days later, when Isoleri brought the design plans, Wood had changed his mind. He told the astonished Isoleri that Bishop Neumann had made a grave mistake in allowing the building of a church for Italians, that there had never been any need for it, and that the Italians were wrong in attempting to keep it in their name. Although opposed to nationality churches, Wood would tolerate the Italian church, however, if it repaid the money that had been loaned to it. Wood added that the church lived on the shoulders of the Irish, that Isoleri had no right to ask for contributions from them, and that Isoleri lived at the expense of nearby St. Paul's. The bishop then issued an ultimatum. If the Italians protested, as they had done a few years ago, and if he had to close the church once more, then he would close it forever. He would consult the two diocesan vicars for his final decision without any input from the Italians.

Wood's abrupt change, Isoleri believed, had been brought about by his lingering resentment about the problems that had closed the church earlier. But recalling that the bishop had forgiven the Italians and had even offered them his blessing, Isoleri was convinced that some Irish priests, envious of his success, must have spoken against him. He was equally certain that there would never be a recurrence of any disturbance as long as the Italians had a priest who knew how to manage them as well as he did. And he refused to believe that his jealous rivals would ultimately influence Wood's decision in administering the diocese.

Isoleri also objected, however, to every point that Wood had raised about the Italians. As to who owned the land on which the church was located, Isoleri contended that Neumann had bought the property only as the agent for the Italians. And while they had never renounced their ownership, Wood had not understood or accepted that aspect of the situation. This fundamental difference exacerbated other issues. While the bishop doubted the ability of the church to meet its debt, Isoleri held a more optimistic view. Acknowledging an outstanding debt of about $1,300, he had paid about $300 in the past year, without being asked, and was confident that the rest would be met without great difficulty. But Isoleri was especially adamant in his belief that further disturbances by Italians would not occur.

Isoleri's greatest concern was for the spiritual well-being of the 3,000 Italians whom he estimated were living in Philadelphia. While Wood was uncertain about the depth of their faith, Isoleri argued that more than 500 Italians had received the sacraments at a recent mission. If their church were taken from them and converted into a chapel for the Irish in the neighborhood, Isoleri asked, what would happen to the Italians? Moreover, if Italians spread throughout the city could be received by other parishes, why could he not receive the Irish who attended his church, listened to his sermons, and made their confessions to him in English as members of his congregation? With enough Catholics to fill another church if it were built in his area, Isoleri pointed out that rather than lose money, parishes could only prosper from voluntary offerings and free charity.

With little hope that Wood would change his mind, Isoleri expected even less from the bishop's vicars, Charles J. H. Carter and Maurice Walsh, who had consistently opposed the Italian Mission. But he was also aware of an incident that clearly confirmed their hostility toward Italians. According to Isoleri, Walsh had told an Italian girl that she ought to be ashamed of working at the parish fair; then, after asking her if the Italian church were as Catholic as his own, he dismissed her with a small donation. The incident also illustrated growing tensions between the Italians and the Irish.

According to Isoleri's account, the situation deteriorated further at a meeting in May, when Wood ordered him to halt the building project. When Isoleri asked him what all the Italians and Catholics as well as the Protestant contributors would say, Wood replied that he really did not care; they could say whatever they wanted. When Isoleri asked him what he should tell those people who were eagerly waiting for the start of construction, Wood left the answer to Isoleri's prudence. And when Isoleri asked him what to do with the money that had been collected, Wood angrily told him to hold it for something else.

Although Wood had been demeaning, Isoleri tried to bring him to his own point of view, but their conversation took an unfortunate turn. The priest reminded the bishop of his promise to visit the church on the first Sunday in June to bless the statue of the patron saint that had been ordered from Genoa. After replying that he did not know whether he would come, Wood added that he might do so in order to give a final lesson to the Italians. Wood declared that it was not they, but the Holy Spirit, who had made him a bishop; and if they could not follow his rule, then "we shall see." With these words, he tried to walk Isoleri out of his office.

Before leaving, Isoleri made a final appeal. While all was peaceful at the moment, Isoleri told Wood that he had kept the decision a secret by not informing his people. The bishop again replied that he did not care. Now convinced that Wood had been waiting for an excuse to close the church, Isoleri believed that most Italians would not be submissive. But why had he been recruited for

Philadelphia's Italians, if Wood had always intended to close their church? However, if the bishop did not regard him as a serious hindrance to the plan, Isoleri was unwilling to be a passive witness to it. Wood had neither approved a useful and necessary project nor had given satisfactory reasons for his refusal. If Isoleri was to find a solution, he had to gain the financial support that would ensure the building project as well as overcome the opposition of an imperious bishop and his vicars.

On the day after his acrimonious meeting with Wood, Isoleri launched a new strategy by drafting a letter to Cardinal Alessandro Barnabò, the prefect of Propaganda Fide. As "un figlio ad un Padre," that is, a son to a father, he asked for permission to complete the building project and promised, while waiting for the reply, to keep secret Wood's refusal. To end the agony from the danger of being closed, Isoleri requested that the church be removed from episcopal control and placed under the direct authority of either the Holy See or Propaganda Fide. He sought to have the church declared not only as primarily for Italians but also as a mission, thus allowing its priests to preach in Italian or English, to baptize whoever attends, and to minister to the sick. Isoleri wanted to accommodate what he estimated as nearly two-thirds of his congregation who were "Cattolici Americani." He promised to use the rescript, if granted, only in the case of an emergency, that is, if the bishop wished arbitrarily to close the church or to restrict it to Italians. Fearing that if this letter to Propaganda Fide became known, Wood would persecute him for as long as he remained in the diocese, Isoleri asked for discreet silence about the correspondence. He concluded with a statement of renewal of his priestly obligations and then asserted the interests of a church that had been "cosi stranamente e ingiustamente perseguitata," that is, so strangely and unjustly persecuted.[19]

Instead of immediately mailing the letter, however, Isoleri renewed his efforts with Wood. On May 6, after going to the bishop's residence but failing to meet with him, he drafted another letter that began deferentially: "I was at your residence this morning a little before 10 o'clock and I am sorry I was not in time to find your Reverence in. But I hope this letter will do just as well." After requesting a marital dispensation on behalf of two Italians, Isoleri resumed his argument about the needs of his church. Asking Wood to reconsider a project that he had allowed to proceed for a year and for which money was now available, he wrote: "I can't see how you changed your mind so suddenly as to forbid me absolutely to build a decent and healthy parsonage with some accommodation for a school." Nevertheless, willing to accept whatever decision was reached, Isoleri asked: "I would like to know whether you persist unconditionally in the one you gave to me on the 2nd . . . in order that I may be able to prudently manage the people according to the circumstances." He closed by inquiring whether Wood still intended to come to the church on the first Sunday in June and asked for his blessing on both the mission and himself. After several changes, Isoleri's final version displayed the proper tone of etiquette but adroitly jabbed at the bishop for his inconsistency.[20]

When Wood replied that they could meet again, Isoleri saw a ray of hope. But at the meeting, Isoleri was greeted by Carter and Walsh, who informed him that they had been placed in charge of the matter. After making some small objections, which Isoleri answered easily, they told him that he would have to pay off the debt to the bishop before the project could be considered, and that he should also pay off the principal owed on the land. Isoleri answered that the debt and $140 annual land rent had always been paid in the past and would be in the future, without any difficulty for the original owner or obligation to pay the entire capital sum. As for any debt to the bishop, while insisting on his right to pay a little each year, Isoleri intended to satisfy the entire amount. (Isoleri actually had doubts about the amount and terms of the debt, because without documentation he could only rely on what the bishop claimed.) But having solicited money specifically for the building project, it was neither just nor convenient to spend it in any other way. Yet the matter was being put "alle calende greche," that is, delayed forever. If he had to pay the debt with this money, he would do so gladly, for at least he could proceed with the building plans. Believing that the vicars were satisfied, when they told him to go ahead with the designs and promised to speak with the bishop again, Isoleri left them. As he passed the bishop's office, Isoleri stopped, but Wood said that he had no time for him and closed his door.

On the following day, with his prospects diminished, Isoleri wrote to Wood to give his version of the meeting with the vicars, who had "kept me talking, and made several objections to the contemplated project; all of which, it seemed, I answered to their satisfaction." Once again, Wood did not reply.[21] On the same day, Isoleri also wrote to the vicars. In his letter to Walsh, "in talking to you yesterday, I felt as if I should place a particular confidence in you; it seemed that you took more interest in listening to me." Inviting Walsh to examine everything himself, Isoleri continued: "If the Church where I am is to be at some future time a really italian Church, there is no other way to come to it, than a school. And I can't see anything better than a school of their own to give the poor souls of the rising generation of so many italian children." He then hoped that Walsh would attend the blessing of the new statue in early June. But as with the bishop, neither vicar answered.[22]

Now even more distressed, Isoleri's next letter asked Wood to allow him to resume the project. Saying that it deserved encouragement rather than opposition, he repeated his earlier points. A better rectory was needed. Italian children had the same right as others to a good parochial school. Even if Italians could not contribute much, their priest should try his best to fund it. People of every nationality should lend their generous help. Trying to ingratiate himself, Isoleri stated his certainty that opposition had not come directly from the bishop himself. And even Protestants had shown their interest at the fair, from which he now expected $8,000 in profit. He also informed Wood that the church required a new roof and interior work. With a little humor even in this bleak moment, Isoleri noted that the statue had not yet arrived, thus forcing him to postpone the blessing ceremony: "I don't know whether it is still on the sea, or under the sea already." But his wit could not hide his concern over the growing impatience of his people.[23]

When Wood wrote that Walsh would convey the decision reached by his vicars, but approved by him, Isoleri found the message to be "secco secco," that is, very dry. On the same day, Walsh advised Isoleri to pay $1,300, then the entire debt on the land, another $2,500; and if it pleased Wood, they would talk again about the project. Isoleri protested that this demand was the same as prohibiting him from building at all. If he paid these amounts, only two or three thousand dollars would be left, and he could not expect any more from his people, who, once they saw that he could not proceed, would no longer have any confidence in him. Isoleri warned that it would be unwise to inform them of this situation, because even if their contributions increased, they would know that Wood did not intend to endorse the project. The bishop's message and Walsh's advice arrived on May 24, only a few days before the feast day of Saint Mary Magdalen dePazzi. Wood and his vicars had to be aware of the proximity of their action to the annual celebration. If Isoleri expected fairness, their insensitive and mean-spirited gesture now dashed any hope of it.

When the statue of Saint Mary Magdalen dePazzi finally arrived from Genoa, Isoleri, accompanied by other Italian priests, led an elaborate celebration at the church in early June. A reporter described it as "an eventful day at the Italian Church," but he gave no indication that the bishop or vicars were present. Citing the unprecedented success and $5,000 profit from the recent fair and the plans for a school, Isoleri was praised for having "infused new life into his people." Another account pointed out: "So ended a day that the Italians of this city will never forget. Never was there greater enthusiasm and unity among them." But the statue of the kneeling saint was accompanied by cherubs whose hands held ribbons, inscribed with her motto both in Italian, "Pati non mori," and in English, "Let me suffer but not die." Her words were especially appropriate, for the troubles that had once closed the church had not ended, and Wood now included its rector among those Italians to whom he intended to teach a final lesson.[24]

Placing the Case before Rome

Unable to find a solution in Philadelphia, Isoleri turned to Rome. In another letter to Propaganda Fide, along with the one drafted but not sent a month earlier, he placed his case before Barnabò. For a year and one-half, Isoleri had told the public that contributions were for the building project, but now, if that money were spent for some other purpose, all hope would be lost. He warned the cardinal that the building committee was not at all disposed to recognize any debt to the bishop, and even less to pay it.[25]

Placing more details before Barnabò, Isoleri wrote that the new building was greatly desired and necessary, that he would be able to pay the debt afterward, that the people were ready to lend their assistance, and that the land was actually free of any debt to the bishop. While the document proving that Mariani had bought the land for the Italians had to be filed in the bishop's office, Isoleri could not say anything more about it. Even if Isoleri were able to persuade his committee to pay the debt, Wood intended to obstruct the project at any cost; he was only tolerating the Italian church until the debt was paid. The interests of the church and the Italians required an appeal to Rome. And even if the debt were paid today, Wood might use the slightest provocation to close the church tomorrow. Although reluctant to write in this manner, Isoleri saw it as the inevitable result of the bishop's actions.

Isoleri implored Barnabò to take to heart the interests of his poor church. He deftly described "tanti poveri ragazzi Italiani," that is, so many poor Italian children, who were growing up without religious education, from which they took flight on Sunday, to forget by Monday in city streets where they learned indescribable debauchery and in Protestant schools where they learned heresy. For clothes and food they exerted themselves in the making of money by any means; thus, they also lost their souls. If one-half or one-third of them could be educated in a good Catholic school of their own, they would grow to honor their religion and society. By the same means they could even win over their fathers, who perhaps for years had worn the chains of membership in secret societies, and their mothers, who lived indifferent to or even frightened by religion. Isoleri insisted that if Wood did not support a school for the Italians, then he neither wished to save adults or children nor cared whether Catholicism flourished or deteriorated.

Repeating the need to keep open St. Mary Magdalen dePazzi and his willingness to meet its financial obligations, Isoleri added that it would be difficult to maintain his earlier level of zeal without some assurance that, having been sent to the mission, he would not be torn in half by his dedication to a people who greatly loved him. He would stay as long as there were no legitimate reasons for him to be removed, the doors of his church remained open, and the building project was allowed to proceed. Isoleri asked Barnabò for a favorable decision, promising again to keep secret Wood's prior decision and warning that the people might find it the cause for the further disturbances that he himself had always sought to avoid.

Isoleri included the names of priests as personal references or sources of information, which also identified his supporters.[26] While noting that Barnabò had certainly considered who would teach at the school, he suggested the Missionary Sisters of St. Francis, who were already working among immigrants in New York City. There was no other way to save young Italians growing up in America, since lay teachers, who could instruct both in Italian and English, had to be paid more than nuns and thus more than the school could afford. But he left the entire matter in Barnabò's hands.

By appealing to Rome, Isoleri had placed himself in a position of considerable risk. As a former student at the College of Propaganda Fide, and now a bishop and benefactor of the papacy, Wood had enormous influence. But Isoleri was convinced that he had no other choice than to present his case before the ecclesiastical authorities in Rome. He identified himself as an alumnus of the Collegio Brignole Sale. He emphasized the special plight of the Italians, and particularly their children, as Catholics in Philadelphia. And he believed that he understood them better than the Anglo American Wood did. Rather than acquiesce in what would be a lost cause, Isoleri thought it was a risk worth taking.

Throughout the summer of 1872, the disagreement between Isoleri and Wood remained unresolved. Isoleri appeared to have gained an edge in July, when Propaganda Fide asked Wood to explain why he had refused to allow the Italian colony to erect a new rectory and parochial school, despite the availability of funds and his previous approval. Wood knew that the request had to be based on information supplied by Isoleri. It was also clear, however, that Isoleri was unable to match what Wood could place before Propaganda Fide in support of his side of any argument.[27]

In early August, as he sent his usually generous Peter's Pence to Rome, Wood informed Propaganda Fide that he was preparing a report on the financial condition of St. Mary Magdalen dePazzi. When Barnabò conveyed the Holy Father's gratitude for the donation, he also urged Wood to reply on the matter. When Wood's answer reached Rome, it contained no surprises. His brief letter, accompanying the report, indicated that since Isoleri had been unwilling to follow his wise counsel, he had to turn the matter over to the vicars. Wood was certain that Barnabò would find it prudent to limit the project to current needs and means in order to avoid further financial difficulties. But neither Isoleri nor Wood intended to allow Barnabò to reach a decision on his own.[28]

Wood's two-page report, prepared by Carter and Walsh, claimed that only a minority of people attending St. Mary Magdalen dePazzi were Italians. Most were Irish Catholics, belonging to St. Paul's parish but permitted by the bishop to attend the Italian church in order to sustain it. After examining the building plans as well as the explanations of the rector, the vicars concluded that the project exceeded the spiritual needs and financial resources of the Italian church. Already burdened by a debt of $6,500 and ground rents of $11,270, it should first pay off the nearly $18,000 and then submit a plan more suitable to its spiritual needs and financial means. The vicars had no doubt that the bishop would approve whatever was truly in the spiritual and temporal interests of the congregation. On its final page, they reported an estimated $60,000 needed for construction, $25,000 collected from the parish fair, $18,000 in current debts and ground rent obligations, $7,000 available for the project, and $53,000 more needed. The report gave neither a favorable nor a promising picture.[29]

By September, Isoleri's efforts appeared to have failed when Propaganda Fide advised him to accept the recommendations of the vicars. Despite this setback, he was determined to prevail. With Wood still willing to endorse the building plan if the financial obligations to him were met, Isoleri's next move largely depended upon settling the debt. But if the buildings were to be what Isoleri believed were necessary, he also had to demonstrate that the spiritual needs of the Italians were greater than the vicars had claimed. Refusing to capitulate to Wood and the vicars, Isoleri renewed his efforts.[30]

Success in Philadelphia

Isoleri realized, however, that some cooperation, if not submission to Wood, would facilitate the desired outcome. But he still had to convince Wood as well as the authorities in Rome of the need to expand the Italian church. He undertook a census of Italians in Philadelphia to determine the size of their population and the magnitude of their spiritual demands. The results were essentially unchanged from information that he had sent earlier to Barnabò. Isoleri reported that some 3,000 Italians were spread throughout the city, including two hundred children with their relatives and another two hundred children, imported by Neapolitans, as he put it, to make money by playing music. He intended to show the existence of a substantial number of children who would be exploited unless the Church protected them.[31]

In early November, bringing the financial ledger to Wood, Isoleri paid a modest sum of $20 on the debt. The bishop was pleased by the payment, and their relationship finally began to move in a favorable direction. Isoleri came again a few days later, and Wood returned the account book, remarking that all seemed to be going well. When Isoleri asked how much of the debt remained, Wood replied $693, which appeared to be correct as long as the bishop did not add any interest. Isoleri seized the moment to inquire about the building plan. Wood's surprising answer was to go ahead; he had never prohibited it in the first place, he said, and if Isoleri returned with the modified plans, everything could be settled. Momentarily confused by the unexpected reply, Isoleri became elated as he realized what had actually happened, feeling that a great weight had been removed from his mind and that the deep wound between him and the bishop had been healed.

Isoleri's reaction, however, was premature. At their next meeting, Wood postponed discussion for a few more days. When they met again, Wood became evasive, informing Isoleri that the vicars had not made any decisions and that it was too late in the year to begin construction. Isoleri argued that the foundation could be dug, but Wood wished to reexamine the architect's plans and proposed another meeting in the following week. Isoleri returned several times, but Wood had no time for him. When Isoleri went twice on the same day and finally found him alone, Wood said that he had not been able to speak with the architect. The bishop clearly was stalling.

During the entire ordeal, activities at St. Mary Magdalen dePazzi seemed to contradict the underlying tension and conflict, as if to prove that it could acquit itself as well as any other parish in the diocese. Despite meager resources, the congregation donated modest sums to the yearly seminary collection and to special campaigns for the pope and for the victims of the great Chicago fire. In August 1872, Isoleri initiated an annual picnic. In September some one hundred fifty members of the San Giuseppe Society, along with Isoleri, participated in a public event for the first time when they carried the papal flag to much applause at the cornerstone laying for St. Elizabeth's, a new German parish in North Philadelphia. At Thanksgiving a holiday festival at the Italian church honored its patroness with vespers, a Solemn High Mass, and a procession of San Giuseppe Society and Society of the Holy Child members.[32]

By January 1873 the dispute suddenly and inexplicably ended. Wood approved construction, "as soon as the weather permits," of a rectory and parochial school. Isoleri had somehow paid off the debt, which would allow work to begin in March. With this unexpected turn, Isoleri and his church entered into a flurry of activity. He was conspicuously present when Father Patrick Moriarty, the distinguished Augustinian scholar and Fenian sympathizer (who had also clashed with Wood), spoke on the question of Ireland at Philadelphia's Horticulture Hall in January. After elaborate Forty Hours Devotion in February, Isoleri led the Feast of Saint Joseph's observance in the next month. A Catholic newspaper noted: "Such a condition of things as this at the Italian Church is in the highest degree edifying and gratifying." An auxiliary bishop, in place of Wood, administered the sacrament of confirmation, and the feast day of Saint Mary Magdalen dePazzi was observed with vespers, a High Mass, and Benediction, with a Plenary Indulgence in May. In June, after similar ceremonies, the Keystone Band and singers from six parishes ended an even more elaborate celebration with a grand concert of sacred music to benefit the building fund.[33]

Three years after coming to Philadelphia, Isoleri once again raised his voice to secure the place that he had made for himself and his church in a letter to the *Catholic Herald* in July 1873. In response to a lecture on the "Reformation of Italy" to be given for the benefit of an Italian Sunday school, he wrote: "As there is but one Italian Roman Catholic Church in town, and here I try to gather all the poor Italian children I can, I don't know what other Sunday school that other gentleman had in mind." He noted that some of the "generous-hearted Christians" who purchased tickets for the event had previously supported the efforts to evangelize Italy being made by Alessandro Gavazzi, who, Isoleri claimed, was "now playing billiards in Rome." As for the featured speaker, who had failed to appear for the lecture, "What disappointment! And he pretended to be a Captain! Well, I pretend only to be a sailor, or a soldier; but if any of your readers should meet him, let them be kind enough to direct him to me. I will give him his dues for the interest he takes for the Italians of this country, and more especially for the Italian children of this city."[34] Isoleri also noted that another newspaper had recently reported that an Italian, after preaching to his countrymen in New York City, had disappeared with money obtained from them for tickets to Rochester where they were to find employment.[35] Isoleri persisted in his role as spokesman and guardian.

By July, with the project nearing completion, Isoleri had written to Wood to ask him to make arrangements with the Missionary Sisters of St. Francis, or to indicate if he should do it himself, to begin teaching in the autumn. Isoleri's revision of his final sentence from "Hoping to have an early and favorable answer" to "Waiting to have an early and favorable answer," along with his tone throughout his brief note, suggested that he was now venturing to tell Wood what was to be done next.[36]

Wood's prompt response confirmed their changed relationship. The bishop had already written to the mother superior in Peekskill and to the vicar general of the Archdiocese of New York. The sisters would come as soon as their living quarters were prepared. When he learned this news, Isoleri said that his joy knew no limits. He informed Wood that he was giving the entire new building to the sisters for their dwelling and school until a residence could be built for them at the east side of the church, and he would continue to live in the old rectory. Since he lived alone, without another priest or sacristan, he had no need for more space, and assigning the sisters only a warehouse for the school, as was first planned, embarrassed him. As for himself, "Ma io ero troppo contento," he was very satisfied.[37]

Out of the Ashes

More difficulties for Isoleri were about to come from a new source. He later described the incident as a challenge sent by his Lord: "and He tested me by allowing a most bitter drop to fall in the chalice of my contentment. Blessed be His Holy Name." It also indicated the personal strength with which Isoleri responded to adversity and the determination with which his people supported his efforts.

Late on the evening of August 7, 1873, as he inspected the nearly completed four-story brick school and rectory, Isoleri was greatly pleased by what had been accomplished. But early on the next morning, a woman looked from her bedroom window on the other side of Marriott Street to see flames leaping from the building. And from his own room in the rectory, Isoleri, awakened by a dry and stifling sensation, saw the schoolhouse wrapped in fire. Although the alarm had been quickly given, the spreading flames destroyed almost all of the building. Because the fire appeared to have started in each of the three stories at the same moment, arson was suspected, but careless vagrants who, despite a fence around the site, had been sleeping there may have caused it. Along with the destruction of the main building, the fire damaged the roof of the church and scorched eight housefronts across the street. While no Italians owned or resided in the damaged homes, the fire inflicted a great loss on their community. It had almost totally destroyed the project intended for "neglected Italian children and destitute Italians." But neither the people nor their priest accepted this setback to their cause.[38]

Isoleri promptly wrote Wood to inform him of the fire, but he received no reply. The priest sent another message on the next day, but the bishop again failed to answer him. After waiting several more days, Isoleri went on August 18 to the episcopal residence, where a secretary said that Wood was ill and unable to speak with him. But if Isoleri thought that Wood had reverted to his earlier opposition to the Italian church and its pastor, he was mistaken. For later in the same day Wood, appearing truly conciliatory, finally visited Isoleri and instructed him to go ahead with the rebuilding. However, he had already written to inform the sisters that everything would be ready for them by Christmas. When Isoleri reminded him of the plan to put the sisters in the new house temporarily, Wood indicated that he would not oppose the purchase of land to build a permanent residence for them.

When local residents met two days after the fire, the reported damage was about $8,000; with insurance covering $5,000 of the loss, another $3,000 had to be raised. Isoleri could not explain the motive of the person who was responsible for the fire. While his church had a half-dozen enemies, he said, it also had a half-million friends. Although the school had been destroyed, it would rise from its ashes. This "meeting of the Italian residents of the city," called to order by Isoleri, elected J. C. Greenfield, an attorney, as chairman; John L. Mellon, as a vice president; Harry Young, as secretary; and two Italians, Agostino Lagomarsino, a prominent businessman, and Dr. Domenico A. Pignatelli, a pharmacist, also as vice presidents. Lagomarsino, Pignatelli, and Mellon along with John McKenna, Stefano Ratto, William Gill, Thomas Rocks, Roger Sweeney, and H. S. Pizagno (probably Antonio J. Pizagno) were selected for a committee to receive pledges and contributions. Although Pignatelli confidently declared that $400 would be easily collected, the meeting generated just under $350 for the rebuilding program. The parish women now met to elect their own committee to raise funds, and non-Italians also came to the aid of the Italian Mission. In the midst of crisis its congregation, refusing to succumb to disaster, resumed their routine activities and even found the means to collect the respectable sum of $106 for the Holy Father on the Feast of the Assumption on August 15.[39]

The success of these efforts was immediately apparent. At their next meeting, the men reported that they had collected $421 more, while the women had raised nearly another $200. After a unanimous vote of appreciation to the United Firemen's Association for its prompt payment of the insurance policy without any reduction, the audience learned that proposals had been tendered for the removal of the fire-damaged walls. But saving its most important news for the end, the committee announced its intention to start rebuilding on the first day of the next month. Not much more than three weeks after the fire, the many friends of St. Mary Magdalen dePazzi were ready to implement Isoleri's promise to raise the schoolhouse from its ashes.[40] Moreover, on the day that the rebuilding was to begin, the committee announced that it had collected nearly $985. Pignatelli, with unflagging enthusiasm, pledged the voluntary participation of his musician friends and proposed a benefit concert. After other reports were presented, over $322 more was contributed, making the total for three weeks about $1,307.[41]

Following a picnic that had generated more money, "the friends of Father Isoleri" held their final meeting. Chairman Greenfield praised Isoleri for his self-denial and courage. A newspaper account added: "Many a man would have sunk under his heavy blow, but he stood it as brave as the bravest." Reporting that no less than 8,000 persons had attended the picnic, and congratulating him on his vast number of friends "from Kensington to the farthest part down town," it concluded that "Father Isoleri will be successful in anything that he puts his hands to."[42]

By November, St. Mary Magdalen dePazzi had recovered with astonishing speed as Rolando, Pila, and Alizeri joined Isoleri in ceremonies to bless a banner for the San Giuseppe Society. With the rebuilding of the school well under way, Isoleri had informed Barnabò, in a letter that amplified details of the fire, that reconstruction was already completed. Not only had the quick arrival of firemen prevented more serious damage, but Isoleri had also secured the $5,000 insurance policy only three weeks before the fire. It was still widely believed to have been an act of arson. Some people accused Protestants; others implicated jealous priests; still others blamed Neapolitans, who, as Isoleri noted, "had something against me, fearing that I would take their children in order to educate them."[43]

Isoleri had written Barnabò not so much to report on the fire but to again defend his mission. Believing that he had won the struggle with Wood, Isoleri asked not to be judged as bothersome for raising the issue of the mission once more, before adding that Barnabò's last reply had given him great consolation and unlimited confidence. He claimed that Wood had opposed the building plans not because of any defect with the project but because of Isoleri's appeal to Rome for support. Then, in his own defense, he described in detail his efforts to reach an accord with Wood without indicating how their dispute had been resolved.

With great regret, Isoleri also informed Barnabò that no Irish or American priest had visited him or sent him a message of condolence after the fire. Although he was sometimes called to minister to the Irish when they were unable to find other priests, their clergy now took little account of him. This negligence stood in sharp and terrible contrast to the charity of lay Catholics, and even of Protestants, who had given more than $200 to the rebuilding campaign.

Isoleri proudly noted that even if the entire property had been lost, sympathy and support—not only from Italians but also from Americans and Protestants—had been so great that he would have been able to rebuild. Nonetheless, he declared, "it was for me a terrible blow!" He had also discovered that ethnic differences among Catholics, rather than between denominations, could jeopardize his plans, and that Protestants were sometimes willing to help Catholics even when their fellow Catholics were not. It was, particularly with ecumenicism so far in the future, a remarkable discovery for a Catholic priest, especially one who had recently criticized Episcopalians for their views on religion in Italy.

Although asking for permission to raise only two issues, Isoleri placed several matters before Barnabò. He repeated his request that St. Mary Magdalen dePazzi be declared a mission church under Propaganda Fide. He pointed out that only one-third of its members were Italians, but two-thirds were Irish or Americans. While Wood was willing to allow persons to become members by renting pews, this option had only brought a dozen or so families to the church. Isoleri hoped to gain affluent non-Italian members while freeing himself from the administrative control of Wood.

In the same letter to Barnabò, Isoleri also resumed his criticism of Wood but disguised it as an appraisal of his priestly colleagues. With enough Catholics to fill existing churches as well as new ones, he asked Barnabò why other priests should regard his church as an anomaly, a stumbling block, a "hole in the wall," or even a stable (as one of them did), without giving great scandal. He identified his opposition as young priests, "pieno di Americanismo, e di se stessi, burlantissi di Roma e del collare Romano," that is, full of Americanism and full of themselves, ridiculers of Rome and of the Roman collar, who acted as if American Catholicism would soon act alone, believing that Rome wanted everything for itself and everything to be done in the Roman way. He feared that this type of priest or bishop would restrict the Italian Mission only to Italians, eventually forcing it to close, as their people alone could not support it. Why were non-Italians who lived nearby not permitted to join his church? However, he was confident that Barnabò not only understood this situation very well but also would do what was best for "la povera Chiesa Italiana di S. M. M. deP in Philadelphia," that is, the poor Italian church of St. Mary Magdalen DePazzi in Philadelphia.

With the expected arrival of the sisters, Isoleri restated his need for an assistant, for the good of Italians scattered "qua e là," here and there, throughout the city or in case he became disabled or died. He had been reluctant to raise this matter, fearing that Ascheri, whom he knew from the seminary as a good young man but a bit rough, imprudent, and not well suited to Philadelphia, would be appointed. He urged that Ascheri instead be assigned to an older pastor who would know how to direct him. Having already asked the Collegio Brignole Sale for someone else, who then had been assigned to Jerusalem, Isoleri now reminded Barnabò that if it were designated as a mission, two priests could live quite well at the church. Then Isoleri, rankled that Ascheri had already received it, asked to be granted the biretta of an Apostolic Missionary. Despite the support of a cleric from Spoleto, now living in Philadelphia, who had written on his behalf, it had not yet been awarded.

Barnabò's answer, which came quickly, informed Isoleri that neither designating the church as a mission under Propaganda Fide nor assigning an Italian priest as an assistant could be considered without the assent of Bishop Wood. But despite these setbacks, Isoleri's negotiations had produced results. In placing his case before Rome and seeking confidentiality in his dispute with Wood, Isoleri had believed that his persuasive skills were sufficient to challenge his bishop. The factors that explain Wood's sudden shift to cooperation at the end of 1872 and Isoleri's confidence by the following July remain unknown. But in petitioning Barnabò, besides referring to himself as an Italian, Isoleri had emphasized the needs and interests of immigrant Italians. And if identifying himself at the beginning and end of the letter as an alumnus of Brignole Sale was not a part of formal protocol, what was its purpose? By playing his "Italian card," Isoleri had gambled and won.[44]

Triumph, Tragedy, and His "Buon Irlandesi"

St. Mary Magdalen dePazzi had fully resumed its liturgical programs by early 1874. In February the arrival of the Missionary Sisters of St. Francis marked the opening of the school for orphans and children of immigrant families. It had about seventy children by the end of its inaugural term, when Bishop Wood attended the blessing of the rebuilt school. While the growing participation of children in parish activities soon required the formation of the Sons and Daughters of Mary in May, even more significantly, Wood's reappearance reflected a détente that was confirmed by subsequent events.[45]

Social activities, such as the annual summer picnic, which generated income for church and school, were also growing in size and importance. But the yearly spring fair, usually held soon after the feast day of the patron saint, captured the renewed spirit and ambiance of parish life more than any other event. The interior and exterior of St. Mary Magdalen dePazzi were decorated with evergreens and flowers; its main altar and sanctuary were resplendently lit; and the saint's statue, supported by angels, was surrounded with lights, flowers, and Latin, Italian, and English mottoes, with papal and American flags. Isoleri celebrated a Solemn High Mass, with Alizeri delivering a panegyric on the saint urging imitation of her virtues, and with a choir rendering music by Haydn and Mozart, on a Sunday morning in early June. After vespers in the afternoon, the schoolchildren, San Giuseppe Society members, and other parish groups carried the patroness's statue in a grand procession through neighborhood streets. At night the church remained illuminated. By 1875 the event had been extended to ten nights of entertainment, with "ice cream and refreshments . . . furnished in abundance" at Kelly's Hall at Eighth and Christian Streets, literary and abstinence societies attending from other parishes, and music provided by the St. Augustine's, Southwark, and several Italian bands. All proceeds went to the building fund.[46]

After learning that Monsignor Cesare Roncetti, the papal ablegate, was coming to Philadelphia, Isoleri invited him to attend "la festa della nostra patrona" in May 1875. Again introducing himself as an alumnus of the Collegio Brignole Sale, Isoleri stated that the Italians wished to give some special testimony of their veneration. But when Roncetti came in June to deliver the pallium, the symbol of an archbishop's authority, thus elevating Philadelphia to an archdiocese with Wood as its first archbishop, Isoleri was also protecting himself against the expanding power of a former adversary. After its rector and sodality members participated in ceremonies at the cathedral, St. Mary Magdalen dePazzi honored Roncetti and his secretary, Ubaldo Ubaldi, with an elaborate reception. Following a grand procession and other speeches, Roncetti addressed the congregation in Italian, before the Solemn Benediction of the Blessed Sacrament and a Te Deum closed an occasion that marked the beginning of a more secure situation for St. Mary Magdalen dePazzi and its rector.[47]

While increasingly resembling territorial parishes, St. Mary Magdalen dePazzi retained some distinctive features. From the time of his first homily, Isoleri had recognized the place of the Irish in his congregation. His efforts to solicit their friendship and support were rewarded when an Irish impresario organized a benefit program for him in October 1873. McEvoy's "Hibernicon" projected a panorama of views of Ireland, and the proceeds went to St. Mary Magdalen dePazzi. The performances of St. Paul's abstinence society's band each night, with its Pioneers attending in their uniforms one evening, added a very visible Irish dimension to the winter festival at the Italian church a few months later.[48]

Isoleri further capitalized on the Irish component with an art exhibit at the Assembly Buildings at Tenth and Chestnut Streets to benefit his church in July 1874. It featured an oil painting of "The Death of Daniel O'Connell," the Irish patriot (which ironically had occurred in Genoa), and it reappeared as a prize at the 1875 winter fair, where Michael Patton, secretary of the Celtic Association, won a steamship ticket to Europe, and John Mellon, the local agent of the Red Star Line, won the painting of O'Connell. Led by St. Paul's brass band, fair-goers marched to Kelly's Hall to continue their celebration. In a letter published by the diocesan press, Isoleri wished Mellon a long and happy life as well as the perpetuation in his family of "the religious and patriotic spirit of which O'Connell's heart was overflowing, and finally a meeting of us all with the great Irishman in Heaven."[49] While the $2,000 realized by the church partly explained his effusiveness, Isoleri had cemented bonds with his "buon Irlandesi."

The peculiar character of his congregation was evident in 1875, when services and instruction in Italian were followed by similar programs for "a number of persons who attend this church, born of Italian parents, or the children of Italians marrying Americans as well as pewholders who understand English better than Italian." Italians and non-Italians, especially the Irish, had a complicated, symbiotic relationship with St. Mary Magdalen dePazzi. Unlike later "duplex parishes," its two-tiered format accommodated Italians as the dominant sector in an ethnically split congregation, as its members adjusted to the acculturation of the younger generation. As noted earlier, the Irish members provided a level of material support that the Italians by themselves could not. And when the fire nearly destroyed the church, the Irish contributed generously to its recovery. Isoleri recognized this situation from the beginning; and in later years, when Italians all but displaced the Irish, he would not forget their unique role during this difficult period.[50]

The success of the Italian Mission did not preclude sad reminders from the past. In March 1874, Isoleri led mourners to the cemetery grave of Father Mariani, where he announced a plan to rebury their first rector at the church itself. Shortly afterward, after news of Cardinal Barnabò's death reached them, Isoleri celebrated a Solemn Requiem Mass for their benefactor. Although Isoleri initially hoped to gather the twenty-five alumni of the Collegio Brignole Sale now serving in the United States to rites at St. Mary Magdalen dePazzi, he had to abandon the plan. In the next year, on the day before his own birthday, he received news of the death of his father. Friends in the priesthood, his congregation, its schoolchildren, and parish societies along with Alonzo M. Viti, the Italian consul, and Frank Cuneo and Agostino Lagomarsino, two community leaders, crowded the church to mourn with Isoleri at a special mass. In his homily, Vassallo, who had suffered a similar loss in the previous year, spoke of the sacrifice of a father who gives up his son for the foreign missions with little hope of ever seeing him again.[51]

By now, familiar with triumph and tragedy, Isoleri was reconciled to the challenges of life in Philadelphia. Almost from the moment of his arrival, he had faced and overcome obstacles that would have defeated a weaker person. He had mastered English, refuted Protestants, defied his bishop, paid off the church debt, built a school and rectory, recovered from a devastating fire, and ingratiated himself with Irish Catholics. He had also been tested as his people's spiritual and temporal leader. Writing in the third person, Isoleri later reflected on his responses to these early challenges: "He encountered difficulty, but it did not stop him; crosses, but he carried them; opposition, but they were only pathways with the grace of the Lord, with indomitable courage and a totally Ligurian tenacity." Isoleri's steadfastness demonstrated that his earlier favorable assessment of himself was not an egocentric exaggeration but rather a self-portrait that contained more than a grain of truth.[52]

CHAPTER FIVE

Saving the Children

With apparent success in his struggle with the bishop, at least for the time being, Father Antonio Isoleri turned his attention to another serious threat to his fragile mission. His concern would range from saving slave children on the streets of Philadelphia to educating school children of families within his own congregation. His plan involved three principal steps: first, wresting child musicians from the control of their *padrone* masters; second, securing peace with the nuns who had assumed responsibility for the parish school; and third, allowing the sisters to do what they had been brought to St. Mary Magdalen dePazzi to do, that is, establish a suitable program of instruction. But he was not alone in having recognized the issues that disrupted the immigrant community. As its population increased, the plight of abused and exploited children had become impossible to ignore by the early 1870s. Moreover, as a local newspaper noted, "in all of our large cities Italian children are held in the same sort of bondage, and nothing has yet been done to reach the evil, the excuse for which may be, until recently, that its existence was scarce suspected by the public generally. . . . It is disgraceful to a civilized community that such a state of slavery should be allowed to exist, and . . . it is proper to ask what are we doing here in Philadelphia about this evil, which notoriously exists among us."[1]

The Campaign to Save the Slave Children

As what they colorfully called "a large influx of Italians" crowded into South Philadelphia, the city's newspapers increasingly reported acts of violence and crime within the immigrant colony. Itinerant musicians, bootblacks, "street Arabs," and newsboys, accompanied by well-dressed and well-fed padrones, had reportedly left New York City, where arrests and prosecutions made it too difficult for them to remain, for Philadelphia. While New York authorities acted to break up "the abominable system of child slavery," it was becoming a greater problem for Philadelphia: "The unfortunate victims have been brought here to escape the vigilance of the metropolitan police, and where they can ply their trades with more security."[2]

By the summer of 1873, newspaper accounts focused on the plight of "the little Italian musicians, who may be found scattered all over the country, though more particularly in our great cities." Brought under false pretenses or even kidnapped, torn from parents and home, shipped like cattle, held by captors or other ruffians in brutal and heartless bondage, they were sent into the streets "to attract the pity of the passer-by with their haggard little faces and doleful music, and their master is supported in idleness, if not in luxury, by the charity they obtain."[3] While such accounts seemed melodramatic, the press had not entirely invented the situation. Leaders of the Italian colony also decried the condition of the "slave children." As one newspaper pointed out, "None felt more keenly the disgrace attaching to this pernicious business than the respectable Italian citizens of this community, all of whom have been long anxious for its abatement or abolition." In a letter to the chief of the city detectives, the Italian consul, Alonzo M. Viti, whose family had been prominent since the early years of the century, declared: "I do not recognize the authority of those persons who control by force and with such a mode of life the direction of those orphans or other children."[4]

While long seen mainly as a nuisance but now becoming a criminal matter, the situation continued to exert pressure on city authorities to react. On the early morning of September 15, 1873, a detachment of forty policemen, armed with search warrants, quietly surrounded nine houses on Carpenter, Christian, and South Eighth Streets before crashing through their doors in a sensational raid. The local press, vividly reporting the raid to the public, described the houses as filthy and disorderly, "with men, women and children being herded together in rooms and beds like swine." In one cellar, eight naked boys were discovered on two beds. And in every house the police found "a superabundance of old clothes, fiddles, harps and other instruments by which the pockets of the people are appealed to through the ears."[5]

Arresting 152 men, women, and children, the raiders marched them to the Second Police District station house on Second Street, above Christian, where they were held in the basement to await a hearing in the late afternoon. As the hour of the hearing approached, a large crowd that included many Italians gathered at the station house. When the prisoners were brought out, some observers found them "more like a herd of sheep . . . than like anything else. Men, women and children of nearly all ages huddled together, most of them being extremely untidy and unclean looking in their persons."[6] But in another account, "nearly all of them were well clad, were hearty looking and the children bore no appearance of cruel treatment."[7] The contrasting perceptions by the two principal newspapers of the city also reflected their different views on the politics of the mayor and his administration.

Some leaders of the Italian community, such as Agostino Lagomarsino, a prominent and respected businessman who served as the court interpreter, were not about to abandon the street musicians in the proceedings that followed. Lagomarsino was probably the saloonkeeper who had obtained the dismissal of some cases earlier in the day by his assurance that no crimes had been committed.[8] And when the magistrate opened the afternoon hearing by asking if there were more individuals to come, he learned for the first time that some of them had already been released. After questioning several others without much success, the magistrate then asked for testimony from the arresting officers, but they had none to give. At this point, he declared: "Then I'll end the farce; let them all be discharged."[9]

With the dismissal of the charges, the Italians ran from the hall. The children laughed, shouted, and threw up their caps as they reached the street, while the adults, happy but puzzled over why they had been arrested in the first place, poured out of the courtroom and marched together back to their neighborhood. Despite the warrants and arrests, the police had lacked evidence that could be used as grounds for criminal charges against the Italians.[10]

Nevertheless, Mayor William Stokley intended to continue his campaign to rid Philadelphia of the street musicians.[11] Reacting to the magistrate's use of the term "farce" in dismissing the case, the *Inquirer* repeated the word in the title ·of a blistering editorial on the next day: "It would be folly to attempt to show the monstrous wrong against humanity, of the stealing or buying away from their sunny Italian homes the little children, bringing them to our inclement climate, subjecting them in all kinds of weather, in the most meagre clothing, to the cruelties of hunger and exposure of body and soul. This barbarous traffic in children has been carried on so long under the eyes of our citizens, its humanity has been so often and so fully exposed, that there is but little left to be said about it."[12] Claiming that authorities had eradicated the padrone system in New York City and commending Stokley for his efforts in Philadelphia, the same editorial raised a critical voice toward the magistrate before identifying what it saw as the source of the problem in this case:

> We do not know, nor do we care to know, why the attempt to destroy this infamous trade of child torture was to this judicial dignitary a mere farce. He is too insignificant a figure in the whole wretched business to engage attention. . . . He is not the culprit to arraign here. The real culprits are

those citizens of Philadelphia, who, in mistaken charity, toss their pennies to the childish musicians of the streets who stop to play their disjointed tunes beneath their windows. They alone are responsible for a wrong so monstrous that its continuance would be a disgrace to any community where it was fostered, as it is in this one; for there is not a little child wandering about the streets playing for money, that is not the cruelly beaten, improperly clothed, badly sheltered and underfed slave of a Padrone. Not a penny that is tossed to them that does not bind their chains faster; not a penny that is given them goes to make their hard lives brighter or happier. All that they gather goes to make rich a Padrone, too lazy to work or beg, and too cowardly to steal. If men and women would but remember this, they would throw no more pennies to the street musicians, for just so soon as they cease to collect pennies, the Padrones will let them go free. They only want them while they make money.[13]

The remedy was clear. The two city councils (the Select Council and the Common Council) could solve the problem by passing an ordinance to prohibit children from playing music for money on city streets.[14] Two days after the raid on the Italians, the police, relying upon a rediscovered vagrancy ordinance, were ordered to arrest all persons playing fiddles, flutes, harps, and other instruments on the streets.[15] While repeating its support for the mayor, the *Inquirer* concluded with a sarcastic recommendation: "We believe there is in Philadelphia a regularly organized society of sentimental ladies whose business it is to provide aromatic baths and shelter for neglected canines. We would respectfully suggest that, as the dog-days are over for 1873, they employ their superfluous energy and benevolence in looking after the little children stolen from Italy to play and sing in our streets. The field is a fine one for tillage by genuine philanthropists."[16]

Although the city councils failed to implement the suggestion, the General Assembly of Pennsylvania, partly at the urging of Viti, passed an act of legislation in May 1874 to prevent traffic in children "for the purpose of singing, playing on musical instruments, begging . . . in the streets, roads and other highways of this commonwealth."[17] Despite these efforts, the problem remained unresolved, and a similar campaign against the abuse of Italian children, still being arrested for playing music on city streets, would be waged ten years later.

This particular case and the overall situation had several implications. The dismissal of all charges in the original incident suggested that the raids owed more to impending municipal elections than to any genuine concern for the welfare of immigrant Italians. The raids also reflected the undeniably difficult conditions of Italians living in or near poverty. Furthermore, the intervention of Viti and Lagomarsino marked the emergence of shared interests and leadership within a community that now itself addressed problems that threatened its existence.

Street Musicians and Secret Societies

In his frequent warnings about the dangers facing immigrant children, Isoleri recognized the plight of the street musicians in particular: "Disgracefully, we also have here many boys and girls abandoned by their relatives, and sometimes even sold. . . . Children abandoned day and night; girls that play music at every hour everywhere." But he sought to connect their spiritual welfare to their material condition: "when they rise again by the grace of Baptism and are made to practice religion, they do well, and they console me. And yes, in many cases they make their First Communion, on the occasion of marriage, and sometimes in instructing them, I must begin by teaching them how to make the Sign of the Cross."[18] The raids and arrests gave Isoleri the opportunity to improve temporal life within the immigrant community. And while his efforts could only strengthen his position and the role of his church among Italians, he could also recognize the implications of any success for his reputation with the ecclesiastical authorities in Rome. But before he implemented his plans for children, he had to contend with some formidable opposition in Philadelphia.

Isoleri found new issues that he used, at least rhetorically, to broaden his view of the evils that threatened Italian Catholics, whether children or adults, in the city. One was Freemasonry, for which Philadelphia had served as a center since colonial times.[19] When some 11,000 Freemasons paraded for the dedication of a temple in late September 1873, Isoleri wrote a stinging condemnation of secret societies for his congregation. He began his "Discorso sopra Le Società Segrete" with the words, "Man was not made to live alone, but has a natural instinct that brings him to social life."[20] Declaring that Rousseau had erred on the original condition of mankind, Isoleri presented the Creation and Fall of Adam as having given a place to perverse persons, sons of the demon, and agents of darkness against the sons of God. In this epic struggle he found the origins of secret societies and their deleterious effects upon family, state, and religion as they spread ruin throughout Europe. He painted the death of hope for the Freemason without a priest, using Voltaire as his example. And for what reason did the Church condemn these brotherhoods of Satan? It did not condemn Protestant union, fraternal love, mutual aid, and organized labor but the evils, abuses, and vices of secret societies. Referring to the bloody events in another city only two years earlier, Isoleri pointed out that Paris was still burning, while ghostly specters roamed its streets with a dagger in one hand and kerosene in the other. Socialism, Communism, Internationalism, Nihilism, and Anarchy, all unleashed, now exulted in orgies on the edge of the abyss that they themselves had dug. But what these movements called themselves did not matter, since the plot had been woven in Masonic lodges. Urging Catholics not to replace rosaries and scapulars of the Virgin Mary with the jewels of Freemasonry and the chains of the devil, Isoleri concluded: "We remain in the Church and with the Church and we will be with God . . . happy in our time and happy in eternity."

While Isoleri's account of human origins relied on Scripture, it was no more mythological than the version of Enlightenment rationalists whom he challenged. And while the movement that he condemned could be seen more favorably, the damage that it inflicted on Catholicism was undeniable. But Isoleri soon found more proximate difficulties, as his efforts to save the children, which had begun with padrone masters as his adversaries, shifted to a battle to save himself against some formidable and worthy sisters.

The Missionary Sisters of St. Francis

While the fire of the previous summer had postponed their coming, three Missionary Sisters of St. Francis finally reached Philadelphia on February 16, 1874. Their school for thirty children and five or six orphans of the neighborhood opened on March 7. Isoleri had sought the order because he assumed that Italian nuns would be sent from the mother house in Gemona. Sister Lucrezia Platter, the mother superior of the group, while fluent in Italian, was an Austrian who had entered the order in Gemona. Distinguished, dignified, and gentle, she would labor on behalf of hundreds of Italian children for some time before Mother Frances Xavier Cabrini began her more celebrated efforts. But her Austrian birth made Sister Lucrezia a liability for the Italian Mission, especially because of the ardently patriotic sentiments of its rector. Moreover, both Sister Philippina Casey, who had Irish origins, and Sister Antonia Del Angelo, who had Italian origins, but was only a postulant, had come from Peekskill rather than Gemona. And when school opened for its first full year in September 1874, Sister Francis Dobbins, another Irish member, joined them.[21]

Almost from their moment of arrival, Isoleri found the sisters unsuited for the assignment. In a lengthy letter to Father Gregorio Fioravante, the Franciscan superior general in Rome, he expressed the fear that his congregation would not receive them and would be angry with him for having promised that they would be Italian. He claimed that the children did not respect Sister Antonia because she was not yet a *monaca*, that is, a professed nun. Sister Gertrude, their Peekskill superior, whose plans called for a *scuola scelta*, that is, a private academy, along with the parish school and Irish- or English-speaking sisters—but not another Italian one—had not understood or did not wish to understand the problem. Isoleri objected to another academy because several already existed in the city. When Bishop Wood's secretary, learning that the same sisters were still there, remarked that only one was Italian, Isoleri felt wounded.[22]

When Isoleri met with Sister Gertrude, matters deteriorated further. To her news that Sister Antonia might complete her novitiate in the city as a special favor, he angrily replied, "*E che grazia*," that is, "by what special grace?" As for a "German" sister teaching Italians, he warned that "*gli Italiani farebbero rivoluzione*," that is to say, the Italians would start a revolution. And when he asked for another sister from Italy, Mother Gertrude seemed to be surprised by his request. Isoleri admitted that he was unable to pay the expenses for her voyage, but then he made his position clearer. He completely opposed opening an academy. Moreover, if three sisters were assigned to the school, at least two should be Italian; if five were assigned, at least three should be Italian. And it mattered little to him who was sent if she could not speak Italian. The undertaking had to be seen, like St. Mary Magdalen de Pazzi itself, as being Italian and for Italians, which Sister Gertrude was still unwilling to acknowledge.

When Isoleri again wrote to Sister Gertrude, he introduced a new problem. In his eyes, Sister Philippina had not only become intractable and haughty with him and with her own superior, but she had also acted so much like a madwoman that the children and neighbors had been scandalized. Moreover, her belief that she was in good standing with Sister Gertrude had increased her duplicity and disobedience.[23]

Despite their differences, however, Isoleri sought to reach an accord with Sister Gertrude. Instead of being adversaries, he proposed that they agree on the interests of the Italian Mission, adding, "Non ho ancora i capelli bianchi, ma ho già un po d'esperienza e conosco qualche cosa" (I do not yet have white hair, but I already have some experience and I know something). But, while appearing conciliatory, he had initiated another strategy. If his proposals were not accepted, he was ready to turn matters over to the authorities in Gemona. He had actually presented his case to Father Gregorio nearly six weeks earlier.

In July, Isoleri wrote to Mother Angela, superior general of the order in Gemona. He included a copy of his letter to Sister Gertrude, commenting that her failure to reply had left him filled with anguish. Identifying himself as an alumnus of the Collegio Brignole Sale and the nephew of three uncles in the Franciscan order, Isoleri told her that he feared that, having left for their annual retreat in Peekskill and now away for some time, the Missionary Sisters did not intend to return to Philadelphia at all. While he may have erred in asking Sister Gertrude not to send another nun, lest she assign more Irish sisters, Isoleri claimed that he only meant someone other than the original three. This misunderstanding might now leave him with none at all. Turning the solution over to Father Gregorio and Mother Angela, Isoleri continued to build his case against Sister Gertrude.[24]

Three days after writing to Mother Angela, when Isoleri wrote again to Father Gregorio and included the reply from Sister Gertrude for which he had been waiting, his tactics became evident. In corresponding with Sister Gertrude, Isoleri had baited a trap, and it now appeared that he had caught her in it. He would not comment on her letter or on the spirit of her reply because "si commenta da se stessa," it spoke for itself. Asking for a judgment from Father Gregorio, he presented more information. Having agreed to pay $200 per year or more for fuel and water costs for the sisters' residence, Isoleri charged that Sister Lucrezia had spent some of the money for a round trip to Peekskill. He claimed that if either of the other sisters were permitted to write, Father Gregorio would see a point of view different from Sister Gertrude's. Aware that the sisters would stay in Peekskill out of obstinacy until the end of August, he thought that they should return to Philadelphia sooner to prepare for the reopening of the school.[25]

While Isoleri expected Sister Gertrude's reaction to strengthen his position, her feisty reply challenged him point for point. He should have known, she said, that she was unable to answer anyone during her retreat. She declared that she was willing to send as many Italian sisters as Isoleri wanted if he would meet their expenses. With this meager income, how was she going to feed and clothe three sisters for two months? And to the question of how would they return to Philadelphia, she suggested, "By a coal train, perhaps?" Moreover, since the superior general made assignments, it was not her fault that someone already professed or better educated than Sister Antonia had not been sent.

To Isoleri's charge that other sisters could testify to her pride, Sister Gertrude suggested that he save his opinion; she was accountable only to God and to her superior. She then summed up her feelings about Philadelphia as a source of many tears and a *hosanna* that never gave her any joy.

Despite Sister Gertrude's strong reply, when Isoleri again wrote Father Gregorio in September 1874, he appeared more confident than ever before. Father Gregorio had expressed his hope that the opening of the school had gone well, and that it would have been the most beautiful thing in the world if it had been possible from the start to have three good Italian teaching sisters in Philadelphia. Seizing the opportunity, Isoleri astutely quoted Father Gregorio's own words before declaring: "in that case, the school would already be going not merely well, but very well."[26] He wanted to persuade Father Gregorio to remove authority for the staffing of the school from Sister Gertrude. Pointing to what Father Gregorio himself had referred to as "debolezze femminile" (feminine weaknesses), Isoleri accused Sister Gertrude of acting capriciously: "What would you say if a Superior was all tenderness with some people, but Bismarck with others?"

Hinting at other charges against Sister Gertrude that had to remain confidential for the good of the order, Isoleri focused on the issues at Philadelphia. He would not compromise on two matters. He refused to accept any more sisters, above all Irish ones, without more Italian sisters; and their residence could never be left unoccupied. (His memories of the fire were still vivid.) Seeking to separate the local mission from Peekskill and Sister Gertrude's control, he proposed that a new province be organized, in view of the importance of Pennsylvania as a state and Philadelphia as a diocese.

On the day that he wrote to Father Gregorio, Isoleri prepared a letter to Mother Angela, with more accusations against Sister Gertrude. Complimenting Mother Angela for her ingenuity and charity in answering Sister Gertrude, he believed that the latter still owed him an explanation or retraction. He was particularly annoyed by her remark that only tears had come from the mission in Philadelphia and by her questions of how the sisters were to be supported and whether they were to return from Peekskill in a coal train. He indignantly noted that Sister Gertrude could pout as long as she wished.[27] When Sister Gertrude finally answered his letters, he added, she informed him that four sisters would leave in late August for Philadelphia. When they arrived, he contended, one of them was only skin and bones and nearly always bedridden, and, in the judgment of physicians, not only unable to work but also not even likely to live much longer. Had this unfortunate one been sent to spite him?

Isoleri had once believed that his demand that another sister, especially an Irish one, not be sent without another Italian, had been too strong. Referring to himself as "il minchione" (the very gullible one), he now thought that it had not been strong enough. Made to swallow a sister so ill that she required attention from all the others, it did not matter whether she were Irish or American, for they were all the same to him. And when Italians spoke of the nun whose illness made her unable to speak to them, they called her "the mute sister." They wanted to know what was going on between Isoleri and Sister Gertrude.

Isoleri renewed his campaign against Sister Gertrude in another letter to Mother Angela in January 1875, when he expanded his version of the situation. An Irish sister, who had been sent to keep watch on another nun, often acted in a diffident or authoritarian manner. Furthermore, the efforts of poor Italians to speak, when they found themselves before the Irish, not only often died in their mouths, but they were also losing their esteem and affection for the sisters. With antipathy between the Italians and the Irish and with most sisters not being Italian, matters would never improve. And as the people became displeased with these developments, they talked and their pastor suffered. So Isoleri depicted the state of affairs.[28]

Then he posed more questions that remained unanswered. Why had Sister Gertrude not replied to his letters? Why was the residence of the sisters left unoccupied? And after he asked for Italians to staff the mission, why had she sent two more Irish nuns? The delay in sending Italian sisters had damaged the school. Families had withdrawn their children, and instead of the expected two hundred students, only about one hundred of them remained enrolled. Isoleri incisively observed: "If out of three sisters, two had been Italians, or of four, three, things certainly would go better, or ought to go so; and the people would not be able to say: they are Irish sisters, or American, but they would say they are our sisters. That is so far what they do not say and are not able to say."

While his school languished, Isoleri was unable to overcome the repugnance in his heart. Although willing to do all that he must for the sisters, he was unable to spend three minutes with them, except for what was absolutely necessary. They might think that he was disappointed, but he denied it, saying that he felt only grief. Italian sisters and an Italian superior as soon as possible were not only what the people wanted, but they were the only means by which the mission would flourish. And not permitting the sisters' residence to be left unoccupied would hold the interests of the mission ahead of those of the mother house at Peekskill.

Isoleri sympathized with Mother Angela's efforts to govern the members of her order in America without a true superior. And while still critical of Sister Gertrude, he sought to win Mother Angela as an ally. Certain of Mother Angela's cooperation, he offered to defray travel expenses for the sisters for the greater glory of God, the good of the mission and of "our sisters." He suggested that the nuns already at the mission, instead of asking Sister Gertrude for money, could raise "*un migliajo di scudi*" (a thousand dollars) with one or two collections per year. And if the sisters took responsibility for the school, then contributions would more easily come to them. His plan would not only make them more stable and independent, he wrote, but also would enable him to enlarge the church.

Reaching an Agreement

In April 1875, when Isoleri next replied to Mother Angela, his opening words, "Quanto mi abbia consolato non glielo posso esprimere" (I cannot tell you how much it has comforted me), indicated that a solution was within reach. Having been informed that she was coming to Philadelphia, Isoleri offered to defray her travel expenses. The other sisters would not be subjected to the humiliation of collecting donations for the voyage but might pay, if they wished, for her return passage. Wistfully expressing his own longing for Italy, he added, "e chi sa che io non le sia compagno nel medesimo" (and who knows if I might not accompany them at the same time).[29]

Isoleri provided Mother Angela with letters of introduction to facilitate her trip through Antwerp and Liverpool and with information on shipping companies and ports of destination. He proposed that her departure be in early May, so that she could arrive in time for the feast day of Saint Mary Magdalen de-Pazzi. And if she informed him of the date of departure, he would meet the ship on its arrival. He concluded by asking Mother Angela to pray for his father, who had died on January 23, the day when he had written his previous letter to her.

The negotiations subsequently produced a formal agreement, dated April 16, 1876, on the issues that had plagued the development of the school and the relationship between him and the sisters for over two years. Placed under his authority in regard to the school and its students, the sisters remained under the direction of their mother house in all other matters. While the assignment of sisters still originated with a request by the local superior to the superior general, the final decision required the agreement of the rector. The superior at the mission had to be an Italian. The sisters assumed full responsibility for the operation of the school, receiving nothing more from the rector than the fees paid by its students. The same condition stated: "The sisters will do all in their power to get as many Italian scholars as they can so that they may labor more for the benefit of their neighborhood."[30]

The agreement also stipulated that the sisters, united to the wishes of Isoleri, were "to open an orphan asylum for the present for the benefit of the Italian girls with the idea of opening in time one for the Italian boys." While first renting a suitable house and equally sharing the cost with the rector, the sisters were expected to collect money in order to buy it. The maintenance was to be taken from the funds intended for the house and whatever the rector wished to give. Any improvements or repairs would be paid for by whatever the sisters could collect or earn "by means of some respectable and holy industry permitted in this country" and approved by the rector and their local superior. The property would become the possession of the Church, with the bishop as its principal protector and with the sisters retaining its permanent use and the right to make improvements. This consideration ensured that "it may serve for the object for which it was bought, and the sisters cannot be removed by anyone, if they continue to provide for the teaching in Italian and English of the parochial school and the orphans."

The agreement took up the status of the sisters directly. No nun could become a permanent member of the mission "unless she be an Italian or a European who speaks Italian." No "Postulanti Inglesi" would be received unless they were able to teach at the school. Italian women seeking a religious vocation could be received with the permission of the superior. Whether American or Italian, they had to take their novitiate training in Italy, unless they obtained a dispensation from the superior allowing it to take place in Philadelphia. The final condition provided $50 annually to each sister for habits, journeys, or other expenses, and an obligation to the mother general of the order. Any savings were to be used only for the benefit of the orphans or for improvements to the house.

Isoleri had prevailed on nearly every point, at least for the moment. The only issue that had not been addressed was the vacating of the residence by the sisters during their annual spiritual retreat in Peekskill. He had to be very satisfied with what had been achieved, but especially for shifting the source of the sisters to the mother house at Gemona, thus almost ensuring that they would be Italians.[31]

St. Mary Magdalen dePazzi School

By the end of 1876, while also engaged in visiting the ill and imprisoned, the sisters mainly devoted themselves to instructing children at the parish school and caring for the girls at the orphanage. The program for the school rested on the need to convince parents of their obligation to send their children to a school that was Italian and Catholic. Since it provided instruction in religion and other subjects in Italian, it almost ensured that only Italian children were to be admitted. While families of other ethnic origins could apply for special permission from the pastor to enroll their children, few, if any, ever did.[32]

The plan for St. Mary Magdalen dePazzi School combined a course of study, curriculum, and daily schedule, along with rules and regulations for teachers and students, that had been adopted from a similar program at a school in Gemona. The school year lasted from the first week of September until final examinations in early July, with secular and religious holidays and lengthier vacations at Christmas and Easter. After a morning session from 8:30 to 11:30 A.M., students were dismissed for lunch; classes resumed at 1:30 P.M. and lasted until 4:00 P.M., with special arrangements for bad weather. The routine included prayers in Latin, attendance at mass on certain days, and reception of the sacraments. The children were expected to conform to standards of neatness, cleanliness, and physical condition as well as of conduct and manners while at school. Teachers were given suggestions on how they should discipline their charges.

The school's program required Italian and English during morning and afternoon sessions, with dismissal of any student who refused to study both languages. Along with reading, writing, and composition in Italian, the curriculum included grammar, geography, arithmetic, some Roman history, a compendium of Italian history, some Italian literature for the highest-level class, Church history, and catechism. Daily exercises of memory and composition in Italian and English on familiar, patriotic, commercial, and sacred subjects were also required. For a half-hour on Tuesday and Friday mornings from October to Christmas and from Easter to June, instruction was given to girls in such "feminine work" as sewing and embroidery, which was graded and recorded on certificates.

The highly organized program also included a general review, then examinations. The performance of students, along with the condition of books, desks, other furniture, and stairways, determined seating arrangements for the next session. A daily register of attendance, study, piety, and conduct was to be read publicly each month and given to parents every other month or more often, if requested. Final examinations, both written and oral, were scheduled for the first Monday in February, then again just before the Fourth of July. The rector and sisters attended examinations together with parents and other invited persons. Final reports were prepared for the rector and parents.

An annual celebration, either on Columbus Day or the nearest Saturday, recognized academic achievement and good conduct. Statues, devotional pictures, and books were awarded to the four students with the highest grades, and honorable mention to other children who had made a good effort. A prize was given to the boy and girl with the highest averages as well as to students with the best conduct. Children who recited prose or poetry or sang in English and Italian provided entertainment for the occasion, which was also a fund-raising event. While parents of children who received awards were given complimentary tickets, others were expected to pay to attend.

The ceremony also dedicated the school year both to a patron saint and to a notable, as models of inspiration and emulation for the students. Isoleri spoke briefly on the saint in English; another speaker, invited for the occasion, lectured on the secular figure in Italian. Students honored these subjects by singing or reciting appropriate tributes. The paired choices of figures to be honored, which were made by Isoleri, were often predictable but sometimes surprising. While Saint Thomas Aquinas and Christopher Columbus, or Saint Bonaventure and Dante, or even Saint Francis of Assisi and Petrarch, might be expected, Saint Teresa of Avila and Boccaccio were a more curious coupling. Political or cultural personages who reflected Italian culture but who hardly might be anticipated from a Catholic institution showed Isoleri's capacity to celebrate Humanism as well as to defy parochialism. Along with the annual ceremony, the program throughout the year offered formidable resources for Italian families and their children.

The recurrent themes in Isoleri's correspondence with Father Gregorio, Sister Gertrude, and Mother Angela reflected his plans for the mission. With the sensational episode of the "slave children," by exposing their plight and linking the Italian Mission to the community, Isoleri saw the parish school as a crucial means of reaching immigrant families and saving their children. He regarded the presence of Italian sisters as indispensable to the endeavor, but he had no intention of relinquishing his control over the church's property or its activities.

Although Isoleri had tied much of his efforts to the immigrant community, whether involving child street musicians or ordinary families, his problems reached beyond the immediate neighborhood. His troubles with Bishop Wood had not really been resolved and would have to be faced again. If prejudice existed in the chancery, then Isoleri would have to confront it. And if, as once before, he sometimes seemed to be playing an ethnic card with the Church authorities in Italy, he was now ready to deal the entire deck. While it might appear that he was pursuing a devious agenda, Isoleri had shrewdly displayed his own sense of how the game of ecclesiastical politics was played. But the harmony that had been reached within his mission was, as the lingering tensions with the sisters would remind him, precarious and temporary. Nonetheless, he had established a foundation upon which he could build what he hoped to achieve at St. Mary Magdalen dePazzi.

CHAPTER SIX

Columbus and Other Heroes

The Search for Identity

From the moment of their arrival in America, immigrants from Italy faced powerful forces that began to transform them. In shops and factories, in schools and churches, and on the streets, they were stripped of the inner values and outer behaviors of their traditional culture. Although often retreating to the security of family life and friendships, they could not fully isolate and insulate themselves, but inevitably only become more American. Out of older retained fragments and newly acquired elements, they were creating a hybrid culture and identity as Italian Americans. In urban America, as they sought continuity with the past, survival and stability in the present, and hope in the future, their success depended upon establishing a cohesive community and a finding a coherent sense of self. It became essential for them to take pride in Italian antecedents that would also connect them to their American-born children. Philadelphia's Italians were participants in these processes, and their religious life played a major role in guiding them through this difficult rite of passage.

In the ancestral land that these immigrants had left, Pope Pius IX responded to the loss of the Papal States by issuing his "Non expedit" decree of 1870, which prohibited Catholics from seeking office, voting, or assuming any political role in the new Italy without incurring excommunication. But papal policy quickly waned in application. By the time of the pope's death in 1878, the Church not only found itself in internal disorder but also in difficulty with almost every other government. Upon his election, Pope Leo XIII almost immediately began efforts to heal relations with other states.[1]

If Italian Catholics, whether in Italy or in the immigrant colonies of American cities, found new problems, patriotic priests faced an even more delicate situation. Isoleri's role as rector of St. Mary Magdalen dePazzi, along with his personal values, encouraged him to seek reconciliation of divergent views. As the only church for Philadelphia's Italians—even those with political differences with the Holy See—it remained an important institution for many, if not all, of them. Isoleri had the task of succeeding where others before him had struggled, and where at least one of them, Gaetano Sorrentini, had failed. If he either lacked ability or made a serious blunder, Isoleri's fate would be the same.

Identity and Celebration:
Columbus as Immigrant and Icon

While seeking to integrate the religious and secular needs of his people as a part of his strategy to stabilize the Italian Mission, Isoleri led their search for an appropriate sense of self in a new society. But America offered complicated choices to Italians, and American Catholicism often made matters even more troublesome. Opinion by other Catholics about Philadelphia's Italians contained hints of character deficiency and an overt emphasis on the need for religious indoctrination: "There are between 2,000 and 3,000 Italians in this city, to be increased shortly, to 5,000 or more. Everyone knows what difficulties the Italians have had to contend with, of late years, their beautiful country torn to pieces by revolutionary passions, and impoverished by taxation. There are few works so necessary as the training and Catholic education of the Italian children here. They must be trained to habits of steady industry, and they must be educated *as Catholics*."[2]

At St. Mary Magdalen dePazzi, such events as the Washington's Birthday Tea Party, with its tables for the Irish, Italians, and Americans displayed a prescient sense of the options of identity and adjustment for Italians.[3] But Catholicism in Philadelphia was embracing a more derogatory depiction, widely shared by the rest of American society, along with a specious comparison of Italians to the Irish. As one Irish American priest declared, "I behold the Italians, like the Irish, full of faith, devotions, and beautiful conceits, but these from time to time, dwindled into puerilities, whilst among the Irish they were ever strong, vigorous and enterprising."[4]

In their search for a new identity as well in defense against calumny, the Italians in Philadelphia turned to community organizations and public ceremonies. After the founding of the first secular beneficial society seven years earlier, the religious Confraternity of San Giuseppe was organized at St. Mary Magdalen dePazzi in 1874 with many of the same members. The candidates for election as its officers included Agostino Lagomarsino, Giuseppe Mangini, Antonio Repetto, Stefano Ratto, Giuseppe Raffetto, Bartolomeo Lavezzo, Pietro Castagnola, Bartolomeo Ferretti, Tomaso Chiapellone, Giuseppe Chiapellone, and Antonio Capelli. At least one, Lagomarsino, had been a trustee during the interdiction in 1867. These leaders of the Italian community had greatly contributed to his church, and Isoleri needed to retain their confidence and cooperation.[5]

Isoleri was continuing to assume a larger role in the civic, as well as religious, life of the immigrant community. Facing the potential loss of an important advocate with the resignation of Alonzo Viti as the vice consul of Italy in March 1875, Isoleri accepted the task of articulating its interests. As a prominent businessman and leader, Viti had led the campaign against the exploitation of the child musicians. After one hundred eighty members of the Società di Unione e Fratellanza Italiana had unanimously approved a motion by its president, Dr. Domenico A. Pignatelli, Isoleri drafted a letter asking Ferdinando DeLuca, the consul general in New York City, to reject Viti's resignation. Citing the long service by Viti as well as that of his highly esteemed father and predecessor in the post, Vito Viti, Isoleri stated that the motion reflected not only the ardent wish of the Società but also of the entire Italian colony. He implored DeLuca to persuade Viti to withdraw his resignation or at least to stay in office until after the impending centennial of American independence. The effort succeeded, and Viti became chairman of the Columbus Monument Association as well. The result also indirectly confirmed Isoleri's stature in the Italian community.[6]

Isoleri again stepped forward in the first major event staged by Philadelphia's Italians, as they dedicated a statue of Columbus that was said to be the first public monument to the explorer in America. On July 5, 1875, after more than two years of planning, residents of the Italian colony joined other citizens at the site in Fairmount Park on which the statue was to be erected. While the Bersaglieri Society's band played, some four hundred members of the Italian Beneficial Society listened to speeches by Nunzio Finelli, the president of the Columbus Monument Association; Alonzo Viti, the vice consul; John A. Clark, a local attorney; and Giovanni Francesco Secchi deCasali, publisher of *L'Eco d'Italia*, the principal Italian newspaper in New York City.[7]

For Philadelphia's Italians, who had been strangely inconspicuous when other residents had demonstrated their support for Italy's independence in years past, this event marked a turning point. As they finally announced their communal presence by celebrating Columbus, it was remarkable in other ways as well. Finelli, a Freemason, and Secchi deCasali, a Protestant, anti-Catholic, and exile supporter of Italian republicanism, shared the platform and podium with Isoleri, a Roman Catholic priest and Savoyard monarchist. Secchi deCasali noted the significance of the day by praising Philadelphia's Italians for uniting. He referred specifically to the Bersaglieri band and a strongly supported beneficial society, contending that neither could be found in New York City.[8]

Concluding the event, Isoleri addressed the Italians and Americans in the audience but spoke only in Italian, as he renewed a plea for sainthood for Columbus. Extolling the explorer as a son of the Church, Isoleri could not deny himself a small gesture of regional pride when he pointed out that Columbus was also the son of a free land, namely, the Ligurian Republic. Reminding his audience of its obligations, he declared that the practice of Christian and civic virtues would make them worthy citizens of the land that Columbus had discovered. He then called for God's blessing upon America and Italy.[9]

Isoleri, however, carefully guarded his ideas and messages, even in their details, at this moment as he would continue to do in the future. When a newspaper incorrectly reported his speech in Fairmount Park, quoting him as saying that Columbus was "perhaps the discoverer of this land," Isoleri cited the error in a letter denying that he had used the word "perhaps" and asked the editor to reprint the entire sentence in the next issue. Isoleri could not ignore a matter as significant as the place of Columbus in American life.[10]

Not willing to restrict himself to religious matters, Isoleri's participation in community affairs had its risks. Some critics saw scandal in a Catholic priest who appeared in ·public with Protestants, anticlericals, liberals, Freemasons, and Italian nationalists, but he had found these occasions to be an opportunity to reconcile his political and religious views. In the summer of 1876, with Isoleri and the Italian colony eagerly anticipating the arrival of the long-awaited statue from Leghorn, the Columbus Monument Association invited the Reverend Edward McGlynn, the noted orator from New York City and later a highly controversial figure, to deliver a lecture on "The Life of Columbus" at the Academy of Music to aid its fund. Plans called for a gala reception for some seven hundred members of the Christopher Columbus Society of Genoa, who would not only take part in the dedication of the statue but would also renew their bonds with Ligurians and other Italians in Philadelphia's Little Italy in early July. But as expectations grew, the seeds for further discontent over Isoleri's role in these events were being sown.[11]

In October 1876, when Philadelphia's Italians finally dedicated the Columbus statue, they heard themselves described by one speaker as "her absent children, sympathizing with the people among whom you have voluntarily cast your lot." But with the governor of Pennsylvania, the mayor of Philadelphia, and Italian delegations from Boston, Richmond, Baltimore, and Washington in attendance, Isoleri gave the principal speech for the occasion in Italian. He began by saluting Columbus with an imaginative account of his own adjustment to a new society and of that of all Italians as immigrants to America. Now thirty-one years old, he was growing beyond his earlier, more cautious manner. Having had the opportunity to reflect on his experiences over six years as well as on his place within the Italian colony, Isoleri thanked God for allowing him to come as a missionary to Italians in America, where he could also remain an Italian. Indeed, as long as the sun shone upon his head and until he drew his final breath, he would remain an Italian. After addressing his audience as Genoese, Tuscans, Neapolitans and Sicilians, Isoleri abruptly corrected himself: "Oh! che dico?" (Oh, what am I saying?) With a new formula for group identity, he then declared that they were no longer Genoese, Tuscans, Neapolitans, or Sicilians but Italians. The ancient divisions were to be condemned and forgotten forever. In contrast to a conspicuous failure in Italy, Isoleri sought to erase regionalism and unite Italians in Philadelphia.[12]

He, however, had only begun to present the argument that he had prepared for the event. Assuming his now familiar role as apologist and patriot, he spoke of the relationship of the new Italy to pagan Rome and to Christian Rome. Adroitly attacking the motives for French involvement in Italian politics, he offered his own view of Italy's interests: "France protected Christian Rome for its own political interests. A day will come when Italy will protect it by a deep conviction to fulfill its own divine mandate; and it will see that by protecting Christian Rome, it protects the greatest of its national glories, it protects itself." But even this argument was not enough for Isoleri, whose devotion to Italy elevated his judgment of its destiny still further. He implored his audience: "Do not be afraid, Italians! Italy is among God's favorite nations, God's smile."

Placing Columbus at the center of a litany of historical figures who had brought greatness to Italy, Isoleri linked the explorer to the experience of the immigrant audience listening to him. Rhetorically asking what had spurred the explorer, he unsurprisingly answered that it was a religious motive. Despite urging cohesion only moments earlier, Isoleri again revealed his own regionalism by identifying Columbus's papal benefactor, Innocent VII, as "genovese" and Columbus as "da Genova." He stated that Columbus's failure to win support from Genoa and Venice, thus forcing him to find it elsewhere, had contributed to Spain's ascendancy among the Western powers. And because Italians eventually made so many contributions to other countries, he argued that a complete history of Italy should have the title "Storia degli italiani 'fuori d'Italia'" (History of the Italians "Outside of Italy").

With the emergence of Italy as a nation, Isoleri declared that it had not abandoned its Catholicism. He urged the Church to recognize Columbus by elevating him to sainthood and to place his remains in Santa Croce in Florence, next to Dante's tomb. And where Dante's epitaph reads "Onorate l'altissimo Poeta," that of Columbus should be inscribed, "Onorate l'altissimo Ammiraglio."

Isoleri now addressed the more immediate situation facing Philadelphia's Italians. With great emotion, he recognized the meaner circumstances of their lives in a new world: "And among immigrants of all nations, if there is any one who has the right to tread on this land, no one has a greater right than the

Italians, when they seek to honestly earn their daily bread; whether as miners, or as railroad laborers; whether they go around playing musical instruments or selling fruit on street corners." Then, turning to the future, Isoleri declared that Italians, by emulating Dante and Columbus, not only would ensure that the name of Italy would be honored everywhere but also that "I figli vostri, e I figli dei vostri si vantaranno sempre di essere Italiani" (your children, and their children will always boast of being Italian). He dramatically pointed to the Italian flag: "They, your children, will often wave this flag from the windows of their houses; and they will tell all with noble pride: Italian blood runs through our veins! You and I have Italian blood in our veins: Let us boast of it!—To that task, I say again, Italians! We are called by God: good Christians and citizens; and we will be blessed by God and men, in this life and in the next." He concluded by calling for cheers for Columbus, for Vito Viti, for King Victor Emmanuel, for Italy, "nostra patria," and finally, for America, "nostra seconda patria."

While Columbus's canonization may appear ludicrous to later critics, Isoleri's proposal seemed plausible to the public of his day. But aspects of his speech were provocative even in his time. Although loyal and obedient to the Holy See, he espoused the political interests of Italy and impugned the motives of France in its defense of Rome. And while the Church had not yet accepted reconciliation, Isoleri sought to heal the separation of the Italian state from the traditional religion of its people.

Although enthusiastically received by his audience, Isoleri's remarks invited criticism from ecclesiastical authorities, which the Catholic press initially confirmed with an attack on Protestant misrepresentation. In contrast to favorable accounts by other newspapers, the *Catholic Standard* claimed that no one hearing the speeches at the dedication would have known that Columbus was a Catholic or that his religion had anything to do with his exploration and discovery: "No one learned from any word dropped by the speakers . . . at least, as we may judge from the full newspaper reports of what they said, now before us—that religion and the spirit of discovery went hand in hand with COLUMBUS on his expedition, or that his first act on landing was the erection of the Cross, the sacred symbol of salvation. There were no allusions—not the slightest—to any of these facts."[13]

These charges had ignored Isoleri's eulogy to Columbus and Catholicism. The same paper in the next week, accurately quoting Isoleri, corrected itself but accused the secular press of being "in full sympathy with the Liberalistic, Infidel spirit of the age, which seeks to ignore Catholicity in the past, as it would drive it from the earth in the present and future, if it could." Criticizing other papers for not translating Isoleri's speech and New York's Italian paper for not even mentioning it, the editorial praised Philadelphia's Italians for frequently applauding him.[14]

Isoleri's speech had also amply testified that even before the era of mass immigration, Italians in Philadelphia and elsewhere were already mired in a difficult adjustment to a new society. And if American perceptions would complicate their lives even more in future years, Isoleri had recognized their current plight. Convinced of the legitimacy of their presence and honorableness of their labors, he not only perceived but was well prepared to minister to their needs.

Isoleri's sense of the future gave an added dimension to his words. He had sought to galvanize his listeners by addressing their origins and destiny. By expressing his belief that he would retain his own identity as an Italian, he asserted that adjustment to America did not require one to cease being an Italian. Children now and in the future would still acknowledge with pride that Italian blood flowed in their veins. He was arguing that ethnicity not only could, but should, persist in present and later generations. Before an Italian crowd, he also knew what cues stirred a fitting mood of celebration.

Speaking to them more as a group than as individuals, Isoleri was cultivating their collective identity and group cohesion. Echoing the well-known words of Massimo d'Azeglio, "We have made Italy; now we must make the Italians," he called upon them to see themselves as Italians rather than in terms of their regional origins. He knew that if their living conditions were to be improved, it was necessary to change how they saw themselves and related to each other. Since power required unity, Isoleri recognized the value of a nationalistic ethnicity. What d'Azeglio had said of Italy was no less true for Italians as immigrants in Philadelphia. But it was also a pluralist rather than an assimilationist vision.

The dedication in Fairmount Park had been more than an occasion on which to honor Columbus and for Italians to enjoy a holiday. It had also provided aspirants to positions of community leadership with a public forum. Isoleri, as rector of St. Mary Magdalen dePazzi, already occupied an important niche, but it did not guarantee his success. Oratorical skills could help to validate his position, but any kind of failure could impair it. By his consistent eloquence at public events, Isoleri was widening his role in the Italian community.

"We Mourn as Italians; We Mourn as Catholics"

In subsequent days, the people of St. Mary Magdalen dePazzi again enjoyed their annual sacred music concert, patronal feast, and summer picnic as well as the Papal Jubilee and the dedication of a statue of Saint Anthony of Padua. Isoleri's influence, meanwhile, continued to grow with his participation in events within his parish and immigrant community. As 1877 neared its end, he blessed a new bell, cast in Venice and finely decorated with bas-relief images of saints and sacred scenes, which had been displayed at Philadelphia's Centennial Exhibition. Donated by the San Giuseppe Society and other parish groups, it was raised into the tower on Christmas Eve and first rung on Christmas Day "to the great delight of the pastor and congregation and all the neighborhood as far as its silver toned voice could be heard." On the same day, the Society of the Holy Child celebrated its seventh anniversary with over two hundred members treated to cakes and candies by a pastor "who seems perfectly at home and happy when among his poor children."[15]

While these events suggested a healthy future for St. Mary Magdalen dePazzi, others soon plunged the parish into sorrow as well as its pastor into controversy. When Victor Emmanuel II died in January 1878, Italian Catholics, despite his problems with the Holy See, grieved for their king. Against a disparaging Catholic press in Philadelphia, Isoleri planned a memorial service at his church. Two days beforehand, however, Isoleri and his people learned that Pius IX had also died. While anticlerical residents of Rome, with obscene and blasphemous songs, attempted to dispatch his body into the Tiber with no interference from the *carabinieri,* Philadelphia's Italians now mourned their pope as well. Isoleri seized the opportunity to unite the two men as well as state and Church.[16]

Nearly two hundred Italians marched from Columbus Hall to St. Mary Magdalen dePazzi, where they joined Mayor Stokley, Consul Galli, Vice Consul Viti, and Secchi diCasale, the journalist and outspoken critic of the papacy, on a Saturday morning in early February. Isoleri began his eulogy by announcing what everyone already knew: "Italiani! è morto il nostro Re!" With his own deep sorrow, he consoled them: "He died with the Lord's kiss and with the blessing of the Vicar of Christ, which ought to end once and for all the lips of slander." With praise for Piedmont and the House of Savoy, he declared that it was difficult to know who was more to be admired: Victor Emmanuel for his humility in asking for the final sacrament of the Church or Pius IX for his charitable love in sending a priest to the king's deathbed.[17]

Isoleri recalled how, at the age of three, when placed on a chair by his uncle, a Capuchin priest, he had sung a popular song that wove together the name of Pius IX with that of King Carlo Alberto of Piedmont. Now the time had come for Italian muses to compose an elegy in which the reconciled Pius IX and Victor Emmanuel would be joined together for eternity. Who would have expected this outcome? "Is it not possible for us to hope that Italy and the Church will be reconciled on these two tombs?" Echoing his duality of "patria e religione," Isoleri poured out his emotions for secular Italy and sacred Rome: "My motto always was and still is: My church and my God! My country and my king!"

Isoleri himself, however, had not yet found sufficient consolation. In a poem composed on the same day as the service for Victor Emmanuel, his opening words—"king without kingdom, son without father"—expressed a sense of loss as if the king were his own father. Away from his family for eight years, he felt a profound sadness. If Italy's immigrant children, flung to Philadelphia and other corners of the world, found sorrow for her, she also cried for them: "Italy cried . . . and then said: 'What did I do? My crying was in vain. Does a father cry if a son stays?' Thus, Italy spoke, and wiped her eye."[18]

Isoleri's poem reflected the plight not only of Italy but also of its author. Still grieving for his own father, Isoleri wept, but he recognized, as the spiritual father to Philadelphia's Italians, that he was not allowed the luxury of self-pity.

Only nine days after the ceremony for their king, Philadelphia's Italians gathered at St. Mary Magdalen dePazzi to mourn for Pius IX. Another procession left Columbus Hall on Eighth Street to honor their dead pope. At the church, where banners proclaimed, "We mourn as Italians" and "We mourn as Catholics," Isoleri delivered the eulogy. He praised the role of Pius IX in the history of Italy and his place in the hearts of Italians. For Isoleri, it was not difficult to describe the accomplishments of the late pope.[19] Elected in 1846, Pius IX had served longer than any other pontiff except for Saint Peter. His early reforms gave as much constitutional progress in the first two years as England had achieved over a period of two centuries. Widely expected to play an important role in Italian politics, he did not take the role that others had anticipated. Instead of becoming the head of a new state, as some early supporters had hoped, Pius IX became one of its major obstacles.[20]

Seeking again to connect the fate of Italy and the Church, Isoleri interpreted recent events: "Brothers, here is the finger of God who wishes to save Italy with the Church, the Church with Italy." And if the timing of these deaths was mere coincidence, then he could no longer find meaning in any human event. Reminding Italians of their obligations to faith and country, he implored them to weep now for Pius IX, as prodigal sons who had shed tears upon the tombs of their fathers and altered their own lives: "Italians! Pius IX was our father." He told them to approach the catafalque, prostrate themselves and repent, shed their tears, and return to God and the Church. Asking that the period of mourning for Catholics and for Italy be brief, he entreated Italians to pray particularly for "un Papa Italiano" as glorious, as long-lived, and as loving of Italy as Pius IX had been. His little Italian church could then cease its mourning, dry its tears, and begin a grand celebration in anticipation of the election of the next pope. As he asked Italians to find their place as Catholics, however, Isoleri was also provoking critics who objected to his politics.

Liberalism, Patriotism, and Fidelity

In the summer of 1878 an unknown observer of recent events in Philadelphia sent a letter to Cardinal Giovanni Simeoni, the prefect of Propaganda Fide, accusing Isoleri of liberal ideas in public and private statements that deviated from declarations of the Holy See and caused scandal among Catholics and Protestants. It charged that he had not missed any opportunity to speak in support of the newly united Italy; had given a patriotic speech at the Columbus statue dedication, which was applauded by an audience in great accord; had run through the streets with the tricolor badge and rosette of Italy; had traveled some forty miles to greet the Italian navy's frigate, *Vittorio Emanuele;* had declared his ardent support of Victor Emmanuel at a meeting in Columbus Hall, which was a Masonic lodge; had held a funeral observance for the king that was actually a political demonstration; and had said that the new pope ought to recognize Italy as an accomplished fact and reconcile himself with the present government for the good of the nation. When he passed these charges on to Bishop Wood in Philadelphia, Simeoni reserved the right to take action but only after giving Isoleri an opportunity to respond. He indicated that the informant did not wish to reveal his name, clearly showing that it had not been Wood. But whoever had known enough to write directly to Simeoni was most likely another priest or a nun, or someone writing on behalf of one, and probably an old enemy rather than a new one.[21]

After Wood disclosed the accusations, which similarly implicated a friend and fellow priest, Giovanni Vassallo, Isoleri sent a respectful, but firm, reply that also addressed the broader dilemma facing Italian Catholics in America. It began with the flattering ploy that since Wood had written in Italian, which he knew very well, Isoleri would respond in the same language. Although the accusations had surprised and saddened him, he argued that they were rather old ones that should not be taken seriously. Thanking Wood for allowing him to explain points that, if wrongly reported or misunderstood, could create a bad impression, Isoleri appeared to be sending a congenial message to an old friend.[22]

To the charge of liberal sentiments, while admitting to having expressed his views in private and having alluded to them in public, Isoleri contended that he had argued that the Italian government had no right to seize the Temporal Power, but now that it was done, the interests of Church and state required them to find a compromise. And with most Italians being Catholics, if allowed to vote, they could remedy the evil already done, impede new evils, and elect deputies to the parliament who would replace bad laws with good ones and restore the assets of the Church. Isoleri reminded Wood that after the taking of Venice from Austria in 1867, Catholics were permitted to vote for deputies who took an oath that they would not approve legislation that was contrary to the laws of God and the Church. But, he continued, prohibiting Catholics from voting only left government open to evil persons and to the passage of perverse laws, which Isoleri greatly deplored both as a priest and an Italian.

To the charges of being an honorary member of the sponsoring organization, riding in a carriage, delivering a speech, and wearing the tricolor badge and rosette at the dedication, Isoleri argued that it was possible to have several different viewpoints on the issue of religion and politics in Italy. He then gave his own colorful description of what had occurred. While the good Italians of Philadelphia had listened with attention and respect and applauded, others who had stood alongside them represented the so-called official world, as he put it, which was grinding its teeth and making as much noise as it could. (A scratched-out section of his first draft identifies Consul Count Galli as a part of "the so-called official world"; and a note refers to some disruption resulting from Isoleri's being too Catholic in his speech and that an attempt had been made to prevent him from speaking.) But Dr. McGlynn and two Passionists had assured him that his speech had contained nothing objectionable.

To the charge that he had traveled some distance to meet the Italian frigate, he admitted that he had done so, but it was at the invitation of Dr. Pignatelli rather than the consul, and more out of curiosity than anything else. Since the vessel represented Genoa's maritime college, he had gone in search of old friends who might be on board without thinking that a sinister interpretation could be made. But he added that if another Italian vessel came in the future and he was unable to overcome the temptation to visit it, he would probably do so incognito.

To the charge that the ceremony for the king had been more political than religious, Isoleri conceded that the Italians had made some noise, but they had been religiously disposed in general; and if some of them had been politically inspired, it was not his fault. Since most participants had once belonged to "the old kingdom of Piedmont" and had read in newspapers of a last confession and a solemn funeral in Rome, they only intended to honor their Christian king and themselves. And when asked to invite Wood, the archbishop had authorized him to proceed with the event. Isoleri accused the newspapers of talking nonsense for reporting that the cost of the service had exceeded several thousand dollars, when it actually had not been more than $400, mostly paid by the consul, without the church spending even "un soldo." But for Pius IX, Isoleri noted that with himself in charge of a more solemn ceremony, all expenses had been paid, and a beautiful throne could be bought with the money that remained.

Again correcting the newspapers, Isoleri claimed that he merely had said that the Lord, wanting Italy to be united, was able to ignore the remarks of priests such as himself in such sad times. And as for himself, he would love his king and country as much as ever. He insisted that the newspapers had erred by reporting that he had said that if all other priests had opposed unity, he was still in favor of it. And returning to what he had said about Victor Emmanuel, since the king had died a Christian, we had the right to hope that his soul was saved, but that we still must pray for him. Isoleri added that he would always pray first for the Church and the pope, then for his country and its king, and he then quoted a psalm that he applied to Italian politics.

To the final charge about advice to the new pope, Isoleri denied that he had ever given any. Having heard so many persons praise Leo XIII as a moderate with profound knowledge of the times, Isoleri only hoped that the pontiff could reach a modus vivendi with the state. Conditions had already become less tense. Successful negotiations with Germany and other nations, along with the truce and relative peace enjoyed by the Church in Italy, made it possible to hope for more in the future. He poetically summarized his position: "because I was, I am, and I hope to always be in the future by the grace of God an obedient son of Holy Mother the Church and submissive to its head, the vicar of Christ on earth." From his opening flattery of Wood's fluency in Italian as *benissimo*, the letter was another exercise in *furbismo*, that is, cleverness.[23]

While Isoleri hoped that Wood would find the reply satisfactory and asked humbly for his blessing, the matter had already gone beyond Philadelphia. Isoleri did not know that Simeoni had sent the charges to Wood, nor did he know that Wood was preparing a reply to Simeoni. Wood had not given Simeoni's entire letter to Isoleri, but only a summary of the charges. Less than a month later, when Isoleri answered correspondence from Simeoni, he had either realized that it would be futile to try to defend himself or he already had done so. Expressing submission and repentance, Isoleri asked Simeoni to excuse him so that he could continue his work, as he himself intended, without going astray in the apostolic vineyard, for the greater glory and salvation of souls. It was language more florid than Isoleri usually used, but he was obviously embroiled in a situation more serious than ever before. He promised to stay far removed from any politics and the liberalism condemned by the Church. Beyond love of country and king, Isoleri wrote that there remained in his heart, and rightly so, the love of the Church and its head. Moreover, many good priests and laymen in Italy and Philadelphia could amply testify on his behalf.[24]

Pastor in a New World

In the glare of public occasions, while addressing the lingering problems of their homeland, Isoleri had sought to strengthen the resources of Italians in a new world. While Italy still suffered, he asked Italians to forget the conflict between Church and state and to link their identity as Italians to that as Catholics. He urged them to replace their regional consciousness with a nationalistic ethnicity as Italians. And while leading them in cheers for Columbus and Victor Emmanuel, Isoleri asked them to raise their voices for America. If he were in some sense a new type of priest, it was partly by embracing a new role in developing an Italian American community with a solidarity more easily and earlier reached in foreign lands than in Italy.

While some observers—victims of their own progressive dreams—had once believed that the Church could join the Risorgimento as a partner in a new state, Pius IX had opposed nationalism, particularly when it meant the loss of papal territory and power. After the election of Leo XIII, some moderating efforts suggested the prospect of reconciliation between Church and state. But having lost the Temporal Power, the papacy was not ready to concede the ideo-logical struggle. Isoleri, meanwhile, flushed with euphoria, had joined the ranks of hopeful celebrants of a new order. But his conspicuous participation in the Columbus Monument dedication and in mourning for the deceased king re-vealed political sentiments that were inappropriate and unacceptable to some minds. By stepping forward in secular activities, he had taken a risky course for a priest. Forced to defend himself before his superiors in Rome, Isoleri still had two strong cards that he had previously played: his affiliation with the Collegio Brignole Sale, and his identity as an Italian. But an unknown adversary with an apparently stronger hand had momentarily prevailed.

The future of St. Mary Magdalen dePazzi, as the end of the 1870s drew near, depended more on what occurred in Philadelphia than in Rome. The willingness of its Ligurian founders to accept newcomers from other regions of their homeland was more important than the reconciliation of Church and state in Italy. The faith of a congregation within its own walls and its veneration of saints on Philadelphia's streets were more significant than events in Italy's cities. More than anything else, Isoleri was demonstrating an astute talent as a juggler. When Wood arrived to administer confirmation in April 1878, Isoleri, accompanied by the members of his parish societies, warmly greeted his for-mer adversary. He had recently procured a statue of Saint Patrick, replacing one that had occupied a curious, but strategic, location since Father Mariani's time. By modest but regular financial contributions to archdiocesan appeals, the "poor Italian church" found the means to assist not only yellow fever suf-ferers in the American South but famine victims in Ireland as well. While pro-voking the sisters, Isoleri placated the archbishop. While inspiring Italians, he honored the Irish. While nurturing Catholicism, he mingled with and allowed Protestants and anticlericals to occupy pews in his church. By all these devices, Isoleri was orchestrating the delicate balance between congregation and com-munity. Despite his recent reprimand from Rome, as he recovered from a long, painful illness just before Christmas in 1878, Isoleri's position was becoming more secure.[25]

General events and changing conditions around his parish would further strengthen church and priest in the neighborhood. With rapidly increasingly numbers of new arrivals seeking a life in Philadelphia, the Italian colony, as it developed, was meeting their needs. Pursuing personal gain and control of civic affairs, Italians were establishing retail businesses, mutual aid societies, labor unions, and political clubs while they emulated other Philadelphians in attempting to restore a social order unraveled by industrialization and urbani-zation. By these efforts, Italians nourished their own resources as they evolved from an inchoate population to an embryonic colony and then to a mature community. The church of St. Mary Magdalen dePazzi was playing a central role in building the "institutional completeness" of Little Italy.

As businessmen, politicians, and protoprofessionals in law and medicine assumed positions of visibility, wealth, honor, and influence, Isoleri took his own place within an emerging elite. While guiding his congregation in its spiritual journey, he applied his indefatigable energies to its material well-being. But he now had to mute the nationalistic fervor that had incurred censure as well as find a narrower path of religious and political orthodoxy, lest he again place his own future as well as that of the Italian Mission into jeopardy.

CHAPTER SEVEN

Building Parish and Community

By the 1880s, St. Mary Magdalen dePazzi and Philadelphia's Italians found themselves in a rapidly changing environment. The first factor for this change was the increasing and shifting character of Italian immigration as well as the American reaction to it. With immigration reaching an unprecedented "flood-tide," as one newspaper noted, Southern European countries were "sending their people to us in larger numbers than ever before." For its part, Italian immigration was shifting to new sources in Southern Italy and Sicily. But public sentiment and legal policy in this country had become less hospitable for all immigrants. The United States began to close its Open Door policy by passing restrictive legislation against the Chinese in 1882. With less favorable perceptions of immigrants in general, attitudes eroded toward the Italians, who themselves were testing the physical boundaries and resources of Philadelphia's Little Italy.[1]

The second major factor originated within the Italian colony itself. South Philadelphia's Italian-born population had numbered about 500 residents in 1870, before growing to about 1,200 in another decade and reaching almost 15,000 at the end of the century.[2] With immigrant life becoming a public concern, the members of the Italian community, rather than evolving without direction, pursued deliberate efforts to determine the course of their future. Against non-Italian benefactors and reformers from external organizations who were eager to intervene and improve social conditions among the foreign born, St. Mary Magdalen dePazzi represented an indigenous effort in the impending struggle for immigrant minds, hearts, and souls. As its pastor, Antonio Isoleri would address the adjustment of Southern Italians: the education of their children, the struggle against dishonest employers, the temptations of urban life, and the preservation of their faith as Catholics. But he once again found contention from sisters of his own faith and proselytizers of other denominations. While initiating plans for a new church to enhance the spiritual life of his congregation, Isoleri also extolled the secular glories of the new Italy that had been left behind. By these efforts, he kept his parish engaged in the affairs of the community emerging around it.

New Immigration: Survival and Faith

As rector of Philadelphia's only Italian church, Isoleri was well situated to serve as a witness to, and commentator on, these changes. In 1881, recognizing the ordeal faced by the youngest members of the community, he warned: "But for the love of God, their relatives in Italy should take care of their little children, and not send them around the world as many have until now done." He perceptively summed up the complex conditions that increasingly drove Italians from their homeland: "Is it not possible that they are able to obtain in Italy their daily bread?" He not only knew the answer to his question but also offered a solution: "Then, if it is not possible, entire families should emigrate, instead of being divided. And above all they should not send little children with persons well known for having little or no religion or morality—whose aim is only to enrich themselves at any cost."[3]

Adjustment in a new land, however, required not only protecting children from exploitation but also shielding families in general from abuses in America. Isoleri proposed a broad strategy for how these problems could be solved:

> As for emigration, the entire family should emigrate together when it is not possible to live and to improve their lot in their native country . . . and it is even better that the wife comes with her husband, rather than the husband or wife alone. But here where the common language is English, Italians must be prepared to come with a little money, or with some trade, such as tailor, or cabinet maker, mason, etc; if they cannot be so situated it will be bad for them. And if they should not have it they are guilty of imprudence. It is also good if no one goes to a foreign country where he cannot find a relative or friend that can help him.[4]

Isoleri obviously regarded the family, language, money, and work as important, but he also recognized the part that informal relationships among relatives and friends—or what scholars would later call "migration chains"—played in the experiences of Italians as immigrants. It was another instance in which he showed his understanding of the sociology of immigrant adjustment, which was to remain a major concern for him throughout his life. And as later reformers would propose, he believed that Italians would adjust more successfully by establishing rural colonies, particularly in the South and West, where good farmworkers with some capital could easily find fertile land to cultivate, as the Irish had done in Minnesota and Kansas. But Italians, beyond the language problem, also had to find practical and honest persons to direct them in these colonies. What Isoleri had in mind in this regard was not surprising: "And it must always be accompanied by a good priest, ready to share the joys and sorrows of the colony, and with the means to build at least a log cabin chapel, attached to which would rise as if by magic a village." Whether it be in a rural or urban settlement of Italians, firmly convinced of the indispensable role of religion, he asked: "But what is a colony without a priest?" His clear answer: "It is better to die of hunger in Italy than to come to America to get rich, but then lose one's soul."[5]

Among the many risks that immigration posed to Italians, Isoleri was preoccupied with the damage that it might do to their faith as Catholics. He asked: "How many lose it in this country, because where they are, there is no Italian Church? But also many do not go to church, even where there is one."[6] It was not long afterward that this issue was formally recognized by the American hierarchy in the Third Plenary Council in Baltimore in 1884. Perhaps Isoleri's warnings had been heard.[7]

The shifting sources of immigration from Italy, however, would have the most immediate impact on St. Mary Magdalen dePazzi at this moment. For its first twenty years its congregation had mainly derived from the Ligurian hill towns overlooking the city of Chiavari. By the late 1870s, the areas near Catania and Messina in Sicily and towns in southern regions of the mainland such as Marsico Nuovo, Marsicovetere, Sant'Angelo le Fratte, Calvello, Laurenzana, Accettura, and Spiniso (in Basilicata); Castellamare di Stabia and Auletta (in Campania); Barletta (in Puglia); and Atessa (in Abruzzo-Molise) now were the roots of couples being married at the church. But it was only the start of the deluge of migration from Southern Italy that soon followed.[8]

By the early 1880s, St. Mary Magdalen de Pazzi, along with the rest of South Philadelphia, was being overrun by new arrivals from the Mezzogiorno and Sicily. Marriages joined natives of San Lorenzo del Vallo, Spezzano Albanese, Rocca Imperiale, San Costantino Calabro, Soveria Mannelli (in Calabria); Sant'Angelo d'Alife, Vietri sul Mare, Campagna, Atena, Montella, Bagnoli Irpino, Solopaca, San Mango, Polla, San Mauro Cilento, Celso, Casamicciola d'Ischia, San Lorenzo Minore, Paternopoli, Calabritto, Massalubrense, Cardile, Castelnuovo Cilento (in Campania); Atessa, Agnone, Monteroduni, Tornareccio, Civitella Messer Raimondo, Torricella Peligna, Venafro, Casalanguida, Longano, Lama Peligna, Gessopalena (in Abruzzo-Molise); Anzi, Ruoti, Viggiano, Salandra, Paterno, Castronovo Sant' Andrea, Colobraro, Trivigno, Vaglio, Tursi, Corleto Peticara,

San Mauro Forte, San Chirico Raparo, Brindisi di Montagna, Garaguso (in Basilicata); Alberona (in Puglia); and Palermo (in Sicily). The migration of Southerners had reached the church and the neighborhood.

This diversity of origins required a response from Isoleri and other leaders of the immigrant community. Despite his earlier efforts to encourage a shared identity and greater cohesion, he recognized that the disparate regional origins of Italians still separated them. As Isoleri succinctly put it in 1881, "he who knows the Italians who emigrate, knows how difficult it is to gather them and to save them because of their material and moral conditions—as well as by that sense of misery and the ancient divisions that dominate them, such that they neither seek to do themselves honor before other peoples, nor do they consider themselves brothers and co-nationals among themselves."[9]

Isoleri was powerless, however, to solve this problem alone. Italians as a group had to decide how they would address it. And with the growing presence of Southern Italians, another factor had emerged. While marriages had usually involved couples from the same town or region, they now showed a different pattern as Italians found mates in the immigrant colony. For immigrants in Little Italy, it was now easier—and perhaps necessary, if one wished to marry at all—to lower the barriers that had once separated them than to restrict themselves to spouses from the particular villages and regions of Italy that they had left behind. They had not only left their ancestral places, but they were leaving behind their old folkways as well.

In little more than a decade, Isoleri had stabilized St. Mary Magdalen de-Pazzi and his position as its rector. Having resolved most of his problems with Archbishop Wood, who was now elderly and in failing health, Isoleri was well prepared to lead his parish toward further growth. Along with enlarging the chapel, as well as directing routine spiritual activities, his plans called for a greater response to the temporal problems—marginal employment, low wages and poverty, congested and dilapidated housing, and exploitation of children—that afflicted his people.

Isoleri had also adjusted on a more personal level to life in America. By 1880, he was delivering his sermons in English, as well as in Italian, with graceful fluency.[10] But his words almost always carried special meaning for Italians who were seeking to adjust to life in America. On Trinity Sunday in May of that year, Isoleri joined other priests in a grand procession from the archbishop's residence to the cathedral for the First Provincial Council of the archdiocese.[11] On the next Sunday, he explained its significance in a sermon in English to his congregation. Drawing on the words of Saint John, "You shall be made sorrowful, but your sorrow shall be turned to joy," he summarized the history of Christianity, then of Catholicism in Philadelphia. Describing how joy was restored after the sorrow of the Reformation, Isoleri identified two great figures, Saint Francis Xavier and Christopher Columbus. He had all but ascribed sainthood to the latter, the only secular Italian hero whom the Church accepted and with whom immigrants identified. Recalling the visit of Cardinal Cesare Roncetti five years previously, he reminded his audience: "And you well remember how respectfully he was received everywhere—and how he was honored by the Italians of Philadelphia—who thus repaired the faults of their New York brethren in their treatment of Monsignor Bedini—and you well remember how he honored us and this little church by coming here to preach and officiate."[12]

Isoleri had resumed his efforts to integrate political patriotism and religious fidelity. But despite his exhortations, he did not gain all that he sought when he was away from his pulpit. Although Wood now regularly participated in confirmation rites, not all of his opposition to Isoleri had ended. When Isoleri's petition for an appointment as an honorary chamberlain at the papal court was remanded to Philadelphia, Wood's failure to support it helped to deny him the position.[13]

Isoleri had better results in other endeavors. In October 1881, he initiated a children's festival to celebrate Columbus Day and to benefit the orphanage. With the increasing popular piety of the times, he instituted a special novena of All Saints. As the Society of the Holy Child, ten years after its founding, reached two hundred members, he organized the Sons and Daughters of Mary for young persons and the Mount Carmel Society for women, as noted earlier. And, as Isoleri wished, the San Giuseppe Society, now with one hundred members, including many prominent leaders of the community, received the sacraments several times each year and marched in special procession on the third Sunday of each month, expressing their intention to retain cultural ties with the homeland, which, as their pastor pointed out, was "as they do in Italy."[14]

Isoleri's efforts had won wide support, which included such non-Catholic neighbors as the "Protestant gentleman" who had presented an arch for the patronal feast, as well as the "enthusiastic Catholic spirit and devotion" displayed by Philadelphia's Italians at its celebration in 1882. But parish growth had made the old church too small in any season and too damp, cold, and unhealthy in winter. As the diocesan newspaper reported, the building was "entirely inadequate and unfit," making its replacement "an imperative necessity"; preliminary steps were taken to erect a new church.[15] But while the mission was deemed "a most deserving one," Isoleri's financial resources remained limited. Brief newspaper items now regularly described the physical needs of the parish along with its meager income. However, they praised the energetic work of its pastor and favorably assessed the fidelity and support of its Italians, succinctly capturing the situation of St. Mary Magdalen dePazzi at Christmas in 1882: "Father Isoleri, though having the poorest congregation and church in the city, is always the equal to his fellow pastors as far as the limits of his means will allow him. . . . He must have been deeply gratified at the piety shown by his people, who seem to be warmly devoted to him. At all the Masses the little building was packed, and a proportionately large number of those present received holy communion."[16]

Despite the praise for his unstinting efforts, Isoleri's requests for an assistant priest remained unfilled, leaving him with prodigious pastoral tasks. Although other priests participated in the parish mission or the patronal feast, he usually found himself alone on ordinary occasions to preach, administer the sacraments, instruct adults and children, advise the confraternities and sodalities, and manage the financial affairs of St. Mary Magdalen dePazzi:

> For my part, I try to do what I can—with confessions every Saturday and on the vigils of feast days. After mass I go on to evenings, sometimes to late hours. I do not have, however, only Italians, but Irish, Americans, and even some French and Spanish.
>
> On Sundays, mass is said at 8 am with two sermons or instructions, alternately in Italian and English. At 10 am, mass is sung in Italian and English. After mass, baptisms—at 2 pm, Christian Doctrine for boys and girls—at 3:30 pm, vespers and catechism for adults, alternately in Italian and English. The preaching in two languages is necessary, not only for the many non-Italians who attend the church, since in fact the congregation has always been mixed, but also for the Italians born and growing up here who understand English better than the language of their fathers.[17]

Meanwhile, despite the reprimand for participating in the Columbus Monument dedication, Isoleri had not abandoned his interest in politics, particularly when his people needed guidance on life in their new country. When President James A. Garfield died in September 1881, three months after being wounded by an assassin's bullet, Isoleri returned to his rectory after hearing confessions and composed a sermon on the tragedy. He began his eulogy by asking, "Is there any man in the land who has shed no tears?" With palpable sorrow, Isoleri continued: "And whilst I would much prefer to grieve in silence, and bow my head before the altar of God on this sad day, yet as you may expect me to address you on this occasion, I will try to make a few appropriate remarks."[18] And these remarks did not greatly differ from other orators on this occasion. Like a modern Saint Paul, Isoleri stated the obligations of family members toward one other, advising parents to give their children a moral education and to raise them in the love of God, and charging children to obey their parents. He urged his listeners to respect authority and reminded public officials, from the policeman to the new president, to remember that authority came from God. Thus, not much more than ten years removed from his own arrival, Isoleri commented on an American event as any other American might do. While his eulogy for a dead president offered a manifesto for the native born as well as for immigrants of their moral and civic responsibilities as citizens, it also conveyed Isoleri's own credo as a priest to his people in a new land.

Another Crisis with the Sisters

Isoleri's success continued to depend on his ability to meet the spiritual and material needs of his immigrant flock. Almost immediately on his arrival, he had recognized the urgency of a school for the children. Opened in March 1874, under Sister Francesca and the Missionary Sisters of St. Francis, the school enrolled 35 boys and 48 girls for its first full year. After Isoleri's dissatisfaction over the performance of the superior, Sister Giuseppa assumed the position for 1875–76, and enrollment increased to 45 boys and 50 girls. Recognizing another need, Isoleri rented a house at Seventh and Marriott Streets for an orphan asylum for Italian girls, also directed by the sisters, in July 1876. In 1876–77 enrollment at the parish school fell slightly, with 40 boys and 45 girls, taught by six sisters. During the next three years it remained steady at 45 boys and 55 girls, with five sisters, until reaching 60 boys and 70 girls, with only four sisters, in 1880–81, then 69 boys and 75 girls, with five sisters, in 1881–82. In 1881, Isoleri obtained land east of the church primarily for the site of a larger orphanage. Meanwhile, trouble was looming, and it could not have been entirely unexpected.[19]

At the end of the 1881–82 school year, Isoleri's difficulties with the sisters, which seemed to have been resolved in 1874, boiled over again. Ironically, Mother Angela, whom he had cultivated as an ally in the struggle against Sister Gertrude, would become his adversary. On an earlier visit, Mother Angela, the Franciscan superior, had reached an agreement with Isoleri to sever all ties between Peekskill and the parish school and to staff it with sisters from Gemona. Only five years later, when Mother Angela returned to Philadelphia, she decided that the only solution was to withdraw her order entirely from the school. Isoleri had to defend himself once again before Archbishop Wood, but it was mainly over how money obtained for the support of his mission was to be divided with the departing sisters.

Isoleri explained his position in a letter to the archbishop in August 1882, which showed clearly why the sisters had left the mission. After reviewing the original agreement, he described a decline in church revenues, claiming that it was due to a recent national economic panic, before adding: "I saw the impossibility of continuing to pay the sisters what I did pay them, of my own accord, since they had first come." He did not want to overtax the congregation, especially with a church to be built. Then, taking up the issue of the sisters, he repeated his previous complaint of:

> the failure of the sisters, as teachers, both in Italian and in English. In Italian they commenced with one! and this queer and sickly . . . one has been nearly all the time in charge of the school, with another one who is not even an Italian . . . the school in the meantime failing more and more every year, [and] my insisting for some competent sister to teach italian being, so far, of

no avail. In English, with the exception of the first 4 months, we went from bad to worse, as long as the sisters taught; so much so that the last one sent from Peekskill was an ignorant irish servant girl etc. sent here *under the very eyes of Mother Angela* on the occasion of her first visit to this country, and who could be kept in the school a whole week.[20]

Both he and Mother Angela desired no longer to be "at the mercy of Peekskill," Isoleri noted to Wood. Now, Italian nuns, subject to the mother house in Gemona, would staff the school, except for a lay teacher of English, in order "to avoid the troubles of mixed nationalities." Without having to go to Peekskill for the annual summer retreat, the sisters could fully devote themselves to the school. For his part, Isoleri was willing to help by sponsoring picnics, lectures, concerts, and other fundraisers for the school. The agreement included the development of the orphanage. As proof of the feasibility of the plan, Isoleri asserted that "the sisters with God's blessing, through my cooperation, [and] their exertions, have not yet been in want of anything, and made some savings besides."

On her return to Philadelphia in 1881, Mother Angela sought some changes in her agreement with Isoleri. The residence for the sisters should belong to the order and be independent of the parish; she should have the right to send as many nuns and of any nationality as she might choose; and the sisters should have the right to organize concerts, lectures, and other events without having to consult him. Isoleri was willing to abandon his opposition on a few points. Although convinced by past experience that it was not a good idea, he accepted the assignment of a sister from Peekskill to teach English. He also would allow Mother Angela to send a non-Italian European as superior, as long as she spoke Italian, as a temporary expedient.

As Isoleri and Mother Angela struggled to resolve these differences, their negotiations rapidly deteriorated. In an effort to reach a solution, Mother Angela had even placed her own sister in charge of the mission in Philadelphia. But when Mother Angela replaced her with an Italian-speaking European, after several visits to the mission without any more proposals to him, Isoleri thought that they were still in accord. He claimed that her decision to end their agreement came at a moment when he was unable to give his attention to the matter. And when she left the city without notifying him, Isoleri maintained that he had not had the opportunity to communicate with her or with the archbishop about the situation.

Isoleri believed, however, that he finally understood Mother Angela's strategy. If he still found the sisters unsatisfactory as teachers, she planned, by separating the orphan asylum from the school and making it independent of the parish, to give up the school but keep the orphanage, leaving him with the awkward choice of either bringing in another religious order or hiring lay teachers.

He accused Mother Angela of abandoning the objective for which her order had been brought to the mission, namely, to support it in saving Italian children. But lacking his usual firmness, and perhaps sensing that Mother Angela had the stronger position, Isoleri now offered to meet the sisters' demands, at least "as much as I can for the present." And at the archbishop's suggestion, he agreed to prepare some counterproposals.

Isoleri presented the counterproposals to the archbishop two days later. He offered to pay the rent on the sisters' residence until they could provide a sum of money with which a new rectory could be built; at that point, the sisters and the orphans would move into the old rectory, and, if necessary, an adjoining lot could be purchased. And when the time came for him to no longer pay their rent, he would give them $400 per year for their services at the school. He added, "I may do more in the course of time, if able, with the help of God." He included some further details to carry out the modified agreement. But in contrast to the conciliatory position that he seemed to have taken, Isoleri's final point indicated that he intended to hold his ground: "Of course, the Orphan Asylum, as well as the parochial school, [is] to be attached to the parish of St. Mary Magdalen dePazzi, as it has been from the beginning, under the direction of the archbishop and the pastor of said parish."[21]

By early September, Archbishop Wood had turned the dispute over to a committee of three priests for arbitration. Since the sisters had already left the mission, the only remaining issue was how certain funds amounting to $2,500, currently held by the archbishop, were to be distributed. It was not merely a matter of settling accounts with the sisters, but also of protecting the meager financial resources of the parish from the archbishop himself. Only a few years after accusing Wood of wanting to drive the Italian church into insolvency, Isoleri now faced the same likelihood. While presenting his case to the archbishop, Isoleri sought to leave the matter to the arbitrators. One of them, Father James Rolando, who had briefly served as rector of St. Mary Magdalen dePazzi, advised him to prepare a statement for the committee. Isoleri's detailed reply was entrusted to Rolando's discretion and conscience. (As on other occasions, when he attempted to remind a correspondent of a special bond, he began it in Italian before turning to English.) Because the money had come entirely from activities initiated by him and was intended to provide a permanent residence for the sisters and orphans as well as to support the parochial school and orphanage, Isoleri argued that these funds belonged "equally and jointly" to all of them. He proposed that $500–600 be given to the sisters, a government bond worth about $1,000 to the archbishop for the benefit of the orphans, and the balance to himself for the parish school. After noting that the share for the orphans might be excessive, since their number was expected to decline from twelve to six within a month, Isoleri cleverly seized the opportunity to add: "Now it is evident that if their number should be soon considerably reduced, it would not be well for the archbishop to be placed in the position of one who took advantage of our troubles etc. which certainly he would not like, and does not intend to."[22]

In his response to Rolando, Isoleri introduced other aspects of his problem. The people knew that about $2,500 had been accumulated by the sisters, and "therefore it will be necessary for me to say what was done with it to prevent talking." He imperiously noted that the arbitrators only had to decide "to give the sisters a decent sum to get back to Italy with; to give the archbishop a reasonable amount for the orphans; [and] to give me the rest for the school." But beyond any settlement with the sisters and archbishop, Isoleri realized that his accountability to his people was being tested.

On the day after writing to the arbitrators, Isoleri sent another message to Wood in which, along with an interest payment on the bond on the orphanage held by the archbishop, he described a disturbing incident. A young reporter, intent on writing a provocative article, had come to the rectory with the news that someone had claimed that the sisters had left suddenly, taking money with them, and that the rector had denounced them from the altar. Isoleri denied the charges, telling Wood: "I got rid of him as best as I could." But fearing that the reporter would call on the archbishop, Isoleri wrote: "As far as the Congregation is concerned the thing passed off quickly and is over; except some paper wishes to keep it up."[23]

Isoleri also reported an attempt by a certain Dr. Nardyz, whom he described as "a greek-italian-garibaldian fraud," to start a Protestant Italian school, but he assured the archbishop that the project would again fail, as it had in the previous winter, "when it was like a still-born affair." He depicted Nardyz as "notoriously bad, [and] his object would be to pocket american protestant money, under the appearance of starting [and] keeping up a school for the Italian children." Isoleri had identified another challenge that would eventually have to be met.

In the meantime, the arbitrators had reached a verdict in regard to the balance of the funds from the mission. A bond of $500, along with one-half of the proceeds from a fundraising program scheduled for the end of the month, would be given to the archbishop for the support of the orphans. While this decision favored Isoleri, the next matter went against him. All money held for the benefit of the parochial school and the orphan asylum, currently in a bank account under Isoleri's name, was to be given to the sisters for their past services. Although the actual amount was not indicated, it appeared to be a generous sum. But with a bond of $1,000 awarded to Isoleri for the benefit of the parochial school, the outcome appeared to satisfy all parties, despite a slight reprimand by the committee to Isoleri.[24]

Anxious to resolve matters, when Isoleri wrote Wood to accept the arbitrators' recommendations, he reported that the school had opened on the past Monday with about as many children as in the previous year. Despite the departure of the sisters, he believed that little damage had been done. Although Isoleri had not been able to secure an Italian teacher, he was hopeful that one could be hired soon. The only applicant so far, a woman with neither religious training nor standing as a Catholic, could not have been more inappropriate. But even worse, she had been one of "the four unfortunate [and] foolish virgins, weeping at the mock funeral of Garibaldi." During the winter, after being offered a position at a Protestant Italian school, she had come to Isoleri to ask his advice, and he told her to have nothing to do with the undertaking. He now wondered if she might go "in the wrong direction." He dismissed the question: "But, I think we may say, that we will be blamed." Despite his own nationalistic fervor, Isoleri's characterization of this unfortunate young woman as well as of Dr. Nardyz revealed that some heroes of recent Italian history remained unacceptable.[25]

Labor Troubles and Protestant Influences

From the autumn of 1882 through almost the entire next year, Isoleri faced old and new troubles that tested his leadership. Despite the information that he had recently conveyed to Wood, its absence from the annual *Catholic Directory* suggests that the school was closed during 1882–83. And if the departure of the teaching sisters was not enough of a problem, the threat of Protestant endeavors among the Italians became a reality. The growing number of Italians had gained the attention of Episcopalians, who established a board of trustees to develop a plan and to find a building suitable for religious instruction. On March 19, 1883, ironically the feast day of Saint Joseph, newspapers reported the organization of the Episcopalian Mission for Italians at Dupont Hall, on Christian Street, just east of Eleventh Street, near the center of the immigrant colony. Under the direction of the Reverend Michele Zara, a native of Rome, a graduate of its university, and a former Catholic priest, it was drawing upward of one hundred children and young people to nightly gatherings. With plans calling for a permanent chapel and a dispensary, a women's committee was holding weekly meetings to develop a program for the Italians of the city. Meanwhile, the Catholic press, reporting programs by such social service agencies as Charles Loring Brace's Children's Aid Society of New York, which sent the "street Arabs" of eastern cities to families in western states for adoption, increased the awareness and urgency to protect Catholic children from Protestant influence.[26]

Protestant efforts to reach Italians soon grew beyond the preliminary stage in Philadelphia, partly in response to the emergence of labor problems. In May 1883, a small army of about two to three hundred Italian railroad laborers, mainly hired in New York, who had received little or no pay for over two months, gathered at the office of a contractor near Fourth and Chestnut Streets to seek their wages. By the second day, the company had enough funds to provide for the immediate needs of the protesting workers, who now numbered about eight hundred. But after hearing an announcement that they would only be paid at Fernwood in Delaware County, when the police attempted to disperse them the men scattered and then reassembled in Independence Square in center city. These disturbances attracted the attention of the Episcopal clergy.[27]

During the second day, the laborers informed the Reverend Samuel Durborrow of the Protestant Episcopal City Missions that they were without food and money. Taking up their cause, he described their situation to Joshua L. Bailey, the proprietor of the Model Coffee House, who agreed to provide dinner for the men. With the assistance of Zara, his Italian colleague, Durborrow led one hundred twenty-five strikers to the coffee house, "where they were supplied with as much as they could eat." Zara urged the workers to remain calm and to refrain from any further disturbance. But a large number of Italians, who refused the food, asked only for their earnings. While railroad officials tried to shift blame to the construction firm, many men, still without lodging, returned to the street near the company office.[28]

By the third day, when only about fifty strikers assembled at the office, the dispute appeared, at least for the time being, to have ended. The money distributed on the previous day and Zara's efforts at persuasion had been enough to keep others away. The company claimed that $10,000 had been allotted to the Italian subcontractor to pay the workers whom he had recruited. Still fearing the possibility of a violent attack against the company office, the police assembled a reserve force.[29]

When the Episcopalians again attempted to relieve the distress of the Italian workers, their efforts fell short. Zara had hoped to provide another dinner for his countrymen at Dupont Hall, where he could deliver what the press described as "a friendly talk." Although some supporters made generous contributions, Zara did not have enough time to organize the effort. When a reporter interviewed him, Zara stated: "My poor countrymen did not strike; they are simply trying to get their wages, their lawful due, and nobody seems to help them to this simple justice. They have most of them gone now, four or five hundred of them, out to their tents and shanties about twelve miles from the city, where they have a sort of camp. They have been staying down at Carpenter street, below Eighth, with their countrymen, who live there. Of course they are not starving, as they have been with their countrymen, but they are having a hard time."[30]

Several other incidents illustrate why the Italians had not supported Zara's program. On the Sunday of Zara's failed plan, another crowd of men, women, and children, along with "an admiring body guard of some half dozen policemen and a score of Irish nursemaids," had gathered near the corner of Seventh and Marriott Streets. The *Inquirer* printed a colorful version of this scene, as well as the character of life among Italians, which was becoming familiar to readers:

The area in front of the Roman Catholic Church of St. Mary Magdalene di Pazzi, of which Rev. Antonio Isoleri is pastor, was thronged, and the interior of the church was so well filled that children hung over the window sills, and the bright hues of the Italian female headdress gleamed from every doorway. It was the fete day of St. Mary Magdalene di Pazzi, the Patron Saint of the Church, and was being celebrated with appropriate ceremonies. Few of the men who had been at work on the Philadelphia and Chester County Railroad, and who have been denied their just wages, were present among the throng of celebrants. An empty stomach is not a great incitant [*sic*] to devotion. One or two of them stood about the doors with hollow cheeks and heavy eyes, their enforced hardships having not yet been sufficient to drive all the color from their swarthy faces, or to destroy in their eyes the attractiveness of the gay attire which delights the dark eyed children of sunny Italy.[31]

On the following day the men with empty stomachs, hollow cheeks, and heavy eyes returned. The railroad claimed that the troubles had ended; the men were back at their jobs, waiting quietly for their wages. But having heard a rumor that their fellow countrymen intended to take measures for their relief, about two hundred workers had walked from their barracks at Fernwood into the city to attend a rally at Independence Square. Giovanni Francesco Secchi deCasali, the publisher of *L'Eco d'Italia*, told them that there was no need to march into the city each day; their immediate needs would be met. Domenico A. Pignatelli, the local pharmacist and social activist, announced that with the aid of John D. Raggio, another prominent leader, a relief fund had been started and that $160 had already been collected. When someone in the crowd shouted that the workers did not want charity, Pignatelli replied that the contractors were expected to have $5,000 with which to pay them at that moment. Urging the men to remain orderly, Count Galli, the Italian consul, told them that he had engaged an attorney to secure their claims. After about fifteen minutes the meeting ended, and the men began the walk back to their barracks. By that night the strike fund, including a $25 contribution from Isoleri, had reached more than $200. As with the celebration of Columbus and political events in their homeland, the hardships of immigrant life had brought Italian Protestants and Catholics, atheists and believers, nationalists and ultramontanists together, if only for a moment, in a common cause.[32]

The condition of poor Italians continued to attract the attention of reformers throughout 1883. When renovated baths at the Bedford Street Mission on Alaska Street were opened in July, announcements printed in Italian were widely distributed to residents of South Philadelphia. In September, an agent of the Society to Protect Children from Cruelty arrested an Italian harpist and two boy violinists for violating the state law prohibiting the employment of children as street musicians. On the basis of testimony by the boys that they were earning 75–80 cents per day, the defendant, despite his plea that he had only been a short time in this country and knew nothing about the law, was convicted and sent to prison. In December the Bedford Street Mission reached out with a Christmas dinner, along with prayers, preaching, and hymns, for over two hundred American, Irish, German, Italian, and African American children. But of all the agencies that offered services to Italians, the energetic efforts of the Episcopalians were the most immediate threat to Isoleri's aims.[33]

By the end of 1883, Isoleri had ever greater reason for concern over the growing influence of Episcopalians on the Italians. They had extensively improved a recently purchased building on Christian Street, with Italians eager to show how well they could paint it, at a cost of $7,000. It was dedicated as the Chapel of the Emmanuello in December, and Zara as its rector led services in English and Italian. Its agenda called for regular worship and preaching in Italian, English lessons for adults and children, and a Ladies Committee assisting in activities. With the purchase of an organ and the launching of a monthly Italian newspaper, the church pursued an ambitious program. As Bishop William B. Stevens pointed out at its dedication, the Episcopalians had opened missions for the French-, Spanish-, Chinese-, and Italian-speaking peoples of the city.[34]

The Episcopalian presence grew stronger in the next year, when Bishop Stevens confirmed thirty-five persons at the chapel. Zara, who was praised for "doing much to improve the moral and temporal condition of his fellow countrymen," had two assistants to help with the nightly English classes. Plans for his mission, supported entirely by contributions, already called for expansion. An assessment of the work being done by Zara and his associates praised not only them but the Italians as well, for results that seemed, despite more than thirty years of ministering to them, to have eluded similar efforts by the Catholic clergy: "the Italians are increasing rapidly in this city, and, not having had heretofore a Protestant missionary speaking their language, their actual wants and conditions have not been made known; but it is claimed that the present work among them proves that they are intelligent and industrious, and anxious for more improvement and education."[35]

When its 1886 report was issued, the Episcopalian Mission had become "a means of doing much toward the uplifting of a class that has long been neglected in this city [whose] results each year, so far, have exceeded expectations." At its night school, established in September 1885, attendance reached as high as 150 adults and children. Its day school, opened in 1866, instructed and, when necessary, fed and clothed girls and boys who had been gathered from the streets. The trustees hoped that these efforts would develop into an industrial home for indigent Italian children. Although the monthly newspaper, *L'Emmanuello*, was said to be reaching Italians throughout the country, financial support had been insufficient to cover its expenses. A reading room with Bibles, tracts, and periodicals in Italian was opened; and a sewing class for younger girls begun. The report also listed fourteen baptisms; two marriages; twenty confirmations; 290 visits to the sick and poor; 100 hospital visits; five prison visits; 150 services; 475 Italians attending the chapel; 47 Sunday school children; 69 Bibles and Testaments distributed; and 150 day and night school children.[36]

The report, however, showed the contrasting approach that separated Zara and the Episcopalians from Isoleri in serving Italians in the city. It noted that the night and day schools of the Episcopalian Mission were not only important instruments of spiritual ministration, but also were a means by which "to accustom the attendants to American ways and habits." While the Emmanuello's program saw a need to Americanize the foreign born, Isoleri sought to enable the members of his congregation to retain their identity as Italians. The increasing volume and changing sources of immigration in general, from Northern to Southern and Eastern Europe, had generated this concern. Episcopalians and other Protestants advocated a social service strategy based upon preserving their own cultural and social hegemony in a society that they saw as threatened by vast numbers of foreign newcomers, and an Irish Catholic hierarchy often shared these reservations. Isoleri, of course, was not dismayed by an influx of more Italians, even from Southern Italy. As a result, while Protestants advocated an assimilationist policy, Isoleri espoused a pluralistic one. In the long run the Protestant emphasis on assimilation set an unforeseen limit on influence among the Italians.

A New Church for St. Mary Magdalen dePazzi

In the face of Protestant efforts to attract Italians, Isoleri moved ahead with his own plans for a new church. In 1881, when he purchased ground just east of the old church, where a lumber yard had stood, a newspaper account declared: "The growing state of this parish has rendered a larger church necessary." The design, by Edwin F. Durang, the prominent church architect, called for an Italianate building with Corinthian elements on its interior and exterior, a central nave divided by eight bays, columns supporting vaulted side aisles, a domed ceiling, two towers flanking the main entrance, and a facade of blue and white marble. In the spring of 1883, a few days after the plan was announced, despite a labor conflict occurring at precisely that point, the parish celebrated the feast of Saint Mary Magdalen dePazzi with its traditional procession of children and adults on Marriott Street in front of the old church, which was decorated with flags and religious banners.[37]

About three months later, with the sisters gone, it appeared that matters had collapsed, leaving Isoleri with a new crisis. But when the school reopened with lay teachers and fifty boys and sixty girls enrolled, it had not only survived but Isoleri had again prevailed. The dedication of the cornerstone and a massive public celebration for the new church rewarded his efforts. After three days of events the actual dedication took place on an October Sunday that began under clouds and heavy showers. In the morning, two masses drew a large number of communicants to the old chapel. By the afternoon, when a bright and dry sky appeared and four bands playing "cheerful airs" marched to the church, some 5,000–6,000 people crowded the streets.[38]

After the placing of the cornerstone, with speeches in English, Italian, and Latin, the program reached its climax with the reading of a cable from Pope Leo XIII, which conveyed his blessing upon the church and its benefactors. Members of a special committee passed through the crowd to collect contributions. While a "handsome sum" had been gathered for the building fund, the *Catholic Standard* noted: "Now that so auspicious a start has been made, we hope Father Isoleri will continue to receive generous support, so that no delay may take place in the carrying out to completion of this great undertaking."[39]

Religious sodalities and secular beneficial societies marching with their distinctive banners and regalia joined a diverse mix of persons in the celebration. The *prominenti* of the Italian community, such as John D. Raggio, Joseph Malatesta, Agostino Lagomarsino, Stefano Ratto, Antonio Pizagno, and Ferdinando Bartilucci, served on the Committee of Arrangements, while other men, including some who were not of Italian origin, participated in the planning as well as in the actual event. Count Galli, the Italian consul; Marchese Luigi Taffini d'Acceglio, an artillery officer and honorary aide-de-camp to King Victor Emmanuel; and Vito Viti, the longtime Philadelphia businessman and former consul, occupied places on the platform for distinguished guests.

The physical expansion of parish facilities continued in subsequent years. In February 1885, after working "as quickly as means at hand would allow," St. Mary Magdalen dePazzi dedicated a new basement chapel before another large crowd, which, despite an admission fee, occupied every seat and almost all the standing room. Archbishop Patrick John Ryan, installed less than a year earlier as Wood's successor, enthusiastically congratulated the congregation on the progress of the building. He urged them to keep the faith of their fathers, the chief glory of Italy, on this side of the Atlantic and to help their pastor to complete the project. As Ryan, a native of Ireland, flanked by statues of Francis of Assisi, a Franco-Italian; Anthony of Padua, a Portuguese; Vincent dePaul, a Frenchman; and Patrick, an Irishman in later life if not by birth, addressed a largely Italian crowd, the setting reflected not only the support that Irish members had given to St. Mary Magdalen dePazzi but also the pluralism within which immigrant life was unfolding.[40]

While physical growth at St. Mary Magdalen dePazzi had given Italians a larger church, it had other implications. The resettlement of immigrants inevitably tested the strength of their traditional culture and social institutions, but the church afforded them a hospitable environment in which to renew their identity and allegiance as Catholics. The participants at regular services and special ceremonies who were members of other ethnic groups indicated that it was not an exclusive institution for Italians only. Similarly, the presence of Italian government officials suggested a diplomatic détente, which allowed Isoleri to play a role in public events without the censure that had followed the Columbus Monument dedication seven years ago. And for Philadelphia as a whole, the building initiative signified a change in the motives and intentions of Italians as a part of the local population. In contrast to their earlier itinerant and transient character, Italians had become a permanent component of the city's landscape and were taking their place as a community among others in Philadelphia.[41]

The Daughters of Charity

With the school again open and church construction under way, there were still problems to resolve. Lay teachers were only a temporary expedient. After fifty boys and sixty-four girls in 1884–85, enrollment declined slightly to fifty boys and sixty girls in the next year. Isoleri needed the services of a religious order of women for the type of education that he wished to offer. When he arranged for the Daughters of Charity, or the Canossian Sisters as they were commonly known, to take over in the autumn of 1886, his reception seemed to promise a long and successful tenure for them. Mother Rosa, the superior of the order, Mother Giuseppina, a veteran of five years in the China missions, Sister Rosa, Sister Lucia, and Sister Helena left Italy in late August. On September 15, informed by wire that the *Switzerland*, a Red Star Line vessel from Antwerp, had arrived at the mouth of the Delaware River, Isoleri set out to greet them accompanied by Vassallo and a committee led by Raggio. Sailing on a U.S. Customs tugboat, after about one hour they reached the steamer at Horse-shoe Bend, where they welcomed the sisters. But this greeting hardly compared to their landing. When the sisters reached the Christian Street wharf, Italian girls in white dresses, directed by Miss Annie McGuire, an English teacher at the school, presented them with fruit baskets and bouquets, and a committee of Italian women ushered them into carriages. Despite rain as they reached the church, along with the still excited group of little girls, a crowd welcomed them to their new assignment. A newspaper account noted, "But if all were happy on that occasion, we dare say that the pastor was the happiest of them all, and marked the day with a Red Letter in the parish Calendar."[42]

With the coming of the Daughters of Charity, St. Mary Magdalen dePazzi had reached a propitious moment. As the new rectory was nearing completion, Isoleri had temporarily moved his own quarters to the floor above the church sacristy, where he occupied a parlor, study, and bedroom. The sisters, housed in the former rectory, took over instruction in the Sunday school and parochial school, which reopened on October 2, the Feast of the Guardian Angels. They also assumed responsibility for the orphan asylum, which had recently received a bequest from the late Francis A. Biddle, a prominent Philadelphian. In support of these programs, two major events were planned. On October 12, the 394th anniversary of another arrival, "Columbus Day, as it is called by the Italians," declared one newspaper, would be celebrated by "a children's festival . . . on the grounds around the old Italian church, for the benefit of the orphans and to provide school-books for the poor children of the parish." Preparations also called for a fair on Thanksgiving Day, a few weeks later, to pay off the debt and hasten the completion of the church. As on previous occasions, the rector's efforts were recognized: "Rev. Father Isoleri has been working hard and steady for many years, and is justly entitled to generous assistance, which we hope will be given to him, as his needs are pressing and the object a most worthy one."[43]

Isoleri now sought not only to avoid a repetition of the problems that had ended the tenure of the Franciscan sisters but also to block any further interference from the archbishop. While enrollment reached sixty boys and seventy girls, as well as a few orphans, in 1886–87, the Canossians, after only one year, suddenly left the school for reasons that remain unclear. Even more surprising, in the next year, five Franciscan sisters, with Mother Gabriella as their superior, returned. With this change, enrollment for 1887–88 fell slightly to fifty boys and sixty girls. But within two years, with eight sisters teaching, it climbed to ninety boys and one hundred ten girls, the highest numbers so far.[44]

"Isabella da Marsicovetere"

Although Isoleri had somehow made enough peace with the Franciscan sisters to secure their return to the school, the completion of his new church would take much longer than expected. But his successes, after nearly twenty years as rector of St. Mary Magdalen dePazzi, had duly earned him a reputation as its "second founder." And along with his other skills and accomplishments, Isoleri's intellectual interests carried his influence to its people. He often redirected his energy into efforts that allowed him to rediscover his proclivities as a writer, or perhaps it is more accurate to say that he had never lost them. Throughout his life he continued to manifest the rhetorical and literary talents that had first been displayed during his seminary years.

During this period of Isoleri's life, the Lyre of the Leronica was evolving into the Lyre of Marriott Street. As early as February 1870, not long after his arrival, he had transcribed some ideas for a melodrama, "L'Orfano Italiano in Philadelphia d'America," concerning the plight of the child street musicians.

In July of the same year he reflected on a possible novel, "Riccardo e Romeo o gli Emigrati per genio." By January 1875 he was drafting a five-act play about Gennaro and Lucia, who were sold by their father to the *padroni* for a life of servitude on Philadelphia streets. Although details and names varied, these tentative efforts usually had the same basic plot and characters.[45]

Isoleri left only one complete script, "Isabella da Marsicovetere o i Piccoli Musicanti in America," a drama set in Philadelphia in 1876. Although beginning the work on a visit to Vassallo's parish in New Jersey on July 4, 1881, Isoleri did not complete it for another four years. While he embellished some aspects, his vivid depiction of the street musicians serves as a documentary of their experiences by a contemporary observer.[46]

Isabella Trafficante, seven years old, has been sold with her twin brother by their parents for a period of six years to Gennaro Durante, a padrone importer of young musicians. A few months after arriving in Philadelphia, Isabella's brother dies of smallpox. For several years, Durante sends the annual price of the contract to the Trafficante family through his own wife, Silvestra, in Marsicovetere. When he finally brings his wife and son to America, Durante no longer sends any money or information to Isabella's parents, who now go to Philadelphia themselves to search for their daughter and seek their fortune. Durante soon dies from a wound in a tavern brawl, but not before a priest absolves him in his final moments. Durante's son, meanwhile, leads a dissolute life.

Isabella wishes to run away from all of this, but the priest, whose name happens to be Antonio Isoleri, advises her to be patient. When her parents arrive, the padrona does not want to give Isabella up, but finally agrees to do so. Although she hates the padrona, Isabella neither loves, nor wants to recognize, the parents who sold her. And now with anger toward them, she runs away with her harp to seek a life alone. When she meets Leone, her former master's son, he reveals his love for her. But on another day, while in a cemetery to pray, Isabella picks a rose as she leaves and is arrested by a half-drunken policeman. Samuel Scott, the son of a Protestant minister, secures her release. When a romance develops, he proposes marriage, but Isabella resists. Instead, she persuades him to become a Catholic and brings him to Father Isoleri for instruction and baptism. But then Isabella is placed in the orphan asylum. When Samuel and Isabella eventually marry, she is reunited with her parents. At the play's end, they all return happily to Italy.

From its opening scene, Isoleri depicts the sad circumstances of the slave children. Isabella, while playing her harp, sings:

> All by myself in a foreign land, I search for some money,
> And if I do not, I am certain my master
> Will give me supper by using a stick.
> With harp on shoulder, the little wretch

Goes around—Oh, oh, Isabella!
What a hard life!
What a lousy way to make a living
Every morning! Every evening![47]

After someone throws a few coins to her from a window, Isabella resumes her lament:

I am poor and unhappy
But my heart tells me
That there is in heaven no God
Of greater kindness
Than this one, who someday
Will take pity on my life.[48]

Although the only surviving text of "Isabella da Marsicovetere," a hand-written draft, contains no evidence that it was ever performed, it melodramatically portrays the situation facing some Italians. Having presided at burial services for immigrant children, Isoleri had seen the results of the temporary indenture or even outright sale of children by impoverished parents in Italy. For Isabella's and other such parents, Isoleri saw himself as their chief protector, here to improve their lives and save their souls. Despite his efforts, their experiences took an enormous toll on family life, in particular encouraging dissolution in the young people. Lured by immoral pleasures to taverns, for example, youths were preyed upon by less than honorable policemen and were subjected to imprisonment, alienation from their parents, dissipated lives, disillusionment, violence, and premature death.

For a Catholic priest willing to engage Protestant ministers in debate, Isoleri's depiction of Protestantism in his play was rather mild. While Samuel Scott was not particularly strong in religious observance, Protestants were basically of good character. Nonetheless, interfaith romances, such as that between Samuel and Isabella, contained dangers, and the conversion of Protestants to the true faith remained essential. In Isabella's confinement to the orphanage, Isoleri presented his parish as a defense against the temptations offered by urban America. But when Samuel and Isabella finally marry, Isoleri also recognized the inevitability of mixed marriages and the assimilation of Italians in America. In this case, however, the play concludes with Samuel and Isabella, her parents, Leone, and even Silvestra the now reformed padrona, returning to their homeland. Their departure suggests that the author believed it to be the only real solution for immigrants in America. The land of their origins was where they belonged, the only place where they could find true contentment. It is not difficult to recognize what was buried in Isoleri's own mind and heart.

From the Pulpit:
Parents, Children, Drunks, and Death

In contrast to the relative subtlety of his play, Isoleri used his homilies to speak even more directly about temporal matters. In September 1882, after the departure of the Franciscan sisters had left immigrant parents alone to care for their children, he took up the responsibilities of family life in his sermon on the Fifteenth Sunday after Pentecost. He had seen a death, a funeral, and the tears of mothers, but it was the many deaths and funerals of young people, morally speaking, to which he was referring. They were not only spiritually dead but good for nothing as well. While admitting that some parents were not to blame, Isoleri asked why so many young men in this country were failures, before he went on to argue that the evil causes also suggested the remedies. He did not let parents off lightly and offered a litany of their faults. They did not send their children to Catholic schools and, when they did, it was only for a short time; moreover, they did not cooperate with the teachers but found fault and believed all of the complaints of their children. Instead of providing them with a wholesome family life, they gave their children too much liberty in too many things: in coming and going, in associating with others, and in their reading. Children were compelled to make money at too young an age for lazy and idle parents, who failed to recognize the natural inclinations of their children that might enable them to choose a profession or trade. Parents often failed to set a good example in resisting such vices as drinking, quarreling, and cursing. They neglected the mass and sacraments. They spoke disrespectfully about priests and Church authorities. Their ill-timed pride blinded them to the faults of their offspring, whom they defended in everything, right or wrong. He concluded with the charge that parents did not pray enough for their children.[49]

Isoleri similarly indicted the children for their shortcomings. They suffered from a lack of obedience to their parents as well as of insufficient prayer and infrequent taking of the sacraments. They associated with companions who led them into bad habits. They read books and papers that corrupted their minds and weakened their faith. They had too much love of pleasure and hatred of restraint and mortification. And they engaged in too much "company-keeping." Although sociologists would not describe the problem of "marginality" until much later, Isoleri had incisively identified the intrusions on immigrant family life and tensions between generations.

Isoleri's sermons sometimes revealed unexpected aspects of life among the Italians. In contrast to the belief that the Irish had problems with alcohol but the Italians did not, his vigorous condemnation of public intoxication painted a different picture on Pentecost Sunday in 1886. Speaking in Italian, he began with the words of Saint Paul: "neither fornicators, nor idolators, nor adulterers, nor the effeminate, nor sodomites, nor thieves, nor drunkards, nor the evil-tongued,

nor the greedy will possess the kingdom of God." Comparing drunkenness to the
Great Flood, Isoleri depicted a staggering queen who walked the land in an obscene and disgusting spectacle. Men and women, young and old, rich and poor,
here today and there tomorrow, he argued, are nearly all affected by this leprosy.
As he reached its relevance for his own people with the words "E gl'Italiani"
(and the Italians), Isoleri parenthetically asked in Latin, "Oh! What has changed
them?" Italians who once boasted of being temperate were no longer able to do
so, as taverns multiplied before their eyes and drunks grew in equal proportion
among them. Isoleri then detailed the damaging effects of drunkenness upon
the human body, the soul, the ability to reason, the family, society and the state,
and even religion.[50]

On the following Sunday, Isoleri resumed his attack on public intoxication. He took his opening words from Ecclesiasticus: "Wine taken with sobriety
is equal life to men: if thou drink it moderately, thou shalt be sober. . . . Wine
was created from the beginning to make men joyful, and not to make them
drunk. . . . Sober drinking is health to soul and body." He then drew upon Saint
Peter: "Be sober, be watchful! For your adversary the devil, as a roaring lion,
goes about seeking someone to devour." With these scriptural guides, Isoleri
turned to the use of alcohol by Italians. His message was simple and straight-
forward. While this vice could be found among all classes, Italians, no longer
models of sobriety, now shared it too, and what good could come from denying
it? The Italian dealers in alcohol, who once could be counted on the fingers of
one hand, were rapidly multiplying in an evil competition to become equal to
the Irish or Germans or to exceed them in number and in infamy.[51]

Isoleri decried the tavernkeepers who put the cross as well as the Savoyard
coat of arms and national colors of Italy, vividly painted, on their doors and
windows. He thunderously punctuated his outrage against "bars, really, that is
to say, biers—places of death and perdition." While the glorious colors of the
Italian flag—white, green, and red—signified faith, hope, and charity, they denoted irony and sacrilege on tavern doors, which ought to be painted black and
yellow for sin and death, where throughout day and night, but especially on
Sundays, men, women, and the tender young found diabolical diversions. He
then recounted a recent experience that had profoundly disturbed him. On the
past Sunday night, as he gave the last rites to a young woman who died near
a corner tavern, an Italian, so drunk that he could hardly remain on his feet,
stood by and blasphemed the blood of God and the Virgin Mary. It was, Isoleri
declared, a mere drop in a sea of filth, infamy, and perdition.

Noting Church, as well as state regulation of these matters, Isoleri added his
own observations to the conclusions of the Third Plenary Council on taverns.
It would be better if ninety-nine out of every hundred places closed forever,
or at least on Sundays, which would no longer be profaned and which would
allow saloonkeepers to go to church for mass and vespers rather than only for

funerals. (He also mentioned here that it was good that the archbishop had prohibited funerals on Sundays.) And what could be said of taverns that were also bordellos or brothels? Musicians should not in good conscience continue to play in such places. Taverns should not stay open all night or allow gambling but instead should serve food as well as drink, as was done in Italy, thus promoting temperance. And tavernkeepers who waited for those who wanted beer alone were "true acolytes of intoxication, perfect courtesans of His Satanic Majesty."

On the next Sunday, Isoleri resumed giving his recommendations for tavern patrons and the use of alcohol. If other groups formed temperance societies, he asked, why should we not wage war against the slavery of intoxication? Temperance meant moderate use, not total abstinence, but if merely tasting alcohol led to intoxication, as he was sure it did for some persons, then moral law dictated a complete avoidance of liquor. Against beliefs that whiskey and brandy were good against the cold or in the heat or against illness, Isoleri declared that they did no good at all. Similarly, wine, beer, and even tobacco, except when used moderately (and only after food, clothing, and education had been provided for the children), brought nothing but sickness, disgrace, and unemployment. Advising his listeners never to set foot in a tavern, he cited Dante's words over the Gates of Hell: "Abandon all hope, ye who enter here." For love of temperance and mortification, he continued, never drink between meals. Drink as little as you can with a meal for your family, and, if not every day, then only on Sundays and holidays. If it is only one glass, share it with your wife or children. Let he who is strong enough drink no beer or wine during Lent and Advent, except on Sundays, or the vigils of holy days, days of fasting, Fridays in honor of Christ's Passion, or Saturdays in honor of the Madonna, as penitence and satisfaction for the sins of intoxication and the conversion of drunkards.[52]

Isoleri declared himself ready to be the first to observe these admonitions. Returning to a metaphor in an earlier sermon, he described the courage of the three hundred Spartans under Leonidas at Thermopylae and the thousands of young Italians in more recent battles. With his usual eloquence, he ended by noting: "How rare intoxication is, the flowering of temperance would be. We are men and Christians; as men we should eat and drink in order to live, rather than live to eat and drink. We are men, and we should not become beasts by intoxication, nor commit suicide. We are Christians and we should be temperate and mortifying men, do penance for our past sins, and avoid falling into new ones."

Welcoming the new year of 1887 by a mass with the members of the Società di Unione e Fratellanza Italiana occupying the front pews in what had become an annual event, Isoleri preached on the value of time. After complimenting them for their participation at mass, he spoke of solemn concerns: "Today we are living, tomorrow we will be dead! How many began the last year and did not end it? How many who see the beginning of this one will not see the end of it? Today in good form, tomorrow in the tomb!"[53] The meaning and purpose of Isoleri's sermon were as clear as the bright sky of the morning of the dawning new year. If intoxication posed a serious problem that might be addressed on ordinary Sundays, the uncertainty of life itself represented an even greater issue that warranted being placed before his congregation on the most special occasions.

Patriotism in the Pulpit:
"Italy Cries, and We Cry with Her"

Within a few weeks, somber news from abroad soon jolted the mood of the community. Toward the end of January 1887, nearly five hundred Italian soldiers had been annihilated in ferocious combat against thousands of Ethiopians at the battle of Dogali. Only a month later a tremendous earthquake on Ash Wednesday took about two thousand lives in Liguria. In commemoration of both tragedies, Isoleri led a grieving population in a Requiem Mass at St. Mary Magdalen dePazzi in late March. Members of the Società di Unione e Fratellanza Italiana, with its president, John D. Raggio, and vice president, Stefano Ratto; the newer Società Italiana di Mutuo Soccorso, under its president, Pompeo Scalella; and the Bersaglieri Society, along with others, once again gathered in their church, now draped in mourning. Speaking in Italian, Isoleri began his eulogy for the fallen victims of the war in Africa in verse:

> Our soldiers have fallen at Dogali; they fell fighting the Abyssinians.
> Our soldiers have fallen at Dogali; they fell fighting as heroes.
> Our soldiers have fallen at Dogali; they fell facing the enemy

Praising the gallantry of these men, Isoleri counseled their loved ones not to await their return: "Mothers and wives, sisters and sweethearts, do not wait for them: they will never return from Africa." As for the fallen men themselves, he declared: "They were sons of strong Piedmont; of noble Venice and gentle Tuscany. Indomitable Ligurians, courageous Lombards, intrepid Romagnolans, bold Calabrians, and undaunted Sicilians. All sons of Italy, all brothers: all fought as heroes."

While his view of Southern Italy remained selective, Isoleri sought to embrace all his countrymen in his praise. Perhaps if he had been able to find more synonyms for bravery, he would have included other regions. And while proclaiming their unification as a people, Isoleri now viewed the life that Italians had found in an immigrant colony through the prism of American experience. Having been quieted for his political views only a few years earlier, he now broke his silence: "Our soldiers have fallen at Dogali. May our cry be: Always forward, Savoy!"

In a homily later on the earthquake, Isoleri similarly poured out his emotion for Liguria and its people along with his lingering bonds with the region of his birth. In his poem, "Liguria," he referred to "You blessed land, patch of paradise." In "Terraemotus," written partly in Latin, he added, "Oh, Liguria, once enchanted land, but by earthquake now destroyed." In the oddly titled "Charitas," he further affirmed his devotion to the region. Although separated from it for nearly two decades, even as he voiced his perception of a larger, unified Italy, Isoleri still remembered the "enchanted land" of his youth and the Riviera di Ponente as his "patch of paradise."[54]

By the end of what had been a particularly tragic year, Isoleri fused together his spiritual themes and secular concerns for his people. On the afternoon of December 28, 1887, he began to transcribe his thoughts, and two days later he carefully revised the final words that he intended to deliver in his next sermon. On January 1, 1888, members of the Società di Unione e Fratellanza Italiana, San Giuseppe Society, the Sodality of the Holy Sacrament, and other worshipers took their places to listen again to their pastor at St. Mary Magdalen dePazzi.

In the first part of his lengthy sermon, Isoleri confined his remarks to religious themes, briefly reflecting on the passing of the years before taking up human mortality as his subject. Asking his audience how many more years they could expect to live, he reminded them that worldly existence was only a preparation for a future life. He declared that having spoken to them as Catholics, he now intended to address them as Italians. In their native language, he affirmed his devotion to the land that they had all left behind:

> I have spoken to all of you until now as Catholics; now I address you as Italians; or rather I invite you to give a look with me to our country, Italy: a country that all of you love, I know, as a child loves his mother, and loves it more because you are so far away: a country, if I may be so bold to say, few love more ardently than I do. Oh, my Italy, Mother of Saints, Geniuses, and Heroes! After the very holy name of God, Mary and of our most sacred religion, your name, Oh my Italy, is the sweetest that can resound on the lips. And to you my thoughts go often, for you have always ignited the love in my heart, since the day, eighteen years ago, that I left you, and a father and mother that I saw no more, nor will ever see again here on earth. My Italy, garden of Europe, as well as the world, smile of God, object of admiration and even of envy by other nations, he who among the Italians does not love you has no heart; and as one, who truly loves you, proudly rises with your glory, and at the same time exalts in it, not only rejoices in your glory, but also is saddened by your sorrows? What of the glory that is your abundant and eternal heritage, if the joy did not last in the year just past, if the cup of sorrows was more than once tasted by your lips. . . .[55]

As Isoleri reviewed the year, he added other catastrophes to the defeat at Dogali and the devastation in Liguria. Another earthquake had devastated parts of Calabria; plague had taken many lives in Sicily. Far more than a routine homily, his words conveyed affection, pride, and fidelity for his country of origin while also reflecting his unstinting efforts for the people of his congregation. Above all, Isoleri expressed the anguish that immigration inevitably imposed, which he shared as well, on all those who were separated from family and homeland. This son, knowing that he, too, would never again see the land that few loved more ardently than he did, or the parents whom he loved even more, indeed drank from a bitter cup of sorrow.

Isoleri had to ignore his own afflictions, however, if he were to meet his pastoral responsibilities. He had to tend to the temporal situation of his people while bringing them to and keeping them in his church. In particular, he recognized their need of a common identity and cohesion. As he continued his homily, he repeated his tribute to the fallen men at Dogali, comparing them again to the Spartans at Thermopylae while also connecting Italy and its immigrants: "The one hundred cities of Italy, its innumerable towns and villages, all ignited by the sacred fire of patriotism, and the Italians spread over the face of the earth, and especially those here in America, honor them, these 500 heroes."

Despite their separation, or even more so because of it, Isoleri argued that immigrant Italians remained strong in their loyalty to their homeland. In regard to the events of the year, he declared: "And Italy cries; and we cry with her, because we would not be true children of Italy if we were insensitive to the sorrow and tears of our mother." While those who remained in Italy would label as Americans those who had migrated, Isoleri had a different point of view. From their reactions to the misfortunes suffered by Italy, Isoleri contended, "in their noble and most charitable undertaking, Italians in America were certainly not less than Italians in Italy. And so the tears of children and the mother are dried; and sorrow is eased."

Isoleri repeated the same theme throughout his remarks on this day, seeking to unite his people as Catholics and Italians. He maintained: "We are always proud to be Italians and Catholics; we are always worthy of the name of Catholics and Italians." In his own way, Isoleri was reacting to the simultaneous threats represented by assimilation, secularism, and proselytization. At the end of his long sermon, he focused on the significance of Pope Leo XIII and reiterated his argument: "Today in spirit we are in Rome, and our heart beats in unison with the heart of 300 million Catholics. . . . Leo XIII, as I have said, is Italian: Italian blood runs through his veins; and you Italians have with him a common country, language, and traditions; and the great light that today surrounds him, will reflect, as I already said, on the Italy that was his mother, and even a little on us, that are brothers to him."

The presence of the Società di Unione e Fratellanza Italiana and other beneficial societies on these occasions reflected their importance in Philadelphia's Little Italy as well as their place in the parish. Mindful of the passing years, Isoleri had taken the theme of time to remind their members of what they had endured and accomplished together. No longer the recently ordained young priest who had arrived in 1870, he was now nearly forty-two years old and had served them for seventeen years. He had confronted hostile priests, an obstructionist archbishop and uncooperative nuns, proselytizing ministers of other denominations, the spiritual indifference of his own flock, and the tavernkeepers and padroni who preyed on immigrants. By prevailing against these challenges, he had become the respected rector of a struggling mission that nevertheless had a promising future.

The centerpiece for the future of parish and pastor at St. Mary Magdalen dePazzi, however, rested on the plans for the construction of the new church, which remained an uncompleted task. During the late 1880s, parish fairs, lectures, dinners, picnics, concerts, and the sale of Isoleri's own writings generated income for the building fund. LaSalle College students staged theatrical productions and Raggio's furniture factory employees performed in a concert to benefit the project. Catholics throughout the city, "irregardless of nationality," were urged to support these programs. The *Catholic Standard* reported that "no honest effort is being spared to obtain the means necessary for carrying this new church to completion"; moreover, "Father Isoleri deserves great credit for his energy and the work he is doing should be regarded as monumental." Although he had undertaken a broad agenda to finance construction, it was not enough. The roof and cross were put into place in late 1884; the basement chapel was dedicated in February 1885; six Genoese parishioners presented a painting of Saint Catherine of Genoa, by an artist of that city, in 1888. After its auspicious start, however, the project appeared to have stalled.[56] While Isoleri, from his first days in Philadelphia, had never been timid about debating from his pulpit and wading into public controversy, by the end of the 1880s, Protestant initiatives, increasing alcohol use, and the assimilation of Italians were forcing him to confront their problems even more. But he was not alone. In an era in which both pastor and parish were evolving in American Catholicism, Isoleri had become a visible presence as a leader among his people and his church an important institution in their community.

CHAPTER **EIGHT**

The Nineties

New Problems and Solutions

By the 1890s, with a widely visible increase in the foreign born, such problems of American cities as unemployment, poverty, slum housing, and crime were easily ascribed to immigration rather than to urbanization itself. The diminishing confidence in America's capacity to absorb the newcomers elicited demands for public policy that would sharply reduce, if not entirely halt, immigration, especially from Southern and Eastern Europe. But Philadelphia's nearly seven thousand Italians, largely concentrated in South Philadelphia, whether welcome or not, had established a colorful and enduring community. A wide range of neighborhood businesses, labor unions, political clubs, and beneficial societies, founded to meet the needs and protect the interests of Italians, brought stability to their lives and to their neighborhoods. Within this local network of enterprise and organization, St. Mary Magdalen dePazzi offered spiritual comfort to successive generations of older families as well as to recent arrivals. Despite the success, or perhaps because of it, soon to be reflected by an impressive new church, the parish was reaching the limits of its capacity to serve them. Beyond celebrating such events as Columbus's discovery of America and its pastor's jubilee as a priest, it would renew the defense against Protestant work among Italians. By the end of the decade, however, it was not the presence of Protestants but of too many Italians, particularly poor ones from the South of Italy, that brought St. Mary Magdalen dePazzi to that point.

The Limits of Parish Growth

Amid great transition in the Italian colony of Philadelphia, Father Antonio Isoleri had become an important liaison between his people and the larger social order, whether it was the city, Catholicism, or simply a public seeking to know more about Italians. After the lynching of eleven Italians in New Orleans in 1891, which precipitated a serious diplomatic crisis between Italy and the United States, the local press sought Isoleri's opinion on the matter. When a reporter asked him about the recall by the Italian government of its minister in Washington, "the reverend gentleman declined to talk upon the subject," expressing only his belief that it would not result in any difficulty between the two countries. But Isoleri's views were of more than academic interest for the press and public, and his influence was needed when Italians in Philadelphia, as in other cities, protested the affair. While the incident increased rancor against Italians and raised demands for immigration restriction, it also confirmed Isoleri's stature among the city's Italians.[1]

At St. Mary Magdalen dePazzi, Isoleri finally acquired long-needed assistance with the appointments of Father Giovanni B. Pambianco, a sixty-three-year-old Ligurian from Savona in 1889, who remained at the parish until 1896; Father Stephen Bonnetto, from 1891 to 1892; and Father Matthew Vacchero, from late 1896 to 1911. But these assignments were only temporary, as the archdiocese had other plans for the Italians. For the moment, St. Mary Magdalen dePazzi, without formal boundaries, served all Italians, wherever they lived—with masses at 6:30 A.M., 8:00 A.M., 9:00 A.M., and 10:30 A.M. and vespers at 3:30 P.M. on Sundays, masses at 6:30 A.M. and 7:30 A.M. on weekdays, and special devotions during Advent, Lent, and in the month of May.

Isoleri's annotated annual reports provided a healthy profile of parish activities.[2] In 1897, an especially productive year, he noted 1,088 baptisms, 270 confirmations, and 200 First Communions (nearly all children but also adults); some 141 marriages; and 4,800 adults meeting their Easter obligations. But Isoleri added that it was hard to tell how many of the "thick and scattered" flock had failed to meet their sacramental duty, had attended English-speaking churches, or had made confessions at his church but instead took communion elsewhere. Six parish confraternities had 250 regular and 285 nonregular members, while seven or eight beneficial societies had 675 members, often only nominally attached to the church and only occasionally joining in some religious feast. They were neither regular nor generous in their support. In explanation, he offered: "especially on account of many outside societies cropping up like mushrooms, bleeding all around . . . wherein a few aim at handling money [and] bossing, camorra-like, in the wrong spirit [and] prevailing for years on the other side."[3]

Although Isoleri was the only pastor in the archdiocese who regularly annotated his annual reports, his remarks, in keeping with his contentious character, were incisive and provocative. In 1897 he referred to a "floating class" of
15,000 Italian Catholics "scattered in and about the city" and made a scathing
assessment of their relationship to the church:

> It is hard to tell; but this much can be said that these people who had
> no struggle like others, with Protestants, at home [and] look upon public
> schools as sufficient for all as they were formerly at home ([and] are about
> the only ones still) will neither support a parochial school, nor appreciate
> it, or send their children to it (the majority of them) poor Catholics, as they
> are; except some for the sake of their native language, some for the sake of
> the English, in the beginning . . . [and] very few indeed for the religious
> interests of their offsprings. Moreover they do not keep them at school long
> enough to repay for the trouble [and] to reap any practical benefit (with
> very few exceptions); because out of need or greed they send them to work
> at anything whilst very young.[4]

Isoleri also ventured into a debate, characterized by Church historians as "the
war of the prelates," that revolved around whether parishes should have their
own schools and whether Catholic parents were obligated to send their children
to them.[5] His misgivings over the lack of Italian support for religion did not
deter him from making efforts on this issue in his own parish, where he achieved
what must be regarded, in view of the turmoil of the previous decade, as a remarkable accomplishment. After resuming their role as teachers, the Franciscan
sisters would remain at the school for nearly a century more. Enrollments that
before 1889 had never exceeded 130 students, with 50–60 boys and 60–70 girls,
steadily increased, reaching 467 students (204 boys and 263 girls), and 20 orphan
girls by 1897. Before their earlier departure in 1882, only five or six sisters had
taught but, after returning, ten sisters with Mother Dominic as their superior
were teaching by 1897.[6]

Parish growth, however, culminated in the opening of the long-needed new
church. Having outgrown the church rebuilt after the fire in 1873, the congregation initially called for its enlargement, but the project eventually became more
ambitious. After the basement chapel was opened in 1885 and a new rectory was
constructed on the east side of the site in the next year, further work proceeded
slowly until it was completed in June 1891.[7]

The new church, described as "beautiful and well proportioned," was 65 feet
wide and 110 feet long, with a neo-Baroque design by Edwin F. Durang and a
massive, ornate front with four columns of granite and blue marble that might
have been found in any Italian city. A wide stairway led to a spacious basement
chapel. In the upper church two rows of Corinthian columns supported the

roof, richly ornamented molding adorned stucco walls, and three handsomely carved altars graced the sanctuary. Above the main altar, a painting of the Crucifixion, a statue of Saint Mary Magdalen dePazzi in a niche, and a life-sized golden crucifix faced the pews, while a skylight held a representation of the Holy Spirit. Above the smaller altar on the west aisle were a large painting donated by six Italian gentlemen, depicting purgatory, and statues of Saints Joseph, Francis of Assisi, and Vincent de Paul. While the wall behind the east altar remained undecorated, plans called for a painting, imported from Genoa, of Mary Magdalen dePazzi among other saints, with its lower part depicting suffering humanity seeking relief as well as Columbus opening up the New World to the needy of the old one. Beneath this unfinished area, already completed niches held statues of the Blessed Virgin, Saint Patrick, and Saint Anthony of Padua. Along the side walls were stained glass windows representing other saints as well as the Stations of the Cross. In the sacristy were stained glass windows portraying two previous pastors, Gaetano Mariani and James Rolando.

As impressive as the structure was, the dedication ceremonies emphasized its significance for the Italian community. Spectators packed neighborhood streets and filled the church, while many others were turned away. Isoleri's old seminary friend, Father Giovanni Vassallo, as master of ceremonies, led the hierarchy and clergy in procession. Inside, "in the presence of a great crowd of Italians, sprinkled with a few Americans," a choir of fifty voices sung Haydn's Second Mass. In his short homily delivered in Italian, another fellow alumnus of the Collegio Brignole Sale, Bishop Winand Wigger of Newark, the celebrant of the mass, complimented Isoleri on his accomplishments and urged the congregation to support his efforts.

After congratulating Isoleri and his people on their beautiful church, Archbishop Ryan spoke to them as immigrants and Italians. He declared that the Lord, by instructing the apostles to go and teach all nations, had recognized the distinctions among them, and that Pope Gregory the Great, in sending Saint Augustine of Canterbury to preach in England, had encouraged him to learn the habits and customs of the people. He cited both cases as examples of the unity and diversity that coexisted within the Church. He then praised free speech and the opportunities that enabled immigrants to become citizens in America. The combining of nationality differences with unity of worship was not only essential to the Church but also recognized by God and blended into one in America. He urged his listeners to adopt American manners and customs but not to forget the traditions of their native land. In a convoluted manner, Ryan added that Italy, "the footstool of Rome," was the spiritual center of the Church and respected throughout the world. And if Italians remained faithful to their traditions and the Church, the salvation of Italy ultimately would be brought about. He noted that America had been discovered by an Italian Catholic whose main objective was to establish Catholicism in this land.

After a grand dinner for the clergy, the public program resumed in the late afternoon. With police controlling the exuberant crowd that had gathered in the streets, the grand marshal, Stefano Ratto, and assistant marshal, Antonio Raggio, led a procession of other officers, cross bearers, and acolytes; boys of the Society of the Holy Child, dressed in sailor suits; girls of the orphanage, strewing flowers along the route; sisters who staffed the orphan asylum; teachers and students of the Sunday school; boys of the Christopher Columbus Society; adult members of the Societies of Saint Michael the Archangel, the Holy Savior, Saint Peter Celestine, San Rocco, the Blessed Sacrament, and Confraternity of Saint Joseph; musicians of the Roma Band; and clergy. The festive paraders marched west on Marriott Street to Eighth, Christian, Seventh, Carpenter, and Eighth again to Marriott for vespers that ended the day.

In reporting the event, newspapers noted the position now held by Saint Mary Magdalen dePazzi in the Italian community. With much of its debt paid, "the crowning point was reached," and "the church favorably compares with any of the other Catholic churches in the city, both in architecture and ornamentation." Its history as the first church for exclusive use by Italians in the United States was repeated, along with praise for Isoleri for being "most successful in his missionary work among the Italian colony."[8]

Celebrating Columbus:
Becoming Italian American

As grand as the dedication ceremonies had been, they were surpassed a year later by the celebration of the 400th anniversary of Columbus's discovery of America. With flags of the United States, Italy, Spain, South American nations, the papacy, and Genoa decorating Saint Mary Magdalen dePazzi; candles, flowers, and palms adorning the aisles; and a bust of Columbus, framed by statues symbolic of America and Italy, greeting visitors at the entrance, the Feste Colombiane began on Sunday, October 9, 1892. Into the church there first came the consul general of Italy, Cavalier Raybaudi-Massiglia, and Emmanuel V. H. Nardi, president of the United Italian Societies, followed by Charles C. A. Baldi leading the Società di Unione e Fratellanza Italiana; then came the Società Italiana di Mutuo Soccorso e Beneficenza, the Sartori, the Bersaglieri La Marmora, the Bersaglieri Principe di Napoli, the Società Italiana Artiglieria di Campagna, the Legione Umberto I, the Legione Garibaldi, the Società Operaia, and the Società Gessopalena. Overflowing its front half, the members of the procession spilled into the sanctuary, while the nave, balconies, and temporary platforms erected for the event "regurgitated" with Italians and Americans in a "truly edifying and imposing spectacle." The momentary harmony among rival factions was made even more astounding by the presence of Garibaldi supporters in

Isoleri's church as ethnic pride allowed tolerance even for radical red republicans, at least for this occasion.[9]

After blessing a banner of the Confraternity of San Giuseppe, Isoleri celebrated Solemn Vespers, with a choir of one hundred children accompanied by the new organ. He then spoke once more on Columbus's life, voyages, and religious faith, and their implications for Europe and its people. Punctuating his remarks with poetic extracts from Seneca, Petrarch, and Torquato Tasso, but especially from Dante's *Divine Comedy,* Isoleri, still proudly Ligurian, again alluded to his native region as a little "patch of heaven." He proclaimed Columbus as a new Moses, who was pointing out a place to the poor and oppressed, forever free from slavery whether of soil or of human tyrants, and as a new Joshua, who was leading them to a promised land. Isoleri concluded his tribute by asking for a blessing on Genoa and Italy, on Spain and America, and especially on the Italians of Philadelphia. After the Benediction of the Blessed Sacrament and a Te Deum, the Italian societies exited to the playing of marches two hours after the ceremonies had begun.

After the entire program for the next day was canceled, ostensibly because a painting of Columbus had not arrived, events resumed when 10,000 students from the entire archdiocese, with bands and banners, paraded from the baseball field at Broad and Huntingdon Streets to the Cathedral of Sts. Peter and Paul, where Archbishop Ryan preached and gave the benediction on October 11. None participated more proudly than the one hundred students in sailor suits, carrying the banner of the Saint Mary Magdalen dePazzi School, who marched behind their pastor and the Italian Marine Band to the cathedral, where they presented Archbishop Ryan with a framed photograph of the Columbus Monument in Genoa.

In the evening an estimated 30,000 Catholics and many bands joined a torchlight procession of historical and allegorical floats. Despite Isoleri's more modest figures of his annual reports, nearly 1,000 marchers from his inexplicably increased parish carried banners and flags decorated with slogans from Dante and with heraldic insignias of the pope and the archbishop of Genoa, Italy, Spain, Brazil, and the United States. Behind Antonio Pizagno, its grand marshal, the Columbus Centennial Society float depicted a young Columbus on board a small boat in his native port. Other marchers, behind their own bands, included the Sodalizio dei Figli di Maria Santissima, the Società di San Michele Archangelo, the Società di San Pietro Celestino, the Società del San Salvatore, the Sodalizio del Santo Sacramento e Mutuo Soccorso, the Congregà di San Rocco, and the Confraternità di San Giuseppe. The final group consisted simply of "italiani," behind Ferdinando Bartilucci, another prominent member of the community. Isoleri, Pambianco, and Vassallo, who had come from New Jersey, rode in a carriage to the viewing stand at the Catholic High School at Broad and Vine Streets, where they presented Ryan with a model of Columbus's ship, the *Santa Maria,* composed of roses and carnations, to great applause from the crowd. The three Italian priests evidently celebrated the occasion as much as the other participants. Having left the rectory at 7:00 P.M., they did not return until 2:00 A.M. on the next day.

On Wednesday, October 12, activities resumed in the church, when Isoleri, assisted by Vassallo and Pambianco, after only a few hours of sleep, celebrated mass at 8:00 A.M. Vassallo's sermon offered a spirited defense of Columbus as the true discoverer of America in response to recent scholarly skeptics. As he thanked Isoleri for inviting him to take part, Vassallo also referred to himself "come Italo-Americano" (as Italian American), a new identity, not only for him, but for his listeners, which captured the spirit of the celebration. After another Te Deum, the United Italian Societies marched through the city again, with floats representing Columbus before Queen Isabella, the countries of Spain and the United States, and a replica of the *Santa Maria.* While the societies passed in review before Consul Raybaudi-Massiglia, Mayor Edwin S. Stuart, and other officials on their way to Fairmount Park, girls from Saint Mary Magdalen dePazzi opened a program of songs, recitals, and tableaux at the Academy of Music. Isoleri, following the men's parade by carriage as far as the Academy of Music, stopped to praise the girls before rejoining the large crowd of dignitaries and Italians assembling in the park.

After other speeches before the Columbus Monument, which he had helped to dedicate sixteen years ago, when Isoleri took the rostrum, he did not disappoint his listeners. Speaking in Italian, he greeted his "dearest fellow countrymen" and then complimented them before connecting himself to them: "I have seen it with my own eyes; I have heard it with my own ears! You have honored yourselves. We have honored ourselves, I will say it better: because even I am still Italian; I am, after nearly a quarter of a century in America; I am, and I boast of it. I boast of it most of all on this most fortunate day! On this day, on which the entire world celebrates *our* Columbus!"[10]

Isoleri recalled the earlier occasion when Italians had dedicated the monument in 1876, how quickly the intervening years had passed, and how the hands of participants at that celebration stretched across those years to clasp the hands of those now present. He mentioned Baron Blanc, who had represented the Italian government sixteen years ago, and Baron Fava, presently serving in the same capacity; and Vito Viti, the first Italian consul in 1872, and Count Raybaudi-Massiglia, now holding the post. Isoleri then stirred the crowd by describing the immigrant experience:

> There were few Italians then, but they were united. They were few, but resolute. They were few, but perseverant, and full of sacred zeal. They were the vanguard, and now they have become an entire army. And I now invite this army to applaud the vanguard that knew how to hold so high, and

through difficult times, the honor of the Italian name in the City of Brotherly Love.

Italians! United Italian Societies! Come together! And henceforth, it will be auspicious and good for us, if we come often to these stones [that is, to the Columbus statue] to seek inspiration.

An army of Italians from every province of Italy now follows this vanguard, and here learns to honor and to admire it. Poor, but honest; poor, but sober; poor, but industrious, and by the sweat of their brow bathed this land discovered by their Countryman, to seek their daily bread for themselves and for their families both near and far.

And under their rough clothes, and under their shoulders bronzed by the sun always beats a heart, warmed by love for the country that gave them birth—and for their adopted country that gives them bread.

I read on your banners: "Union, Brotherhood, Mutual Aid, Welfare," and so on. Ah! May the ill-fated day never come, Italians, when your actions contradict these words; but instead may peace, joy, full prosperity be the everlasting heritage of this Italian colony of Philadelphia; and it will be pointed out as a model. . . .

Come together, Italians, and come often to these stones to be inspired. Come here especially to gain strength, courage in times of danger, perseverance in undertakings, faith in the future; here the sacred love of religion and nation will be rekindled, so that it never goes away, cools, or is extinguished.[11]

As Isoleri expressed his empathy for immigrants as well as the need for cooperation among them if they were to prevail in their struggle in America, he continued to reaffirm his own role among them. In the evening of this festive day, Catholics from the entire city convened at the Academy of Music for more poetry, speeches, and a talk by Archbishop Ryan on Columbus. In the streets of the gaily decorated and brightly illuminated immigrant quarter, musicians played through the night to the sounds of fireworks and gunshots. In his own notes, Isoleri wrote, "E così dovrà essere," "this was the way that it ought to be." "The celebration was nothing less than the discovery of America, done by an Italian; and the Italians in America were celebrating it." He emphatically concluded, "Benone! Evviva!!!"[12]

Parish groups again gathered at Saint Mary Magdalen dePazzi on Sunday, October 16, for a High Mass composed by Mercadante, with a large choir and orchestra. Isoleri, preaching in English, spoke of events taking place in America, Spain, and Italy honoring Columbus, of the explorer's character, and of lessons to be learned from his life before calling again for his canonization. Then, promising to be brief and asking for their usual courteous attention, he shifted to Italian in order to describe the past glories of the homeland and the future obligations of Italians in a synthesis of history, literature, and religious instruction.

In the afternoon a procession entered the church once again, with men's societies followed by the Daughters of Mary, girls from the orphanage, the Society of the Holy Child, boys of the parish, and the rest of the girls. Isoleri blessed a statue of Saint Peter, donated by parishioners from Civitella Messer Raimondi in the province of Chieti, and a statue of Saint Paul, given by the pastor himself. After Solemn Vespers, Pambianco thanked Isoleri, again praised Columbus, greeted the parish societies, saluted the Italians, and reminded everyone of the underlying religious precepts. A choir of one hundred girls sang old, familiar hymns and then a new piece, before the final Benediction and Te Deum. But while Italians filled the pews, the choir loft above held participants from other ethnic backgrounds. The regular choir and organist, joined by additional voices as well as by the choirmaster, largely consisted of an ensemble with Irish American names. While Isoleri later wrote that an Italian band could not have made this event any merrier, his "Italian church," during its exuberant celebration of *Italianità*, had been anything but an exclusively Italian enclave.

The Feste Colombiane of 1892, far more than any other occasion for Saint Mary Magdalen dePazzi and its pastor, affirmed the elevation of Columbus to a national hero, at least during this innocent age of American popular culture. But that was not enough for Isoleri. When he later assessed the Feste Colombiane, noting how Italians and Catholics had celebrated the 400th anniversary of the Great Discovery, he added that while others will observe its 500th anniversary here on earth, "all of us will celebrate it in heaven, with Christopher Columbus." Isoleri, of course, would not live to see later efforts to remove Columbus not only from an honored place in American history but from heaven as well. But for the moment, these events had testified to the role of parish and pastor in the assimilation of Italians as American citizens and as American Catholics. Their participation, moreover, demonstrated that they had a place in their adopted land not merely as Italians but also as Americans, as they reshaped themselves and their community into components of a broader America. And by finding an undeniably Italian hero and emphasizing his faith as a Catholic, they asserted that religious fidelity did not threaten secular loyalty and that Roman Catholicism could support allegiance to America.

"Tu es sacerdos in aeternum, secundum ordinem Melchisedech"

In the midst of these happy days, Isoleri learned in August 1893 of the death of Father Giuseppe Alizeri, a native of Genoa as well as an old friend and frequent participant in events at Saint Mary Magdalen dePazzi, who had taught theology and sacred scripture at the Vincentian seminary in Germantown before joining the faculty at Niagara University. Despite this loss, Isoleri and his parish looked to the future when another event, not quite so grand as the Feste Colombiane, gave him the place of honor.

Interrupting himself during an evening Lenten service in March 1894, Isoleri suddenly asked: "Have I been the Habakuk under God's dispensation to bring spiritual food to the people of this congregation?" With this reference to the prophet who had been commanded by an angel to bring food to Daniel in the lion's den, he revealed that it was the twenty-fifth anniversary of his ordination. Although said to have been a surprise, the three-day celebration that followed indicated that his congregation had been well aware of the impending anniversary. It began on Easter Monday, a traditional day of festivities in Italy, when a cheerful crowd filled the church basement. Isoleri sat in front of members of the parish organizations with their bright regalia and badges, and American, Italian, and papal emblems decorated the stage along with a large crayon portrait of him.[13]

After a chorus sang "Welcome to Our Pastor," Harry Gandolfo, a recent graduate of LaSalle College, recited an ode written for the occasion by a well-known Catholic poet, Miss Eleanor C. Donnelly, which saluted the priest, the parish, and its people:

> In exile from his native shores, he came when life was bright,
> And youth, its witching glamor, about his fancy flung:
> He trod the land his own Columbus hailed with glad delight,
> And found celestial music in Columbia's stranger-tongue.
>
> Here, stood the lowly little shrine that Mariani reared
> To the glory of De'Pazzi, the sainted Carmelite;
> Here Sorrentini labored, and Cicaterri cheered,
> And, (in turn,) the two Rolandos—were loyal to the right.
>
> But now, the tiny mustard-seed by moldering fingers sown,
> In by-gone days, within this soil, (so fruitful and so blest,)
> God helping Isoleri, to a mighty tree hath grown,
> And thousands cluster round its trunk, or in its branches rest.[14]

The girls of the parish, in a cast still dominated by Ligurian family names, performed "The Silver Jubilee," a play written by Miss Donnelly. The gifts presented to Isoleri included a surplice from the Columbus Society, a gold-headed walking stick from the Children of Mary Sodality, a silver tea set from the Blessed Sacrament Society, a gold-mounted chalice from Father Pambianco, a silver set and humeral veil from the sisters and schoolchildren, a chasuble from old friends Dr. and Mrs. Wilson, a silver pitcher from Consul Raybaudi-Massiglia, a silver bowl from the St. Rocco Society, and a silver pitcher from the St. Joseph's Confraternity. After more entertainment by younger members of the parish, John Harold, the local representative to the City Council, gave a special gift from the pewholders, English-speaking friends, and congregation. Stating that Isoleri was not another Habakuk but rather "the 'Alter Christus,' the Good Shepherd going after the sheep that was lost," Harold apologized for being unable to bring with him the "small gift," a set of bedroom and parlor furniture that had been sent to the rectory.

As Isoleri thanked his benefactors—first in Italian, then in English—he spoke of his struggles and accomplishments during the twenty-three years since his arrival in Philadelphia. To the Italians, he confessed that whenever he was preoccupied by his thoughts, the sight of the new church sometimes made him think that he was dreaming and he had to reassure himself that it was a reality. But how much more might have been done if only some others had met their obligations. In his English remarks, he was more gracious and acknowledged the contributions of non-Italians: "all those noble people . . . [who] . . . helped the young and inexperienced priest to accomplish what we now see and admire . . . the big-hearted Irish, German, and American Catholics of this city, and particularly of this neighborhood." On the next evening, parish children presented songs, recitations, precision drills, and plays at the Christian Street Hall. The girls staged a two-act drama, "The Vision of St. Agnes"; the boys performed "Handy Andy," also in two acts. After a tableau, "The Martyrdom of St. Agnes," the program ended with a march as the young performers made their exit.

On the following day, Isoleri celebrated a Solemn High Mass, assisted by Vassallo and Pambianco and a large choir. Before Archbishop Ryan and many other priests in the church, Vassallo recited words of the ordination rite, "Tu es sacerdos in aeternum, secundum ordinem Melchisedech" (Thou art a priest forever, according to the order of Melchisedech). Speaking in Italian, he advised parishioners: "Your hearts should be full of gratitude for the noble sacrifices that your pastor has made and is continually making for you." Implying that their own sacrifices had somehow been less than those of their pastor, Vassallo reminded them: "Father Isoleri left his homeland [and] relatives in order to come to work and sacrifice himself for his countrymen who live in a foreign land." Ryan similarly praised Isoleri for building the new church, orphanage, rectory, and school and for his ministry to the sick and poor and the young and old. He hoped that Isoleri might reach his golden jubilee, always standing without reproach as a good and holy priest before God's altar. Ryan's words showed that Isoleri, once mired in deep conflict with a previous archbishop and his vicars but now quietly weeping as he listened, had come a long way as a member of the archdiocesan clergy. In a lighter vein, clergy and laymen toasted Isoleri at a midday meal. In the evening, parish women provided a banquet in his honor at the Christian Street Hall with the proceeds going to the debt fund of the new church. Isoleri presided over the event. An Italian band enlivened the occasion and concluded with a serenade that evoked nostalgic thoughts, even for a priest, of a distant homeland.

While esteem and affection came from many friends and admirers, another gift brought recognition from beyond Philadelphia. Although unable to attend, Archbishop Francesco Satolli, the apostolic delegate and the highest papal official in the United States since 1889, sent a gold chalice along with an invitation for Isoleri to join him on a visit to the Benedictine monastery of St. Vincent's, near Pittsburgh. Since he had preached an eight-day retreat at St. Mary Magdalen dePazzi in March 1893, Satolli's friendship with Isoleri had grown. His gift was not a perfunctory gesture but rather an expression of genuine amity with parish and pastor.[15]

Newspapers also paid tribute to Isoleri. A Catholic paper declared that he had "identified himself so thoroughly with the cause of his people that his name is a watchword in Philadelphia whenever Italian interests are in question." While the local press provided extensive coverage, newspapers beyond Philadelphia similarly saluted him. An Italian newspaper in New York City declared: "Full of zeal and energy, conquering every obstacle, the young priest has worked indefatigably all these long years for the spiritual good of his countrymen, as all of Philadelphia can testify." From San Francisco, with its large Genoese community, another Italian paper wrote: "To the worthy Italian priest, son of Liguria, and therefore our compatriot, we send our most sincere congratulations, hoping to be able to join Father Isoleri, when God allows him to celebrate his golden jubilee." Describing his achievements, it added: "Besides his intelligence, Father Isoleri possesses an unmatched apostolic zeal. To this most zealous apostle of God's cause, the Italians of Philadelphia owe the establishing of an orphanage and a parochial school."[16]

As his parish continued to grow, Isoleri knew that St. Mary Magdalen dePazzi would require further expansion of its physical facilities. To accommodate the increasing number of families and children, plans called for a larger school at a projected cost of $12,000 to be built between the church and the convent. These efforts sometimes drew distinguished visitors who offered support for such projects, but not without complications. When Satolli came to preach in 1893, he stayed for a week as Isoleri's guest. While newspaper stories reported that his sermons attracted large crowds, one paper warned that if English-speaking people filled the church, thus excluding Italians, the purpose of the visit would be defeated.[17]

Isoleri knew that he could rely on Satolli as a resource in developing the church, but their friendship was also enhancing his own reputation. After his elevation to archbishop and cardinal, the prelate returned to participate in another week of spiritual exercises at St. Mary Magdalen dePazzi, "preaching morning and evening to his compatriots" in early 1896. Reportedly visiting

Philadelphia more often than any other diocese in the United States, Satolli forged a special bond with Isoleri, who was now recognized as an important, well-regarded, and trusted member of the local clergy. The press routinely took note of even minor events in his parish, such as the forty-first anniversary of the laying of the cornerstone of the first church, but it also reported Isoleri's presence at graver events, such as the execution in June 1893 of an Italian who had murdered an Irish American nun. This coverage enabled a wider public to become acquainted with the colorful and capable pastor of the Italian church: "Father Isoleri in the pulpit displays remarkable oratorical and intellectual ability; he is a gifted poet and has written volumes of sonnets, odes, canzones and dramas in Italian, besides compiling a number of religious books of instruction for the use of his Italian parishioners."[18]

Piety and Protestantism

While more Philadelphians were becoming aware of Isoleri, his own people were learning to adjust their traditional customs to the American environment. Italians regularly celebrated the patron saint's feast day with a High Mass in the morning, then afternoon vespers, followed by a street procession by the members of parish societies carrying the statue of Mary Magdalen dePazzi decorated with gold earrings, rings, and necklaces. In June 1895 an observer described this event, "to which is always attached a peculiarity, novel in itself, and which tends to bring crowds of people from different parts of the city, excited most probably, more by curiosity than by devotion." He then added: "But there is always a deep piety and devotion on the part of the people whose celebration it is." An elderly woman, for example, weeping and praying aloud, approached the main altar after the morning mass and claimed that her total blindness, from which she had long suffered, had been cured by prayers that the saint had answered on that day.[19]

Traditional beliefs and practices often had a less favorable reception in America than in Italy. Italians customarily placed some token on the statue of the interceding saint in return for a favor that they believed had been granted. Thus, the statue of Mary Magdalen dePazzi was covered on her feast day with "many silent but eloquent proofs of favors received." At that celebration in 1895, the crowd, awed and inspired by their belief in miraculous acts but restrained by the solemnity of events, remained orderly throughout the day, leaving the police an unnecessary presence. But critics of Catholicism, particularly anti-clerical Italians, regarded these observances as superstitious and exploitative practices designed to separate the faithful from the little money they had. And even Catholic authorities objected when the revenue-generating icon and its gleanings were not controlled by the parish itself but by private interests.[20]

Church officials also questioned other Italian religious customs. At the dedication of a parish school in October 1895, Archbishop Ryan denounced the Italian tradition of having a separate sponsor for each child at confirmation. Pointing out the inconvenience when the number of candidates was large and stating that it was unnecessary for the validity of the sacrament, he indicated that hereafter his diocese would follow the American practice of one man acting as sponsor for all the boys and one woman for all the girls. Beleaguered by negative reactions to their folkways, Italians were learning what it meant to become American.[21]

Isoleri and the Catholic Church were not alone in their attempts to respond to the needs of Italians. Protestants shared the belief that "of all the vast army of aliens who daily pass through the portals of our United States, no one nationality deserves more attention and study than does the Italian." They therefore were increasing the efforts that they had begun in the previous decade. Since 1882 the Church of the Emmanuello, claiming to be the first Episcopal church for Italians in the United States and the only organized Protestant mission for them in Philadelphia, had held services in the heart of Little Italy. When reporters, after the New Orleans lynchings in 1891, sought opinions on the Italian character, the Reverend Herman L. Duhring, pastor of All Saints Episcopal Church at Twelfth and Fitzwater Streets, replied: "My association with the many Italians, of whom there are fully 20,000 in this neighborhood, has led me the more to like them as I know them better, particularly those who belong to the Episcopal Church, who are my nearest neighbors."[22]

Bishop Ozi W. Whitaker of the Episcopal Diocese of Pennsylvania personally supervised the Emmanuello Mission, which received no aid from diocesan missionary boards but depended on special contributions from other parishes. Whitaker expressed his attitude toward Italians during a cornerstone-laying ceremony for the mission in 1891: "It is built for those who have come to our land from Italy; it is an expression of our regard for them, and that every blessing we enjoy shall be extended to them. The Church and school stand as a witness that we welcome them as brothers, and offer them equal opportunities that we enjoy."[23] When the Emmanuello observed its eleventh anniversary in November 1893 with a special service at St. Stephen's Church at Tenth and Chestnut Streets, the program included a report to its benefactors. The Reverend Dr. S. D. McConnell stated that most of the 35,000–40,000 Italian residents of the city were very poor but frugal, ignorant, and superstitious and that the Emmanuello provided the only Christian standard for them. As to why his church was concerned with them, he maintained that only about 1,000 Italians regularly attended mass as Roman Catholics: "The great bulk of them have their children baptized in a formal manner, and have their rites after death performed in a formal manner, and there the work of the Roman Church begins and ends. The work of the Protestant Episcopal Church does not include proselytizing, but simply aims to bring Christ to a large and thrifty section of our population."[24]

With about two hundred members at most, the Emmanuello probably did not irritate Isoleri as much as his Episcopalian rivals had done thirty years ago. And if he read the newspaper account, the celebration would not have bothered him as much as McConnell's remarks on the weak fidelity of Italians to Catholicism, even though Isoleri had often expressed the same sentiment. But the Catholic press rallied to his defense by citing his accomplishments at St. Mary Magdalen dePazzi and praising him for "indefatigably working for his countrymen for a quarter of a century . . . at the bedside of the dying, in hospitals, in the dark and dirty alleys, in the prison, [where] he has been and is still doing his work."[25]

The Episcopalians, however, were neither united in their course of action toward Italians nor in their attitude toward the pastor of St. Mary Magdalen dePazzi. One faction, with affinities for Roman Catholicism that eventually produced conversions from its ranks, strongly dissented on the matter of a mission and could be seen almost as allies of Isoleri. Their monthly magazine, *Evangelists,* edited by Henry R. Percival, rector of the Church of the Evangelist, on Catharine Street between Sixth and Seventh Streets, warmly praised Isoleri and his parishioners. It noted that the Episcopalian chapel was surrounded by Italians in a neighborhood that was aptly called "Little Italy," whose residents did not neglect their religious duties:

> We gravely doubt whether anywhere, among an equal number of Americans, so many men and women can be found who are careful and observant of the duties of religion. To a simple and childlike faith they unite a zeal for God and an ardent love of the Church. From their distant homes across the sea they have brought with them their religion, and although they are for the most part uneducated, as education is reckoned in this country, they are wise enough with regard to salvation to repel and reject any and every attempt to lead them to abandon their faith and be false to their religion. It is true that they are, some of them, very poor, and that, urged by need, they sometimes appear to apostatize [*sic*] and even attend the services and perhaps receive the sacraments from ministers of an alien church, but this is at the most a natural (although of course sinful) concession to the needs of the body and a yielding to a cunningly-devised temptation. But when the hour of death comes they repent of their wickedness, they send for the minister of their own faith, they die strengthened with the life-giving sacraments, and are buried with the rites of the Church of their birth and nation.[26]

The same writer maintained that the Episcopalian effort to reach Italians, "an attempt backed by all that money and hatred to the Catholic religion can give," had buried only one person, because "the religion people believe is the religion they wish to die in." This extraordinary accolade advised anyone who wished to see how religious the Italians actually were to stand on Seventh Street at seven o'clock on any Sunday morning, near Marriott Lane, where "their beautiful Church of Santa Maria Magdalena DePazzi is situated, and he will find the street literally full both sides of the way with men and women coming from service." While some Protestants might expect them to remain in bed until Sunday was half over, "then to eat a heavy breakfast and afterwards decorously resort to a 'Church' to hear a sermon and sing a hymn or two," the writer added:

> Thank God, our Italian neighbors have brought with them a better religion than that. While Protestants are tucked in bed, these foreigners, to whom, forsooth, in the pride and conceit of their hearts. some would send a "Mission," are in their church, with Jesus, adoring Him in the mystery of the altar and uniting in that sacrifice which He has instituted for the propitiation of God to His people.
>
> Our Italian neighbors are quick-tempered, with warm Southern impulses. They do many things which to our cold, Anglo-Saxon natures seem odd enough. But little as in many respects their ways are like ours, an irreligious people they certainly are not, and those who have come to teach them "a better way" might well take lessons from them on the constancy of faith and devotion to the Church of their birth.
>
> God forbid that we should do anything to weaken their faith. If we find any of them wavering or neglecting their duties, we, at least of this parish, shall do our best to get them to go to their own faithful pastor, Father Isoleri, and if in any way we can be of any assistance or comfort to them we shall always be ready most gladly to show our good-will towards them, praying that the time may soon come when our unhappy divisions shall be done away, and there shall be visibly as there is and only can be really "one fold and one Shepherd."[27]

Despite an occasional compliment to Catholicism, several Protestant denominations persisted in their efforts to reach Italians through neighborhood missions, chapels, and settlement houses as well as through seminaries and divinity schools with specialized programs to train them as ministers and to teach the Italian language.[28] Although Episcopalians, Methodists, and Presbyterians opened missions or churches in the Italian quarter of Philadelphia, they had only limited success. While Italians could be indifferent and negligent as Catholics and overtly hostile at times to the papacy, Protestantism had not become a widely popular alternative for them. One writer, signing himself as "an Italian Catholic," summed up the religious orientation of his countrymen in a letter to a local newspaper:

It is true . . . that some are cold or indifferent. Some think that it is "up to the times" to show indifference in matters of religion—an indifference that they do not feel. Some are "free thinkers," so-called, but these people do not believe any more in a Protestant minister than in a Catholic priest. The majority of the Italians are Catholics at heart. They will (without scarcely any exception) have their children baptized in the Catholic Church. They teach them to say the "Ave Maria" and the "Salve Regina." They teach them to love the "Madonna" . . . and without these elements of their faith they do not understand religion at all.

If some of them send their children to Protestant missions, it is not because they believe in them, but because the children get nice presents. Most all these children wear scapulars around their necks and carry rosary beads, and you will see these and other sacred emblems in most all their houses. The Italians get married at the church by a priest, and if some of them get married in some other place or by someone else, they do not feel any respect for each other; neither husband nor wife feels assured that their lives will be happy. When they are in trouble they go to the priest; very few (in fact, I never saw or heard of any) at the hour of death fail to send for the padre.[29]

Although this anonymous Catholic apologist overstated some points, his letter contained more than a grain of truth. And Protestants who recognized the importance of continuity knew the value of designing churches and services that mimicked forms of Catholicism that were familiar to Italians, if they were ever to be weaned away from that faith.

"We are God's Poor—We ask for Bread"

While not seriously weakened by Protestant endeavors, St. Mary Magdalen dePazzi encountered a new threat from a source that could be inferred from a newspaper account of its pastor's efforts: "The work which he has accomplished assumes gigantic proportions when the difficulties with which he has had to contend are taken into consideration. The Italian population of the district of which his church is the centre is not less than 10,000, and though by far the great majority of that number are members of the faith, the active and contributing members of the congregation form a very small percentage. Serious loss to the pastor results from the line which appears to have been drawn between the prosperous or well-to-do Italians and the lower class."[30]

The flood of Southern Italians into Philadelphia at the end of the century provided a serious basis for cleavage within the immigrant population. Although Isoleri and others had urged Italians to unite two decades earlier, the unresolved problem of unification now caused cracks in Little Italy that were not easily mended. The situation also tested Isoleri, whose character left him ill suited for what was about to occur. What supporters viewed as "a countenance indicative of intelligence and strength," his critics saw as a haughtiness that was a pastoral liability. And while this new threat basically stemmed from the deluge of Southern Italians, it was complicated by the limited capacity of the parish to care for them as well as by the otherwise modest efforts of the Protestants. But it was aggravated even further by the demands of insurgent Italians who claimed to have felt the sting of rejection both from the Ligurian pastor of St. Mary Magdalen dePazzi and from the Irish priests at St. Paul's.[31]

Only one year after the Silver Jubilee celebration of Isoleri's ordination, which had been marked by the congregation's great respect and affection for him, a contrasting attitude began to emerge. In March 1895 a group of dissidents, alleging that their spiritual needs were not being adequately met, petitioned Archbishop Satolli, the apostolic delegate, for a new parish. Not wishing to offend his friend Isoleri or to intrude on episcopal authority, Satolli advised them to submit their request to Archbishop Ryan along with their plans for financing another church. But Ryan had already refused to meet with the group and had forbidden its priest, who had reportedly left Italy without permission, from saying mass.[32]

When Archbishop Ryan asked Isoleri to tell Satolli what he knew about two principal participants in the matter, more details unfolded. Isoleri described Loreto Cardarelli as a "pseudo-priest," often pretending to be a priest, whose involvement in a sex scandal in Italy had led the bishop of the Diocese of Sora, in the province of Caserta, to forbid him from entering any church. After coming to Philadelphia in November 1894, Cardarelli sent for his brother, Clemente, who actually was a priest. Isoleri blamed the latter Cardarelli for the petition to Satolli and for stirring up the "elemento meridionale," or Southern element—an unfortunate choice of words considering that he had earlier attempted to unite the immigrant population. While Cardarelli had apparently received permission to leave his diocese for two months, he was supposed to be in Naples rather than seeking to organize a parish for Italians in Philadelphia. Isoleri concluded his report by arguing that neither the number of Italians nor the prospect of financial support was great enough to warrant another parish.

Clemente Cardarelli, meanwhile, had increased his efforts among the Italians of the city. Defying an order from his bishop to return to Italy, with Ryan willing to pay the fare to get rid of him, he opened the chapel of Our Lady of Pompeii at Sixth and Fitzwater Streets in 1896. Although Cardarelli claimed to have received permission from Rome for his chapel, Ryan asked Isoleri to write Satolli again, to seek a letter condemning the project. Ryan believed that if Satolli's response, along with a letter of his own, were read from the pulpit at St. Mary Magdalen dePazzi, Cardarelli's followers, informed of the true status of the chapel, would abandon him. But Satolli again refused to become involved and advised Ryan to settle the matter by asking Cardarelli for proof that Rome had authorized him.

Cardarelli was not alone in pleading his case. Edward L. Aves, a center-city architect, offered a strong apology on behalf of Cardarelli and his flock in a letter to Ryan in December 1896. Aves wrote that Ryan probably already had had some communication with the people of Sixth and Fitzwater Streets, "where in a poverty stricken corner, they go every Sunday to the number of about 900 to hear Mass said by Rev. C. Cardarelli." If what had occurred was in any way distasteful to Ryan, Aves blamed himself, although the matter had been forced upon him. He had seen it as "a chance of staying further scandal and helping to make peace."[33]

Aves presented his own version of the dispute. He contended that a group of Italians had sought his advice on obtaining property and making alterations to their present premises. After asking them who they were, he also inquired, in an attempt to determine the name of their pastor, "Who sent you?" Aves refused to help them unless they were willing to meet certain conditions: first, they had to form a society in a regular manner, with the archbishop included on its board; and second, its pastor had to be a priest with legitimate authority. To Aves's surprise, the group accepted both stipulations, and they began to organize their society and to seek incorporation. Aves had also asked that the new society submit an appropriate petition, which he would translate, to the archbishop. After a three-week investigation to verify the facts, Aves persuaded Cardarelli to write his own letter in submission to the archbishop.

Aves believed that much sorrow and scandal could have been avoided by "a little common humanity, not to say Christian Charity." Convinced that Cardarelli had never had the least intention of being rebellious, Aves thought that the priest had been the victim of "many deliberate misrepresentations . . . by interested parties" made to the archbishop. In a letter to Ryan, Aves found Cardarelli "in absolute want and suffering, without means in the coldest of weather even to make a fire, a bed to lie down on, unfit for a stable boy; and what was worse the Blessed Sacrament in a dirty poverty stricken hole and 900 people attending Mass there every Sunday. Surely something can be done?"[34]

Cardarelli, meanwhile, defended himself in an undated letter to Ryan, written in perfect English (evidently by someone else but signed by him), probably at Aves's urging. After conveying his respects and submission to the archbishop, Cardarelli asked for "the fullest pardon, if I have seemingly transgressed the discipline of your diocese," on the grounds that he had been unacquainted with the language and community. He claimed to have been unaware of the impression, presumably given to Ryan, "by the harsh and unjust action toward me, on my arrival on the part of Rev'd Isoleri," and offered his explanation of the underlying circumstances. On his arrival, Cardarelli had first met with the archbishop and then at Ryan's instruction had gone to see Isoleri. According to Cardarelli, after five days, Isoleri expelled him, saying that the newcomer should have come to him before going to "my bishop" (underlining these last two words in his letter). By his account, Cardarelli had offended Isoleri, which no priest recently arrived from Italy could afford to do. It was unclear, however, whether he had written an accurate or exaggerated account of his encounter with Isoleri.

Responding to other charges, Cardarelli contended that the accusation that his departure from Italy was without proper authorization was untrue, because he had no parish there and was only a simple professor in a college. Claiming that he remained on friendly terms with the bishop of his former diocese, he denied that Satolli had ever ordered him to return to Italy. Cardarelli then described the conditions that he had found among the Italians in Philadelphia, along with his own reactions, at the time of his arrival. At least 15,000 were without spiritual care, but an average of 900 of them were coming to mass "in the poverty stricken home I possess." He plaintively concluded: "I cannot leave my people who cry out for sympathy and help, and who ask now for your kindness and sanction."[35]

The members of the Church of Our Lady of Pompeii, however, provided the most compelling statements of their cause in a petition, probably the same document that Satolli had received, which they sent to Ryan at Christmas in 1896. They declared themselves to be "Italian Catholic citizens of Philadelphia [and] from our birth children of Holy Church, Catholic Apostolic and Roman, . . . recognizing the authority of that Church, as vested in the office now held by your Grace." The signers argued that their petition contained facts that had been verified "by those who kindly consented to speak for us," obviously alluding to Aves, and suggested that others had rendered similar support. They begged the archbishop "to remove the injustice which is inflicted on us, by want of proper spiritual attendance and church accommodation."[36]

Their petition gave further details on the situation. They claimed that their signatures were only a part of 3,000 that represented the interests of at least 15,000 Italians, mainly from Naples, the Abruzzi, and Sicily, and including many who had not attended mass or received the sacraments for ten years. The only Italian church, they contended, was not only one-third American and Irish in its membership but one where Italians were publicly told that "they were not wanted because they were unable to pay the regulation price for a seat, as though God's sanctuary were a theatre or concert hall." The petitioners made an even more serious accusation against its pastor: "With the priest in charge there we cannot have any sympathy, for he has none with us." Their problems, however, did not end with his attitude, for they noted that the church could only accommodate 1,000 persons. Having been driven from St. Mary Magdalen dePazzi, many of them had tried to attend nearby St. Paul's but were expelled by its sexton, whose standing orders, presumably from its Irish American pastor, were "to turn us from the door, unless dressed beyond our means."

Because of these rejections, the group had banded together in a religious society under the patronage of Our Lady of Pompeii. Having elected officers and twelve other members to its council, they sought a charter of incorporation under the laws of their adopted country. The petitioners insisted that they had not intended to defy the wishes or policy of the archbishop but rather to strengthen his position, as well as their own, in the matter, "wishing always to remain loyal faithful children of the Church." They adhered to the two conditions recommended by Aves that the archbishop be a member of their board and that their pastor be a legitimate priest. The petitioners also noted that they had found refuge for the past year in the home of a priest who had come as a stranger, but, by working and caring for them without remuneration, had now "found himself through misrepresentation and unjust treatment unwittingly placed as though in opposition to Your Grace's policy." They asked for the removal of all hindrances and for the granting of full approval and patronage from the archbishop, so that they and their priest might erect a church of their own.

The names of sixty-six men and sixty-six women—many of them marked only by the "X" of an illiterate signer—in support of the petition bore mute testimony to their plight. (Some names, which were not Italian, suggested intermarriage, Americanization, or an Irish-American presence even here.) Under the more familiar title and address of their society, they identified themselves as the Chiesa Maria Ss. del Rosario. Their final words contained a pithy message, worthy of any radical polemicist of their times, but still echoing and haunting: "We are God's Poor—We ask for Bread."

The document sent to Ryan by the members of the Society of Our Lady of Pompeii exposed a widening fissure between Northern Italians and the recent immigrants from Southern Italy and Sicily as well as the tensions between Italians and other Catholics, particularly the Irish. It disclosed conflicts based on class-based lifestyles both within the Italian population as well as between it and other groups. The petition reflected the difficulties that the American clergy and hierarchy had with the traditional culture of Southern Italians. The formidable charges by the petitioners of the Society of Our Lady of Pompeii also indicted the leadership and personal character of Isoleri.

Ryan met with Cardarelli in an attempt to resolve the situation. Afterward, Ryan informed Satolli that Cardarelli claimed that he had been granted permission to organize the chapel by the apostolic delegate himself. Ryan again asked Satolli for a written condemnation of the chapel and renewed his plan to have the two letters read from the pulpit. He believed that Cardarelli was unwilling to alter any plans and remained under the influence of his brother, who still pretended to be a priest. But Ryan also feared that if he sent a letter to the defiant priest, as Satolli had suggested, Cardarelli would misrepresent it to his illiterate followers as a document authorizing the chapel. He concluded his report to Satolli by proposing the organizing of another parish for the Italians.

Despite Isoleri's objections, Ryan believed that the project was feasible, and he had already initiated discussions with the Oblates of St. Francis de Sales about undertaking it. He also sent Satolli a notice, which had been circulating in the Italian community, announcing that Our Lady of Pompeii was a church that served the poor, with no pews reserved for the wealthy. However, Satolli still chose not to interfere, and the chapel remained open in 1897.

After succeeding Satolli as apostolic delegate, Archbishop Sebastiano Martinelli, O.S.A., provided Ryan with the support that he had failed to obtain from his predecessor. In a jointly issued pastoral letter to the parishes of the Italian quarter in January 1897, Martinelli and Ryan declared that Cardarelli was not a priest of the archdiocese, and they condemned his chapel. Ryan then halted the incorporation petition by the Society of Our Lady of Pompeii in September 1897. In a local court, two judges concurred with Ryan that granting the charter would imply that the archdiocese had approved the chapel when it had actually condemned it as schismatic.

The members of the Society of Our Lady of Pompeii continued to wage their campaign on behalf of Father Cardarelli and his chapel through letters to Archbishop Martinelli. They contended that Cardarelli had indeed been granted permission from his bishop in Italy to minister in Philadelphia, and that he had brought many Italians who had not practiced their faith for years back to the sacraments. Throughout 1898, subsequent letters argued that many Italians had stopped attending mass because of neglect by their own church or of abuse by another. Rejected at St. Mary Magdalen dePazzi because they could not pay pew rents, they had been turned away from St. Paul's because they did not dress well enough for its sexton. And while the Society of Our Lady of Pompeii was willing to include Ryan on its board, they defended Cardarelli as a legitimate priest who had been misrepresented. But Martinelli bluntly informed them, "I cannot and do not intend to interfere in any way."

While Cardarelli's supporters had been unable to prevail, both Ryan and Martinelli still recognized the urgent need for another Italian parish despite Isoleri's opposition. They believed that the Cardarelli affair would not have occurred if such a parish had already been established. After an attempt to bring in the Salesians failed, the Augustinians were invited to organize the new parish, and the Society of Our Lady of Pompeii finally vanished from the scene. As for their priest, Cardarelli corresponded with Martinelli until 1900, when he asked for permission either to say mass or for money with which to go back to Italy, since he had no other means of support. Much like Angelo Inglesi, who had brought turmoil in earlier decades, Cardarelli left Philadelphia at this point, but he would continue his priestly career in New Jersey and Missouri.[37]

Although in Philadelphia since founding St. Augustine's Church in 1796, the Augustinians were a curious choice for the new parish, as several other religious orders also ministered to Italians in American cities. It was not irrelevant that

Martinelli, before becoming apostolic delegate, had been superior general of the order and the person to whom Ryan now found himself indebted for support in the Cardarelli case. Despite their many parishes for Italians elsewhere, Franciscans, Servites, Pallotines, Stigmatines, and Scalabrinians would remain conspicuously absent as the Augustinians became the only male religious order with an enduring presence in the parishes of South Philadelphia.

The Augustinians and Our Lady of Good Counsel

"God's Poor" received the bread that they had sought when Archbishop Ryan announced in April 1897 that St. Mary Magdalen dePazzi parish was to be divided. While the old church would serve Italians living east of Eighth Street, west side residents would have a new parish, Our Lady of Good Counsel, staffed by Italian Augustinians. While awaiting the assignment of their pastor, Italians organized services at St. Paul's Church under the direction of Father Nazareno Casacca, of Villanova College. The new parish was not formally inaugurated until the arrival from Genoa of Father Guglielmo A. Repetti.

Born on the Feast of the Assumption, August 15, 1872, in Cabella Ligure in Alessandria province, Repetti had entered the seminary just after his thirteenth birthday. Ordained in 1895, he served nearly two years at Our Lady of Consolation in Genoa before being sent to America. Observing Christmas while on their Atlantic crossing, Repetti and two other Augustinians reached Philadelphia on December 30, 1897, where he assumed his responsibilities at the age of twenty-five. At the first service on Sunday evening, January 9, 1898, in a chapel at the former school of St. Paul's, Repetti urged his congregation to cooperate in the great work that they had undertaken and promised them a church of their own in the near future. The archdiocesan newspaper, referring to "a division of St. Mary Magdalen," claimed that the exceedingly large congregation of the new church included some of the most prominent families among the 40,000 Italians in the city.[38]

Despite Repetti's great enthusiasm, he struggled to resolve the financial problems of Our Lady of Good Counsel. While the old school building had been purchased for $25,000 from St. Paul's parish, only $2,000 had been paid by November 1898, when another Augustinian, Father Joseph A. Coleman, a former president of Villanova College who had recently returned from twelve years in Australia, was placed in charge of the project. Recognizing the need to go beyond the limited means of the community, Coleman appealed to Catholics throughout the city on November 1, 1898, the Feast of All Saints. He had the difficult task of convincing "English-speaking Catholics to save the Italian Catholics." He pointed out that although the Italian Augustinians since their arrival had devoted themselves to visiting families and giving spiritual instruction, their people were not providing financial support. In their defense, Coleman stated: "as they have not been habituated to support their Church at home, they do not comprehend the necessity of contributing abroad." He added: "They are accordingly less censurable for not supporting more generously religion than people of other nationalities who have been accustomed by force of training and habit to do so."[39]

In making his appeal, Coleman appraised the Italian character and the situation in which the immigrants found themselves. He maintained that "the Italians in America are a poor, but thrifty race" whose ignorance of the language and customs of their new country, along with the utter neglect of spiritual agencies, had left them in a lamentable religious and intellectual condition. Coleman called on religion to improve their deplorable spiritual state and on education to rescue them from the stigma of pauperism and place them in the broad arena "where honest labor meets its just reward." He laid out an ambitious plan for the future: "To accomplish this beneficial work for the poor Italians, we are necessitated to provide a suitable church, schools and a parochial residence, even after the debt on the present humble building has been liquidated; and to accommodate the particular exigencies of the congregation, composed entirely of working people, we must establish permanently night schools as well as day schools."[40] Echoing the sentiments of Cardarelli's former followers, Coleman declared that it was necessary to leave "in the hands and hearts of all benevolent persons the cause of the children of the poor." He ended his plea with a line from Saint Peter: "Be ye all of one mind, having compassion one of another, being lovers of the Brotherhood." Coleman's carefully chosen words had not only been sensitive to the plight of the Italians but also transcended the boundaries of ethnic differences. He had sought the support of other Catholics while avoiding insult to the Italians.

Coleman's persuasive efforts bore fruit when a decision was soon reached to extensively remodel the old school. Only sixteen months since the coming of the Augustinians, and seven months after Coleman's appeal, on Pentecost Sunday in May 1899 an estimated crowd of about 10,000 jammed Christian Street for the laying of the cornerstone of the Church of Our Lady of Good Counsel, on the site where St. Paul's parish school had once been. The entirely renovated building had a stone facade of Romanesque design, with a basement chapel, and there were plans for a large church on the first floor and a parish school on the second. Some fifty priests, among them parish pastors, seminary faculty, and Augustinians from Villanova College as well as *prominenti* including the consul general of Italy, Count D'Aste Brandolini, joined together in procession. Archbishop Martinelli, assisted by pastors of two nearby churches, Father M. C. Donovan of St. Paul's and Father Antonio Isoleri of St. Mary Magdalen dePazzi, presided over the program. The Società Italiana di Mutuo Soccorso, the Blessed Sacrament Society of Isoleri's parish, and the Santa Lucia Beneficial Society, with their members wearing badges and carrying banners, were among the organizations representing the Italian community.[41]

The dedication ceremonies gaily celebrated the Italian presence in Philadelphia. It was manifested by the exuberance of the crowd and by the religious and beneficial societies, along with Martinelli and the many Italians who sought to kiss his ring. It was shared by its sister parish, whose pastor, Isoleri, had donated $100 in support of the project that he had once opposed and that now was carving its membership out of his own congregation. It was exalted by the choir directed by Mrs. Joseph Solari with soloists Madame Barilli, Signor Giannini, and D. J. Santoro. And it was confirmed by the Italian Augustinian friars in the first church placed under their care in the city.

The occasion also signaled the growing attention by the Church to the "Italian problem," that is, the challenge that immigrant Italians placed before American Catholicism. While Church authorities had been concerned about the defection of Italians from the faith for some time, the situation had been recently aggravated by increasing tensions between Italians and the Irish. It had been stirred by the rejection of Italians at the doors of territorial parishes such as St. Paul's and by Irish American priests who had expressed their doubts about Italian fidelity from the pulpit. Monsignor James D. Loughlin, chancellor of the archdiocese, now had the task, without being condescending or offensive, of asking Italians to give more in financial support than they had previously been accustomed to do. Speaking first in English, he attempted to explain the difficulties of Italians in remarks that seemed aimed at other Catholics:

> For several reasons the Italian Catholics have been placed at a disadvantage in respect to the other Catholics of the city. Brought up in a country where for ages it was the glory of nobles and the rich to embellish and adorn the church instead of lavishing their wealth for selfish purposes, it has come harder for them to give of their hard-earned wages for the support of the Church and its schools than to those of us whom centuries of persecution had accustomed, not only to support our churches and schools without the aid of the Government, but in spite of the penal laws which prevented their worship and their education in the faith.[42]

While Loughlin elevated the motives of the Italian nobility (and ignored their abuse and exploitation of the peasantry), he similarly oversimplified his depiction of Irish history. But even worse, he drove the same wedge between Italians and the Irish that other Irish American priests had been accused of doing, often more bluntly, when they addressed the differences between the way that their own people acted as Catholics and the way that others did. It was a theme that offended Italians. They had heard it from the pulpit too often, and it embittered them against priests who claimed to know them. And it was a theme that they would continue to hear in the years ahead.

After Repetti addressed his countrymen, calling upon them to remain faithful, Loughlin spoke again, but in Italian. He declared that the happiest days of his life had been spent in Rome, where the beauty of the language had won his heart. After extolling the Church, he concluded by calling attention to what Italians ought to be. While his fluency in Italian elicited the compliment from Father Angelo Caruso, O.S.A., that Loughlin was a "true alumnus of the Propaganda," the impact of his remarks on the Italians remained difficult to assess. Although he had attempted to ingratiate himself with them, they had again been instructed on their character and faith by one more Irish priest.

At the end of the dedication ceremonies, the clergy gathered for a private dinner as the guests of the Augustinians, where Father Donovan of St. Paul's summarized conditions among Italians in the city. Comparing the number presently in the area to the entire population of Catholics in New York City fifty years earlier, he asked what would have been the spiritual condition of souls if the Church had not cared for them. What the 30,000–40,000 Catholic Italians of the neighborhood will become in fifty more years, he answered, depended on the care and opportunities afforded to them. Not only were they here to stay, but Donovan also noted that immigration and an unusually high birth rate, which gave "a strong proof of their virtuous family life," were rapidly increasing their numbers. As for their future, he maintained:

> They have all the qualifications to secure success from a temporal standpoint. They are honest, sober, industrious, intelligent, devoted to their families and their offspring. They have some difficulties to contend with, but they have all the characteristics necessary to cope with even greater difficulties. They will surely form an important and influential element in the future population of this land. Their future attitude towards the Church depends largely upon the efforts of the bishops and priests of to-day, upon the attitude of the Church to them to-day.[43]

Assuming that one-fifth of any population was of school age, Donovan estimated that 6,000–8,000 children were in the Italian colony. With 469 pupils at St. Mary Magdalen dePazzi's parish school and another 100 at St. Paul's, he asked where the other 5,500–7,500 Italian children were. He doubted that they could be attending Sunday schools; the combined facilities of the three area parishes did not have enough room for them. "Even our boasted public school system has not provided accommodation for these children," he said, "even while enacting the farce of a compulsory education law." Noting further that the "enemies of the faith" were not indifferent to these children but were making strenuous efforts to recruit them, he listed Protestant facilities: an Episcopal church and school on Christian Street, a day school conducted by the Epworth League on Ninth Street, another branch of the Episcopal Church and a Sunday school on Ninth Street, and a branch of Bethany Church at Sixth and Christian Streets. Baptists and Methodists were also seeking to evangelize in the neighborhood. Donovan maintained, however, that despite the efforts of apostates and proselytizers, with the same methods that were used "to pervert the Irish in famine days," all attempts to reach Italians were doomed because "in religion the Italian is, if anything, Catholic."

Donovan, recognizing the need for more priests and schools, saluted those who labored in this cause—Repetti, Caruso, Coleman, and particularly Isoleri: "Before I sit down, I desire to say one word more, and it is this, that I would not have one syllable of what I have uttered construed into any reflection on the zeal or priestly character of my neighbor, Father Isoleri." But Donovan's praise had been curiously worded. Describing Isoleri's accomplishments during the past thirty years, he added: "Of all the hard-working priests in the Diocese of Philadelphia there is none more over-worked, none more devoted to duty, none more constantly at his post, in season and out of season, than Father Isoleri." Donovan continued in the same vein: "Much as he has done, the Italian population has outgrown the capacity of his church and school, and it would be unfair to expect him to start all over again." In response to Isoleri's earlier view that another parish was not needed, Donovan's message offered consolation, as his domain was being dismantled. Isoleri's long and successful efforts were now being rewarded by the imposed sharing of his inheritance with newly found younger brothers. Donovan's praise could only bear witness to compromise and chagrin, not triumph, for Isoleri, who had lost his battle not with Cardarelli or the Protestants but with the archdiocese.[44]

The entire history of Our Lady of Good Counsel, however, was to be marked by persistent difficulties. Two months after the cornerstone laying, its first pastor, Father Repetti, not quite twenty-seven years old, died of typhoid fever, and Isoleri preached his funeral sermon on the warmest day of the summer in August 1899. Although Repetti's untimely death prefigured the demise of the parish itself only thirty-two years later, Our Lady of Good Counsel, during its brief life span, became the principal parish for Italians in the area. But if this church had been meant to supplant the Society of Our Lady of Pompeii, its site did not make much sense, because Cardarelli's chapel, at Sixth and Fitzwater Streets, had been on the east side of St. Mary Magdalen dePazzi, while Our Lady of Good Counsel was on the west side. If, however, it was intended to serve the growing population radiating west and south block by block, then its location had been well chosen.[45]

St. Mary Magdalen dePazzi, meanwhile, located in what had once been the center of the Italian colony, had been boxed into an area with limited potential for future growth. On its east, toward the Delaware River, Jews and Eastern

European Catholics, occupying their own neighborhoods, formed as much of an enduring presence as the Italians. But on the west, toward Broad Street, and to the south, older residents were vacating blocks that were being rapidly filled by Italians. This redistribution of population left St. Mary Magdalen dePazzi to face a serious threat of atrophy and to risk becoming merely a relic of an earlier time, with its pastor reduced to only a symbolic role in community life.

The Augustinian Conquest

With the dividing of neighborhood territory, Our Lady of Good Counsel, almost from its inception, served a far larger congregation than did St. Mary Magdalen dePazzi. In 1900, priests at Our Lady of Good Counsel baptized 962 children and two adults and officiated at 196 weddings, while clergy at St. Mary Magdalen dePazzi christened 533 children and performed 98 marriages. This almost 2:1 ratio, both for baptisms and marriages, remained fairly constant in subsequent years. The size of the Catholic population, as reported in the pastor's annual report, confirmed the relative difference between the two parishes. While Father Agostino Cogliani, acting as pastor after Repetti's death, calculated 32,000 souls in his area, Isoleri reported only 7,000. The disparity between the two parishes also suggested their future significance in South Philadelphia.[46]

Behind a new church for Italians, and beneath parish rivalries, other factors shaped the relationship between the two churches. Philadelphia's Italian population, as noted earlier, had been sharply altered from its early Ligurian character by the huge volume of newcomers from Southern Italy and Sicily in the late nineteenth century. At the same time, the struggle for leadership within the community had been resolved by the emergence of individuals with Southern Italian origins. In some sense, Isoleri, while not mortally wounded, was a casualty in a religious struggle that ran parallel to this secular conflict. Along with its greater size, Our Lady of Good Counsel, with echoes of the Cardarelli affair still reverberating, was seen as being for Southern Italians, while St. Mary Magdalen dePazzi was identified as "the Genoese church."

None of these changes, however, was entirely unexpected. With Italians moving away from Little Italy's original center, the Church had responded to their needs in other locations. During his brief tenure as pastor of Our Lady of Good Counsel, Repetti had preached missions to Italians at Manayunk and Germantown in the city and at Lenni in Delaware County.[47] The clusters of Italians in these places, often colonies of railroad and construction laborers, became parts of outlying urban neighborhoods or suburban communities. Even Isoleri had recognized these settlements in his annual reports. But by repeatedly describing the Italian population as both thick and scattered, with many people attending religious services elsewhere than in his church, and by blaming "outside societies" independent of his parish, "cropping up like mushrooms," he was admitting that he could no longer remain the only pastor serving them.[48]

Isoleri was well aware of the congestion and its consequences in his district. Mindful of the agrarian origins of Italians, he proposed that one-half of them, for their own moral, hygienic, and economic improvement as well as for the benefit of their new society, resettle in rural areas where there was land for them to cultivate. Isoleri also asked city officials to open two or three small parks below South Street to relieve the congestion that caused idleness nine months of the year, bred disease, crime, and socialism, and encouraged Protestant proselytizing. The era of St. Mary Magdalen dePazzi as Little Italy's only church had reached its end.[49]

Another aspect of Our Lady of Good Counsel, however, remained hidden from public knowledge. In February 1899, the Congregation of Propaganda Fide had granted the Augustinians not only the new church "in perpetuum" but also the care of all Italians in Philadelphia, except for those who were currently members of St. Mary Magdalen dePazzi. In July 1900, Archbishop Ryan added to the contract that the parish and property of St. Mary Magdalen dePazzi, upon the death of its present pastor, would be assigned to the Augustinians. With an estimated 30,000 Italians in Philadelphia at this time, the arrangement appeared to be feasible, but subsequent population growth, along with a new archdiocesan policy of establishing its own churches, would eventually negate it. And some thirty-four years after the original agreement, Archbishop Dennis J. Dougherty's suppression of Our Lady of Good Counsel would provoke the most turbulent events in the archdiocese since the Hoganism schism a century earlier.[50]

CHAPTER NINE

The "Italian Problem"

Catholic and Protestant Responses

By the late nineteenth century, the saga of St. Mary Magdalen dePazzi and its pastor had transcended local history to become part of an important chapter in American religious history. Whether speaking to his people as Catholics or as Italians, Father Antonio Isoleri, from his pulpit at St. Mary Magdalen dePazzi, addressed not only questions of faith but also secular matters facing Italians in America. At these moments, he sought to guide them through what was becoming known to prelates, scholars, and activists as the "Italian problem." As immigrants adjusting to a new society, Italians had to deal with a multifaceted array of challenges, but three in particular held the most relevance for them as Catholics: their willingness and ability to financially support their faith; their distinctive forms of popular piety; and above all else, their defection, or "leakage," as it was commonly called, as practicing Catholics, especially in response to the initiatives of Protestants and secular reformers. Along with secret societies, the labor movement, the need for a national university, the school controversy, Cahenslyism, and Americanism, the Italian problem took its place as another urgent issue confronting American Catholicism at a time aptly characterized as its "age of problems."[1]

While the "Italian problem" was being defined and debated in the higher councils of Catholicism in Rome and elsewhere, however, St. Mary Magdalen dePazzi would provide its own answer as a test case to the dilemmas facing leaders and laity. Although its core issues were not at all new to Isoleri, they now linked his parish and others like it to broader concerns and Church authorities in a way that would alter his congregants' future in America. For what engaged Isoleri was not only an administrative problem for the hierarchy, but one that also affected the everyday life of parish and pastor. As the dialogue about the "Italian problem" continued to unfold, it also had to be implemented in the rectory, at the altar, and even in the street at places such as St. Mary Magdalen dePazzi. It provided a context for all nationality parishes that served to drive the development of archdiocesan policy toward them. To understand what happened at St. Mary Magdalen dePazzi and similar parishes in the years ahead requires an examination of that larger context.

Early Responses to the "Italian Problem"

The "Italian problem" originated largely as a result of conditions and perceptions of immigrant life in New York City. Protestant reformers had provided material and spiritual aid to needy Italians for some time before the first church for Italian Catholics in that city was founded in 1867. And when a Catholic response finally came, it was sometimes seen more as an instrument of reactionary opposition to Italian nationalism than as stemming from a true concern for people in need. If favorable character traits were found among Italians, credit was given to secular or Protestant agencies, while the role of the Catholic Church was regarded as harmful or absent. Moreover, the political situation in Italy helped to shape prevailing views on the influence of Catholicism on Italians. The same factors that prevented Catholics from being good citizens in Italy supposedly carried over and conditioned their religious attitudes after immigration. At the same time, government policies in Italy, particularly the unresolved "Roman question," antagonized Irish Americans and other Catholics toward Italians. However unfairly, they were also considered more ignorant and superstitious in religious matters than any other Catholic immigrant group, as well as unable and unwilling to support their Church.[2]

The American hierarchy, concerned over the faith of immigrants, had recognized the need for priests from the same backgrounds as their flock as early the Fourth Provincial Council of Baltimore in 1840. The Second Plenary Council of Baltimore in 1866, without specifically mentioning immigrants, similarly heard a call for "well trained and zealous priests" to protect the faith of the people. But it became a pastoral crisis when Italians poured into America as the first immigrant Catholics to arrive without an adequate number of their own priests.[3]

The "Italian problem" was formally recognized in preparations for the Third Plenary Council of 1884. When American archbishops convened in Rome in the autumn of 1883, they placed the spiritual needs of Italian immigrants on the agenda for their impending meeting in Baltimore, believing that the problem could be resolved by absorbing them into existing parishes. They unanimously agreed that societies to care for Italian immigrants, modeled on the St. Raphael Society for Germans, should be established in principal cities of destination in America and in such ports of departure as Genoa and Naples. The prelates also identified the Collegio Brignole Sale in Genoa and the Salesian fathers of the Don Bosco Institute as the main sources for suitable priests.[4]

The preliminary deliberations in Rome, however, were not marked by complete accord. When Archbishop James Gibbons of Baltimore noted that some American cities already had Italian churches staffed by Italian priests, the coadjutor archbishop of New York, Michael Corrigan, objected. Arguing that Italians were unaccustomed to attending church, were dispersed throughout the cities, and contributed nothing in support of their priests or their churches, Corrigan opposed establishing special parishes for them. After another prelate suggested that priests at larger parishes could be assigned to care for Italians, the delegates concluded that they should be urged to attend wherever clergy fluent in their language could instruct them.[5]

More problems emerged when Cardinal Giovanni Simeoni, the prefect of Propaganda Fide, convinced that Italians suffered more than other immigrant groups, encouraged Gibbons to develop a plan for their spiritual and temporal care. While Gibbons supported the program, first discussed at the meeting in Rome, for immigrant societies and their own priests (but not rural colonies for Italians), responsibility for drafting the chapter, "De Colonis Italianis," for the Baltimore Council fell upon Archbishop William H. Elder of Cincinnati. But Elder, more interested in other issues, asked to be relieved of this duty. When disagreement erupted over the "Italian problem" at the Council, Corrigan contended that few Italians in his city attended mass or received the sacraments. Moreover, they were being confirmed by a heretical bishop, several of their priests had been expelled from Italy for crimes, and Southern Italian peasants, in particular, were abominably ignorant in religious matters. Corrigan argued that efforts to provide religion to Italian immigrants in New York had completely failed. With support from other bishops, a revision to the plan took up immigration in general, praising German and Irish societies, calling for more priests in seaport cities, noting the needs of women and the desirability to encourage rural settlement, but not specifying Italian immigrants. The "Italian problem" had been momentarily erased by issues such as parish boundaries, nationality missions, "chapels of ease," and the rights of priests as irremovable rectors.[6]

By failing to resolve, or even to address, the "Italian problem," the American bishops had complicated their relationship to Rome. After eliminating any references to Italians but now apprehensive about papal reaction, they agreed on the need to send an explanation to Rome. Reluctant to convey to Pope Leo XIII the "delicate matter," as it was termed, of "how utterly faithless the specimens of his country coming here really are," they sent their message to Cardinal Simeoni.

Repeating Corrigan's views, now shared by other prelates, that Italians were not only derelict in their practice of religion but also geographically dispersed and generally unsupportive, the bishops blamed inadequate religious training in Italy and called for stronger spiritual care in the homeland.[7]

Within the American hierarchy, differences of opinion could be found. Mindful of successful efforts with Italians in Baltimore, Gibbons remained convinced that nationality-based churches, restricted to the members of a particular ethnic group within the boundaries of regular parishes, could be developed to care for immigrants. Anticipating reduced immigration as the result of stringent laws being enacted in Europe, along with the assimilation of immigrant children, Gibbons held a more optimistic view of the future of Italian life in America than did other prelates.[8]

The opposition of German Catholics to assimilation, along with the demand for their own clergy, carried matters to the next stage. When German American bishops sent Father Peter Abbelen, vicar general of Milwaukee, to Rome in 1886 with a petition for separate parishes (also conveyed to Gibbons), his arrival brought the Holy See into the controversy. At the same time an American bishop asked Cardinal Simeoni to make an authoritative ruling on nationality parishes, which were being challenged as illegal, quasi-parishes. Simeoni endorsed the legitimacy of these parishes in his reply to Gibbons in the summer of 1887.[9]

As German American bishops waged their campaign, they pursued a course that reached beyond their own people to the concerns of other immigrant groups. After a hasty meeting of archbishops in late 1886, Corrigan's opposition, provoked by the plight of German immigrants, to nationality churches in general had serious implications for all groups. But Italian immigrants, lacking religious leaders willing to make demands, did not challenge assimilationists such as Corrigan. If they were dissatisfied with the American Church, they quietly defected from membership, thus confirming the gist of the "Italian problem."[10]

The first positive response to the "Italian problem" came with the founding of a missionary college in Piacenza by Bishop Giovanni Scalabrini in 1887 and the establishing of the Congregation of St. Charles Borromeo, an order dedicated to a special ministry among Italians in the Americas in the next year. The Italian clergy in the United States, meanwhile, emulating the Germans, began a campaign for greater autonomy in their ministry. After the bishops opposed apostolate vicariates for Italians, their strategy shifted. Monsignor Gennaro deConcilio, pastor of St. Michael's Church in Jersey City, in a pamphlet widely distributed among the hierarchy in Italy, proposed an ambitious plan for an independent "Mother Church," offering social services in every major American city with a large immigrant population, and chapels in smaller colonies, staffed by Italian priests and funded by Propaganda Fide. Corrigan again led the opposition to the proposal.[11]

In December 1888, Pope Leo XIII appealed to the American hierarchy for help in ameliorating the plight of Italian Catholics in the United States. After decrying the poverty, dehumanization, and exploitation accompanying immigrant life, he focused on pastoral problems. He noted the lack of familiarity with the Italian language, the shortage of priests, and the contracting of marriages outside of the Church, which contributed "everywhere with this people [to] a decay of Christian morality and a growth of wickedness." Depicting Italians as "wandering like sheep without a shepherd through steep paths and dangerous places," the pope expressed his concern for "men sprung from the same soil as ourselves." Having already asked Propaganda Fide to provide remedies, especially by sending more priests "accustomed to the language of their countrymen" to teach the faith, administer the sacraments, and guide the young, he announced the founding of the missionary college in Piacenza as a means of achieving these goals. The Holy Father urged American bishops to recruit "young men from your own country, children of Italian parents," who, after ordination, would work in dioceses with large immigrant communities, but under episcopal authority and experienced pastors. He also asked that any further proposals be directed to Propaganda Fide.[12]

Despite the solicitous and conciliatory tone of the pope's document, secular and religious leaders disagreed over his proposals. In Italy, while the leftist former prime minister, Agostino Depretis, praised Leo XIII for his concern with Italians overseas, the current head of state, Francesco Crispi, believed that it was intended to implement a plan to put immigrants under priestly control. Similarly, the pontiff's recommendations were received neither with unanimity nor full enthusiasm by the American bishops. Bishop Bernard McQuaid of Rochester, who vigorously objected, thought that other Americans would oppose the proposals. He also believed that the papal message was based upon exaggerated figures and, contrary to deConcilio's data, that only a small number of temporary migrants were living in his diocese.[13]

While deConcilio sought support for his proposals from Bishop Scalabrini, the American bishops renewed their attention to the demands that had been initiated and long espoused by the Germans. Convening in Lucerne, Switzerland, in December 1890, representatives of the St. Raphael Society chapters from seven countries revised a plan, first formulated by Scalabrini's followers, for immigrants to have their own parishes, priests, and bishops, before submitting it for papal approval. Peter Paul Cahensly, the founder of the St. Raphael Society, who had devoted himself to immigrant care for twenty years, delivered the so-called Lucerne Memorial to Leo XIII in April 1891. If one can say that the Abbelen petition had dropped an earlier shoe, the second one fell in the form of the Lucerne Memorial five years later. But its message was badly distorted in the American press by claims that it espoused a double jurisdiction, with American bishops for American Catholics and ethnic bishops for immigrant Catholics.

In fact, its main principles had already been widely accepted in the American Church.[14]

The actual situation was not only more complicated, but its essential parts were also changing. While the Holy See did not intend to give each ethnic group its own prelates, neither did it believe that immigrants should abandon their ethnic origins. Meanwhile, with the growing immigrant population in New York, Corrigan, although still opposing the Lucerne Memorial, had become an officer of the St. Raphael movement and a supporter of the work of Bishop Scalabrini and Mother Frances Xavier Cabrini. Corrigan and Scalabrini, personal friends who trusted one other, exchanged several messages in their attempt to resolve the newspaper distortions of Cahenslyism, as it had come to be known. Similarly, at the installation of Archbishop F. X. Katzer of Milwaukee in 1891, which at first appeared to be a great triumph for German Americans, Cardinal Gibbons, no longer seeking compromise, strongly espoused the Americanist position while also attempting to refute the misconceptions of the press.[15]

American Catholicism, seriously divided on pastoral policy and practice, had to decide between how much emphasis to place on what immigrants had been in their homeland against what they were likely to become in America. Paradoxically, along with the possibility that non-Catholics, confused by Cahenslyism, still perceived Catholicism as a foreign institution, it also feared that many immigrants had defected from a Church that, by being American, was alien to them. While advocates of pluralism misunderstood the consciousness emerging among immigrants, Americanists underestimated the increasing volume of immigrants and the persistence of ethnic identity and culture among them. And if the "Italian problem" could be seen apart from these issues, it was closely tied to the more general problem of reconciling diversity with unity.

Although American Catholicism sought to solve the "Italian problem" in various ways, the principal means was the parish. Three alternatives in parish structure, with different formats and degrees of belonging, brought Italians into Catholic communal life. First, the "duplex," or "annex," model put Italians and their religious services into a basement chapel of a main church while granting them "second-class membership" in a parish controlled by another ethnic group. Second, the nationality parish gave Italians their own church, usually with an Italian pastor and priests as well as greater autonomy and support for cultural pluralism within Catholicism. And third, the canonical or territorial parish, with Italian priests in residence and some services in their own language but within a main church, offered gradual integration into a larger congregation while almost denying cultural differences and encouraging eventual assimilation as Catholic Americans.[16]

These alternatives reflected the continuing debate over such related issues as whether Italians could support their own churches, whether enough Italian priests could be recruited to serve the immigrant population, and whether priests of suitable character could be found. After Leo XIII again addressed these problems in 1890, an Italian pastor in Cleveland, Father Pacifico Capitani, proposed establishing a specialized seminary in America. Skeptical of the Scalabrini program, which allowed the recruitment of seminarians who did not initially speak English, permitted priests to return to Italy after five years, and left them accountable to an Italian bishop as well as to an American one, Capitani sought a more suitable program for the American missions. Aware that the future depended upon American-born children who knew little or no Italian, he proposed educating Italian seminarians in the United States where, by learning English and mixing with Americans, they would be better prepared for the priesthood. But by the end of the century, the "Italian problem," despite the attention that it had received, remained "the great Catholic question in this country."[17]

The "Italian Problem":
St. Mary Magdalen dePazzi

Immigrant Italians placed two principal issues before American Catholicism: how to save their immortal souls, and how to keep their temporal fidelity while the material exigencies of their lives generated concern. How could the Church ameliorate the impact of social and economic conditions that loosened religious affiliation? How could the Church respond to poverty, padrone, and Protestant in the immigrant community? The basic question remained: Should Italians have their own parishes? The answer largely depended on several factors: the shortage of Italian priests, the willingness and ability of Italians to financially support their parishes, the degree of belief and type of piety reflected by their folk religious practices, the potential divisiveness of nationality parishes to American Catholicism, the threat of foreign allegiance especially to Nativist Americans, and prejudice among Irish Americans against Italians.

The problem of saving the faith of immigrants did not pertain to Italians alone, of course, but was shared by other immigrant groups within the broader context of Catholicism in America. Were salvation and fidelity more likely to be achieved through assimilation or pluralism? Would Catholics be better off as one people with a shared culture or by remaining different groups in separate structures? German bishops and priests in the Midwest, where large numbers of their people formed strong communities, were hesitant about assimilation, which they believed should be gradual. Convinced that foreign language and identity would persist, they sought to use their culture as a means of transmitting the faith. Irish American bishops believed that assimilation was not only inevitable and desirable but would also occur quickly, and that Americanization was appropriate in preserving faith while avoiding expressions of nationalism that confirmed Nativist suspicions. But American bishops, failing to recognize that group life went beyond the retention of foreign languages and cultural practices, also underestimated the discontent of Catholics who thought that they had not been fully accepted and who resented Irish control of the Church.[18]

Although initially opposing any cultural partitioning of the Church, American bishops gradually accepted the formation of nationality parishes. While their change of thinking partly resulted from concern over immigrant defections from the Church as well as from the legacy of the Lucerne Memorial and Cahenslyism, it included a concession to the advocates of the dreaded threat of equal representation by ethnic bishops within the hierarchy. The Holy See, meanwhile, concerned since the time of Archbishop John Carroll that American bishops, imbued with republican sentiments, could end up with enough power to be self-governing, now sought the appointment of a permanent apostolic delegate to the United States. In the aftermath, American Catholicism accepted a parish form that organized religious worship and communal life for immigrants as well as provided an expedient response to the "Italian problem" in American cities throughout the early twentieth century.

The attitudes of bishops toward Catholics who were neither English nor Irish in origin also influenced religious life in Philadelphia and elsewhere. While earlier bishops had difficulties with Germans at Holy Trinity Church, Bishop John Neumann, an immigrant from Bohemia, had a more sympathetic response to the foreign born, which was expressed by his intention to build a hospital for them. He also showed his understanding of the importance of language and customs when he founded St. Mary Magdalen dePazzi for the Italians. But Neumann's tenure lasted less than eight years before Bishop James F. Wood, who had been assuming episcopal duties for some time, succeeded his saintly predecessor. The ensuing erosion of the situation for Italians became evident first in Wood's interdict of their church and then in his later conflict with the young Isoleri.[19]

The larger dialogue over the "Italian problem," however, generally ignored St. Mary Magdalen dePazzi. When the bishops met in Philadelphia in 1886 to prepare their defense against the demands of the German clergy, they recalled only that St. Mary Magdalen dePazzi had needed the support of English-speaking Catholics at the time of its founding and that Wood had later attempted to close it. Although it was cited by the hierarchy as evidence of the difficulties in efforts to maintain Italian parishes, Isoleri surely would have rejected the applicability of their conclusions to his church at this time, and he would not have been alone. Similar cases suggested not only that Italian parishes could succeed but that they could also provide an acceptable solution to the "Italian problem." An observer in New York noted "a superior class of Italians, all apparently prosperous and at peace with their surrounding" at the Franciscan church of St. Anthony's in 1881. And when Cardinal Gibbons endorsed the formation of nationality parishes in 1886, he had been partly influenced by the success of Father J. L. Andreis at St. Vincent's Church in Baltimore. But why had the bishops not regarded the first and oldest Italian church in America—the flagship of Italian American Catholicism—more favorably or even as a model for a solution to the "Italian problem"?[20]

Both the broader history of immigration and the particular case of St. Mary Magdalen dePazzi provide clues to the answer to this question. When Italian immigration soared in the late nineteenth century, with New York City as the principal port of entry, government officials, religious authorities, and scholars rightfully riveted their attention on this great center of immigrant settlement and community life. This preoccupation with New York City, which has sometimes skewed the interpretation of the Italian experience in America, affirms the necessity of examining other locations.

From its beginning the Italian Mission in Philadelphia never fully fit the pattern of the Italian parishes of later years. In its case, immigrants had organized, or were given, their own church long before they were part of any "Italian problem." Its congregation, moreover, had a very short prelude, if any, as an annex church within a larger territorial parish. Father Mariani's note on the eve of its opening indicated that St. Mary Magdalen dePazzi had been intended as an Italian church from its inception. Although their names almost entirely comprised its first building committee in the 1850s and appeared later on similar lists, the Irish never controlled church affairs. While it was sometimes identified as a church for the French, St. Mary Magdalen dePazzi remained the Italian church. And although it encountered serious threats to its existence, its early history clearly demonstrated that Italians could organize and maintain their own parish. And by the 1890s, far from its poor and precarious condition during its formative years, its accomplishments, under Isoleri, which included a new church building, a parochial school, an orphanage, a rectory, and a convent, indicated solvency and stability.

As another part of its formula for success, St. Mary Magdalen dePazzi and its pastor established a strong relationship, marked by affinity and cooperation, with secular organizations and Philadelphia's Italian community in general. The oldest and most important fraternal and benevolent society, the Società di Unione e Fratellanza Italiana, despite venerating the anticlerical Giuseppe Garibaldi, to whom it had offered an honorary presidency in 1867, regularly participated in church activities. At mock funerals for King Victor Emmanuel II and Pope Pius IX or at the annual mass on New Year's Day, Società members, in their ceremonial regalia, occupied front pews. Similarly, Isoleri stood alongside them on such civic occasions as the Columbus Monument dedication. If more subtle tensions between voluntary associations and organized religion existed, their visible traces have faded from the record. With financial solidity, increasing membership, and a conspicuous presence in the community, St. Mary Magdalen dePazzi became, as such parishes elsewhere, a place where "immigrant Italians who were on the religious and social periphery of society, could fulfill their religious needs, find opportunity for self-expression, and preserve their self-perception of being human in the face of an unknown social environment."[21]

The "Italian problem" had its nuances. Pastors who allowed Italians to worship in a basement chapel made room for them in the institutional Church but not in their upstairs church. While some skeptics doubted that Italians could successfully maintain their own parishes, others simply opposed their having any parish at all. In a further complication, the real issue was not simply an "Italian problem" but also a "Southern Italian problem." And not only American priests but Italian priests also faltered on this matter. Despite his speech at the Columbus Monument dedication in Fairmount Park in 1876, when he called for his audience to forget regional differences and become united as Italians, even Isoleri later stumbled over the swelling "elemento meridionale."

The "Italian Problem": Popular Piety

Beyond parish organization and governance, another dimension to the "Italian problem" elicited ecclesiastical and secular attention. In their homeland, Italians often faced a threatening natural environment that had shaped religious beliefs and practices, before eventually encouraging many of them to migrate elsewhere. But, encountering perils after immigration that stemmed from their new social milieu, Italians found a powerful resource for adjustment, protection, and comfort in the piety that they had brought with them. For Italians, whether in the towns of an ancestral homeland or in the immigrant enclaves of American cities, their distinctive forms of piety provided the core of Catholicism for them.[22]

Although Catholicism may have shown less regional variation at the beginning of the modern era than in the late nineteenth century, religious customs that were frequently attributed to Southern regions were also found in the North.[23] As more Southern Italians arrived in Philadelphia, their forms of piety neither differed nor threatened the religious culture of their predecessors. Moreover, at St. Mary Magdalen dePazzi, Isoleri recognized the benefits to be derived from saintly patrons. Along with the memory of his own mystical experience some years before, when the eyes of a Marian icon moved, he believed that the intercession of Mary Magdalen dePazzi had brought his recovery from a painful and serious illness that had kept him on "the brink of the grave" from June to December 1878. In a devotional work, Isoleri described thirty-three other instances of "special graces and favors," modest words for miraculous results, that attested to the efficacy of veneration to the patron saint of his parish. Stating that devotion to the saint "has increased wonderfully here," Isoleri described the procession on her feast day in May, with its "many votive offerings in gold . . . money, etc., made for graces received."[24]

While not identical to the devotional practices of other Catholics, the street processions of Italians were not entirely different from the public demonstrations of other groups, whether religious or secular, who were marching behind their own banners and musical bands in other areas of the city. But bemused accounts by the press, or the begrudging tolerance of other Catholics, reflected the inability of outsiders to understand the functions that a patron saint performed for Italians. One aspect was the protection that the patron brought to Italians by living among them. The saint was so closely connected to their place that, on its feast day, it was brought out of the church, which only housed it, to pass through the streets of the urban village that it protected. Along with providing a sense of security amid the calamities that threatened human lives, these celebrations liberated individuals and promoted community.[25] Consequently, the participants of the feast day procession of Mary Magdalen dePazzi venerated her and thanked her for the guardian powers that made the streets of Little Italy both safe and sacred. The event also declared to the rest of Philadelphia that this part of the city belonged to them.

In sum, the distinctive forms of piety that Italians followed, even in their most public moments, represented far more than simply another unwholesome dimension of the "Italian problem." These practices, which revolved around the veneration of patron saints and which often mattered more than other aspects of the organized Church and its precepts, enabled Italians to remain observant Catholics. And while Joseph and other saints, the benefactors of parish sodalities and protectors of immigrants from various parts of Italy, also took their place in processions, Mary Magdalen dePazzi remained the patron of Philadelphia's Italian community, at least until 1898.

The Protestant Crusade:
Missions and Settlement Houses

While Catholic authorities tried to clarify their understanding of the "Italian problem," Protestant and secular agencies had already decided what it meant and how they should respond. Critics of Roman Catholicism held that the Church had not only opposed independence and deterred progress in Italy but had been an unhealthy influence on immigrant life in America. Protestants relied on two principal instruments to reach Italians: churches and missions that sought to convert them; and settlement houses and other agencies that offered social services to them.

Protestant efforts in Philadelphia's Little Italy began with the Episcopalian Church of the Emmanuello, which by the early 1880s offered weekday and

Sunday services, day and night schools, a nursery and kindergarten, sewing classes, a sick diet kitchen, a dispensary, fresh air fund, and other means of poor relief as well as the services of an Italian doctor. It fed about twenty-five children at noonday meals in the winter, with the support of the Ladies' Italian League, while the Brotherhood of St. Andrew and the Circolo Galeazzo sponsored loftier cultural activities. The Italian and French Methodist Episcopal Mission, founded in 1890 at 721 South Ninth Street, included the Circolo Diodati for young members and the Dante Alighieri Association for literary and musical events. Along with English classes each evening, the mission sponsored a sewing school, mothers' meeting, reading room, cooking class, and kindergarten. Its Benevolent Association offered aid to the ill, poor, and strangers; interpreters and legal aid in the courts; and care for abandoned children. The Italian Presbyterian Church, organized in 1903, at 724 South Tenth Street, provided a night school, free reading room, and sewing school as well as a club for young men. The Woman's Home Missionary Society of the Philadelphia Conference of the Methodist Episcopal Church, concerned with immigrants and industrial issues since 1883, developed plans for its Italian and French Mission on South Ninth Street. The Methodist Missionary and Church Extension Society had worked among the French, Jews, Poles, Russians, and Italians since 1892.[26]

Protestants expanded their work among immigrants in the new century. The Reverend T. D. Malan solicited contributions of clothing and money in 1901 to support programs at the Methodist Mission on Ninth Street. Baptists planned a church in Camden, New Jersey, for the growing Italian colony that had overflowed from Philadelphia. In January 1903 the Presbyterian Evangelistic Committee opened a 3,000-seat tabernacle for Italians at Tenth and Washington Streets, with services under the Reverends M. Nardi and Felix Santilli. Six months later the Italian Tabernacle initiated a summer missionary campaign for anyone who did not regularly attend religious services. Even the Hebrew Education Society, which offered classes, a reading room, and a free public bath at Tenth and Carpenter Streets, reported forty-one Italian pupils in educational programs in 1903.[27]

While Protestants held ambivalent attitudes toward immigration in general and Italians in particular, they offered a variety of proposals. In the Arch Street Methodist Church a preacher claimed that promulgating the Christian gospel through the "Home Missions" was the only way to save America from the perils of the foreign born. The secretary of the Baptist State Missionary Society warned a gathering at the First Baptist Church at Seventeenth and Sansom Streets that Slavic immigration was driving Protestantism out of some areas of Pennsylvania. Describing Presbyterian successes among Bohemians, he maintained that many Italians and others were very difficult to assimilate, and that the only possible remedy, from a religious and political point of view, was to spread the gospel among foreigners. Another minister, at the Wayne Avenue Baptist Church in Germantown, asserted that despite the flood of immigration, which brought "vices, ignorance, superstitions, and continental Sabbaths," there was no need for alarm, if a way into what he called the "Ideal City" could be found.[28]

Some Protestant leaders offered less favorable views and harsher solutions. Only a week after the "Ideal City" proposal, in what must have been the high season for reflection on the immigration question, the Reverend J. Madison Peters, speaking on "Unrestricted Immigration" at the Broad Street Baptist Church, argued that the first arrivals had come with republican sentiments, an open Bible, and the cross, but the current immigrants had left their homeland for its own good, with dynamite in one hand and a stiletto in the other, and they were providing more than their share of insane asylum and almshouse inmates. Claiming that three-fourths of all immigration since the Civil War were from the lowest strata of European society, he added that 70 percent of them came from the "most unfavorable recruiting grounds under the sun for American citizenship" in the most recent year. In the next week, Peters warned that lax laws had not only let in impoverished, diseased, illiterate, vicious, and criminal immigrants but gave them the power and authority "to violate the traditions and deface our fair history." If allowed to continue, Peters feared, this immigration was nothing less than a crime against humanity for which posterity and a righteous God would someday hold us guilty. Peters's Nativist ideology delivered in a respectable setting and reported by responsible media sharply contrasted with the sympathetic views of more liberal Protestants who sought protection for immigrants.[29]

Protestant efforts in the early twentieth century failed to achieve much greater success than in previous decades. In 1911, the Episcopalian Board of Missions reported that the Church of the Emmanuello was prosperous; all its agencies were growing vigorously, to much satisfaction and improvement; two deaconesses, appointed during the year, were working well among the children; the Sunday school had reached its highest record of attendance so far; and a mission worker at the Immigration Depot was doing splendid work among newcomers. While the report concluded that "every line of work is very promising and encouraging," its figures indicated only modest results. With 69 families, 142 communicants, about 75 in regular attendance, claimed as its congregation, and 190 students in the Sunday school, the Emmanuello recorded only eleven baptisms, thirty-one confirmations, three marriages, and three burials for the year. Nevertheless, with similar figures for the next year, Episcopalians saw favorable results from their endeavors. Calling for greater efforts among Italians, they also welcomed the obligation to assist immigrants toward citizenship and a better life. But after thirty years of labor in the vineyard of Italian immigration, the Emmanuello was reaping a scant harvest compared to the numbers served by Catholic agencies at the same time.[30]

If Protestant missions, with only limited success in gaining converts, did not sufficiently alarm Catholic authorities, the settlement house movement posed another threat to the fidelity of Italians. In fact, it was sometimes difficult to separate the ostensibly secular programs of these agencies, among the forerunners of modern social work, from their Protestant origins or from a covert agenda based on Protestant culture. Usually seen as originating at Toynbee House in London's East End in 1884 before reaching New York City two years later, local antecedents dated back to the House of Industry, at 716 Catharine Street, founded in 1847 to aid Irish immigrants and their children in acquiring work skills and employment. While social reformers used various approaches, perhaps none had greater promise than the settlement house in dealing with immigrants' adjustment to urban America. Young adults, recruited from more educated classes, settled as resident workers in city neighborhoods to instruct and inspire members of immigrant families to follow the ways of American society. In these settlement house programs, adult immigrants learned how to speak English, cook American foods, and prepare themselves for citizenship. They joined thrift clubs, sewing classes, and fuel cooperatives. Their children, meanwhile, learned the rudiments of basketball and baseball and attended summer camps in rural areas. By the time that the College Settlement, the first in Philadelphia, was established in 1892, the movement had already appeared in several other American cities. By 1911, similar neighborhood centers existed at thirty sites in Philadelphia. Larger ones, such as the College Settlement, offered activities and services not only at various locations within the city but also at the New Jersey seashore. While some settlement houses offered a broad range of activities, others, such as the Settlement Music School, were specialized.[31]

Some programs clearly pursued aims beyond material assistance. In 1897 the Starr Kitchen of the College Settlement admitted that its work only began with such concerns of the poor as "where to live, what to eat, and wherewithal to be clothed," before adding: "But the Kitchen and other branches of practical work could not justify their own existence were they not a fitting foundation on which to build character, a training, a foundation for goodness and for those things as Lowell expresses it 'which are out of sight,' but toward which we are all aspiring."[32]

Although often presented as nonsectarian, settlement house programs could be found under Baptist, Presbyterian, Quaker, Methodist, Episcopal, and nondenominational auspices (but clearly Christian or Jewish in orientation), while similar centers started by Unitarians or by the Ethical Culture Society also had implications for religious belief and practice. Founded by the Episcopal Diocese of Pennsylvania, St. Martha's House, near Eighth Street and Snyder Avenue, offered a medical and dental clinic, milk distribution center, savings bank, library, and kindergarten. After 1918 the influx of Italians to the neighborhood made them the predominant clients of St. Martha's House. If proselytizing did not occur, insensitivity sometimes accompanied efforts to shape young patrons along cultural and religious lines. When two outstanding young scholars were denied the customary prizes because they were not baptized Christians but instead were given pictures of scenes from the life of Christ, we can surmise that the Glazier family had ancient reasons for not baptizing their daughters, Yetta and Elizabeth, as Christians. Similarly, the Reed Street Neighborhood House, after evolving out of the St. James Industrial School for Girls and supported by the Episcopalians until 1919, more subtly encouraged conversion to Protestantism. But the Baptist Settlement House, on Passyunk Avenue above Eleventh Street, with a kindergarten, Sunday school, industrial school, kitchen garden, language classes, and youth clubs, openly offered religious instruction to Italians.[33]

Settlement house programs unavoidably affected immigrant culture and group life. After the Starr Centre, founded to care for African Americans, reorganized in order to reach immigrants, it sought to reduce the infant mortality rate in South Philadelphia, ascribed to unpasteurized milk ladled from unsanitary cans, by a highly successful initiative to supply families with a safer product. From 1904 onward, Italians comprised the largest number of participants in the milk program, which often led to broader contact with client families: "From the detailed report which follows, it will be noted that the majority of the patients treated were Italians, and after these the colored people. All of the Italian patients came originally through the modified milk department. The nurse visits all the babies to whom milk is distributed. If sickness is found in any member of the household, medical assistance is advised, and if there be no physician in attendance, a visit to the dispensary or a call from the doctor is the natural result."[34] As the Starr Centre reached into immigrant family life by emphasizing the "betterment of the home" through cooking, sewing, and kitchen garden classes, it declared: "We try to make easier the adjustment of foreigners to their new environment and to lessen the friction which often results out of the aptitude of the child for the new language and his ability to adapt himself to the ways of a new country—thus placing the parent at a disadvantage."[35]

Settlement house workers sought not to disrupt families or exacerbate intergenerational conflict but rather to improve the quality of life among immigrants by reaching into their homes. The Starr Centre emphatically stated: "In all our departments we are going into the home, and each department is measured by its influence in the home."[36] But even programs that only sought to improve immigrant living conditions carried the risk of altering cultural patterns and disturbing social relations within families.

In late 1907 the Starr Centre established a branch at Casa Ravello, at Seventh and Catharine Streets in the heart of Little Italy. Built four years earlier by the Octavia Hill Housing Association, it was intended to provide "model tenements" for Italians in a neighborhood where several immigrant groups had "strongly entrenched themselves." Describing the newcomers as "both industrious and frugal, but . . . exceedingly poor," one observer added that they were kept poor "partly by their ignorance and partly by their efforts to bring relatives over from

Europe to share what they regard as their good fortune." And as they altered living quarters to accommodate relatives, Italians "unused to living in houses of the American style" were seen as "exceedingly destructive of property." Along with a "baby saving station" that provided safe milk, the Starr Centre offered various other services, but its underlying perception of Italians was not much different from that of other agencies.[37]

The settlement house movement often served other objectives, as the 1908 report of the Starr Centre revealed: "The selling of milk especially prepared for babies and the problem of assimilation of the foreign immigrant do not at first seem to have a very close relation to each other. The huge problem of the Americanization of the immigrant is approached from an infinite variety of sides, and the providing of pure honest milk to a helpless mother in the hour of her baby's greatest need affords an avenue of approach not likely to be ignored, and that road leads one straight to the immigrant's heart."[38]

The settlement house movement emphatically espoused democratic values, and it claimed to have more empathy for immigrants and to offer a more benign alternative to other ideologies and programs for them. In 1913, however, a political economist from the University of Rome, who recognized the ethnocentrism of the settlement movement, urged workers to be more sensitive to Italian customs, habits, employments, amusements, and traditions. He advised them to feel the spirit of Italians and to see things from their point of view. Moreover, they were to help them to retain the good traits of their families, if the settlement houses were truly to become centers for the whole neighborhood. Despite such warnings, settlement workers still sought, in their own way, to alter immigrant life and character. And while these alterations might be called Americanization, they imposed cultural standards of earlier Northern European groups, modified somewhat by their American experience, on later arrivals. But the implications were not lost on Catholic observers, who were concerned about the underlying agendas of such secular agencies as the Starr Centre as they sought to ameliorate the corporal and temporal problems of immigrants. And when religion was openly introduced as a part of the solution, it could only connote Protestant proselytization. Although Catholicism eventually embraced its own version of the settlement house movement, its apprehensions about Protestant interest and influence among Italians were indeed warranted.[39]

The "Italian Problem": Fidelity and Assimilation

If American Catholicism were to find a solution to the "Italian problem," it could not be limited merely to the issue of apostasy. It went far beyond abdication of practice and defection from membership, because Italian immigrants greatly varied in their identity with, affiliation to, and observance of Catholicism. While many of them were devout adherents, others attended mass only on a couple of holidays, if at all, and many of them venerated patron saints in a manner that bordered on idolatry to some observers. Moreover, while some Italians were Protestant before migration, others were agnostic, atheistic, or anticlerical. For most Italians, it was not the soundness of theological arguments but the exigencies of survival that really mattered.

While Catholic prelates, priests, and laymen engaged in their dialogue on the "Italian problem," Protestant activists attempted to ease the material needs of immigrants in American cities. Although Italians were willing to accept aid from churches, missions, and settlement houses that might make life easier or better for them and their families, they were less inclined to change their traditional religious identity and affiliation. If the Catholic effort to solve the "Italian problem" were to succeed, it necessitated entering into programs similar to those of the Protestants. It required replacing the exploitation and alienation that immigrants often encountered with economic opportunity and emotional security in their own community, which eventually could bring assimilation in the larger society. If the Church had a role to play in the life of immigrants, it would achieve its spiritual objectives only by taking its part as another institution in the building of their earthly community.

The "Italian problem" could not be separated from issues of material and cultural adjustment faced by Italians as immigrants. The Catholic response began to set in place an ambivalent view, implemented by an ambiguous policy toward Italians. Incorporating both continuity and change, it allowed Italians to retain their traditional devotional culture and nationality parishes while also delivering them by a strategy of assimilation to secular America. Its implementation would sometimes be aggressively and insensitively conducted. The solution to the "Italian problem," that is, the task of saving the faith of Little Italy, would increasingly depend upon assimilating its people as Americans. And while institutional Catholicism struggled with the "Italian problem," much of the burden of achieving its complicated task fell on pastoral shoulders. At St. Mary Magdalen dePazzi, Isoleri would construct his own solution by addressing the delicate relationship between fidelity and identity in the years ahead. It would require the recasting of his familiar theme of "patria e religione" for new generations of Italian Americans.

CHAPTER TEN

A New Century

Shortly after beginning a special midnight mass, Father Antonio Isoleri, pastor of St. Mary Magdalen dePazzi Church, approached his pulpit early in the morning of January 1, 1901, the first day of the twentieth century. As he looked out at his congregation, seated in the pews, Isoleri greeted them with the words of Saint Paul: "He that regardeth the day regardeth it unto the Lord. For none of us liveth unto himself and no man dieth unto himself. For whether we live or whether we die, we die unto the Lord. Therefore whether we live or whether we die, we are the Lord's."[1]

It was a theme that Isoleri used year after year in his homily for New Year's Day—the gift of life, as short as it was, and how we were to use it by service to the Lord. On this unique occasion, as one century ended and a new one began, he then shifted from Saint Paul to Shakespeare:

"What fools these mortals be!" Strange, but true! What should be an occasion for serious reflection is seized upon as an opportunity for the greatest pagan-like dissipation. A few minutes, and another year, another century will come to an end, and another year, another century will begin. Life is short and fleeting, like a shadow—it lasts no longer than the flower which blossoms in the morning and withers in the evening! And yet people rush madly on, thoughtlessly on to their grave—to eternity. But this life is not our own; this present time is not our own: ". . . because whether we live or die, we are the Lord's." It is from the Lord we received this life—and all the years we have already spent, and the years—or the days we be allowed to spend here below. Therefore we should spend all our life—in God's service! Perhaps we have squandered many days and years already! We should redeem the time—at once—and constantly, as the Apostle tells us! Think of those who have no longer time . . . because they died, have been judged and already entered eternity; for them *tempus non erit amplius.*

Ah! if but one day—one hour were granted to the lost souls . . . they would give for it all the treasures of this world! And we? We throw away days and months and years! We have time for everything, except for God, for our immortal souls. . . . "They spend their days in wealth . . . and in a moment they go down to hell" (Job 21:13). Let us make some good resolutions to serve God for the remainder of our lives. The new year may be our last here on earth . . . death may come suddenly . . . as we live so shall we die. . . . Life is not ours, neither is time! For—"whether we live, or whether we die, we are the Lord's."[2]

In his notes, Isoleri wrote: "For midnight mass dec.31–1900–Jan'y 1 1901—the beginning of the 20th Century," adding the Latin words: "Regi immortali saeculorum omnis honor et gloria in saecula saeculorum!" Disturbed by the "pagan-like" way in which revelers usually welcomed a new year, he reminded his parishioners that it might be their last one. Isoleri was beyond the midpoint of his own mortal life and about to enter his own gloomy woods. Almost fifty-six years old and a pastor for over thirty years, his church was no longer the only one for Italians in Philadelphia. After unsuccessfully contending that another parish was not necessary, he had to wonder what the future held for his church and for himself. Isoleri could be certain, however, of at least one thing—he would continue to serve his Lord.

The Great Migration and Little Italy

While Isoleri's deep faith gave him the strength to face the future, many immigrants entered the new century with much less certainty. Immigration to America had climbed after the Civil War and reached its peak in the first decade of the twentieth century. It remained high until World War I halted Atlantic passage, and then it resumed after the Armistice. With the National Origins Quota Acts of the 1920s, immigration steadily declined to its modern nadir during the Depression of the 1930s. Italian immigration reflected a similar pattern before restrictive legislation, along with poor economic conditions, brought it almost to a complete halt.[3]

During the Great Migration the Italian population in Philadelphia, as in other major destinations, continued to grow. By 1890, it was about 7,000; then nearly 18,000 by 1900, slightly over 45,000 by 1910, and almost 64,000 by 1920.

Calculating the total number of immigrants and American-born members of their families was more difficult. In the late 1890s estimates varied from slightly over 20,000 in Philadelphia to almost 50,000 in New York City and Brooklyn. Claiming 80,000 in Philadelphia and 20,000 more in its surrounding areas in 1906, the principal Italian newspaper of the city contended that many of them, already naturalized or with some knowledge of English, were passing themselves off as Americans. While the U.S. Census reported 76,734 first- and second-generation Italians in 1910, and 136,793 in 1920, another newspaper estimated the Italian population at about 200,000 in 1917. Exceeded by other groups during the previous century, Italians were second only to the Irish in Philadelphia by 1920.[4]

With peak immigration, more Italians than ever before had become residents of Philadelphia. Largely from the Abruzzi and Sicily but also from other regions of the South, and with a modest number of Tuscans and Genoese, they reportedly occupied ninety blocks of South Philadelphia. Italians toiled as farmhands and ditchdiggers; as laborers in bridge, street, and railroad construction, sent from Philadelphia to wherever their work was needed; or as barbers, tailors, bricklayers, stonemasons, and carpenters, and even as physicians and in other professions in the city. Their presence had exacerbated a debate over the personal character and desirability of Italians. The consul general of Italy reported that the Italian was generally well regarded and that his amply demonstrated energy, sobriety, and honesty made him preferred above other types of workers. But the majority of Philadelphians, who did not appreciate the Italian imprint on what they regarded as their city, did not share this view. When a prominent writer returned after a long absence, she declared: "To be honest . . . I do not like to find Philadelphia a foreign town. . . . I do not like to find streets where the name on almost every store is Italian."[5] Nevertheless, displaced from distant origins, transplanted to new soil, and now deeply rooted, Italians had built an extensive community of their own in Philadelphia—families and households, immigrants who had resettled there, children who were born there, adults who were spending their lives there, and the elderly who would die there. After a half-century of gestation, and despite some recent dispersion of population, their institutional and commercial life remained concentrated near Christian Street between South Sixth and South Eleventh Streets.[6]

Italians shopped at the many groceries owned by their countrymen in Little Italy. They bought meat at the large butcher shop that slaughtered two hundred sheep, thirty steers, and fifty calves each week, or in other smaller markets. While milk, butter, and eggs were sold in stores, they were also delivered by horse and wagon. Italians, similarly, bought produce in stores, or hucksters delivered fruit and vegetables to homes. Each morning, fresh bread came from the ovens of bakeries. Italians seeking specialties from their homeland found rustic sausages and cheeses, true Neapolitan pasta, and Sicilian-style bread. And most of them knew the formidable macaroni factory of Guano and Raggio on South Seventh Street, just east of St. Mary Magdalen dePazzi Church.

Italians slaked their thirst at places owned and operated by other Italians, who brewed their own beer, sold imported and domestic wines and liquor, and served customers in saloons or restaurants. Perhaps mindful of the dangers of alcohol, some of them also sold tea or produced their own *acqua gassosa*. They dined at Italian oyster houses, where they might also play billiards. They satisfied their appetite for gelato, soft drinks, and candy at confectionaries and "ice cream saloons" owned by their fellow countrymen. They found a wide range of goods and services provided by their own community, which included barber shops, laundries, shoe stores and shoe repair shops, hatters, jewelers, custom tailors, fabric and notions stores, leather goods, and even bookbinding. And they shopped in stores whose now-enterprising proprietors had once been street musicians.

To seek employment, deposit their earnings in a savings account, remit money to families in Italy, or buy steamship tickets to return themselves, Italians dealt with the Italian Exchange Bank. There were also the Banco Torino, Banca Cantoni, Banca d'Italia, Banca Napoli, Banca Calabrese, Banca Alessandroni, and Banca Provinciale Romana as well as agencies whose names were intended to inspire confidence but actually varied in stability, honesty, and dependability. Some banks competed with other firms by offering wireless communication with steamships on the Atlantic. While banks were often also employment agencies, one firm limited itself to finding jobs for barbers. If Italians wanted to rent or buy property, they had their own real estate dealers. If they needed mortgages, they applied for loans from the First Italo-American Building Association. They could fill their newly acquired homes with furniture and adorn rooms with statuettes made by Italian firms in the community. If they needed home improvements, Italians hired Italian carpenters and other tradesmen. If things required repair, they relied on the abilities of Italian mechanics. To protect their property and families, they bought fire and life insurance from Italian agents of major companies in the community. And if they wanted images of themselves in their new life, they were photographed at studios in Little Italy.

Newly arrived immigrants found rooms in Little Italy at a hotel with a restaurant and beer saloon or in one of the many smaller *pensioni* and private homes, where their relatives or *paesani* already lived. More distinguished or prosperous newcomers stayed at Abramo Personeni's Basso Hotel in center city. And if Italians wanted to board or hire horses, they could find several livery stables.

Italians found security within the network of their own labor unions, political clubs, beneficial societies, and women's auxiliaries, which the Italian Federation of Philadelphia now attempted to coordinate. Based on town of origin, occupation, or some shared interest, often under the protection of a patron saint, voluntary associations had rapidly proliferated among Philadelphia's Italians in the late nineteenth century. These organizations offered congenial companionship, emotional support, and distractions from the rigors of immigrant life. In these communal activities, with the declining influence of the older Ligurian founders, leaders with Southern Italian roots emerged. Charles C. A. Baldi, born in Castelnuovo Cilento in the province of Salerno, typified the new *prominenti* of the twentieth century. After working as a fruit vendor, then as an interpreter for railroad laborers, Baldi and his brothers opened a coalyard, then a funeral home, livery stable, and real estate office in Philadelphia. Before long, C. C. A. Baldi Brothers & Co., valued at $350,000, had taken its place among the leading firms in the city. In 1903 the Baldis organized, in partnership with another family, the Italian Exchange Bank, with C. C. A. Baldi as its president. Three years later, Baldi launched *L'Opinione*, a daily newspaper for Italian readers. As a founder or as president of several mutual aid societies as well as of the new Italian Federation, he took a conspicuous part in almost every major event in the immigrant community. Staunchly Republican, he sealed the indebtedness and allegiance that delivered Italians to the political machine that governed Philadelphia almost without interruption for seventy-five years. Standing at the vortex of communal and commercial affairs, Baldi was acclaimed as the person who "prepares the future for the Italians of Philadelphia."

For information and amusement, Philadelphia's Italians found many newspapers in their own language in the early twentieth century. Among weeklies and dailies they read *Battaglia, Il Corriere della Philadelphia, Il Corriere della Sera, La Forbice, Il Giornale Italiano, Italica Gente, La Libera Parola, Mattino, Mastro Paolo, Il Momento, Pensiero, Sera, Sigaretta, La Verità, Vero, La Voce della Colonia, La Voce del Popolo,* or *Il Vesuvio.* From 1906 onward, however, *L'Opinione,* for which readers paid "un soldo" for an eight-page daily and "due soldi" for the twelve-page Sunday edition, with the latest news telegraphed from Italy, represented the dominant voice in the community.

In their leisure time, Italians attended plays, concerts, and other entertainments at Verdi Hall, one of the most impressive theaters to be found in the Italian colony of any American city, with a capacity of 700, on Christian Street between Seventh and Eighth Streets. Its proprietor, Ferruccio Giannini, a widely acclaimed operatic tenor, had also organized the Verdi Italian Orchestral Society. Italian musicians, ranging from renowned professionals to amateurs who shared a love for music and a passion to perform, filled the orchestra for Verdi Hall programs as well as played in the many bands who sought their talents for events in Little Italy and elsewhere in the city.

Italian audiences paid twenty-five cents for general admission, and ten cents extra for reserved seats, to see moving pictures and to hear music by Rossini and Verdi—sometimes for the benefit of St. Mary Magdalen dePazzi Church—at the New Pennsylvania Hall at Sixth and Montrose Streets. Parents sent their children to an afternoon program with a ten-cent admission in the same theater. The members of Dante Court of the Foresters of America bought tickets at twenty-five cents to attend its concert and dance. Those who aspired to perform studied "bel canto Italiano" at an uptown studio or at a "scuola di musica" in their own neighborhood. They bought pianos and organs made by the largest Italian manufacturer in the nation at either of two factories as well as other instruments at music stores in South Philadelphia.

If Italians had health problems, they had access to a wide range of medical practitioners who spoke their language and shared their origins. If Italians needed a specialist, they could find surgeon, obstetrician, gynecologist, pediatrician, dermatologist, dentist, or eye doctor in their own community. If they preferred to treat an ailment on their own, they found imported medicinal oils and digestive tonics, as well as perfumes to make their bodies smell better, at pharmacy shops. They could pay an Italian druggist $1.00 for a bottle of his own Ferro China, "a perfect chemical combination of quinine and iron tonic, completely assimilable by every organ." If they required greater care, they entered the Fabiani Italian Hospital, adjacent to St. Paul's Church, on Christian Street. And when they were willing to risk less conventional approaches, Italians could find Professor Napoli in his "electrotherapeutic office," where he specialized in "illnesses of the nervous system, stomach, teeth, rheumatism, or any other of life's sorrows." When new life was imminent, Italians asked an Italian midwife to deliver the infant. And at life's end, Italian funeral parlors buried the dead.

If Italians sought spiritual guidance, two Catholic churches, with their own schools and an orphanage, and several Protestant churches, with a wide range of programs, now served them. Although eclipsed by a much larger congregation at the Augustinian church, St. Mary Magdalen dePazzi, nevertheless, retained an important role in the Italian community. If its stores, restaurants and cafés, banks, employment agencies and real estate offices, hotels and boardinghouses, labor unions, political and social clubs, newspapers, theaters, doctors, pharmacists, funeral parlors, and churches now provided "institutional completeness," thus making the immigrant enclave virtually a city within a city, then St. Mary Magdalen dePazzi remained at its center as the "cathedral of Little Italy."

Assimilation and Faith

Whether in their "cathedral" or elsewhere, the residents of Little Italy had captured the attention of Catholic authorities, who continued to regard the religious beliefs and practices of Italians as a problem. The Holy See had addressed ethnic diversity in 1897 when a Propaganda Fide decree conveyed to American bishops through the new apostolic delegate, Archbishop Sebastiano Martinelli, its concerns on nationality, language differences, and parish membership. Two years later a papal encyclical, *Testem Benevolentiae,* took up similar issues. Defining and clarifying these problems as well as finding solutions required training priests, reshaping parish life, and extending religious programs beyond parochial boundaries.

As the dialogue continued, the varying interpretations of the instructions from Rome reflected underlying differences of opinion within American Catholicism in regard to Church structure as well as more secular political ideology. One view held that Propaganda Fide allowed foreign languages in caring for immigrants but sought to bring all Catholics together in America by also encouraging the use of English. Immigrants and their adult children, once they understood English, were free to join English-speaking parishes and were enjoined to avoid perpetuating differences that obstructed assimilation. While foreign languages fostered separation and antagonism, the use of English voiced national sentiment, promulgated law, and represented the recognized medium of public institutions and international relations. Ignorance of English was not merely an inconvenience but also caused crime and lawlessness; accordingly, law-abiding citizens were taxed for the protection of stable government. Nationality parishes, consequently, were "justified only by necessity and expediency," but amalgamation was the ultimate goal, "even if it implies the eventual elimination of all foreign national traditions such as is indicated and fostered by separate churches and educational service in a foreign tongue." This view also noted that "a parish priest who has ministered to a foreign population in their own language might see his parish dwindle down to narrow limits as the younger generation and those who prefer the English language drift away, and leave their pastor with a mere handful of his former flock."[7]

Not all authorities—so far away in time but even more distant in spirit from the enculturation and the liturgical use of the vernacular that Vatican II would eventually endorse—shared such xenophobic views. A more tolerant observer admitted the indifference of adults but asked what could be done for younger Italians. Rather than seeing Italians as "greedy and stingy" but as "thrifty and provident," he asked with great empathy: "Place a million persons who have resided for fifty years in a foreign country, in the same conditions under which Italians find themselves in America, and would we make more or even as much of our opportunities as the Italians are making?" And if Italian priests were limited by regional differences, American priests who went to Italy returned too educated, too cultivated, and too ambitious "to be sent to insignificant parishes with the task of working among the poorest from whom little pecuniary compensation can be expected and still less received." The solution was a special type of priest trained for "Italian missions" in America: "They need to be priests not so much of big heads as of big hearts, not so much of noble intellects as men of deep religious sentiment and zealous activity, men not destined for degrees but eager to learn the dialects of Italy, especially the Neapolitan and Sicilian; men

Rev. Gaetano Mariani (1800–1866). Founding pastor (1852/53–1866) of St. Mary Magdalen dePazzi Church. From Isoleri's "Souvenir and Bouquet," a privately printed (1911) collection of documents on parish history. Courtesy of Rev. Alfred M. Natali, O.S.A.

Page from sacramental ledger recorded by Rev. Mariani on October 23, 1853, noting the founding of the Italian chapel dedicated to "Santa Maria Maddalena dePazzi." Courtesy of the Philadelphia Archdiocesan Historical Research Center.

Old St. Mary Magdalen dePazzi church and rectory. Courtesy of Rev. Alfred M. Natali, O.S.A.

(*above*)
Rev. Antonio Isoleri (1845–1932). Sixth rector, often regarded as the second founder, of St. Mary Magdalen dePazzi. He served as its pastor from 1870 to 1926. Courtesy of Rev. Alfred M. Natali, O.S.A.

(*facing*)
Rev. Antonio Isoleri, standing, 1876. Courtesy of Rev. Alfred M. Natali, O.S.A.

(above)
Villanova d'Albenga. The ancient walled town near the Ligurian coast where Isoleri was born on February 16, 1845.

(facing)

Sisters and young scholars of the St. Mary Magdalen dePazzi orphanage and parish school, 1878. Courtesy of Sister Francis Marie, Archivist, Missionary Sisters of Saint Francis, Peekskill, New York.

The new
church and
rectory of
St. Mary
Magdalen dePazzi,
early 1890s.
Courtesy of
Rev. Alfred M.
Natali, O.S.A.

A portrait of Rev. Antonio Isoleri near the time of the opening of the new church and rectory, early 1890s. Courtesy of Rev. Alfred M. Natali, O.S.A.

Early efforts of secular and Protestant agencies at the "Baby Saving Station" of the Starr Centre Association, providing pure milk to meet the needs of immigrant families in South Philadelphia (ca. 1910). Courtesy of the Urban Archives, Paley Library, Temple University, Philadelphia.

Rev. Pietro Michetti, pastor of St. Donato's Church in West Philadelphia, blesses members of his parish as they prepare to leave for military service in World War I. Courtesy of the Philadelphia Archdiocesan Historical Research Center.

A crowd of angry parishioners surround their pastor, Father Aurelio Marini, O.S.A., at Our Lady of Good Counsel, seeking to prevent his departure after the archdiocese announced the closing of their church in South Philadelphia in May 1933. Courtesy of the Philadelphia Archdiocesan Historical Research Center.

In an almost operatic scene, the parishioners of Our Lady of Good Counsel defy the archdiocese and city police officers in an attempt to prevent the closing of their church in May 1933. Courtesy of the Augustinian Archives, Province of St. Thomas of Villanova, Villanova, Pennsylvania.

who are anxious to acquire sympathy for the Italian people without which no work can be done . . . men who are willing to sacrifice themselves in their own country, for the sake of the hundreds of thousands of souls they can be instrumental in saving to the Church in the United States."[8]

With lavish praise for the Italian character and for a people destined to become the greatest force in America in another generation, the writer declared that their imminent assimilation was no less certain: "In a generation or two the children are likely to become thorough Americans." But this vision rested upon a Celtic cure: "Where Italian men have married Irish wives the issue seems to be blessed with the good characteristics of both nations. The Irish wives wish to get away from Italian quarters. The Italian husbands trust implicitly their Irish wives. The children are enthusiastic Americans who know and love the religion of their parents."[9]

Rejecting the conclusion that proselytizers had converted many Italians, the same observer contended: "They make poor Protestants." Although the Italians were willing to accept provisions and assistance, once these gifts ceased, their Protestantism ceased with them. But with Protestants and other benefactors taking great interest in the children, the need to guard their faith dictated that each diocese and religious order send men for training in Italy as well as implement similar plans for other immigrant groups.[10]

With Catholic opinion never monolithic, some clergy confidently expected and supported assimilation, while others rejected it. A pluralistic approach urged some remedy for the isolation of Italians and Slavs without asking them to forget their past or offering them bribes to abandon their ideals. The slow development of interest until "our almost hopeless situation in planning for their assimilation only then dawned on us," along with the exploitation of immigrant workers and the limitations of parishes and parochial schools, required that more social service agencies be organized. Another appraisal warned, "Do not, however, try to assimilate them too soon; otherwise they will be lost to the Church." Praising the clannish feeling that forms colonies, it held that "as soon as they get away from that center they get away from the Church and from the faith." Too much Americanism spiritually harmed immigrants and their children.[11]

Bishop Regis Canevin of Pittsburgh greatly contributed to the debate by a demographic analysis of "leakage." Rejecting previous figures as exaggerations of defection, which had become widely accepted, Canevin reported a much higher American Catholic population that included about 2.3 million Italians. With not more than 30 percent of later immigrants and their children counted by parish censuses, he argued that the underenumerated population remained as Catholic in America as their counterparts in Europe. Besides nominal Catholics missed by the census, Canevin noted that: "there is a very large number of real Catholic immigrants, 'foreigners' as they are called, scattered all over the United

States, yearning for the Bread of Life, but having no priest, or none whom they can understand, to minister to them."[12]

Pointing out that deaths and return migration had also reduced the figures for recent years, Canevin concluded: "It was a decade of great immigration and of great emigration. These are facts which many writers and speakers have not considered in their estimates of Catholic leakage and losses." To Canevin, the causes of leakage were the shortage of priests, churches, and parochial schools; scandals and schisms resulting from trusteeism; intemperance and poverty; discrimination and persecution of Catholics; proselytizing of orphans and adults of weak faith; but, most of all, mixed marriages. Citing poverty, lack of religious education, indifference, and apathy as factors enabling proselytizers to lure Italians to Protestantism, he noted signs of change among younger ones. Using a widely shared sense of the religiosity of earlier groups, Canevin added: "Had the sons of Italy the robust faith of the Irish and German immigrants of seventy and eighty years ago, or the militant Christianity of their fellow immigrants from Northeastern Europe, the story of our loss and gain in recent years would be vastly different."[13]

With Canevin's findings, the "Italian problem" shifted away from an irredeemable adult generation to its more salvable offspring. A Jesuit priest who had served Italian neighborhoods in Chicago and St. Louis asked: "To whom will the Italian immigrant hand on the pick and shovel with which he now builds the nation's drainage systems and traffic ways?" Convinced of imminent assimilation and upward mobility, he was not so sure of their fidelity to the Church: "Religious indifference is a ravaging contagion among them, and all but inherited." What assurance was there for millions born to parents who themselves were "being turned into the camp of irreligion by default of instruction and emphasis of bad example"? After nearly a half-century of discussion, some observers had only recently discovered the "Italian problem" as an issue for American Catholicism.[14]

Relying upon an oversimplified view of the Catholicity of earlier groups, Italians could not be favorably compared to Irish, Polish, and German immigrants who had come "heroically attached to their religion, well instructed in it, faithful in the use of its Sacraments, and ready to die for it." Unlike peoples for whom the Church was the center of life, Italians were seen as marked by widespread religious ignorance and anticlericalism. An assessment of their piety indicted their frequent celebrations of patron saints as occasions for missing Sunday mass, their street music and cannonading as a temptation to even well-instructed children to stay outside of church during services, and their participation at mass as a reflection of respect for a custom or rule rather than as evidence of real religious conviction. Lacking knowledge and true love of Catholicity, Italians were supposedly unprepared to resist those sects who offered services and activities but aimed ultimately at proselytization.[15]

Similarly, since the Italian home was believed to inflict more harm than help, other agencies had to save the children. And contrary to previous observations on religious indifference, priests could do very little because they were too busy administering the sacraments and other services to Italians. But lay apostolates offered similar services at the settlement houses for children of all ages. Despite ambiguity and ambivalence in these assessments of culture and character, the emphasis on saving the children signaled a new direction in Catholic efforts on behalf of Italians.[16]

On the eve of an attempt by the Archdiocese of New York to carry out a systematic study on dealing with Italian children, a preliminary report asserted that they were more remiss in meeting their religious obligations. But while parental indifference and inability, along with a lack of adaptation between parish and child, were cited as basic causes, instead of blaming Italians alone, it perceptively declared: "The fact of the matter is that [the] Italian portion of the flock has run beyond us; has grown so fast as to confuse us; has made demands which, under the pressure of other work, we have called too exacting; and has tempted many of us to believe that the task of adequately meeting these demands is so clearly impossible as to be not worth our while to attempt."[17]

Seeking to avoid the debate over nationality parishes for Italians, the report called for parishes "specifically adapted to their needs." The pastor who "holds the Italians in the hollow of his hand," with gentleness and patience, incongruously testified to the need for methodical supervision. The report sensitively described how immigrant occupations, high birth rates and large families, scandals (whether real or the propaganda of anticlericalism), rejection by other Catholics, and their own failure to grasp such new customs as money offerings discouraged Italians from meeting their religious obligations. But despite failures and imperfections, the Italian whose personal and cultural traits remained conducive to Catholicism was "not ready really to abandon his religion, at the behest of the institution that tries to bribe him to commit this baseness."[18]

The author of the report found that the plight of Italian children presented special problems. Unlike in English-speaking cases, the child in immigrant families had a peculiar "moral disadvantage" of knowing more than his parents about the language and customs of their new society: "This inevitably secures for him both a power to defy and an opportunity to deceive, which is impossible in the case of the average child. Consequently, the worker who is looking after the child's interest will have to take more than ordinary pains to keep in touch with the home and to control the false impressions which arise in the mind of the parent, with regard for instance to places of amusement, or school regulations, or the rules and demands of the parish."[19]

This perception captured a key problem in the immigrant family—what sociologists would call "marginality," or "the dilemma of the second generation." But such efforts as a Catholic settlement house program that reportedly had won back five hundred children in one neighborhood exemplified the more practical solutions for working with Italian families and their offspring. Although parents were not disposed to educating children beyond the minimum prescribed by the law, plans for industrial schools and candidates for the priesthood particularly deserved greater support. Above all, the specially trained pastor was identified as the final answer to the problem. As a member of the Italian apostolate in New York City had claimed, "other things being equal, it is the Italian priest who is best adapted to provide for all the spiritual needs of his fellow-countrymen." With this refocusing, the "Italian problem" was no longer so much a matter of the Holy See, bishops, and petitions as it was of priests, parishes, families, and children.[20]

At the annual meeting of the American Federation of Catholic Societies in 1915, Father Francis C. Kelley, president of the Catholic Extension Society, made a distinction between "self-supporting groups" and "missionary groups" that had great implications for subsequent thought on immigration. Early Catholic immigrants, mainly the Irish and Germans, as well as later French Canadians, Poles, and Slavs, had been "self-supporting" groups who usually settled together and took care of themselves. By building churches and schools, training priests, and organizing teaching orders for women, they developed the Church for their own protection. Kelley added: "It was not so much a question as to what the Church did for them as what they did for the Church." Wherever these groups settled, they solved by themselves the problem of religious care, became assets to the Church, and did not suffer great losses. With a memorable metaphor, Kelley declared that "the salt water of the Atlantic has not tainted the freshness of their Faith."[21]

Kelley asked what was needed to ameliorate the religious condition of immigrants while America was improving them in other ways. His answer was that Catholics themselves, like secular and non-Catholic groups, had to do more to alleviate the crowding, congestion, and bad housing that brought disease and delinquency in the city. By "practical praying" and the practice of civic virtues, he called for the establishing of Catholic social settlements and clubs, day nurseries, and the training of workers. Kelley urged Catholics to reconsider their attitude, "one of too much suspicion without investigation," toward nonsectarian agencies that helped immigrants and the poor by opening playgrounds, free libraries, and free bathhouses. He cited a priest who had said, "We ought to find out the good in these agencies, and see if we can't cooperate more." Denying that salaries destroyed the ideals and efficiency of charity work, Kelley exhorted Catholics to embrace professional social work and praised the graduates of Chicago's Loyola University: "They are the beginners in a field we have scarcely touched, and they will become more important to us as the years go on."[22]

While faulting Catholics for ignoring recent immigrants, Kelley refuted objections to the retention of the language of the homeland by eloquently defending cultural pluralism:

The mother-tongue is doomed to die in America, and yet it cannot be killed. It is a tie that binds the immigrant to the very best that was in his native land. It is a good thing that it dies hard. It is no burden to carry around. To lose it too quickly means that an immigrant people tends to feel contempt for their parents and the Faith of their fathers. The immigrant should be taught his language, should be encouraged to preserve it. It is safer to let his great-grandchildren lose it than to let his children forget it. The man who is ashamed of the country from which he came is not likely to be bound to the new country by anything but self-interest. It is better for us to have immigrants with hearts right than to have them singing the Star Spangled Banner; for what the Star Spangled Banner represents will be loved more by the man who respects the land of his forefathers than by the one who has forgotten it in his love for money and position.[23]

His concept of the "missionary group," which included Italians, Mexicans, and some Slavs, referred to peoples who had not been trained to help themselves or who did not do so for other reasons. He believed that Italians were no less Catholic in America than in Italy; indeed, they were even more so because they attended church out of choice. In contrast to the war on religion in Italy, education offered hope in America, but quick action was needed because among all immigrants, the Italian was "the least tenacious of the language and traditions that bind him to the best that was in his own country."[24]

Kelley even found opportunities in the limitations of immigrants. If their religion had too much emotion, it could be used as a foundation on which to build something better. If their priests did not come to America, many American pastors had learned their languages. And if some peoples did not understand American conditions, it was because we did not try to make them understand. The overall answer was clear: "Schools, schools, schools and more schools; sisterhoods that will sacrifice themselves; priests that will starve for them; a press to speak for them and money to support them all. Are you trying to find a solution for your home missionary difficulties? There is no need to look long and far for it. It has been in front of you for fifty years. It is money: cold cash and personal service."[25]

Kelley proposed establishing an immigrant department within the Church Extension Society that would be financed by a "missionary quarter," an annual collection in every parish and diocese in the country. He ended with an impassioned plea: "Let this night be a new Holy night. Let Toledo be a new Bethlehem.... Make a slogan of the 'missionary quarter,' and you will solve the immigrant problem."[26]

Father Frederick Siedenburg, S.J., another pioneer in Catholic social work as head of the sociology program at Loyola University of Chicago, also addressed the 1915 meeting of the federation. Asking whether immigration was an asset or a liability to the nation, he summarized data on its volume, number of Catholics, motives, geographical distribution, occupations, and social, economic, and religious conditions. While other groups remained strong as Catholics in America, the Italian situation was less hopeful. Not as reliant as either "the persecuted Pole or the sturdy Slav," Italians in their churches and organizations were "often weak if not altogether wanting, while the Italian parochial school is still lost in the land of the future."[27] Siedenburg quoted Peter Roberts, a noted social scientist and reformer, on the unprecedented task ahead: "Never in the history of the world has a religious organization faced an obligation such as that confronting the Roman Catholic Church of the United States." Siedenburg emphatically rejected objections to immigration by noting that false arguments on assimilation, once used against Germans and Irish, had no more validity when applied to Italians, Jews, and Slavs.[28]

While priests, scholars, and activists debated the problem of how to meet the needs of immigrants, they were also reconstructing American Catholicism. And they increasingly recognized that the parish eventually would be not enough by itself or in its familiar form. While the efforts of American Catholicism had not been well appreciated, sometimes even by immigrants themselves, modern social work had now become an imperative part of the solution.

Popular Piety, Socialism, and a Murder Plot

As American Catholic scholars and policymakers pondered threats to the fidelity of immigrants, another aspect of Italian piety attracted the attention of less sympathetic observers in Philadelphia. It was not concern over losing one's faith but the undesirability of having it at all that prompted the critics of what organized religion, especially Catholicism, did to its adherents. On the occasion of a visit to Villanova College by Archbishop Diomede Falconio, apostolic delegate to the United States, in May 1904, a speaker alluded to "the fierce conflict between capital and labor that is giving strength to the destructive principle of socialism." On the next day, police arrested several reputed Italian Socialists at the feast day celebration of Mary Magdalen dePazzi. Taking aim at the *festa*, leaflets distributed to the crowd demanded, "Down with the priests! No more buffoonery! Down with superstition!" Other flyers, written in Italian, referred to "clowns and hypocrites, infected with rottenness," and called the Church "a big barracks." Other notices declared: "Make a show of your puppets, for the Sunday has come to pocket money," and "Down with the assassins of Giordano Bruno! Hurrah for Free Thought!" Warned of an impending plot against Isoleri, police mingled with the crowd as the procession began. As one man, throwing leaflets from an Eighth Street trolley, was arrested, two others, one carrying a loaded revolver, who began blowing whistles, were also taken into custody.

While no further disturbance took place, policemen closely guarded Isoleri until the procession reached the church.[29]

After mass, the procession left the church to wind its way through neighborhood streets. Behind American and Italian flags, a band, acolytes, boys and girls with candles, and parish sodalities, some 2,000 participants bore the statues of saints past the estimated 20,000 spectators who were lining the sidewalks. Behind a man who staggered under the weight of a crucifix that he carried alone, Isoleri walked with two other priests. In the final unit, sixteen men escorted a statue of Mary Magdalen dePazzi, which was so heavy that the group was relieved every half block. Men and women forced their way through the crowd to affix tributes to their favorite saint. By the time the procession returned to the church, the statues were covered with bills of various denominations and items of jewelry. Along with the patron of the parish, the statue of Saint Rocco, another popular icon, was completely cloaked in money.[30]

On the day after the celebration, Isoleri declared that the report of a murder plot by Italian Socialists was actually due to overzealousness by the police. He acknowledged that some tension with Socialists had persisted for several months before culminating in the events of the previous Sunday. When he had denounced them as atheists and deep-rooted anarchists a few weeks earlier, they sent a petition with about two hundred signatures to city officials asking them to stop the procession, which they described as a "mercenary scheme, concocted by the priests to fill their pockets with money earned by hard-working Italians." After considering their objections, Mayor John Weaver had granted a permit for the parade three days before it was to take place. The police assigned extra men to protect the priests, with six of them staying close to Isoleri throughout the ceremonies, and to arrest anyone who might interfere with the parade. Isoleri maintained that the Socialists, after their failed attempt to prevent the parade, had sought revenge by denouncing the clergy, but their arrests led police to conclude that they had intended to murder him. Despite Isoleri's disclaimer, the incident disclosed the existence of radical politics and internal tensions in the Italian quarter.[31]

While anticlerical observers saw only superstition and exploitation, some Catholics also made unfavorable assessments of this sort of folk religion. In contrast to accounts in the secular press, the *Catholic Standard and Times* reported that the procession was witnessed by a respectful crowd, without any disorder marring the solemnity and joy of the day, and denied what other newspapers had said. It stated that the amount of money offered to the various saints had been greatly exaggerated and that police protection could not have been better and deserved thanks. But the emphatic denial of disorder could not obscure an implicit defensiveness about public celebrations of folk piety by Italians. Although quaint and colorful, they were being called into question by other Catholics, who preferred more dignified expressions of faith. Yet the *festa* was a part of Italian Catholicism that could not be easily eliminated without risking the further alienation of Italian Catholics themselves.[32]

In the next year the parish observed the feast day of its patron saint without any public disruption or threat of violence against Isoleri. One newspaper linked its account of the event to the May Day procession of the Virgin Mary at the Church of the Gesú, a Jesuit parish in North Philadelphia. The similarities between the two events suggested the difficulties that archdiocesan authorities might face if they attempted to curb such celebrations of the saints. Although these exuberant expressions of piety were not far removed from similar programs by other Catholics, the Italian display of religiosity on city streets, which often attracted reporters and photographers of the secular press, elicited chagrin from more straightlaced coreligionists. After Germans had first challenged the cultural uniformity of Irish American Catholicism, Italians had become a later source of diversity. But while American Catholicism had to decide what type of faith was to be preserved, it also had to choose *whose* faith was to be preserved. And in attempting to integrate its ethnic components, American Catholicism deemed the expression of popular piety as one more part of the so-called "Italian problem."[33]

Preserving the Faith:
Rhetoric and Action

In the early twentieth century, with the number of new arrivals increasing and Protestantism eager to serve them, American Catholics still had to find an effective strategy to meet the challenge posed by immigration from Italy. The eventual solution expanded organizations and activities within the parish while introducing social services by agencies outside of it. Whether within or outside of the parish, these programs often followed a course that vacillated between cultural preservation and assimilation. When based on the premise that language meant faith, some efforts retained an emphasis on traditional culture. When laced with gratuitous references to "sunny Italy" by American priests on public occasions, however, such utterances had the appearance, without the reality, of pluralism. Other programs more clearly advocated assimilation. And if Presbyterian or Methodist proselytizers sought to make Italians more like Protestant Americans, Catholic advocates of assimilation often seemed to be trying to turn them into Irish Americans.

With a new century, the Archdiocese of Philadelphia initiated an ambitious plan that eventually included the founding of parishes and parochial schools, the opening of membership in older parishes, a special apostolate for priests, and the extension of social service agencies and programs. It also involved a sharp, sometimes bitter, verbal war waged from the pulpit as well as by newspaper articles and editorials and at nearly every groundbreaking, cornerstone laying, and building dedication at which bishops and priests addressed the public. The archdiocese not only used these means to serve Italians but also to secure its own future by attempting to offset the perceived threat of the dreaded proselytizers. With this phase of the campaign to solve the "Italian problem," the issue of immigrants and "leakage" did not disappear but simply moved to new arenas.

The first step occurred when the Missionary Sisters of St. Francis opened a day nursery and sewing school at 744–746 South Tenth Street in June 1901. After many years at St. Mary Magdalen dePazzi's parish school and girls' asylum, the nuns had found "a fresh outlet for their zeal" through new charitable and educational work that introduced Catholic social services to Philadelphia's Italians. By 1904, this work included an industrial school, with nineteen sisters caring for 500 children in the nursery, along with a kindergarten, evening classes for girls, and another 500 pupils at Our Lady of Good Counsel School. Although their building was dedicated on the Feast of Saint Joseph, it would have been more appropriate two days earlier on the Feast of Saint Patrick. Archbishop Ryan blessed each room while a choir of Italian girls sang hymns. Assisted by priests from Our Lady of Good Counsel, Ryan ended with Solemn Benediction in the chapel, where a statue of Saint Joseph, adorned with shamrocks and an Irish flag, denoted the teaching staff of thirteen sisters of Irish descent (but only six Italian members of the order). A newspaper account captured the moment: "Thus Ireland is endeavoring to repay Italy for the faith sent her from Rome by aiding in preventing the little ones of sunny Italy from being robbed of their faith."[34]

Whether the Irish were sisters only harmlessly showing some ethnic pride or whether their decorations meant something more serious, such events had underlying nuances and unanticipated consequences. On such occasions, Italians were given an ambiguous message about their own ethnicity when they were both praised and criticized by the same speaker. When many Italians, including the consul, gathered for the blessing of Our Lady of Good Counsel School in September 1901, Monsignor Daniel I. McDermott, pastor of Old St. Mary's Church, objected to the false patriotism that asked immigrants to forget their past, and he declared that their language enabled them to preserve the best sentiments of their race. Another Irish American priest urged them neither to be blind to the necessity of Christian education nor to be surpassed by other Catholics in their efforts to preserve the faith of their children. Cardinal Martinelli, before an audience standing out of respect for him, asked them to emulate Germans and French Canadians, whom he praised for their support of parish schools. Whether by Irish American priests or by a cardinal from their own country, Italians were being invidiously compared to other groups. And by emphasizing the exemplary behavior of others while denigrating the beliefs and practices of Italians, these clergymen also demeaned them. For these missionary efforts as well as the attempt to define Italian character, it was only the beginning.[35]

While the archdiocese opened new parishes for Italians, it could not easily provide schools for them. Italians could neither afford nor understand the wisdom of paying to send their children to parochial schools, as had the Irish. But if the Church was to succeed in preserving the faith of Italians, it had to enable young people to find wholesome and instructive activities. In the summer of 1902, Father Michael C. Donovan, the pastor of St. Paul's, organized a night school in manual arts along with catechetical instruction at his parish. Two years later the Knights of Columbus asked that two financial contributions, which it had made to the archdiocese, be used for a mission house or "settlement" in the Italian section of the city. Using the term "proselytizers" to identify the threat, the largely Irish American Knights were actually continuing their defense against Protestantism. Responding to the Knights' request, Father Henry T. Drumgoole, a St. Charles Borromeo Seminary professor, placed the newly established Catholic Settlement Society into a recently obtained fifteen-room building, the Madonna House, at 814 South Tenth Street in September 1904. In the next month, when Archbishop Ryan presided at its first meeting, the society appointed a laywoman as resident manager and another as a visiting nurse. Emulating its secular and Protestant counterparts and initiating a far more extensive program than any previous effort, the Madonna House, also known as the Italian College Settlement, became the first Catholic settlement house in Philadelphia.[36]

In November 1904, Archbishop Ryan called for a mass meeting to discuss the situation facing "the children of our Italian brethren in the city of Philadelphia." Seven priests at two churches were deemed inadequate to minister to the estimated 115,000 Italians in the city, or to the 85,000 in the most congested district. But even well-organized parishes with sufficient clergy were no longer enough for a faith put in jeopardy "in this age, and in the circumstances of American life the growing generation is forced to breathe." Similarly, the parochial schools were unable to accommodate more than one-tenth of the 15,000 to 20,000 children. Ryan was also concerned over sectarian groups "ministering formally and solely to Italians" with generous financial and moral support from organizations and wealthy coreligionists. He noted a new Episcopalian venture, St. Martin's College, at Eighth and Catharine Streets in the heart of Little Italy, where boys, admitted as residents and students, would be given religious instruction. Ryan hoped that the Catholic Missionary Society, with continuing support from the Knights of Columbus, could follow the model of non-Catholic organizations.[37]

As Ryan's plan unfolded, the task was made more urgent when the handful of priests tending to the needs of Italians was reduced by the sudden death of

Father Agostino Cogliani, a young Augustinian at Our Lady of Good Counsel, following surgery for appendicitis. Only a few days after Cogliani had taken part in the blessing of the bells at St. Mary Magdalen dePazzi, Isoleri delivered a eulogy at his funeral. As a native of the province of Avellino, Cogliani's Southern Italian origins made him a priest whom the community could ill afford to lose.[38]

The archdiocese, meanwhile, prepared to implement its settlement house plan. Answering Ryan's call, priests and laity gathered in November 1904, at the Catholic High School, where they sought to preserve the faith in Little Italy from threats posed by "proselytizers and propagandists of infidelity, socialism and anarchy." Declaring that settlement workers in New York City, by going into homes and showing practical sympathy to the people, were doing more than ten priests could do, Ryan gave an impassioned plea for the Italians:

> One cannot look into the black eyes of these little children and see the soul shine forth without feeling that there is something good in them. The Church is one great family and we must not draw the line of nationality in our good works. Our hearts should bleed because these children are growing up without that Christian education which has made their land glorious in history. Therefore you are summoned to this glorious task which should be dear to every Catholic heart, and, in fact, even to non-Catholics, for if these children grow up to be good Catholics they will be good citizens, having respect for legitimate authority.[39]

After Ryan's remarks, Drumgoole described the Madonna House program, which included a kindergarten; sewing, drawing, manual training, and English-language classes; catechism and religious clubs; and trips to local parks for six hundred children and smaller numbers of adults. He praised the resident manager for giving up a better position and studying other settlement houses in Philadelphia and New York before assuming her duties at the Madonna House. Proposing that it become the center for lay activity, its workers would bring the best artists, entertainers, and teachers to the colony to accomplish what no priest or nun, or missions and sermons, could do.[40]

After Isoleri, then Angelo Caruso, the Augustinian pastor of Our Lady of Good Counsel, and other priests spoke briefly, Father Donovan of St. Paul's gave the most noteworthy address. As pastor of a parish where three hundred Italian children attended its school, he was regarded as an authority on the immigrant community. Donovan declared it a privilege "to second the appeal of my Italian brethren in behalf of their extensive flocks and to speak a word in favor of the inhabitants of 'Little Italy,' in whose midst I have resided during the past ten years." Condemning prejudices held even by other Catholics, he averred that Italians had "many excellent traits of character which their American brethren could do well to emulate." Moreover, they belonged "to a race that has never been tainted by heresy." And even when he turned to their flaws, Donovan strongly defended them: "As an Irishman, I cannot afford to be too severe on the occasional breaches of the peace of which they are accused, but justice demands of me to say that the acts of violence, sometimes laid at their doors, are rarely if ever premeditated. but provoked on the spur of the moment by suddenly aroused passion."[41]

Donovan saw the great defect of Italians "to a man of my cloth" to be that "they do not appear to good advantage on collection Sunday." Echoing a popular misconception, he claimed that Irish and German Catholics had practiced generosity to the Church for four hundred years, although they had "not yet attained to such a degree of perfection that we do not occasionally complain of the number of collections." Since Italians were victims of ancestors who had lavishly endowed the Church, Donovan asked "their brethren in the faith, only to have a little patience with them and help them to bridge over the present crisis in their spiritual affairs."[42]

Donovan described Protestant efforts near his own parish that sought "the perversion of the Italians from the Catholic faith." He listed an Episcopalian church and school at Eleventh and Christian; the Italian Presbyterian Mission kindergarten and school at Tenth and Washington Streets; St. Martin's College at Seventh and Catharine; the Chiesa Italiana Cristiana at Sixth and Catharine; the Bedford Street Mission and school at Sixth and Kater; the City Gospel Mission at Sixth and Kater; and a nonsectarian school that occupied an old market house in the past summer at Eleventh and Fitzwater. Among their deceptive, almost coercive means, Donovan included the use of "nonsectarian" as a pure and simple fiction that really meant "hatred and opposition to the Catholic Church"; the nightly display of an illuminated cross at a mission; devotions to the Virgin Mary during the month of May; visits to Italian homes by agents promising "temporal gains"; and even entering St. Paul's during mass in an attempt to lure children away.[43]

Donovan contended that the Presbyterians were the most aggressive, opening "their tents and tabernacles in the very heart of the colony." He offered his appraisal of the situation: "it is vain for us to deceive ourselves by saying that these people are not succeeding. . . . For every convert we receive we lose hundreds of [our] own baptized children, and our non-Catholic friends can well afford to laugh at us. . . . These people are willing to pour out their money like water in the Italian colony today, knowing that in a few years the Italian will be thoroughly Americanized and will contribute his full share to church support, as every other American citizen."[44]

"While we sleep the enemy is awake," Donovan declared. The enemy was not just Protestantism but also the indifference, materialism, socialism, and anarchism as well as the secret societies that had sprung up "like foul weeds in an uncultivated garden" in the Italian colony. He was not surprised that its seven or eight weekly newspapers were anti-Catholic in spirit and tone. But six worthy priests labored in an "impossible situation" among their countrymen: "Had they the tongues of angels and of men they could not reach the whole flock." Indeed, two Augustinians had sacrificed their lives "in the bloom and vigor of early manhood," while another was still being mourned. Among Italian priests, however, Donovan noted: "One of them has borne the burden of the day and the heats of the night in this arduous field of labor for thirty odd years."[45]

Calling for more practical assistance for priests in the Italian colony, Donovan praised the work of the Catholic Missionary Society. The significance of his message, however, was found not only in its substance but also in his place on the program over the lesser role given to the two Italian pastors, thus confirming the direction of archdiocesan policy. With the pastor of St. Paul's speaking about Italians, the archdiocese was expanding its program for them. For Isoleri, with his congregation partitioned by the opening of Our Lady of Good Counsel, his long tenure as the only spiritual leader of the Italians had ended. And despite its immediate and impressive growth, even the Augustinian presence was now compromised, as St. Paul's, at times almost as a special project of the archbishop, increasingly reached out to Italians. The ensuing abutting and overlapping of territorial and nationality parishes, secular and religious priests, and archdiocesan bureaucracy and religious communities left a delicate situation for the future.

The Catholic Missionary Society, meanwhile, increased its solicitation of support for its work in the Italian community. Shortly after the meeting at the high school, Ryan sent a letter thanking participants and inviting them to increase their donations beyond the one-dollar annual membership fee. By Christmas in 1904, the Madonna House was directly seeking contributions along with two older, already existing facilities: the orphan asylum for girls at St. Mary Magdalen dePazzi and the day nursery of the Missionary Sisters of St. Francis on Tenth Street. Their programs also shared the intention to make their young clients less Italian. In their own search for funds, the Missionary Sisters stated:

> We are trying to educate and Americanize the rising generation—to educate these little ones to be good, loyal residents of this city of "Brotherly Love," as well as to train them for a happy citizenship hereafter. The salvation of souls is the greatest work in which we can be engaged, and you can be a helper in this most noble work by aiding us materially to carry it on. We are very much in need of means at the present time, and an offering no matter how small will be gratefully received. The nursery affords an opportunity to poor mothers to seek employment, and have the pleasure of their little ones' company in the evening. We make no distinction in nationality or creed.[46]

Similar nursery programs for Italian children spread to other locations. For example, from its inception in 1907, St. Rita's, a "duplex parish" for Italian- and English-speaking Catholics, planned a day nursery with its new church on Broad Street.[47]

Although later research would confirm that the actual defection of Italians from religious practice as a result of immigration had been exaggerated, Catholics continued to raise their voices against the threat of Protestantism. In December 1909, Monsignor McDermott of Old St. Mary's Church again brought the message to the heart of Little Italy in a lecture delivered to an evening gathering at St. Paul's. While seeking converts on purely spiritual grounds by demonstrating that the superiority of a new faith was commendable, he argued that a newer form of proselytization was tempting the poor by offering them bread and clothing. It was the same strategy, McDermott added, that had been used in the attempt to convert Catholics to Protestantism in Ireland. But by adopting crosses, images of the Madonna, devotions in honor of the Virgin and Saint Anthony, vestments on higher clergy, altars and masses, it relied on what he called "counterfeit Catholicism." And by employing fallen priests and "escaped nuns," McDermott contended that it found its prototype in Judas Iscariot.[48]

McDermott's spirited attack on Presbyterians, however, could not obscure his somewhat inconsistent view of the Italian character. As Catholics, Italians possessed "true doctrines and sound moral principles, religious habits and traditions that are the outgrowth of centuries of Christian teaching and devotion." Yet, he noted, "at times many Italians are not remarkable for the fervor of their piety or fidelity to their religion." McDermott explained that "all the enemies of religion have done their utmost to uproot piety and faith in Italy, and that immigration has freed Italians to a great extent in this country from domestic, social and even religious influences; that their language and character are not understood; that their provocations to violence have been great and their temptations in other directions have been many."[49]

While it was questionable whether Protestants ever exploited the presumed religious indifference of Italians, McDermott had correctly described something else about their activities. Protestants had responded, while Catholics had lagged, in recognizing the temporal needs of immigrants. Moreover, if Catholic efforts were to go beyond the spiritual emphasis of parish life, they had to follow the model of Protestant agencies in offering social services. But McDermott's assessment of the Italian character also resounded with patronizing, if not demeaning, accusations that risked alienating the clientele of such programs.

By 1909, five years after opening the Madonna House, the Catholic Missionary Society provided Sunday schools, sacramental preparation classes, night schools, sewing and singing classes, manual training, fifteen clubs, a gymnasium and sports program, free baths, a library, and a savings bank. In related programs, the Dorcas Society distributed 889 garments, the Shoe Fund gave out 108 pairs of shoes, and a summer program organized outings for children. At the Madonna House, a manager, one assistant, and two residents supervised more than 125 nonresident workers, with slightly more than $10,500 in expenditures from May 1907 through December 1908. By 1909, the Catholic Missionary Society reached well beyond South Philadelphia to initiate similar programs for Italian children in Germantown and Ambler, and it also garnered nearly $16,000 in contributions for the relief of earthquake victims in Southern Italy and Sicily.[50]

As Italians continued to challenge the will and resources of the archdiocese, Archbishop Edmond F. Prendergast asked his pastors for more support in March 1912:

> We are confronting a very grievous situation in the large Italian colony of this diocese. The continuous stream of immigration that has poured into this city in the last ten years has caused a condition of great congestion, making it quite impossible to supply by the usual parochial methods the religious needs of many thousands of these people. Especially is this true of the Italian children who are attending the public schools and receive in their homes no religious care and attend no church or Sunday school. Reaching the age of fourteen, they enter a life of hard work and come thus to manhood and womanhood without religious conviction, ignorant even of ordinary Catholic practice. Yet the vast majority of these children are baptized in the Catholic Church.
>
> We cannot see this sad defection of a large and increasingly important part of the flock entrusted to our care without feeling our sacred duty compelling us to an earnest and efficient solution of this very difficult problem. The work of the Catholic Missionary Society in this respect must be known to you. From its centre in the Madonna House, it has been for the past eight years a force for good, reaching an ever increasing number of these little ones. We have decided that our purpose can best be served by multiplying its activities until it is reaching and caring for all who need its services. As the work of the Society is limited only by its resources, we will increase its means by an appeal to the body of our faithful people. Such an appeal will depend for its success on a proper understanding by the people of the pressing need of this our great Home Mission. Therefore we have thought it best that the Society's work be explained to them, and that they be asked to become contributing members of this missionary movement. We have accordingly empowered the Superintendent of the Society, the Rev. Dr. Corrigan, to carry out these our purposes throughout the diocese. You will therefore of your charity grant him a hearing before your people and an opportunity to seek their aid.[51]

Prendergast's message marked a new phase in the Catholic settlement house movement that had begun with the appointment of Father Joseph M. Corrigan as Drumgoole's successor as director of the Catholic Missionary Society. Having served as an assistant, then as head, at the Madonna House since 1909, Corrigan had introduced its programs to the Germantown section of the city and to Ambler in the suburbs. But the Madonna House also expanded with the founding of L'Assunta House at 1208 Reed Street in January 1912. By the end of 1914, Catholic social services for Italians, beyond South Philadelphia, included the recently opened L'Annunziata (sometimes called La Nunziata) House at Wayne Avenue and Logan Street in Germantown, which was primarily staffed by lay workers.[52]

Religious orders already had or were about to assume new responsibilities. The Missionary Sisters of St. Francis, a long-familiar presence in Little Italy, were the largest contingent. Under Sister Laurenza as superior, twenty-five Missionary Sisters served 152 boys and 128 girls at the Italian Industrial School, Kindergarten, and Day Nursery in its fifteenth year on Tenth Street. Ten sisters tended twenty-six residents of the St. Mary Magdalen dePazzi Asylum for Orphan Girls, where their community, with only a slight break, approached a half-century of service. Some twenty-two Missionary Sisters also taught at Our Lady of Good Counsel School, while ten other members of the order instructed at St. Rita's School.[53]

In February 1914, Prendergast invited the Salesians to take over a building formerly occupied by the St. Francis de Sales Industrial Home at 507–09 South Ninth Street. In August the Don Bosco Institute, under Father Peter Catori, began to provide religious instruction and recreational activities for the public schoolboys of the neighborhood. Through clubs for the spiritual, intellectual, physical, and social improvement of the members, it offered classes in religious and literary subjects along with an evening trade school. Although intended mainly for young Italians, the Don Bosco Institute, located on the border rather than in the heart of the Italian district, accepted other Catholics as members and officers in its programs. In this setting, interacting with other young people, Italians were becoming more acculturated as Americans, if not more Catholic.[54]

Three years after Corrigan's appointment, Father Edward J. Lyng succeeded him as head of the Catholic Missionary Society in September 1915. In the next month, its board of directors, at their meeting to confirm Lyng's appointment, also proposed the Sisters of the Immaculate Heart of Mary to manage the settlement houses in South Philadelphia, where they would serve for the next nineteen years. As support increased, the Catholic Missionary Society further developed its program, quite innovative for Philadelphia Catholicism, at the Madonna Catholic Club. Actors, singers, a mandolin ensemble, and a club orchestra offering dance music entertained when some twenty applicants were admitted. Basketball, pool, and pinochle remained popular activities for other members in October 1915.[55]

While expanding in services and activities, the main objective of the Catholic Missionary Society continued to be the strengthening of the faith among Italians. Social and debating clubs, athletics for boys and young men, along with classes in reading, domestic science, sewing, and home economics for girls and young women, attracted young people and also exposed them to programs for "the spiritual betterment of our Italian children." Its library offered "young ladies and matrons" a reading course taught "by ladies well versed in literature." Similarly, "eminent laymen, doctors, and clergymen" instructed young men in citizenship, English, and elementary branches of education. While "subjects of practical benefit" embraced secular knowledge, the entire program still rested upon religious instruction. The Madonna Guild offered inspirational talks, reports, and assessments of efforts by teachers, workers, and others staffing the Madonna House and L'Assunta House. The agenda of the Catholic Missionary Society in its nursing program to the sick and needy at home offered a striking parallel with that of the secular Starr Centre: "Oftentimes the defection or the salvation of a soul in our Italian colony is traceable to the sick room or to the death bed of one of the family. Misery is quick to remember kindness, and frequently from an outside source kindness results in the abandonment of the old faith."[56]

The Catholic settlement house was an innovation that required new roles and actions. Departing from their traditional labors, the sisters at the Madonna House and L'Assunta House distributed clothing to the poor, found employment for members of families, and advised probation officers, charity visitors, and other social service workers. But whether religious or laity, like their counterparts at other agencies, Catholic settlement workers went outside their own facilities to serve clients and claimed to have made an average of 10,000 home visits each year. Workers were told to become acquainted with district physicians and nurses and to enlist their skills when medical needs were discovered through home visits. The overall program, however, as indicated in a 1919 report, retained its religious priorities: "Its main objective is to afford catechetical instruction to the children of the surrounding district and thus to preserve them from Protestant influence. To facilitate the accomplishment of this purpose, instruction is offered free in sewing, embroidery, knitting, cooking, etc. Music is offered at the nominal sum of ten cents a lesson. A playground affords recreation to thousands of children during the summer months."[57]

In response to public schools, neighborhood settlement houses, and other proselytizing threats, Catholics continued to make catechetical instruction, the preparation of sacramental candidates, and the preservation of the faith the principal objectives of their work among Italians. Despite its earnest enthusiasm, the Catholic program suffered from limitations of information, perception, and application. Even Lyng, the director of the Catholic Missionary Society, stumbled when he declared that the large immigration from "sunny Italy" would produce "a sturdy race of American-Italians, in whom shall be combined the poetic and active imagination of the Tuscan with the aggressive spirit of the American." Lyng's hyperbolic view of regional origins—by this time overwhelmingly Southern Italian—put his authority on immigrant life into question. But another priest, speaking on Church history, offered an even more dubious view by declaring: "Again it is a monk from the 'Isle of Saints and Scholars' who brings both faith and learning to far-off Northern Italy."[58]

Under Irish American priests at St. Paul's parish, the Madonna House, intended for Italians but with a mixed constituency, faced potential ethnic conflict in staffing and programs. With W. A. S. Lapetina, president, and Joseph A. Lombardi, secretary, the Madonna Catholic Club had George H. Bonner as its director and other Irish Americans as officers. Similarly, Miss McGrath ran the Circolo di Sant'Agnese, the young ladies' guild, while Irish American women guided other activities at the Madonna House. Among the inherent risks of seeking to preserve the faith of Italians by Irish Americans, the Catholic Missionary Society had to neutralize its own ethnocentrism.[59]

When Irish Americans showed insensitivity, their efforts only offended Italians. For St. Patrick's Day in 1916, the members of the Circolo di Sant'Agnese decorated the Madonna House "in emerald hue and the entertainment included songs, recitations, monologues and stories relating to Ireland and Irish subjects" as well as performances of "Robert Emmett," a drama on the life of the Irish patriot, for the benefit of St. Paul's Church. Whether wanting to be Irish was only an Irish delusion or an actual aspiration of some Italians, such means of reaching young Italians were at least tenuous, if not offensive.[60]

The Catholic Missionary Society pursued its social and spiritual programs by aligning them with territorial parishes. While the Madonna House became affiliated with St. Paul's in 1912, L'Assunta House was assigned in 1915 to Annunciation Church at Tenth and Dickinson Streets, with Father Victor Strumia, recently arrived from Italy, as its spiritual director. The energetic Strumia immediately organized the Benedict XV Italian Catholic Club at L'Assunta House. Within two weeks its fifty members had elected officers and begun a campaign for contributions, assisted by young women of the Santa Lucia Club, to benefit Italian soldiers in the war raging in their homeland. But like the Madonna House, L'Assunta House harbored a mix of participants. While Miss Dowd gave classes in English and stenography, Miss Flocco taught art needlework. Under Strumia's influence, L'Assunta House projected a different ambiance than the more Irish-tinged Madonna House. Unfortunately for its Italians, however, Strumia was soon appointed pastor of a parish outside of the city. But even with leaders such as Father Strumia, Catholic agencies still faced a huge challenge.[61]

When the Catholic Missionary Society met in April 1916, speakers called for increased efforts among Italian children whose unmet spiritual needs placed them "in imminent peril of losing their faith." Public officials blamed crime and delinquency on the lack of adequate religious instruction. Moreover, they described experiences with young Italian offenders in the Juvenile Court of Philadelphia and urged more support by the laity for Catholic Missionary Society programs. But other efforts were already being made in the Italian quarter of the city.[62]

While the Catholic Missionary Society pursued an assimilationist approach by thrusting Irish history and culture upon Italian children, another effort took a different course. In December 1910, a group of prominent Italians, seeking to purchase a recently vacated building with a very unusual history at the southwest corner of Tenth and Bainbridge Streets, initiated plans for a temporary shelter for new arrivals from Italy. Formerly the residence of a wealthy Catholic woman whose plan for a new religious order, with herself as its superior, had been rejected by Pope Pius IX, it had been willed, along with most of her estate, to Archbishop Ryan. After he sold the building in 1900, it became the Home for Hebrew Orphans. But with the king of Italy and his government rumored to be involved, another plan for the property was now emerging.[63]

The Society for Italian Immigrants dedicated its new building in January 1912 with the claim that its charities and educational programs were the first of their kind among Italians in Philadelphia. Its previous work had already been awarded a gold medal at the Turin Exposition in 1911 for "doing the greatest good for the Italians in foreign countries." While Joseph P. Bartilucci, president of the society, delivered the opening address at the dedication, other speakers included Archbishop Prendergast, Vice Consul Carlo DeConstantin, and John DiSilvestro, a community leader. Reportedly holding a special interest in the day nursery, Prendergast blessed the building and its departments and commended the objectives of the institution. Officers of the society and other leaders in the Italian American community—Emmanuel V. H. Nardi, Henry DiBerardino, Harry B. Gandolfo, Antonio Raggio, John M. Queroli, Frank Rosatto, and Frank Travascio—also participated. While the project appeared to be mainly controlled by Italians, the presence of Prendergast along with his chancellor, Monsignor Charles F. Kavanagh, priests from Our Lady of Good Counsel, and other clergy indicated that the archdiocese had more than a symbolic role in the project.[64]

The Society for Italian Immigrants planned a broad program with a day nursery for over one hundred children, under the Missionary Sisters of St. Francis; a free medical dispensary and pharmacy staffed by "twelve of the best Italian-American doctors and two druggists"; a naturalization school; and an information bureau for immigrants. Its building was also intended to house the Italo-American Alliance of the United States, the Philadelphia Section of the Italian Colonial Institute, the St. Vincent DePaul Society chapter of Our Lady of Good Counsel Church, and the Italo-American League of Philadelphia. The Società di Unione e Fratellanza Italiana pledged a six-dollar yearly membership tax together with contributions to fund the work of the society. Despite broad support from the Italian community, with the outbreak of the World War and the cessation of immigration, this once promising project failed after only a few years. The Society for Italian Immigrants was forced to cease its activities and sell the building.[65]

With the collapse of this project to aid Italians, the momentum swung back to programs under religious auspices. The Catholic Missionary Society retained its role in the "congested district" with social services that still entrusted the care of Italian children to Irish Americans, the self-proclaimed keepers of the faith in America. As Italians spread beyond their original neighborhoods, the archdiocese organized parishes for them with authoritative reminders of the exemplary standards set by Irish Catholics. But parishes that reaffirmed personal identity and facilitated group cohesion remained bunkers of persisting ethnicity for Italian Americans. And one parish, in particular, was assuming a crucial place as their religious experience continued to unfold in Philadelphia.

CHAPTER ELEVEN

Saving the Faith of Southern Italians

In its early years, St. Mary Magdalen dePazzi Church had played a unique role while a small immigrant population, mainly of Ligurian origin, was building its communal life in Philadelphia's emerging Little Italy. By 1898, however, when a larger population required another church, the archdiocese founded Our Lady of Good Counsel. But along with the increased number of Italians, their changing regional origins gave the newer parish its significance. As Italians from Southern Italy and Sicily flooded into South Philadelphia as well as made their way to other locations within and beyond the city, for the Archdiocese of Philadelphia the task of meeting their spiritual and temporal needs was not only becoming greater but also more complicated. And in the older area of settlement, if St. Mary Magdalen dePazzi remained in some sense the titular cathedral of Little Italy, Our Lady of Good Counsel became almost immediately the more popular parish for the newly arrived masses from the Mezzogiorno.

Rather than being some sort of institutional parvenu, Our Lady of Good Counsel had roots that reached as far back as the dispute that had placed St. Mary Magdalen dePazzi under interdict a generation earlier. For example, of the trustees who had challenged Archbishop Wood's authority in 1867, Agostino Lagomarsino, now among the *prominenti* of Little Italy, emerged as a benefactor of Our Lady of Good Counsel. Whether his support was intended to ensure that Southern Italians would be contained within their own parish or whether it represented a more sincere effort on its behalf, Lagomarsino's Ligurian origins did not keep him away from the "meridionali" at Our Lady of Good Counsel. And even though St. Mary Magdalen dePazzi was known as the Genoese church and

Our Lady of Good Counsel as the parish for Southern Italians, Lagomarsino was probably not the only Ligurian to find his way between the two. At his death in 1906, his funeral, by being held at the newer church, confirmed his place in its history, and the Augustinians continued to acknowledge his generosity a decade after he died.[1] The plight of the ill-fated Chapel of Our Lady of Pompeii under its enigmatic pastor, Clemente Cardarelli, undoubtedly was an even broader link to the past. But if that stormy encounter renewed a provocation that the archdiocese had to resolve if it were to keep the peace as well as to maintain its own authority, it also presaged the unfortunate demise that ultimately awaited Our Lady of Good Counsel after a brief, meteoric trajectory among Philadelphia's Italians.

"One of the most picturesque in the city"

The comparative volume of activities demonstrated that the opening of Our Lady of Good Counsel altered the position that St. Mary Magdalen dePazzi had long held within the immigrant community. Despite boundaries drawn by the archdiocese, the new church and its older neighbor, only two blocks away, represented at least mildly invidious alternatives of membership as well as an inevitable competition for limited local resources. At first the two churches, by offering similar services on different dates, shared primacy in the community. When Leo XIII died in 1903, Our Lady of Good Counsel held a Requiem Mass attended by the consul general of Italy and members of Italian religious and beneficial societies. With Father Matthew Vacchero, an assistant at St. Mary Magdalen dePazzi, acting as subdeacon, Isoleri also participated in the mass. On the next day some fifteen hundred men and women, representing eighteen Italian organizations, paid tribute to the pope with a massive street procession and a service at St. Mary Magdalen dePazzi, where Father Angelo Caruso, pastor of Our Lady of Good Counsel, assisted Vacchero at the mass. In the next year, when Father Agostino Cogliani, an Augustinian, died, Vacchero acted as master of ceremonies for the Requiem Mass at Our Lady of Good Counsel. This cooperation suggested that Catholic ministry to Italians would be shared by the diocesan priests at the older parish and Augustinians at the newer one.[2]

Our Lady of Good Counsel, however, almost immediately became the greater provider of services to the Italian community (see Table 11.1). By 1901, while St. Mary Magdalen dePazzi still had a larger school enrollment, Our Lady of Good Counsel recorded nearly twice as many baptisms, First Communions, and marriages. By June 1903, despite its limited space, the number of students at Our Lady of Good Counsel (427) exceeded St. Mary Magdalen dePazzi (335) for the first time. An early assessment claimed that children born in this country quickly adopted American ways while their parents remained "clannish in the

TABLE 11.1. Participation in Parish Activities, 1901–1913:
St. Mary Magdalen dePazzi and Our Lady of Good Counsel

Year	Baptisms		First Communions		Marriages		School Enrollments	
	StMM-deP	OLGC	StMM-deP	OLGC	StMM-deP	OLGC	StMM-deP	OLGC
1901	595	1,021	139	250	85	221	495	422
1902	638	1,203	162	228	116	242	352	320
1903	677	*	171	*	121	*	335	427
1904	718	*	168	*	117	*	447	805
1905	677	*	190	*	110	*	491	921
1906	693	*	159	*	109	*	473	1,002
1907	713	*	166	*	128	*	424	1,128
1908	701	*	114	*	106	*	412	1,123
1909	643	*	140	*	112	*	466	1,029
1910	724	*	179	*	109	*	482	894
1911	660	*	384	*	143	*	396	1,030
1912	653	2,000	241	640	129	458	438	948
1913	617	2,072	176	624	114	547	449	924

Source: Questiones: Annual Report (submitted by pastors of each parish, January 1, 1900–January 1, 1901, to January 1, 1913–January 1, 1914); *Annual Report of the Superintendent of Parish Schools of the Archdiocese of Philadelphia* (1901–1913), PAHRC. An asterisk means that no data were reported. The school figures represent the enrollment reported at the end of the year given.[3]

extreme"; indeed, "this may be readily seen at their churches." Placing the newer church "in the centre of the Italian quarter," which had shifted westward, the same writer, while distorting the composition of its membership, depicted its colorful ambiance:

> The congregation is one of the most picturesque in the city. On Sunday mornings or holidays may be seen congregated at the entrance of the church typical Italians, from Genoa, Venice, Rome, Florence, Sicily and other parts

of the Italian kingdom. To an experienced eye costumes indicate the exact spot from which the wearer comes. As a rule, bright colors and massive jewelry predominate, and, curious as it may appear, the men are generally better dressed than the women. For that matter, many Italian women follow the custom of the Papal court of going to church without a hat, the head being covered with a "mantilla." Young girls, however, disport the hat of their American sisters. The interior of the church also is thoroughly Italian in the style of architecture and decorations. A great deal of ostentation may be seen everywhere, but above everything the sacred music and songs are scarcely to be equaled anywhere else in Philadelphia.[4]

By December 1903, when another newspaper reported that more than two hundred pupils occupied fourteen small rooms in Our Lady of Good Counsel's school, the actual number was already much higher and rising rapidly. Seeking more space, Father Caruso, after purchasing two properties on Montrose Street, announced plans for a remodeled building, with the Young Italian Catholic Association on the first floor and classrooms on the upper two floors. By June 1904, the superintendent of parish schools reported 805 pupils at Our Lady of Good Counsel, almost twice as many as the 447 pupils at the older parish. When the annex was dedicated in March 1905, Isoleri and Vacchero, further refuting any visible rivalry, joined with the Augustinians in the opening ceremonies.[5]

By 1912, the sacraments at Our Lady of Good Counsel were administered about three times more often and the school enrollment had become more than twice as large as at St. Mary Magdalen dePazzi. Our Lady of Good Counsel had now eclipsed St. Mary Magdalen dePazzi, at least by these measures of its presence in the Italian population. This pattern would not merely persist but would also grow much larger in the future. At the same time, for St. Mary Magdalen dePazzi, while the number of baptisms, First Communions, marriages, and school enrollments fluctuated from year to year, parish activity generally remained almost as high at the end of the period as it had been in previous years.

Student enrollments followed an even more consistent pattern for both schools throughout the early years of the century (see Table 11.2). Although kindergarten appears to have been accepted by immigrant parents, the largest numbers of children attended school in the first or second grade, but there followed a noticeably sharp and steady decline thereafter.

The preponderance of pupils in the early grades may have reflected variations in age distribution in the population, with many more younger children in these families, and some families may have moved to other areas as their children grew older, but the stable pattern over the years indicates that there were two other factors. Unlike the Irish, who strongly supported parochial schools, Italians were much more inclined to prefer public schools for their offspring. But the declining number of Italian children in later grades was even more likely

TABLE 11.2. School Enrollments by Year, 1906–1915:
St. Mary Magdalen dePazzi and Our Lady of Good Counsel

Grade	1906		1909		1912		1915	
	StMM-deP	OLGC	StMM-deP	OLGC	StMM-deP	OLGC	StMM-deP	OLGC
K	101	194	0	170	0	129	0	100
1	220	463	251	225	224	197	201	211
2	46	192	100	254	57	253	74	245
3	60	102	34	195	56	234	45	242
4	21	25	41	125	62	86	26	68
5	23	22	25	22	25	23	21	41
6	0	4	15	18	8	16	13	34
7	0	0	0	8	6	10	10	24
8	2	0	0	12	0	0	0	12
Totals	473	1,002	466	1,029	438	948	390	977

Source: Annual Report of the Superintendent of Parish Schools of the Archdiocese of Philadelphia (1901–1916).

to have resulted from their early entrance into the labor force. Families who expected their children to contribute to household income did not support long-term education.

While a large congregation, reflected by enrollments at its school, secured the place of Our Lady of Good Counsel, other aspects increased its influence in the community. First, unlike efforts to secure the faith of Italians through Americanization or through Irish American models of character and culture, Our Lady of Good Counsel offered to its people a different basis for consciousness and cohesion. And by being under the jurisdiction of the superior general of the Augustinian order in Rome rather than under the archbishop of Philadelphia, it had another advantage. Despite some early misbehavior of its priests that led to the appointing of an American provincial, the archbishop's powers were limited, and all personnel decisions were made in Rome. In contrast to a diocesan parish, with only a pastor and one assistant, dependent on the archdiocese, the monastery of Our Lady of Good Counsel had seven or eight members and the resources of its religious order. Even more important, it may have been a transplanted version of the relatively autonomous type of parish known as a "chiesa ricettizia," long found in Southern Italy and in this case somewhat modified as an immigrant institution, which gave it greater sovereignty.[6]

The place of Our Lady of Good Counsel was further enhanced by the agreement made by Propaganda Fide, Archbishop Ryan, and the Augustinians in 1899, which assigned all Italians in Philadelphia, except for members of St. Mary Magdalen dePazzi, to the care of the Italian Augustinians. This exception only remained until Isoleri's death, when his parish and church building were to be transferred to the Augustinians. As the Italian population grew from about 30,000 to 160,000 by the mid–1920s, the archdiocese ignored the agreement by establishing new parishes under its own control. But the agreement, despite being abrogated, had undeniably invested the Augustinians with the care of Italians in Philadelphia.[7]

Our Lady of Good Counsel initially enjoyed the protection of a powerful patron, Archbishop Sebastiano Martinelli, the apostolic delegate to the United States from 1896 to 1903 and previously superior general of the Augustinians. He had invited the Italian Augustinians to organize the church in 1898, presided at its cornerstone laying in May 1899, sang the High Mass at its dedication in December 1899, and blessed its new school in 1901. When Martinelli confirmed eight hundred children at Our Lady of Good Counsel in 1902, it was one of the largest groups ever to receive the sacrament in Philadelphia. But a telegram recalling him to Rome made it one of his last public acts in the United States. Almost to his final days as apostolic delegate, Martinelli's support for Our Lady of Good Counsel ensured its importance in Little Italy.[8]

While Martinelli's presence raised the status of Our Lady of Good Counsel, so did visits by other church dignitaries. When the new apostolic delegate, Archbishop Diomede Falconio, a Franciscan, visited Villanova College in 1904, the parish modestly received him. It provided an even grander reception two years later when some thirty-one Italian Catholic societies, with the church, school, cloister, and neighborhood homes decorated with papal banners and American flags, greeted him. Escorted by Father Caruso, Falconio joined Archbishop Prendergast, secular clergy, Augustinians, and Salesians in the ceremonies. One account captured the moment: "Handsome girls, with great black eyes and dark complexions, shriveled old women wearing large gaudy handkerchiefs for head coverings, youths and old men whose general appearance indicated the laborious occupations by which they earn their living, craned their necks and gazed at the scene."[9]

Beyond the colorful, but patronizing, accounts that newspapers often gave of events in Little Italy, this occasion marked the first time that a papal delegate had been entertained by a union of religious societies in America, as Pope Pius X noted in a letter to them. On the first evening, Henry Croce, president of the Young Men's Sodality, provided the reassurance that the apostolic delegate perhaps had sought on this occasion: "We are Catholics and proud of it, and I know that I speak for all the societies represented here when I say that the hands of heretics cannot tear the Catholic faith from our hearts. Whatever is said of the progress of the Protestants among the Italians, we know it is false. We know that the Italian who has gone among the Protestants is unhappy because of his state and his treason. Tell the Holy Father that the Italian youth of America are and always will be Catholic."[10]

On the next morning, when Falconio offered mass, assisted by two Augustinians, he was the first papal delegate to officiate in a First Communion program in any American parish, distributing the sacrament to 350 children. In the afternoon, when he confirmed 1,400 children, an unanticipated moment added drama to the event when efforts to remove a woman who had fainted—amid shouts of "Fuori! Fuori!" (Outside! Outside!), first misunderstood as "Fire! Fire!"—caused a brief panic before calm was restored to the crowded church. As important as these ceremonies were for Philadelphia's Italians, they also were unprecedented in American Catholic history. Yet, only an assistant priest represented St. Mary Magdalen dePazzi, since another engagement had summoned its pastor, by a convenient coincidence, out of town. When Isoleri finally came to pay his respects to Falconio, he was symbolically surrendering the primacy of his own church to the Augustinians.[11]

The priests at Our Lady of Good Counsel extended their ministry both within and beyond Little Italy. Since 1902, Father Caruso had offered mass and other devotions in the camps of Italian construction workers on the edge of the city. By the end of the decade, not to be outdone within South Philadelphia, the parish was holding its own street procession, followed by a High Mass, on the Feast of Our Mother of Sorrows. Its priests were also celebrating masses on Sundays in the Chapel of the Holy Rosary at the Society for Italian Immigrants on Tenth and Bainbridge Streets. By 1916, while the activities of its Circolo Cattolico Italiano included visits to the poor and hospitalized of the parish, Father Thomas Terlizzi, now pastor, offered a week-long mission for 125 Italian inmates at Eastern Penitentiary. As Our Lady of Good Counsel ambitiously embraced its role in the Italian district, further recognition came when the Italian consul general, vice consul, and a visiting captain of the royal navy presided at closing exercises at the parish school in June 1914.[12]

As the largest nationality parish for Philadelphia's Italians, Our Lady of Good Counsel recorded over 10,000 marriages and 75,000 baptisms during its thirty-five-year life span. As a social service center, it offered English-language instruction and an employment bureau. It provided the anchor, after the founding of St. Rita's (1907) under the American Province of the order, and St. Nicholas of Tolentine (1912), as its own mission, of an "Augustinian triangle" in South Philadelphia. Through priests who promulgated a strong sense of *italianità*, Our Lady of Good Counsel sent a clear message to immigrant families. While the Catholic Missionary Society sought to preserve the faith of Little Italy by making its residents more like Irish Americans, the Italian Augustinians encouraged them to retain their own culture and identity. Father Caruso, undeterred by Prendergast's presence, thus spoke in his native language to urge Italians to preserve their traditions at the dedication of the parish school in 1905. But by consistently delivering a similar message, the Italian Augustinians challenged archdiocesan authority and invited trouble in the future.

The founding of Our Lady of Good Counsel had undeniably encroached upon an older parish and its esteemed pastor, who had disagreed with the need for another mission. The immigration of Southern Italians, who favored the new church, had left the future of St. Mary Magdalen dePazzi uncertain. But while residents may have regarded St. Mary Magdalen dePazzi as a parish for Northern Italians, its congregation also included Southern Italians. And although Church authorities defined parish membership by street boundaries, Italians could still ignore them. Isoleri's response, however, to Our Lady of Good Counsel—especially by delivering the sermon at the funeral mass for Repetti, its first pastor, in 1899, as well as on numerous other occasions—was clear. Despite his misgivings, the Augustinians had eased the pastoral burden at his own church. Whether disturbed by the partitioning of his flock, Isoleri accepted the Augustinians and shared their concern for the temporal and spiritual needs of Little Italy. In return they not only deferred to him but also provided the companionship that had been denied to him for nearly thirty years. But Our Lady of Good Counsel neither completely erased the presence nor the influence of the older church and its pastor, it had reduced the place of St. Mary Magdalen dePazzi in the Italian community.

An Old Church in a New Era

As Italians exceeded the capacity of a single church to accommodate their spiritual needs, St. Mary Magdalen dePazzi entered into a new chapter of its history. No longer the only Italian church nor the largest one, with each passing year the increasing disparity between St. Mary Magdalen dePazzi and Our Lady of Good Counsel in the number of persons receiving the sacraments or children attending parish schools attested to a changing situation. If St. Mary Magdalen dePazzi had approached some kind of twilight, it rested upon the shift to Southern Italian immigration. More than just another church for new arrivals, it required a clergy responsive to the "elemento meridionale," which could neither be ignored nor absorbed by a community previously dominated by Northern Italians. Although Ligurians had practiced their own "folk Catholicism," the religiosity of Southern Italians posed a new challenge. While the first pastor of Our Lady of Good Counsel, Guglielmo A. Repetti, was from the North, his successors tended to be, like most of its congregation, Southern Italians. But if his parish reflected change, then the older St. Mary Magdalen dePazzi, despite more Abruzzese and Neapolitan members even there, retained its historical primacy as the first Italian church, with its Ligurian founders and prosperous residents of Little Italy, while its pastor remained a spokesman for all Italians in the city.

St. Mary Magdalen dePazzi endured other threats during these years. In February 1903, when a candle ignited altar hangings at vespers, some parishioners fled while others stayed to fight the rapidly spreading flames until firemen reached the building, but not before the main altar and ceiling had been destroyed. Resuming the activities that made other Philadelphians take notice, some fifteen hundred marchers, following three musical bands in "an event that would have impressed even the most casual spectators with its importance," celebrated the patronal feast only three months later. Behind flag bearers, marshals, and acolytes with their emblems of Catholicism, Italy, and America, the Society of the Holy Child and parochial school students led parade units. Parish societies carried statues of saints "almost hidden under the votive offerings that had been attached to them," with San Giuseppe, the favorite, cloaked in the dollars of the devout. After more acolytes came Isoleri, Vacchero, and a lone Augustinian, then the girls of the orphanage. Four men in teams bore the great statue of Mary Magdalen dePazzi, weighing over 1,200 pounds, as the procession made its way over Montrose Street to Eighth, then Fitzwater, Seventh, Carpenter, then Eighth, Montrose, and Seventh again, before returning to the church. With children and women at the upper windows of houses, an estimated 20,000 spectators lined the sidewalks. A newspaper reported: "Little Italy reposes its affairs in the keeping of numerous saints, some of them almost unknown to those who consult only church calendars printed in English." St. Mary Magdalen dePazzi, rising from the ashes of a devastating fire for the second time in its history, had recaptured the attention of the city with its street procession.[13]

In July 1903, when its people grieved over the death of Leo XIII, some fifteen hundred solemn mourners and eighteen Italian societies preceded a dirge-playing band, which was followed by members of the Society of the Holy Child and women dressed in black. Inside the church, Father Vacchero, assisted by the Augustinian Caruso, with Isoleri giving the sermon, celebrated a mass with a symbolic catafalque and silver casket, and with Verdi's *Requiem* sung by the choir. In the next year, after escaping the alleged assassination plot, Isoleri again led the celebration of the Feast of Mary Magdalen dePazzi. And in 1905, "thousands of Italians from all parts of the city" watched a procession "conducted with the enthusiasm and fervid piety of the Latin race."[14]

While Isoleri was the most consistent benefactor of St. Mary Magdalen dePazzi, others contributed to its renewal after the 1903 fire. Isoleri first honored the saint for whom he was named by endowing a statue of Saint Anthony of Padua and then his own father by one of Saint Francis of Assisi. After the death of his friend, Father Joseph Alizeri, Isoleri obtained a statue of Saint Joseph and later, in memory of Father James Rolando, a statue of Saint Vincent dePaul, the founder of the Vincentian order. Parishioners from Civitella Messer Raimondo in the Chieti province of Abruzzi donated a statue of Saint Peter for the main altar, before Isoleri obtained Saint Paul as its appropriate companion. He honored the Irish with a statue of Saint Patrick along with the transfer of a $2,000 bequest, made long ago by a benefactor named Patrick Quinn, to the building fund. Two bells were added to the church towers in October 1904. One bell, donated by Isoleri, weighed over 2,000 pounds and was placed over the side altar of Anthony of Padua, for whom it was named. The other bell, weighing 700 pounds, a gift from two converts, Mr. and Mrs. P. Harton, in memory of their deceased daughters, Frances and Magdalen, was placed over the altar of Francis of Assisi and carried his name. The participation of Fathers Cogliani and Donati from Our Lady of Good Counsel in the dedication ceremonies indicated the ongoing amity between the two Italian parishes. Two weeks later, Isoleri expressed his gratitude for his recovery from an illness twenty-five years earlier by presenting a statue of Saint Mary Magdalen de-Pazzi for the main altar of his church. Then, in August 1905, newspapers reported the start of excavation for a parish hall, gymnasium, and library, but only a modest facility was opened on Beulah Street behind the rectory later in the year.[15]

Isoleri's efforts culminated in the simultaneous celebration of the 300th anniversary of the death of Saint Mary Magdalen dePazzi (in 1607), the fiftieth anniversary of the original "chiesa vecchia" (1857), and the consecration of the renovated "chiesa nuova" in May–June 1907. Not even heavy rains dampened spirits as the congregation and the community joined in the "triple anniversary." Members of founding families—Bartilucci, Berretta, Lapetina, Raggio, Lagomarsino, Mangini, Pizagno, Repetto, Dondero—as well as more recent arrivals comprised the planning committee, which also included Captain Thomas Furey, who represented not only the veterans of "la guerra per la liberazione degli schiavi" (the war for the liberation of the slaves) but also, in Isoleri's words, "the good Irish who attended the Old Italian Church, and did so much for the building of the old and new one, until the always growing number of Italians and Jews forced them, against their will, to leave this neighborhood."[16]

After a novena that began on May 18, Archbishop Ryan, Bishop Prendergast, local pastors and priests, and clergy from other dioceses participated in ceremonies over the next two weeks. Fathers Caruso, Paolo Gentile, Pietro Michetti, and Lamberto Travi represented other Italian churches in the archdiocese, while Father Giuseppe Ascheri came from his parish in Lodi, New Jersey. Along with Count Attilio Fabbri, the delegate of the Italian government, members of the Società di Unione e Fratellanza Italiana joined in the celebration.[17]

The principal event was the consecration of the renovated church, with its main altar a gift from Isoleri himself in memory of his parents. On the evening of May 25, after meeting Archbishop Falconio's train at the Broad Street Station, Isoleri escorted him to the church, where the apostolic delegate blessed a large crowd of clergy and laity to the ringing of its bells. After a procession carried the relics of saints to an altar, Isoleri joined several priests and Franciscan seminarians in reciting morning prayers, and then an honor guard took up an all-night vigil. At 5 A.M. on the next day, the bells began to peal again. From 5:30 A.M. onward, Isoleri and other priests celebrated masses at the altar of the lower church. At 6:30 A.M., Falconio, assisted by Isoleri, said mass in the chapel of the Missionary Sisters. Shortly after 7:00 A.M., undeterred by dark skies and a steady downpour, Falconio began the consecration ceremonies, which continued for three hours. At 10:00 A.M., Ryan and Prendergast led another procession to the upper church, where, accompanied by an Italian orchestra and mainly Irish chorus, they celebrated a Solemn Pontifical Mass by Mercadante.[18]

In his sermon, Father Serafino Pierotti, a Franciscan from Newark, New Jersey, praised Isoleri for building the school, convent, orphanage, rectory, parish hall, and library. Despite limited means and difficult sacrifices, Pierotti asserted, as Isoleri himself frequently had, that the intercession of the patron saint had brought success to these projects. Pierotti noted that Isoleri, after carrying her reliquary from Italy, had purchased her statue for the church, now admired for over thirty-eight years, with his own money. The congregation saw the usually stoic Isoleri weeping throughout the sermon. But his tears, as Isoleri later noted, were sweet: "Dolci lagrime!"[19]

After a dinner in the parish hall, Falconio exhorted Italians at Solemn Vespers to emulate American Catholics by supporting the Church. He urged them to be worthy of their ancestors, to increase their honor and glory in a foreign land by living as good Catholics and citizens in their adopted country. A Te Deum, Benediction, and veneration of the saint's reliquary ended the program. Falconio had displayed his sensitivity to the plight of immigrant Italians, who were currently demeaned and disparaged by the mounting calls of Nativist Americans for restriction, if not total exclusion. He had, instead, proposed that the solution was to be found in the retention, rather than in the eradication, of their Italian identity.[20]

After bringing Falconio to the train station the next morning, Isoleri rushed back to his church for another mass, with its own sense of what it meant to be Italian and Catholic in Philadelphia. Offering it for living and deceased benefactors—David Botto and Agostino Lagomarsino for donating side altars and Patrick Quinn for leaving $2,000 in his will to the pastor—he also remembered the Carrolls, Greenfields, McKennas, Gallaghers, Sweeneys, Scotts, Fureys, Devines, Drurys, Morrises, Haggertys, Cochrans, and Wilsons, among others. These were the "buon irlandesi" who had supported the Italian church, especially during the struggle to keep it alive in defiance of the bishop and vicar general.[21]

The "triple anniversary" auspiciously ended on Sunday, June 2. After Isoleri presided at a Solemn High Mass in the morning, he and his fellow clergy sang

Solemn Vespers later in the day. Several hundred persons—young members of the Society of the Holy Child, leaders of other parish organizations, and a band of musicians—filled the church with their banners and floral tributes. Despite rain so heavy "come se mai fosse piovuto" (as if it had never rained before), as Isoleri observed, a crowd eagerly awaited another procession through the streets of Little Italy. While the children had confidently insisted throughout the morning that it would happen, in Isoleri's eyes it was nothing less than a miracle when the rain finally stopped just before the start of the procession.[22]

Under still cloudy and menacing skies, the huge procession uniquely demonstrated the strength and permanence of the Italians and their community in Philadelphia and also proclaimed their Catholicism. After seven bands leading the parade, acolytes with crucifixes and censers carried its real meaning. The Society of the Holy Child, four women's sodalities, fourteen men's societies, all with banners and statues, and then the girls of the orphanage preceded the many clergy. A contingent of men carrying a statue of Mary Magdalen dePazzi in a state of ecstasy brought the parade to its final stage. Two more women's sodalities protected the statue from behind. Then, barefoot supplicants, bearing torches in testimony to favors granted by the intercession of the saint, provided the conclusion.[23]

Isoleri's reflections on these events give us a sense of how far his faith and parish had come in their American journey. Remarking on the money and jewelry placed as offerings on the statues and recalling earlier disruptions, he noted that a solemn manifestation of Italian Catholic faith had taken place in a foreign and Protestant country without the least disturbance. Aware of the still unresolved Church-state problem in his homeland, Isoleri added that a similar celebration could not have occurred in Italy or even in Florence, the saint's own city.[24] He also wryly assessed the piety of his flock:

> No one, however, can say, (alas), with St. Mary Magdalen dePazzi that in regard to Italians *may their faith follow the path of the sun.* Despite what is preached to them, many people have too much regard for processions and parades, and neglect the more essential obligations of their religion; and often place the whip and the broomstick in the hands of the enemies of religion. And what can be said about the drunkenness, rapes, blackmail, and homicides that are increasing in frightening numbers everywhere in the United States? And they still dare to pretend to be moralists, people that methodically make war upon priests and negate God, rendering themselves accomplices to crimes committed by their disciples, without law and without belief! *What little intelligence they have!* This procession of St. Mary Magdalen dePazzi grew from little, like the mustard seed; and the reason therefore that so many statues are carried in it is to prevent the various societies from celebrating their own annual feast day and carrying the statues of their own respective saints on the streets; that would render religion, almost

each week, ridiculous; . . . as has already been done by extravagant funerals with their carriages, flowers and bands, even on the part of the poorest people, sometimes dying in a hospital, and whose children on the very next day must be put into an orphanage.[25]

Despite their specious piety, Isoleri found better behavior among the Italians in America than in their homeland. The many police on the scene only had to deal with ordinary misbehavior or to prevent the great crowd from impeding the passing of the procession. Protestants, he added, who respectfully observed this spectacle of Catholic Italy transported to America wanted to be informed each year of the day when it would take place. The procession meant that while Italians found freedom in America, they did not in Italy, which appeared to him to be falling into barbarism or worse. Once again, citing the famous words of Massimo D'Azeglio, "We have made Italy; now we must make the Italians," Isoleri addressed the political situation in his native land. In his judgment, many Italians still obstructed unification. This failure to seek unity and concord based on the religious faith, blessed by God and his earthly vicar, that defended it from foreigners and united all of its territory, made Italy into a "servant" or a "house of sorrow." And with hostility toward religion along with class hatred, no nation could prosper. With these words, Isoleri concluded his own appraisal of the "triple anniversary" of 1907.[26]

The View from the Outside

While Italians expressed their religious and ethnic patrimony in street processions, other Philadelphians found opportunities to form their own judgments of them. In October 1908, a newspaper article marking the 225th anniversary of the city's founding focused on "Philadelphia's Great Italian Colony." It placed churches at the center of the community, with a drawing of St. Mary Magdalen dePazzi, a large photograph of the newly opened St. Rita's, and pictures of their pastors along with Father Caruso of Our Lady of Good Counsel (but without his church) across the top of the page. The local press had evidently concluded that religion not only represented an important aspect of life in Little Italy but also provided readers with a means of becoming better acquainted with its people.[27]

The place of St. Mary Magdalen dePazzi in the Italian community as well as its visibility to the rest of the city remained reflected in its public celebrations. By 1910, when the Feast of Saint Mary Magdalen dePazzi had become even greater in size and importance for Philadelphia's Italians, another newspaper account, reporting a crowd of worshipers in the church and a throng on the street, described the event as "longer, more solemn and more magnificent than ever before." It was made "exceedingly picturesque" by "all the colorful bits of apparel and drapery that came from Italy for just such occasions . . . visible here and there, both on personal apparel and on the shop and house windows." The scene gave observers "a glimpse of the real municipal feast day in the convent towns of Girgenti and Castrogiovanni on the sun-lit bay of Naples." Some "two score of flags, Italian and American," led the procession, followed by altar boys, a thousand girls in bridal array, and finally four young men with the statue of the saint on their shoulders. The bearers frequently lowered the statue so that "one of the white-frocked fanciula [*sic*] might bow her pretty brown head" and affix an offering. As "the figure of the Magdalen" was carried to the altar and the church bell rang, "thousands on the streets and pavements lifted their hats and inclined their heads, breathing a prayer for forgiveness, for forgiveness is the great teaching of the life of the saint whose memory was being celebrated." The final paragraph related the conclusion of the day: "And the feast was not at an end after the procession either, because there was a general merrymaking in the colony all evening, and the hundreds of guests were regaled with the much-loved cicoria in brodo, which, in English, is nothing more than a kind of spinach soup, and lingua di manzo inumido [*sic*] and polpettine alla Napoletana."[28]

In depicting life in the Italian district, the press was not merely describing events and conditions but was also defining Little Italy and its people for other Philadelphians. Faulty facts, such as equating the biblical Mary Magdalen with the Florentine Mary Magdalen dePazzi, sometimes muddled reality but still served to put an image of Italians into place. Almost everything about them was colorful. They now came from the "sun-lit bay of Naples"; they could be alternately Italian and American; their religion was highly expressive and somewhat exotic; foreign terms still disguised their food and cooking. Exaggeration and distortion, clichés about culture and character, and an almost operatic libretto of community life did not merely portray Italians but also assigned them to their place in the city.

The Lyre of Little Italy

Now adjusting to the changing circumstances of his parish, Isoleri continued to find, as he had since his seminary years, great satisfaction in his literary endeavors. A few years after arriving in Philadelphia, he published his three-volume *Lira Leronica* (1876–1878) to raise funds for the girls' orphanage at the Italian Mission. In later years he sought diversion from his pastoral burdens and his efforts brought him private comfort and public recognition. His six-part book, *Un Tributo di Divozione a Santa Maria Maddalena dePazzi*, consisting of a biography, sayings and miracles, indulgences and privileges, and prayers, devotions, and a novena, was described by an American bishop as "a treasure of spiritual reading" when it was published 1883. In the next year its English translation drew high praise in a scholarly periodical on Catholic affairs. In the same year, Isoleri also published *La Strenna,* a catechism and prayer manual in Italian, to counteract Protestant proselytization. While usually sold to generate financial support for parish projects, these publications were distributed without cost to indigent Italians.[29]

Martin I. J. Griffin, the most prominent intellectual in the Philadelphia laity, recognized Isoleri by inviting him to become a charter member of the American Catholic Historical Society in 1884. Although endorsing Griffin's plan for the society, Isoleri refused the invitation because of "other pressing business." But Griffin still sought Isoleri's opinion on several issues. In 1897, when the *Catholic Citizen,* the archdiocesan newspaper of Milwaukee, published a controversial series on "The Neglected Italians," Griffin wrote Isoleri for his views. Isoleri replied that he was unaware of the articles but believed that "the Ecclesiastical authorities would know best what to do." He gave a stronger response to another issue raised by Griffin. Underlining his words, Isoleri stated that he never knew, nor could he ever conceive, of any Irish influence that obstructed Italian American applicants to the local seminary. Turning to his own financial support of prospective seminarians, he wrote that parents, whether rich or poor, "were too anxious to use their children to make money," while in other cases "the signs of Ecclesiastical vocation vanished." Through their occasional exchanges, when Griffin sought answers on Italians as Catholics, Isoleri's intellectual authority clearly reached beyond his immigrant audience.[30]

In subsequent years, Isolari continued his literary efforts. In 1900, he translated from Italian into English, *The Life and Works of St. Mary Magdalen de Pazzi,* a biography by another author that had served as a basis for his own writings on the saint. Nine years later, he translated *The Life of St. Leonard of Port Maurice,* which paid homage to a native of Porto Maurizio, on the Riviera di Ponente about twenty kilometers from his own hometown of Villanova d'Albenga. In fulfillment of a vow, he paid the publication costs for these works, which were sold to benefit the church, parish school, and orphan asylum of St. Mary Magdalen de Pazzi. He ensured that his work in Philadelphia was noticed at higher ecclesiastical levels by sending handsomely bound copies to Pope Pius X and Cardinal Rafael Merry del Val, the Vatican secretary of state, in Rome. In reply, along with his own appreciative comments, Merry del Val wrote: "His Holiness heartily thanks you and blesses you, together with your mission."[31]

Isoleri's unpublished writings not only served as personal exercises but also disclosed, as when he had looked on the pines near Albenga, a poetic sensitivity to the world of nature. In the lingering winter of 1906, as Isoleri peered from a train window, he painted what he saw in classic sonnet form. Although after writing it in Italian, he never left his own English version, it loses little if we offer it in translation here:

On the Train

Be gone now, cruel winter, tyrant
That scourged fields with its storms,
And even silenced their sounds,
And was cause of even more misfortune.

Let spring come to take away the sorrow
Of the morning and the boredom of evenings,
The spring that is the best time of the year
With flowers, and songs and honest pleasure.

And yet, as the night brought rest
To our tired limbs, so that the next day
We can return to our usual work,

So winter itself gives even to the earth
The rest owed to every thing,
That spring, like Midas, then changes quietly into gold![32]

His *Souvenir and Bouquet,* although intended as a memoir of the "triple anniversary" of 1907, contained far more when it was published four years later. It included a parish history, newspaper articles, church documents, photographs of priestly comrades along with Isoleri's poetic tributes to them (as well as by them to him), and sermons, essays, and devotions to the patron saint. Many of these items testified to Isoleri's reputation. The archdiocesan newspaper lavishly praised him in its account of Little Italy's triple festival. The American correspondent of an Italian newspaper identified him as the "patriarch of Italian priests in North America." What Isoleri wrote on its title page succinctly conveyed what his years as a priest had been about: "Reverente e grato depose, come un mazzo di fiori ai piedi della Santa" (Reverently and gratefully placed, as a bouquet of flowers at the feet of the Saint). The artful juggler of words had placed his bouquet of panegyrics at the feet of Mary Magdalen dePazzi.

Isoleri expressed much about himself in messages from his pulpit. For Sunday masses, he meticulously prepared long texts that were carefully transcribed onto handwritten pages. While the seeds of creativity easily burst from his fertile mind, he revived the scripts of past performances after the intervening years allowed his flock to forget what they may have already heard. Many of his homilies bore both an earlier date and a later one. On occasions such as funerals, Isoleri jotted his thoughts on cards, scraps of paper, or even between the printed lines of his business correspondence.

In funeral services, Isoleri, disregarding the grief of family members, bluntly reminded mourners of their religious duties. At the funeral of Mark Malatesta, an Atlantic City hotel owner and the scion of a family who had helped to build the Italian community in Philadelphia (but who had not always met his obligations as a practicing Catholic), Isoleri raised such concerns. He revealed that after receiving last rites shortly before his death in August 1903, Malatesta had declared

> that he very much regretted his past neglect of his religious duties and sincerely intended, had God restored him to health and spared him longer, to lead in the future the life of a practical Catholic . . . [But] in the city we must die! In the country we must die! At the seashore we must die! . . . People may become renowned . . . reach high places, yet one day, they must die. But alas! Very few think of it. . . . It is a sad thought and most men wish to call it off. . . . In this case, it is certainly remarkable that whilst in my experience I did not see the imminent danger, and even the family doctor could not exactly tell, yet death came so swiftly.[33]

He sometimes addressed the profligacy of younger members of the immigrant community in the face of the temptations that they found in American cities. But Isoleri also emphasized the redemptive role that religion offered, as in one instance in February 1904:

> How many lives are cut off in their midst? And oh! How many lives, if longer, would only be a heavier curse! For with many young men, it is not as with wine, which the older it gets the better it becomes; but just the reverse . . . the son of a good mother, the first-born and the pride of his mother . . . one of the altar boys in the old Italian church, a fairer, a more pious and providing boy than he, there could not easily be found at the foot of the altar . . . he may have wandered away a little. . . . But, oh! God is good! A long and painful sickness, patiently borne, with the strengthening grace of the Sacraments, often received, in the midst of his days, brought him to the gates of death, nay, to his grave. But we hope he was able to say on his death bed: Thou hast delivered my soul, Lord, that it should not perish.[34]

The spiritual risks, for Isoleri, far outweighed earthly pleasures in immigrant life. And at the death of a young person, when mourners were likely to include others of a similar age, Isoleri called attention to the redeeming grace offered by the sacraments, while he also sternly warned them of the eternal consequences of a sinful life: "we must make some sacrifices to save our souls. . . . By a terrible sickness, patiently borne, and sanctified by the Sacraments, the deceased has atoned for past neglect—in part at least—and God only knows what would have become of him if he had been taken off . . . do not build your hopes on a death-bed repentance. Do not lead a careless life . . . to neglect Mass on Sunday, or to neglect the Easter duty once is amply sufficient to send one to hell."[35]

In other cases, however, Isoleri provided comfort to mourners. Extolling Matilde Berretta for leading "the life of a good, practical Catholic, faithful at her prayers, at Mass, at the Sacraments," he declared that she had left "to all who knew her, but more particularly to her children a precious legacy," which "they should endeavour faithfully to imitate," as he conducted her services in December 1903. On another occasion, he remarked on the poignancy of life and death in the immigrant community at the funeral for Teresa and Giulia Barbieri, a mother and daughter who both died in August 1908. Speaking in Italian, Isoleri contrasted the daughter's sudden death at the beach with the mother's death on her bed of sorrow after a lifetime of anguish, and then he dramatically reenacted their bittersweet reunion before the tribunal of God. In these moments, he usually returned to the essential lesson of his New Year's Day homily at the start of the new century, which always remained the dominant theme of his own life and message to his congregation—the gift of life and the need to serve the Lord.[36]

While St. Mary Magdalen dePazzi was losing its once-unique position within the Italian community, its pastor's influence was now reaching a broader public. When the *Ettore Fieramosca,* an Italian cruiser, docked at Philadelphia in November 1906, Isoleri spoke at a reception for its officers at the Hotel Walton before an audience that included the Italian ambassador and other dignitaries. Having only been asked "at the eleventh hour," Isoleri declared that he had not expected to speak at the affair, but as "part and parcel of them for over one-third of a century," he could hardly refuse. With candor, he boldly added, "What I don't know, pardon me, about the Italians of Philadelphia is hardly worth learning."[37]

Promising to be brief, because a great crowd of Italians had gathered on Broad Street to greet the officers, Isoleri recalled similar celebrations in previous years. Mentioning the 1876 Columbus Monument dedication and the visit of another Italian naval vessel, the *Vittorio Emanuele,* he saluted the memory of the king with the words, "God rest him!" Although as a priest he had long agonized over the "Roman question," Isoleri now toasted the king who had helped to bring it about. Shifting in his remarks to the character and status of the thousands of Italians residing in Philadelphia, he maintained that they had earned the respect of city authorities "by their thrift, hard work, honesty and patriotism." Comparing them to the celebrated and victorious knights led by Ettore Fieramosca in the early fifteenth century, Isoleri argued: "Many of them landing here the poor sons of a glorious mother had a harder task than the memorable thirteen of the *disfida di Barletta*; but by hard work and sober living, they acquited themselves nobly, conquering their ground inch by inch, and earning every day more the respect of those of their fellow citizens who know them well."[38]

With some hyperbole he maintained: "There are not wanting today, and there were never wanting in the past, well educated people, artists and literary men, of whom any nationality might be proud." But the distance from their native land as well as the trials in their adopted one had only intensified Italians' energies and love for both countries. He urged the commanding officer of the *Ettore Fieramosca*, "when you return to the Bella Italia . . . bring this good tiding to Italy: the Italians of Philadelphia love the country of their birth!" Then, turning to John Weaver, Isoleri intoned: "Mr. Mayor, the Italians of Philadelphia love the country of their adoption!" Although he had first written into his text that they "are trying to become good law-abiding citizens," Isoleri deleted this phrase from the final version.

Nearing his conclusion, Isoleri made an oddly prophetic promise. Proposing that if it ever became necessary to fight either for the Italian green, white, and red, or for the American red, white, and blue, then asking for both banners so that he might entwine them, Isoleri assured his listeners that Italians would prove themselves to be again like the knights of Ettore Fieramosca. Moreover, he himself would serve as their chaplain if he were still "living and not too old." He then raised his glass to the President of the United States, the King of Italy, the State of Pennsylvania, the city of Philadelphia, the army and navy of Italy, the officers and crew of the *Ettore Fieramosca,* and to "all the Italians of Philadelphia."

In his notes on his remarks, however, Isoleri revealed that tensions had lurked behind the occasion. Only two days earlier, Italian American leaders, including Charles C. A. Baldi and Emmanuel Nardi, had invited him to speak. Frank J. Bartilucci, a parish supporter, provided a ticket and, along with Rocco DiNubile, escorted him to the affair. But by giving his address in English, he had rejected the request that he speak in Italian. And his notes concluded with an especially bristling comment. When the Italian ambassador, accompanied by Consul Giacomo Fara Forni, paid a visit to him on the day of the reception, Isoleri remembered that, "tired of waiting all day, I had gone out."

Two years later, Isoleri found another occasion to assert his convictions and position when Philadelphia observed the 225th anniversary of its founding. In attempting to celebrate ethnic diversity in October 1908, the city's Founders' Week actually expressed a somewhat racist and European-centered view. One event presented English, French, Swedish, Dutch, Irish, German and Welsh music, with several Italians only performing as singers of grand opera. The program included African Americans in "Negro jubilee and dance pastimes" intended to introduce "the old-time Plantation Melodies, sung by real African Negroes and followed with a dance." As for Native Americans, "the advent of the white men in any country has meant civilization or the annihilation of barbarians. . . . The North American Indian has always been a barbarian and he has rapidly lost his identity."[39]

Not to be excluded from ethnocentric revelry, the Italians celebrated Columbus Day with a huge parade and the dedication of a monument to the memory of Giuseppe Verdi in Fairmount Park. Isoleri, meanwhile, prepared a homily for a mass and Te Deum at St. Mary Magdalen dePazzi. He began with a long quotation from a letter by William Penn, an extraordinary device for a Catholic priest who had often vigorously defended his faith against Protestantism. But, shifting to a more familiar theme, Isoleri declared that "Colombo è il nostro" (Columbus is our own), when he resumed his familiar salute to the historical and spiritual significance of Columbus.[40]

In 1909, when Columbus Day was officially observed for the first time by the city, Italians staged another large parade to honor the Genoese explorer. On the same evening, at a Knights of Columbus banquet at the Bellevue-Stratford Hotel, Archbishop Ryan called for the canonization of Columbus. Governor Edwin S. Stuart commended the "Latin races," adding that he had never seen more orderly men than the members of the Italian societies in the earlier events of the day. Amid the praise for Columbus and despite the compliments for Italians, not one Italian was listed among the guests attending the event. By 1912, when Columbus Day had become a legal holiday in thirty states, the archdiocesan newspaper claimed that it was nowhere more appropriately observed than in Philadelphia. Italian churches celebrated with special masses. Italian fraternal societies, with their bands and banners, paraded through neighborhood streets to the Columbus Monument in Fairmount Park. But at the very moment when Italians held these events, Columbus was being expropriated from them.[41]

Italians and their community, however, were losing more than their venerated hero under the impact of Irish American Catholicism, mainstream patriotism, and assimilation. For along with the acculturation of Italians as American Catholics, Isoleri and his church, which had once been their only spiritual home, would be among the casualties. The "triple anniversary" and similar events, which symbolized the place of church and pastor in Little Italy, were becoming gestures to a rapidly fading past. With the growing size and influence of Our Lady of Good Counsel, St. Mary Magdalen dePazzi had taken a reduced role in South Philadelphia. And as employment and housing opportunities redistributed Italians, Isoleri, who had long pleaded for assistance, would now receive it—but not in the form that he had sought. Rather than by the assignment of new priests to his own church, it would be by establishing new parishes. And as his parish, no longer the only church for Italians, diminished in influence, Isoleri, like an earlier Genoese navigator, also had to find a new course across an uncharted parochial sea.

CHAPTER TWELVE

Beyond South Philadelphia

Before the twentieth century, while Italians had settled in locations within and outside of Philadelphia, most of them had gathered together in the vicinity of St. Mary Magdalen dePazzi. With the next century, as the core community expanded, its periphery pushed well beyond the old boundaries. Clustered with their relatives and friends to find employment, their own shops and stores, beneficial societies and fraternal groups, amusements and recreation, and a sense of place, Italians formed pockets of settlement farther afield. Varying levels of "institutional completeness" produced a spectrum of differing ties between these Italian colonies and the older, original center of settlement. Some "satellite communities" still depended to a degree upon activities and services found in the hub of South Philadelphia, while more autonomous enclaves had less relationship, if any at all, to it. But these newer communities also found themselves enmeshed within the more immediate context of their surrounding localities.

When the Archdiocese of Philadelphia responded to the growth of the Italian population as well as to its own sense of the "Italian problem" by opening Our Lady of Good Counsel, it was the first step in a larger plan. Only six years later the two Italian churches would find themselves "unable to accommodate the throngs anxious to attend services."[1] Under Archbishop Patrick J. Ryan and then his successor, Archbishop Edmond F. Prendergast, the archdiocese undertook an unprecedented proliferation of new parishes on the fringes of the old district and in other areas, along with an expansion of social services to meet the needs of Italians.

More churches, parochial schools, and other facilities for Italians were not to be achieved without difficulty. Despite the meager success of Protestant efforts, Catholic authorities still feared that proselytizing threatened the fidelity of Italians. Pastors, moreover, disputed parish boundaries and contended with each other for parishioners. Diocesan clergy sometimes clashed with religious orders, particularly the Augustinians, over similar issues. New tensions between Italians and the Irish exacerbated old sources of ethnic conflict. Financial support for Italian parishes proved to be an ongoing and constant problem. And finding adequate social services for needy Italians challenged Catholic resources.

It was no longer simply a matter, as it had been just a few years earlier, of Antonio Isoleri as the lone Italian pastor versus the archbishop, or versus the sisters, or versus the Episcopalians. Now it had become a complicated configuration of institutions, personalities, and issues. At the same time, these problems echoed the earlier chapters of the history of St. Mary Magdalen dePazzi in many respects and in their own manner reflected Isoleri's legacy to his church and priestly heirs.

Leaving the Neighborhood

With their great increase in numbers, Italians in locations beyond South Philadelphia offered a new pastoral challenge. Since the summer of 1902, Father Angelo Caruso, rector of Our Lady of Good Counsel, had offered mass for nearly two hundred construction laborers at a water filtration plant on Belmont Avenue at the western edge of the city. The firm of Ryan and Kelley, employers of Italians and guardians of their Catholicism as well, had erected a temporary frame building to house what they called the Chapel of the Sacred Heart. When Archbishop Ryan visited this site on a July afternoon, an Italian band and about 1,000 persons greeted him. Father Caruso, now joined by Father Matthew Vacchero of St. Mary Magdalen dePazzi, led the archbishop to the chapel, where a chorus of workers sang "Salve Regina," which, according to tradition, was the evening hymn of Columbus's sailors. Ryan reminded his audience that Saint Joseph was, like them, a worker who had sanctified labor. He asked them never to forget that they were Catholics and, despite their humble chapel, that they were, as Italians, from "a land of splendid churches." Reminding them that Michelangelo could draw a beautiful angel from a rough block of marble, Ryan urged his listeners to free their souls from the bondage of sin by chiseling away the impediments to a righteous life. As the workers cheered "Viva la nostra santa religione, e viva il nostro Arcivescovo!" Ryan's visit presaged the expansion of Italian parishes beyond South Philadelphia. Italian communal life and religious experience in Philadelphia were never again to be contained.[2]

When Fathers Ottavio Lionne, C.P., and Nicola Rufo, C.P., preached a mission for Italians at St. Patrick's in Norristown, on the Schuylkill River about twenty miles from Philadelphia, they galvanized support for a new church in the spring of 1903. Only a few months later, after Father Michael Maggio, with a committee of representatives from several communities, developed a plan for an Italian mission, Ryan laid the cornerstone of Holy Savior for the estimated 3,000 residents of the area. While this parish, with Maggio as its first pastor, rapidly grew in membership, it also suffered from debt. By 1907, under Father Lamberto Travi, evidently a financial wizard, income far exceeded debt, thus allowing the building and the dedication of the new church in the following year. For Travi, who would remain its pastor for another twenty-seven years, it was equally auspicious.[3]

The dedication of Holy Savior provided a prototype that guided archdiocesan policy toward Italians. Accompanied by a host of priests, Archbishop Prendergast was met at the DeKalb Street train station in Norristown by hundreds of people, several Italian societies, and three bands on a Sunday morning in late September. Escorted to a site where a larger crowd awaited them, Prendergast, assisted by the pastor of St. Patrick's, blessed the Italian church. Following its dedication, Father Caruso of Philadelphia's Our Lady of Good Counsel sang a High Mass with two other Italian priests, Father Antonio Orlando as deacon and Father Joseph Matera as subdeacon, and an American priest from St. Charles Borromeo Seminary as master of ceremonies. Father Vito Veralli preached in Italian, while Father William J. Garrigan preached in English. After Father Antonio Isoleri celebrated Solemn Vespers in the afternoon, local Italian societies held a reception. The basic format of the day—the archbishop leading a parade in celebration of local Catholicism, a symbolic exodus of Italians from the old church to the new one, homilists alternately speaking in English and Italian to a mixed audience, and Italian clergy sharing the ministry with American colleagues—would be repeated in future years.[4]

Father Garrigan, pastor of St. Columba's, a largely Irish parish in North Philadelphia (soon to launch its Italians toward their own church), delivered the principal message of the day. After congratulating Travi, he turned to "the Italian situation in our country as it strikes me." Contrasting the "beautiful simple life" of their homeland with the difficulties encountered in a new land, Garrigan said that the Italians would be rescued by their natural virtues. Besides their sobriety, industry, and morality, he noted their lack of vagrancy, low rate of alcoholism, and the fidelity of their women before adding: "we are not unsensitive to their faults." These were chiefly apathy, indifference to religious practice, and the lack of financial support for their churches in America.[5]

Then, Garrigan railed at the "misguided efforts of our separated brethren, bent on perverting the Italian immigrant from the faith of his fathers." He attacked the use of icons and symbols as well as veneration of the Virgin Mother "to deceive and allure these poor people." Moreover, he criticized the deployment "as missionaries among their less educated countrymen of renegade Italian perverts whose whole stock in trade is abuse, calumny and blasphemy of all that is good and holy and sacred in our Catholic religion." Urging Italians to be loyal to their Church, pastor, and faith, Garrigan warned them not to fill "the place made vacant by the perfidy of the Jews," by being blinded by pride and falling into infidelity. Exhorting his listeners to follow lives worthy of the traditions of their native land, so that future generations would speak of them as they spoke of their own ancestors "with sincere Catholic pride," he painted a vivid image of their character, the threats that Italians faced in their adopted country, and instructions on how they should live as Catholics. Conspicuously featured by the archdiocesan newspaper, Garrigan's message loomed over the dedication of the new church.[6]

The dispersion of Italians from Philadelphia's Little Italy did not inevitably lead to the establishing of a new parish. In Chestnut Hill, in the northwestern part of the city, Our Mother of Consolation, an Augustinian parish, included in 1904 about one hundred Italians who never secured their own church. While its pastor was aware of their needs, the solution found Father Daniele Scallabrella, an Augustinian from Our Lady of Good Counsel, conducting mass for them at 10 A.M. on Sundays and hearing confessions in their own language. They also formed a strong-enough component of parish life to warrant, at least once, "an Italian jubilee celebration" with masses, sermons, confessions, and home visits. But without sufficient presence or power to demand anything more, they remained within Our Mother of Consolation.[7]

The spiritual needs of Italians led to the founding of sixteen parishes within the present-day boundaries of the archdiocese between 1903 and 1917. Holy Savior (1903) was followed by St. Lucy's (1906) in Manayunk; St. Ann's (1907) in Bristol; Our Lady of Angels (1907) in West Philadelphia; St. Rita's (1907), another Augustinian church, in South Philadelphia; Our Lady of the Assumption (1908) on the upper Main Line in Strafford; St. Anthony's (1908) in Chester; St. Donato's (1910) in West Philadelphia; St. Mary of the Eternal (1911) in North Philadelphia; Mater Dolorosa (1911) in Frankford; St. Nicholas of Tolentine (1912), also Augustinian, in South Philadelphia; Sts. Cosmas and Damian (1912) in Conshohocken; Our Lady of Pompeii (1914) in North Philadelphia; Our Lady of Consolation (1917) in Tacony; Our Lady of the Rosary (1917) in Coatesville; and Immaculate Conception (1917) in Marcus Hook. Except for St. Rita's and St. Nicholas of Tolentine, all of them were outside South Philadelphia, and seven of them were outside the city.[8]

The sites of these parishes reflected changes in locations of work and residence for Italians. St. Rita's and St. Nicholas of Tolentine were in neighborhoods where Italians had displaced other ethnic groups and had marked boundaries for their own community. The other churches were situated in sections within

Philadelphia or outside the city where employment opportunities in local industries had encouraged the establishment of colonies of Italian laborers and where the structure of their religious experience was reshaped.[9]

While each parish had its own history and presented different issues for the archdiocese in dealing with Italians, some aspects of development often overlapped from one case to another. For example, St. Lucy's, near the Belmont Avenue filtration plant, where workers had serenaded the archbishop, accommodated Belmont Hills (or West Manayunk) on the suburban side and Manayunk on the city side of the Schuylkill River. In 1905, when asked by Archbishop Ryan to form another congregation, Father Antonio Orlando first gathered members in a basement chapel at St. John the Baptist Church in Manayunk. But in December 1906, St. Lucy's, with about 160 families in its congregation, moved to a newly finished basement chapel at Price and Jefferson Streets, on a bluff on the west bank of the Schuylkill in West Manayunk. At its dedication, Father Caruso, of Our Lady of Good Counsel, preached at a mass, as did Father Travi, of Holy Savior, at vespers as Italian rectors supported each other's efforts. The archdiocesan press reported that "Father Orlando in his earnest labors among the Italian people of Manayunk has met with encouraging success."[10]

The extent of Orlando's success, reflected in his annual reports for these early years, followed a pattern found in other parishes. It began with a cluster of Italian worshipers in an older, territorial, largely Irish parish. Either by their own request or by its pastor, the archbishop appointed a priest—often Italian, but sometimes Irish—as their provisional head to obtain property. In the interim the Italians became a subcongregation, literally and figuratively, with services in their own language in a basement chapel of the parent church. The pastor of the original parish, with support from his congregation, usually played a major role in establishing the Italian church, which often remained semi-autonomous. This sequence became as familiar for Italians in Philadelphia as it was elsewhere.[11]

A similar pattern was followed by St. Ann's, far up the Delaware River in Bristol. Although an Italian family was believed to have settled in the area as early as 1868, it was almost forty years later that Italians attending St. Mark's had their own church. In April 1906, the archdiocese named Father Paolo Gentile to form St. Ann's parish. After a period not only of growth but also of debt, its future brightened on St. Patrick's Day in 1907 when parish groups from Philadelphia, Bristol, and nearby towns together with a brass band, about 3,000 spectators, and Italian priests from South Philadelphia, Norristown, Reading, Manayunk, Trenton, Atlantic City, and Camden, convened for the laying of the cornerstone. Archbishop Prendergast praised the work being done among Italians and urged parishioners to aid Gentile in completing the edifice.[12]

Although the dedication of the finished church in October 1907 signified progress, parish activities only modestly increased, income and expenses declined, but property debt remained high. Rectors such as Gentile, with tight budgets balanced to the penny or with deficits, documented the fragile financial condition of their missions and the vicissitudes facing them. They sometimes denoted their own marginality, as the pastor of St. Ann's did, by altering his signature in his annual reports from "Paul Gentile" in 1907 to "Paolo Gentile" in 1908. With the stress of precarious ventures taking its toll, several rectors served at St. Ann's from 1910 to 1916. After Gentile, Father Orlando stayed briefly before Vito Veralli replaced him. When bad health forced Veralli to resign, he was succeeded by Gerardo deVecchis in April 1914. Two years later, when Father Isadore Jenne, a Trinitarian, became rector, and the cornerstone for the upper church was laid in November 1916, St. Ann's finally found stability as a parish.[13]

While St. Ann's grew in Bristol, another Italian mission was incubating at Our Mother of Sorrows in West Philadelphia. When Italians began emerging as a group, Father John J. McCort, its pastor, scheduled mass for them in the mortuary chapel at the nearby cemetery. During this period, Father Daniel Dever, of St. Charles Borromeo Seminary, also served them. As their numbers grew, the mass was moved to the school hall before a new church, Our Lady of Angels, was dedicated in December 1907 on a site obtained by McCort at Fiftieth and Master Streets.[14] This parish was seen as "part of the organized movement to supply Catholic churches . . . for the increasing Italian population."[15] By July 1907, its congregation was believed to have reached 1,000 members. When the cornerstone for its chapel was laid, Father James A. Mullen, pastor of nearby Our Lady of Lourdes Church, expressed a widely shared perception of the Italians before a crowd of about 5,000 spectators: "They are a noble people. . . . With their industry, their religious fervor, their morality and their sobriety they are a useful addition to the community. They have their peculiarities, which have been caused by the excessive taxation and persecution that drives so many of them from their native country. Priests like Father McCort and Father Dever, who have welcomed them to their churches have done a great good. The growth of our Italian parishes gives the lie to the assertion that Italians are indifferent to the faith."[16]

Italian priests had played prominent roles at the cornerstone laying, but by the time of the church's dedication a few months later, they had almost entirely disappeared. With Bishop Prendergast presiding, only one Italian, Father Lamberto Travi, had the opportunity to respond to Irish American views on the religiosity of his countrymen. In a homily in Italian, Travi praised McCort for his interest in the Italians. After all, Travi noted, McCort had found a place for them in the mortuary chapel. But he urged Italians to be faithful to their religious duties and to generously contribute to the Church, since it received no aid from the state in America. On this public occasion, Travi's views were not noticeably different from Mullen's.[17]

While the early history of Our Lady of Angels remains vague, neither the parishioners, who allegedly paid for the new church, nor McCort seemed ready to relinquish control. The archdiocesan newspaper asserted that the Italian church had been erected by McCort, remained under his charge, and was attached to his parish, and McCort similarly continued to submit the annual report for Our Lady of the Angels as an appendix to his report for Our Mother of Sorrows. By stating that the parish had 800 Italian members, but that some 1,200 others had left in 1908, McCort left a clue that they may not have fully embraced him as their pastor.[18]

In November 1909, Our Lady of Angels welcomed Father Pietro Michetti, a native of Cossignano, near Ascoli Piceno, as its pastor with a gala celebration that included speeches and a parade. But in July 1910, less than a year later, Michetti left for another parish. In January 1911, Paolo Gentile, formerly at St. Ann's in Bristol, signed the annual report as rector of Our Lady of Angels. Whatever lay behind these events has not remained in the historical record.[19]

Displacing Others in South Philadelphia

While the Italian presence grew in new locations, it also expanded at the fringes of its original center to displace other groups in South Philadelphia. By 1904, St. Mary Magdalen dePazzi and Our Lady of Good Counsel, so near each other in a heavily congested area, were no longer able "to administer to the increasing number of Italian Catholics in the district below their respective boundaries." The same pressure was building in other directions as Italians moved west and south from their earlier concentration. The archdiocese initially attempted to establish more churches for Italians by buying property from older Protestant congregations that were abandoning the area. And if Italian families moved into areas where Catholic churches already existed, the archdiocese sometimes simply incorporated them into these existing parishes.[20]

Italian migration that was too large to be accommodated by merely assigning another priest, however, could overwhelm an older parish. While forcing the opening of new churches as nationality parishes in outlying areas, the encroachment of Italians now also co-opted older territorial parishes and converted them in some neighborhoods into de facto Italian churches. Founded in 1843, St. Paul's, at Christian Street just west of Ninth Street, faced a situation in which whole streets once occupied by Irish American families were now populated by Italians. The events that transpired at this parish brought into vivid relief what faced the archdiocese in reconciling ethnic differences within the Catholic population.[21]

The conversion of St. Paul's to a predominantly Italian parish partly sprang from the needs of the children of immigrant families. When Archbishop Ryan convened clergy and laity in November 1904 to discuss ways of preserving the faith in Little Italy, few participants spoke with more authority than Father

Paul C. Donovan, pastor of St. Paul's, who had concluded his address by calling for a practical plan for the education of Italian children. Three months later, its implementation began when Ryan dedicated an annex for 400 more pupils in addition to the 1,000 already attending St. Paul's parish school. He also announced plans "to further provide for the wants of 'Little Italy'" by a new school of thirty rooms for 2,000 more pupils, to be erected on Montrose Street behind St. Paul's present school. But the needs of the children could not be met by St. Paul's alone. In the next month the archbishop returned to dedicate an annex to Our Lady of Good Counsel's school as well.[22]

The cornerstone laying for St. Paul's new school in May 1905 was "a gala day in the neighborhood," with American and Italian flags flying from houses while spectators filled streets, windows, and rooftop grandstands. The Total Abstinence Society of St. Paul's, mainly Irish in its membership, was joined in a procession by the parish societies of Italian churches. A prominent Catholic lawyer, in the principal speech of the day, claimed that 100,000 Italians who lived in the city included 20,000 school-age children—three-fourths of them attending St. Paul's and the two nearby Italian schools—who must not be allowed to drift away from their faith.[23]

When the new St. Paul's school was dedicated in December 1905, it signaled a shift in archdiocesan strategy. Nationality parishes were no longer the only means of solving the "Italian problem," especially when Italians displaced earlier groups in areas with older territorial parishes. By penetrating the neighborhood around St. Paul's, these families presented another kind of problem, but the parish itself provided a solution. And while Fathers Isoleri and Caruso participated in the dedication ceremonies, both of them must have seen that a new vessel with a different keel had been launched at St. Paul's.[24]

This alternative to the nationality parish had great implications for Italian Catholicism. Whether through conscious planning by Church authorities or as an unintended result of their own mobility, Italians would have less control of parishes. And instead of transplanted traditions, Italians would encounter a different cultural experience in parish life. In the next year, when Archbishop Ryan returned to St. Paul's school, the program in his honor emphasized "the assimilating power of the Catholic Church in America." Although most pupils and spectators were Italians, children of Irish, Syrian, and English descent also participated. Referring to them as "Americans all," the archdiocesan newspaper boldly asserted that the program proved "that talent is not confined to any nationality." The priests who witnessed the events included two Donovans, Ring (a visitor from Ireland), McKay, who spoke in Italian to the students, and Sheehan, but not Isoleri, Caruso, or any other Italian cleric. Congratulating the sisters and pupils, Donovan thanked Ryan for building and maintaining the annex. Then, declaring a holiday, the archbishop promised to send candy to the students. Father Ring urged them to remember such kind friends and benefactors as the archbishop and pastor in their daily prayers. But while an emphasis on assimilation had gained momentum, ethnic diversity persisted at St. Paul's.[25]

When St. Paul's entertained Ryan in 1908, the program still celebrated nationality differences, but they were subordinated to American and Catholic unity. While ethnic groups expressed separate identities, they also were establishing a new order among themselves. When an orchestra played an Irish air entitled "St. Patrick's Day," the archdiocesan newspaper claimed that "the little Italians could scarcely keep their feet still." But Italian girls, wearing sashes in their national colors, also sang an Italian song and carried the papal flag for "the Holy Father in the Vatican, whose children from Italy are in the care of the Archbishop." The boys wore sashes of the national colors and carried an American flag, but their old patriotic song had new words that saluted America, the papacy, the archbishop, and the archdiocese. The newspaper account commented: "The greatest comradeship seemed to exist between those of Irish, Italian and Syrian blood, who were in the majority, though there were other nationalities represented." Stating his pleasure at seeing these various groups united as Catholics and Americans, Ryan urged Italians to be especially proud of the pope and to love all peoples as children of God. It is unclear whether the tapping feet of Italian children reflected the emergence of Irish cultural hegemony or were merely an unconscious reflex in response to an engaging tempo. It is also unclear how much of the description in the newspaper was a projection by an observer constructing his own version of social reality. But Ryan's remarks were less ambiguous. By asking Italians to submerge their ethnic identity into a broader sense of self and group, he clearly sought to engage himself in the difficult task of uniting the many into one.[26]

After succeeding Ryan, Archbishop Prendergast visited St. Paul's school in December 1911, where a student orator, speaking for his 1,700 schoolmates, described Ryan as a father figure, frequent visitor, and generous benefactor who had enabled them to receive a Catholic education. The youth then asked the archbishop for his continued support. Prendergast replied that Ryan had been full of religious zeal and love for the Italian children. Urging them to be proud of their sunny ancestral land and their adopted one as well, he added that America offered opportunities for success that no European country could extend. To become good Americans and to win respect could only be accomplished by being good Catholics, with a love of Italy, the land of their parents, and of America, their own land. But in his remarks, Ryan had actually reversed the direction of the formula for Italians that American Catholic leaders had previously proposed. Instead of becoming American as a means of preserving their faith, they were now exhorted to be good Catholics in order to become good Americans. As Prendergast attempted to uphold the agenda of his predecessor with this twist, St. Paul's continued to evolve. From only a handful of Italian children in attendance when it opened another classroom building in 1898, the parish school grew to an enrollment of 1,460, with all but twenty students being Italian, by 1920. Thus, Italian children took over the school, as their families did the parish, while they were themselves being absorbed by a dominant culture. School and parish had both become caldrons of assimilation for Italians.[27]

West of Broad Street

Although some Italians feared that crossing Broad Street—Philadelphia's principal north-south artery—meant reprisals from the Irish, an increasing number of families took that risk in their search for housing. When the archdiocese opened St. Rita's Church, Irish American Augustinians erased that boundary altogether. Neither a nationality parish nor a co-opted territorial parish, St. Rita's was marked by anomaly and ambiguity from its inception. It began with a legacy from a wealthy layman to the archdiocese that directed the Augustinians from Villanova College to build a church in nearby suburban Bryn Mawr. Since one already existed there, the archdiocese sought to use the bequest in another manner, but the Augustinian role still had to be resolved. In 1905, recognizing the urgent need for another Italian church, the archdiocese began securing properties on the west side of South Broad Street below Ellsworth. Unlike Our Lady of Good Counsel with its Italian clergy, St. Rita's, staffed by American priests, rested on a compromise between the archdiocese and the American Province of the Augustinians.[28]

An ambitious plan called for other facilities as well as a church for the community. The energetic pastor of St. Rita's, Father James F. McGowan, O.S.A., bought a house on Broad Street for a day nursery, kindergarten, and parish center under the direction of Augustinian brothers. Behind quickly demolished houses on Broad Street, he renovated a former stable as a temporary chapel in the spring of 1907. By autumn, the congregation had exceeded its capacity. A Protestant neighbor provided an almost providential solution. Eschewing the usual discord between denominations, the Reverend Frederick W. Smith, rector of the Messiah Protestant Episcopal Church, extended the use of his parish house without charge to the Augustinians. From this exemplary act, McGowan was able to offer six masses on Sundays. Reciprocating this precocious ecumenicism, McGowan invited Smith to the dedication of the basement chapel in 1908.[29]

The ambiguous status of St. Rita's as a parish represents a puzzling aspect of its early history. Although termed an Italian church as well as "Italian-English," St. Rita's was intended to serve not only the Italians west of Twelfth Street but also the English-speaking Catholics on both sides of Broad Street. When an estimated 10,000 spectators gathered for the cornerstone laying-ceremonies, Italians staked their claim. A large procession from Little Italy, led by older people, then children's sodalities, and other religious societies, marched from Our Lady of Good Counsel to St. Rita's in the celebration.[30]

When the basement chapel opened in September 1908, newspaper accounts referred to St. Rita's as an Italian church or as one for the Italian colony, but it was more diverse than other congregations in which Italians found themselves:

> The congregation, mainly composed of persons of Irish and Italian birth or ancestry, included also representatives of half a dozen other nationalities and a sprinkling of Colored Catholics. Among those present were some of the recent converts of Episcopalianism, as also members of the Messiah congregation of that denomination, which so kindly placed its parish house at the disposal of St. Rita's pastor and people pending the completion of the new basement. There were two sermons, one in English and one in Italian, the latter paying tribute to the faith and fidelity of the Irish race. The celebrant of the Mass bore a name redolent of the Old Sod, the deacons were sons of Sunny Italy, the master of ceremonies suggested France and a minor officer "bleeding Poland."[31]

Despite the tendency of the archdiocesan press to celebrate the "unifying power of the Catholic Church" as a fait accompli, St. Rita's had to reconcile a largely Italian congregation with an Irish American clergy as well as with the ethnic diversity within its parish. Father Joseph Bizzarri, a priest from Rome, helped to settle differences at the chapel dedication. Speaking in Italian, he described traits shared by the Irish and Italians. Praising the Irish for their fidelity, he spoke of their persecution in Ireland and their ostracism in America. He then applauded them for overcoming these obstacles and for winning respect for their Church and themselves in their new country. With Italians coming in large numbers, he asserted that the lack of their own priests posed a problem, but they would, if cared for, be as faithful as Catholics as the Irish had been. And both groups, united by the Church, would resist socialism and anarchy by elevating citizenship through religion. Bizzarri had shown a remarkably prophetic sense of the future for Italian and Irish Catholics in America.[32]

From the Main Line to Chester

At almost the same time that Italians crossed Broad Street, they formed new churches in Strafford, in the Main Line suburbs to the west, and in Chester, the industrial city to the south of Philadelphia. The origins of Our Lady of the Assumption Church in Strafford have been attributed to a woman from Teramo, who wrote to her uncle, a monsignor in Rome, seeking a priest to hear confessions in her native language. In early 1908, Archbishop Ryan asked Father Amilius Landolfi to organize a parish for Italians in the area, who perhaps included the persuasive letterwriter. Securing a $1,500 loan from the archdiocese and support from local Italians, he obtained Strafford Hall, a former Protestant Sunday school, which was moved on railroad ties to a site on Old Eagle School Road. In June some 400 people, wearing badges combining the American and Italian colors, attended the dedication. Father Caruso of Our Lady of Good Counsel preached the homily.[33]

The early years of Our Lady of the Assumption were marked by turmoil. After only a year, Landolfi was reassigned to a church in upstate Pennsylvania at Bethlehem. Fathers Louis Fiorillo and Carmine Cillo alternated as its priest until Father Antonio Scialabba became rector in August 1911. In September, when a dispute over parish finances reached Ryan, the archbishop advised Fiorillo to present them in a substantiated form. Meanwhile, in his defense, Scialabba submitted a letter that he claimed had been sent by Fiorillo to a layman in Strafford. With only blank pages for the 1908–1910 annual reports, the archdiocesan consultors, in their capacity as advisers to the archbishop, urged that priests be reminded of their obligation to keep careful financial accounts. After deferring further action on the case, the consultors never returned to it. Later figures of increasing numbers of parishioners and sacramental activity, along with persisting financial deficits, confirm its early difficulties. Scialabba remained pastor, however, and the parish eventually achieved stability.[34]

Pastor and parishioners similarly struggled in founding St. Anthony of Padua in Chester, although conflicting accounts muddle the picture of its early years. In one version, meetings of Italian immigrants in a basement room at St. Michael's Church, which had opened in 1908, culminated in Father Antonio Garritano's appointment as first pastor of a new Italian church four years later. But Father Pietro A. Pillarella's annual reports for St. Anthony of Padua from September 1907 to December 1912 contradict it. A turbulent episode gives some indication of later disagreements over the years.[35]

A petition supported by 125 signatures, which was sent to Archbishop Ryan in April 1909, cited an effort seeking Pillarella's removal as the work of a faction of "discontented and malicious Italians" that included "in some inconceivable manner the names of many illiterate Italians." The priest's supporters declared that "the more enlightened members of the Italian Colony and those interested in the work of the Rev. P. A. Pilarella [sic] are indignant at the action of the parties responsible to this petition." Describing the opposition "as devoid of sense as it is of decency," they declared that its charges were false and that other petitions had borne the names not only "of minors, evangelists and Socialists, but also of uneducated persons" to whom matters had been misrepresented. Pillarella's defenders indicted this "floating colony [who] are here to-day and away to-morrow, and who lead Godless lives, without Church or Sacraments and whose names can easily be had at any time for a glass of beer; the majority have never seen Father Pilarella [*sic*] or had any connection with him in any way." His advocates contended that Pillarella was held "in the highest esteem by the people of Chester, irrespective of creed or nationality."[36]

After arriving at St. Anthony of Padua in late December 1912, Garritano apparently attempted to discredit Pillarella to archdiocesan officials. Garritano reported that the size of the congregation was not only much lower than his predecessor had claimed, but that Pillarella had collected the Christmas donations, usually the largest of the year, just before he left, and taken them with him. Along with debts, Garritano inherited an unfurnished church and residence, requiring him to spend "every cent of my money" to furnish them. He was, moreover, unable to find any financial or spiritual records and believed that they had been either destroyed or retained by his predecessor.[37]

Garritano soon sought permission to build a church, for which ground was broken in April and the cornerstone laid in October 1913. By year's end, his parish had about 5,000 Italians scattered in Chester, Marcus Hook, Eddystone, Avondale, Upland, Rockdale, Lenni, Media, and other towns. Significantly, his baptisms included six children previously baptized by Italian Presbyterians. Despite the debts that Pillarella had left and an ongoing deficit, Garritano won financial support and approval for his efforts from the consultors.[38]

Not only the first church for Italians in Chester, St. Anthony of Padua was also the first one in Delaware County. At the dedication in June 1914 the archdiocesan newspaper gave a highly favorable appraisal of its situation:

> When Father Garritano came here, a year and seven months ago, he found a small frame structure and a scattered, neglected Italian congregation, a great many attending the Presbyterian mission a square away, and the rest with no inclination to serve God in this new world. They were truly a neglected people, preyed upon by proselytizers with promiscuous gift-making, lured by all kinds of social entertainment, deceived by a cross over the portal of a sectarian meeting house and statues within, and mercilessly deprived of love for the sacraments by discourses by the minister in charge, formerly a priest. . . . Frequent missions were given, conducted in the old Italian form, which directly appealed to his countrymen.[39]

Whether in Chester or elsewhere, the argument was common by now that Protestant proselytizers, working among Italians and imitating symbolic forms of Catholic culture to induce them to convert, had made more Catholic churches necessary. Although the results of Protestant efforts remained a moot question, the contention that "an Italian is Catholic or nothing" added another dimension. While Protestantism made an easy target for Catholic criticism, it was not, however, the main threat to Italian Catholicism. As noted earlier, the greater source of Italian apostasy was anticlericalism, disbelief, and indifference, without the influence of any other denomination.[40]

Garritano's efforts earned him great affection in Chester, as was seen in August 1915 upon his return from a visit to Italy, when a welcoming committee escorted him from the Reading Railroad Terminal in Philadelphia to an exuberant and joyful celebration at his parish. But he also gained the respect of archdiocesan officials. After fourteen years at St. Anthony of Padua, he would be appointed to succeed Antonio Isoleri as pastor of St. Mary Magdalen dePazzi in May 1926.[41]

More Growth in West Philadelphia

Only three years after the founding of Our Lady of Angels, the growing Italian population in West Philadelphia required another church. This need dated back to Italians who had been attending Our Lady of the Rosary at Sixty-third and Callowhill Streets since 1896. Its pastor finally invited an Italian priest to preach the first mission to them nearly a decade later. As this colony grew, Irish American priests offered mass on Sundays for the Italians, with a sermon in their language, first in the school hall and later in the church.[42]

When Archbishop Ryan asked for more Italian priests for the archdiocese during a visit to Rome, Propaganda Fide sent Father Pietro Michetti to serve Italians in Pottsville and smaller missions in December 1905. Reassigned to Our Lady of Angels in October 1909, Michetti was asked by Ryan to organize another parish four months later. On land purchased in February 1910, the cornerstone for St. Donato's Church at Sixty-fifth and Callowhill Streets was laid in June of that year.[43]

In a now familiar scene, the ceremonies began with a procession of priests and acolytes, musicians, and societies carrying Italian and American flags along streets decorated for the occasion, before an Italian priest delivered a homily to his countrymen in their own language. Father Joseph M. Corrigan, superintendent of the recently formed Catholic Missionary Society of Philadelphia, then followed it with the kind of message that Italians were hearing on almost every public occasion. Alluding to the oddity of a new church in the shadow of an existing one, Corrigan praised Father John Lynch, pastor of nearby Holy Rosary, to whom the care of souls in the district had been committed, before stating the real problem that Catholics were facing: "We all know the conditions created in this community by the great influx of immigration. A people alien to us in language, customs and traditions has sought in a free country the freedom that is the glorious gift of this Republic. They have only one thing in common with American Catholics—their common altar, their common faith."[44]

Corrigan called for the recognition of brotherhood between immigrants and Americans in a shared faith: "This unity is to be their strength and your pride." For immigrants weakened by the circumstances that "beset the stranger in a strange land," he asked Americans to stand by them:

> all others are to take notice by this demonstration that you stand side by side with Italian Catholics for their strength and their defense. Therefore, who insult these weak ones of Christ's Church insult you also; who seek to rob the Church of God of these members offend you also. Once this is well understood there will be an end to the baiting of souls and the wooing away to false creeds of these poorly-instructed immigrants. There will be an end of such scoundrelly efforts as unnamed cowards put forth to-day, when they circulated printed lies about the one thing of value the poor Italians bring with them from their fatherland—the religion of Jesus Christ.[45]

While reminding American Catholics of their obligations, Corrigan had much more to say. Revising the reasons for Italian migration from economic motives to political ones, he placed their lives in a religious context. Depicting their deficiencies as Catholics, Corrigan exhorted Italians to resist those who sought to lure them away from Catholicism. Indeed he warned, Catholic unity would prevail against Protestant proselytizers.[46]

Michetti, the new pastor at St. Donato's, vigorously responded. A few weeks after the cornerstone laying, a basement chapel was dedicated on the Feast of Our Lady of Mount Carmel in July 1910. A detailed plan called for the main church, in Renaissance style, designed by a leading architect of the city. Michetti had charge of an estimated 3,000 Italians, many employed by construction companies, in his own congregation along with 2,000 more at Our Lady of Angels. Only a week later, the naming of Father Paolo Gentile as his successor at Our Lady of Angels enabled Michetti to devote himself entirely to St. Donato's. In 1911, he opened a kindergarten and brought the Missionary Sisters of the Sacred Heart to the parish, and in 1913, he began construction of a new school building. But by 1914, despite 400 families in the parish and 220 children enrolled in the kindergarten, there was still no main church.[47]

As St. Donato's pursued an intensive fund-raising effort, articles in the archdiocesan newspaper, rare for other parishes, announced euchre games for the benefit of the school building fund. When the school was dedicated in August 1914, Corrigan, again the speaker, assailed his audience: "It is a useless task to ask why the Italian people here have not the same standard of religious activity as our people have . . . what does matter is that the Italian children are blameless." Then in early 1916, Italian businessmen and civic leaders from South and West Philadelphia and some non-Italians sought to raise $50,000 in a ten-week campaign for St. Donato's. From March through May, the names of individuals and organizations who had pledged $100 to $2,000 appeared in the archdiocesan newspaper. Although Italians had generously contributed, the campaign did not reach its goal.[48] Nevertheless, when the upper church was finally dedicated in 1922, Michetti was praised for building a convent, orphanage, rectory, school, and church "in the short space of 10 years . . . single-handed and alone." Although the church had taken twelve years and its cost had risen from the $25,000 first projected in 1910 to $160,000, his accomplishments could not be denied.[49]

Besides West Philadelphia, smaller waves of Italians had radiated into other sections of the city. In July 1910, when Archbishop Ryan asked Father Joseph Matera, a native of Albano di Lucania in the province of Potenza, to organize a church, the spiritual needs of Italians in North Philadelphia were recognized. Matera first held services in the school hall at St. Columba's, a largely Irish parish on Lehigh Avenue. After six months his flock was identified in his first annual report merely as the "Italian Congregation—meeting in St. Columba's Parish."[50]

After a year at St. Columba's, ground was broken for a chapel for Italians in July 1911. In September, Archbishop Prendergast laid the cornerstone of St. Mary of the Eternal (sometimes called Our Lady of the Eternal) at Twenty-first and Toronto Streets before a festive crowd. Some 260 Italian families remained at St. Columba's for three more months until services at their own church were first held on Christmas Eve of 1911. In November 1912, after the formal dedication in the morning, the confirmation of 216 persons, including 37 adults, attested to the enthusiasm of Italians for their new church.[51]

As on previous occasions, Prendergast reiterated a familiar message. Praising their pastor's efforts, he warned Italians to be wary of proselytizers who sought to rob their children of the faith. Later, in describing the event, the archdiocesan newspaper noted that Father Matera, in addition to organizing parish sodalities and clubs, had been pursuing "every means to offset the baneful influence of the [Protestant] sects by increasing the number of devotions and by labor in the homes of the members of his flock, urging parents to be on their guard against the snares used by misguided persons who are paid to rob, if possible, the Italian children of their primitive and true faith."[52]

Matera's 1912 annual report offered a profile of his pastoral problems, which included too many children attending public schools, parishioners failing to meet their Easter duty, insufficient parish income, and debt due to the mortgage on the new church. He also wrote: "The rector had no possible way to take a salary. All his personal income was a part of the perquisites at the amount of $360.85." He was referring to the practice of treating fees from baptisms, marriages, and funerals as personal income rather than as parish revenue, which produced only a modest sum for him to live on.[53]

Father Matera departed in August 1915 to serve Italy as a military chaplain in the World War. The next pastor, Father Thomas Barra, a native of Coassolo Torinese in the province of Turin, found discrepancies in the parish records. At year's end, Barra reported 550 families as well as 400 boarders in a population of 3,300, although he was unable to provide much other information. Confirmations had been not administered in the past three years. For First Communions, he recorded a series of question marks. For the Easter obligation of his parishioners, Barra could only write: "I think 80% failed."[54] He was thus forced to submit an incomplete annual report to the archdiocese. A mortgage debt of $21,534.53 puzzled him the most: "I can not understand why the Rev. Matera not only did not pay a cent on the capital but since 1912 augmented it of $2,752.31." Implying malfeasance by his predecessor, Barra struggled with the unresolved financial problems at St. Mary of the Eternal.[55]

As they spread into other neighborhoods, Italians eventually organized several parishes in North Philadelphia. In February 1908, the archdiocese assigned a priest to find property for a parish in Frankford. According to parish lore, the roots of Mater Dolorosa began with Father Ernesto Santoro holding services at a store on Unity Street near Griscom, in the Grocers' Association Building. In the next year, Archbishop Ryan obtained a house and lot at 4330 Paul Street, first called St. Peter's, until another chapel became St. Rocco's in April 1910. With Santoro's transfer, Father Cosmas Bruni became rector there in September 1911. Only three months later, the chapel was dedicated as Mater Dolorosa (but often referred to as Santa Maria Dolorosa) in December 1911.[56]

Father Bruni reached out at Mater Dolorosa to as many as 3,000 Italians scattered from Frankford to Wissinoming, Tacony, Holmesburg, and Torresdale. As other Italian pastors had found it necessary to do, Bruni met deficits with his own money, although the increasing sacramental numbers indicated that his parish was coming to life. It provided, however, a meager living for its pastor, who could report in 1912 only a bookcase, a rug, and a sofa as his personal possessions.[57]

By December 1913, Mater Dolorosa's chapel was "entirely too small to accommodate the increasing numbers of the Italians." As the archdiocese launched a plan for a church, Italians were reported to be "enthusiastic in their cooperation with their pastor, the Rev. Cosmas Bruni." In January 1914, a concert and dance, with a modest admission fee of 35 cents, brought aid to Mater Dolorosa. In August, the cornerstone laying for the new church on ground at Paul and Ruan Streets brought a "day of rejoicing for Frankford Italians" in a celebration that transcended ethnic boundaries. Italian beneficial societies marched with their own bands together with the Ancient Order of Hibernians, the Holy Name Society, and groups from several other parishes.[58]

The speakers again reminded Italians of what was expected of them as Catholics in America. Father Francis Castellano, a priest from Brooklyn, who addressed them in Italian, declared the importance of religion in general and Catholicism in particular to the health of the nation. After arguing that Catholicism, with its festivals, flowers, music and processions, was the only faith that appealed to the

Italians' temperament, he urged them to emulate American, Irish, German, and Polish Catholics in supporting the Church.[59] Father James E. Flood, the superintendent of archdiocesan schools, speaking in English, then argued that keeping their faith made Italians good citizens of their new country. But, quoting Scripture, he warned them about Protestant proselytizers: "Be steadfast in your faith, then, my dear Italian brethren. Let not strange customs in a strange land nor lying tongues deceive you. Spurn the bribing hand that would rob you of your birthright. Love your Church. Be guided by your lawful pastors."[60]

When Mater Dolorosa was dedicated in December 1914, the neighborhood turned out in celebration. A Gothic altar of dark wood finished in gold had been donated by St. Joachim's, its previous location, after serving as a part of the French exhibit at Philadelphia's 1876 Centennial Exposition. Father Bruni spoke of the joy that the occasion gave to Italians and Americans, whom he was particularly glad to see together. Along with Bishop James McCort, Bruni thanked Father Francis P. Fitzmaurice, pastor of St. Joachim's, for being like a father and brother to him, and especially for his great encouragement over the past three years. Bruni urged his congregation to show its appreciation by living "as one fold with one shepherd."[61]

While Bruni's gratitude to his Irish colleagues showed that religious priorities could overcome ethnic differences, his success also came from his own efforts within the archdiocesan bureaucracy. When he sought support from the consultors, his petition had been referred to two priests, one of whom was Fitzmaurice. They obviously had endorsed his plan, as they would do again in the future. At the dedication of Mater Dolorosa, Bruni thanked Fitzmaurice for the favorable response by the consultors as well as for his understanding of what was required in negotiating with them.[62]

Bishop McCort, who had emerged as an important figure in archdiocesan planning on Italian matters, complimented the congregation for an edifice that compared in beauty and architecture to any Italian church in the archdiocese. He praised other Catholics who offered sympathy and encouragement to Italians. McCort then congratulated the Italians for having another church where teaching, hymns, and devotions in their own sweet tongue could preserve the faith for their children. But, for McCort, Italians still had to be taught what it meant to be Catholic in America; they had to learn to make sacrifices for the Church. Having scolded them, he could also bless the Italians, before a choir closed the ceremonies with hymns.[63] Despite his attempt to make them better Catholics, the Italians had not allowed an Irish American bishop, if they paid any attention his words at all, to dampen their festive celebration.

By having a church of their own, Italians found comfort and self-respect as Catholics, regardless of what any Irish American priest or bishop might say about them. While they attested to the role of Mater Dolorosa by their active participation in parish life, income remained a problem, with its pastor again making up the deficit from his own funds. But Mater Dolorosa had become and would remain an important institution in Frankford for many years.[64]

Like some of his peers, Father Bruni exemplified the second generation of Italian pastors. Educated at the diocesan seminary of Ripatransone in the Marches, near where he was born, he had first come to St. Donato's in 1910. Not quite a year later, Archbishop Ryan asked him to form Mater Dolorosa, the only church for Italians between Girard Avenue and the northeastern limits of the city. Knowing that the spiritual needs of Italians in nearby Richmond and Kensington could not be met by his church alone, Bruni also opened St. Rocco as a mission at Ontario and Amber Streets in 1918. He further distinguished himself by his high-spirited letters in defense of the faith to the *Catholic Standard and Times,* when Protestant proselytizers sought converts among Italians. During his thirty-four years as a pastor, Bruni built a church, school, rectory, and convent and became a leader for Italians across the entire city. Father Antonio Isoleri had pioneered this role alone, when his St. Mary Magdalen dePazzi had been the only refuge for Italian Catholics in Philadelphia. Now there were other colonies, other parishes, and other pastors.[65]

Expansion to the South

As Italians moved farther in a southern direction in South Philadelphia, Archbishop Ryan assigned Father Edmund Fitzmaurice, recently ordained in Rome, to take charge in 1904 in the area of Annunciation parish, at Tenth and Dickinson Streets. At the end of the year, after an unsuccessful attempt to buy a Presbyterian church at Ninth and Wharton Streets as a chapel for Italians, the archdiocese considered other plans. While the opening of St. Rita's had established a church for them on the west side of Broad Street, the needs of the Italian population on the east side remained unmet.[66]

In parts of South Philadelphia, with Italians displacing earlier residents, older Protestant churches faced the prospect of dwindling congregations. In April 1912, after the Augustinians bought a substantial chapel, only eighteen years old, with a seating capacity of 400 persons, and an adjoining house at Ninth and Watkins Streets, Italian societies, behind brass bands and banners, once again marched to the opening of another church, St. Nicholas of Tolentine, as a succursal parish (i.e., mission) of Our Lady of Good Counsel. With some irony, the American Augustinian provincial, preaching in English, praised Italians for founding a church where they would be served by priests who spoke their language.[67]

Less than three months after the dedication of St. Nicholas of Tolentine, Father Emiliano Bartolozzi, O.S.A., pastor of Our Lady of Good Counsel, claimed 2,000 members for the new church in June 1912. Although Father John

Cerruti, O.S.A., was only thirty-two years old when he was appointed as its first administrator, illness soon forced his replacement and he died in 1919. With renewed growth under Father Alfonso Baldassarre, O.S.A., who became administrator in November 1914, St. Nicholas of Tolentine acquired more property on Ninth and Pierce Streets. In 1916, the original chapel was demolished and replaced by one completed less than two years later, followed by a parochial school in seven more years. By any measure, the mission had quickly achieved stability and found its place among neighborhood churches. Also, St. Nicholas of Tolentine now anchored the third corner of the "Augustinian triangle" that covered a large area of South Philadelphia.[68]

Hill Town on the River

At the turn of the century, Italians went to work in the steel mills and quarries of Conshohocken, a town nestled on the slopes above the Schuylkill River about twenty miles west of Philadelphia. As their numbers increased, joined by others from Norristown, Italians attended mass at Little's Hall, a theater at First and Fayette Streets. In March 1912, the archdiocese named Father Nicholas Coscia, a native of Carlantino in the province of Foggia, already a priest for twenty-six years, as the rector of Sts. Cosmas and Damian Church. Quickly organizing his congregation, he performed baptisms and marriages in the spring and summer before construction began in the fall on a temporary chapel at Fifth and Maple Streets, with plans for a permanent structure toward the front of the property.[69]

In his first annual report for what he identified as the "Italian Congregation, Conshohocken," Coscia, with a hesitant use of an unfamiliar language, recorded 1,000 members in 1912. In the familiar pattern for such public events, when a small basement chapel was dedicated, Italian fraternal societies and bands escorted Bishop McCort from the train station in the spring of 1913. With the outbreak of the World War, Coscia deferred plans for the upper church. After its completion in 1926, joy was soon tempered by sorrow over his death in the next year. Succeeding Coscia, Father Victor A. Strumia would shepherd Sts. Cosmas and Damian, at its site above narrow winding streets reminiscent of the Apennine villages from where many of its members came, for the next forty-one years.[70]

Expansion to the North

Since the late 1880s, Italians had lived in Germantown. They were gathering for mass with Father Secundus Lavizeri, C.M., at St. Vincent's Seminary on East Chelten Avenue by the early 1890s. After the establishing of Immaculate Conception as a territorial parish in 1901, Italians attended their own mass on Sunday mornings in its basement chapel. About 1905, Father Peter Montiani, C.M., succeeded Lavizeri as their priest. By 1907, they required two masses on Sunday mornings. While using the Vincentian chapel for regular services and for such special events as a mission preached in April 1912 by Augustinians from Our Lady of Good Counsel, Germantown's Italians remained in a parochial limbo without a church of their own.[71]

Our Lady of the Rosary, also known as Holy Rosary, remained an ambiguous entity until a school in a renovated mansion at East Haines and Morton Streets was blessed by Monsignor Philip R. McDevitt in November 1913. With lay teachers as its staff, Father James Lavezzari, C.M., a recent arrival from Genoa, preached in Italian at its opening. In September 1914, when Bishop McCort blessed the school again, the archdiocesan newspaper referred to Holy Rosary as an Italian parish.[72]

While the 1915 archdiocesan directory no longer listed a mass for Italians at Immaculate Conception, it included Our Lady of the Rosary among parishes and missions for the first time, with Montiani as rector and Lavezzari as his assistant, and with both men as well as Lavizeri as residents at the Vincentian seminary. But no pastor's report was submitted to the archdiocese, nor was it mentioned in the Immaculate Conception parish report. Although Our Lady of the Rosary now regularly appeared in the directory, no founding date was given for some time, thus reflecting the uncertainty even of archdiocesan authorities. Nevertheless, the parish existed in some manner, even if not in the fullest official sense.[73]

Secundus Lavizeri, the first priest of Germantown's Italians, died at nearly ninety years of age in 1915. He was a native of Asti in the Piedmont region of Italy and had been ordained in 1848. A Vincentian since 1851, he had served at the Barrens, the noted frontier seminary in Missouri, and in St. Louis; Niagara, New York; and Emmitsburg, Maryland. He first came to St. Vincent's Seminary at its opening in 1868. During his long priesthood, he played an important role in the life of Germantown's Italians.[74]

The ambiguity of Our Lady of the Rosary as a parish ended with the purchase of a former Methodist chapel at Haines and Musgrave Streets, which finally gave Italians their own church, under Father Dominic Nepote, C.M., in May 1928. Constructed of Germantown stone, renovated by architect Giovanni Sindoni, and embellished with stained-glass windows from the well-known Nicola D'Ascenzo studio, Our Lady of the Rosary Church, with a capacity of 500 worshipers, became a reality. Although the archdiocesan newspaper reported that the dedication of the church completed the parish plant, it would have been more accurate to say that it completed the parish.[75]

Although references to "the old temporary church in the basement of St. Vincent's Seminary" reminded Italians that the temporary could become nearly permanent, especially in regard to their place within American Catholicism, the dedication was made significant by the presence of a distinguished guest. The principal officiant at the dedication as well as the celebrant of the Solemn High Mass that followed was an eighty-three-year-old priest from South Philadelphia—Father Antonio Isoleri. The pastor of the oldest Italian parish congratulated the members of the newest Italian church in their own language. He was, after all, another immigrant who had come to America uncertain whether his stay would be temporary but for whom it became permanent. He was now making one of his last public appearances.[76]

Italian colonies had made similar demands on the Archdiocese of Philadelphia across North Philadelphia. In early 1914, for three hundred families scattered beyond Mater Dolorosa, east of Broad Street, it opened Our Lady of Pompeii as a mission at Sixth and Erie Streets, with Father Paolo Gentile as rector. Gentile, a native of Cosenza in Calabria, had come to America in 1903 and served in several places before succeeding Pietro Michetti at Our Lady of Angels. It was his task to organize the mission in North Philadelphia. Seventeen months after its founding, Our Lady of Pompeii dedicated a newly constructed church in September 1915.[77]

The dedication of Our Lady of Pompeii brought together in the sanctuary Bishop McCort, assisted by two Irish American priests; the Reverend Walter P. Gough, pastor of St. Columba's Church, with Fathers Antonio Orlando as deacon and Cosmas Bruni as subdeacon; and Peter Michetti and Gentile, the new pastor. The cast of this ecclesiastical tableau reflected the power structure within the archdiocese, where Italian priests still played subordinate roles to their Irish American colleagues but where Orlando, Bruni, Michetti, and Gentile, a new generation of pastors, formed their own network of prestige and influence. But this occasion was made notable by the conspicuous absence of Isoleri, the patriarch of Italian priests in Philadelphia.[78]

The message to Italians at the dedication reiterated the usual themes. It called upon them to be grateful to the archbishop, who had always shown "a deep regard for the spiritual welfare of all foreign Catholics, but especially the Italians," and who now provided them with their own church. It identified other benefactors. It specified how Italians could express their gratitude by following the precepts and practices of Catholicism. It urged them to send their children to the mission for religious instruction and to avoid "the false teachings and alluring inducements that are snares to the foreign Catholic, but especially to the Italian." And it advised them to imitate and practice "the faith and piety to be found throughout your country, sunny Italy." It also sought to elevate spirits, darkened by the factory tainted skies that hovered over North Philadelphia in the early twentieth century.[79]

At almost the same time, some thirty Calabrian families who were seeking "to work out the destiny of their lives" formed the core of another Italian community in Tacony. They were first accommodated by Father Bruni, pastor of

Mater Dolorosa, with masses in the chapel of St. Vincent's Orphan Asylum. In October 1915, Archbishop Prendergast named Father Alfredo Procopio as pastor for a population that had grown to about 150 families living between Frankford and Bristol. Procopio, a thirty-six-year-old native of Centrache, below Catanzaro, who had served in Filadelfia, a Calabrian town named for a faraway American city, was said to have only limited fluency in English and few friends in this country. Standing before houses decorated in the American, Italian, and papal colors, an estimated 5,000 persons watched as Bishop McCort presided at the cornerstone laying in August 1916. After Flood, the school superintendent, spoke in English, Procopio addressed them in Italian. Several Italian rectors, including Fathers Orlando, Michetti, Gentile, Garritano, and deVecchis, also participated at the church first identified as Our Lady of Mount Carmel. Four months later, on the day before Christmas of 1916, with a membership of 300 persons but now called Our Lady of Consolation, its basement chapel was dedicated. McCort again exhorted his listeners to meet their religious duties and to help their pastor in paying the debt incurred by its construction.[80]

Expansion Farther West and South

As the archdiocese founded new churches in the city, more distant areas remained a similarly fertile field. With Italians recruited by railroad company agents as track maintenance workers, labor camps became incipient immigrant communities. In October 1916 ground was broken for an Italian church, at a reported cost of $12,000, in Coatesville, about forty miles west of Philadelphia, with Father Cajetan (Gaetano) Diana, from Palermo in Sicily, as its pastor. Before an estimated 2,500 spectators, McCort delivered his usual plea for support. When subsequent days at Our Lady of the Rosary became difficult, Diana was replaced in January 1918 by Father Victor Donati, a native of Gradoli in the province of Viterbo. Despite lingering financial deficits and debt, Donati remained its pastor for ten years.[81]

At almost the same time as in Tacony and Coatesville, the archdiocese inaugurated an Italian church in Marcus Hook, near Chester. Older members claimed that it had grown out of their gathering for mass on the Feast of the Assumption at Holy Savior Church in nearby Linwood, as well as out of the efforts of an American midwife who proposed a church at a meeting with Father Garritano, pastor of St. Anthony's in Chester, early in 1916. Shortly afterward, Italians met at Cadorna Society Hall to form a building fund committee. In November 1916, ground was broken on land donated by wealthy industrialist Howard J. Pew for Immaculate Conception of Lourdes Church as a mission from St. Anthony's. On August 15, 1917, two years after the plan was first launched, Italians celebrated the opening of their church. Immaculate

Conception remained a mission of St. Anthony's until it was designated a parish in July 1924. Despite the earnest clamor for their formation, churches such as the Italian mission in Marcus Hook often remained in a precarious situation in their early years.[82]

Ethnic Parishes:
An Early Assessment

As the United States moved toward public policy to restrict further immigration from Italy and other undesirable sources, the Archdiocese of Philadelphia suspended its building program for Italians in 1917. After sixteen new parishes and missions for Italians, along with the hybrid St. Rita's for Italian- and English-speaking Catholics, as well as the absorption of Italians into existing territorial parishes, efforts came to a momentary halt. While basement chapels would be replaced by completed upper churches, no more Italian parishes were begun in the next seven years until the archdiocese resumed its program with six more from 1924 to 1932. But, for the time being, it was over.

Although the churches established between 1903 and 1917 left Italian parishes in neighborhoods and communities throughout the Philadelphia area, they varied greatly in size, sacramental activity, and stability. In 1918, for example, while Our Lady of the Assumption in Strafford had only sixty-four baptisms, Our Lady of Good Counsel in South Philadelphia, the largest Italian parish in the archdiocese, recorded 2,024 baptisms. Similarly, while only two marriages were performed at Our Lady of the Rosary in Coatesville, some 185 took place at Our Lady of Good Counsel. Meanwhile, the need for Catholic education posed a special problem, as pastors who reported the number of children in public schools added their hopes for parochial schools. After examining the annual parish report, the archdiocesan auditor often concurred by such notations as "ought to have a school."[83]

Parish finances provided particularly urgent concerns for pastors and the archdiocese. Like the volume of spiritual activities, the amount of money flowing through rectory coffers greatly varied. While Our Lady of the Assumption collected only $861 in 1918, Mater Dolorosa in Frankford took in $15,423, but expenses were greater than income in both cases. And the Augustinian order had to rescue Our Lady of Good Counsel from its deficit for the same year. Several Italian parishes regularly faced annual deficits. And no Italian church approached such affluent territorial parishes as St. Patrick's, near Rittenhouse Square in center city, whose income in 1918 not only exceeded $65,000 but produced a surplus of over $18,000. While Italian pastors struggled to keep their parishes alive, the financial problems of a few especially troubled outposts were temporarily hidden by their failure to submit annual reports. Although Italian parishes could anticipate a potentially huge spiritual harvest, they did not find themselves in an abundant financial vineyard.[84]

The frequent charge that Italians in America had to learn to contribute to the Church oversimplified a complex situation. While religious authorities were willing to concede that Italians had emigrated from a nation in which their government financially supported religious institutions, they ignored two other factors. Most Italians, only recently arrived as immigrants to America, were not earning at prosperous wage levels and were barely able to survive in their new land. If they had any surplus income, it was often intended to be sent as remittances to families left behind in Italy. They also were being asked to finance the development of new churches rather than already established parishes, and the initial costs for these new churches were substantial. The problem was unlikely to be solved by the constant haranguing by American priests and prelates.

Few pastors of fragile missions and parishes, who were the most strategically placed witnesses to the situation, ever recorded their observations. Father Pietro Michetti, pastor of a church once within the Archdiocese of Philadelphia but later a part of the Allentown diocese, left a glimpse of the difficulties of pastor and parish in an Italian community in a letter to Archbishop Ryan in 1908:

> Called to the spiritual care of this community, I came trusting with the help of God, to do all the good I could and on the 27th day of Dec. 1905 I arrived in Pottsville where I found the Italian people scattered in different parts, having neglected their duties and interesting themselves only in their temporal needs and leaving their souls to be forgotten; they were drifting away from God because they did not have a Church nor a priest to guide them; with a thousand pretences and excuses they did not hear Mass in the American Churches.
>
> I found a colony without faith, without religion. My whole energy was to bring them back to God and to the Church.
>
> As I did not have a Church I rented one from Rev. Father Longinus, the rent being $150 per annum; finally, I decided to buy the Church and it was sold to me for $2500; but, I had no money and the congregation offered me only $250. What should I do?
>
> Rev. Father Longinus made the condition that if I did not pay $650 (the capital and interest) every April for five years, I should have to give up the Church.
>
> Not wishing to do wrong I borrowed the money from a Bank in Philadelphia and paid Father Longinus at once.
>
> Everyday I searched the streets to find the Italians to invite them to come to Church; God knows what work I did and what humiliations I suffered; I was sad but not discouraged when my work was not crowned with

success, the usual number in Church being only twenty or thirty persons; but, with faith in God and with prayerful lips, I continued my work and gathered them into the Church, sometimes by force and sometimes of their own free will.

After a year I was satisfied to see more than two hundred of the faithful at the Mass on Sundays and last year at the solemnities of the Church there were more than three hundred persons.

Those who come regularly are not able to pay their monthly portion. In the beginning it was possible to collect a trifle but since the financial crisis I have not been able to collect anything.

A good part of the regular attendants [*sic*] has gone away and while, formerly, I collected enough to pay the expenses of the Church itself, now there are days when not more than two dollars are collected.

But, with all this I should have been able to go on with the work if, when an assistant, Rev. Thomas Atteni, was sent to me I had not felt that it was necessary to build a house which building was sanctioned by Your Excellency through Father Travi.

To acquire this I suffered many disappointments and sacrifices. Now, the offerings for the Mass and the perquisites are used to help pay the expenses of the house.

Although I have spent for the Church, cemetary [*sic*] and house about $9000, I am glad to be able to say that the value of the property of this congregation has increased to about $14000.

All the actual difficulties are caused by the congregation not paying anything and there is, at present, no hope of collecting anything until the present financial condition of the country shall become brighter.

I do not know how I shall pay the bills amounting to $790; these embarrassments being removed it will be possible for me to proceed better.

Some persons have tried to disparage my work, saying that I have made useless and superfluous expenses; for this reason I pray your Excellency to do me the favor and send someone here to examine my work and to refer to Your Excellency what I have done and if he should find that I have been extravagant I shall be glad to pay for it myself when I am able.[85]

Michetti's letter was intended to serve his own case, but it identified several issues facing many Italian parishes. Rather than simply being a response to a large number of neglected Catholics clamoring for their own parish, it implied that the archdiocese had overextended itself in seeking to reach a relatively small and indifferent population before apostasy permanently separated it from Catholicism. Michetti's financial difficulties, moreover, tested his relationship with a neighboring pastor, whose assistance was crucial for his own success. He also had to recruit very nominal Catholics, alienated from their faith, for his congregation. With the inability of his congregation to contribute, his financial difficulties not only continued but increased with the acquisition of new property, while a slumping national economy only added to the distress of parishioners and parish alike. Michetti had unveiled the underlying reasons for his letter when he asked the archbishop to send someone to examine his work, thus answering critics who had accused him of incurring "useless and superfluous expenses."

A congregation unable or unwilling to provide material support, indifference to religion, expenses increasing rather than diminishing, strained relations with fellow clergy, and disparaging critics all defined the pastoral situation. But it was complicated further by the growth and spread of the Italian population as well as by the Catholic response to it. After a period of intense parish proliferation, Father Amilius Landolfi, in an appendix to his annual report for 1915, described conditions at his parish in West Philadelphia:

> The Church of Our [Lady of] Angels is working under peculiar circumstances. The congregation has been almost scattered by the war, and the ones left behind are either too poor, or religious once in a year.
>
> The Church needs outside help to have a right to life. But unfortunately she can't scarcely breathe between two big American Churches, and the few Americans, residing in the neighborhood, have moved elsewhere.
>
> The Italian Colony amounts to three hundred families, of which one hundred are near 40th and Girard Ave, and consequently too far. Of them 10% attend religious services, and 5% give some help. It is not a local fact; it is the index of conditions all over. Specifically this Colony is not formed by the best specimens of Italian race [*sic*]. At any rate a Colony that contributed only $240 in building an edifice of $20,000, can't be depended on for its keep.
>
> The Parochial School was the last card to build up the congregation. But lack of funds, the war and other reasons have compelled us to give up the idea. And this may be the worst page of the history of Our Lady of Angels Church!
>
> There is no parish house. This means that the priest must depend upon the good will of self appointed patrons, and the damage that comes from them to the Church interests is not at all irrelevant. And it means also additional monthly rent.
>
> There are a few little things that handicap our progress. For instance.
>
> Some individuals encourage the Italians to go to other Churches. Occasionally baptisms, funerals and marriages have been performed in other Churches. We have however the burden to assist all Italians from the River to 58th Street, with five hospitals to be attended.
>
> As West Philadelphia has two Italian parishes, it is supposed that each one should, in collecting, mention its own name, and not suppress the name

and collect for the Italians of West Philadelphia. The Missionary Sisters, I am told, collect, occasionally, under the name of Our Lady of Angels Church. And I am also been told, that somebody tells people at large that Our Lady of Angels Church does not need financiary assistence, for the simple reason that has near Our Mother of Sorrows' Church [*sic*].

All these things, of course, are trifling matter; but they hurt the interests of Our Lady of Angels Church, which is in need of improvements, and has a mortgage of $10,000.

And hurt the interests of the priest too. He can't make his salary, and can't save anything for the rainy days, or in case of sickness. The only thing he can make is a very poor living that often is not sufficient to meet the exigencies of life.

But there is the certitude that Our Lord and our Superiors will arrange the things in the way that all, sooner or later, get their good chance in the life.[86]

In his poignant comments, Landolfi indicated that the archdiocesan response to the situation did not guarantee the prosperity and well-being of all parishes. At his parish, attendance and financial support were not growing. Plans for a parochial school were already in jeopardy, and it still lacked a rectory. Sacramental events that might bring desperately needed stipends were being performed in other churches. Confusion and perhaps deception diverted money to other beneficiaries. The mortgage was quite large, and the pastor's income insufficient for even "the exigencies of life." The sources of difficulty were only partly to be found in the limitations of the people; they also came from another parish and several religious agencies. Eight years after its founding, Our Lady of Angels was not only still struggling for its survival, but was also withering before the later established, but already more successful, nearby St. Donato's.

Despite the precarious condition of some parishes, more Italian churches had been opened throughout Philadelphia and in outlying communities. But the growing Italian population had also gained the attention of Protestants in the northern and western sections of the city, as it had in South Philadelphia. In April 1910, the Christian Italian Mission had been reorganized as the Second Italian Presbyterian Church of Philadelphia, at Simpson and Callowhill Streets in West Philadelphia. Its founder, A. A. Scott, was reported as saying that he began his efforts among Italians only after being informed by a priest at a Catholic parish that they were not wanted there. When Father Joseph Corrigan addressed the issue of proselytization at the cornerstone ceremonies at St. Donato's, he was expressing his concern about a threat that had encouraged the founding of this parish as well as other ones. Although their earlier efforts had achieved only limited success, Protestants, especially with former Catholic priests of Italian origin as ministers, still posed a troubling problem to all levels of the Archdiocese of Philadelphia.[87]

The archdiocese reacted to this proselytization by Protestants in various ways. Through its weekly newspaper, for example, it criticized the Presbyterians for seeking converts by the misleading use of such symbols as the cross and by promising jobs. Among its Italian priests, whose position made them especially well suited to respond to Protestant efforts, Cosmas Bruni, rector of Mater Dolorosa, emerged as the principal apologist for Catholicism. In a letter to *La Verità*, an Italian-language newspaper, he argued that Scott and the Presbyterians had greatly exaggerated the success of their endeavors. In another letter to the archdiocesan newspaper, Bruni declared that the only members of the Presbyterian mission in West Philadelphia were a half-dozen young men who had obtained "good jobs" at the large department store where Scott was employed on the condition that they join his church. Bruni also insisted that the annual reports of the Episcopalian Mission in South Philadelphia had inflated its accomplishments. He claimed that after spending more than $100,000 in less than twenty-five years, it actually had only thirty-two members. Bruni particularly objected to the use of former priests, "the outcasts of the Catholic Church," as ministers among the Italians. He charged that Scott, perhaps carried away by his zeal, had declared, "Let us unite all Protestants, Socialists, Anarchists, and the Popery will be destroyed." Bruni indicted this coalition of radicals and anticlericals as the result of proselytism. By engaging in the vitriolic debate that often characterized the interfaith dialogue of Philadelphia Christians at this time, Bruni had joined Antonio Isoleri in declaiming and defending the interests of Italians as Catholics.[88]

Unlike the long years when Isoleri had labored alone, the issues afflicting Italian pastors now included the consequences of parish proliferation and growth. At the dedication of St. Rita's church building in 1915, Archbishop Prendergast commented on the significance of the day's events: "It is not so long ago since there was only one Italian church in the city, a little brick building on Marriot Street. Now there are many Italian churches, some of them fine buildings, and many others are going up in different parts of the diocese."[89]

While Prendergast could have added that in the earlier period to which he had referred there was only one Italian priest, he had succinctly summarized the situation facing Italian nationality parishes in Philadelphia. But beyond the "bricks and mortar," the new parishes meant that issues of human relationships had to be resolved—pastors and bishops, Catholics and Protestant proselytizers, Italians and Irish Americans, Northern Italians and Southern Italians, zealous priests and indifferent parishioners. Moreover, there was another factor—the relationship of these many priests and their parishes to one another. St. Mary Magdalen dePazzi was not just the first and sole Italian church, but was also the prototype for all the Italian parishes in Philadelphia that came afterward. And with its aging pastor, Antonio Isoleri, advancing toward the twilight of his own life, his younger brothers in the priesthood now struggled with the legacy that he would leave them.

Any attempt to assess the outcome of the archdiocesan program of expanding Italian parishes, however, finds consequences that go beyond its explicit intentions. The founding of nationality parishes did not resolve the "Italian problem" and in some respects may have actually exacerbated it. In particular, while the founding of their own parishes was welcomed by Italians, the dedication ceremonies became occasions when they were likely to be impugned. Even on these festive occasions, the principal speakers with predictable regularity described the inadequacies of Italians as Catholics and scolded them for their laxity in spiritual practices and financial support. But by their indictments of Italian Catholics, the representatives of archdiocesan authority were also constructing an unflattering public image of Italians in general, which could only fuel further hostility from other Philadelphians.

And perhaps even worse, these dedication events followed a consistent pattern. What Italians saw and heard was not a matter of mere coincidence but a clear reflection of archdiocesan policy. At the critical moment of celebration, the archdiocese was reversing an older formula by which American Catholicism had previously sought to solve the "Italian problem." While the earlier strategy had been to preserve their faith by making them good Americans, the message now shifted to a newer formula—that by being good Catholics they would become good Americans.

CHAPTER THIRTEEN

Final Years of a Priest

After a long period of intermittent turbulence and lingering tensions, the assassin's bullets that killed Archduke Ferdinand in Sarajevo in June 1914 jolted all of Europe. By autumn, most major European powers as well as Japan and the Ottoman Empire had declared war on some other nation. Eventually the United States also entered "the war to end all wars." When it finally ended, the world and the nation faced the unprecedented economic, political, and social challenges of a new era: foreign war and a just peace, internationalism and isolationism, economic prosperity and depression, Bolshevism and capitalism, totalitarianism and democracy, modernity and hedonism, morality and the Jazz Age. And religious institutions, whether entire denominations or merely particular congregations, were not immune.

In Philadelphia, local government officials and archdiocesan authorities sought to restore peace, prosperity, and progress in the postwar period. This goal required not only extracting the city from foreign wars and politics but reducing the influence of alien cultures and ideas as well. It encouraged public support for immigration restriction and for programs of Americanization directed to the foreign born and their children who were already here. It also cautioned against groups, organizations, and individuals who could divide citizens. And if it did not embrace truly integrating all Americans, it did seek to bring them under control. At the beginning of the war, state and Church had joined together to make America more American. When the Armistice brought the troops home, the exigencies of the postwar era encouraged the continuation of that goal. For an aging, foreign-born pastor of an immigrant parish, who had found a bicultural identity for himself and sought pluralism for his people, these conditions posed their own challenge.

War Comes to Little Italy

Although Italy did not enter the war until 1915, its military forces engaged the armies of the Central Powers in a line of combat broader than the Western Front. After a long and bitter stalemate in treacherous mountain terrain and weather as well as the disastrous setback at Caporetto, an Italian counteroffensive finally broke Austro-German defenses at Vittorio Veneto. And when the Armistice came in November 1918, the Italians were the only Allied forces that ended the war on enemy soil.[1]

While other Philadelphians concerned themselves with French and Belgian battlefields, Italian residents turned their attention to the bitter struggle on the Austrian front. Even before America joined the Allies, Little Italy already was a distinctive home front where residents gathered in cafés and on street corners to argue the role of their native land in the European conflict. The church of St. Mary Magdalen dePazzi served as a center of activities, where familiar religious pageantry took on new concerns. When the parish held its annual May procession in 1915, an estimated 8,000 residents marched behind American and Italian flags. Members of religious and military societies, along with hundreds of schoolchildren, participated in a massive display of religious faith and political support for their *madrepatria*. Inside the church, Father Antonio Isoleri, its pastor, led prayers for Italy.[2]

An auction to determine flag bearers for the parade captured the significance of the day for the community. A bootblack who operated a stand near City Hall won the privilege of carrying the Italian flag with his bid of $100. But when the bidding for the American flag reached only $5, angry spectators protested before someone exclaimed, "The United States is Italy's friend, and the one who carries the Red, White, and Blue shall pay the same sum as the bearer of the colors of Italy." One bidder, who refused to identify himself, then matched the offer. While customary devotions and donations were still made, the sentiments of the crowd now included politics in Italy as well as religion in America. As a newspaper account pointed out, "most of the prayers were made for the safety of relatives abroad, who soon will be in battle." On almost the same day, Italy declared war on Austria.[3]

No less patriotic than his parishioners, Isoleri responded to the war with fervor. While other priests, such as Father Joseph Matera, returned to Italy to serve as chaplains, Isoleri, now seventy years in age, was too old for military service. But after the Italian parliament declared war on Austria, he took up his pen on the day following the procession to write a poem calling the sons of Italy to war, "Il 24 Maggio 1915—Viva L'Italia!" Aware of the unresolved problem of Church and state as well as the territorial claims of Italy, he inventively linked pope and king together in the Italian cause and called for the inclusion of Trieste and Trento within the desired boundaries of an expanded nation. Beginning his final stanza with "O Guerra Santa, Guerra Benedetta" (O holy war, blessed war), Isoleri ended his bellicose poem by linking the cross of Savoy to that of Calvary. And if his words were not enough, he claimed to have recently seen "the extraordinary spectacle" of the Italian tricolor radiating around the sun.[4]

After some uncertainty about what was required of them, Italian reservists began registering at the consulate in Philadelphia, and the *Duca degli Abruzzi*, the first ship, carrying a vanguard of 3,000 men to serve their homeland, left New York in early June. In mid-June over 500 more Italians boarded the *Ancona* in Philadelphia and, after taking on other reservists in New York, sailed for Naples to join their countrymen in the war against Austria. At the same time, a large group of Italians in the New England states were ready to answer the call to arms.[5]

Italians who remained in Philadelphia responded in other ways to the war. In late May 1915, community leaders announced plans for poor relief to families of military reservists. From its headquarters on South Tenth Street, one group, claiming to have already collected $3,000 of its goal of $50,000 for the War Relief Fund, called for a mass meeting at the Musical Fund Hall. Meanwhile, the Order of the Sons of Italy in America sought to raise $100,000. In June, after parading through South Philadelphia behind Italian and American flags, Italians crowded Lyric Hall at Sixth and Christian Streets for a program sponsored by the Italian Federation. With Charles C. A. Baldi, Emmanuel V. Nardi, and other *prominenti* as well as Gaetano Poccardi, the Italian consul, in attendance, a supper provided as "the principal dish . . . the traditional spaghetti," and Ferruccio Giannini, the popular tenor, entertained them by singing his own composition, "A Trento e Trieste."[6]

Philadelphia's Italians again expressed their support of the war effort in late July. After Italian-language newspapers published the royal decree ordering reservists overseas to register for military duty or face prosecution as deserters, some 700 of them, mostly between twenty and twenty-three years old, prepared to depart from the Vine Street Municipal Pier on the *Ancona*. Along with them, the *Ancona* carried 30–40 cars of canned meats loaded in Philadelphia as well as more meat for the Italian army, horses, and 700 to 800 more men who had boarded in New York. Although the *Ancona*'s buff funnel had been painted black, her name obliterated, and her characteristic markings altered, the threat of enemy vessels on the Atlantic presented dangers to her passengers long before they reached the battlefields. The sinking of the *Ancona* four months later confirmed these fears.[7]

The call for mobilization put Little Italy in "a fever of excitement" as Italians demonstrated support for their homeland. About 30,000 men, from an estimated

Italian population of 80,000 in Eastern Pennsylvania, Southern New Jersey, and Delaware, were believed to be eligible for military service. When the consulate issued its final call in July 1915, some 3,000 reservists from the Philadelphia district were said to have already returned to Italy. As advertisements placed by "Neapolitans" eager to sell their belongings before departing filled pages of the Italian-language newspapers, the largest exodus of reservists was expected soon. And any man, whether an alien, a naturalized citizen, or American-born of Italian origin, who refused to answer the call was branded a "traitor."[8]

By August 1915, patriotic fervor was still growing among Philadelphia's Italians. On the Feast of Saint Rocco on August 16, Italians tempered their customary celebration with a more subdued observance. Special masses were held at St. Mary Magdalen dePazzi, Our Lady of Good Counsel, and St. Rita's, and about eight hundred members of the first two parishes paraded together through the streets. Money ordinarily intended for social events was collected for the War Relief Committee. As one observer noted, "For many of the Italians of this State, New Jersey, and Delaware, this will be the last celebration of any kind they will take part in before their departure for Italy, on Thursday next, when the reservists will sail from this city to join the army. . . . Prominent members of the colony here say practically all those subject to this call have responded and there will be few laggards."[9]

For men willing to serve their country, the return trip to Italy had its complications. On the day after the Saint Rocco celebration, upward of six hundred reservists gathered at the consulate on Spruce Street, carrying passports and other identification papers. The crowd soon overflowed from the steps onto the sidewalk and into the street. Inside the building, the shorthanded staff, augmented by temporary workers, processed applicants. This army of immigrants, not yet in uniform, then moved on to the Frank DiBerardino Company on Christian Street or to the Agenzia Generale di Navigazione on South Ninth Street to settle matters of money exchange, transportation, and dates of sailing. On the next day the *San Guglielmo*, with 2,000 reservists aboard, then in another two days, the *Stampalia* of the Veloce Line, and in early September, the *Sant'Anna* of the Fabre Line were scheduled to leave New York for Naples. Men with families, who began selling their household belongings, learned that they could only depart for Italy with their wives and children from New York, as ships no longer sailed from Philadelphia.[10]

As war in Europe drew closer to America, Italians gathered at St. Mary Magdalen dePazzi on a Sunday afternoon in May 1916. Greeting them with the Latin words, "Domine, da propitius pacem in diebus nostris" (Lord, with favorable peace in our times), Father Isoleri proceeded to speak in Italian, but his message followed a circuitous path. He talked of moving the body of Father Mariani, the first pastor, from St. Mary's Cemetery for reburial alongside of the church, and of replacing the cross on the old outer wall that protruded through its roof, which he greatly wished could have been carried in the day's procession. Abruptly changing the topic, he said that he preferred that it had been a day of thanksgiving for final victory and peace as well as of prayer and penitence. He praised "i nostri soldati" (our soldiers), who had fought heroically on the Isonzo, the Carso, at Monte San Michele, and at other places to the astonishment of the entire world, before reaching the boundaries assigned by God to the "bel paese, che Apennin parte, il mar circonda e l'Alpe" (beautiful land, parted by the Apennines and surrounded by the sea and the Alps), in an allusion to Dante. He declared that the Carso, bathed in so much Italian blood and now the tomb of so many sons of Italy, had become a sacred place where others would come in search of inspiration. Isoleri beseeched God to bless these soldiers, to free Italy from foreign enemies, to make her prosperous and happy again, and to bring her soldiers safely back to their homes and families.[11]

Isoleri then asked the patron saint of his parish to protect those in America, but especially in Philadelphia, who answered the homeland's call by offering their blood and lives to a patriotism that would be recorded in gold in the annals of the Italian colonies. While professing love for America, the land that had hosted Italians (before adding his inevitable gloss that it had been discovered by one of them), Isoleri reasserted that "we will always love our dear Italy." After other intercessions and a call for both flags to be brought to him to be intertwined and kissed, he declared: "for all of you, as well as for me, still Italian, after 46 years in America . . . we all know that if we love Italy, we also love Columbia, and we wish that the peace and friendship between them never be disturbed, but may endure as long as the world."[12]

After Isoleri's speech, a large but orderly crowd marched under the nearly perfect skies of the late afternoon through the streets of the neighborhood to affirm their faith, patriotism, and ethnic identity. But it was already too late. Rather than yield to the supplications of Italians in Philadelphia, the war could only come more fully into their lives. While many reservists had returned to Italy, other Italians would eventually serve in the American forces after the United States entered the war. Whether in uniform or on the home front, the war had already thrust America into the lives of Philadelphia's Italians.

The impending involvement of the United States in the World War had unprecedented implications for the Italians in Philadelphia. Many Americans felt an urgent need to resolve loyalty and allegiance issues resulting from a highly diverse population that included large numbers from countries with which their nation would soon be at war. A deliberate and accelerated Americanization program had to replace the undirected acculturation and assimilation of past years. When the National Americanization Committee began a two-day conference in Philadelphia in January 1916, its task was "the patriotic business of driving the hyphen out of life in America, now and in years to come." While participants differed on means and goals, the *Public Ledger* saw a clearly defined agenda:

"A definite campaign for Americanization is to be launched along lines laid down by men and women whose business it is to see that the United States assimilates the human ingredients of all nations in the melting pot."[13]

The Americanization conference culminated in a banquet that featured several main speakers. Father Joseph M. Corrigan, of the St. Vincent DePaul Society, presented the views of Cardinal James Gibbons, the country's leading Catholic prelate. From his days as a student in Rome to a more recent time as director of the Catholic Missionary Society of Philadelphia, Corrigan had come to know Italians well. In his speech, he declared that "God made this a shelter house for all nations." Defending the immigrant, he added: "He comes, indeed, in poverty; but we would have departed from our ideals if poverty was a bar to him." Before an audience eager to make Americans out of the foreign born, if not to exclude them entirely, Corrigan asked for kindness, patience, and consideration.[14]

The next speaker, Theodore Roosevelt, had enthusiastically applauded Corrigan, but he now launched into a rebuttal. In his far-ranging remarks, Roosevelt criticized the "promise everything and do nothing policies of the Democratic Administration," before referring to pacifists as "persons of indeterminate sex." Reaching his real target, he stated that hyphenates made America "a polyglot boarding house." Then, turning to face Corrigan at several points, Roosevelt declared that "the hyphenate is incompatible with patriotism." The former president's views, probably shared by most of his audience, foreshadowed increasing difficulties for the foreign born, whether of origins in nations aligned with or against America in the expanding war.[15]

For Isoleri and many Philadelphia Italians, Americanization meant even less than Roosevelt realized. When their pastor spoke to them, he spoke as an Italian in America, not as an Italian American. And when they paraded in the streets of Little Italy in support of troops at the Austrian front, they did not march as Italian Americans, but as Italians. And while other citizens might know what a hyphenated American was, many Italians did not. In an ethnic enclave where their language, family and friendship ties, religious worship, street life, and other experiences were defined and confined by Italian parameters, they could not anticipate the changes of later decades. Regardless of what other Americans believed, the residents of Little Italy expected, if they thought about it at all, that future generations would be as Italian as they were.

Disputing Parish Boundaries

Isoleri's long years of service were formally recognized when he was named a Domestic Prelate with the title of Right Reverend Monsignor by Pope Benedict XV in August 1916. Nearly two months later, the archdiocesan newspaper

announced the appointment in a first-page article and photograph of "the venerable rector of St. Mary Magdalen dePazzi's." As an honorary member of the pontifical household, entitled to wear the purple sash and other accouterments of a
monsignor, Isoleri was described as "one of the best known and most highly
esteemed Italian ecclesiastics in this country," whose elevation would please all
who knew of "his long, self-sacrificing and fruitful labors for the preservation
and advancement of the faith among his fellow countrymen."[16]

While these years brought further acclaim to Isoleri, his parish was declining in the Italian community. As new ones were being established in other areas,
Our Lady of Good Counsel increased its role in the old Italian district. In the estimates provided by the pastors' annual reports, Isoleri cited between 5,000 and
6,500 in the Catholic population of the area from 1914 to 1919, while Our Lady of
Good Counsel claimed 20,000 Catholics (except for 1917, when it gave an oddly
precise figure of 13,343). But both churches scaled down their later numbers.
From 5,000 in 1920, Isoleri's figure fell to 2,500 in 1925, while Our Lady of Good
Counsel reported only 10,000 to 12,000 for these years.[17]

Sacramental participation and school enrollments also recorded much
larger numbers for Our Lady of Good Counsel than for St. Mary Magdalen
dePazzi from 1914 to 1925. While baptisms and marriages remained high at the
Augustinian church, they steadily declined at St. Mary Magdalen dePazzi. By
1925, Isoleri's last full year as pastor, with only ninety baptisms and seventeen
marriages for St. Mary Magdalen dePazzi, some 1,210 baptisms and 389 marriages were recorded at Our Lady of Good Counsel (see Table 13.1).[18]

Despite surpassing its neighboring parish in the size of its congregation,
the volume of sacraments, and school enrollment, Our Lady of Good Counsel
encountered its own difficulties. While Isoleri long ago had retired the debt at
St. Mary Magdalen dePazzi, Our Lady of Good Counsel underwent an expensive
phase of development. With affluent Northern Italians remaining in Isoleri's
parish, more recent, poorer arrivals from Southern Italy comprised the congregation of the newer church. Consequently, in contrast to Isoleri's consistently
balanced budget, Our Lady of Good Counsel often showed deficits at the end
of the year. Although the congregation of St. Mary Magdalen dePazzi modestly
contributed to special collections, the archbishop formally excused Our Lady of
Good Counsel, because of its lack of funds, from these obligations in 1919. Yet,
Our Lady of Good Counsel had another resource—the financial support of the
Augustinian order, which St. Mary Magdalen dePazzi and territorial parishes
lacked, that routinely erased parish deficits.[19]

With the numbers of Italians increasing throughout South Philadelphia,
the juxtaposition of territorial and nationality parishes blurred their boundaries. While Isoleri could not dispute the assigning of Italians in more distant
parishes, he could contest two cases close to home. In February 1915, when Father Thomas Hurton, pastor of Annunciation Church, asked for jurisdiction

TABLE 13.1.   Participation in Parish Activities, 1914–1925:
St. Mary Magdalen dePazzi and Our Lady of Good Counsel

Year	Baptisms		First Communions		Marriages		School Enrollments	
	StMM-deP	OLGC	StMM-deP	OLGC	StMM-deP	OLGC	StMM-deP	OLGC
1914	567	2,103	*	695	118	527	440	1,033
1915	550	2,115	212	256	78	432	390	977
1916	470	2,273	176	302	94	*	396	1,095
1917	390	2,189	192	209	84	412	356	1,031
1918	369	2,024	148	164	52	185	380	1,031
1919	305	1,589	273	263	87	385	453	965
1920	287	1,499	140	247	80	387	474	950
1921	222	1,538	160	234	52	385	475	1,000
1922	238	*	160	*	45	*	*	*
1923	188	1,450	115	340	52	234	420	1,021
1924	145	1,550	89	250	19	345	437	1,095
1925	90	1,210	147	330	17	389	389	1,080

Source: Questiones: Annual Report (submitted by pastors of each parish, January 1, 1914–January 1, 1915, to January 1, 1925–January 1, 1926); *Annual Report of the Superintendent of Parish Schools of the Archdiocese of Philadelphia* (1914–1925), PAHRC. An asterisk means that no data were reported. The school figures represent the enrollment reported at the end of the year given.

over Italians living in an area east of Broad Street, near his parish, the archbishop's consultors initially postponed any decision until they could discuss the matter with pastors affected by the outcome. In the next month, Hurton also asked for $2,500 in compensation for the fees of Italian children attending his parish school, whose families were too poor to contribute anything themselves. The consultors again withheld their answer until the questions of boundary and jurisdiction in the neighborhood were settled.[20]

The consultors, however, already had responses from some pastors on the boundary issue. While Father Charles H. Driscoll, newly appointed at St. Rita's, did not like the plan, he did not intend to resist any decision by the archbishop.

On the other hand, Father Thomas Terlizzi, of Our Lady of Good Counsel, objecting to the loss of parishioners, strongly opposed it, and he was convinced
that the Augustinian General in Rome would do the same. The consultors now
agreed to send Auxiliary Bishop John J. McCort to seek a decision from the
papal delegate in Washington, DC. But while needing help on the boundary
question, the consultors did resolve the other issue. When Hurton again asked
for $2,500 for the four hundred Italian schoolchildren, the consultors dismissed
his request on the grounds that they lacked money for such a purpose.[21]

On McCort's return from Washington, he informed the consultors that the
papal delegate intended to submit the boundary question to authorities in Rome
later in the year. McCort had identified the specific issue as the division of Our
Lady of Good Counsel parish. Entering into the dispute, Isoleri sent a complaint
to the consultors in December 1915 that the Augustinians at Our Lady of Good
Counsel were taking away baptisms and funerals that belonged to his church.
The consultors found his charges to be vague and requested more information.
In January 1916, Hurton resubmitted his previous plea on behalf of Annunciation
parish, adding that the departure of English-speaking Catholics made it impossible to educate Italian children without an annual subsidy, now reduced to $2,400.
In contrast to their earlier rejection, the consultors now "favorably considered"
his request, without clarifying the meaning of their choice of words. These events
showed that establishing new parishes for Italians, or absorbing them into older
ones, became difficult when pastors sensed that their territory was being invaded,
their parishioners were being captured, or financial support was not forthcom-
ing. And despite nearly twenty years of apparent harmony, they also revealed a
less amicable relationship between Isoleri and the Augustinians.[22]

Isoleri's annual reports further confirmed his problems with the Augustinians. He declared that the actual size of his population was difficult to know. It
greatly fluctuated with Italians who went off to work outside of the city in the
summer, or who neglected their religious obligations, or who attended other
churches. In his 1916 report, he noted that they were going to mass and having
baptisms, marriages, or funerals, against the rules, at the Augustinian church.
Isoleri again complained that religious societies, which he had founded in the
parish, had evolved into benevolent societies that still observed annual feast
days of patron saints but did nothing more for the church.[23]

The parish of St. Mary Magdalen dePazzi witnessed the end of a much older
presence in July 1916, when Isoleri learned that the Franciscan sisters, who had
gone to their mother house in Peekskill, New York, then had decided not to
return to oversee the orphan asylum. While Isoleri disputed their charges and
impugned their character with words reminiscent of his battles with them forty
years earlier, his efforts were to no avail, and thus closed an institution that had
been a part of the parish almost from its beginning. But while Isoleri struggled
with these issues, a more lethal threat suddenly loomed over his community.[24]

The Influenza Epidemic

In the summer of 1918, as the war in Europe entered its final months, the worldwide influenza epidemic made Philadelphia another kind of battlefield. Gaining momentum in late September, it soon tore at the fabric of the entire city. In early October, the Board of Health closed all public and private schools, churches and Sunday schools, theaters, music and concert halls, dancing studios and halls, billiard and pool parlors, boxing arenas, skating rinks, and saloons. Archbishop Dennis J. Dougherty instructed pastors to open church buildings, parish halls, and schools for use as hospitals and permitted 2,000 uncloistered sisters to serve as nurses in hospitals and private homes for the duration of the crisis. City officials assigned physicians to police stations to facilitate immediate house calls in the congested districts. Patrolmen carried prescriptions to pharmacists to be filled at public expense and then delivered medications to the afflicted in their homes. At its peak, when the toll exceeded seven hundred deaths in a single day, policemen assisted overworked undertakers in removing the bodies of deceased victims from their homes, and some two hundred students from St. Charles Borromeo Seminary volunteered to bury the dead.[25]

At the height of the epidemic, Isoleri again reached for the instrument which had so frequently brought solace to him in the past, but now to restore health and peace to his people. He was seeking not only an end to the influenza but to the war as well. On October 24, he composed "Deprecatio," a remarkable poem and prayer in which each stanza in Italian ended with the plea in Latin, "A peste, fame et bello, libera nos, Domine" (From disease, famine, and war, deliver us, Lord).[26]

By the end of October, the epidemic had run its course, restrictions were lifted, and life began returning to normal in the city. The archdiocese reopened its churches in late October and parish schools in early November. But the final toll was devastating. Some city authorities believed that the official count of over 49,000 persons stricken by the disease was only one-fifth of the actual number of cases. The reported deaths from influenza and related causes varied from 13,500 to 17,000 for the year, with nearly 7,500 in October alone and 13,000 in seven autumn weeks. Not only had more deaths occurred than in most other American cities, but more Philadelphians had died from influenza than on foreign battlefields during the war.[27]

During its brief duration, the epidemic inflicted severe losses on Italians in the heavily congested districts of the city. Of the 1,457 deaths in 1918 from all causes among Italian-born residents, influenza had killed 422, while others had died from probably related causes (98 from broncho-pneumonia and 268 from pneumonia). Undoubtedly, the deaths of American-born children of Italian parents further augmented these numbers but were not separately reported by city agencies. Altogether, some 597 children, less than one year old, of Italian-born mothers, died during the year. This figure, representing 21 percent of infant deaths for all foreign-born mothers, was higher than for any other immigrant group, and more than 10 percent of all infant mortality in the city. Whether from an epidemic or from chronic conditions, death was never far away from life in the immigrant community.[28]

A Declining Role

When his poem "Deprecatio" was printed, Isoleri added a note that his supplication had been granted with the simultaneous cessation, as if by a miracle, of both the epidemic and the war on November 3, 1918. While his choice of date in regard to the epidemic was arbitrary, Isoleri had accurately denoted the end of hostilities on the Austrian front. Undeterred by the recent public health crisis, Italians in Philadelphia celebrated Italy's victory and the restoration of peace with ceremonies at Independence Square, while Isoleri reclaimed his role as their spiritual leader and patriotic bard.

When the *Conte di Cavour*, an Italian cruiser, visited Philadelphia in October 1919, Isoleri prepared a sermon for a special Columbus Day mass on the vessel. Although he had not seen his homeland for nearly a half-century, Isoleri wrote that he still carried "La Bella Italia" in his mind and heart. Being on board would be almost like being there, because the ship truly was, as he again used one of his favorite phrases, a "lembo d'Italia" (patch of Italy). On the next day, when he led parish children on a tour of the ship, he was to celebrate mass in place of the archbishop whose great love for Italy had supposedly made him "half-Italian." Drafting remarks for his sermon, Isoleri recounted in detail Columbus's voyages, reaffirmed his own love of religion and nation, and asked for God's blessing on King Victor Emmanuel III. Although bad weather forced cancellation of the ceremony, Isoleri's undelivered text, nevertheless, showed his persistent affection and allegiance for Italy as well as his talent for finding ingratiating words on nearly every occasion.[29]

Now cast in an increasingly ceremonial role, Isoleri could not yet be ignored as a leader of the Italian community. Recognizing his many years of experience as a pastor, the archbishop in September 1921 named him as a consultor, a position that he would hold for the rest of his life. In contrast to his early clashes with Archbishop Wood, his appointment underscored his accomplishments and the respect that he had earned within the archdiocese. He had also arrived at some accord with agencies in his neighborhood, and the Starr Centre sought his financial and moral support for its programs to aid children of foreign ancestry. Similarly, the U.S. Department of Labor's Employment Bureau, writing to him as "Monsignor Salera," solicited his help in recruiting laborers for New

Jersey's truck farms. How Isoleri responded to such pleas remains unknown, except that, mindful of his own scarce resources, he parsimoniously outlined his sermons on the same pages that brought this correspondence.[30]

Entering his final years as a pastor, Isoleri's role among Italians had been altered both by his advancing age and broader changes within the community. After a half-century in Philadelphia, while he still saw himself as an Italian, his congregation, especially its younger generation, swept up by acculturation, was increasingly American. And if he had once railed from his pulpit about the evils tempting his people, he now faced a far more materialistic and hedonistic society. In some ways, Isoleri had become a priestly relic of an earlier time, compatible more with the religion and culture of the previous century than with the present era. Although his physical strength had slowed a bit, his spiritual zeal had not; and he was still the pastor of St. Mary Magdalen dePazzi. But another instrument of assimilation, much closer to Isoleri, had emerged. Secular, Protestant America was no longer alone.

Americanization in the Parishes

Almost immediately with the U.S. entry into the World War, Catholic social thought and public policy rushed to offer staunch support for Americanization at all levels. Twelve days after the United States declared war on Germany in April 1917, the archbishops met in Washington, pledged the loyalty of the clergy and laity, and offered their services to the government. In August a meeting at the Catholic University of America organized the National Catholic War Council (NCWC), composed of the fourteen archbishops and an administrative committee of four other bishops, with the Knights of Columbus and the Committee on Special War Activities as subordinate bodies. It assumed a major role in forging the official position of American Catholicism on the foreign born.[31]

The postwar Church continued to address the issue of immigration. Several NCWC civic education programs, initially fostered by wartime exigencies, stressed the need to teach the fundamentals of democracy to the foreign born and their children. The Americanization plan began with English lessons, then moved on to naturalization and the acquisition of the attitudes and ideals of American citizenship. In September 1919, the Catholic hierarchy issued a pastoral letter stating: "In making them its own, America has shown a power of assimilation without precedent in the temporal order"; but it admitted that much remained to be done for those who "like our forefathers, come from other countries to find a home in America." Immigrants needed help in understanding the American system of government, assuming citizenship duties, and avoiding the contagion of evil influences. Above all, the letter called for a Christian sympathy that saw possibilities rather than defects and that was based on charity instead of distrust in dealing with immigrants: "Since many of their failings are the consequence of treatment from which they suffered in their homelands, our attitude and action toward them should, for that reason, be all the more sympathetic and helpful."[32]

The American hierarchy had become no less assimilationist than anyone else. In January 1920 the renamed National Catholic Welfare Council claimed that the hierarchy, speaking on behalf of twenty million American Catholics, was the first religious body to pledge "whole-hearted and unreserved support to the President and the National Government" at the start of the war. Citing it as "the fulfillment and embodiment of that promise," the NCWC described its work during the war years. In reporting on the Committee on Special War Activities, the NCWC presented its slogan, "MAKE AMERICA 100 PER CENT AMERICAN," in capital letters. Its publication office printed thousands of copies of a pamphlet, *The Fundamentals of Citizenship*, in English, Polish, Italian, and Hungarian for civic education classes. Another NCWC publication, *Civics Catechism on the Rights and Duties of American Citizens*, posed questions and answers based on an extensive section on naturalization. It seemed as if Theodore Roosevelt had finally made converts of the members of the American hierarchy.[33]

Despite embracing an assimilationist program, however, the hierarchy had not entirely abandoned the spirit of Corrigan's earlier remarks at the Philadelphia conference on Americanization in 1916. At the NCWC meeting in September 1920, Archbishop Edward J. Hanna reported that representatives of the Polish, Italian, Lithuanian, and Slovak communities, serving on various committees, knew that "they are welcome to have a voice in these councils." Archbishop Dougherty of Philadelphia described an Americanization bill, expected to be the most important matter in the next Congress, that afforded an opportunity "to lift the curse of illiteracy."[34]

While old issues were still evolving, however, new ones were also appearing. At a convention of Catholic men, Father John J. Burke, the NCWC's general secretary, outlined some dimensions of immigration in late September 1920. Of 100,000 immigrant arrivals in the previous month, the majority were Catholics. Of one million immigrants expected in the next year, at least 60 percent would be Catholics. Yet, while Evangelical Protestants ran ten of the fifteen agencies allowed on Ellis Island, only one Catholic group, mainly for English-speaking arrivals, provided services to newcomers. Moreover, Young Men's Christian Association (YMCA) agents worked at ports of embarkation, traveled with immigrants on ships, met arrivals at Ellis Island, and conducted them to their final destinations.[35]

Burke declared that Communism posed an even greater threat to immigrants, who came not as violent radicals but as law-abiding peasants seeking opportunities. After offering jobs and housing and ingratiating themselves with new arrivals at Ellis Island, the Communist "begins to sow the seed of discontent, of radicalism, in the immigrant's heart by telling of the cruelty of the capitalists; of how financial interests control our Government." Then, Burke continued, brought to radical gatherings, where fellow immigrants are found and all good, hopeful beliefs about America are undermined, they soon join the "revolutionary" party.[36]

With the American hierarchy now endorsing Americanization, the Holy See renewed its efforts to ensure pastoral care for Italian immigrants. In 1920, Benedict XV revived a plan, first sought by Pius X but postponed by the war, to establish a college in Rome to train Italian priests to look after the moral and spiritual welfare of emigrants, supervise the work of these priests, assist them by seeking help and cooperation from local bishops, and coordinate all efforts toward immigrants. No Italian priest of the diocesan clergy would be allowed to minister to immigrants unless he had been trained at the college. It was also expected that the bishops of foreign countries would cooperate by assigning the care of Italians only to priests trained at the college. Other provisions of the plan, which focused on the dangers of migration itself, sought to establish a social service system for new arrivals that was ready at all times "to receive them kindly, help them, direct them, accompany them, and save them from the intrigues of the vampires who in Italy and elsewhere try to exploit these poor emigrants." Although NCWC support was anticipated, the plan implicitly challenged Americanization and threatened the control of American bishops over parishes and priests.[37]

Three years later, Bishop Edward M. Dunne reiterated NCWC policy on assimilation. Echoing Nativist views, he wrote that Southern and Eastern Europeans had been unwilling or slow to give up their customs and languages as well as reluctant to amalgamate with other peoples. While keeping immigrants faithful to Catholicism and retaining their native tongue as long as necessary, the Church wanted to make them good American citizens. And although never seeking to erase ethnic characteristics, they could not be indefinitely maintained. But immigrant communities could not isolate themselves from other Americans, as it was neither good for the common country nor for the immigrants themselves. Arguing that the Church had long assimilated divergent races, Dunne noted that new canon law prohibited any further formation of parishes based on language or nationality without special permission from the Holy See. He concluded: "The Church is contributing her full share towards the Americanization of the immigrant."[38]

Catholic opinion included some dissent to this emphasis on assimilation. Father Nicola Fusco's filio-pietistic survey of contributions from Columbus to those of present-day laborers praised Italians without even slightly implying that their assimilation was desirable. Father Aurelio Palmieri, an Augustinian, defended the popular piety and fidelity of Italians but recognized the inevitability of assimilation: "I am convinced that after another half century there will be no longer 'Italian' churches in the United States. The children of immigrants will no longer talk Italian nor preserve remembrance of Italian life or traditions. They will be completely 'Americanized.'"[39]

When passage of the Johnson-Reed Act in 1924 solidified restrictive federal immigration policy, an observer argued that "our Catholic immigration problem enters upon a new phase." A spirit of Nativism throughout America dictated "that this country shall become more and more one homogeneous nation, built upon one political tradition of government and one language." With amalgamation of foreign groups an unmistakable and unmixed blessing that could not be opposed on any grounds, the "melting pot" was no longer an option but a legal and moral imperative. The new law also affected Church policy, but since Catholics had always been "wholeheartedly loyal to America," Catholicism could now offer its own version of Nativism. As one priest observed,

> Foreign Catholics are no exception to this rule. There is danger, however, that if the latter insist overmuch on setting themselves aside into permanently isolated national groups, they will contribute to intensify that feeling of distrust. There can be no room of course in the American Republic for colonies of European countries or anything that even remotely amounts to that, such as language groups where a foreign spirit, foreign ideas and foreign customs are clung to tenaciously. There is no need for casting any aspersion on their loyalty. However there is need for serious thought and reform when statistics such as those recently published by our Secretary of Labor show that one of our largest national groups—Catholic to the core—has a naturalization record of only 28 per cent., where other national groups have a record of 60 to 72 per cent.[40]

The same writer predicted the implications of immigration restriction for religious life in America. First, "our national parishes will gradually decline in number and importance." But the foreign priest, ministering to a foreign flock, was also advised not to obstruct this natural evolution, as he stands to lose nothing and gain everything. In a curious choice of words, "the imperious need of foreign priests will also decrease as the number of immigrants decreases." (One can only wonder how Isoleri, after fifty-four years in America, might have interpreted this sentence.) Canon law now allowed the children of immigrant families to abandon their nationality parish and to join one where English was preached. The rationalization for policy that not only reduced nationality parishes but also undermined other institutions that preserved immigrant culture was readily available: "Very often the younger generation takes advantage of this privilege. To them their parents' tongue has lost its interest and value. Brought up in American surroundings, with the English language as the vehicle of their education, imbued with the heroism that gave rise to the American Republic, using the English language in their daily life in business and at play, they have a natural and rightful predilection for it and for the country it represents. No foreign speech, not even that of their parents, will arouse in them the same enthusiasm, or appeal to their innermost soul."[41]

This strategy and its underlying ideology fused Catholicism and Americanism. Its proponents argued that no antagonism could ever exist between "sane patriotism and true religion." They believed that a gradual natural process, without undue pressure toward unhealthy assimilation, would determine the outcome, while legislation would serve as a catalyst. But with immigration restriction and an aging first generation, Italian colonies in urban America were becoming Italian American neighborhoods. As the Church waited out the anticipated demise of nationality parishes, the Archdiocese of Philadelphia pursued a different course by founding St. Michael of the Saints (1924) in Germantown; Our Lady of Mount Carmel (1924) in Bridgeport, Montgomery County; King of Peace (1926) in Gray's Ferry; Mother of Divine Grace (1926) in North Philadelphia; St. Lucy's (1927), long a congregation in Manayunk; Our Lady of the Rosary (1928), already with its own school in Germantown; and Our Lady of Loreto (1932) in Southwest Philadelphia, the last parish intended for Italians in the city. As population growth and parish expansion continued in other areas, the archdiocese, whether by conscious design or unintended consequence, pursued a course of action in South Philadelphia that was isolating St. Mary Magdalen dePazzi, about to eliminate Our Lady of Good Counsel, and strengthening St. Paul's as the principal church. And for an old priest at Little Italy's first church, the future was coming quickly.

The Catholic Missionary Society
and the Don Bosco Institute

In addition to parishes, the Catholic Missionary Society sought to reach young Italian Americans through the Madonna House and L'Assunta House in South Philadelphia. Father Edward J. Lyng, after seven years as director, described efforts to bring about the Americanization of Italian children in 1922: "The keen observer in the Settlement work of an Italian district becomes daily conscious of gradual changes and visible spiritual improvement. This has particular reference to the children of these immigrants. The reason is not far to find. They are essentially the children of the land, growing up in a thoroughly American atmosphere, imbibing principles of American conduct, adapting themselves, consciously or unconsciously, to American standards, learning American aggressiveness, and evolving themselves into dependable citizens of the future."[42] Along with Americanization, Lyng identified the other aim of settlement work as the reclaiming of immigrant children, particularly public school students, for Catholicism. Catechetical instruction would enable children "to combat the insidious errors so prevalent in this day, to resist the attractions of proselytizing agents and institutions, and to give forth in their future lives the evidence or the 'reason for the faith that is in them.'"[43]

In the summer of 1923, the Catholic Missionary Society announced plans to construct a new building, costing $60,000, for the Madonna House at 926–930 Christian Street. The Renaissance-design structure would house a library, staff offices, and social services on the first floor; six classrooms and a large clubroom for girls on the second floor; a similar pattern of rooms for boys on the third floor; and a playroom for older children and a kindergarten in the basement.[44]

At their meeting in October 1923, Archbishop Dougherty and the Missionary Society's board of directors discussed current work and future plans. According to one account, Dougherty "showed a thorough grasp of the situation by his display of intimate knowledge of many of the difficulties connected with religious work among the Italian people." Along with plans for a new L'Assunta House at Tenth and Dickinson Streets, he expressed concern for public school students who were being deprived of religious instruction. Declaring that the need for work among Italians had become more apparent, Father Lyng then reported on what had been accomplished. Almost 300 children, who might otherwise have been neglected, had been baptized, and 100 others were almost ready for the sacrament. He stated that workers had made 10,000 home visits in South Philadelphia and Norristown in six months, which had led to 250 baptisms, 500 First Communions, and 3,000 enrolled in catechism classes. These workers also visited sick persons at home or in hospitals, found jobs for the unemployed, and placed destitute and orphaned children in Catholic families. By such work, Catholic settlements had become "household words in the Italian colonies," and their workers were "greatly appreciated by those in whose spiritual behalf they have labored."[45]

At the same meeting, Lyng announced another program for Italians. After eight troubled years the Salesians had closed the Don Bosco Institute, and the archdiocese now sought to relocate the participants in its programs to a building, obtained and renovated at Dougherty's request, at 609 South Tenth Street. Lyng asserted that "the new Don Bosco Club is destined to do great good among the youth of the Italian colony and its membership is on the steady increase"; moreover, such organizations provided "a means of solving the perplexing Italian problem." His remarks as well as the retaining of an old name for a new effort implicitly deprecated the work of the Salesians, whose departure had not only ended their presence among Philadelphia's Italians but would also foreshadow the controversial termination of Our Lady of Good Counsel a decade later.[46]

Even before the Salesians had arrived, the planning for a new undertaking among Italians had been marked by disagreement over objectives, programs, and facilities. In 1910, a local priest had informed the Salesians that he could secure a building suitable for college and community work. Nearly four years later, Louise Drexel Morrell, the younger stepsister of Mother Katherine Drexel, expressed her wish·to support efforts among young Italians, and her husband, Edward Morrell, stated his intention to convey ownership of a building to the archdiocese in a letter to Prendergast. But while the Morrells, generous benefactors to various causes, had envisioned a Catholic version of the YMCA, the Salesians anticipated a more ambitious program. The Salesians also disagreed with the archdiocese over whether their chapel should be available to the public for mass on Sundays and Holy Days. By 1916, the Salesians had already considered terminating their work at the Institute. And, in another year, the Morrells themselves questioned the transfer of property ownership to the Salesians.[47]

Salesian dealings with the archdiocese deteriorated further after Dougherty became archbishop of Philadelphia in July 1918. In the next year, when the original agreement with the Morrells neared its end, the Salesians turned to the archdiocese. But the consultors concluded that the Institute did not warrant their support and recommended a reorganization of the Salesian project. Meanwhile, Mrs. Morrell was making her final contribution.[48]

Financial issues were not the only problem between the Salesians and the archbishop. In August 1920, Father Ernest Coppo, director of the Don Bosco Institute, while attending a meeting of Italian clergy in Atlantic City, was asked to conduct a survey to determine whether Italian priests would join Buona Stampa, a society seeking to organize them in Philadelphia, as well as support the *Giornale Italiano,* a daily newspaper, and the *Almanacco,* an annual guide for Italians in America. While Dougherty was not pleased, he took no immediate action. In December, however, electrical inspectors abruptly descended on the Don Bosco Institute and found fifty-three violations and other matters needing attention. In emphatic words typed in red, their report described the condition of the building as "extra hazardous to life and property." For the Salesians, the situation was to become even worse.[49]

Although the Salesians believed that they had regained Mrs. Morrell's support, Dougherty still opposed their plans. Early in 1921 he refused their request to relocate in another part of the archdiocese. In September, Father Peter Truffa, newly appointed as director of the Don Bosco Institute, wrote to Father Emmanuel Manassero, the American provincial, asking if the influence of Cardinal Giovanni Bonzano, apostolic delegate to the United States, might enable them to gain Dougherty's support in obtaining St. Paul's parish. In his reply, Manassero indicated his hope that a Catholic high school might also be in their future. Now antagonized even more, Dougherty informed Truffa of his dissatisfaction with the Salesians. Believing that they had achieved very little, Dougherty intended to deny them any further financial support and to expedite the closing of the Institute. But he even more strongly opposed any Salesian involvement in parish work while they waited for a parish of their own.[50]

By late 1921, Truffa recognized two major problems. First, the limitations of its building seriously hindered the work of the Don Bosco Institute; second, while it served younger members and families of St. Paul's, the Salesians could not exercise religious or moral control over them, which remained the right of the parish. Truffa proposed that either the youth program be reorganized within a parish or, even better, that St. Paul's be granted to the Salesians as their own parish.[51]

Truffa described the rapidly deteriorating situation in another letter to Manassero in May 1922. While indicating that more help was needed, he reported that Dougherty had abruptly ended a recent meeting. Beyond the archbishop's lack of enthusiasm, the building housing the Don Bosco Institute was not only ill-suited for its program, but the Morrells had also finally given it to Dougherty rather than to the Salesians. Truffa declared that only a miracle could save the Salesians.[52]

Rather than a miracle, Manassero brought the situation to its final stage by stating the Salesian position in a letter to Dougherty in August. Unless they were allowed to expand their efforts in the community, other plans should be made for the Institute, thus freeing the Salesians to be sent to other work. But Dougherty neither responded to the letter nor to a delegation that included an archbishop who supported the Salesian cause. Realizing that Dougherty had no intention of providing financial assistance or access to any other institution, parish, or church, the Salesians "turned the lock for the last time on the doors of Don Bosco Institute" sometime between August and November 1922.[53]

Unresolved disagreements had doomed the Don Bosco Institute from the start. While the Morrells wanted a recreation program, the Salesians preferred to undertake spiritual and religious work. After accepting the building, they found it inadequate for their efforts. When they sought to transfer the building to their own control, the Morrells lost confidence in them. When Dougherty wanted them to teach catechism, visit the sick, and call upon families to persuade them to attend church, the Salesians believed that this work would conflict with that of existing parishes and their priests. And when they sought to attach their work to a church, Dougherty refused to give them either a parish or to allow them to relocate elsewhere. As a Salesian scholar succinctly stated, "There was no room for dialogue, explanation, or discussion of the wishes of the Salesians."[54]

Underneath these issues, other factors had separated the Salesians and the archbishop. In believing that "Father Coppo had lost himself in the useless undertaking of founding an Italian Catholic newspaper," Dougherty had actually misrepresented Coppo's role at the Atlantic City conference of 1920.[55] But as an archbishop who espoused Americanization, he could not ignore the threat of an organized, nationalistic clergy within his own domain. Moreover, along with the Augustinians already there, the Salesian presence further threatened archdiocesan influence among Italians in South Philadelphia. While an elderly diocesan priest such as Isoleri posed no threat, the Augustinians might have to be dealt with in the future. Consequently, the outcome of the Don Bosco Institute controversy reflected the will of a prelate who did not intend to share one more parish or any more influence within the Italian community with any religious order whose members were not under his direct control.

With the Salesians gone, the Catholic Missionary Society resumed its role as the principal Catholic agency providing social services to Philadelphia's Italians. As the new Madonna House neared completion, the society thanked the Irish-dominated Knights of Columbus for supporting its work among Italians. At its semi-annual meeting, Catholic Missionary Society members and Cardinal Dougherty discussed Church efforts "to bring her blessings to her children of Italian extraction." At the Madonna House dedication, it became a shared Irish and Italian project when the Knights of Columbus, Italian societies, Irish American clergy, Archbishop Dougherty, Consul Luigi Sillitti, and Henry DiBerardino, a prominent banker, all played conspicuous parts.[56]

The Missionary Society held a highly flattering mirror to its work among Italians in a 1925 report. In the last six months its activities included 3,500 home visits as well as visits to 200 sick persons, some of whom were dying; some 68 children baptized; another 100 more prepared for baptism; and several hundred children instructed at the Madonna House and L'Assunta House in South Philadelphia and the Catholic Settlement House in Norristown for their First Communion. The society also encouraged children to attend parochial schools, helped the poor to find employment, aided older children and adults, and distributed food and clothing. It offered special activities at Christmas. It cooperated with district nurses and legal aid services and ran a dispensary and clinic under the direction of a physician at the Madonna House. And it had also organized the Don Bosco Catholic Club for young people. Despite the need to reduce debt, and persistent proselytization efforts by outside groups, the society optimistically assessed its own programs. With increases in the work at the settlement houses, it noted that the good accomplished among hundreds of children was not only helping to solve the "Italian problem," but also "doing inestimable good towards the instilling of genuine principles and ideals of Americanism." Besides DiBerardino, previously the only Italian member, Joseph P. Bartilucci, a lawyer, and Emmanuel V. H. Nardi, a businessman, now represented their community on the board.[57]

By its twenty-fifth year, in 1927 the Catholic Missionary Society claimed a staggering 14,000 home visits, 500 First Communions, 500 confirmations, 500 more candidates for both sacraments, and some 3,000 children under instruction. Although the volume of house visits was "a matter for very grave reflection," it had brought many families "into closer association with religion . . . who might otherwise have been neglected in the great conquest of souls." It was a moment of "spiritual revival and re-interest by Italians" whose children were coming "to a gradual consciousness of their religious obligations." Meanwhile, the society's medical and social services, mainly through the ear, nose, and throat clinic at the Madonna House under Dr. A. A. S. Giordano, had treated more than 200 patients during the year. Its report asserted that the Madonna House facilities were unsurpassed by any of the "proselytizing institutions," thus making it the chief settlement house in the entire Italian district. The new Bosco Catholic Club, moreover, had never appealed for financial support for any building project or activity, but took pride in being self-supporting and eager to assume its own financial obligations. But this gratuitous slap at the Salesians was not the only invidious aspect of the report in its relationship to other efforts among Italians.[58]

The Missionary Society did more than surpass "proselytizing institutions"; its programs had implications for Catholic parishes as well. In meeting the challenge of the settlement house movement, the society provided services and activities that might have otherwise been offered by parishes. Rather than supplement parish life, the society diminished it. By assuming the needs of Italian families and their children, which even in the heart of Little Italy could not be left to their own parishes, it assigned their care to Irish American control. And while the society's programs assumed a joint Irish and Italian character, there was little doubt about their emphasis.

When the Missionary Society celebrated its twenty-fifth anniversary with a banquet at the Bellevue-Stratford Hotel in January 1928, older and newer factors that defined Irish and Italian relations, as well as the problems facing the archdiocese, became apparent. The principal speakers included Giacomo Nobile deMartino, Italian ambassador to the United States; Mayor Harry A. Mackey; Monsignor Henry T. Drumgoole, founding director of the Missionary Society and the Madonna House; and Father Joseph M. Corrigan, the second director and current rector of St. Charles Borromeo Seminary. Henry DiBerardino served as master of ceremonies. Among Italian Americans who addressed the gathering, the Honorable John J. Freschi of New York spoke on "The Italian in America," Judge Eugene V. Alessandroni on "The Italian in Philadelphia," and John DiSilvestro, grand venerable of the Sons of Italy, on "The Italian in Pennsylvania." The music for the evening included Irish and Italian pieces. On this occasion, which marked archdiocesan efforts in Little Italy, the oratory of co-opted laymen, without even one Italian priest in any visible role, could not entirely disguise Irish hegemony within the religious life of its citizens.[59]

Cardinal Dougherty, in the main event of the evening, further attested to the direction of ethnic power in the activities undertaken by the archdiocese. In his profile and assessment of the Italians, he described the size and location of the local population, the reasons for its immigration, its cultural traits and contributions, the role of women, the poverty and needs of the colony, and the futility of sectarian settlement houses seeking to proselytize within it. As he depicted the Italians, Dougherty noted the increasing complexity of Little Italy: "In that section one may hear not only Tuscan, but also nearly every Italian dialect; and see reproduced the charming customs, so dear to Italians and all lovers of Italy." Beneath his ostensible sensitivity to Italians, it was evident that Dougherty, with his commitment to Americanization, was actually patronizing them.[60]

Dougherty then traced the history of the Madonna House, paying tribute to leaders, staff, and the Italians whom it served but especially to its lay workers, "whether Italian or of other nationalities." His remarks could not hide the fact that the Madonna House, as a neighborhood institution, now impinged upon the material, religious, and cultural roles of Italian priests and nationality parishes. Agencies such as the Madonna House, largely Irish American in leadership, staffing, and program content, offered an alternative cultural pathway, particularly to young people in their religious expression as well as in their adjustment to urban life, which reflected the triumph of Irish American Catholicism as the dominant form of American Catholicism.[61]

At the same time, the Missionary Society's celebration openly displayed a recently emerged dimension of international politics that impinged on the religious life of Italians in Philadelphia as well as in Italy. In his address at the banquet, Ambassador Nobile deMartino spoke of the political situation in Italy since the end of the war: "under the constructive genius of Mussolini, the threatened evil of anarchy and chaos springing from the menace of Bolshevism had been averted." He declared Italy's need for Catholicism, extolling the special place of the Virgin Mary in popular piety. While Italians would be joined by many Americans in believing that il Duce's Corporate State offered a viable program for the future of Italy, these convictions cemented an unfortunate liaison between Catholicism and Fascism as a bulwark of defense against "Godless communism."[62]

While the Italian clergy moved cautiously, prominent Italian American laymen endorsed the Church and archdiocese by their own words and actions. In the week before the Madonna House banquet in 1928, Judge Alessandroni celebrated the renewal of his own faith as a Catholic at a meeting of the Knights of Columbus. A newspaper item described his speech as "more in the nature of apologia for the return to the Faith of his fathers." As he looked into the depths of his soul, Alessandroni declared that he had to travel on the same path "in which my fathers and forefathers before me had traveled and had placed me." Beyond his return to Catholicism, he claimed that for Italians, no other institution was "more adapted to their needs; more suitable to their aspirations; more essential for their spiritual salvation." But Alessandroni would have been more accurate if he had recognized that he was traveling on a path of fathers and forefathers from Galway, rather than from Abruzzi. And his public confession, much like the once-popular practice of the Catholic press of reporting conversions of prominent Protestants, made him a newly earned trophy of the archdiocese as well as its prized role model for other Italians.[63]

In the Twilight Years

By the 1920s, as Italians and their American-born children adopted the culture of a new society and, along with other Americans, struggled with rapid change and readjustment, they also became immigrants to modern times. In the ethnic ghettos of American cities, social change and assimilation posed a double challenge to residents and institutions. Now, St. Mary Magdalen dePazzi, which as the only Italian church had long served to define Little Italy until it was diminished by other parishes, shared its people and place. Similarly, Isoleri's pastoral role had not only reached its final stage but also reflected this altered context.

As technology transformed American life, Isoleri sought to guide St. Mary Magdalen dePazzi, as its pastoral shepherd, into the modern era without rejecting traditional beliefs and practices. When electricity first lit the church in January 1922, he began his homily at the dedication ceremony by referring to God's illumination of the world, before noting the contributions of Italian genius—Volta, Galvani, and Marconi—as well as "il nostro Franklin." Asking that God's gifts be not abused by man, Isoleri stated his hope that intellect and faith, bodily senses and divine grace, and the sun and moon as well as electric lights would together illuminate the steps to the eternal rest and perpetual light for which we were all created. His brief but eloquent remarks, while linking technological progress with ethnic pride, at the same time captured the efforts of his ancient faith to enter the contemporary world.[64]

A week after the electric lamp ceremony, Isoleri returned to the familiar theme of the sacredness of matrimony in his Sunday homily. Citing remarks by Theodore Roosevelt on "race suicide," Isoleri condemned birth control as an aspect of a society of sensuality. He then gave a detailed outline of what the Church asked of its members as they prepared for marriage. On the next Sunday, Isoleri sorrowfully eulogized the recently deceased Benedict XV while remarking on the national origins of 259 popes. He admitted his hope for the election of another Italian. From birth control to papal succession, Isoleri was caught up as much as anyone else by the issues confronting Catholicism.[65]

The past, however, was not forgotten, nor was the future being ignored. In November 1923, five years after the Armistice ended "the war to end all wars," a grand parade wound through South Philadelphia to celebrate the fifth anniversary of the pivotal Italian victory at Vittorio Veneto. At ceremonies for military veterans at the Armory at Broad and Wharton Streets, Isoleri's brief patriotic address, filled with vivid memories, intense sentiments, and subtle allusions, noted the blessings bestowed on Italy by its modern history. He remembered the ineffable joys of early victories in the struggle for Italian independence. He recalled the loss of Nice and Savoy at the time of his final exams in the seminary, when his professors lamented the impending prospect of "un altra guerra per liberare questa Italia nostra" (another war to liberate our Italy). He deplored the ceding of Venice to France while the old emperor, Franz Joseph, held Trento and Trieste for Austria. Isoleri even granted that the old mocking observations of Metternich and others long ago held some truth.[66]

Shifting to Italy's role in the World War, Isoleri remembered the reservists on the *Ancona*, whom he had blessed as they departed for military service in their mother country. Along with three long years of tears, prayers, and fears by families left behind, he poignantly depicted the Italian soldiers who had bathed the Alps with their blood and turned red the waters of the Piave River. But their ultimate success, he declared, had etched in gold the name "Vittorio Veneto" forever in history. He urged the veterans to wave the tricolor banner of Italy intertwined with the Stars and Stripes of their adopted land. And while praising one Italian who discovered America and another who named it, Isoleri again used Dante's celebrated phrase to refer to Italy as "il bel paese che . . . il mar circonda e l'alpe."[67]

Isoleri's other topics were almost lost in his concluding and disconnected remarks. Thanking God "che un figlio della forte Romagna, un' ex-combattente fa finalmente valere e rispettore questa Italia nostra" (that a son of strong Romagna, a war veteran [i.e., Mussolini], is finally making our Italy worthy and respected), he recognized a new reality in modern Italy and its politics. Resuming his main theme and extolling veterans as second only to martyrs of the faith, he exhorted his listeners to ignore the insults of traitors and Bolsheviks. He then returned to the need to resolve "the fatal divorce between Church and State." Isoleri concluded with his familiar gesture of kissing the two flags to cries of "Viva l'Italia, viva l'America!" But while still capable of stirring an audience, he was nearing his end as a political prophet in the Italian community. It was a good thing. For despite his tribute to the "son of strong Romagna," the rise of Fascism would prove to be a fantasy of national power and respectability for Italians in America that ultimately would lead only to disaster.[68]

Pastor Emeritus

In May 1926, at the age of eighty-one, Isoleri resigned after fifty-six years as pastor of St. Mary Magdalen dePazzi. Subsequent events indicate that some persuasion may have encouraged his decision. Four days later, the archdiocese named Father Antonio Garritano, a Calabrian, as pastor. Garritano, previously pastor at St. Anthony of Padua in Chester, was accompanied by Father Agnello J. Angelini, who was also transferred from the same church to St. Mary Magdalen dePazzi. Garritano almost immediately began to reorganize the parish with a new schedule of confessions, masses, baptisms, devotions, and sodality programs. In July, 200 girls joined the Sodality of the Blessed Virgin Mary and boys met to form their own clubs, thus "illustrating the progressive spirit of the parishioners under Father Garritano's guidance," while he claimed that large numbers now crowded all services. For priests arriving from Italy, it also served as a temporary refuge before they were assigned to other parishes. Activities in October included a mission preached by a Vincentian, the opening of a shrine to Saint Teresa of Avila, and the induction of 400 members into the Children of Mary and 175 men to the Holy Name Society. Garritano claimed that all indications pointed to a flourishing religious life for the future. These results, regularly reported in the archdiocesan newspaper, projected an image of a recently languishing parish that had been revived by an energetic new pastor.[69]

The renewal of parish life at St. Mary Magdalen dePazzi and harmony within its rectory as well as with the archdiocese were, however, more illusion than reality. Isoleri, as pastor emeritus, was not quietly fading into retirement but was remaining a formidable presence, almost giving the parish two pastors. In July 1927, when St. Mary Magdalen dePazzi observed its seventy-fifth anniversary by placing the cornerstone for a new school, Cardinal Dougherty attempted to mediate the delicate relationship between past and present pastor. After Isoleri celebrated mass, Dougherty, the principal speaker, commended both priests "for their untiring efforts in the upbringing of the spiritual and temporal edifice of the parish." He saluted Isoleri as its second founder and the only Italian secular priest in the diocese, in charge of about 3,000 Italians scattered throughout the city and nine other counties upon his arrival in 1870. But now, with some 160,000 Italians in the city alone, Dougherty called them "for the most part good citizens, hard working men and women, a credit to their mother country, an honor to their adopted land." Objecting to new immigration laws, he hoped that "before long this country will realize its mistake and lift up the bars, so that we may have more helpers in the development of this land."[70]

Despite his praise, Dougherty's remarks also contained a warning. Commending Garritano on his zeal for the school and his flock, "so loved by him and so attached to him in return," Dougherty enjoined the congregation: "I plead with you to give him the support, which he needs. I trust that you will not permit him to undermine his health by worry over the debt contracted in the construction of this building. Let all put their shoulders to the wheel, in order that before long this debt be liquidated."[71] Moreover, the cardinal undoubtedly recognized that the "Italian problem" transcended any single parish and remained an issue throughout the archdiocese. For St. Mary Magdalen dePazzi, the solution only partly involved a new school as well as renovation of the old church.

As parish renewal at St. Mary Magdalen dePazzi reached a new stage, Isoleri continued to take a major part. At the opening of its new school at Seventh and Christian Streets in early December 1927, he addressed its classes. One week later, after its pupils entertained the public, Elvira Cavalieri, the talented young soprano and pride of the local community, and her husband, pianist Ferdinand

Tito Manlio, were featured performers in a concert inaugurating the school auditorium.[72]

When Isoleri again conspicuously participated in ceremonies at the school a year later, the occasion produced a surprising new appraisal of Italian religiosity. The *Catholic Standard and Times* now extolled the attitudes and behavior of Italians as Catholics:

> Firm conviction on the part of the Italian people that the Catholic school is the place for their children and that no personal sacrifices are too great for the maintenance of the parish school, were strongly expressed last Sunday afternoon on the occasion of the dedication of the newly-completed school of St. Mary Magdalen de Pazzi's parish. . . .
>
> The route of the procession was through a densely crowded section. On all hands were evidences of the deep piety and faith of the Italians The reverent attitude of the women was especially noted; they knelt to implore the episcopal blessing as the Cardinal passed by; nor were the men less ardent in their public profession of faith. . . .
>
> . . . appreciation was voiced for the zeal, devotion and self-sacrifice of the Italian people in erecting the new school. Particular emphasis was laid on the fact that the school was concrete evidence that the Italian people realize that the most important thing in life is the salvation of the soul.[73]

In contrast to past allegations directed against Italians as well as unfavorable comparisons with the Irish in the practice of their faith, these remarks now implied, almost as if by a miracle, that the "Italian problem" had finally disappeared. Italians had not only become as observant as other Catholics, but they were also especially supportive of parochial education. But neither public assertions nor newspaper accounts of this revised view resolved the underlying challenge faced by the archdiocese in reaching, ministering to, and accommodating the needs of Italians as Catholics.

The renovation of St. Mary Magdalen dePazzi's church reflected strong support by the archdiocese to a parish with considerable physical needs. Less than forty years after its dedication in 1891, the building required extensive improvements. After an almost complete renovation of the interior, it was reopened amid much fanfare in March 1928. The capitals of its Corinthian columns had been decorated with gold leaf, and gold mosaic inlays had been added to the Stations of the Cross. A marble altar rail and a terrazzo floor had been installed. New statues had been purchased and old paintings restored. A modern electrical system provided direct and indirect lighting throughout the church. The sanctuary had been entirely renovated and the marble steps to the altar repaired. In a statement of parochial "boosterism," Garritano declared that his parishioners had demonstrated great enthusiasm about the restoration. Lenten services were reportedly crowded, and parish societies flourished with increased membership. With some 700 children registered at the reopened school, enrollment was expected to reach 1,600 pupils in the next school year. But instead of Garritano, it was Isoleri who celebrated the Solemn High Mass at the reopening ceremonies.[74]

Inside the church, before a large gathering of prominent Church and community figures, speakers delivered remarks that subtly exposed conditions that were more interpersonal than physical, but no less important to the parish. Garritano almost obsequiously pledged loyalty, affection, and devotion and thanked Dougherty for his kindly and fatherly interest in the Italian people, who would try to be worthy of his confidence. The cardinal then delivered an instructive commentary on priestly character and achievement as well as on tensions in the rectory. After reviewing the parish's history, he cited Isoleri's many accomplishments from the time of his arrival to his retirement:

> It is amazing that, after fifty-nine years in the Priesthood (fifty-six of which have been spent as rector of your congregation), during which he was obliged to rear so many structures, care for such great numbers of Italian exiles, and administer to three generations, he is today the celebrant of the High Mass; not broken in health, not decrepit with age; but with undimmed mind, in the full use of his senses, his heart still beating with love of his people, and with zeal for the spread of the Faith. To him is primarily due the status of your parish; to him must be paid the tribute of having provided you with one of the most beautiful churches of the diocese.
>
> In blamelessness of private and public life, he has been a pattern to his flock and his fellow-priests. With those set over him by God he has been a co-worker; during his long sacerdotal career he has never given them one moment of concern; but, on the contrary, has been to them an encouragement and inspiration.[75]

This assessment had understandably omitted any reference to Isoleri's early clashes with Archbishop Wood, but it also offered a subtle contrast between the present and former pastors of the parish. As he shifted to Garritano as his subject, Dougherty made a circumspect appraisal of the younger man: "In body he is frail; his health has been shattered under the burden laid upon him; nevertheless, in view of his inexhaustible zeal and energy, he was deemed a fitting successor to your beloved Monsignor Isoleri. Although he has been in your midst but a short time, he has fulfilled the expectations reposed in him. In spite of hard times, he undertook the construction of your magnificent new school, the pride of South Philadelphia and the honor of your congregation. Having completed the school, he has now embellished your church."[76]

Mindful of earlier episodes of conflict in the archdiocese, Dougherty asked that "God may keep priest and people in peace and harmony." He perhaps already knew what few clergy or laity could have foreseen. The most contentious chapter in Italian Catholic experience in Philadelphia was not far in the future, and its foundation was then being put into place. But for now, at St. Mary Magdalen dePazzi, a determined pastor, only two years in his position, was suffering from ill health and, even more, from sharing parish and rectory with his intransigent predecessor.

As part of this celebration, an Italian government official informed Garritano that the prime minister, Benito Mussolini, was donating a school desk to be occupied by the student with the highest rank in academic work and conduct. With a similar gift from Pope Pius XI, Mussolini's gesture demonstrated the interest of the Italian government in what it still regarded as its people overseas as well as the imminent thaw in the relationship of Church and state in Italy.[77]

Political events in Italy soon had a broader impact on Philadelphia's Italian Catholics. In March 1927, when Victor Emmanuel III decorated Cardinal Dougherty with the Order of the Crown of Italy, Mussolini's signing of the document suggested that other matters had been set into motion. In the same year, the Vatican opened formal negotiations with the Italian government on the unresolved "Roman question," the status of the Holy See within the modern nation-state. By 1929, the rapprochement of Church and state in Italy evoked celebrations in Philadelphia's Italian parishes. In February, Isoleri celebrated a Solemn High Mass at St. Mary Magdalen dePazzi, with Garritano as master of ceremonies, in thanksgiving for the Lateran Agreements. Father Gerald P. O'Hara, secretary to the cardinal, in a sermon delivered in Italian, saluted Mussolini as the "young Neptune," who had saved his country from the chaos of Communism, and as the first modern leader to proclaim the religious factor in the life of a nation. The local Italian newspaper, *L'Opinione,* praised the crowd that filled the church for its display of religious devotion and *italianità.* Similar events, which took place at Italian churches throughout the archdiocese, represented the apogee of appreciation for Italian politics, before the next decade ushered in a far less hospitable judgment of Fascism.[78]

The celebration of February 1929 marked a milestone of another kind for Philadelphia's Little Italy. While Isoleri had been able to say mass and preach less than a year earlier at the dedication of Our Lady of the Holy Rosary Church in Germantown, he was now greatly slowed by his age. The venerable former pastor of St. Mary Magdalen dePazzi, an imposing force in religious and secular events for nearly sixty years, was giving his final performance. From this time on, he would be conspicuously absent from public events, whether of the parish or the community, and even from occasions at which his presence would have been deemed mandatory. In October 1929, with Cardinal Dougherty presiding at a Solemn High Mass on the twenty-fifth anniversary of Garritano's ordination, Isoleri was not among the principal celebrants. In this case, his absence was not due merely to advanced age but also to a deteriorating relationship with his successor.[79]

By late 1929, public events reflected the altered conditions within the Italian community. With population redistribution and parishes founded in outlying areas, other communities now assumed the role once played only in South Philadelphia. In November, when St. Mary of the Eternal in North Philadelphia laid the cornerstone for its new church, it commemorated the Armistice that ended the World War. With the participation of DiBerardino, Alessandroni, Baldi, leading Italian Americans, and Consul Luigi Sillitti, the celebration of *italianità* had moved to an "uptown" site far from its former "downtown" setting.[80]

The cast of characters at St. Mary Magdalen dePazzi as well as its part in community life were about to be further altered by other changes in its rectory. In June 1930, Garritano was transferred to King of Peace parish in Gray's Ferry. His tenure as pastor at St. Mary Magdalen dePazzi had lasted slightly more than four years. While observers of parish life undoubtedly had their own opinions on what was behind his transfer, the circumstances remained "in petto" (held in secret). Garritano had inherited an extremely delicate and difficult situation when he succeeded the highly educated, proud, and feisty Northern Italian who had ruled a virtual fiefdom for more than a half-century. Having to share rectory, pulpit, and sidewalk with his predecessor, Garritano found it nearly impossible to ameliorate their relationship.[81]

Death Comes to the Rectory

On Monday, April 11, 1932, St. Mary Magdalen dePazzi suffered an even greater loss. Under cloudy skies, a light rain sporadically reappeared, until the temperature reached its high of 48 degrees in the late afternoon. Inside the rectory at 714 Montrose Street, friends and priests sat at the bedside of the aged servant of God and his people. At eighty-six, he was the oldest priest in the archdiocese. Stricken with influenza three days earlier, he had grown steadily weaker but remained conscious. In the early afternoon, another priest anointed him with the Holy Viaticum of the last rites of the Roman Catholic Church. Shortly before five o'clock, he raised his head for the last time and asked, "What's the date and the time?" Within a few more minutes, Monsignor Antonio Isoleri peacefully entered into eternal life.[82]

Isoleri had come from Villanova d'Albenga, a small town on the Riviera di Ponente, expecting to be sent to the Far East missions; instead, he had been assigned to the Italian Mission in Philadelphia. From the region of Italy, whose principal city of Genoa had long been known as "la Superba," he brought pride and wisdom for his faith, along with passion and patriotism for his native land, as he ministered to his people and enabled them to build their lives in a new country. On the day after his death, the leading newspaper of the city called him the "grand old man of Little Italy," before declaring: "Standing in the narrow little street of Philadelphia's Italian colony are a handsomely decorated church, a rectory, school and orphanage bearing the name of one of Italy's greatest Carmelite nuns—magnificent evidence of the half-century struggle of Monsignor Isoleri."[83]

After describing his early years in Italy and Philadelphia and noting his eventual appointment as a domestic prelate by Pope Benedict XV, the same account continued: "Intellectually, he was gifted with great oratorical power and his ability as a poet is evidenced by three volumes of Italian sonnets, odes, canzonets, and dramas." It described the 1904 incident thought to be an attempt on Isoleri's life and his own conclusion that although some antagonism had existed between the Church and Italian Socialists, he had not believed that any plot against him actually existed and ascribed the trouble to overzealousness on the part of the police. Despite this commendable effort by the local press, no words in an obituary could adequately capture the magnitude of the loss incurred by the Italian community as well as by the city of Philadelphia.[84]

Four days after Isoleri's death, his body was brought into his church and placed on a catafalque before the main altar. The men of the parish's societies and former pupils of its school formed an honor guard that kept vigil throughout the night. Father Joseph M. Pugliese, now the pastor, said an evening mass for the children of the parish. On the next morning, as a huge crowd gathered outside, the church doors were kept closed until the clergy and the members of the parish societies were seated. By then, more than 10,000 mourners had filed through the church. At 9:30 A.M., Cardinal Dougherty began the Office of the Dead, assisted by Auxiliary Bishop Gerald P. O'Hara and one hundred other priests, who sang the antiphons and lessons of the service. Their names—Guasco, Priori, Nepote, Matera, Marini, Montiani, Strumia, Toffolini, and Lanza—paid tribute to Isoleri's role in the life of his people. Dominic Nepote, the Vincentian pastor of Our Lady of the Rosary in Germantown, celebrated the Solemn High Requiem Mass, with Lamberto Travi as deacon, Zaccaria Priori as subdeacon, and Otto Toffolini, temporary rector at St. Donato's in West Philadelphia, as the eulogist. Italian men and women from the now numerous immigrant communities all over the city had come together to mourn the man who had been their leader when they had only one community.[85]

The archdiocesan press commented on the makeup of the crowd: "The obsequies were attended by many old parishioners for whom Monsignor Isoleri had labored during his priestly life. Former boys of the parish, many of them occupying important positions in business and the professions, members of the judiciary and prominent officials were present. Outside the church, within the narrow confines of Montrose street, so great a number of Italians from the neighborhood gathered that a special cordon of police was required to care for the throng."[86] Even after death, however, Isoleri would never again leave St. Mary Magdalen dePazzi. He was buried in a crypt on the left side of the nine steps rising to the church entrance. The remains of Father Gaetano Mariani, its first pastor, would eventually be returned and interred in a similar crypt on the other side. These two pioneers of Italian American Catholicism rest in this location today.

Ten days after Isoleri's death, his last will revealed an estate of about $34,000 to be distributed among beneficiaries in Philadelphia and Italy. Although drawn up on the day before his death, thus making the bequests invalid, the executors agreed to carry out his wishes. He asked that the proceeds from two World War Liberty Bonds go to his three nieces in Villanova d'Albenga. He left money from the sale of City of Philadelphia bonds to St. John's Orphan Asylum, St. Joseph's Female Orphan Asylum, the Columbus Hospital on South Broad Street, and St. Mary Magdalen dePazzi Church. He directed that the money in a bank account be equally divided among the Collegio Brignole Sale in Genoa, the Carmelite Convent of St. Mary Magdalen dePazzi in Florence, the Diocesan Seminary of Albenga in Savona, and a nephew, Agostino Isoleri, who was living in Italy. He requested that masses be said for himself and his relatives as well as for the benefactors and parishioners of his church. He bequeathed a chalice to St. Mary Magdalen dePazzi and another one to the church of Santa Caterina in Villanova d'Albenga. And he left a parcel of land and a building behind his rectory to the parish with instructions that they were to be used exclusively for lectures on history, religion, education, and ethics, with dances and athletic games expressly prohibited. But above any material bequest, the spiritual and cultural legacy that Antonio Isoleri left to Italian Catholics in Philadelphia was beyond calculation.[87]

CHAPTER FOURTEEN

The Dismemberment of
Our Lady of Good Counsel

The death in April 1932 of Monsignor Antonio Isoleri, the former pastor of St. Mary Magdalen dePazzi, undeniably represented a sad event for his parish as well as for Italian Catholics throughout Philadelphia. But if the death of one elderly pastor after a long life and career was significant, the Italians of South Philadelphia soon suffered an even greater loss by the suppression of Our Lady of Good Counsel Church. While both events diminished the community, Isoleri's passing only brought sadness and mourning, but the closing of the Augustinian church would ignite the anger of Italians toward the archdiocese and its archbishop.

The disruption that occurred at Our Lady of Good Counsel had its roots in its inception as a parish. At the founding of Buon Consiglio (as it was familiarly known) in 1898, the Congregation of Propaganda Fide had granted the care of all Italians in Philadelphia, except for those who were members of St. Mary Magdalen dePazzi, to the Augustinians. In July 1900, the contract between the archdiocese and the order was amended to include a clause that the parish and property of St. Mary Magdalen dePazzi, upon the death of its current pastor, be reassigned to the Augustinians. When the Italian population of Philadelphia consisted of an estimated 30,000 souls, the plans for Our Lady of Good Counsel appeared to offer a reasonable strategy for their spiritual care. Founded to accommodate the massive immigration of Southern Italians, it quickly became their cherished spiritual home.

By the early 1930s, when the Italian population reached upward of 150,000, the archdiocese, through its policy of establishing other parishes for them, had long abandoned the original agreement. And after Isoleri's death, instead of the absorption of St. Mary Magdalen dePazzi, Archbishop Dennis J. Dougherty's decision to dismantle Our Lady of Good Counsel parish provoked an unanticipated insurrection in the Italian community that reflected the fealty of its congregation. The ensuing crisis between Italians and the archdiocese would only be settled by the Supreme Court of the State of Pennsylvania after five more years of protests, demonstrations, and legal action. It left a residue of unresolved animosity among Italians in its aftermath that long lingered in their relationship to the archdiocese.

Alongside the long, proud history of St. Mary Magdalen dePazzi is another compelling chapter in Italian American religious experience in Philadelphia—the brief, bitter saga of Our Lady of Good Counsel. During the public furor over the closing of the Augustinian church, neighboring St. Mary Magdalen dePazzi momentarily faded in significance for the community. But, closely located in site and intertwined as institutions, to understand the meaning of either parish for Philadelphia's Italians depends upon some knowledge of the other one. Similarly, any assessment of the nationality parish as a means of solving the "Italian problem," or more generally of Church policy in dealing with ethnic diversity, requires an examination of these two parishes separately and in their relationship to one another. And, in particular, we must ask why the archdiocese chose to dismember Our Lady of Good Counsel rather than St. Mary Magdalen dePazzi.

The Readjustment of Parish Boundaries

From the 1870s through the 1920s, American Catholicism sought to solve what it defined as the "Italian problem": the huge number of new arrivals from Italy who purportedly failed to properly practice their faith or to provide material support to its institutions. Although apostasy as a result of immigration was actually low, some observers believed that many Italians had lost their faith while finding a life in America. The peculiar piety of Italian Catholics, moreover, made them seem only nominal in affiliation, neglectful in observance, and superstitious in veneration. Although subjected to unfavorable comparisons that only encouraged further animosity rather than harmony, Italians were arguably no less observant as Catholics than the Irish immigrants had been before the "devotional revolution" that swept Ireland in the second half of the nineteenth century. But many Italians, like most immigrants from ostensibly Catholic countries, arrived in America with their own customs in matters of religion. Consequently, although similar to the Irish and other immigrant groups as only potential candidates for parish membership, the Italians were almost uniquely defined as a serious pastoral challenge by the Catholic Church in the United States.[1]

Early in the twentieth century, the Archdiocese of Philadelphia, responding to its perception of the distinctive deficiencies in beliefs and practices among Italians, increased its efforts among them, mainly by an ambitious program that was intended to produce spiritually good Catholics and financially sound parishes. Recognizing the desirability of providing Italians with their own parishes, for their spiritual welfare as well as for the future of the Church, it also sought Italian priests willing to emigrate and to serve them. The hierarchy in Rome, meanwhile, included prelates who were as eager as their American colleagues to preserve the faith of these immigrants. After establishing the Italian Mission of St. Mary Magdalen dePazzi in 1852, the archdiocese passed through a long period of inactivity among Italians before opening Our Lady of Good Counsel in 1898. With continued immigration, some sixteen more Italian churches were founded in Philadelphia and nearby communities in an intense period of parish building from 1903 to 1917, followed by a seven-year hiatus before five more Italian parishes were opened between 1924 and 1932. As Italians displaced other ethnic groups in Philadelphia, the archdiocese altogether founded twenty-four Italian parishes in the city and its environs as well as other parishes in places no longer within its present boundaries.

When nationality parishes no longer offered a clear solution to the "Italian problem," the archdiocese recognized that the time had come to reexamine its policy. In particular, it had to address the future of the parishes that had been established to serve Italians. After describing the unresolved issue to his consultors in June 1931, Dougherty, now a cardinal, appointed a committee under Auxiliary Bishop Gerald P. O'Hara to conduct a study that would provide a basis on which to readjust the boundaries, made even more troublesome by their ambiguity, of Italian parishes in South Philadelphia. While the main device would be a census of Italian families served either by nationality or territorial parishes in the area, the committee also solicited comments from their pastors. Three months later, after some preliminary information had been gathered, O'Hara declared that unspecified complications had made further investigation necessary.[2]

As pastors continued to submit reports over the next two years, their comments disclosed several problems. The pastor of St. Patrick's, near Rittenhouse Square, a church with few Italians, knew that the census was a prelude to redrawing boundaries. Having lost four blocks of parochial turf only a few years earlier, he vigorously objected: "I will not be a party, in any way, to have Old St. Patrick's Parish stripped again of its territorial boundaries." Among several pastors who reported the inadequacies of Italians as parishioners, Father Anthony Garritano, now at King of Peace in the Gray's Ferry section, stated: "the class of Italians who are in the vicinity of the church never will be able to pay interest or principal." He proposed "a parish of mixed nationalities" as a solution. The pastor of St. Anthony's, with only 160 Italian families within its borders, complained: "Some of these Italian families say they are Protestants, and there is not one really Catholic family amongst them, according to Irish standards of Catholicity."[3]

Even before all of the responses were received, O'Hara had already submitted his final report and the consultors had approved the readjusting of parish boundaries. Whether providing a basis for a new direction in policy or a rationalization for decisions previously made, it had profound consequences for Italians. Although the consultors appeared to have consented only to a general idea rather than to the details of its implementation, their earlier deliberations had already put some specific actions into motion. At the same meeting, Cardinal Dougherty announced that the Augustinians had agreed to reassign the parish facilities of Our Lady of Good Counsel to St. Nicholas of Tolentine, even though further data from pastors continued to trickle into the Chancery in subsequent months. Somewhat ironically, as the dismantling of Our Lady of Good Counsel began, the consultors were making plans for the founding of Our Lady of Loreto in Southwest Philadelphia, the last Italian parish established in the city. But the aged Antonio Isoleri, who as the only Italian consultor might have acted as the advocate for these parishes and their pastors, had become too ill to attend most meetings.[4]

The archdiocesan study of parishes provided important information. As seen in Table 14.1, St. Rita's had the largest number of Italian families, while

TABLE 14.1.   Italian Families in South Philadelphia Parishes, 1931–1933

Parish	Number of Families
St. Rita's	8,172
St. Paul's	5,240
Annunciation	4,023
St. Nicholas of Tolentine	3,322
St. Mary Magdalen dePazzi	3,184
St. Thomas Aquinas	2,519
King of Peace	2,180
Epiphany	2,055
Our Lady of Good Counsel	1,369
St. Monica's	1,110
St. Edmond's	838
St. Gabriel's	722
St. Teresa of Avila	137

Source: Italian Parish Study File, PAHRC.

St. Paul's and Annunciation, both territorial parishes, came next, then St. Nicholas of Tolentine, St. Mary Magdalen dePazzi, St. Thomas Aquinas, King of Peace, Epiphany, Our Lady of Good Counsel, St. Monica's, St. Edmond's, St. Gabriel's, and St. Teresa's. Several other parishes had only a negligible number. Many more Italians, despite the founding of nationality parishes, had already moved into territorial parishes with mixed congregations. Somewhat unexpectedly, several parishes had more Italian families than Our Lady of Good Counsel. And even more surprising, St. Mary Magdalen dePazzi, contrary to earlier pastors' annual reports, was one of them.

The total number of Italian families for eight territorial parishes in South Philadelphia was 16,652, while the number for the five nationality parishes in the area was 18,227. The territorial parishes were now serving the spiritual needs of these families almost as much as the nationality parishes were. If the archdiocese still sought Americanization as a goal, then Italian families, by joining territorial parishes, whether they were aware of it or not, were moving toward assimilation. And the archdiocese intended to facilitate this process.

When archdiocesan officials analyzed the census, their apprehensions, or perhaps their preconceptions, were confirmed. Bishop O'Hara's final report began by noting that great changes had taken place in the English-speaking parishes of South Philadelphia over the past twenty years, mainly from "the growth of the Negro population and by the large influx of Italians." While Italian parishes were supposed to care for their kind, the report, assuming an average of five members to each family, estimated an Italian population of 91,135 living in the area south of Market Street, between the Delaware and Schuylkill rivers. Noting that Italian priests had acknowledged that they neither knew nor could know all of their people, the report added, "Much less are they in contact with them."[5]

Among its findings, O'Hara's report concluded that Italian parishes were not paying proper spiritual attention to members, normal parish life did not exist, and enrollment at none of their parochial schools reached a level of 90 percent or more of parish children, in contrast to what was usually found in English-speaking parishes. The findings clearly implied that territorial parishes had been more successful than nationality parishes in caring for Italian families. As provocative as these conclusions were, the underlying causes were even more so. Indeed, the explanation contained potential dynamite: "The faith has suffered here, 1st because of the inactivity for so many years of Msgr. Isoleri; 2nd because the Italian Augustinian Fathers were given and hold these parishes in South Philadelphia."[6]

While the boundaries of Italian parishes in South Philadelphia made "real pastoral contact between priests and people impossible," the report singled out the three Augustinian parishes—St. Rita's, St. Nicholas of Tolentine, and Our Lady of Good Counsel. If the confines described in the report were accurate, each of them had a very peculiar shape. The boundaries of St. Rita's swept down Broad Street from Market Street in a swath eight blocks wide to Tasker Street, then six blocks wide to the Navy Yard, to overlap with eight English-speaking parishes. In a width of four blocks, St. Nicholas of Tolentine ran from Tasker Street to the Navy Yard and overlapped with two English-speaking parishes. The boundaries given for Our Lady of Good Counsel, with a width of only four blocks, extended from Girard Avenue in North Philadelphia to Wharton Street in South Philadelphia and gave it a pattern that can only be described as bizarre.

The report continued with the information that Italians living at the edges of these parishes did not attend the churches originally intended for them; if they went at all, they attended the nearest English-speaking parish. This produced confusion as well as frequent disputes in regard to the proper site for baptisms, funerals, and marriages. Stating that new boundaries were clearly needed, the report asked: "What new arrangements should be adopted? It is difficult to answer this question." As Monsignor Hugh Lamb had suggested, when he first wrote to O'Hara on the desirability of an investigation, the report concluded that a series of meetings of the pastors affected by these conditions "might bring to light a happy solution of the problem." But a happy solution, unfortunately, was not to come.[7]

While the Italian parishes and their pastors waited for further action by the archdiocese, the Augustinians, in particular, had cause for concern. Father Lorenzo Andolfi, pastor of St. Nicholas of Tolentine, believed that a reasonable limitation of its boundaries would help the work of its clergy and eliminate problems with nearby parishes. Similarly, in a note to the chancellor of the archdiocese, Father Joseph A. Hickey, the assistant general of the Augustinian order, had expressed his eagerness to sign whatever documents were necessary for the reorganization of Our Lady of Good Counsel before he returned to Rome. But archdiocesan officials had proposed a drastic solution to the "Italian problem." The blame, moreover, previously placed on the defects of lay Italians as Catholics had now shifted to the defects of the Italian clergy. The only possible answer, consequently, required reorganizing Italian parishes and shifting control over them.[8]

The principal means to implement this strategy would be a redefinition of parish boundaries that reassigned families mainly from nationality parishes to territorial ones. A prior proposal had called for the shifting of 950 families from St. Rita's, 333 families from St. Mary Magdalen dePazzi, and 856 families from St. Nicholas of Tolentine to Annunciation parish. But when the final plan was announced, although new boundaries provoked only timid objections from a few priests, a drastic call for the elimination of one parish precipitated the most serious revolt by laity since the dispute over trusteeship at St. Mary's a century earlier.[9]

Since its earliest days, Our Lady of Good Counsel had endured a succession of serious difficulties. Its congregation had always included a large number of poor Southern Italians who were unable to provide much financial support. In correspondence with their superiors in Rome, its priests frequently mentioned their efforts to obtain donations for building programs and other projects. With subsidies from the Augustinian order erasing year-end deficits, along with gifts from an occasional Irish American benefactor, Our Lady of Good Counsel struggled onward.[10]

If financial problems were not enough to threaten its existence, the small monastery at Our Lady of Good Counsel suffered from individual misconduct and internal dissension. While parishioners complained about priests who did not respond to calls, priests in turn deplored shameful behavior by the faithful. When his superiors requested that one pastor not resign, he insisted that he must do so. And as parishioners sought a pastor with a wide knowledge of the English language and American customs, other difficulties arose from not only improperly keeping accounts but also from accusations that one pastor had even lost his faith. Meanwhile, charges of scandalous behavior, which implied sexual misconduct, were also being made. By 1912, as one faction perceived a need to break up a clique formed by other priests within the monastery, these problems led it to be without procurator, prior, and vice prior at one point. In short, a contentious band of Augustinian friars was running its Italian mission in Philadelphia.[11]

What eventually provoked the rage of the community, however, was the matter of church ownership, which had plagued Philadelphia Catholics since the time of the disputes with Holy Trinity's Germans and St. Mary's English and Irish. When a new pastor, Father Thomas Terlizzi, sent from Rome to also serve as head of all Italian Augustinians in the United States, arrived in 1914, Our Lady of Good Counsel appeared to have become more stable. Despite past troubles, it appeared to be in a healthy condition in November 1917, with a parish census reporting 2,587 families and a total of 13,343 members, divided almost equally between Italian immigrants and American-born persons of Italian descent. But with Archbishop Prendergast seeking clarification from the Holy See on the matter of his control over the church, new troubles were emerging for the Augustinians. In the next year, when Terlizzi, taking a more visible public role, offered the invocation at an Italian Liberty Loan program, he also took up the defense of Augustinian interests in the community. In a later report to the Italian Augustinian General Office, he rejected the contention that the involvement of the consultors was necessary to settle the claim of his order to St. Mary Magdalen dePazzi. Terlizzi based his argument on the original agreement with Archbishop Ryan, copies of which were held by the Augustinians. The document had not only clearly granted control of Our Lady of Good Counsel in perpetuity to the Hermits of St. Augustine, but it also stated that St. Mary Magdalen dePazzi was to be turned over to them upon the death of Father Isoleri.[12]

When Dougherty was installed as archbishop of Philadelphia, the dispute over the future of St. Mary Magdalen dePazzi remained unsettled. Having served as a bishop for twelve years in the Philippines, where the Augustinians had a strong presence, Dougherty now faced them again in his new assignment. He held that the Augustinians had no valid claim on St. Mary Magdalen dePazzi because no contract existed in the archdiocesan archives. Furthermore, if any agreement had been made by Ryan and the Augustinians, Dougherty still rejected it on the grounds that the consultors had not given their approval.[13]

The precarious financial situation of Our Lady of Good Counsel required the Augustinians to make careful use of their limited resources. A 1926 report, written in Italian, described the parish as very poor and composed of immigrant Italians who, besides being poor themselves, were not accustomed to the idea of supporting their church through their offerings. Since the parish was unable to pay salaries, its priests depended on stipends received from officiating at baptisms and funerals and from collections at masses. Although certain that the next generation would become more accustomed to the "sistema americana," the report added that the parish had not yet arrived at the level of American parishes. Its next lines provided the crux of the Augustinian problem: "The Augustinians have principally developed the school, providing only little care for the church, with the faith that the parish of St. Mary Magdalen dePazzi, would be given on the death of its old pastor, according to the decree of canonical foundation."[14]

With the number of Italian Catholics in Philadelphia growing to an estimated 150,000, Father Aurelio Marini, rector of Our Lady of Good Counsel and commissary provincial of the Italian Vice Province, reiterated the Augustinian position. In reply to Dougherty's contention that the agreement granting the church to them had been made without the advice of the consultors, Marini noted that five other parishes had already been established without any objection in areas assigned to the Augustinians. While admitting that two or three scandals (perhaps an understatement) had happened in his religious community, he stated that although the Augustinians were willing to concede territory to the archdiocese, they would hold firm to their claim to St. Mary Magdalen dePazzi. Marini also reported to his superiors in Rome that no reply to these matters had yet come from the archdiocese.[15]

Dismemberment and Dissent

When the Augustinian claims were rejected by the archdiocese, they were replaced by more serious action by the people, whose intense affection and attachment to Our Lady of Good Counsel was soon to become evident. As early as January 1933 some Italians already knew that the parish was to be taken from the Augustinians, although the archdiocese would not announce it until four months later. In March, Cardinal Dougherty provided a preview of a broad plan for the Italian parishes in a personal letter to Judge Eugene V. Alessandroni. He expressed his intention "to give the English-speaking parishes of St. Paul's and the Annunciation to the Italians with all the parochial property." His peculiar wording conveyed the impression that the archdiocese was returning to the days of lay trustees as legal owners of Church property. He also alluded to the necessity of readjusting the boundaries of the parishes in the southeastern section of the city to provide better care for the Italians. But Dougherty's final point provided the most important change. While compensating the Augustinians by elevating their mission at St. Nicholas of Tolentine to a parish, he also intended to abolish Our Lady of Good Counsel.[16]

The purpose of Dougherty's letter, however, was not merely to inform an Italian supporter of his plan for the parishes. Knowing that Italians were already mobilizing in opposition to his decision to "dismember" the parish, as it would be quaintly termed, he was preparing his own defense. In his letter he thanked Alessandroni for his willingness to recruit prominent Italians to speak at an upcoming meeting. Hoping that the judge might help him put an end to the agitation that was mounting in the community, Dougherty added: "When I am trying my best to help the Italians, I meet with this unreasonable opposition." But the cardinal would be unable to avoid the confrontation with the Italians over the suppression of their parish.[17]

The archdiocese officially announced the details of its plan for what it saw as a much-needed readjustment of several Italian parishes in a news release sent to major newspapers on May 4, 1933. Its rationale was that it had long been clear, based on migration in and out of the congested districts, that many Italians lived at great distances from their parish churches and parochial schools. After much deliberation by local pastors, the plan consisted of three main recommendations. First, St. Paul's and the Annunciation parishes would be placed under Italian rectors. But while the appointment of Italian pastors at the two churches made sense in view of the changing ethnic composition of their congregations, it could also be construed as a compromise to avert a negative reaction to other aspects of the proposals. Second, since Our Lady of Good Counsel was close to St. Paul's but had inadequate parish buildings and a rapidly dwindling population—reportedly falling to about one-fifth of what it had been in 1920— Augustinians would be transferred to St. Nicholas of Tolentine. And third, the latter church, which had once been a succursal church or chapel of Our Lady of Good Counsel but now exceeded it in size, would be raised to the full status of a regular parish with expanded boundaries. The statement concluded that the action was being taken for the benefit of the Italians, who would now have the well-equipped parishes of St. Paul's and the Annunciation. Those who lived at a great distance would be cared for by Italian priests or Italian-speaking priests attached to local English-speaking parishes. But the parishioners of Our Lady of Good Counsel understood clearly what it all meant for them.[18]

Recognizing that they were about to lose Our Lady of Good Counsel as their parish, Italians rose up against the archdiocesan decision in a protest that would take several more years before it ended. On May 3, the day before the archdiocese formally released the announcement of the euphemistically termed "dismemberment" or suppression of Our Lady of Good Counsel, with its members to be absorbed by other parishes, the community had already begun mobilizing its opposition. As leaking news of the impending decision spread through the Italian quarter, a crowd began assembling in the afternoon before converging to begin an all-night vigil at the church.[19]

Italians who had first sought only to take a firm stand against the transfer of the Augustinians at Our Lady of Good Counsel were now battling for the survival of their church. Several hundred children paraded in the streets with banners and placards amid shouts of "We want our church!" Someone carrying a large crucifix appeared on the front steps, and the crowd became quiet as many people knelt down. By nine o'clock the throng grew to upward of 3,000 protestors and, despite the presence of the police, the situation deteriorated. The crowd now prevented Father Marini and his assistants from leaving the rectory for their new residence at St. Nicholas of Tolentine. When the beleaguered pastor attempted to enter the church, police cleared his way to the altar. Speaking to his parishioners with tears in his eyes, Marini implored them, "Go home. Go to sleep. I am tired. I want to go to sleep. We must do what we are told." Ignoring his plea, the defiant crowd refused to disperse, and a police escort eventually rescued him. In the ensuing confusion, while two Augustinian brothers fled through a side door, two other priests remained inside. Meanwhile, protestors surged into and outside of the church, tolling its bell and carrying black crosses in mourning, and a band of musicians joined the effort with the intention of playing through the night. At almost exactly midnight the bell cracked under strain of the incessant tolling, but determined parishioners continued to pull its rope, sending forth a "dull, metallic clack" that continued as a muffled protest on the next day.[20]

With the morning, the crowd, now refreshed by a few hours of sleep, expanded its protest. When a funeral procession attempted to enter the church, the throng slammed shut the entrance gates and surrounded the mourners. From an upper window, Father Simpliciano Gatt, the assistant pastor, implored the protesters to allow the funeral party to enter the church, but the crowd surged forward and pushed the grieving mourners away. At this point, the funeral director wisely announced that the cortege would move to St. Mary Magdalen dePazzi. With the police clearing the way and a band of musicians playing a dirge, the mourners retreated, and the elated crowd broke into cheers. Throughout the day the musicians, taking up positions on the steps of Our

Lady of Good Counsel, continued to encourage the demonstrators by playing "Onward, Christian Soldiers" as well as the Italian national anthem and the "Star Spangled Banner." But more anger was about to unfold.[21]

Later in the day, when Father Marini reappeared, accompanied by Father Otto Toffolini, whom he sought to introduce as their new pastor, the two priests parked their cars a safe distance from the demonstrators. But as they approached the church, both men were greeted with jeers and the entrance gates were slammed shut again. One woman attempted to scratch Marini's face. When a police officer asked why they were repudiating their own pastor, who had merely come for his belongings, a spokesman for the crowd explained: "If he wants them, we'll send them to him. He left us last night, and we don't want him back. We asked him to stay and he refused." Another voice interjected, "If he tries to get in again, we'll kill him." To the hostile crowd, Marini had over-night become the scapegoat for the parish's demise. And having rejected Marini as their pastor, the protestors also recognized that another priest could not be allowed to escape: "Father Gatt is here and we love him and we will not let him leave. . . . He is a prisoner." Gatt, in dismay, told a reporter: "I don't know what I can do. I left here and when I came back with an empty suitcase to get some belongings they would not let me leave."[22]

Throughout the day, however, the police provoked the crowd even more. When they shoved their way into the vestibule of the church, the demonstrators pushed them back. Two mounted policemen rode their horses up the steps to clear a path for their fellow officers when, swinging their clubs, they retreated from the building. With the gates closed once more, the evicted police, forced unto the sidewalk, regrouped and reconsidered their strategy. In the afternoon, police reinforcements arrived, armed with tear gas, and formed a phalanx three lines deep from curb to curb on Christian Street in front of the church. But these Italians, whose ancestors had defended their villages before the terrifying attacks of Saracens, Turks, and other invaders, were not ready to back down and cede their turf to mere Philadelphia policemen. As one demonstrator indicated, "We plan to stay forty-eight hours. If forty-eight hours aren't enough, we'll stay one hundred and forty-eight hours. . . . We will camp here a year or longer if it is nec-essary, but we are going to win, and we won't give up until we do."[23] And another man explained, "The chief point of the protest is that we want the Augustinian order of priests to remain in the neighborhood. The Augustinians have been in charge of this church since it was built thirty-six years ago. If the Augustinians could be sent to St. Paul's Church . . . , the people would be satisfied, because they could attend mass there." Then he poignantly added, "This church was built not only with the funds contributed by the people, but by their labor. They worked, actually labored to erect it, after they had done their regular day's work."[24]

Despite their bold defiance, the actions of the resolute parishioners were des-tined to end in failure. After the first night of protest, a committee, formed almost immediately to seek the reopening of the church, sent a cablegram to Pius XI, asking him to intervene on their behalf. Informing the pontiff that "2,500 Italian Catholics are in revolt because the Church of Our Lady of Good Counsel is to be closed," the message called upon him "to save the church for the people and to avoid real trouble." The committee also sought to carry its demands to a meeting with Dougherty. But the pope would not intervene, nor would the cardinal revoke his decision, and the situation would grow even worse.[25]

In subsequent weeks, the protesting committee expanded its tactics. In late May, it organized a general demonstration throughout the Italian community. Signs placed in store windows announced "as a testimonial of sorrow for the order to abolish the Church of Our Mother of Good Council [*sic*] and for the eviction of the Augustinian Mission," that they were closing for several hours on Monday, May 22. In July, as the "strike" continued, a delegation, that included the president of the Committee of Thirty-six, representing parish societies, the president of the Committee of 500, the secretary of the united committees, and a newspaper editor met in Washington, DC, with the Italian ambassador. A few days later the supporters of Buon Consiglio initiated legal proceedings to restore their church.[26]

As parishioners continued to occupy the church, the crisis persisted with intermittent flareups of protest throughout the summer and into the autumn of 1933. After Father Marini escaped from his confinement, Father Gatt assumed his duties as rector. But the guard of parishioners held the unfortunate Gatt a virtual prisoner for nearly five months before finally consenting to his release in late October. Learning that Gatt's inability to meet Augustinian regulations could result in his suspension from the order, the parishioners held a "peace meeting" at which they voted to allow him to leave the rectory. To demonstrate their regard for Gatt, they held a farewell reception in the rectory and then escorted him to his next assignment in Vineland, New Jersey. These actions clearly showed that the protestors' anger over what had befallen them was directed against Cardinal Dougherty and the archdiocese rather than against the Augustinians.[27]

While Dougherty's suppression of Our Lady of Good Counsel had antagonized the Italian community, it damaged him even more. He had once written that he took "a special delight in helping our Italians, whom I got to know during the four years of my residence in Italy and my numerous visits later on to Rome; and for whom I have a deep esteem and affection." However, after closing the church, when Dougherty made his next visit for confirmation rites at a nearby parish, Philadelphia policemen closely guarded him from possible harm. Any high regard that the Italians may have once held for him was now gone.[28]

Dougherty's critics now seized the opportunity. Leaflets addressed "To the Italian People of South Philadelphia" flooded the community to denounce Church authorities, especially the cardinal. One circular rhetorically asked,

"Must a priest, even if a prince of Holy Mother Church, tell the truth?" It accused Dougherty of not heeding the demands and requests of thousands of his children as well as ignoring the Gospel and "the sweet words of Christ." It charged his secretary of promulgating seven serious lies, among which were that the Augustinians were satisfied to abandon the church and the Italians would be better cared for if the church was suppressed. It vehemently argued that Dougherty had oppressed the Augustinians through unwarranted tax assessments on parish properties and through demands for contributions in support of the archdiocesan seminary. And it singled out a prominent layman as a collaborator for forcing the Augustinians to pay $26,000 for a house worth no more than $4,000, which had already been donated to the archdiocese, as a residence for the sisters: "The Italians have plenty to thank Mr. Henry DiBerardino, who had the nerve of estimating said home at such a pitched price solely and merely to please, as usual, the Prince."[29]

The same leaflet offered much more in its interpretation of the situation. Claiming that the "whole truth in a nut-shell" was much simpler than the explanations given by the archdiocese, it provided an alternate view: "The Prince of the Holy Roman Church has solemnly given this sentence: I DO NOT WANT THAT THE ITALIAN AUGUSTINIANS WILL HAVE MORE THAN ONE CHURCH IN MY DIOCESE." Asserting that the boundaries of both St. Nicholas of Tolentine and St. Rita's had also been reduced, it argued that the plan would take the first of these two churches from the Italians at a later time, before asking: "Oh, Prince where is your shame!" But the leaflet's writer offered a solution: "It is therefore evident that the Prince lies in his pockets, when he says that all this took place for the welfare of souls. It is nothing more than personal revenge. Will he get away with it? It's up to you Italians." And against assertions that gangsters were behind the resistance, it exhorted: "March on fighting my friends as you had never fought before. . . . You are facing a man or rather a Prince . . . who in the midst of much sorrow caused to the thousands of Italian hearts, dares come forth with his lips full of lies and his heart full of hatred, anxious only to tire the Italians and see them give up the fight. Fight on brave Christian soldiers against such an unworthy Prince of your Church."[30]

Similar leaflets were distributed throughout the Italian district in subsequent months. One accused Archbishop Amleto Cicognani, who had recently become apostolic delegate to the United States, of being a co-conspirator in the betrayal of the Italians. Stating that Dougherty had suspended Father Gatt without warning for saying mass privately for the rebellious parishioners, the pamphleteer asked: "Has the Archbishop of Philadelphia any faith left?" The writer asserted that both Cicognani and Dougherty were allowing the Eucharist to be abandoned and corrupted by their refusal to allow any priest to celebrate mass. Another leaflet flatly declared: "Our church will not be taken away—we have nothing to worry about."[31]

When the parishioners turned to the courts in their struggle to regain control and reopen the church, their suit ironically had to be brought against the Augustinians as the property owners. After several hearings in the Court of Common Pleas, *L'Opinione* summarized the situation in October 1933. According to the newspaper's account, Father Aurelio Ciantar, a Maltese Augustinian and pastor of a church in Vineland, testified that canon law required that the people affected by the dismemberment of a parish had to be consulted, but in this case it had not been properly done. Father Marini, the longtime former pastor who had fled Our Lady of Good Counsel on the first night of the protests, declared that the prescribed canonical reason for dismemberment—namely, that the faithful had great difficulty in reaching the church—did not exist. He maintained that indeed it was easily reached on foot from every part of the neighborhood. (Contrary to his testimony, its actual northern boundary, Girard Avenue, was far away but accessible by public transportation.) When Marini asked for the baptismal registers, which the parishioners had taken into their possession when they occupied the church, one of their leaders replied that the records could not be returned without consulting his committee. The presiding judge decreed that nothing would be removed from the church before the court reached its decision.[32]

It was generally understood, *L'Opinione* declared, that the entire situation might have been avoided if the intensity of passion felt by the people toward their church had been initially recognized. But even the simple matter of scheduling the next court session made it clear that everything had now become much more complicated. When an attorney for the people asked for a three-week delay to allow the interrogation of Father Angelo Caruso, one of the parish founders and believed to be living in Italy, Father Mortimer Sullivan, the Augustinian provincial at Villanova College, who was thought to be opposed to the request, informed the court that the old pastor was dead. The newspaper, however, declared that Caruso was not only still alive but also in good health. (Caruso actually had died in 1921.) The judge introduced old correspondence from Cardinal Martinelli instructing Caruso to collect money from Italians to build the church and indicating that the trustees, rather than the Augustinians or the congregation, would be the true proprietors. It seems that *L'Opinione* had offered its own interpretation of the court documents to readers in the Italian community.[33]

Although street demonstrations had ended, the dispute remained unresolved. When dissident parishioners challenged ecclesiastical authorities in the courts, the archdiocese attempted to bury the situation. As historian Richard Varbero has aptly described it, the secular press extensively covered the "comic opera scenario," but the archdiocesan newspaper failed to mention it at all.[34] The protracted struggle finally ended when the Supreme Court of Pennsylvania ruled against the parishioners in April 1936. The plaintiffs handed over the keys of the parish property to officials of the archdiocese on April 5, 1937. A few years later, the church building was torn down to make way for a parking lot. The public demonstrations in the streets of South Philadelphia had lasted for six months; the legal action against the Augustinians in the courts of the city and state continued for nearly three years. But hostility toward the cardinal and archdiocese on the part of Italians who fondly remembered their parish would linger for many more years to come.[35]

The Aftermath

Many questions about the closing of Our Lady of Good Counsel remain unanswered to the present day. Why was it closed? Did the Italians, who so long and vigorously resisted its closing, have reasonable and legitimate objections? What impact did this affair have on other nationality parishes, particularly on St. Mary Magdalen dePazzi? And what was its significance for Italian Americans? Like the issues that had disrupted their community but remained unresolved, these questions cannot be fully answered, but some reflection on them is instructive. And that enables us to address the broadest question: What was the place of Our Lady of Good Counsel in American Catholic history?

The official reason given by the Archdiocese of Philadelphia for closing Our Lady of Good Counsel was based on the general need to readjust the boundaries of Italian parishes in the southeastern part of the city in order to better serve Italian Catholics. Beyond that starting point, however, the archbishop and his advisers had concluded that the Italian church had inadequate parish buildings and a dwindling population. While the solution dislodged and redistributed the congregation from a church that no longer existed, the subsequent destination of its former members remains unclear. In 1932, in the last annual report submitted to the archdiocese before the suppression of the parish, its pastor stated that Our Lady of Good Counsel had 1,203 families and 5,088 individuals as members. But the annual reports by the pastors of other parishes give some sense of what happened to its members (see Table 14.2). Although their figures may be questioned, they represent the only source for such information.

From the annual reports of the pastors, several changes in the size of congregations stood out as the readjustment of parish boundaries was being implemented. St. Paul's, for instance, grew from only 214 families and 2,074 individuals in 1931 to 2,060 families and 9,600 individuals in 1934. As the nearest territorial parish, about one block away from the suppressed Our Lady of Good Counsel, the increase was not surprising. It also was one of the parishes for which an Italian pastor, Father Otto Toffolini, was designated in 1933. Annunciation parish similarly grew from only 115 families and 459 individuals in 1931 to 2,500 families and 7,600 individuals only two years later in 1933, before a slight decline in the next year. It had also received its first Italian pastor, Father John V. Tolino, in 1933. What

TABLE 14.2.   Reported Populations of Five Parishes, 1931–1934

	1931	*1932*	*1933*	*1934*
Our Lady of Good Counsel				
Families	1,195	1,203		
Individuals	4,980	5,088		
St. Paul's				
Families	214	671	1,500	2,060
Individuals	2,074	3,051	7,500	9,600
Annunciation				
Families	115	N/A	2,500	2,350
Individuals	459	N/A	7,600	7,250
St. Nicholas of Tolentine				
Families	900	900	1,207	2,386
Individuals	4,500	4,500	4,817	11,930
St. Mary Magdalen dePazzi				
Families	2,650	2,594	1,238	1,249
Individuals	15,200	14,411	5,627	5,714

Source: Annual Reports (1931–1934), PAHRC.

was anomalous in both cases, however, were the very small numbers reported for 1931. But the previous pastors of both parishes had evidently provided only the number of properly registered congregants, mainly drawn from the declining population of non-Italians still residing in these neighborhoods, and excluded Italians, who were expected to be enrolled, if anywhere, in nationality parishes. While the practice prompted the 1931 parish families census, which showed very different figures, the easing of the requirement itself brought Italians into territorial parishes. But in the aftermath of the closing of Our Lady of Good Counsel, St. Nicholas of Tolentine, the newly elevated Augustinian parish, still held the largest congregation. From 900 families and 4,500 individuals in 1932, it had climbed to 2,386 families and 11,930 individuals, probably far more Italian members than any other parish, in 1934.

The growth of these parishes could have been partly due to a natural increase, that is, the excess of births over deaths for the general population during this brief period. The appointment of the Italian pastors to the two territorial parishes may also have contributed to their desirability for some Italians. The transfer of the Augustinian priests to St. Nicholas of Tolentine similarly attracted some more parishioners. With the cessation of foreign arrivals, sharply reduced by the National Origins Quota Acts of 1921 and 1924 and discouraged by economic depression, new immigration certainly did not contribute at all. More than anything else, the formidable increases experienced by all of the parishes undoubtedly reflected the dismemberment of Our Lady of Good Counsel.

The one exception to the overall pattern of growth among the parishes serving the Italians was found at St. Mary Magdalen dePazzi. From 2,594 families and 14,411 individuals reported in 1932, the figures for the oldest church in the area fell to 1,249 families and 5,714 individuals in only two years. The high numbers for 1932 appear to be inconsistent with information for previous years. But if the figures are valid, St. Mary Magdalen dePazzi appears to have been the only parish that did not benefit by an increase in the size of its own congregation from the suppression of its neighbor.

Whether the redesign of parish boundaries produced the desired spiritual effects is a question that transcends worldly knowledge and is gladly left to another kind of judgment. It is appropriate, however, to attempt to assess the temporal consequences of, as well as the underlying motives for, the dismembering of Our Lady of Good Counsel. Several factors may have contributed to its suppression, but it is difficult to conclude that any single one of them was sufficient in itself to warrant the closing of the parish. First, some members of the parish had raised serious allegations of improprieties and scandalous conduct against its priests in correspondence to the archbishop. However, the removal or transfer of an accused miscreant to another assignment would have quietly solved the problem without risking any reaction by parishioners. But this type of issue seldom, if ever, has resulted in the suppression of an entire parish. Second, the archdiocese presented the financial difficulties of the parish, along with Cardinal Dougherty's attempt to introduce efficient managerial practices, as the "official" reasons given for the decision. Although the Augustinians, who evidently believed that the parish was worth saving, had previously subsidized any shortfall at Our Lady of Good Counsel at year's end, this support was apparently no longer deemed feasible. While the parish could hope to improve in financial health in the future, the Great Depression had caused widespread job layoffs and reduced incomes among immigrant workers. Third, when the Italian population reached a number that was five times as large as it had been when Propaganda Fide and Archbishop Ryan had first given its care to the Augustinians, it was probably too large to allow that agreement to continue. And finally, the possibility that Cardinal Dougherty now hoped to expand archdiocesan control over parishes, which required regaining some power from the Augustinians, provides another plausible reason for the decision to close Our Lady of Good Counsel. It was convenient for Dougherty to claim that no agreement approved by the consulters could be found. The decision was made more interesting by the Augustinians' insistence that an agreement did exist, an argument that is supported today by documents still in their archives. But perhaps there is even more to all of this.

Another aspect of the situation, which historian Peter D'Agostino has identified, may be found in the special role that Italian religious orders played in attempting to maintain the ethnicity of their congregations during the Fascist era.[36] By separating from the jurisdiction of American provincial offices and shifting to direct control from Rome, they made themselves even more independent of local hierarchical authority. The Augustinian order enabled the friars at Our Lady of Good Counsel to achieve exactly this result by establishing the Italian Vice Province in late 1925. If their intention was to defy Cardinal Dougherty, who, despite the personal recognition that he had received from Mussolini, was deeply committed to Americanization, then the actions of the Italian friars may have fueled the eventual demise of their church.

When evaluated, weighed, and fitted together, however, these circumstances return to an older issue in the Italian religious experience in America that remained a concern for ecclesiastical authorities. Neither giving Italians their own parishes nor introducing social services by agencies beyond the parish had solved the "Italian problem." Like Protestant efforts to aid and convert them, the Catholic strategy to save the faith of Italians now required their acculturation and assimilation as Americans. But by what it had become almost from the moment of its founding, Our Lady of Good Counsel was a real and symbolic obstacle to that objective. Because its size, location, and importance made it a bastion of Little Italy, the parish embodied, far more than any other, the persistence of ethnicity, whether in religious beliefs and practices or in secular matters. It also was the parish that was least likely to favorably embrace either Americanization or the Irish American surrogate of religious identity. Consequently, Our Lady of Good Counsel represented a clear test of Dougherty's own policy toward Italians as Catholics and as Americans. With his personal commitment to an Americanization agenda, he removed its congregation from an institutional setting that was a much greater deterrent to assimilation than that of any other parish under diocesan clergy. The subsequent defiance on the streets and in the courts to the suppression of their parish confirmed the resistance of Italians to assimilation.

In the final analysis, the reasons for the closing of Our Lady of Good Counsel remain shrouded in time, and the argument offered here is more of a hypothesis than a confirmed conclusion. But some consequences were visible in the aftermath of its closing. At the root of the controversial decision made by the archdiocese, there was a convergence of several issues. The founding of nationality parishes had created a fundamental redundancy by establishing overlapping parishes. While nationality parishes with boundaries that merely encroached on territorial parishes could be adjusted and permitted to continue to serve their congregations, Our Lady of Good Counsel faced a different situation. Its boundaries fully overlapped the space already occupied by older parishes. Whether its physical facilities were indeed inadequate, as claimed by the archdiocese, it had become superfluous as a parish. The archdiocese chose to implement a risky policy that ignored the wishes of parishioners and underestimated what they were willing to do to defend the existence of their parish. The decision to close Our Lady of Good Counsel reverberated widely and loudly throughout South Philadelphia in the years to come.

The suppression of Our Lady of Good Counsel also gave Dougherty the opportunity to redistribute its population among St. Paul's, the Annunciation, and St. Nicholas of Tolentine. But for the most part, the former parishioners of Our Lady of Good Counsel—at least those who had not been alienated by the conflict with the archdiocese from Catholicism in general—augmented the congregation of St. Paul's. And whether Irish American ushers approved of how Italians who appeared on Sundays at the doors of St. Paul's or other territorial parishes were dressed, the newcomers were there to stay.

At St. Mary Magdalen dePazzi the consequences were far less because Eighth Street remained the boundary defining its limits. Its old pastor, Antonio Isoleri, might have played a larger part in the controversy over Our Lady of Good Counsel if it had occurred at an earlier time. Although he had expressed his reservations about the degree of religious fervor among the "elemento meridionale," Isoleri could also rise above his own provincialism and parochialism. But he had died in the year previous to the closing of the Augustinian church. Both the death of Isoleri in 1932 and the closing of Our Lady of Good Counsel in the next year symbolized the end of an era for Italians as immigrant Catholics in Philadelphia.

In the larger context of American Catholic history, the suppression of Our Lady of Good Counsel has various implications. This case showed that controversy over trusteeship was not a matter of the distant past but had persisted into the twentieth century. It similarly revealed that Church policy had clearly shifted from supporting immigrant culture through the founding of nationality parishes to one of strongly promoting Americanization. In this shift, American Catholicism had joined other religious bodies and secular agencies in the effort to assimilate its population, while it also sought acceptance as an institution that was a thoroughly integrated part of the national culture. Its means of achieving this objective, however, produced casualties. While other circumstances, such as the alleged misconduct of its priests and its precarious financial condition, contributed to the difficulties of Our Lady of Good Counsel, the suppression of the parish reflected the altered direction of Church policy. What Italians had sought was a refuge from the storm of assimilation, and this refuge had been unequivocally provided by Italian priests at this Italian church. And for years afterward, the suppression of Our Lady of Good Counsel would be remembered not only with sadness at the loss of their parish, but also with anger toward the archbishop by its former parishioners, who would emphatically say that "He took our church away from us."

Parish, Priest, and People

The preceding pages have presented the story of a parish, a priest and a people. These three dimensions—institutional, biographical, and sociocultural—cannot easily be separated from one another, nor should they be. The threads of the story of St. Mary Magdalen dePazzi parish; the life of Antonio Isoleri, its longtime pastor; and the history of Italian Catholic immigrants in Philadelphia form a tightly woven tapestry. But the story may also be seen as a case study within the larger context of American Catholic history, and thus it is also about parishes, priests, and people in a collective sense. In this final section, these three aspects will be addressed along with some related issues that others may want to explore further.

From the time of the Reformation, Roman Catholicism faced the need to reexamine and reconstruct its forms and practices. In the sixteenth century the Council of Trent began the restoration of Catholicism in its reply to Protestantism. Not long afterward, the Enlightenment presented a new threat that was secular in origin but equally disruptive to religious authority. As Catholicism sought to regain its place among European peoples and societies, it also had the complicated task of introducing itself to America.[1]

The diffusion of Catholicism to America eventually required a synthesis of the old and the new that would characterize it until the time of the Second Vatican Council. Traditional rituals had to be enriched by innovations in devotion, prayer, and instruction. The relationship of clergy and laity, while maintaining ecclesiastical discipline, had to develop roles and boundaries that were appropriate to the society of the New World. The traditional hierarchical structure and centralized control had to be reconciled with the values and aspirations of a republican culture. American Catholicism also had to build ramparts of defense against Nativist prejudices and movements as well as against the seductions of secular life that endangered the fidelity of its members. And the Church in America had to resolve the complicated problem of ethnic diversity and unite its constituents in a common culture, shared identity, and community of worshipers. The varying peoples who not only comprised the faithful but also increasingly interacted with each other had to be aligned and integrated without any appearance of particularism or favoritism.

Although Church authorities, whether defenders of tradition or proponents of innovation, were conducting this great experiment in the bureaucracies of Rome and the chancelleries of the New World, American Catholicism was also being forged in its rectories and churches. In this process, the parish became the principal instrument that organized religious experience, provided the setting for new forms of liturgy and piety, altered relations between clergy and laity, and presented Catholicism in a manner that facilitated acceptance by other Americans. But if the Nativist riots of 1844 had encouraged Philadelphia's Catholics "to carefully and deliberately wrap themselves together within the warmth and security of the parish,"[2] even more was required from its immigrant churches faced with the need to ameliorate the adjustment of immigrants to America.[3]

While Italians have long lived in Philadelphia, their chapter in local religious history remains to be told. Italian families appear in the early pages of sacramental ledgers for the city's oldest Catholic churches. Along with the laity during the same period, Italian priests were also serving in the area as members of the Jesuit community at Old St. Joseph's Church, as Augustinian friars at Villanova College, and as instructors at the diocesan seminary of St. Charles Borromeo. But the founding of St. Mary Magdalen dePazzi in 1852 turned a new page in this story. Under Father Gaetano Mariani, its saintly first rector, the struggling mission reached a precarious foothold in the twelve years before his death in 1864. After a brief but turbulent period that left the church under interdict, the recently ordained Antonio Isoleri was appointed rector in 1870. During the next fifty-six years, St. Mary Magdalen dePazzi grew, prospered, and stabilized under Father Isoleri, who was widely recognized as its second founder.

The story of St. Mary Magdalen dePazzi, however, was never far from broader issues of social and religious experiences. As their numbers grew, Italian immigrants chose not merely Philadelphia but also the city's Little Italy as their eventual destination. The process began with "migration chains," that is, the patterns of kinship and friendship based on origins in the same towns of Italy, that facilitated the Atlantic passage. These interpersonal networks in turn linked immigrants to ethnic neighborhoods in American cities that were near the points of arrival, where there were employment opportunities and inexpensive housing as well as the prejudices of other groups about where foreigners should be allowed to reside. But once established, the Italian colony provided the locus of daily life for its people in the urban environment. Within the confines of this urban village, Italians found familiar experiences and personal security. If the ethnic ghetto eased the acculturation of immigrants to America, then its institutions served as the instruments of that process. The narrative of St. Mary Magdalen dePazzi, the life of its pastor, and the people who made up its congregation and much of the immigrant colony must be viewed in this context.

Italians offered a distinctive challenge to Catholicism when they relocated to the cities of America. When the Church deemed them deficient in their religious life or feared losing them as communicants, it attempted to solve the "Italian problem" by providing them with the nationality parish. While primarily intended as a means of saving their faith, it was warmly embraced by its members. For analogous to what Little Italy represented in its relationship to the society surrounding it, this solution coincided with what Italians themselves sought for their religious life in America—to worship together, to maintain their own form of piety, and to hear the sacred message in their own language. At St. Mary Magdalen dePazzi, as at other nationality parishes subsequently founded in the Archdiocese of Philadelphia, this dimension of institutional life was a major part of a larger story of Italians as immigrants and as Catholics. Solving the "Italian problem" became synonymous with saving the faith in Little Italy.

The Parish:
St. Mary Magdalen dePazzi as a Community Institution

An influential scholar once noted, "A colony must have attained a certain size and stability before it can maintain a priest."[4] But if this is true of a priest, it must be even more true of a parish. Moreover, if the growth and stability of an immigrant colony determined the appointment of a priest and the establishment of a parish, these consequences became factors that encouraged its further development. And if the immigrant ghetto eased the transition from the homeland to the adopted society, then the Church also served that end. Despite their conflict with the Papal States during the Risorgimento and their sometimes tepid practice of religion, Italians remained a largely Catholic people and part of the Church in Italy and America.

The Italian Mission of St. Mary Magdalen dePazzi was founded when the Italian population of Philadelphia was quite small. Situated where Italians had already begun to cluster, it became the ceremonial hub of immigrant life, and its presence declared the existence of an embryonic Italian district. Beyond the liturgical calendar, important events in Italy, whether religious or secular, were usually celebrated with a mass in the church and a parade afterward. And whenever its congregation took to the streets in procession, it was marking its core and boundaries, sanctified by the blessings and power of its patron saints, as Little Italy. Such moments attested to Genoese dominance in early years, along with the lingering perception of St. Mary Magdalen dePazzi as the "Genoese church," even as its membership changed. Yet, as a beacon to later arrivals who sought to live with their own people, the church acted as a catalyst for further growth and diversification of the Italian population. By helping to sustain personal identity and promote group cohesion, it also became another means of transforming an aggregate into a community. And by visibly asserting itself before the entire city, it reinforced the claim that Italians had staked to their place in Philadelphia.

For its Genoese founders and later arrivals, St. Mary Magdalen dePazzi erased the distance between Italy and Philadelphia by maintaining the continuity between their Old World origins and their destination in urban America. The interior of the remodeled church reflected the Baroque style that was popular in many areas of Italy. Its faux marble columns, ornate entablature, modestly arched domes, and statues of familiar saints could be found in churches not only in Liguria and Tuscany but also in Abruzzo-Molise, Campania, Basilicata, Calabria, Puglia, and Sicily. The staging of rites, through reenactments that could have been in the churches of ancestral towns, enabled immigrants to remember their native land. Although the sound of old dialects was replaced by the nasal tones of a Ligurian pastor preaching in standardized Italian, it was more easily understood and embraced than the English or brogue of an Irish American priest. By these powerful allusions to—as well as illusions of—Italy, St. Mary Magdalen dePazzi served as a cultural and psychological refuge within a mainly Anglo-Saxon and Protestant city. Indeed, as an Italian journalist speaking of a similar parish has said, it was "an umbilical cord to the motherland."[5]

More than any other institution, the parish anchored the immigrant community. By meeting the needs of individuals throughout their entire lifespan, it cared for the population at all ages. In some sense, the parish was like the great cathedrals of towns in the Middle Ages. It provided the setting for the rituals—sanctifying birth, marriage, and death—that gave deeper meaning to daily life. Beyond spiritual life, it provided temporal assistance of the sort that has now come to be called social services—medical, educational, and legal—and that enabled people to endure everyday life. And in a city replete with bars and brothels, it offered wholesome forms of amusement, entertainment, and recreation. Thus, the parish maintained the continuity of its members' cultural heritage, perpetuated their personal identity, demarcated their neighborhood, and promoted cohesion. The parish, in short, provided a sense of past, of self, and of community as it nurtured life among Italians in Philadelphia.

For nearly a half-century, St. Mary Magdalen dePazzi did this work alone. Its religious activities, along with other functions, showed that Italians themselves, with good leadership, could solve the "Italian problem" even before it was identified as such by ecclesiastical authorities. But it eventually became apparent that it could not be done by a single parish. It was, however, not the failure of the old parish or its pastor but rather the volume and pattern of Italian immigration that altered the situation. With the growth of the immigrant population, Isoleri faced the "pastor's dilemma." If he failed to report an increase in membership, it would reflect unfavorably on him. Moreover, having sought the appointment of an assistant for years, he could only justify his need by citing a heavier pastoral burden. On the other hand, if he reported too large a number of parishioners, he was revealing to archdiocesan authorities the need to divide the parish and to establish a new one. Complicating matters further, ethnic diversity at St. Mary Magdalen dePazzi, which had once meant Italian and Irish members, embraced Italians of different origins, with Ligurians, Abruzzese-Molisani, and Neapolitans by the 1880s. But immigrants from Southern Italy contended that Isoleri was neither sympathetic nor suitable. When migration swelled from the Mezzogiorno and Sicily, the new arrivals petitioned the archdiocese for another church. Although it could have expanded the resources and facilities at St. Mary Magdalen dePazzi, the archdiocese chose to open other nationality parishes. By this course of action, it implicitly recognized that St. Mary Magdalen dePazzi was not a failure. Instead, it was a model for a successful strategy, at least for the immediate future, in the effort to save the faith of Italians as Catholics.

The Priest:
Isoleri as a Spiritual and Secular Leader

Only eighteen years after its founding, St. Mary Magdalen dePazzi weathered the serious crisis of being placed under interdict. With permanent suppression still threatening its future when Antonio Isoleri arrived as the rector, a recently ordained, twenty-five-year-old priest hardly seemed the appropriate candidate to save the troubled Italian Mission in Philadelphia and guide it to calmer waters. But he did. And not only did he save it, but he preserved it, nurtured it, and transformed it from a precarious mission to a stable parish over the next fifty-six years.

Assigned to restore peace within the Italian Mission as well as between its congregation and the diocese, Isoleri almost immediately led it into controversy. While early differences and debate with Protestants had undoubtedly gained the favor of local Catholic authorities, Isoleri's challenge of hierarchical power within his own church seriously risked his position. But here was a young priest with the audacity to appeal to Rome for relief from perceived injustices by his immediate superiors. Because ecclesiastical regulations were ambiguous on many matters until the modern codification of canon law, Isoleri was relatively free to set his own course.

But what kind of man was Isoleri? Often combative when he had to be, he was also proud, intellectual, creative, and deeply spiritual. From his early years he displayed academic and literary talents that, if he had remained in his homeland, might have led him to a career as a seminary professor at the Collegio Brignole Sale or at a similar institution. His impressive grasp of literary and scholarly texts not only included Scripture but also classical Greek and Roman writers, Renaissance Humanists, contemporary Italian authors, and even Comtean Positivists. His personal papers reveal that he had read Virgil, Dante, Shakespeare, Manzoni, and Pellico. But the same erudition and aesthetic sensibility could have distanced him from the needs of his people. His congregation included literate, ambitious, and even affluent entrepreneurs, as well as less skilled workers who struggled desperately merely to survive. Without compromising his character, Isoleri applied his formidable talents to the material improvement and spiritual salvation of his people. When he alluded to Dante or to some other Italian writer, as he often did in his sermons, he was not displaying conceit but was instead using the power of words to inform his listeners, awaken their religious fervor, and preserve their cultural patrimony. Above all else, Isoleri knew who he was as well as who his people were, or what he strongly believed they ought to be.

Like other pastors of his time, Isoleri led people into the "devotional revolution" that erupted in the mid-nineteenth century. They crowded into the church for the Forty Hours Devotions that Bishop John Neumann had introduced to the diocese, and Isoleri welcomed them to the annual parish mission, usually preached by Italian Passionists. He urged the use of rosaries, medals, crucifixes, and scapulars to encourage private worship and veneration. He promoted the formation of parish confraternities and sodalities for children and adults. His prolific writings on devotional exercises grafted traditional sensibilities to the exigencies of immigrant life. But newer forms of piety did not obviate older practices that still resonated with religious and cultural meaning. Although he objected to *feste* when they were organized outside of his control, Isoleri conspicuously officiated at all major and sanctioned events. And he retained the feast day of Saint Mary Magdalen dePazzi as the main occasion to bind his people together not only as a "household of faith" but also as a community of immigrants.

Isoleri's enthusiastic support for traditional expressions of popular piety as well as for newer forms of devotion facilitated this outcome. His efforts erased the gap of two-tiered religiosity that could separate the elite from the common and divide his congregation. He also channeled the deeper values and perceptions of the people, or what Robert Orsi calls "what really matters," to the normative control of the institutional Church.[6] Isoleri's extensive devotional writings were a rich feast for readers seeking to nourish their own spiritual appetites. In these writings he shaped devotional resources to the particular needs of Italians as Catholics in America. In this role, Isoleri became a modern version of what Peter Brown calls an "impresario" of the "cult of saints."[7] As he collaborated with the organized Church in co-opting traditional piety and repositioning it, Isoleri redeemed himself in the judgment of his ecclesiastical superiors. He had gone from early maverick to esteemed pastor.

From the outset, Isoleri demonstrated his strategy to forge a constituency that would ensure the future of the Italian Mission. Pew rentals brought affluent English-speaking residents, primarily Irish Americans, into his church. By enlisting their support, Isoleri secured the viability of his parish during its formative stage. By employing his Ligurian version of blarney to defuse potential sources of tension and division, he gained Irish support for his Italian Mission. And by promoting cooperation between the two ethnic Catholic groups, who could have easily found themselves in conflict with each other, Isoleri invited harmony and integration.

When available resources were not enough, Isoleri sought other means of consolidating his congregation and community. Almost immediately after becoming rector, he recognized the urgency for establishing an orphanage and parish school as well as for securing a staff of teaching sisters at St. Mary Magdalen dePazzi. But Isoleri's dealings with the Missionary Sisters of St. Francis, together with his demands that only Italian sisters be sent to his parish, provoked their abrupt departure in 1882. His willingness to welcome them back, however, brought about a reconciliation and their return to the parish five years later. After weathering this storm, the Franciscan sisters not only outlasted Isoleri but remained as fixtures of parish life for another fifty years after his death. By his successes in other matters, however, Isoleri tempered the contention that Italian immigration, tending not to include priests or sisters, led to a less institutionalized form of Catholicism. Nor did he offer a folk Catholicism, and certainly not the anticlericalism, imputed to later Italians, that conflicted with more voluntary organizational patterns developing in America. To the contrary, his version of Catholicism, in its theological substance, liturgical forms, and social relations, was as contemporary as that of any other Philadelphia pastor.

As much as Isoleri devoted himself to the spiritual needs of his people, he also sought to ameliorate their material condition. From his pulpit he helped to initiate the campaign against the exploitation of "slave children" as street musicians by padrone masters. He opened his church on the feast day of its patron saint as a sanctuary for striking railroad laborers. In his sermons he offered advice on such personal issues as the mutual obligations of parents and children, the dangers of alcohol abuse, and the value of a good education. He emphatically endorsed the necessity of enabling family members to migrate together and the desirability of resettling them in rural areas. He used public occasions to comment on, or sometimes to lament, political and military events in Italy. Albeit from a distance, he especially sought the reconciliation of Church and state in his native land. From such platforms as the dedication of the Columbus Monument in Fairmount Park, he called for unity among Italians in America. And he rallied his community, first in support of Italy but then in the cause of the United States, in the patriotic frenzy surrounding World War I. By word and deed before his people, Isoleri sought to protect, inspire, and improve their lives in this world as well as in the next one.

Isoleri's influence undoubtedly transcended altar, pulpit, and confessional to reach into the larger community. Besides the sodalities and confraternities of his parish, secular organizations found St. Mary Magdalen dePazzi to be a hospitable site. The Società di Unione e Fratellanza Italiana, the oldest voluntary association among the city's Italians, regularly participated in a mass on New Year's Day at the church. Such occasions exposed these organizations, at least for the moment, to Isoleri's persuasive rhetoric and instruction. And by connecting himself and his parish with the *prominenti*, Isoleri cemented the relationship between the secular and sacred domains of the Italian colony. Together their leadership gave the material opportunities and satisfactions, political consciousness and protection, and spiritual comfort and consolation that stabilized life within Little Italy. During a public life that spanned more than a half-century, Isoleri maintained his position. Addressing Italians far longer than anyone else, even as the community changed, he spoke a message that provided continuity between its past and future.

Isoleri certainly had his imperfections. In the glare of public life he could be arbitrary, inconsistent, and imperious. He had come, after all, from that region of Italy where both a republic and its principal city had been known as "La Superba." But in Philadelphia, after exhorting Italians to rise above their regional differences, he would offend Southern Italians by his disdain for the "elemento meridionale." He may have even sufficiently antagonized anticlerical Socialists and Anarchists, who obviously had little appreciation for religion or priests, to make them willing to attempt his assassination. And even those who faced Isoleri in what should have been a benign relationship had their difficulties with him. The Missionary Sisters of St. Francis had found him to be demanding and disagreeable. Father Antonio Garritano, his successor as pastor, admitted that he had left St. Mary Magdalen dePazzi because of Isoleri; and that if he had not, he might have committed an act of violence against the old priest.[8]

The few living informants who once knew him still remember his flaws. A former parishioner recalled that her family, convinced that Isoleri did not want Southern Italians in his parish, left for St. Paul's, only to find Irish nuns who treated them even worse. (They finally became Episcopalians.) But the vulgar phrase that she used to describe Isoleri only made her remarks and his image even more indelible. And elderly parishioners, the last generation to have known him, depict him as a haughty pastor who inspired more fear than genuine affection.[9] Yet, none of these recollections erases his accomplishments and significance. In the final analysis, he began his career as a priest in Philadelphia as the young gadfly who challenged the authority of his bishop and ended it as a diocesan consultor to a later cardinal archbishop, saluted at his death as the "Grand Old Man of Little Italy."

Isoleri's tenure as pastor is arguably unmatched in American Catholic history. It occurred during a crucial phase of the Italian experience in the United States. Starting when the number of immigrants from Italy was only a handful, it ended shortly after Congress enacted a restrictive policy that all but ended immigration from Italy. It spanned an era when the area around his church evolved from Little Italy to simply another ethnic neighborhood in the city. It extended over at least two generations in which his people went from being immigrants to being an American ethnic group. It occurred during a period when this population also went from being street musicians and plaster-statue vendors to being members of the working and middle classes. And it extended from a time when the Catholic Church in America found it desirable to establish new parishes for the foreign born to a later moment when it closed them. Isoleri's ministry in Philadelphia began in the same year that Italian troops defeated papal forces, ending the Temporal Power of the papacy, captured the city of Rome, and unified most of the modern Italian state. It ended shortly after Benito Mussolini and Pius XI reached accords in the Lateran Treaty and the Vatican Concordat, which resolved the tensions between Church and state, restored freedom and power to Catholicism, and implicitly endorsed Fascism.

Through these years, by serving as a model for the priest and pastor of the nationality parish as well as for any lay leader of the ethnic community, Isoleri defined the challenges of life for foreign-born Catholics and the terms of their assimilation in their adopted land. He was one of the principal architects of the Italian community in Philadelphia. Yet, throughout his sixty-two years in America, Isoleri retained his self-consciousness as an Italian and his genuine affection for Italy. In his overt expression of dual identity and his loyalties to his homeland and to America, Isoleri was able to be at the same time both an Italian and an American. His adjustment, however, was not a unique and private experience, relevant only to the life of one man; it had implications for all Italians in America.

The People:
Saving the Faith of Little Italy

When St. Mary Magdalen dePazzi first opened its doors, it welcomed the dawning of a new era in American Catholic history. Having survived the assaults of American Nativism, the Catholic Church, despite the threat of lingering hostility and discrimination, was approaching imminent acceptance as an institution in the United States. From a fundamentally Protestant nation and culture, but now with the increasing presence of Catholics and Jews, America was moving toward the pluralism that would characterize religion until nearly the end of the twentieth century. And as Catholicism in America was being reshaped by its own national leadership and by ecclesiastical Rome to better fit this situation, St. Mary Magdalen dePazzi served as an incubator.

Although the Italian Mission was officially organized by Bishop Neumann, nevertheless, it was as a sociological reality created and sustained by its own people. In simple terms, the people were the parish and, conversely, the parish was the people. As it called them together to praise God, to deliver the gospel and sacraments, to console them in times of sorrow, to lead them to salvation, and to celebrate their faith, their parish also affirmed their identity and solidified their cohesion. As a major social institution of the immigrant community, it mediated their entrance into and relationship with the larger society.

While each immigrant group posed a unique challenge, its integration into a common faith and new society at the same time presented an even greater one for Catholicism in America. The Italians, perceived less favorably rather than welcomed warmly as co-religionists by Catholics already here, found themselves at the core of the multifaceted "Italian problem." Despite eventual findings that immigrant apostasy had not been great, Church leaders became preoccupied with the issue of "leakage." But the financial difficulties of congregations largely made up of low-income workers and their families threatened the efficacy of the nationality parish as a solution. Ecclesiastical authorities had to convince Italians to increase their financial contributions to the Church, and to their parishes in particular, something that they had not been required to do in Italy. In this precarious setting the Church also had to protect Italians from the Protestant proselytization that responded to their material needs while offering them an alternative to Catholicism.

When the Archdiocese of Philadelphia recognized that spiritual care required greater attention to material care, the response to the "Italian problem" entered into a new phase with the establishment of agencies beyond the parish. In some sense, these policy initiatives acknowledged that Protestant and secular welfare agencies had met needs that could no longer be ignored if the fidelity of immigrants was to be secured. And when Catholic efforts began to adopt this strategy, essentially emulating the Protestant model, they similarly moved toward an assimilationist ideology. Among other facets of "assimilative shock" in their adjustment, whether abetted by Protestant or Catholic efforts, Italians were threatened with the loss of their secular and spiritual culture.

Further aggravating the "Italian problem" was the "devotional revolution," when the Church introduced the forms of piety that widely characterized Catholicism from the mid-nineteenth century to the Second Vatican Council. But for Italians at St. Mary Magdalen dePazzi and other nationality parishes, their faith had long rested on an older "affective spirituality" whose sacred traditions had roots reaching back to late antiquity. With its emphasis upon the "cult of the saints," their religiosity was derived from beliefs and practices in native towns not only in the South but in all regions of Italy where peasant peoples for centuries had struggled to survive. As in the ancient Roman world, its momentum derived from "the need to play out the common preoccupation of all . . . with new forms of the exercise of power, new bonds of human dependence, [and] new, intimate hopes for protection and justice in a changing world."[10] Rather than being an aspect of recent innovation first encountered in the religious system at their destination, they had carried it along with other tools of survival in their cultural baggage as immigrants to America.[11]

Italians unpacked and reconstructed their "household of faith" after their arrival. In Philadelphia, as in other cities where Italian immigrants formed communities, they found security by continuing to pay homage to the patron saints of the towns and villages of their homeland, as their ancestors had done for centuries. An immigrant New Yorker declared: "Our Italians, and I mean the old folks, feel that without the guardianship of their former patron saint, life would be next to impossible." According to Orsi, this "theology of the streets" depended at its core on a very personalized and reciprocal relationship between client and patron. As another of his sources put it, "I'm sure that the Madonna will listen to me, because I fight with Her, I get angry with Her, and then I always ask Her pardon—this is the best system." This intercessory dialogue was not in a language directed at a remote deity but rather in the vernacular of domestic disputes between parents and their children or between brothers and sisters. But if Italians already had a profound "affective spirituality" within their own "household of faith," it interacted with the altered conditions that they found in America.[12]

When Isoleri described younger Italians as knowing virtually nothing about Catholic devotions, he had implicitly subscribed to the oversimplified belief that made the Irish the standard bearers of religious practice in America. But as with the Irish before them, the parish became the setting where immigrant Italians could come to be more Catholic.[13] And when their lack of knowledge in religious matters is linked to the temporal objectives that they often sought, their piety became more visibly related to the ordeal of adjusting to life in America.

With some irony, some aspects of traditional Italian religiosity were already pointing in the direction toward which the "devotional revolution" was pulling American Catholics. Public celebrations on city streets, such as the *feste*, threatened to spill outside of immigrant ghettos, disrupt public order, and, by their emotion and exuberance, embarrass Church authorities. But if participants behaved well, the local newspapers described these events as colorful, noisy, peaceful, and full of rustic charm. The media construction of reality not only defused the situation but also welcomed Italians as Catholics to the archdiocese and as residents to the city.

When American Catholicism turned itself to the issue of saving the faith of immigrants, the search for a solution brought controversy and divisiveness rather than agreement and unity. Although the German American hierarchy and clergy believed assimilation to be inevitable, they had supported a gradual process that allowed their people to retain their traditional language and identity. Irish American prelates and priests, on the other hand, tended to see rapid acculturation and integration as the answer. Meanwhile, the spiritual needs of Italians required the founding of nationality parishes in which they could remain Catholic while becoming American.

As St. Mary Magdalen dePazzi facilitated immigrant adjustment, Isoleri saw his congregation as a part of an enduring Italian colony in America, even as the Philadelphia hierarchy sought to transform ethnic parishes into tools of Americanization. While other Catholics marched only behind American and papal banners, his parishioners also routinely carried their Italian tricolor. On these occasions, Isoleri emphatically affirmed in his speeches that while becoming good Americans and faithful Catholics, they remained Italians. But contrary to his intentions, these public events could not offset stronger forces that swept Italians farther from their native land and its culture while co-opting and reshaping them into Americans. Whether by expressions of piety or manifestations of ethnicity, whatever differences distinguished Italians as a group, it was difficult to keep them apart from other Catholics. Subjected to Irish American ecclesiastical authority and cultural hegemony, Italian Catholics could only become more like their co-religionists in America and less like their fellow countrymen left behind in their native land. As Italians became American Catholics, they also became Italian Americans as their acculturation increasingly unfolded under Church policy and in religious experience.

Within such vessels as St. Mary Magdalen dePazzi, the Church had recognized Italians as a homogeneous population even before Italy established itself as a nation. But seeing them as a distinct "people" was an oversimplification. As such, "Italians" had not yet been created but remained separated by the regional cultures, linguistic variations, and political differences of their native land. So while the Church disregarded what separated Italians from one another—treating them instead as if they had a common background and character and imposing a shared identity on them—it was encouraging a unified and nationalistic ethnicity among them, both as Italian Americans and as Americans. The effort to solve the perceived and presumed deficiencies of Italians as Catholics, predicated on a strategy that by becoming American their faith could also be preserved, led to a reciprocal corollary—that by becoming better Catholics, they also became better Americans. From acculturating Italians as Americans to save them as Catholics, the Church had shifted to using their faith to make them better Americans. Ironically, this formula, in effect, also co-opted Isoleri's old motto of "patria e religione," but it altered the "patria" from Italy to America.

In the final analysis, the nationality parish had a limited life span and influence that eventually had to come to an end, thus making it a relic of an earlier time. By adopting assimilation as a strategy, the Church was remaking Italians into Americans as well as into American Catholics, often along the Irish Catholic model. Meanwhile, pluralists who believed in the value of preserving and retaining one's original culture, such as Antonio Isoleri at St. Mary Magdalen dePazzi as well as the Augustinians at Our Lady of Good Counsel, wanted Italians to become not only better Catholics but also to remain Italians. Although neither ideology could foresee the future, pluralism was especially blind to it because assimilation was, as we now know, inescapable. And even Isoleri, a cultural nationalist who refused to allow his people to step blindly into the "melting pot," was a realist who knew as well as did the assimilationists what inevitably awaited Italians in America.

Before mass migration, a handful of Ligurians and Tuscans, posing no serious challenge to other ethnic groups, found themselves appreciated and accepted in a Philadelphia that was far more alarmed by the threat of a possible Celtic flood. Members of the small Italian community found it necessary to find spouses in other ethnic groups. The early records of St. Mary Magdalen dePazzi, when it was still proclaimed as the Italian Mission, reveal the names of Irish members along with evidence of harmony between the two groups, without any effort by the Irish to control parish life.

With mass migration from Southern Italy and Sicily at the end of the nineteenth century, nationality parishes afforded an institutional setting that enabled Italians to maintain their faith as Catholics. But the situation of Italian Catholics remained only one case of the larger need to integrate all immigrants into a common Catholicism. And if Italians represented a problem, its roots went back to Archbishop John Carroll's much earlier efforts to establish a form of Catholicism for all of its adherents that was compatible with American culture and society—and acceptable to other Americans. If there eventually was an "Italian problem," it was still contained within this larger framework of a lingering "Catholic problem" that transcended any specific ethnic group. After first defining the "Italian problem" as being that Italian immigrants were not Catholic enough, the Church later decided that they were not American enough. When it finally concluded that this solution may have also retarded Americanization, nationality parishes then had to be "de-nationalized," modified in some way, or even terminated.

The advent of World War I encouraged Americans to reject the slower, organic process by which immigrants had been previously absorbed and to replace it with a more direct program of Americanization. Assimilation could no longer be allowed to occur in a gradual, undirected manner, which would have inevitably happened; it had to be implemented and accelerated by a deliberate strategy. Whether these immigrants fully embraced their old faith, accepted only a part of it, tried to ignore it, or sought escape from it entirely, the Church was always there, lurking somewhere in their consciousness and communal life and teaching important lessons of what it meant to live in America.

As the politics of modern times continued to influence religion, the rise of Fascism in Italy, in particular, not only affected Catholicism but also Italians and their community institutions in the Unites States. After an early, misguided appreciation of Mussolini by many Italians in America, but widely shared by others, sentiment gradually drifted toward opposition. The outbreak of World War II, with Italy on the enemy side, however, enabled Catholicism to join the struggle as well as to give a final thrust to resolving the "Italian problem." At a time demanding loyalty, the Church firmly positioned itself in the mainstream of American politics and culture as a conduit of nationalism and patriotism. The arguments of an Italian American bishop against traditional customs of folk Catholicism confirmed the concluding phase of the "Italian problem," which had once required the dismemberment of the most Italian of parishes and now discredited the vestiges of alien loyalties found in the popular piety of Italians. Ironically, the author was one of the two priests who had been appointed as the first Italian pastors of territorial parishes in South Philadelphia.[14]

The central motif of the Italian experience in Philadelphia as well as in other American cities has been the continuous redistribution of a people in their residential locations, social characteristics, lifestyles, class positions, personal identities, and relations with other racial and ethnic groups. At no stage of this long history have Italian immigrants and their successive generations lived in a static situation. Upon their arrival they found modest levels of employment and housing largely concentrated in Little Italy. But their children and grandchildren soon encountered the rapidly expanding opportunities of an industrial and urban nation. After World War II they joined other Americans in moving from the working class in city neighborhoods to the middle class in the suburbs. And whether they wanted to or not, Italians had also entered into the process of acculturation and assimilation that thoroughly transformed them into Americans. By the end of the twentieth century, while slightly more than 140,000 Philadelphia residents could still identify themselves as being wholly or partly Italian in ancestry, two and one-half times as many could be found in the four other counties of southeastern Pennsylvania.[15] Similarly, a significantly large number of Italian Americans, including many former Philadelphia residents, lived in the nearby counties of South Jersey. They now are widely dispersed in where they work, how they live, how they see themselves, and how others see them.

These changes have profoundly altered the social and religious life of Italian Americans. In suburban communities, intermarried with other groups, they find themselves in families in which ethnic consciousness continues to dissolve, as well as in very diverse congregations where socioeconomic class has become far more important than ethnicity in shaping lifestyle and identity. Their presence also represents the final surmounting of the barriers that once excluded them from such parishes and encouraged Church authorities to establish nationality parishes for them. And in an occasional case, in an area formerly occupied by a "satellite community" in the suburbs, the arrival of other groups has even led to the reorganization of a parish that was once Italian. In 1955, for example, Our Lady of the Assumption, founded forty-seven years earlier as an Italian church in suburban Strafford, along the Main Line, was reconstituted as a territorial parish to accommodate the growth and diversity of the Catholic population in the area.

In older sections of Philadelphia, what Italians once did to earlier residents is now being done to them. In recent years, newer racial and ethnic groups have displaced Italians from their former neighborhoods. Although the archdiocese once attempted to maintain parishes in these areas, it has been closing them in recent years. Between 1972 and 1998, five former Italian parishes were shut entirely, and several others consolidated with nearby parishes. In 1999, the archdiocese announced that St. Mary Magdalen dePazzi, nearly 150 years after its founding, was among six parishes that would be closed sometime in the following year. As the Catholic population continues to grow in suburban areas, it declines in the urban neighborhoods where European immigrants once formed great colonies. Born of necessity, as more Catholics left the city, this policy has dissolved a large number of formerly territorial parishes. At the same time, some pastors heroically struggle to meet the needs of newly arrived Latino, African, and Asian Catholics, sometimes in the same parishes. These newcomers represent as unprecedented diversity of language and culture far more complicated than that of earlier years, and pastoral agendas have replaced assimilation with "enculturation" to maintain their Catholicism. But while the archdiocese once sought to preserve the faith of immigrant Europeans by providing parishes for them, it has shifted its priorities away from potential converts and instead largely directs its resources to schools, churches, and other facilities for affluent Catholics in the expanding outer suburbs of the metropolitan area.

In the wake of this situation, many churches that once housed immigrant congregations face an uncertain future today. Historic institutions, such as St. Mary Magdalen dePazzi, now await the likelihood of sale to a different denomination and resurrection as a house of worship or, like its former neighbor, Our Lady of Good Counsel, of being desanctified and then razed by the wrecker's crane. Like descendants of the immigrants who crowded into them, they have become the beneficiaries of an ambiguous process of assimilation: Americanized to the point of their own cultural extinction and only remnants of the culture that once was theirs. And the communities that they once helped to build have now deserted them, leaving them sad shadows of what they once were, to join other ghost parishes that haunt old neighborhoods. But American Catholicism, by its earlier enthusiasm for nationality parishes as well as by its later abandonment of them, created an institutional legacy whose traces remain in the minds, hearts and souls of those whom they once served.

In June 2000 the Archdiocese of Philadelphia closed the parish of St. Mary Magdalen dePazzi, 148 years after its founding.

NOTES

Introduction

1. Among the more important works on the Italian religious experince in America, see Rudolph J. Vecoli, "Prelates and Peasants: Italian Immigrants and the Catholic Church," *Journal of Social History* 2 (Spring 1969): 217–68; Vecoli, "Cult and Occult in Italian American Culture: The Persistence of a Religious Heritage," in Randall M. Miller and Thomas D. Marzik, eds., *Immigrants and Religion in Urban America* (Philadelphia: Temple University Press, 1980); and Robert Anthony Orsi, *The Madonna of 115th Street: Faith and Community in Italian Harlem, 1880–1950* (New Haven and London: Yale University Press, 1985). Although somewhat dated, for an overview of this area of research, see Silvano M. Tomasi and Edward C. Stibili, *Italian Americans and Religion: An Annotated Bibliography* (New York: Center for Migration Studies, 1978). Beyond Italian Americans as a particular case, the most comprehensive consideration of relevant issues is found in J. J. Mol, *Churches and Immigrants: A Sociological Study of the Mutual Effect of Religion and Immigrant Adjustment* (The Hague, 1961).

2. For the institutions of community life, see the classic studies in American sociology by Robert S. Lynd and Helen Merrell Lynd, *Middletown: A Study in Modern American Culture* (New York: Harcourt, Brace and World, 1920) and *Middletown in Transition: A Study in Cultural Conflicts* (New York: Harcourt, Brace and World, 1937), in which the authors adopted the perspective of anthropologist W. H. R. Rivers.

3. For important studies of these issues, see Colman J. Barry, *The Catholic Church and German Americans* (Milwaukee: Bruce, 1953); Richard M. Linkh, *American Catholicism and European Immigrants, 1900–1924* (Staten Island, NY: Center for Migration Studies, 1975); and Orsi, *The Madonna of 115th Street*. See also Miller and Marzik, eds., *Immigrants and Religion*, for an even wider survey of these issues. For the concept of "institutional completeness," see Raymond Breton, "Institutional Completeness of Ethnic Communities and the Personal Relations of Immigrants," *American Journal of Sociology* 70 (September 1964): 141–46.

4. Barry, *The Catholic Church and German Americans*.

5. See the remarks by Henry Warner Bowden, series editor, Denominations in America, in Patrick W. Carey, *The Roman Catholics* (Westport, CT: Greenwood Press, 1993).

6. Silvano Tomasi, *Piety and Power: The Role of the Italian Parishes in the New York Metropolitan Area, 1880–1930* (Staten Island, NY: Center for Migration Studies, 1975).

7. Jay P. Dolan, "A Critical Period in American Catholicism," *Review of Politics* 35:4 (October 1973): 523–36; Dolan, *The Immigrant Church: New York's Irish and German Catholics, 1815–1865* (Baltimore: Johns Hopkins University Press, 1975); Kathleen Gavigan, "The Rise and Fall of Parish Cohesiveness in Philadelphia," *Records of the American Catholic Historical Society of Philadelphia* (hereafter *RACHS*) 86 (1975): 107–31.

Since the Catholic Church in America had a missionary status, which placed it under the direct jurisdiction of the Congregation of Propaganda Fide until June 1908, under canon law it had, strictly speaking, neither parishes nor pastors. For a discussion of the point, see John P. Marschall, "Diocesan and Religious Clergy: The History of a Relationship, 1789–1969," in John Tracy Ellis, ed., *The Catholic Priest in the United States* (Collegeville, MN: Saint John's University Press, 1971), 385–421. However, since these terms have been long used by historians in describing American Catholic experience and by Catholics themselves during this period, it is appropriate to apply them here.

8. Much of the material on the early history of the parish has been taken from *Souvenir and Bouquet* (Philadelphia, 1911). This invaluable resource was prepared for the "triple anniversary" celebration of 1907. In addition to a history of the parish, it includes reprints of a number of documents, such as newspaper articles, originally published on significant occasions during these years.

The parish was named for Catharine dePazzi (1566–1607), born to a noble family in Florence, who joined the Carmelite order and gained a reputation as a mystic, which led to her canonization as Saint Mary Magdalen dePazzi in 1669. The preferred form is "dePazzi," denoting her to be a member of the Pazzi family. The alternative "de'Pazzi" is acceptable, but it is sometimes incorrectly translated, even in Italian sources, as "of the insane." Religious ecstasy should not be confused with mental illness.

9. John Gilmary Shea, *History of the Catholic Church in the United States,* vol. 4 (Akron, OH: D. H. McBride, 1892).

10. Aurelio Palmieri, O.S.A., "The Contribution of the Italian Catholic Clergy to the United States," in C. E. McGuire, ed., *Catholic Builders of the Nation: A Symposium on the Catholic Contribution to the Civilization of the United States* (Boston: Continental Press, 1923).

11. Dolores Liptak, R.S.M., *Immigrants and Their Church* (New York: Macmillan, 1989), 144–45.

12. Tomasi, *Piety and Power.*

13. Joseph L. J. Kirlin, *Catholicity in Philadelphia: From the Earliest Missionaries to the Present Times* (Philadelphia: John Joseph McVey, 1909).

14. James F. Connelly, ed., *The History of the Archdiocese of Philadelphia* (Philadelphia, 1976).

15. A principal source on Isoleri's life and writings is his *Lira Leronica,* the three volumes of poetry, plays, and other items published in Philadelphia in 1876–1878. The title of this work, which might be put into English as the Lyre of the Lerone (or Lerrone), refers to one of three streams in the area where Isoleri was born, the others being the Neva and the Arroscia, that once came together to form the Centa River, flowed downward to Albenga, and emptied into the Ligurian Sea. See *Enciclopedia Italiana di Scienze, Lettere ed Arti,* vol. 12 (Rome: Istituto de Enciclopedia Italiana, 1934). The Lerrone may have been, however, only a torrent produced by seasonal rains that flowed out of the mountains; it does not appear on the maps available to the author at the present time.

16. C. Wright Mills, *The Sociological Imagination* (New York: Oxford University Press, 1959); R. Baritono et al., eds., *Public and Private in American History: State, Family, Subjectivity in the Twentieth Century* (Turin: Otto Editore, 2003).

17. *International Migrations,* vol. 1, no. 14 (New York: National Bureau of Economic Research, 1931), 384; United States Census Office, *Ninth Census of the United States: 1870* (Washington, DC, 1873); John Maneval, *An Ethnic History of South Philadelphia, 1870–1980: A Research Tool for Demographic Studies,* an unpublished report prepared for the Balch Institute for Ethnic Studies (Philadelphia, 1991).

18. *Sadlier's Catholic Directory* (New York: D. & J. Sadlier, 1870), 257.

19. United States Department of Justice, *Annual Report of the Immigration and Natural-ization Service* (Washington, DC, 1978).

20. United States Census Office, *Fifteenth Census of the United States: 1930* (Washington, DC, 1932); Maneval, *An Ethnic History*, 48–50.

21. *The Official Catholic Directory* (New York: P. J. Kenedy & Sons, 1930), 163.

22. This total has been calculated by the author on the basis of figures provided by the pastors about the size of their parishes in their annual reports to the archdiocese. See the *Questiones* (1930), Philadelphia Archdiocesan Historical Research Center (hereafter PAHRC). In most cases the pastors gave precise figures but in a few instances they only estimated parish population. In one case the pastor provided the number of families in his parish but not the number of individuals. In the latter instance, using the ratio between families and individuals for other parishes, we were able to generate a likely total for in-dividuals. There is no other available source for such information, and a few members of these parishes may not have been Italians. After 1930, only one other Italian parish, Our Lady of Loreto, was founded in Philadelphia; and in 1954, as a result of population changes in its suburban location in Strafford, the Assumption of the Blessed Virgin Mary was re-commissioned as a territorial parish.

23. For a persuasive argument on the importance of the nationality parish, see Tomasi, *Piety and Power;* for a view on the failure of the nationality parish to prevent assimila-tion, see Leonard Covello, "Cultural Assimilation and the Church," *Religious Education* (July–August 1944): 229–35.

24. The earlier view is found in Oscar Handlin, *The Uprooted* (Boston: Little, Brown, 1951); for an important dissent and revision, see Rudolph J. Vecoli, "Contadini in Chicago: A Critique of *The Uprooted,*" in *Journal of American History* 51 (December 1964): 404–17.

CHAPTER ONE.   *The Italian Church in Philadelphia*

1. Mary Maples Dunn and Richard S. Dunn, "The Founding, 1681–1701," in Russell F. Weigley, ed., *Philadelphia: A 300-Year History* (New York: W. W. Norton & Company, 1982), 1–32. Although it must be used with caution, the basic source on early Catholicism in Phila-delphia remains Kirlin, *Catholicity in Philadelphia*.

2. Neale to Charles Shireburn, S.J., April 25, 1741, in Thomas Hughes, S.J., ed., *History of the Society of Jesus in North America: Documents* (Cleveland, 1908), cited in John Tracy Ellis, *American Catholicism* (Chicago: University of Chicago Press, 1956), 28.

3. Ellis, *American Catholicism*, 28.

4. Dale B. Light, *Rome and the New Republic: Conflict and Continuity in Philadelphia Catholicism between the Republic and the Civil War* (Notre Dame, IN: University of Notre Dame Press, 1996).

5. For a more detailed discussion of the problem of determining the actual number of Italians in Philadelphia, applicable to other American cities at the same time, see Richard N. Juliani, *Building Little Italy: Philadelphia's Italians before Mass Migration* (University Park: Pennsylvania State University Press, 1998), 323–30.

6. Giovanni Schiavo, *Four Centuries of Italian American Experience* (New York: Vigo Press, 1957), 107.

7. Giovanni Schiavo, *Italian American History,* vol. 2 (New York: Vigo Press, 1947–1949), 101–2; Fanny Morton Peck, "Roman Consul of the Nineteenth Century," *Historical Records and Studies* 13 (May 1919): 61–83; Leo F. Stock, "The Papal Consuls of Philadelphia," *RACHS* 55 (1944): 178–89.

8. The original boundaries of Philadelphia were the Delaware River on the east, the Schuylkill River on the west, Vine Street on the north, and South Street on the south. The Act of Consolidation of February 1854 joined all of the previously independent districts, boroughs, and townships in the county with the original city to form the present city.

9. For information on this strange episode of Church history in Philadelphia, see Kirlin, *Catholicity in Philadelphia*, 238–39; and Juliani, *Building Little Italy*, 90–94. While some sources give Perugia as his birthplace, Inglesi was born in Rome and later attended the seminary in Perugia. For details on his life, see the materials on the trusteeship controversy at St. Mary's, written by Richard W. Meade and by Inglesi himself, in the PAHRC pamphlet file. The report of Inglesi's death is found in a letter written by Bishop Conwell to Propaganda Fide (hereafter PF), dated March 19, 1826; see PF Docs, vol. 940, fol. 646.

10. This section draws upon several principal sources. For a thorough examination of Bedini's visit, as well as his subsequent report, see Rev. James F. Connelly, *The Visit of Archbishop Gaetano Bedini to the United States of America (June, 1853–February, 1854)*, Analecta Gregoriana, 109, Series Facultatis Historiae Ecclesiaticae: Section B, n. 20 (Rome, 1960). Other efforts to describe the Bedini affair with particular reference to Philadelphia include Light, *Rome and the New Republic*, 322–29, and Juliani, *Building Little Italy*, 156–64.

11. Giovanni Pizzorusso and Matteo Sanfilippo, "Introduction," *Fonti ecclesiastiche romane per lo studio dell'emigrazione italiana in Nord America (1642–1922)*, *Studi Emigrazione*, 33, 124, December, 1996 (Rome: Centro Studi Emigrazione).

12. *Catholic Herald* (March 18, 1852), 1; *Universe* (December 15, 1866); *Catholic Standard* (February 2, 1867), 4; J. Thomas Scharf and Thompson Westcott, *History of Philadelphia, 1609–1884*, vol. 2 (Philadelphia: L. H. Everts, 1884), 1384; Rev. John F. Byrne, "The Redemptorists in America," *Records* 43 (1932): 34–61. The article on the Catholic Church in Philadelphia in Scharf and Westcott was actually written by Martin I. J. Griffin, the leading authority on the subject at the time.

Information on the individual priests involved in the events leading up to the formation of the parish is very limited, sometimes contradictory, and often confusing. In 1851, Antonio DellaNave was at St. Paul's; listed as the Reverend Mr. DellaNave, he was probably still a seminarian, serving his diaconate at the parish, and soon to be ordained. See *Metropolitan Catholic Almanac and Laity's Directory for 1852* (Baltimore: Fielding Lucas, Jr., 1851), 79. DellaNave appears in later editions as a member of the clergy serving in Rock Lake, Pennsylvania. See *Sadlier's Catholic Almanac and Ordo for 1864* (New York: D. & J. Sadlier, 1864), 212. In Kirlin's *Catholicity in Philadelphia*, while not listed among the priests ordained for the Diocese of Philadelphia, C. A. Dellanave appears as the second chaplain at St. John's Orphan Asylum in West Philadelphia and as being responsible for having doubled the size of its chapel in 1853. See Kirlin, 363–64. Peter Folchi, a Jesuit, was a member of the faculty at Georgetown College in Washington, DC, in the early 1850s. See *Metropolitan Catholic Almanac and Laity's Directory for 1853*, (Baltimore: Fielding Lucas, Jr., 1852), 64. Although Griffin identified a Rev. De la Piance as the person who assembled Italian children for religious instruction at St. Paul's Church, no one of that name can be found in the almanacs, directories, or diocesan records for the period. It is possible that Griffin confused De la Piance with Dellanave.

13. "Church for the Italians," *Catholic Herald* (October 21, 1852), 2.

14. "New Catholic Church," *Public Ledger* (June 18, 1853), 1. Contrary to the announcement, other sources give the laying of the cornerstone and the beginning of construction as May 14, 1854. See "Some Historical Notes" and the newspaper items in the commemorative volume, *Souvenir and Bouquet*, published by the parish in 1911.

15. There was another priest with the same family name, who came at an earlier time to Philadelphia to serve as a missionary in the United States, who should not be confused with Gaetano Mariani. From various sources, some details of his life can be assembled that clearly reveal that they were two different persons. In 1818, Giovanni Maria Rossetti, who is sometimes described simply as a priest of the Diocese of Milan but who may have been a Lazarist (that is, a Vincentian), organized a band of missionaries for the United States; among them was Charles Mariani. In July they sailed from Leghorn for the port of Philadelphia. In November 1818, C. Mariani, also identified as a Vincentian, sent a letter from New Orleans, describing certain aspects of the Church in that city, to the Countess Durini in Milan. While Mariani had apparently continued on his journey to a post in New Orleans, Rossetti and other members of the group remained in Philadelphia until 1820, when they finally reached their destination at the Barrens, the seminary at Fredonia, Missouri. Although listed as "N. Mariani" in 1822, Mariani appears again as an assistant at the cathedral in New Orleans.

Frequent references to Charles Mariani can be found in documents in the archives of Propaganda Fide as well as in published accounts that describe the Rossetti mission or other aspects of Church history at this time. For example, see *The Laity's Directory to the Church Service for the Year of Our Lord M,DCC,XXII* (New York: William H. Creagh, 1822); *The Diary of Joseph Rosati* (St. Louis Archdiocesan Archives, n.d.); Joseph Rosati, *Life of Felix de Andreis* (St. Louis: B. Herder, 1900); and Joseph Rosati, C.M., "Recollections of the Establishment of the Congregation of the Mission in the United States of America, IV," translated and annotated by Stafford Poole, C.M., *Vincentian Heritage* 4:2 (1983): 109–39. Although he may be found in other records for later years, there is no need for the present study to go further. The Charles Mariani who came to Philadelphia in 1818 was not the same person as the Gaetano Mariani who arrived in 1851. The latter was reported to have been born on the date used here and to be in his sixty-seventh year at the time of his death in the obituary that appeared in the *Catholic Standard* (March 17, 1866), but he was reported to be seventy years of age by the secular press in the obituary published in the *Public Ledger* (March 9, 1866), which would make the year of his birth three years earlier. It is likely in this case that the Catholic newspaper used a more reliable source.

16. Although no record on his life can be found in the file of priests in the archives of the Archdiocese of Philadelphia, some details on Mariani's life, in particular his early years, can be obtained from obituaries at the time of his death and afterward. For example, see the *Catholic Standard* (March 17, 1866, and February 2, 1867) available on microfilm at the Philadelphia Archdiocesan Historical Research Center. For a brief note indicating the correspondence, but unfortunately not revealing its contents, between Kenrick and Mariani, see *Bishop Kenrick's Journal* (October 7, 1851).

17. For the history of the seminary and its faculty, see Monsignor J. F. Connelly, *St. Charles Seminary* (Philadelphia, 1979). See also Scharf and Westcott, *History of Philadelphia*.

18. *Catholic Standard* (February 2, 1867), 4.

19. St. Mary Magdalen dePazzi, Baptismal Ledger (October 23, 1853), PAHRC.

20. "St. John's Orphan Asylum," *Catholic Herald* (December 29, 1853); "Devotion of the Forty Hours," *Catholic Herald* (December 12, 1853); Scharf and Westcott, *History of Philadelphia*, 1384; *Catholic Standard* (February 2, 1867), 4.

21. Although the sacramental ledger, as it exists today, lists only one baptism, Neumann reported a total of twenty-one in a note on the mission for 1835. Congressi America Centrale, vol. 16, sect. III, fol. 852r–857r (Rome, December 16, 1854), Relatio Status Ecclesiae Philadelphiensis in Toederatis Americae Septentsionati Statibus, AD MDCCCLIV, in PAHRC, Miscellaneous Manuscripts.

22. Baptism Register, St. Mary Magdalen dePazzi (December 1853–January 1866). These figures are limited to entries made by Mariani. While he often provided some information about the families, his successor, Father Gaetano Sorrentini, who made his first entry in March of that year, restricted himself to ecclesiastical information. The figure given here for 1866 represents only the final entry by Mariani and none of Sorrentini's entries afterward. There probably were more baptisms than were listed. Although only thirty cases can be counted on the pages, Mariani noted thirty-one baptized children for Italian parents for 1860. Some pages, now stuck together and unseparable without damage, also appear to contain more cases.

23. For a more detailed examination of this population, see Juliani, *Building Little Italy,* 164–69.

24. *Souvenir and Bouquet,* 22.

25. Ibid.

26. A Statement . . . showing the receipts and expenditures of the Italian Church of St. Mary Magdalen dePazzi, Miscellaneous Manuscripts, M-6, PAHRC.

27. Scharf and Westcott, 1384; for a glowing appraisal of his medical abilities, see his obituary in the *Catholic Standard* (March 17, 1866), 2.

28. *Public Ledger* (March 9, 1966), 1.

29. I am indebted to Jeanne Torre, who found these documents in the death registers in the parish archives of Santa Maria Assunta in San Colombano Certenoli; to Pier Felice Torre, who helped to secure them; and to the Reverend Emilio Jozelli, the present pastor, for granting me permission to use them. *Santa Maria Assunta in Certenoli–Atti di Morti* (1862), no. 23.

30. *Catholic Standard* (March 17, 1866), 2; *Souvenir and Bouquet,* 37.

31. *Catholic Standard* (March 17, 1866), 2; *Public Ledger* (March 12, 1866), 1.

32. Connelly, *St. Charles Seminary,* 55.

33. The various sources on his life provide slightly different details on almost everything. A general biographical sketch is included in the Reverend Thomas J. Peterman's *Priests of a Century, 1868–1968, Diocese of Wilmington, Delaware* (Wilmington, n.d., probably 1968), 8–9. For differences in the place of birth, compare the account in the Necrology section of *The Official Catholic Directory* (New York: Sadlier, 1894), which gives it as Rome (as does Peterman), with a document reproduced in *Souvenir and Bouquet* (p. 27), which identifies him as Neapolitan. Similarly, his date of birth is given in the *Directory* as August 2, 1815, and by Peterman as August 7. For information on citizenship, see the Declaration of Intention (August 13, 1855) and Petition for Naturalization (December 17, 1860), both filed in the Court of Common Pleas, City and County of Philadelphia. An extensive record of his role as Vicar General of Monterey can be reconstructed from documents in the archives of the Congregation of Propaganda Fide.

34. PF Docs, Lettere, vol. 346, fol. 174r, and vol. 347, fol. 578v. Since it maintained jurisdiction over Catholicism in America from the first missionary activities in the colonial period until 1908, these matters had to be placed before the Congregation of Propaganda Fide. In addition to its archives in Rome, the documents cited here from Propaganda Fide are generally available on microfilm under the title: Catholic Church: Congregatio de Propaganda Fide Records, Archives of the University of Notre Dame, Notre Dame, Indiana.

35. Again, there are numerous documents relevant to this situation, but in particular, see PF Docs, Scritture Originali Riferite nelle Congregazioni Generali, vol. 985, fols. 250rv, 251rv, 344rv, and 345r.

36. For Sorrentini's involvement in the dispute, again there are numerous documents in the archives of Propaganda Fide. See, for example, PF Docs, vol. 18, fols. 157rv and 158rv;

Lettere, vol. 349, fols. 159v and 207rv; and Congressi, Collegi d'Italia, Brignole-Sale-Negroni, 1841–1891, vol. 20, fols. 823r and 824v. The Collegio Brignole Sale was the principal seminary preparing missionaries for the United States and elsewhere. It would become especially important for Philadelphia about twelve years later with the assignment of another alumnus, Antonio Isoleri, to St. Mary Magdalen dePazzi.

37. PF Docs, Scritture, vol. 985, fols. 55rv, 77rv, 138rv, 140rv, and 141rv. See also Peterman, *Priests of a Century*, 8.

38. Cajetano Sorrentini, *New Lights and True Light on the Revolution in Italy in 1860* (N.p., 1860).

39. Cajetano Sorrentini, *The Pope, Napoleon III, England, and Italian Carbonaris* (Philadelphia: J. & J. B. Duffey, 1861). 40. Peterman, *Priests of a Century*, 8.

41. PF Docs, vol. 20, fols. 1236rv, 1237rv, and 1248; vol. 356, fol. 296rv.

42. Peterman, *Priests of a Century*, 9.

43. Peterman erroneously wrote that Sorrentini came to Philadelphia to serve as the second pastor of St. Mary Magdalen dePazzi in 1861, but he did not succeed Mariani until after the latter's death in 1866.

44. *Catholic Standard* (June 20, 1891). This account is also included in *Souvenir and Bouquet*, 36–39.

45. *Souvenir and Bouquet*, 22. Even a more recent history by a priest in residence at the parish repeated this point without adding further information; see Rev. Alfred M. Natali, O.S.A., *140th Anniversary—St. Mary Magdalen dePazzi* (Philadelphia, 1991).

46. *Catholic Standard* (January 27, 1866), 2.

47. St. Mary Magdalen dePazzi (April 28, 1866), Document 51.111Ach, PAHRC.

48. *Public Ledger* (May 26, 1866), 1.

49. *Catholic Standard* (June 9, 1866), 5.

50. *Catholic Standard* (June 16, 1866), 5. From this point on, the listings in this newspaper were given under the title of the Church of the Immaculate Conception.

51. *Catholic Standard* (September 1, 1866), 5.

52. *Catholic Standard* (September 15, 1866), 5.

53. *Catholic Standard* (October 20, 1866), 4; as well as October 27, 1866, and December 8, 1866.

54. The charges against Sorrentini are found in the petition of the trustees sent to Rome (June 4, 1867), PF Docs, vol. 22, fols. 319r–321v, 322v.

55. *Catholic Standard* (January 19, 1867), 5. It is ironic that the Italian effort began on the same Sunday that Bishop Amat, in his continuing relations with Sorrentini, appeared at the parish to appeal for financial support for his own diocese.

56. St. Mary Magdalen dePazzi (February 13, 1867), 51.112Ach, PAHRC.

57. *Catholic Standard* (February 2, 1867), 5. It is not clear how much the reconstruction of the meeting in this article represents Wood's views or the comments of its writer. But it appears, and they are being treated as such in my interpretation, that the article attempted to convey Wood's opinion as it was delivered at the time.

58. *Souvenir and Bouquet*, 22. Where he first went upon his departure from Philadelphia is not clear, but in August 1867, Sorrentini resurfaced as the pastor of St. Aloysius Church in Pottstown, Pennsylvania, where he remained until 1871. During this period he had far greater success in his new appointment than he had in his previous one; the two published parish histories praise his leadership as pastor. In addition to the contributions to the development of the parish itself, Sorrentini also pursued a special ministry in his visits to the growing number of Italian laborers in the railroad camps of the area. From the contributions, he was able to purchase a marble statue of the Virgin Mary that remained

in the convent garden many years later. Information on this phase of Sorrentini's life can be found in William Bishop Schuyler, *Historical Sketch of St. Aloysius Parish, Pottstown, Pennsylvania* (1906); and in Charles H. Pickar, O.S.A., *One Hundred Years of Service: The Story of St. Aloysius' Church* (1956).

There is no indication of how Sorrentini and Wood regarded each other during the times of the troubles in South Philadelphia or the later period in Pottstown; and despite his success at St. Aloysius, or perhaps because of it, Sorrentini soon left the Diocese of Philadelphia. He returned to Wilmington, Delaware, as pastor at St. James Church on December 25, 1871, where he remained until 1873 (see Peterman, *Priests of a Century*, 8; and *Sadlier's Catholic Almanac* for 1873). But there may have been more involved. In a letter of January 1872 informing Propaganda Fide of his incardination into the Diocese of Wilmington by Bishop Thomas A. Becker, Sorrentini also complained about Bishop Wood. See PF Documents, vol. 24, fol. 140rv (January 22, 1872). In its reply in the following month, Propaganda Fide provided encouragement and support to Sorrentini. See PF Documents, vol. 367, fols. 234v and 235r (February 20, 1872). In his volume on the clergy of Wilmington, Father Peterman described Sorrentini's rather successful efforts to develop St. James, until his ill-fated tour of Argentina to solicit further financial support in 1873–74. This eleemosynary expedition led first to a disagreement with Bishop Becker and then to Sorrentini's resignation from the Diocese of Wilmington in May 1877. With the old troubles with the Franciscans perhaps forgotten, Sorrentini found his way back to California as the founding pastor of Sacred Heart Church in Salinas City, where he remained until his death in 1893. As with the details of his early life, the sources on this final moment are also contradictory. Peterman says that Sorrentini was buried on the gospel side before the main altar of Sacred Heart Church in Salinas City, but *Souvenir and Bouquet* informs the reader that its controversial former pastor was buried in the Jesuit church of Santa Clara in Salinas City (see p. 22).

59. St. Mary Magdalen dePazzi, 51.113Ach, PAHRC. The date of the meeting in January, as it was reported in the *Catholic Standard* article of February 2, 1867, and the date on this letter make the exact chronology of events confusing. Either the date on the letter is an error, or something had been sent to the bishop earlier, or this is another effort by the Italians to clarify their position. In any case, it remains unresolved. The eight trustees were Paolo Cavagnaro, president; Antonio Sciutti, secretary; Agostino Feretti, Agostino Lagomarsino, Giovanni Raggio, Giovanni Villa, Giacomo Molinari, and Stefano Cuneo.

60. Miscellaneous Manuscripts (May 20, 1867), PAHRC.

61. St. Mary Magdalen dePazzi, 51.115Ach, PAHRC.

62. St. Mary Magdalen dePazzi, 52.83Ach, PAHRC.

63. PF Docs, vol. 358, fols. 790v and 791r (September 13, 1867). The priest mentioned by the Italians was probably Andrew Rossi, a Vincentian and philosophy professor at the seminary in the early 1850s.

64. *Catholic Standard* (July 27, 1867), 4.

65. PF Docs, vol. 358, fols. 790v and 791r (September 13, 1867).

66. Document 52.82Ach (September 27, 1867), PAHRC.

67. PF Docs, vol. 22, fols. 323rv and 324rv. Although no dates are given on this document, from the sequence of previous correspondence and actions it appears that Wood wrote this letter in November 1867.

68. PF Docs, vol. 358, fols. 994v and 995r (December 11, 1867).

69. PF Docs, vol. 22, fol. 162rv (April 3, 1868).

70. *Souvenir and Bouquet*, 22. For Cicaterri's early postings, see the listings in *Metropolitan Catholic Almanac for 1853*, and also for subsequent years; and *Sadlier's Catholic*

Almanac and Ordo for 1864. It is not necessary to trace his career after his departure from St. Mary Magdalen dePazzi, but Cicaterri was in residence at the Church of the Gesu at the time of his death at St. Joseph's Hospital in Philadelphia on November 19, 1895. See *Hoffman's Catholic Directory* (Milwaukee: Hoffman Brothers, 1896).

71. *Catholic Standard* (June 27, 1868), 5.

72. *Souvenir and Bouquet*, 22–23; *Public Ledger* (November 27, 1883, and November 30, 1883). The obituary in the *Public Ledger* gave his place and year of birth as Genoa in 1816, but Rev. Alfred M. Natali, O.S.A., in his history of the parish states that holy cards issued at Father Rolando's funeral provided this information as Pieve di Teco in 1815. In my judgment, Natali's account has more credibility than a newspaper obituary. See Natali's *140th Anniversary—St. Mary Magdalen dePazzi*. Rolando remained in Paris until 1871, when he returned to the United States and became pastor of St. Vincent's Church in St. Louis, Missouri. After two more years he was appointed as visitor or provincial of the Vincentians, an office which he held until 1879. When he died in 1883, Rolando had been serving as president of St. Vincent's Seminary in the Germantown section of Philadelphia. See *Sadlier's Catholic Directory* (New York: D. & J. Sadlier, 1884), 51; and M. A. Drennan, C.M., "The Early History of the Congregation of the Mission in Philadelphia," *RACHS* 20 (1909): 4–21.

73. *Catholic Standard* (January 30, 1869), 5.

74. *Catholic Standard* (February 20, 1869), 5.

75. *Catholic Standard* (January 1, 1870), 5.

76. *Catholic Standard* (May 15, 1869), 5; Martin I. J. Griffin, *Notebook*, 49, Manuscript Collections, M-568, PAHRC.

77. PF Docs, vol. 22, fol. 965r (May 19, 1869); vol. 361, fol. 670v (June 14, 1869); vol. 22, fol. 1028r (June 21, 1869); vol. 362, fol. 743rv (July 7, 1869); PF Docs, Collegi d'Italia 3, Brignole Sale Negroni, 1846–1891, Volume not numbered, fol. 970r (1869). The claim that James Rolando recommended Isoleri to Wood is made in *Souvenir and Bouquet*, 22–23. The ties between Rolando and Isoleri may have been even greater. If Rolando's town of origin was Pieve di Teco, close to Isoleri's birthplace, they shared the strong bonds of place—making them almost *paesani*—that have been emphasized in the study of Italian immigration. Joseph Rolando, the other temporary pastor, returned to the Diocese of Newark, where he served until his retirement as a priest. He died in Madison, New Jersey, on January 13, 1907. See *The Official Catholic Directory* (New York and Milwaukee, 1908), 989.

78. For further information on the Italian community in Philadelphia in its early years, see Juliani, *Building Little Italy*; and for later years, Richard N. Juliani, *The Social Organization of Immigration: The Italians in Philadelphia* (New York: Arno Press, 1980).

CHAPTER TWO.   *European Politics, American Catholicism, and Italian Immigration*

1. *Universe* (July 23, 1864), 5. We can speculate on the principal motives for such urging, but some comments at the end of the article are revealing. The writer states that while Philadelphia is an episcopal city, it could become an archepiscopal one, thus making it one of the most influential Catholic cities in the world. We can add that this result would be far more in the interest of a member of the clergy than for any layman. Could the inspiration for the argument have originated in an ambitious member of the hierarchy?

2. The Catholic press in Philadelphia began with the *Catholic Herald and Register* which expired after the publication of only three issues in 1822. Another *Catholic Herald* appeared in 1833 and lasted until 1857, when it merged with the *Catholic Visitor* and became the *Catholic Herald and Visitor*. Under new ownership in 1867, it became the *Universe: The Catholic Herald and Visitor*, which lasted until its demise somewhere between 1867 and 1870. In 1866 another paper, the *Catholic Standard*, appeared; in 1895 it merged with the *Catholic Times*, founded in 1892, when the two papers became the *Catholic Standard and Times*, which presently remains as the voice of the archdiocese. Some information on the history of the Catholic press in Philadelphia is found in the pamphlet, *Sources for Genealogical Research*, prepared by the Philadelphia Archdiocesan Historical Research Center. Some sense of the Catholic press in the 1860s, with an emphasis on politics, is provided by Joseph George, Jr., "Philadelphia's *Catholic Herald*: The Civil War Years," *Pennsylvania Magazine of History and Biography* 103:2 (April 1979): 196–221.

3. *Universe* (May 14, 1864), 4.

4. *Universe* (May 5, 1864), 4.

5. For an excellent treatment of these events, see Spencer DiScala's *Italy: From Revolution to Republic, 1700 to the Present* (Boulder, CO: Westview Press, 1995).

6. *Catholic Standard* (September 28, 1867), 4.

7. *Catholic Standard* (October 5, 1867), 4.

8. Ibid.

9. *Catholic Standard* (December 14, 1867), 4.

10. Ibid.

11. *Catholic Standard* (April 13, 1867), 5.

12. "Reception of Bishop Wood," *Catholic Standard* (October 5, 1867), 2.

13. Their story has been engagingly told by G. F. H. Berkeley, *The Irish Battalion in the Papal Army of 1860* (Dublin and Cork: The Talbot Press, 1929). Some participants in this campaign later became members of the Union army in the American Civil War and the U.S. cavalry in the Indian Wars. Evan S. Connell's *Son of the Morning Star* (San Francisco: North Point Press, 1984) reveals that at least one veteran of the Irish Battalion died at the Little Big Horn under the command of Col. George Armstrong Custer.

14. *Catholic Standard* (May 9, 1868), 4.

15. Howard Marraro, *American Opinion on the Unification of Italy, 1846–1861* (New York: Columbia University Press, 1932). Although his work remains an indispensable source on the subject more than sixty years after its publication, Marraro focused on the secular press and the earlier period of the Risorgimento. Beyond examination by the press, a treatment of the actual events may be found in William O. Madden, S.J., *American Catholic Support for the Papal Army, 1866–1868* (H.E.D diss., Pontifical Gregorian University, Rome, 1968).

16. *Catholic Standard* (May 9, 1868), 4.

17. PF Docs, vol. 22, fol. 206rv, n.d. [May 14, 1868], fols. 207r, 208rv, n.d. [May 13, 1868], fols. 209r, 210v (May 13, 1868).

18. PF Docs, vol. 22, fols. 220r and 221r (May 21, 1868), 245r and 246rv (June 10, 1868), and 284–287, rectos only (June 24, 1868). Bishop Wood of Philadelphia was not among the correspondents who sent this letter; it would be interesting to know his views on this matter.

19. PF Docs, vol. 360, fols. 742v and 743r (July 22, 1868); *Catholic Standard* (August 29, 1868).

20. For the history of the Peter's Pence, from the Middle Ages to modern times, see *Catholic Encyclopedia*, vol. 11 (New York: Appleton, 1911), 774–75; and *New Catholic*

Encyclopedia, vol. 11 (New York: McGraw-Hill, 1967), 235. For the action at the Provincial and Plenary Council of the bishops, a useful, relatively recent source is Hugh Nolan, ed., *Pastoral Letters of the United States Catholic Bishops,* vol. 1 (Washington, DC: United States Catholic Conference, 1984), 158–59.

21. *Catholic Encyclopedia,* vol. 11, 774–75. The time series data for the U.S. economy that would convert these figures to their equivalents in more recent dollar amounts are not available. The earliest data begin in 1875. If indices for 1875 are used, however, some approximate amounts can be reached. Thus, $1,850,000 would be roughly equivalent to more than $31 million in 1993; similarly, $4 million would be roughly equivalent to slightly more than $67 million in 1993. For time series data from 1875 to 1991, see Appendix A in Robert J. Gordon, *Macroeconomics,* 6th ed. (New York: HarperCollins, 1993); for the 1993 data, see *The Economic Report of the President* (Washington, DC, 1994).

22. *Catholic Standard* (May 9, 1868), 4.

23. PF Docs, vol. 22, fols. 265rv and 266rv (June 5, 1868).

24. These figures were available from the Peter's Pence, 1867 and 1869 files of the archdiocese, PAHRC (51.02–51.03). Information on Wood's mission to Rome in 1867 is provided in the *Catholic Standard* (July 27, 1867). If data for 1875 are used, the $60,000 from the diocese as a whole in 1867 is the rough equivalent of slightly more than $1,007,000 in 1993 dollars. The $363 donation from the parish in the same year would amount to about $6,000 in 1993 dollars, and the nearly $34,000 contribution of the diocese in 1869 would be about $570,000 in 1993. The $148 sum from the parish in that year would be worth about $2,500 in 1993.

25. PF Docs, vol. 24, fol. 388r (August 6, 1872); vol. 368, fols. 1067v and 1068r (August 27, 1872).

26. See the extensive file on the protest meeting, which includes articles from major newspapers in Philadelphia and New York, PAHRC SB-1:49–55 and 64.

27. *Age* (December 5, 1870); *Evening Bulletin* (December 5, 1870); *Morning Post* (December 5, 1870); *Philadelphia Inquirer* (December 5, 1870); *Public Ledger* (December 5, 1870). (Unpaginated newspaper clippings, PAHRC file.) The diocese published its own account in a pamphlet, *Protest of the Catholics of Philadelphia,* edited by Mark F. Vallette (Philadelphia, 1871). Vallette was probably its principal author and likely wrote the lengthy article in the *Catholic Standard* on the day after the meeting. Born in Basel, Switzerland, of French parentage, Vallette migrated to the United States as a child. He became editor of the *Catholic Standard* in 1867 and other papers in later years before continuing his career in journalism and public education in New York City. He also was an active early member of the United States Catholic Historical Society. For a biographical sketch, see Eugene F. Willging and Herta Hatzfeld, *Catholic Serials of the Nineteenth Century in the United States: A Descriptive Bibliography and Union List,* Second Series, Part Five, Pennsylvania (Washington, DC: Catholic University of America Press, 1964), 145. A note on names: A. Antelo, of Portuguese background, and A. Merino, a native of Madrid, who have sometimes been incorrectly identified as Italian, were among the participants.

28. Vallette, *Protest,* 9–29. Campbell's words were slightly altered by Vallette's reporting of them.

29. Ibid., 29–31.

30. *Inquirer* (December 5, 1870).

31. *Age* (December 5, 1870).

32. *Evening Telegraph* (December 5, 1870), PAHRC SB-1:51.

33. *Evening Bulletin* (December 5, 1870).

34. *Morning Post* (December 5, 1870).

35. Ibid.

36. *New York Herald* (December 6, 1870), PAHRC SB-1:56.

37. The daring pastor was the Reverend Thomas Farrell, pastor of St. Joseph's Church in Greenwich Village. A newspaper article on the day after the protest, under the heading "A Liberal Priest—An Ultramontane Audience," gave a vivid image of the affair: "The attendance was wholly male and almost as wholly Irish, presenting a body of about 600 splendid specimens of muscular Christianity." *New York Herald* (December 6, 1870). See PAHRC SB-1:56. In later years, Farrell played a conspicuous part as a member of the Accademia, a small group of remarkably liberal priests in the Archdiocese of New York, who consistently opposed Archbishop Michael A. Corrigan. Some discussion of Farrell and his associates, particularly in regard to the controversy over another liberal-thinking priest, the Reverend Edward McGlynn, who was excommunicated either for his economic and political views or for his defiance of ecclesiastical authority (depending on which side of the controversy is accepted) but afterward was restored in standing as a priest, is available in Florence D. Cohalan, *A Popular History of the Archdiocese of New York* (Yonkers, NY: United States Catholic Historical Society, 1983), 118–38.

38. The letter was written by a prominent layman, M. A. Frenaye, and published in the *Catholic Standard* (December 5, 1870), PAHRC SB-1:59.

39. There is, of course, a large body of scholarly research on Italian migration, but one of the earliest studies remains in many ways the indispensable source. See Robert F. Foerster, *The Italian Emigration of Our Times* (Cambridge, MA: Harvard University Press, 1924).

40. "Pio IX," *Catholic Standard* (December 10, 1870), 4–5, 8.

CHAPTER THREE. *Portrait of a Young Priest*

1. There are two basic sources on Isoleri's early life. Some information is derived from the Record of Priests, Archdiocese of Philadelphia, PAHRC; from this document in Isoleri's handwriting, it seems by the question mark that he placed on the line that he did not know the maiden name of his mother. The other, more detailed source is an autobiographical sketch that Isoleri sent to Professor P. Rossi, C.M., at the Collegio Brignole Sale in January 1889, found in the collection of his personal papers. In the latter document he listed his mother's first name as Geronima.

2. On the document in his own handwriting in the Record of Priests, PAHRC, Isoleri gave his education as "College and Seminary at Albenga, Savona, et Genova, with the Lazarists, in the College Brignole Sale for Foreign Missions." According to *Souvenir and Bouquet*, after pursuing classical studies at the Royal College in Albenga, then philosophy at the seminary in the same city, Isoleri completed his education at the Apostolic College of Brignole Sale; see p. 46. This account is a reproduction of an item on the celebration of the 25th anniversary of his ordination that appeared in the *Catholic Times* (March 24, 1894).

3. The passenger list for the voyage of the St. Laurent, a steamship which departed from Le Havre on December 17, 1869, and arrived at the port of New York City on December 30, 1869, erroneously gives the name of Luigi Isoleri, age forty-one, a priest, traveling first class, Italy as the country of origin and intended final residence. In a memoir composed in 1889, Isoleri wrote that he had embarked from the ship on the evening of December 29, 1869.

4. See "Brignole Sale, Antonio" and "Collegio Brignole Sale Negrone," *Enciclopedia Cattolica* (Città del Vaticano, Rome, 1949), pp. 100 and 1964; for more on Wigger, see

Carl Derivaux, *The History of the Diocese of Newark, 1873–1901* (Ph.D. diss., Catholic University of America, 1963); and Charles George Herbermann, "Rt. Rev. Winand Michael Wigger, D.D., Third Bishop of Newark," *Historical Records and Studies* 2 (1901): 292–320. For Isoleri's notes on Auguste Comte, see Miscellaneous Papers, Isoleri Papers.

    5. See the Record of Priests, PAHRC.

    6. Antonio Isoleri, *Lira Leronica* (Philadelphia, 1876–1878). His three volumes mainly consist of poetry and plays written from 1861 to 1869. Volume 1 contains fourteen sonnets, sixty-seven "liriche diverse," five "carmi," eight "poesie Bernesche," and three "idilli." The "poesie Bernesche," in the style of Francesco Berni, the early sixteenth-century Florentine poet, are playful verses intended to reflect a virtuous life in contrast to the decadence and corruption of the times. See the entry on Berni in the *Enciclopedia Italiana di Scienza, Lettere ed Arti*, vol. 12 (Rome: Istituto dell' Enciclopedia Italiana, 1934). Volume 2 of *Lira Leronica* includes three plays, some brief explanatory notes, and one sonnet, "Al Nuovo Poeta Ligure," written about and dedicated to Isoleri in 1876 by Giuseppe Alizeri, a Vincentian priest and old friend, who was stationed in the Germantown section of Philadelphia. Volume 3 begins with a play in which the plot weaves the Italian struggle for independence into a tale of two families, at first enemies, who are eventually united through marriage, entitled "Il Volontario Fiorentino o I Promessi Sposi." It was inspired by Alessandro Manzoni's celebrated novel. The volume continues with two comedies and an assortment of poems, prose essays, and some speeches and sermons given in Philadelphia. Each volume also includes some remarks that Isoleri wrote as he prepared the work for publication in 1876–1878.

    7. Isoleri, *Lira,* vol. 1, 5–6.

    8. "Essi non si raccomandano per merito letterario; ma l'amicizia e la carità (si vendono a benefizio di un' Orfanotrofio . . .) possono ben farli ricercare e leggere forse con qualche gusto." Isoleri, *Lira,* vol. 3, 157.

    9. Isoleri, "Liriche Diverse I. Pel Giorno di S.M. Il Re Vittorio Emanuele II," *Lira,* vol. 1, 21. Despite his modest denial of any artistic merit, Isoleri's poems, especially when in their original language, are still worth reading after the passage of many years.

> Tutto acceso di nobili ardori,
> Giovinetto sull' orme del padre,
> Muoverà coll' Italiche squadre
> A scacciare i tiranni da te.

    10. Isoleri, "La mia leva," *Lira,* vol. 1, 207–8. Isoleri also discussed this particular poem in his autobiographical sketch of 1889.

    11. Isoleri, "Il Risorgimento d'Italia," *Lira,* vol. 1, 37.

> E la tromba del Rege Sabaudo
> Che già echeggia dal Pò fino a Scilla.

    12. Isoleri, "Per la festa dello Statuto e dell' Unità d'Italia," *Lira,* vol. 1, 54.

> Figli miei, da Milano a Palermo,
> S'alzi un grido, ma libero e forte:
> Viva il patto che Italia ha già fermo
> Con Vittorio Emanuele suo Re!

    13. Isoleri, "Esortazione a liberare la Venezia dai Tedeschi," *Lira,* vol. 1, 70.

> Ma guerra ai Tedeschi!—Corriam alla bajonetta!
> Finche Venezia—d'Italia sarà—

Andiamo pel Mincio—Corriamo sul Po!
Vittorio il Re nostro—Colà ci chiamò.
Savoja! Savoja! Corriam alla bajonetta
Finchè l'Italia—Riunita sarà.
Addio padre e madre—La Patria mi chiamò
Raggiungerò le squadre—Non so se tornerò.
Combatterò da prode—a vivere o morir!
Sarò degno di lode—Perciò voglio partir.
Se morirò, dolenti—Ergetemi un' avel! . . .
Se tornerò, contenti—Benediremo il ciel.

14. Isoleri, "L'Addio del giovane Missionario," *Lira*, vol. 1, 73–74.

Viva Dio! S'Ei chiamommi, in non cale
Io porrò la mia patria e la vita;
Per versare dell' acqua lustrale
Su color che la colpa macchiò.

15. Isoleri, *Religione e Patria o i Martiri Coreani,* in *Lira*, vol. 2, 115–200.
16. Ibid., 187.
17. Isoleri, "Per la partenza del mio compagno di collegio sacerdote Giovanni Vassallo destinato per la diocesi di Newark N.J. Stati Uniti," *Lira*, vol. 1, 161–62.

Se un' Italo scoprì, gl'Itali a Dio
Consacrino la terra Americana!
Coraggio adunque, e fede! o amico mio.
Ogni altra cosa è vana.

18. Isoleri, "L'Emetico," *Lira,* vol. 1, 236. "Esculapio! m'ho rotto la testa!"
19. Isoleri, "Per la visita che mi fe' il Signore il Giovedi Santo, 25 Marzo 1869, quando lo ricevetti per Viatico," *Lira*, vol. 1, 174–76.
20. Isoleri, "Inno Eucaristico," *Lira,* vol. 1, 177–82. It is not clear whether he meant his first mass as a priest or his first mass for the feast day of Easter.
21. Isoleri, "Ode Eucaristica," *Lira,* vol. 1, 185.
22. Isoleri, "L'Addio del Missionario," *Lira,* vol. 3, 158–60. "O gloriosa e magnanima Stirpe Sabauda, Stirpe di Santi e d'Eroi, Addio! Deh! saggiamente governa l'Italia che Iddio volle porre sotto il tuo scettro. Rendila forte, gloriosa, felice, fra tutte le nazioni della terra. Ma tieni certo che renderla tale, dêi recondurla pentita al Vicario di Cristo, affinchè Egli la benedica, e con lei i suoi vessilli e i suoi brandi."
23. Ibid., 160. "Se io non fossi dal ciel chiamato fra le apostoliche schiere, sarei pronto a versare il mio sangue per te, come il più valoroso dei tuoi soldati, miei fratelli;—la mia vita non sarebbe nè dei miei genitori nè mia, si fortemente io t'amo! Ed è perciò che a Te pensando, il mio cuore ognor sì commuoverà; e si commuove nel darti l'*Addio*, o le lagrime m'irrigano le gote."
24. Ibid., 163. "Partiamo adunque per Philadelphia. Benedetimi, o Genitori, e con voi mi benedica Iddio! Maria Santa delle Grazie mi protegga e m'assista! L'Angiolo mio custode mi guidi! I Santi miei protettori intercedano sempre per me. Addio, patria diletta! Addio, parenti ed amici carissimi! Ci rivedremo in cielo!"
25. Isoleri, *Lira,* vol. 3, 99, 103; "Notables Attend Rites for Monsignor Isoleri," *Public Ledger* (April 17, 1932), 12.

CHAPTER FOUR. *The Challenge of Leadership*

1. For a detailed examination of the Italian community at this time, see Juliani, *Building Little Italy,* especially chapter 6, "The 1870 Census: A Community Portrait," 228–53.

2. Isoleri Papers, Nel seminario di Filadelfia (28 Gennaio 1870); "St. Mary Magdalen dePazzi," *Catholic Standard* (January 29, 1870), 4.

3. Isoleri Papers, Traccia ed Appunti pei discorsi che io dovrò fare nella Missione agli Italiani dai 21 ai 27 Marzo '70; "St. Mary Magdalen dePazzi," *Catholic Standard* (March 12, 1870), 4; "St. Mary Magdalen dePazzi," *Catholic Standard* (March 26, 1870), 5.

4. Isoleri Papers, Letter to Prof. P. Rossi, C.M., Collegio Brignole Sale (January 1889).

5. Isoleri Papers, 2° Sermone Inglese del Venerdi di Passione (8 Aprile 1870).

6. Isoleri, "Cristoforo Colombo," *Lira,* vol. 3, 165–98.

7. Isoleri Papers (November 23, 1871).

8. *Public Ledger* (November 16, 1871).

9. Isoleri Papers (November 26, 1871). In contrast to the rest of the Isoleri papers, two versions, one in Italian and the other in English, exist of this particular item. The Italian version, dated November 23, 1871, is also marked with a notation as the final Sunday after Pentecost.

10. This argument has been well developed in a discussion of the fateful events of 1870 by the British historian, Harry Hearder: "In that one year the pope lost the last shreds of his temporal power but secured a spiritual authority which was continually to be reaffirmed over the next century." See his chapter on "Religion and the Church" in *Italy in the Age of the Risorgimento, 1790–1870* (London and New York: Longman, 1983), 283–94.

11. "Reception of Rt. Rev. James F. Wood," *Catholic Standard* (April 16, 1870), 4.

12. These events are documented by frequent articles and announcements in the *Catholic Standard,* the weekly newspaper of the archdiocese, during these years.

13. For Ascheri, see PF Docs, 10:23353, Collegi d'Italia, fol. 1007rv; vol. 23, fol. 1344r; and 10:794, vol. 366, fol. 846rv; "Clerical Changes and Appointments," *Catholic Standard* (March 23, 1872), 4; *Catholic Herald* (August 31, 1872), 4; *Catholic Directory* (1874), 268; and *Catholic Directory* (1875), 379.

14. "St. Mary Magdalena dePazzi," *Catholic Standard* (October 7, 1871), 4; "St. Mary Magdalen dePazzi," *Catholic Standard* (October 14, 1871), 4; "St. Mary Magdalena dePazzi," *Catholic Standard* (November 4, 1871), 4.

15. "Ecclesiastical News—Society Items," *Catholic Standard* (February 3, 1872), 2.

16. "St. Mary Magdalen dePazzi," *Catholic Standard* (February 10, 1872), 5; "Magnificent Altar Reliquary and Tabernacle," *Catholic Standard* (March 30, 1872), 5. See subsequent articles on the fair in the same newspaper (April 6, 1872; April 14, 1872; April 20, 1872; April 27, 1872; May 4, 1872; and June 15, 1872).

17. This section is based on several sources, including notes that Isoleri made after two meetings with the bishop (April 11, 1872, and May 2, 1872) and three letters to Cardinal Barnabò (May 3, 1872; June 3, 1872; and October 14, 1873). Most of this material was written in Italian and is found in the Isoleri Papers.

18. Isoleri Papers, Letter to unidentified priest (c. late 1881).

19. See Isoleri Papers (May 3, 1872) or PF Docs, vol. 24, fols. 270rv–274r (May 3, 1872). Although dated May 3, 1872, Isoleri did not send it until one month later, when he enclosed it with a second letter, which began with an explanation that he had decided to make another effort with Wood before turning his case over to Rome. See Isoleri Papers

(June 3, 1872). The two letters provide a very detailed account of his efforts. The copy of the letter of May 3, 1872, in Isoleri's personal papers, however, is slightly different from the version found in the archives of Propaganda Fide. But since corrections in the former version appear in the text of the latter, it is obviously the earlier draft of what he sent to Rome.

20. Isoleri Papers, Letter to Wood (May 6, 1872).

21. Isoleri Papers, Letter to Wood (May 11, 1872).

22. Isoleri Papers, Letter to Walsh (May 11, 1872).

23. Isoleri Papers, Letter to Wood (May 22, 1872).

24. "Blessing of a Statue," *Catholic Standard* (June 15, 1872), 5; "Santa Maria Maddalena De Pazzi," *Catholic Herald* (June 22, 1872), 4; "Blessing a Statue at St. Mary Magdalene De Pazzi," *Catholic Standard* (June 22, 1872), 4.

25. PF Docs, vol. 24, fols. 275rv–277rv (June 3, 1872).

26. He included Father Giacomo (or James) Rolando, the Vincentian who had been the temporary pastor at the Italian Mission; Father Giuseppe Alizeri, a Vincentian professor at the seminary of the order in Germantown; Father William Lowecamp, the Redemptorist pastor of St. Peter's Church at Fifth and Girard Streets; Father A. M. Grundtner, the pastor of St. Alphonsus Church, a German parish at Fourth and Reed Streets; and Fathers Vincenzo Tranquilli and Nilo Mastroianno, the two Passionist missionaries who had recently preached a retreat at St. Mary Magdalen dePazzi.

27. PF Docs, vol. 368, fol. 841rv (July 1, 1872).

28. PF Docs, vol. 24, fol. 388r (August 6, 1872); vol. 368, fols. 1067v, 1068r (August 27, 1872); vol. 24, fol. 62r (n.d., but probably August 24, 1872).

29. PF Docs, vol. 24, fol. 421rv (August 24, 1872).

30. PF Docs, vol. 368, fol. 1187rv (September 17, 1872).

31. Isoleri Papers (October 14, 1873). In this letter to Cardinal Barnabò, Isoleri's detailed comments are the only source for the account that follows on his efforts during the autumn of 1872.

32. See PAHRC, Griffin, *Notebook*, 49, 108–11; "Chicago Sufferers," *Catholic Standard* (November 11, 1871), 4; "Seminary of St. Charles Borromeo," *Catholic Standard* (April 13, 1872), 4; "The Italian Church—A Picnic," *Catholic Standard* (August 24, 1872), 4; "Corner-Stone Laying—The New Church of St. Elizabeth," *Catholic Standard* (September 28, 1872), 4; "Diocesan News—St. Elizabeth's," *Catholic Herald* (September 28, 1872), 4; "St. Mary Magdalen," *Catholic Standard* (November 30, 1872), 5

33. "St. Mary Magdalene dePazzi," *Catholic Standard* (January 18, 1873), 5; "Moriarty versus Froude," *Catholic Standard* (January 25, 1873), 1; "Santa Maria Maddalena de-Pazzi," *Catholic Herald* (February 1, 1873), 4–5; "St. Mary Magdalene," *Catholic Standard* (March 29, 1873), 5; "Sta. Maria Maddalena dePazzi," *Catholic Herald* (March 29, 1873), 4; "Sta. Maria Maddalena dePazzi," *Catholic Herald* (April 26, 1873), 4; "Sta. Maria Maddalena dePazzi," *Catholic Herald* (May 31, 1873), 5; "St. Mary Magdalen dePazzi," *Catholic Standard* (May 31, 1873), 5; "Santa Maria Maddalena," *Catholic Herald* (June 21, 1873), 6; "St. Mary Magdalene dePazzi," *Catholic Standard* (June 28, 1873), 5; "St. Mary Magdalen's," *Catholic Standard* (July 5, 1873), 5. For further discussion of Moriarty's problems with Wood, see Dennis Clark, *The Irish in Philadelphia: Ten Generations of Urban Experience* (Philadelphia: Temple University Press, 1973).

34. *Catholic Herald* (July 26, 1873), 5.

35. Ibid.

36. Isoleri Papers, Letter to Wood (July 18, 1873).

37. Isoleri Papers, Letter to Barnabò (October 14, 1873), in which Isoleri gives an account of his on-going dealings with Wood.

38. The details of the fire were reported differently in newspaper accounts. The *Inquirer* said that it broke out at twenty minutes after four o'clock, and it listed the damaged houses as 719 Marriott (vacant), 721 Marriott (occupied by William Dougherty), and 725 Marriott (occupied by William Nutz), all owned by Bradley Brothers; 729 Marriott (owned and occupied by Miss Mary Murphy and her sister); 731 Marriott (owned and occupied by Patrick Corcoran); 735 Marriott (occupied by Mrs. Ann Riley) and 737 Marriott (occupied by James Curtis), both also belonging to Bradley Brothers. See "School House Destroyed," *Inquirer* (August 9, 1873), 2. The *Public Ledger* gave the time as shortly before 4 A.M., and the damaged houses as 719 to 733 Marriott Street, without listing names, except for 731 Marriott, owned and occupied by Daniel Strafford, and 733 Marriott, owned and occupied by Patrick Corcorsan [*sic*]; the other buildings were owned by Bradley Brothers. See "Catholic School-House and Parsonage Burned," *Public Ledger* (August 9, 1873), 1. The *Catholic Standard* included Daniel Staffaner at 731 Marriott Street on its list of occupants. "St. Mary Magdalen dePazzi," *Catholic Standard* (August 16, 1873), 5. See also "Burning of the School-house of St. Mary Magdelen de Pazzi," *Catholic Herald* (August 16, 1873), 4.

39. "To Rise Again," *Inquirer* (August 11, 1873), 2; "Meeting at St. Mary Magdalene de Pazzi's," *Catholic Standard* (August 16, 1873), 5; "Collection for the Holy Father," *Catholic Standard* (October 4, 1873), 4.

40. "St. Mary Magdalene di Pazzi," *Inquirer* (August 18, 1873), 2; "St. Mary Magdalen de Pazzi," *Catholic Standard* (August 23, 1873), 5, and (August 30, 1873), 5; "St. Mary Magdalen de Pazzi," *Catholic Herald* (August 23, 1873), 5, and (August 30, 1873), 13.

41. "The Italian Church," *Inquirer* (September 1, 1873), 1; "St. Mary Magdalen de Pazzi," *Catholic Herald* (September 6, 1873), 5.

42. "St. Mary Magdalene de Pazzi," *Catholic Standard* (September 13, 1873), 4–5.

43. "St. Mary Magdalen de Pazzi," *Catholic Standard* (November 29, 1873), 5; Isoleri Papers, Letter to Barnabò (October 14, 1873); also found in PF Docs 10:509, vol. 24, fols. 1081r–1084v.

44. PF Docs 10:1439, vol. 369, fol. 589v, PF to Antonio Isoleri (December 4, 1873).

45. "St. Mary Magdalen de Pazzi," *Catholic Standard* (February 28, 1874), 5; "St. Mary Magdalen de Pazzi," *Catholic Standard* (March 7, 1874), 5; "St. Mary Magdalen de Pazzi," *Catholic Standard* (February 2, 1875), 5; "Easter Services," *Catholic Standard* (April 3, 1875), 4; "St. Mary Magdalen de Pazzi," *Catholic Standard* (June 6, 1874), 5; "St. Mary Magdalen de Pazzi," *Catholic Standard* (June 20, 1874), 4; "St. Mary Magdalen de Pazzi," *Catholic Standard* (May 29, 1875), 5.

46. "St. Mary Magdalen de Pazzi," *Catholic Standard* (August 1, 1874), 5; "St. Mary Magdalen de Pazzi," *Catholic Standard* (May 29, 1875), 5; "St. Mary Magdalen de Pazzi," *Catholic Standard* (June 5, 1875), 1; "St. Mary Magdalen de Pazzi," *Catholic Standard* (June 19, 1875), 3.

47. Isoleri Papers, Letter to Roncetti (April 17, 1875); "The Pallium," *Catholic Standard* (June 26, 1875), 1; "St. Mary Magdalen dePazzi," *Catholic Standard* (June 26, 1875), 5.

48. "St. Mary Magdalen de Pazzi," *Catholic Standard* (October 4, 1873), 5; "St. Mary Magdalen de Pazzi—A Reception and Festival," *Catholic Standard* (February 14, 1874), 5.

49. "St. Mary Magdalen de Pazzi," *Catholic Standard* (July 11, 1874), 5; see the frequent other articles on the painting and exhibit through the autumn of 1874 to February 1875, including Isoleri's letter to Mellon in the issue for January 16, 1875.

50. "St. Mary Magdalen de Pazzi," *Catholic Standard* (February 24, 1875), 5; "St. Mary Magdalen de Pazzi," *Catholic Standard* (April 10, 1875), 5; "St. Mary Magdalen de Pazzi," *Catholic Standard* (April 17, 1875), 5.

51. "St. Mary Magdalen de Pazzi," *Catholic Standard* (March 14, 1874), 5; "Death of Cardinal Barnabò," *Catholic Standard* (March 21, 1874), 5; "News from Rome: Death of

Cardinal Barnabò," *Catholic Standard* (March 28, 1874), 1; "The Late Cardinal Barnabò," *Catholic Standard* (March 28, 1874), 4; "St. Mary Magdalen de Pazzi," *Catholic Standard* (May 2, 1874), 5; "In Memoriam. Francesco Isoleri," *Catholic Standard* (March 6, 1875), 5.

52. Isoleri Papers, Letter to Prof. P. Rossi, C.M., Collegio Brignole Sale (January 1889).

CHAPTER FIVE.   *Saving the Children*

1. "Italian Slave Cases," *Inquirer* (July 28, 1873), 4.

2. "An Influx of Italians," *Inquirer* (August 22, 1873), 2.

3. "The Italian Slave Children," *Inquirer* (August 29, 1873), 4. For a fuller account of the community context of these events, see Juliani, *Building Little Italy.*

4. "Philadelphia and Suburbs: A Raid on Padrones," *Inquirer* (September 16, 1873), 7.

5. Ibid.

6. Ibid.

7. "Local Affairs: Remarkable Police Operation," *Public Ledger* (September 16, 1873), 1.

8. Ibid.

9. "Philadelphia and Suburbs: A Raid on Padrones," *Inquirer* (September 16, 1873), 7.

10. Ibid.

11. Ibid.

12. "The Farce of Inhumanity," *Inquirer* (September 16, 1873), 4.

13. Ibid.

14. Ibid.

15. "The Crusade against Italian Vagrancy," *Inquirer* (September 17, 1873), 2.

16. Untitled editorial, *Inquirer* (September 17, 1873), 4.

17. *Constitution of the Commonwealth; Also Laws of the General Assembly of Said Commonwealth, Passed at the Session of 1874* (Harrisburg, 1874), 179–80. For Viti's role, see John Zucchi, "New Yorkers and Italian Child Street Musicians in the 1870s," in *Italian Americans Celebrate Life: The Arts and Popular Culture,* ed. Paola A. Sensi Isolani and Anthony Julian Tamburri (New York: American Italian Historical Association, 1990), 128. For the later campaign led by Dr. Domenico A. Pignatelli, see "Local Affairs—Denouncing an Anonymous Letter Writer—Concerning Italian Laborers," *Public Ledger* (May 1, 1884), 1; and the articles in *L'Eco d'Italia* (April 21, 1883; May 22, 1883; April 4, 1884; April 20, 1883), cited in Edwin Fenton, *Immigrants and Unions, A Case Study: Italians and American Labor, 1870–1920* (New York: Arno Press, 1975), 99–100. In an article, "Italians in the Labor Movement," in *Pennsylvania History* 26 (1959), Fenton identified Pignatelli as an Italian American physician. Pignatelli, a native of Naples, who operated a pharmacy at Eighth and Fitzwater Streets in South Philadelphia, was licensed for the practice of medicine by the state, but he lacked a physician's degree. See Department of Records, Philadelphia, *Medical Register, Philadelphia County,* vol. 1, 353. For the persistence of the problem in the 1890s see "Music Hath Charms," *Inquirer* (April 6, 1893), 6.

18. Isoleri Papers, Letter to an unidentified priest (c.1881).

19. Dorothy Gondos Beers, "The Centennial City, 1865–1876," in Russell F. Weigley, ed., *Philadelphia: A 300-Year History* (New York: W. W. Norton and Company, 1982), 422–23.

20. Isoleri Papers, "Discorso sopra Le Società Segrete" (October 5, 1873).

21. *Souvenir and Bouquet,* 23; Sr. M. Agnes Gertrude, O.S.F., "Italian Immigration into Philadelphia," *RACHS* 58 (1947): 199; Provincial Archives, Franciscan Sisters, Peekskill, New York. With their arrival at St. Mary Magdalen dePazzi, the Missionary Sisters

of the Third Order of St. Francis were introduced into the Diocese of Philadelphia in 1874. The order had been founded in 1860 in Gemona, in the Veneto, then a part of the French empire, by Laura Leroux, the duchess of Bauffremount, a wealthy Parisian noblewoman. Although she never took religious vows, her great missionary zeal attracted applicants to the order. By the time that she ended her patronage, the order had increased its membership and activities throughout Europe. It was established in the United States in 1865, when Mother Gertrude opened the mother house at Peekskill, New York, to serve hospitals and schools. See *Historical Sketches of the Catholic Churches and Institutions of Philadelphia—A Parish Register and Book of Reference* (Philadelphia: Daniel H. Mahoney, 1895), 100.

22. Isoleri Papers, Letter to Padre Gregorio (June 4, 1874).

23. Isoleri Papers, Letter to Mother Gertrude (July 14, 1874).

24. Isoleri Papers, Letter to Mother Angela (July 24, 1874).

25. Isoleri Papers, Letter to Padre Gregorio (July 27, 1874). Isoleri included a transcription that he had written of Sister Gertrude's letter. Presumably, he provided a full and accurate version.

26. Isoleri Papers, Letter to Padre Gregorio (September 8, 1874).

27. Isoleri Papers, Letter to Mother Angela (September 8, 1874).

28. Isoleri Papers, Letter to Mother Angela (January 23, 1875).

29. Isoleri Papers, Letter to Mother Angela (April 2, 1875).

30. St. Mary Magdalen dePazzi, *Convenzione* (April 16, 1876), 51.117Ach, PAHRC. This document, prepared in Italian and English, remains available in both languages, but the numbering and organization of the two versions slightly differ. In addition, the Italian version ends with the note that copies of the agreement would be consigned to Isoleri, the local superior, the General Hermitage of the Franciscans Minor, and the mother house of the sisters at Gemona. The English version included a two-page addendum with several proposals made by Mother Angela, "with the permission of the Most Rev. Archbishop of Philadelphia." She indicated that she was making these points "to continue the Mission." These conditions, however, varied from the agreement between Isoleri and Mother Angela. She proposed that while the sisters of the Italian Mission would depend upon the archbishop, the observance of their rules would be determined by the superior named by the Father General of the Franciscans and the Provincial Superior at Peekskill. In the future the selection of sisters for the mission would be made by the Provincial Superior with the agreement of the Superior General, but the only criterion was that they would be nuns who would best satisfy the wants of the house and the school. In addition to a dwelling entirely for themselves, the pastor would provide a salary of $200 for each of three sisters, of which $50 would be sent for the novitiate. The same condition also indicated that one of them would be English and the other two Italian. With the consent of the archbishop and under his dependence the sisters would maintain the orphanage for girls as well as its residents, while they themselves would live and clothe themselves by means of pious alms. With the money already on hand and what they could collect, the sisters were also directed to purchase a house for the use of the orphans, which would become the property of the diocese under the protection of the archbishop.

The document containing the proposals by Mother Angela also recorded the laws of the Diocese of Philadelphia for the benefit of the sisters who taught in its schools. The parish priest was expected to provide them with a rent-free house; gas, water, and coal; a stipend of $150 for each sister as well as $50 more for her novitiate; repairs to the house; rent-free pews in the parish church; and a chapel with the Blessed Sacrament. While she noted that the archbishop intended these privileges were to be enjoyed by all the sisters, Mother Angela added: "as Rev. Father Isoleri cannot give so much we content ourselves with that which his conscience judges just." Although the item containing these points is catalogued after the agreement itself, it appears likely that they were proposals with which Mother Angela entered the negotiation rather than considerations that she made afterward.

31. Author's personal correspondence, Records Office, Franciscan Sisters, Peekskill, New York (March 18, 1997).

32. "The Italian Missionary Sisters of St. Francis," *Catholic Standard* (December 12, 1876), 5. For a detailed description of these efforts, see the informative study by Sr. M. Jane Thomas Gorman, O.S.F., "Tertiary Franciscan Missionary Sisters of the Sacred Heart and Catholic Education in the United States" (Ph.D. diss., Fordham University, 1946), 122–30. My discussion is based upon material gathered by her.

CHAPTER SIX.   *Columbus and Other Heroes: The Search for Identity*

1. Harry Hearder, *Italy: A Short History* (Cambridge: Cambridge University Press, 1990), 203–4; Giuliano Procacci, *History of the Italian People* (Middlesex, Eng.: Penguin Books, 1970), 331–32; Anthony Rhodes, *The Vatican in the Age of the Dictators, 1922–1945* (New York: Holt, Rinehart and Winston, 1973), 23–24. The ban on voting in Italian elections would be formally eliminated by Pius X just before the general election of 1904.

2. "St. Mary Magdalen de Pazzi's Italian Church," *Catholic Standard* (May 13, 1876), 5.

3. "St. Mary Magdalen di Pazzi," *Catholic Standard* (February 19, 1876), 5, and issues over the next two weeks.

4. "Irish Characteristics," *Catholic Standard* (April 1, 1876), 2.

5. Isoleri Papers, Anno 1874–75, Candidati per gli Uffiziali della Confraternità di S. Giuseppe.

6. Isoleri Papers, Letter to DeLuca (March 17, 1875).

7. "Fair of the Columbus Monument Association," *Inquirer* (September 30, 1873), 2; "The Italian Celebration—Columbus Monument," *Public Ledger* (July 6, 1875), 1. The figure may have exaggerated the membership of the Italian Beneficial Society. Isoleri's letter to DeLuca, the general consul in New York City, written four months earlier, reported only 180. The four hundred individuals may have been the total number in attendance for the event in the park.

8. His remark may be disputed. The Società di Unione e Fratellanza Italiana was founded in Philadelphia in 1867, but it had been modeled after a similar organization established ten years earlier in New York City. After the latter and a similar one in San Francisco, the Philadelphia Società was the third such organization in the United States. Secchi deCasali was perhaps disappointed with the condition of the Società in New York City. Although its official title was the Società di Unione e Fratellanza Italiana, it was sometimes identified as the Italian Beneficial Society, particularly by the mainstream press.

9. Isoleri, "Un Monumento a Cristoforo Colombo," *Lira*, vol. 3, 198–200.

10. Isoleri Papers, Letter to L. G. Conte (July 13, 1875). The newspaper appears to have been *L'Italia*, which was published in Philadelphia in 1874–75. See Philip F. Mooney, "Philadelphia's Ethnic Press, 1876–1976," *Drexel Library Quarterly* 12:3 (July 1976). The printed version of the speech, when it was published three years later, read: "Colombo, Scopritore di questa terra," clearly supporting Isoleri's claim. See *Lira*, vol. 3, 198–200. The original manuscript version of the speech does not appear to be among Isoleri's personal papers.

11. "Italian Visitors," *Catholic Standard* (April 2, 1876), 8; "St. Mary Magdalen de Pazzi," *Catholic Standard* (May 20, 1876), 1; "The Exhibition," *Catholic Standard* (May 20, 1876), 1;

"The Columbus Monument—Lecture by Dr. McGlynn," *Catholic Standard* (May 27, 1876), 5; "St. Mary Magdalen de Pazzi," *Catholic Standard* (May 27, 1876), 5; "St. Mary Magdalen de Pazzi," *Catholic Standard* (June 3, 1876), 5; "The Columbus Monument," *Catholic Standard* (June 3, 1876), 5.

12. "Unveiling of the Columbus Monument," *Public Ledger* (October 13, 1876), 1; Isoleri, "Del Monumento a Cristoforo Colombo," *Lira,* vol. 3, 200–208. The handwritten draft of the original speech found in his personal papers differs slightly from the published version in the *Lira Leronica.*

13. "Christopher Columbus: How He Is Misrepresented," *Catholic Standard* (October 21, 1876), 4.

14. "Unveiling of the Monument to Columbus," *Catholic Standard* (October 28, 1876), 4.

15. The *Catholic Standard* usually reported these events in its weekly news of parish activities in the archdiocese. For the bell, see "St. Mary Magdalen De Pazzi," *Catholic Standard* (January 5, 1878), 4–5.

16. "Death of Victor Emmanuel," *Catholic Standard* (January 19, 1878), 4; Rhodes, *The Vatican in the Age of the Dictators,* 24.

17. "The Italians and Their Late King," *Public Ledger* (February 11, 1878), 1; Isoleri, "In occasione dei solenni funerali fatti dalla colonia Italiana nella chiesa . . . per il riposo dell'anima di S. M. il Re Vittorio Emanuele II," *Lira,* vol. 3, 215–20.

18. "In morte di S. M. il Re Vittorio Emanuele II," *Lira,* vol. 3, 221–24.

19. "Funeral Services for the Pope at the Italian Church," *Public Ledger* (February 11, 1878), 1; "Requiem Mass Yesterday Morning at the Italian Church to Commemorate the Death of Pius IX," *Public Ledger* (February 19, 1878), 1; "Report of Mortuary Services— St. Mary Magdalen di Pazzi's," *Catholic Standard* (February 23, 1878), 5. For a more detailed description, see "In Occasione dei Solenni Funerali Speciali Fatti dalla Colonia Italiana di Philadelphia, nella Chiesa di S. Maria Maddalena De-Pazzi, in Suffragio dell'Anima di S. S. Pio IX," in *Lira,* vol. 3, 225–37.

20. F. A. Simpson, *Louis Napoleon and the Recovery of France* (1923), cited in Philip Hughes, *A Popular History of the Catholic Church* (Garden City, NY: Image Books, 1954), 241.

21. Wood Papers, Letter from Simeoni to Wood, Document 52.716, PAHRC.

22. Isoleri Papers, Letter to Wood (August 22, 1878).

23. Isoleri also sent Wood his summary of the remarks that Vassallo had made before the mass for Victor Emmanuel. When Vassallo cited the king as the liberator of Italy— calling him the father of his country and the Italian Washington— he was referring, according to Isoleri, to the liberation of Northern Italy from the Austrians in 1859–60. While the king would be kept alive in the tears and prayers of his subjects, his death must teach them to despise human greatness. Along with the hope that the king would find mercy before the Lord, Vassallo expressed the desire that all the political and religious dissensions of Italy would also be buried in the royal tomb. While both Isoleri and Vassallo had shown anguish over being caught between their loyalty to the state and their fidelity to the faith, neither had betrayed his priestly vows or duties.

24. Wood Papers, Letter to Wood from Simeoni (June 25, 1878), Document 52.716, PAHRC; Isoleri Papers, Letter to Simeoni (September 16, 1878).

25. "St. Mary Magdalen de Pazzi," *Catholic Standard* (April 13, 1878), 5; "Contributions for the Sufferers by the Yellow Fever in the South," *Catholic Standard* (October 21, 1878), 4, and subsequent weeks; "Church Collections and Contributions for the Relief of the Distressed Poor in Ireland," *Catholic Standard* (February 21, 1880), 5; "St. Mary Magdalen de Pazzi," *Catholic Standard* (January 11, 1879), 5. Ironically, when Isoleri's old nemesis,

Father Charles J. H. Carter, died in September 1878, his obituary reported that the former vicar general had "never formed a wrong judgment or took a wrong step in dealing with his fellow-priests." Although the sisters from St. Mary Magdelen dePazzi were reported among the mourners at Carter's funeral mass, its rector was not listed among the clergy. See the *Catholic Standard* (September 27, 1878), 1, 4.

CHAPTER SEVEN. *Building Parish and Community*

1. "The Revival of Immigration," *Catholic Standard* (January 1, 1880), 2; "Immigration at Flood-Tide," *Catholic Standard* (July 23, 1881), 2; "Nearly Eight Hundred Thousand," *Catholic Standard* (October 9, 1882), 1; see also the untitled editorials in the *Catholic Standard* (July 30, 1881; May 27, 1882).

2. Maneval, *An Ethnic History.*

3. Isoleri Papers, Letter to unidentified priest (c. autumn 1881).

4. Ibid.

5. Ibid.

6. Ibid.

7. Henry J. Browne, "The 'Italian Problem' in the Catholic Church of the United States, 1880–1900," *Historical Records and Studies* 35 (1946): 46–75. In this important article the author failed to even mention the church of St. Mary Magdalen dePazzi in his discussion of early Italian religious experience, despite the fact that the founding of the Philadelphia church (1852) preceded its counterpart in New York, St. Anthony of Padua (1867), by fifteen years.

8. Marriages—St. Mary Magdalen de Pazzi (1872–1885).

9. Isoleri Papers, Letter to unidentified priest (c. autumn 1881).

10. Isoleri Papers, "2nd Sunday in Lent" (February 22, 1880).

11. *Catholicity in Philadelphia,* 389–91.

12. Isoleri Papers, "In Occasione del Concilio Provinciale Philadelphiense primo" (May 28, 1880). Although the council ended on May 30, 1880, Isoleri had prepared his sermon two days earlier.

13. Isoleri Papers, "Dal Maggiordomato" (31 Gennaio 1882).

14. "St. Mary Magdalen de Pazzi's," *Catholic Standard* (October 22, 1881), 5; "St. Mary Magdalen de Pazzi's Church," *Catholic Standard* (October 29, 1881), 4; "St. Mary Magdalen de Pazzi's," *Catholic Standard* (November 12, 1881), 5; Isoleri Papers, Letter to unidentified priest (c. autumn 1881).

15. "St. Mary Magdalen de Pazzi's," *Catholic Standard* (November 12, 1881), 5; "St. Mary Magdalen de Pazzi's," *Catholic Standard* (February 4, 1882), 5; "St. Mary Magdalen de Pazzi's," *Catholic Standard* (June 10, 1882), 5; "St. Mary Magdalen de Pazzi's," *Catholic Standard* (June 17, 1882), 5; "St. Mary Magdalen de Pazzi's," *Catholic Standard* (May 26, 1883), 5.

16. "St. Mary Magdalen de Pazzi's," *Catholic Standard* (January 6, 1883), 5.

17. Isoleri Papers, Letter to unidentified priest (c. autumn 1881).

18. Isoleri Papers, "For the death and funeral of President James A. Garfield" (September 24, 1881); Letter to unidentified priest (c. autumn 1881).

19. The enrollment figures are taken from *Sadlier's Catholic Directory* for these years. The annual volume provides information for each previous year.

20. Wood Papers, Isoleri to Wood (August 5, 1882), 51.119 Ach, PAHRC.

21. Wood Papers, Isoleri to Wood (August 7, 1882), 52.74 Ach, PAHRC.

22. Wood Papers, Isoleri to Rolando (September 1, 1882), 51.120 Ach, PAHRC.

23. Wood Papers, Isoleri to Wood (September 2, 1882), 51.121 Ach, PAHRC.

24. Wood Papers, Arbitrators to Wood (September 5, 1882), 51.122 Ach, PAHRC.

25. Wood Papers, Isoleri to Wood (September 8, 1882), 52.75 Ach, PAHRC.

26. "The Italian Mission," *Inquirer* (March 19, 1883), 8. Protestant efforts to reach the Italian population were not restricted to Philadelphia. At almost the same time as the Episcopalian program was launched, another newspaper account reported that the Reverend W. C. Vanmeter, "so widely known as the superintendent of the Italian Bible and Sunday School Mission," had returned from Rome to his family in Philadelphia. His nondenominational society was described as having had "great success in the furtherance of Sunday school work in Italy, and in the establishment of night schools in Rome." See "Home from Italy," *Inquirer* (May 14, 1883), 3. For a typical Catholic press item on Protestant work to relocate children at this time, see "The Cry of the Children," *Catholic Standard* (March 29, 1884), 2.

27. "They Meant Business," *Inquirer* (May 24, 1883), 3; "Excited Railroad Operatives Clamoring for their Wages—The Philadelphia and Chester County Railway Company and the Contractors," *Public Ledger* (May 24, 1883), 3; "Still Waiting," *Inquirer* (May 25, 1883), 8.

28. "Dining the Italian Railroad Operatives—Scenes at the Railroad Office," *Public Ledger* (May 25, 1883), 3.

29. "The Poor Italians," *Inquirer* (May 26, 1883), 2; "The Italian Laborers," *Public Ledger* (May 26, 1883), 1.

30. "Suffering Sons of Italy," *Inquirer* (May 28, 1883), 2.

31. Ibid.

32. "The Italians," *Inquirer* (May 29, 1883), 2; "Help for the Italian Railroad Laborers," *Public Ledger* (May 29, 1883), 1.

33. "Bedford Street Mission," *Inquirer* (July 14, 1883), 2; "Acts of Wrongdoers," *Inquirer* (September 3, 1883), 2; "Local Affairs," *Public Ledger* (September 3, 1883), 1; "Protection for Children," *Public Ledger* (September 6, 1883), 1; "The Bedford Mission," *Inquirer* (December 26, 1883), 2.

34. "An Italian Mission," *Inquirer* (December 21, 1883), 8.

35. "Religious News: Episcopal," *Public Ledger* (February 16, 1884), 1.

36. "Local Affairs—The Protestant Episcopal Italian Mission," *Public Ledger* (May 26, 1883), 1.

37. *Souvenir and Bouquet*, 23; "A New Italian Catholic Church," *Public Ledger* (May 25, 1883), 3; "Feast of a Patroness of a Church," *Public Ledger* (May 28, 1883), 1.

38. "Laying a Corner Stone," *Inquirer* (October 15, 1883), 2; "Laying the Corner Stone of the New Church of St. Mary Magdalen de Pazzi," *Public Ledger* (October 15, 1883), 1; "A New Church for the Italian Congregation," *Catholic Standard* (October 6, 1883), 5; "St. Mary Magdalen de Pazzi's," *Catholic Standard* (October 13, 1883), 5; "Laying of the Corner-Stone of the New Church of St. Mary Magdalen de Pazzi," *Catholic Standard* (October 20, 1883), 5.

39. Quoted in *Souvenir and Bouquet*, 26.

40. "Blessing of St. Mary Magdalen De Pazzi's Basement Chapel," *Catholic Standard* (February 14, 1885), reprinted in *Souvenir and Bouquet*, 34–35.

41. In his study of Italian Harlem, Robert Orsi argues that Leo XIII in the late nineteenth century tried to heal the relationship between the papacy and the Italian government while demonstrating that the Church truly cared about the Italian people, whether in their own country or as immigrants elsewhere, by designating the Madonna of 115th Street as an official shrine. See Orsi, *The Madonna of 115th Street*, 63–65. This strategy was similarly evident earlier in support given to the Italian church in Philadelphia.

42. As previously noted, the enrollment figures are found in the annual edition of *Sadlier's Catholic Directory*. For the arrival of the sisters, see "St. Mary Magdalen di Pazzi's," *Catholic Standard* (October 9, 1886), PAHRC SB-2:465.

43. "St. Mary Magdalen di Pazzi's", *Catholic Standard* (October 9, 1886), PAHRC SB-2:465.

44. *Catholic Directory*, 1888 and 1890.

45. Isoleri Papers, "L'Orfano Italiano in Philadelphia d'America" (8 Febbraio 1870).

46. Isoleri Papers, "Isabella da Marsicovetere o i Piccoli Musicanti in America" (July 4, 1881).

47. Ibid.

> Sola soletta in terra straniera
> Cerco dei soldi—per questa sara
> Se no, son certo che il mio padrone
> Mi dará cena—con il bastone
> Coll'arpa in spalla—la tapinella
> Son va girando—Oh! Oh! Isabella!
> Che duro pane! Che rio mestiere
> Ogni mattina! Tutte le sere!

48. Ibid.

> Son povera infelice;
> Ma il cor mi dice
> Che v'è nel cielo non Dio
> di cosi gran bontà
> Che d'esto viver mio
> Un dì pietade avrà.

49. Isoleri Papers, 15th Sunday after Pentecost (September 10, 1882).

50. Isoleri Papers, "Il gran male che è l'ubbriachezza" (June 13, 1886). This sermon and the two that followed on successive Sundays may have been presented at evening services, rather than at morning masses.

51. Isoleri Papers, "Raccomandazioni e Regole per tavernae e gli altri" (June 20, 1886).

52. Isoleri Papers, "Raccomandazioni e Regole" (June 27, 1886).

53. Isoleri Papers, "1 dell'anno 1887" (January 1, 1887).

54. Isoleri Papers, "Del terremoto che devasto la Riviera di Ponente il mattino del Mercoledi delle Ceneri" (23 Febbraio 1887).

55. Isoleri Papers, "Del 1st dell'anno 1888" (January 1, 1888).

56. See the regular reports of parish activities for "St. Mary Magdalen dePazzi" in the *Catholic Standard* during the 1880s. For the comments reported here, see the items for October 13, 1883, and September 27, 1884; for the roof and cross, see December 27, 1884, and January 3, 1885; for the gift of the painting, see October 6, 1888.

CHAPTER EIGHT. *The Nineties: New Problems and Solutions*

1. The local press provided extensive coverage of the incident. Relevant articles can be found almost every day. For Isoleri's cautious view on the matter, see "The Feeling in the City," *Public Ledger* (April 1, 1891), 1. For the protest meetings in Philadelphia, see "An

Italian Protest," *Public Ledger* (March 16, 1891), 1; "Italians to Act," *Public Ledger* (March 17, 1891), 2; and "Mass Meeting," *Public Ledger* (March 21, 1891), 1.

2. For the data and other information presented here, see the *Questiones—Annual Reports* for these particular years held by the PAHRC.

3. St. Mary Magdalen dePazzi, *Annual Report* (January 1, 1897–January 1, 1898), PAHRC.

4. Ibid.

5. Gerald P. Fogarty, S.J., *The Vatican and the American Hierarchy from 1870 to 1965* (Collegeville, MN: Liturgical Press, 1990), 65–66.

6. Information on clerical staffing of the parish and the figures on school enrollment are taken from *Sadlier's Catholic Directory* for appropriate years. For the schedule of services, see *Historical Sketches of the Catholic Churches and Institutions of Philadelphia.*

7. For the details of these events, see the extensive coverage provided by the newspapers of the city: "Dedicated to God," *Press* (June 29, 1891); "Dedication of De Pazzi," *Record* (June 29, 1891); "The Italian Church," *Catholic Times* (June 29, 1891); "A New Italian Church," *Public Ledger* (June 29, 1891); "Church Dedication," *Inquirer* (June 29, 1891); "Italian Church Dedicated," *North American* (June 29, 1891); and "The New St. Mary Magdalen de Pazzi's Church," *Catholic Standard* (July 4, 1891), PAHRC SB-3:347–48.

8. "Italian Catholic Church Dedicated," *North American* (June 29, 1891); "The Italian Church," *Catholic Times* (June 29, 1891), PAHRC SB-3:347–48.

9. The main source of information is the account by Isoleri in *Un Ricordo delle Feste Colombiane* (Philadelphia, 1893).

10. Ibid., 45.

11. Ibid., 45–46.

12. Ibid., 47.

13. The main source of information is *Le Nozze d'Argento or Silver Jubilee of the Rev. Antonio Isoleri, Ap. Miss., Souvenir Notes*, Collected and Edited by a Friend (Philadelphia, 1894).

14. Ibid., 51.

15. Ibid., 60, 71; "Archbishop Satolli in Philadelphia," *Catholic Standard and Times* (February 1, 1896), PAHRC SB-4:278.

16. *Catholic Times* (March 24, 1894), *Cristoforo Colombo* (April 3, 1894), and *La Verità* (April 7, 1894), reprinted in *Le Nozze d'Argento*, 20–25, 69–71, and 72–73.

17. "Satolli Talks to His People," *Inquirer* (November 20, 1893), 3; "Sermon by Satolli," *Inquirer* (March 21, 1893), 5; "Satolli's Sermons," *Inquirer* (March 3, 1893), 3.

18. "Archbishop Satolli in Philadelphia," *Catholic Standard and Times* (February 1, 1896), PAHRC SB-4:278; "News in the State: Six Hundred See Buccieri Hanged," *Inquirer* (June 30, 1893), 4; "First Church for Italians Here," *Press* (April 29, 1895), PAHRC SB-4:131.

19. "St. Mary Magdalen dePazzi's," *Catholic Standard* (June 6, 1895), PAHRC SB-4:.163.

20. Ibid. For the opposition to these practices as well as to nationality parishes by Church authorities in later years, see the articles by a Philadelphia auxiliary bishop, John V. Tolino, "Solving the Italian Problem," *Ecclesiastical Review* 99:3 (September 1938): 246–56, and "The Church in America and the Italian Problem," *Ecclesiastical Review* 100:1 (January 1939): 22–32.

21. "St. Mary Magdalen dePazzi's," *Catholic Standard* (November 2, 1895), PAHRC SB-4:236; for another article on the same event, see *Catholic Times* (October 26, 1895), PAHRC SB-4:238.

22. Sarah G. Pomeroy, *The Italians* (New York: Fleming H. Revell Company, 1914), 9; "The New Orleans Tragedy," *Public Ledger* (March 16, 1891), 2.

23. "The Italian Mission," *Public Ledger* (April 8, 1891), 2.

24. "Work in Little Italy," *Public Ledger* (November 27, 1893), 2; "A Proselytizing Movement," *Catholic Times* (December 2, 1893), reprinted in *Le Nozze d'Argento*, 15–19.

25. "A Proselytizing Movement," *Catholic Times* (December 2, 1893), reprinted in *Le Nozze d'Argento*, 15–19.

26. "Our Foreign Neighbors," reprinted in *Catholic Times* (April 28, 1894) and in *Le Nozze d'Argento*, 74–76. For background information on Percival and the former Episcopalian chapel on Catharine Street, now the Samuel S. Fleisher Art Memorial, by an Anglican priest who converted to Roman Catholicism, see Monsignor Edward Hawks, "The Church of the Evangelists, Philadelphia," *RACHS* 55 (1944): 125–34.

27. "Our Foreign Neighbors," reprinted in *Catholic Times* (April 28, 1894) and in *Le Nozze d'Argento*, pp.74–76.

28. Protestant efforts were described at the time; for example, see Antonio Mangano, *Sons of Italy: A Social and Religious Study of the Italians in America* (New York: Missionary Education Movement of the United States and Canada, 1917); Philip Rose, *The Italians in America* (New York: George H. Doran Company, 1922); and Enrico C. Sartorio, *Social and Religious Life of Italians in America* (Boston: Christopher Publishing House, 1918). Each of these authors was involved in missionary work among the Italians: Mangano, a native of Italy, as pastor of the First Italian Baptist Church of Brooklyn and later director of the Italian Department at Colgate Theological Seminary; Rose as pastor of the First Italian Congregational Church of Hartford, Connecticut; and Sartorio, also a native of Italy, as an Episcopalian.

29. "A Proselytizing Movement," *Catholic Times* (December 2, 1893), reprinted in *Le Nozze d'Argento*,15–19.

30. "First Italian Church," *Catholic Times* (March 11, 1893), reprinted in *Le Nozze d'Argento*, 9–14.

31. Ibid.

32. The principal source on the Cardarelli affair is chapter 4, "The Immigrant Apostolate," in Joseph F. Martino, "A Study of Certain Aspects of the Episcopate of Patrick J. Ryan, Archbishop of Philadelphia, 1884–1911" (Ph.D. diss., Gregorian Pontifical University, Rome, 1982).

33. Letter, Edward L. Aves to Ryan (December 29, 1896), PAHRC, Ryan Papers, 61.112Acl.

34. Ibid.

35. Letter, Cardarelli to Ryan (n.d.), PAHRC, Ryan Papers, 61.113Acl.

36. Letter, Church of Our Lady of Pompeii to Ryan (Christmas 1896), PAHRC, Ryan Papers, 61.111Acl.

37. A few years after leaving Philadelphia, Cardarelli, an assistant pastor at Our Lady of Mount Carmel in Orange, New Jersey, remained a provocative figure. In January 1903, police in that city arrested Father Carmelo Falconi, a priest at the Italian Catholic Orphan Asylum, on charges of assaulting and attempting to kill Cardarelli. See "Priest Accused of an Assault on Fellow Cleric," *Public Ledger* (January 5, 1903), 14. In 1906, Cardarelli served at the Italian mission of Our Lady of the Most Holy Rosary in Port Reading, New Jersey, then from 1907 to 1910 at St. Anthony's Church in the same location in the Diocese of Trenton, although his name is not listed among the clergy for that period in official directory sources. Between 1915 and 1918, Cardarelli was at Holy Rosary, an Italian church in Kansas City, Missouri, but he disappears from church records at the end of that period. See *The Official Catholic Directory* (New York: P. J. Kenedy, 1915 and 1918). For the Inglesi case, see Juliani, *Building Little Italy*, 90–94.

38. "New Italian Parish," *Catholic Standard and Times* (January 15, 1898), PAHRC SB-5:43; for information on Repetti, see "Italian Church Loses its Pastor," *Catholic Standard and Times* (August 5, 1899), PAHRC SB-5:217.

39. "To Build an Extension, Important Improvements in the New Italian Church," *Public Ledger* (November 19, 1898), PAHRC SB-5:126; "An Appeal to the Citizens of Philadelphia in Aid of the New Italian Church of Our Lady of Good Counsel," PAHRC SB-5:141; Kirlin, *Catholicity in Philadelphia*, 504.

40. "An Appeal to the Citizens of Philadelphia in Aid of the New Italian Church of Our Lady of Good Counsel," PAHRC SB-5:141.

41. "Corner-Stone of New Church," *Press* (May 22, 1899); "A Day in the Churches," *Record* (May 22, 1899); "Mgr. Martinelli Officiates," *Public Ledger* (May 22, 1899); "Corner-Stone Laid," *Times* (May 22, 1899); "New Church for Italians," *Catholic Standard and Times* (May 27, 1899). For these articles, see PAHRC SB-5:198 and SB-5:201.

42. "Corner-Stone of New Church," *Press* (May 22, 1899), PAHRC SB-5:198.

43. "Church Work in the Italian Colony," *Catholic Standard and Times* (May 27, 1899), PAHRC SB-5:201.

44. "New Church for Italians," *Catholic Standard and Times* (May 27, 1899), PAHRC SB-5:201.

45. Isoleri Papers, "Pel funerale del Rev. Guglielmo Serafino Repetti, O.S.A."; "Italian Church Loses its Pastor," *Catholic Standard and Times* (August 5, 1899), PAHRC SB-5:217; "Father Repetti's Funeral," *Catholic Standard and Times* (August 12, 1899), PAHRC SB-5:218.

46. Our Lady of Good Counsel, *Annual Report* (January 1, 1900–January 1, 1901); St. Mary Magdalen dePazzi, *Annual Report* (January 1, 1900–January 1, 1901), PAHRC.

47. "Italian Church Loses its Pastor," *Catholic Standard and Times* (August 5, 1899), PAHRC SB-5:217.

48. St. Mary Magdalen dePazzi, *Annual Report* (January 1, 1897–January 1, 1898), PAHRC.

49. St. Mary Magdalen dePazzi, *Annual Report* (January 1, 1898–January 1, 1899), PAHRC.

50. See the document under the name of Archbishop Ryan, "Nos Patritius Joannes Ryan," Augustinian Archives, St. Thomas of Villanova Province, Villanova, PA (hereafter AAVU).

CHAPTER NINE.   *The "Italian Problem": Catholic and Protestant Responses*

1. The initial source on these issues is the essay by Browne, "'The Italian Problem.'" For an excellent study on Catholic policy, see Linkh, *American Catholicism and European Immigrants* For a sociological examination of the "Italian problem," see Tomasi, *Piety and Power*. For the ecclesiastical background to the "Italian problem," see Fogarty, *The Vatican and the American Hierarchy from 1870 to 1965*. See also Vecoli, "Prelates and Peasants."

2. Browne, "'The Italian Problem,'" 49–53.

3. Ibid., 53–54.

4. Ibid., 54–55.

5. Ibid., 55–59. Browne believed that the prelate who made this suggestion most likely was Patrick J. Ryan, then acting as coadjutor in St. Louis, before becoming the archbishop of Philadelphia in August 1884 and serving in this capacity until his death in 1918, an important period of Italian parish formation. See ibid., 56 n. 34.

6. Ibid., 56–59; Gerald P. Fogarty, S.J., "The Parish and Community in American Catholic History," *U.S. Catholic Historian* 4:3 (Fall 1985): 233–57, also in Brian C. Mitchell,

ed., *Building the American Catholic City: Parishes and Institutions* (New York and London: Garland Publishing, 1988), 1–25. "Chapels of ease" refers to small dependent chapels that provided religious services when a main church was not conveniently located or had become overcrowded.

7. Browne, "'The Italian Problem,'" 59–61.

8. Ibid., 61–62.

9. For the definitive source on these matters, see Barry, *The Catholic Church and German Americans.* For the implications of the German experience for Italians, see Tomasi, *Piety and Power,* 74–105.

10. Browne, "'The Italian Problem,'" 62–63.

11. Ibid., 63–64; Tomasi, *Piety and Power,* 86–88. Tomasi provides a biographical sketch of the remarkable deConcilio. A Neapolitan educated at the Collegio Brignole Sale, deConcilio came to America to assist Father Antonio Cauvin in Newark, also becoming a chaplain and professor of logic at Seton Hall University in 1860. He founded two churches in Jersey City and served as the treasurer of the St. Raphael's Society for the Protection of Italian Immigrants. DeConcilio participated as a theologian in the Third Plenary Council of Baltimore in 1884. He frequently acted as an advocate on behalf of Italian immigrants by his writings and letters to Church authorities. His most important accomplishment, however, may have been his writing of the Baltimore Catechism, which was used for religious instruction without revision for fifty years.

12. Browne, "'The Italian Problem,'" 65; Tomasi, *Piety and Power,* 88; "Pope Leo XIII's Plea for the Italian Immigrants in America, December 10, 1888," in John Tracy Ellis, ed., *Documents of American Catholic History* (Milwaukee: Bruce, 1956), 482–85. For a brief but contemporary response, see "Leo XIII and the Italian Catholics in the United States," *American Ecclesiastical Review* 1:2 (February 1889): 41–48.

13. Browne, "'The Italian Problem,'" 66. See especially the footnotes in Browne's article on this point. For the views and policies of Italian politicians on Church-state relations at this time, see DiScala, *Italy: From Revolution to Republic.*

14. Tomasi, *Piety and Power,* 89–90; Barry, *The Catholic Church and German Americans,* 132ff.

15. Tomasi, *Piety and Power,* 90–91; Barry, *The Catholic Church and German Americans,* 152–67.

16. Browne, "'The Italian Problem,'" 67–68. For a more recent discussion of the options as well as the argument that the nationality parish became a "quasi-sect," see Tomasi, *Piety and Power.*

17. Browne, "'The Italian Problem,'" 68–70. For related views, see John T. McNicholas, O.P., "The Need of American Priests for the Italian Missions," *Ecclesiastical Review* 39:6 (December 1908): 677–87; "Diocesan Bureaux for the Care of Italian, Slav, Ruthenian, and Asiatic Catholics in America," *Ecclesiastical Review* 48:2 (February 1913); W. J. Agnew, S.J., "Pastoral Care of Italian Children in America," *Ecclesiastical Review* 48:3 (March 1913): 257–67; Joseph McSorley, C.S.P., "The Church and the Italian Child," *Ecclesiastical Review* 48:3 (March 1913): 268–82; Jerome N. Zazzara, T.O.R., "Pastoral Care of Italian Emigrants," *Ecclesiastical Review* 64:3 (March 1921): 279–84; P. C. Romanus, "The Future of Our Immigrant Parishes," *Homiletic and Pastoral Review* 24:9 (June 1924): 919–26; Rt. Rev. Edmund M. Dunne, "The Church and the Immigrant," in C. E. McGuire, *Catholic Builders of the Nation* (Boston: Continental Press, 1923), 1–15; and Palmieri, "The Contribution of the Italian Catholic Clergy to the United States," 127–49, in the same volume. For a flawed but provocative examination of immigrants and religion, see Gerald Shaughnessy, *Has the Immigrant Kept the Faith? A Study of Immigration and Catholic Growth in the United States,*

1790–1920 (New York: Macmillan, 1925). For a later discussion with relevance to Philadelphia, see Rev. John V. Tolino, "Solving the Italian Problem," *Ecclesiastical Review* 99:3 (September 1938): 246–56; idem, "The Church in America and the Italian Problem," *Ecclesiastical Review* 100:1 (January 1939): 22–32; and idem, "The Future of the Italian-American Problem," *Ecclesiastical Review* 101:3 (September 1939): 221–32.

18. Tomasi, *Piety and Power*, 85–89.

19. Light, *Rome and the New Republic*; Kirlin, *Catholicity in Philadelphia*, 352–69.

20. Charlotte Adams, "Italian Life in New York," *Harper's New Monthly Magazine* 57 (April 1881): 682, cited by Browne, "'The Italian Problem,'" 51 n. 19; J. L. Andreis to James Gibbons, St. Vincent's Church (September 11, 1879), Baltimore Cathedral Archives, 74-R-4, cited in Browne, "'The Italian Problem,'" 61 n. 48.

21. Tomasi, *Piety and Power*, 105.

22. For an analysis of popular piety in Italy, which guides this interpretation, see two exemplary works of sociologist Michael P. Carroll: *Madonnas that Maim: Popular Catholicism in Italy since the Fifteenth Century* (Baltimore and London: Johns Hopkins University Press, 1992), and *Veiled Threats: The Logic of Popular Catholicism in Italy* (Baltimore and London: Johns Hopkins University Press, 1996).

23. See Carroll, *Madonnas that Maim*, especially chapter 5, "Regional Differences," 88–111, and *Veiled Threats*, 41.

24. *Souvenir and Bouquet*, 76–84.

25. Carroll, *Madonnas that Maim*, 138–39 and 38–43. The final point here is a paraphrase of Carroll's translation of an incisive observation by Luigi M. Lombardi Satriani.

26. *A Directory of the Charitable, Social Improvement, Educational and Religious Associations and Churches of Philadelphia*, Prepared by the Civic Club, 2nd (Philadelphia, 1903).

27. "Italian Methodist Episcopal Mission," *Public Ledger* (November 28, 1901), 3; "Proposed Church for Italians," *Public Ledger* (May 21, 1901), 10; "Italian Tabernacle Opened," *Public Ledger* (January 31, 1903), 2; "Opens Missionary Campaign," *Public Ledger* (June 21, 1903), 2; "Hebrew Education Society," *Public Ledger* (June 23, 1903), 2.

28. "Home Missions Urged," *Public Ledger* (January 8, 1903), 2; "Sees Grave Peril in Rush of-Foreigners," *Public Ledger* (October 12, 1903), 2.

29. "Evils of Immigration," *Public Ledger* (November 16, 1903), 3; "New Law for Immigrants," *Public Ledger* (November 23, 1903), 3.

30. *Fifty-Second Annual Report of the Board of Missions of the Diocese of Pennsylvania* (Philadelphia, 1911), 42–45; *Fifty-Third Annual Report of the Board of Missions of the Diocese of Pennsylvania* (Philadelphia, 1912), 5, 45–48.

31. Within the vast literature on the settlement house movement, it must suffice to identify only a few particularly relevant items: Robert A. Woods and Albert J. Kennedy, eds., *Handbook of Settlements* (New York: Russell Sage Foundation, Charities Publication Committee, 1911); Lucy Perkins Carner, *The Settlement Way in Philadelphia* (Philadelphia: Delaware Valley Settlement Alliance, 1964); and Allen F. Davis, *Spearheads for Reform* (New York: Oxford University Press, 1967). For an examination of specific settlements and the Italian community of Philadelphia, see Richard N. Juliani, "The Settlement House and the Italian Family," 103–23, in Betty Boyd Caroli et al., eds., *The Italian Immigrant Woman in North America* (Toronto: Multicultural History Center of Ontario, 1978). Linkh's previously cited *American Catholicism and European Immigrants* is also important.

32. The Starr Kitchen, formerly The College Settlement Kitchen and Coffee House, *Second Annual Report* (Philadelphia, 1897), Urban Archives, Temple University.

33. Woods and Kennedy, *Handbook of Settlements*, 262–81; also see the "History of St. Martha's House," St. Martha's House, Acc.103, Box 1, Urban Archives, Temple University; and Juliani, "The Settlement House and the Italian Family," in Caroli et al., 114–15.

34. *Report of the Starr Centre, Neighborhood House* (Philadelphia, 1904), Urban Archives, Temple University. In addition to the annual reports in the Starr Centre Collection, see also *History of a Street* (Philadelphia, January 1901).

35. *Report of the Starr Centre, Neighborhood House* (Philadelphia, 1910), cited in Woods and Kennedy, *Handbook of Settlements*, 272.

36. Ibid.

37. Addison B. Burk, "The Tenement House Question in Philadelphia," *Public Ledger* (February 22, 1903).

38. *The Starr Centre Association* (Philadelphia, 1908), Urban Archives, Temple University.

39. "The Italian and the Settlement," *Survey* (April 12, 1913), 58–59.

CHAPTER TEN. *A New Century*

1. Isoleri Papers, Sermon for Midnight Mass (December 31, 1900–January 1, 1901).

2. Ibid.

3. U.S. Immigration and Naturalization Service, *Statistical Yearbook of the Immigration and Naturalization Service, 1986* (Washington, DC, 1987).

4. Eighth Census of the United States, vol. 1, *Population of the United States in 1860* (Washington, DC, 1864), 610; Ninth Census of the United States, vol. 1, *The Statistics of the Population of the United States* (Washington, DC, 1872), 369; Tenth Census of the United States, vol. 1, *Statistics of the Population of the United States* (Washington, DC, 1883), 541; Eleventh Census of the United States, Part 1, *Report of the Population of the United States* (Washington, DC, 1895), clxix and 654; Twelfth Census of the United States, vol. 1, *Census Reports—Population—1900* (Washington, DC, 1901), clxxviii; Thirteenth Census of the United States, vol. 2, *Population—1910* (Washington, DC, 1913), 582; Fourteenth Census of the United States, vol. 3, *Population—1920* (Washington, DC, 1923), 1896. For the 1907 estimate, see the report by the Italian Consul in Philadelphia, Cav. Giacomo Fara Forni, "Gli Italiani nel Distretto Consolare di Filadelfia," in Ministero degli Affari Esteri, Commissariato dell'Emigrazione, *Emigrazione e Colonie: Raccolta di Rapporti dei R. Agenti Diplomatici e Consolari*, vol. 3, *America* (Rome, 1908). This estimate was first made by an earlier consul in Philadelphia, Cav. Conte Gerolamo Naselli, and it previously appeared in *La Colonia Italiana di Filadelfia* (Philadelphia, 1906) and in A. Frangini, *Italiani in Filadelfia, Strenna Nazionale, Cenni Biografici* (Philadelphia, 1907), both published by *L'Opinione*, the Italian-language daily in the city. For the 1917 estimate, see the editorial, "Philadelphia's 'Italian Colony,'" *Public Ledger* (October 4, 1917), 10.

5. For a discussion of Elizabeth Robins Pennell's views on Italians in the city, see Juliani, *Building Little Italy*, 318–19.

6. The reconstruction of the community that follows is based on information found in *La Colonia Italiana di Filadelfia*); Frangini, *Italiani in Filadelfia*; and a program of events at the New Pennsylvania Hall (March 1905), in the Isoleri Papers.

7. "Parish Rights of Foreign Catholics," *Ecclesiastical Review* 38:1 (January 1908): 65–69; "Why the Discrimination?" *Ecclesiastical Review* 38:2 (February 1908): 208–11.

8. McNicholas, "The Need of American Priests for the Italian Missions."

9. Ibid., 684.

10. Ibid., 685–86.

11. Paul Sandalgi, "The Catholic Immigrant from a Priest's Standpoint," in *Proceedings, Second Biennial Meeting of the National Conference of Catholic Charities* (Washington, DC: Catholic University of America, 1912), 181–85; Peter Siewierski, "The Catholic Immigrant from a Social Worker's Standpoint," in ibid., 185–89. See also the comments by Father Smetz, in ibid., 189–91.

12. Rt. Rev. Regis Canevin, *An Examination Historical and Statistical into Losses and Gains of the Catholic Church in the United States from 1790 to 1910* (Pittsburgh, 1912), 13.

13. Ibid., 19.

14. Agnew, "Pastoral Care of Italian Children in America."

15. Ibid,, 258–61. For a more recent revision of this early characterization of Catholicity among previous immigrants, see Jay P. Dolan, *The Immigrant Church: New York's Irish and German Catholics, 1815–1865,* 2d ed. (Notre Dame, IN: University of Notre Dame Press, 1983).

16. Agnew, "Pastoral Care of Italian Children in America," 262–67.

17. McSorley, "The Church and the Italian Child," 270.

18. Ibid., 274–76.

19. Ibid., 276.

20. Robert E. Park, "Human Migration and the Marginal Man," *American Journal of Sociology* 33 (1928): 881–93; Everett V. Stonequist, *The Marginal Man* (New York: Charles Scribner's Sons, 1937); Charles F. Marden and Gladys Meyer, *Minorities in American Society,* 2d ed. (New York: American Book Company, 1962), 88–91; McSorley, "The Church and the Italian Child," 277–82.

21. Francis C. Kelley, D.D., "The Church and the Immigrant," *Catholic Mind* 13:17 (September 8, 1915): 471–73.

22. Ibid., 473–74.

23. Ibid., 476–77.

24. Ibid., 479–80.

25. Ibid., 481–82.

26. Ibid., 483–84.

27. Frederick Siedenburg, S.J., "The Immigration Problem," *Catholic Mind* 13:17 (September 8, 1915): 484–94.

28. Ibid., 494–95.

29. "Mgr. Falconio at Villanova," *Catholic Standard and Times* (May 28, 1904), PAHRC SB-7:4; "Police Tell of Plot to Murder a Priest," *Public Ledger* (May 30, 1904), PAHRC SB-7:4.

30. "Police Tell of Plot to Murder a Priest," *Public Ledger* (May 30, 1904), PAHRC SB-7:4.

31. "Denies Murder Plot," *Public Ledger* (May 31, 1904), PAHRC SB-7:5.

32. "St. Mary Magdalen dePazzi's Congregation Celebrate Patronal Feast," *Catholic Standard and Times* (June 4, 1904), PAHRC SB-7:5.

33. "Jewelry and Money Placed on Statues," *Public Ledger* (May 29, 1905), PAHRC SB-7:109; Dolan, *The Immigrant Church,* 6–7.

34. "Day Nursery for Italian Children," *Catholic Standard and Times* (June 19, 1901), PAHRC SB-5:385; "Blessed by the Archbishop," *Catholic Standard and Times* (March 26, 1904), PAHRC SB-4:483.

35. "Blessing of New Italian School," *Catholic Standard and Times* (September 14, 1901), PAHRC SB-5:460.

36. "Second Donation for the Italian Settlement," *Catholic Standard and Times* (July 30, 1904), PAHRC SB-7:26; *Golden Jubilee Celebration of the Madonna House, 1903–1953* (Philadelphia, 1953).

37. "In Behalf of Our Catholic Italians," *Catholic Standard and Times* (November 12, 1904), PAHRC SB-7:51.

38. Ibid.; "Funeral of Italian Priest," *Public Ledger* (November 9, 1904), PAHRC SB-7:50.

39. "To Preserve the Faith in Philadelphia's 'Little Italy,'" *Catholic Standard and Times* (November 9, 1904), PAHRC SB-7:52.

40. Ibid.

41. Ibid.

42. Ibid.

43. Ibid.

44. Ibid.

45. Ibid.

46. Letter from Ryan (n.d.), PAHRC SB-7:63; "Christmas in Our Institutions," *Catholic Standard and Times* (December 24, 1904), PAHRC SB-7:64.

47. Untitled article, *Telegraph* (April 13, 1907), PAHRC SB-7:348.

48. *A Lecture on Presbyterian Proselytism of Roman Catholic Italians delivered by Very Reverend D. I. McDermott in St. Paul's Church, Philadelphia* (December 5, 1909), PAHRC, Pamphlet Collection.

49. Ibid., 9.

50. Untitled article, *Public Ledger* (June 18, 1909), PAHRC SB-8:95; "Catholics Aid Italians," *Catholic Standard and Times* (January 23, 1909), PAHRC SB-8:47; "$15,670.17," *Catholic Standard and Times* (February 6, 1909), PAHRC SB-8:56.

51. Prendergast to pastors (March 25, 1912), PAHRC SB-9:82.

52. *Golden Jubilee Celebration of the Madonna House, 1903–1953* (Philadelphia, 1953); Edward J. Lyng, "Catholic Missionary Society of Philadelphia," *Catholic Charities Review* 6:7 (September 1922): 236–39.

53. *Catholic Standard and Times Almanac for 1915* (Philadelphia, 1915), 43–47.

54. Ibid., 43; "Don Bosco Institute for Philadelphia," *Catholic Standard and Times* (August 22, 1914), 1; "Don Bosco Catholic Club," *Catholic Standard and Times* (December 11, 1915), 10. For a study of the Salesians in Philadelphia, see the unpublished paper by Philip J. Pascucci, S.D.B., "No Greater Love than This: A Brief History of Don Bosco Institute in Philadelphia, Pennsylvania" (1996), PAHRC (1997/05).

55. *Golden Jubilee Celebration of the Madonna House*; Lyng, "Catholic Missionary Society of Philadelphia"; "The Week among Literary Institutes: Madonna Catholic Club," *Catholic Standard and Times* (October 9, 1915), 8, and similar items for October 23, 1915, and October 30, 1915.

56. "The Catholic Missionary Society of Philadelphia," *Catholic Standard and Times* (November 6, 1915), 4.

57. L'Assunta House to Motherhouse of the Sisters, Servants of the Immaculate Heart of Mary, Villa Maria, West Chester, Pennsylvania (August 1, 1919). For a description and assessment of activities along with some figures indicating the volume of services, see Lyng, "Catholic Missionary Society of Philadelphia."

58. Lyng, "Catholic Missionary Society of Philadelphia," 239; "Catholic Boys' High School Alumni Observe Its Twenty-Fifth Anniversary," *Catholic Standard and Times* (January 1, 1916), 1.

59. "The Week among Literary Institutes: Madonna Catholic Club," *Catholic Standard and Times* (October 30, 1915), 8; "The Week among Literary Institutes: Madonna Catholic Club," *Catholic Standard and Times* (January 29, 1916), 8.

60. "The Week among Literary Institutes: Madonna Club," *Catholic Standard and Times* (March 25, 1916), 8.

61. "Benedict XV Italian Club Organized in Annunciation Parish," *Catholic Standard and Times* (June 5, 1915), 5; "Church News: L'Assunta House," *Catholic Standard and Times* (February 15, 1916), 5.

62. "Catholic Missionary Society," *Catholic Standard and Times* (April 15, 1916), 9.

63. "Italians Planning Immigrant Home," *Evening Bulletin* (December 7, 1910), PAHRC SB-8:233.

64. "The Society for Italian Immigrants," *Catholic Standard and Times* (January 27, 1912), PAHRC SB-9:50.

65. Ibid.; *History of the Società di Unione e Fratellanza Italiana* (Philadelphia, 1929).

CHAPTER ELEVEN. *Saving the Faith of Southern Italians*

1. For more on the life of Agostino Lagomarsino, see Juliani, *Building Little Italy*; for the Augustinian assessment of his importance for their parish, see *Almanacco Illustrato della Parrocchia del Buon Consiglio per l'anno 1916* (Philadelphia, 1915), AAVP. The parish almanac, however, erroneously gives the date of his death as May 1, 1896. Lagomarsino died on May 1, 1906. "Deaths of the Day: Augustino Lagomarsino," *Public Ledger* (May 3, 1906), 9.

2. "Requiem Masses for Leo," *Public Ledger* (July 29, 1903), 3; "Italians' Tribute to Leo," *Public Ledger* (July 30, 1903), 8; "Funeral of Italian Priest," *Public Ledger* (November 9, 1904), PAHRC SB-7:50.

3. The figures for school enrollments vary between what was provided in the parish reports and the superintendent's reports. For 1901 and 1905, figures were obtained from the *Questiones;* for other years, from the *Annual Report of the Superintendent.* While the *Questiones* gave only one figure per year without any clear specification to what point it referred, the superintendent's annual report gave separate figures for the beginning and end of each school year as well as the average daily attendance. Where the superintendent's reports are used, the figure represents the reported enrollment at the end of the school year. For example, 447 pupils were reported as enrolled at St. Mary Magdalen dePazzi at the end of the school year in June 1904.

4. "Foreign Churches in the City of Philadelphia," *Public Ledger* (September 6, 1903), 15.

5. "School to be Enlarged," *Public Ledger* (December 15, 1903), 10; "Important Improvements in Our Lady of Good Counsel Parish," *Catholic Standard and Times* (December 19, 1903), PAHRC SB-6:445; "Blessing of Our Lady of Good Counsel School Annex," *Standard and Times* (March 11, 1905), PAHRC SB-7:85.

6. Joseph A. Hickey, O.S.A., Notes on the Italian Vice Province of Philadelphia, n.d., AAVU. For the nature and characteristics of the "chiesa ricettizia," see the seminal work of Gabriele DeRosa, *Chiesa e Religione Populare nel Mezzogiorno* (Rome-Bari: Laterza, 1978); and the studies by Carroll, *Madonnas that Maim,* and *Veiled Threats.*

7. See the document under the name of Archbishop Ryan, "Nos Patritius Joannes Ryan," and notes on the Italian Mission, AAVP.

8. "New Italian Parish," *Catholic Standard and Times* (January 15, 1898), PAHRC SB-5:43; "Corner-Stone of New Church," *Press* (May 22, 1899); "A Day in the Churches," *Record* (May 22, 1899); "Mgr. Martinelli Officiates," *Public Ledger* (May 22, 1899); "Corner-Stone Laid," *Times* (May 22, 1899); "New Church for Italians," *Catholic Standard and Times* (May 27, 1899). For these articles, see PAHRC SB-5:198 and SB-5:201. "New Church for Italians," *Catholic Standard and Times* (December 2, 1899), PAHRC SB-5:268; "Blessing of New Italian School," *Catholic Standard and Times* (September 14, 1901), PAHRC SB-5:460; "Cardinal Martinelli Confirms Eight Hundred," *Catholic Standard and Times* (May 3, 1902), PAHRC SB-5:71; "Cardinal Martinelli Recalled to Rome," *Catholic Standard and Times* (May 3, 1902), 1.

9. "Mgr Falconio at Villanova," *Catholic Standard and Times* (May 28, 1904), PAHRC SB-7:1; "Reception for Falconio," *Public Ledger* (April 30, 1906), PAHRC SB-7:228; "Prayer Gong Rung; Stops Church Panic," *Public Ledger* (May 2, 1906), PAHRC SB-7:229; "The Apostolic Delegate Visits Philadelphia," *Catholic Standard and Times* (May 5, 1906), PAHRC SB-7:230. For this description of the Italian quarter, see "Warm Greeting for Apostolic Delegate," *Public Ledger* (May 1, 1906), PAHRC SB-7:228.

10. "Reception for Falconio," *Public Ledger* (April 30, 1906), PAHRC SB-7:228; "Warm Greeting for Apostolic Delegate," *Public Ledger* (May 1, 1906), PAHRC SB-7:228.

11. "Reception for Falconio," *Public Ledger* (April 30, 1906), PAHRC SB-7:228; "Warm Greeting for Apostolic Delegate," *Public Ledger* (May 1, 1906), PAHRC SB-7:228; "Prayer Gong Rung; Stops Church Panic," *Public Ledger* (May 2, 1906), PAHRC SB-7:229; "The Apostolic Delegate Visits Philadelphia," *Catholic Standard and Times* (May 5, 1906), PAHRC SB-7:230.

12. "Archbishop Ryan to Italian Laborers," *Public Ledger* (July 8, 1902), PAHRC SB-6:115; "Priest and Lay Brother Sent Here from Rome," *Public Ledger* (July 21, 1902), PAHRC SB-6:116; "Italians Observe Feast of Our Mother of Sorrows," *Catholic Standard and Times* (September 25, 1909), PAHRC SB-8:119; *Catholic Standard and Times Almanac* (1917), 23; "Church News: Our Lady of Good Counsel Church," *Catholic Standard and Times* (April 15, 1916), 5; "Mission for Italian Prisoners," *Catholic Standard and Times* (April 22, 1916), 5; "Closing of the Italian School of Our Lady of Good Counsel," *Catholic Standard and Times* (June 27, 1914), 5.

13. "Fire Destroys Church Altar," *Public Ledger* (February 5, 1903), 11; "Statues of Saints Covered with Money," *Public Ledger* (June 1, 1903), 2.

14. "Italians' Tribute to Leo," *Public Ledger* (July 30, 1903), 8; "St. Mary Magdalen dePazzi's Congregation Celebrate Patronal Feast," *Catholic Standard and Times* (June 4, 1904), 6; "Jewelry and Money Placed on Statues," *Public Ledger* (May 29, 1905), PAHRC SB-7:109.

15. "Some Historical Notes," *Souvenir and Bouquet,* 29–30; "Archbishop Blessed Bells at St. Mary Magdalen dePazzi's," *Catholic Standard and Times* (October 22, 1904), PAHRC SB-7:43; "Parish Hall for St. Mary Magdalen dePazzi's," *Catholic Standard and Times* (August 19, 1905), PAHRC SB-7:140.

16. "Parte I, Souvenir," *Souvenir and Bouquet,* 7 n. 1.

17. Ibid., 5–21.

18. Ibid., 11–13.

19. Ibid., 13–14.

20. Ibid., 15–16.

21. Ibid., 16–17.

22. Ibid., 17.

23. Ibid., 18–19.

24. Ibid., 19.

25. Ibid., 19 n. 1.

26. Ibid., 19–20.

27. "Philadelphia's Great Italian Colony," *Public Ledger* (October 8, 1908), PAHRC SB-8:12.

28. "Joyous Parade in Saint's Honor," *Public Ledger* (May 23, 1910), PAHRC SB-8:169.

29. *Lira Leronica* (Philadelphia, 1876–1878). Each of the three volumes of the *Lira Leronica* carried the note: "Si vende a benefizio dell'Asilo di S. Maria Maddalena De-Pazzi, aperto recentemente in Filadelfia per le ragazze orfane italiane, sotto la cura delle Suore Missionarie del 3° Ordine di S. Francesco." For a review of *A Tribute of Devotion to St. Mary Magdalen dePazzi* (Philadelphia, 1884), see *American Catholic Quarterly Review* 9 (January–October 1884): 571–72. See also *Souvenir and Bouquet*, 27–28.

30. For the Isoleri-Griffin correspondence, see the Martin I. J. Griffin Papers, Special Collections, Georgetown University Library, Washington, DC.

31. Porto Maurizio held special meaning for Isoleri for several reasons. It was the birthplace of Father Giuseppe Ascheri, who had attended the Collegio Brignole Sale and had preceded Isoleri as a missionary to America. Ascheri served for many years as the pastor of St. Francis de Sales Church in Lodi, New Jersey, and was involved in important occasions in Isoleri's pastoral life in Philadelphia. They remained close friends until Ascheri's death in 1910. For Merry del Val's message, see *Souvenir and Bouquet*, 29.

32. Isoleri Papers, "Sul Treno" (February 8, 1906). The author has translated this poem into English with the indispensable assistance of Professor Robert Melzi.

33. Isoleri Papers, "In Morte Marci Malatesta" (August 31, 1930). See the obituary for "Mark Malatesta," *Public Ledger* (August 29, 1903), 9; for more on this family, see Juliani, *Building Little Italy.*

34. Isoleri Papers, "Pro Augustino Cuneo" (February 7, 1904).

35. Isoleri Papers, "In funerale, Michaelis Campi" (October 15, 1903).

36. Isoleri Papers, "Pro Matilde Berretta" (December 19, 1903), and "La funerale di Giulia Barbieri e Teresa Barbieri" (August 31, 1908).

37. Isoleri Papers, untitled address to the officers and crew of the *Ettore Fieramosca* (November 19, 1906).

38. Ibid.

39. The newspapers of the city provided extensive coverage of these events. See also *The Book of the Pageant, Philadelphia* (October 9, 1908) and *Official Program—1683–1908, 225th Anniversary of the Founding of Philadelphia,* held at Franklin Field, University of Pennsylvania (October 5–10, 1908).

40. *Philadelphia—Founders' Week* (October 4–10, 1908), Philadelphia Town Printing Company (1908); Isoleri Papers, "Son terminate le Feste Magnifiche" (October 2–3, 1908).

41. "Prelate Calls for Canonization of Columbus," *Public Ledger* (October 13, 1909), PAHRC SB-8:126; "1492—Christopher Columbus—1909," *Catholic Standard and Times* (October 19, 1909), PAHRC SB-8:136. "Columbus Day," *Catholic Standard and Times* (October 19, 1912), PAHRC SB-9:142.

CHAPTER TWELVE.   *Beyond South Philadelphia*

1. "New Catholic Church Needed," *Public Ledger* (December 29, 1904), PAHRC SB-7:64.

2. "Archbishop Ryan to Italian Laborers," *Public Ledger* (July 8, 1902), PAHRC SB-6:115; "Priest and Lay Brother Sent Here from Rome," *Public Ledger* (July 21, 1902), PAHRC SB-6:116.

3. "New Church for Italians at Norristown," *Catholic Standard and Times* (September 5, 1903), PAHRC SB-6:366: "Dedicated Church for Italians at Norristown," *Catholic Standard and Times* (December 5, 1903), PAHRC SB-6:442; *Questiones, 1904, 1907,* PAHRC; "The Italian in America," *Catholic Standard and Times* (September 26, 1908), PAHRC SB-8:2; *Golden Jubilee, San Salvatore Church, Norristown, Pa.,* PAHRC.

4. "The Italian in America," *Catholic Standard and Times* (September 26, 1908), PAHRC SB-8:2.

5. Ibid.

6. Ibid.

7. "Chestnut Hill Italians and the Feast of the Immaculate Conception," *Catholic Standard and Times* (December 17, 1904), PAHRC SB-7:62; *Catholic Standard and Times Almanac for 1922* (Philadelphia, 1922), 42.

8. During the same period, the archdiocese opened fourteen other parishes and missions for Italians in areas that are now outside of its boundaries but within the Diocese of Allentown, which was established in 1962. These sites were: Our Lady of Mount Carmel, Roseto (1897); Immaculate Conception, Kelayres (1899); Our Lady of Pompeii, Bethlehem (1902); Our Lady of Mount Carmel, Nesquehoning (mission, 1904; parish, 1913); Holy Rosary, Reading (1904); Holy Rosary Mission, Reading (1904); St. Joseph, Pottsville (1906); Sacred Heart, Mahanoy City (1907); St. Anthony of Padua, Easton (1909); Our Lady of Mount Carmel, Allentown (1911); St. Barbara, Minersville (1913); Our Lady of Mount Carmel, Shenandoah (1914); Immaculate Conception, Birdsboro (1916); and St. Bartholomew, Tresckow (1917).

9. Dennis Clark described these processes in the formation of Catholic parishes in general in his important essay, "A Pattern of Urban Growth: Residential Development and Church Location in Philadelphia," *RACHS* 82 (1971): 159–70, reprinted in Brian C. Mitchell, ed., *Building the American Catholic City: Parishes and Institutions* (New York: Garland Publishing, 1988), 76–87.

10. Among the extensive collection of parish histories at the Philadelphia Archdiocesan Historical Research Center, see *History of Our Parish—A Brief History of the Parish of St. Lucy, Manayunk, Phila., PA—1927 Golden Jubilee 1977* (Philadelphia, 1977); see also, "Part of Church Consecrated," *Telegraph* (December 10, 1906), PAHRC SB-7:299; "Dedication of Italian Church in West Manayunk," *Catholic Standard and Times* (December 8, 1906), PAHRC SB-7:302; "Blessing of New Italian Church, West Manayunk," *Catholic Standard and Times* (December 15, 1906), PAHRC SB-7:302; and Kirlin, *Catholicity in Philadelphia,* 507. Some twenty-one years after its dedication in 1906, St. Lucy's returned to the city by locating a church building, along with official parish status for Italians in Manayunk, on the north side of the Schuylkill River.

11. *Questiones, 1906, 1907,* PAHRC.

12. *St. Ann's Church 1906–1956,* Parish Histories, PAHRC; *Questiones, 1906,* PAHRC.

13. "Bishop to Lay Church Cornerstone at Bristol," *Catholic Standard and Times* (March 16, 1907), PAHRC SB-7:330; "For Bristol's Italian Catholics," *Catholic Standard and Times* (March 23, 1907), 5; "Bristol's New Italian Church," *Catholic Standard and Times* (October 5, 1907), 5; *Questiones, 1907, 1908,* PAHRC; *St. Ann's Church 1906–1956.*

14. Before Italians lived in the area, Father Cosimo A. Delle Nave served Catholics at a toolshed chapel, later called St. Gregory's, at Old Cathedral Cemetery (before becoming Our Mother of Sorrows), and doubled its seating capacity between 1853 and 1856. He also tended the Italians who later founded St. Mary Magdalen dePazzi. See *Historical Sketches of the Catholic Churches and Institutions of Philadelphia,* 101; "Three New Italian Churches," *Catholic Standard and Times* (January 19, 1907), PAHRC SB-7:306; "Corner-Stone Laying of Italian Church," *Catholic Standard and Times* (July 6, 1907), PAHRC SB-7:363; "Lay

Corner-Stone of New Italian Church," *North American* (July 7, 1907), PAHRC SB-7:364; "Laid Corner-stone of New Italian Church," *Catholic Standard and Times* (July 13, 1907), PAHRC SB-7:363; "Dedicated New Italian Church," *Catholic Standard and Times* (December 7, 1907), PAHRC SB-7:399; Kirlin, *Catholicity in Philadelphia*, 363–64, 507–8; and *Golden Jubilee, Our Lady of Angel's Church, 1907–1957,* Souvenir Program (1957).

15. Kirlin first made this interpretation before it reappeared nearly fifty years later in the souvenir program of the Golden Jubilee celebration in 1957.

16. "Doings of a Day in the Churches," *Record* (July 7, 1907), PAHRC SB-7:365.

17. For Travi's remarks and other comments on the relationship of the new parish to the old one and its pastor, see "Three New Italian Churches," *Catholic Standard and Times* (January 19, 1907), PAHRC SB-7:306; "Corner-Stone Laying of Italian Church," *Catholic Standard and Times* (July 6, 1907), PAHRC SB-7:363; "Laid Corner-stone of New Italian Church," *Catholic Standard and Times* (July 13, 1907), PAHRC SB-7:363; "To Dedicate Italian Church," *Catholic Standard and Times* (November 11, 1907), PAHRC SB-7:396; "Bishop Dedicates Church," *Public Ledger* (December 1, 1907), PAHRC SB-7:398; and "Dedicated New Italian Church," *Catholic Standard and Times* (December 7, 1907), PAHRC SB-7:399.

18. "Corner-Stone Laying of Italian Church," *Catholic Standard and Times* (July 6, 1907), PAHRC SB-7:363; "Laid Corner-stone of New Italian Church," *Catholic Standard and Times* (July 13, 1907), PAHRC SB-7:363; "To Dedicate Italian Church," *Catholic Standard and Times* (November 11, 1907), PAHRC SB-7:396; "Bishop Dedicates Church," *Public Ledger* (December 1, 1907), PAHRC SB-7:398; "Dedicated New Italian Church," *Catholic Standard and Times* (December 7, 1907), PAHRC SB-7:399; *Questiones, 1907, 1908,* PAHRC.

19. In addition to the previously cited sources, see also "Welcome Italian Pastor," *Catholic Standard and Times* (November 27, 1909), PAHRC SB-8:142; "Italian Parish School Corner-Stone to be Laid," *Catholic Standard and Times* (August 23, 1924), PAHRC SB-12:128; and "Rev. P. Michetti Celebrates His Silver Jubilee," *Catholic Standard and Times* (April 28, 1927), PAHRC SB-13:199. Serious disparities sometimes exist among newspaper accounts, parish histories, and archdiocesan personnel records. Some sources contain serious errors. For parish assignments of priests, see the curricula vitae, or Priests' Files, at PAHRC, but even this information should be compared to other sources.

20. "New Catholic Church Needed," *Public Ledger* (December 29, 1904), PAHRC SB-7:64;. Kirlin, *Catholicity in Philadelphia*, 372–73, 467; "New Parishes Formed by Archbishop Ryan," *Public Ledger* (November 25, 1904), PAHRC SB-7:54.

21. Kirlin, *Catholicity in Philadelphia*, 298–99, 449–50.

22. "To Preserve the Faith in Philadelphia's 'Little Italy,'" *Catholic Standard and Times* (November 19, 1904), PAHRC SB-7:54; "School Accommodations for Italian Children," *Catholic Standard and Times* (February 18, 1905), PAHRC SB-7:81: "Parochial School Annex Dedicated," *Public Ledger* (March 6, 1905), PAHRC SB-7:85; "Blessing of Our Lady of Good Counsel School Annex," *Catholic Standard and Times* (March 11, 1905), PAHRC SB-7:85.

23. "Dedicates School; Lays Cornerstone," *Public Ledger* (May 1, 1905), PAHRC SB-7:99: "A Day in the Churches," *Record* (May 1, 1905), PAHRC SB-7:99; "Archbishop Blesses School and Convent," *North American* (May 1, 1905), PAHRC SB-7:100; "New School in Italian Quarter," *Catholic Standard and Times* (May 6, 1905), PAHRC SB-7:102.

24. "Exercises at St. Paul's for the Italian Children," *Public Ledger* (December 4, 1905), PAHRC SB-7:177: "Archbishop Blesses New School Building," *North American* (December 4, 1905), PAHRC SB-7:178.

25. "Archbishop Views Work of Italian Pupils," *Catholic Standard and Times* (July 7, 1906), PAHRC SB-7:259.

26. "Archbishop Guest of St. Paul's Children,"*Catholic Standard and Times* (May 16, 1908), PAHRC SB-7:464.

27. "The Archbishop at St. Paul's," *Catholic Standard and Times* (December 2, 1911), PAHRC SB-9:29; "A Sketch of the Work and History of the Sisters, Servants of the Immaculate Heart of Mary 1845–1920," *RACHS* 31 (1920): 276–338.

28. Kirlin, *Catholicity in Philadelphia*, 508; "The New Church for Italians," *Catholic Standard and Times* (November 11, 1905), PAHRC SB-7:174.

29. "Three New Italian Churches," *Catholic Standard and Times* (January 19, 1907), PAHRC SB-7:306; "Clearing the Ground for St. Rita's Italian Church," *Catholic Standard and Times* (March 16, 1907), PAHRC SB-7:330; Kirlin, *Catholicity in Philadelphia*, 508; untitled article, *Telegraph* (April 13, 1907), PAHRC SB-7:348; "St. Rita's Chapel Blessed," *Catholic Standard and Times* (June 29, 1907), PAHRC SB-7:362; "Catholics Worship in Episcopal Parish House," *Catholic Standard and Times* (November 23, 1907), PAHRC SB-7:396.

30. "Boundaries of St. Rita's Parish," *Catholic Standard and Times* (July 20, 1907), PAHRC SB-7:365; "Doings of a Day in the Churches," *Record* (October 28, 1907), PAHRC SB-7:387; "New Church for Italian Colony," *Public Ledger* (October 28, 1907), PAHRC SB-7:386; "Corner Stone is Laid by Bishop," *Inquirer* (October 28, 1907), PAHRC SB-7:386; "Doings of a Day in the Churches," *Record* (October 28, 1907), PAHRC SB-7:387; "Laid St. Rita's Corner-Stone," *Catholic Standard and Times* (November 2, 1907), PAHRC SB-7:391; "Dedicated New Italian Church," *Catholic Standard and Times* (December 7, 1907), PAHRC SB-7:399.

31. "St. Rita's to Open," *Catholic Standard and Times* (June 13, 1908), PAHRC SB-7:479; "New St. Rita's Catholic Church for Italians," *Public Ledger* (September 19, 1908), PAHRC SB-7:497: "Pastors and People of Philadelphia," *Public Ledger* (September 26, 1908), SB-8:1; "Doings of a Day in the Churches," *Record* (September 28, 1908), PAHRC SB-8:1; "New Chapel Dedicated," *Public Ledger* (September 28, 1908), PAHRC SB-8:1; "Archbishop Blesses St. Rita's," *Catholic Standard and Times* (October 3, 1908), PAHRC SB-8:6.

32. "Archbishop Blesses St. Rita's," *Catholic Standard and Times* (October 3, 1908), PAHRC SB-8:6.

33. *Our Lady of the Assumption Church, 75th Anniversary (1908–1983)*, Parish Histories, PAHRC; "New Italian Chapel at Strafford," *Catholic Standard and Times* (June 13, 1908), 5.

34. *Our Lady of the Assumption Church, 75th Anniversary (1908–1983)*, Parish Histories, PAHRC; Priests' Files, PAHRC; *Consultors' Minute Book*, vol. 1 (February 10, 1908), 73, PAHRC; *Questiones, 1908–1913*, PAHRC.

35. *St. Anthony of Padua Church*, 1983, Parish Histories, PAHRC; *Questiones, 1907–1910*, PAHRC.

36. Ryan Papers, 61.77 Ach, PAHRC.

37. *Questiones, 1908–1912*, PAHRC. Garritano's notes in the 1912 report and the attached letter dated October 30, 1913, are especially informative here.

38. *Consultors' Minute Book*, vol. 1 (March 3, 1913), 144, (April 7, 1913), 147, (June 2, 1913), 151, (April 6, 1914), 169, PAHRC; "Corner-stone Laying at Chester," *Catholic Standard and Times* (November 1, 1913), 5; *Questiones, 1913*, PAHRC.

39. "Chester's First Church for Italian Catholics," *Catholic Standard and Times* (June 13, 1914), 5, Falvey Library, Villanova University (hereafter FLVU); "New Church for Chester Italians," *Catholic Standard and Times* (June 20,1914), 5, FLVU.

40. "Chester's First Church for Italian Catholics," *Catholic Standard and Times* (June 13, 1914), 5, FLVU.

41. "Chester Pastor Home after Visit to Italy," *Catholic Standard and Times* (August 28, 1915), 5, FLVU.

42. "Despite 'Rum, Romanism, Police and Politics,'" *Catholic Standard and Times* (December 13, 1913), 1, FLVU; "Dedication of St. Donato's School," *Catholic Standard amd Times* (August 15, 1914), 1, FLVU; *St. Donato's Parish 1910–1960*, Parish Histories, PAHRC.

43. "The Pastor of St. Donato's," *Catholic Standard and Times* (February 7, 1914), 5, FLVU; "Laid Corner-Stone of Italian Church," *Catholic Standard and Times* (June 25, 1910), PAHRC SB-8:187; "Silver Jubilees Observed by Three Diocesan Priests," *Catholic Standard and Times* (May 28, 1927), PAHRC SB-13:198.

44. "Laid Corner-Stone of Italian Church," *Catholic Standard and Times* (June 25, 1910), PAHRC SB-8:187.

45. Ibid.

46. Ibid.

47. "The Pastor of St. Donato's," *Catholic Standard and Times* (February 7, 1915), 5, FLVU; "Laid Corner-Stone of Italian Church," *Catholic Standard and Times* (June 25, 1910), PAHRC SB-8:187; "Dedication of St. Donato's Basement Chapel," *Catholic Standard and Times* (July 23, 1910), PAHRC SB-8:192; "Clerical Appointments," *Catholic Standard and Times* (July 30, 1910), PAHRC SB-8:192.

48. *Questiones, 1911, 1915,* PAHRC; *Catholic Standard and Times* (November 29, 1913), 5, and subsequent issues; "Dedication of St. Donato's School," *Catholic Standard and Times* (August 15, 1914), 1, FLVU; "St. Donato's Campaign," *Catholic Standard and Times* (March 18, 1916), 9, and similar items in later weeks, FLVU.

49. "Cardinal Will Dedicate New Italian Church Today," *Record* (December 24, 1922), Campbell Collection, vol. 8, Historical Society of Pennsylvania, Philadelphia (hereafter HSP).

50. *Questiones, 1910,* PAHRC; Priests' Files, PAHRC.

51. "Italian Catholics to Have New Church," *North American* (September 11, 1911), PAHRC SB-8:460; "Lay Corner Stone of Two Churches," *Press* (September 11, 1911), PAHRC SB-8:460; "Church for Italians in the Northwest," *Catholic Standard and Times* (November 16, 1912), PAHRC SB-9:152.

52. "Church for Italians in the Northwest," *Catholic Standard and Times* (November 16, 1912), PAHRC SB-9:152.

53. *Questiones, 1912,* PAHRC.

54. *Questiones, 1915,* PAHRC; Priests' Files, PAHRC.

55. *Questiones, 1915,* PAHRC.

56. "Possible New Italian Parish," *Catholic Standard and Times* (February 1, 1908), PAHRC SB-7:406; *Souvenir Program for the Silver Jubilee of the Dedication of Mater Dolorosa Church in Frankford, Philadelphia, PA* (Philadelphia, May 12, 1940), PAHRC, Parish Histories; "Principal Events for 1911," *Catholic Standard and Times Almanac for 1912* (Philadelphia, 1912).

57. *Questiones, 1911, 1912,* PAHRC. The entry was listed under the alternate name of the parish, Santa Maria Addolorata, at this time.

58. "Frankford Italian Parish Acquires New Church Site," *Catholic Standard and Times* (December 20, 1913), 5, FLVU; advertisement, *Catholic Standard and Times* (January 3, 1914), 5, FLVU; "Day of Rejoicing for Frankford Catholics," *Catholic Standard and Times* (August 22, 1914), 3, FLVU.

59. "Day of Rejoicing for Frankford Catholics," *Catholic Standard and Times* (August 22, 1914), 3, FLVU.

60. Ibid.

61. "Frankford's New Italian Church," *Catholic Standard and Times* (December 26, 1914), 1, FLVU.

62. *Consultors' Minute Book,* vol. 1 (June 2, 1913), 151, PAHRC. In 1914, Bruni was denied permission for an unrestricted bond for a loan. See *Consultors' Minute Book,* vol. 1 (September 8, 1914), 175, PAHRC. For the final item, see *Consultors' Minute Book,* vol. 1 (March 3, 1914), 167, PAHRC.

63. "Frankford's New Italian Church," *Catholic Standard and Times* (December 26, 1914), 1, FLVU.

64. *Questiones, 1915,* PAHRC.

65. *Souvenir Program for the Silver Jubilee of the Dedication of Mater Dolorosa Church in Frankford;* "Mater Dolorosa Pastor Dies," *Catholic Standard and Times* (August 24, 1945), 1, PAHRC.

66. "New Catholic Church Needed," *Public Ledger* (December 29, 1904), PAHRC SB-7:64; "New Parishes Formed by Archbishop Ryan," *Public Ledger* (November 25, 1904), PAHRC SB-7:54.

67. "Catholics Buy Salem Church," *Evening Bulletin* (April 11, 1912), Campbell Collection, vol. 8, HSP; "Italian Church Dedicated," *Record* (April 15, 1912), PAHRC SB-9:87; "New Catholic Church," *Public Ledger* (April 15, 1912), PAHRC SB-9:87; "St. Nicholas of Tolentine's Opened," *Catholic Standard and Times* (April 20, 1912), PAHRC SB-9:87.

68. *Yearly Report of the Augustinian Convent of Our Lady of Good Counsel at Philadelphia, Pa. For the year ending June 30th, 1912,* AAVU. For the early history of the mission, see Fr. George J. DeMarco, O.S.A., "St. Nicholas of Tolentine Church, Philadelphia, Pa., Historical Sketch, 1912–1966," AAVU; and *Questiones, 1912, 1913, 1915,* PAHRC.

69. *Ss. Cosmas and Damian Church—Diamond Jubilee of Father Victor A. Strumia, 1907–1977,* Parish Histories, PAHRC; Sr. Helen Constance, "History of Ss. Cosmas and Damian, Conshohocken, Pa. 1912–1971" (1971), Parish Histories, PAHRC; "Dedicated Church for Conshohocken Italians," *Catholic Standard and Times* (May 10, 1913), 5; "Rev. N. Coscia, Rector of Italian Church Dies," *Catholic Standard and Times* (May 14, 1927), PAHRC SB-13:195.

70. *Questiones, 1912,* PAHRC; Sr. Helen Constance, "History of Ss. Cosmas and Damian"; "Dedicated Church for Conshohocken Italians," *Catholic Standard and Times* (May 10, 1913), 5; *Ss. Cosmas and Damian Church;* "Rev. N. Coscia, Rector of Italian Church Dies," *Catholic Standard and Times* (May 14, 1927), PAHRC SB-13:195.

71. *1st Annual Reunion, January 24, 1948, Holy Rosary, Germantown, PA.* Parish Histories, PAHRC; *Catholic Standard and Times Almanac for 1907* (Philadelphia, 1907); *Catholic Standard and Times Almanac for 1908* (Philadelphia, 1908); "Mission for Italians of Germantown," *Catholic Standard and Times* (April 13, 1912), PAHRC SB-9:87; Kirlin, *Catholicity in Philadelphia,* 457–58.

72. "Blessing of Germantown's Italian School," *Catholic Standard and Times* (November 15, 1913), 5, FLVU; "Blessing of Germantown's Italian Parish School," *Catholic Standard and Times* (November 29, 1913), 5, FLVU; "Holy Rosary (Italian) Parish School Blessed," *Catholic Standard and Times* (September 26, 1914), 1, FLVU.

73. *Catholic Standard and Times Almanac for 1915* (Philadelphia, 1915). See subsequent editions of the *Almanac* as well as the Annual Reports, or *Questiones,* of the pastors. Since closing as a parish, the *Almanac* states, from its 1973 edition onward, that Holy Rosary is attended by Immaculate Conception Parish. With some irony, Holy Rosary has returned to its parochial womb.

74. "Double Funeral of Aged Vincentians," *Catholic Standard and Times* (June 12, 1915), 3, FLVU.

75. "Methodist Church is Purchased by Italians," *Catholic Standard and Times* (May 12, 1928), 1; "Edifice Occupied by Italian Parish," *Catholic Standard and Times* (May 19, 1928), 4. More recent editions of the *Almanac* give the founding date of the parish as 1928.

76. "Edifice Occupied by Italian Parish," *Catholic Standard and Times* (May 19, 1928), 4.

77. "New Italian Parish in the Northeast," *Catholic Standard and Times* (August 15, 1914), 5; "Church News: Dedication of Church of Our Lady of Pompeii," *Catholic Standard and Times* (August 28, 1915), 5; "New Church of Our Lady of Pompeii," *Catholic Standard and Times* (September 4, 1915), 1; "Fine Edifice for Italian Catholics," *Catholic Standard and Times* (September 11, 1915), 3.

78. "Fine Edifice for Italian Catholics," *Catholic Standard and Times* (September 11, 1915), 3.

79. "New Italian Church of Our Lady of Pompeii," *Catholic Standard and Times* (January 16, 1915), PAHRC SB-9:357; "Fine Edifice for Italian Catholics," *Catholic Standard and Times* (September 11, 1915), 3; *Questiones, 1915,* PAHRC.

80. *Our Lady of Consolation, Philadelphia, Pa., 50 Years of Parish Progress* (Philadelphia, 1967), Parish Histories, PAHRC; "New Church for Italians of Tacony," *Catholic Standard and Times* (September 2, 1916), 1; Priests' Files, PAHRC; "Happenings of a Day in the City Churches," unidentified newspaper (December 25, 1916), Campbell Collection, vol. 8, HSP; "Church for Italians at Tacony Dedicated," *Catholic Standard and Times* (December 30, 1916), PAHRC SB-9:487; "Bishop Furey Offers Mass for Rev. Alfred Procopio," *Catholic Standard and Times* (January 6, 1961), 1; *Questiones, 1916–1918,* PAHRC.

81. "Break Ground for Italian Church at Coatesville," *Catholic Standard and Times* (October 28, 1916), 5; "Bishop Breaks Ground for New Italian Church," *Catholic Standard and Times* (November 4, 1916), 1; Priests' Files, PAHRC; *Questiones, 1916–1918,* PAHRC.

82. "Ground Broken for New Italian Church," *Catholic Standard and Times* (December 2, 1916), 5; *Fiftieth Anniversary of Immaculate Conception of Lourdes Church, Marcus Hook, Penna. 1917–1967,* Parish Histories, PAHRC.

83. *Questiones, 1918,* PAHRC.

84. Ibid.

85. Ryan Papers, PAHRC, Ach 61.100.

86. *Questiones, 1915,* PAHRC.

87. "Despite 'Rum, Romanism, Police and Politics,'" *Catholic Standard and Times* (December 13, 1913), 1, FLVU.

88. Ibid. For Cosmas Bruni's letters, see "A Man, a Pear Tree, Five Boys and Fifty Cents," *Catholic Standard and Times* (November 29, 1913), 5; and "Why 'So Many' Italians Become Protestants," *Catholic Standard and Times* (December 27, 1913), 5, FLVU.

89. "Archbishop Dedicates St. Rita's," *Catholic Standard and Times* (May 22, 1915), 1–2, FLVU.

CHAPTER THIRTEEN.   *Final Years of a Priest*

1. DiScala, *Italy: From Revolution to Republic,* 204.

2. "Italian Physicians Here Offer Services for War," *Public Ledger* (May 22, 1915), 3; "Italian May Procession Brings Prayers for Success of the Fatherland's Arms," *Public Ledger* (May 24, 1915), 6.

3. "Italian May Procession Brings Prayers for Success of the Fatherland's Arms," *Public Ledger* (May 24, 1915), PAHRC SB-9:382.

4. Isoleri Papers, "Il 24 Maggio 1915—Viva L'Italia!" Isoleri most likely had seen and described the effects of rings caused by atmospheric dust around the sun, which had been reported by other people at the time. For a more scientific view, see the letter "Rings around the Sun," *Public Ledger* (June 27, 1915), 9.

5. "Italian Reservists in U.S. to Register," *Public Ledger* (June 4, 1915), 4; "Italian Reservists Start for Home," *Public Ledger* (June 5, 1915), 7; "Viva L'Italia," *Public Ledger* (June 6, 1915), 1; "3,000 Italians to Sail for War," *Public Ledger* (June 8, 1915), 4; "Italian Reservists Sail for Home Today," *Public Ledger* (June 14, 1915), 3; "New England Italians Ready to Join Colors," *Public Ledger* (June 16, 1915), 9.

6. "Italians Here Raise Aid Fund," *Public Ledger* (May 25, 1915), 3; "Relief Work Begun by 'Little Italy,'" *Public Ledger* (May 26, 1915), 3; "Italians Seek Fund to Aid Colony's Poor," *Public Ledger* (May 30, 1915), 4; "Italians Pledge Aid for $100,000," *Public Ledger* (June 14, 1915), 2; "Italians Collect $3000 for War Relief Fund," *Public Ledger* (June 19, 1915), 3; "Italian Festival in Aid of Poor," *Public Ledger* (June 29, 1915), 3.

7. "700 Italian Reservists to Sail for Home Today," *Public Ledger* (July 22, 1915), 2.

8. "'Final Call' to Italians Here," *Public Ledger* (July 29, 1915), 1.

9. "Italians Observe Feast of St. Rocco," *Public Ledger* (August 17, 1915), 11.

10. "Italian Reservists Hasten to Enter," *Public Ledger* (August 18, 1915), 8.

11. Isoleri Papers, "Peace Sunday" (21 Maggio 1916). Isoleri may have been mistaken in identifying this day as "Peace Sunday," which was the title used a year earlier for a program in Rome. But it does not seem to have been used again when the Archdiocese of Philadelphia sponsored a military mass on May 21, 1916.

12. Ibid.

13. "Conference on Citizen Making to Begin Today," *Public Ledger* (January 19, 1916), 1; "Assimilation Delegates Open Sessions Today," *Public Ledger* (January 20, 1916), 1.

14. "Roosevelt Gives His Preparedness Plans to Philadelphians," *Public Ledger* (January 21, 1916), 1, 11.

15. Ibid.

16. "Father Isoleri a Domestic Prelate," *Catholic Standard and Times* (October 14, 1916), 1.

17. For these figures, see *Questiones: Annual Report* (submitted by pastors of each parish, January 1, 1914–January 1, 1915 to January 1, 1925–January 1, 1926). Although the figure was simply listed as "Catholic Population," it referred to the population in the neighborhood belonging to the parish. In the first year after Isoleri's retirement as pastor, his successor, Father Anthony Garritano, apparently interpreting the question differently, gave a greatly increased total of 15,000–20,000 in 1926.

18. *Questiones: Annual Report* (January 1, 1914–January 1, 1915 to January 1, 1925–January 1, 1926).

19. See the *Questiones* for the period 1914–1925.

20. *Consultors' Minutes*, vol. 1, 181, 183, PAHRC. (This series, also cited in this volume as *Consultors' Minute Book*, varied in title. My citations match the title of given document.) For a discussion of the efforts of Italian pastors to secure assistance from the archdiocesan consultors between 1893 and 1916, see Juliani, "The Parish as an Urban Institution: Italian Catholics in Philadelphia," *RACHS*, 96:1–4 (March–December 1986): 49–65.

21. *Consultors' Minutes*, vol. 1, 184–85, PAHRC.

22. Ibid., 185, 200, and 202.

23. *Questiones* (January 1, 1916–January 1, 1917).

24. Isoleri to Prendergast (July 27, 1916), 71.433 AIorp, PAHRC; Isoleri to Prendergast (August 5, 1916), 71.434 AIorp, PAHRC.

25. *Mayor's Annual Message* (1918), vol. 1, "Department of Public Safety: Bureau of Police," 39. See also Lloyd M. Abernethy, "Progressivism, 1905–1919," 524–65, in Russell F. Weigley, ed., *Philadelphia: A 300-Year History* (New York: W. W. Norton & Company, 1982). For the archdiocesan response to the epidemic, see "Principal Events for 1918," in *Catholic Standard and Times Almanac for 1919* (Philadelphia, 1919), 67.

26. Isoleri Papers, "Il 24 Ottobre 1918—Deprecatio."

27. *Mayor's Annual Message* (1918), vol. 1, "Department of Public Health and Charities," 305–6, "Division of Medical Inspection," 400, 452, and "Bureau of Health," 466, *Catholic Standard and Times Almanac*, 67; Abernethy, "Progressivism," 561.

28. *Mayor's Annual Message* (1918), "Department of Public Health and Charities," 410–19, and "Division of Medical Inspection," 452.

29. Isoleri Papers, untitled (October 12, 1919).

30. *Consultors' Minutes* (1921–1932), PAHRC; Isoleri Papers, sermon (written February 26, 1919, for March 2, 1919), and sermon (May 18, 1919).

31. U.S. Department of Commerce, Bureau of the Census, *Census of Religious Bodies, 1926, Roman Catholic Church: Statistics, History, Doctrine and Organization* (Washington, DC, 1929), 25–26.

32. *Pastoral Letter of the Archbishops and Bishops of the United States Assembled in Conference at the Catholic University of America, September 1919*, National Catholic Welfare Council (Washington, DC, 1920), 32, 65. For NCWC programs, see Reconstruction Pamphlets, *Outlines of a Social Service Program for Catholic Agencies*, no. 7 (June 1919) and *A Program for Citizenship*, no. 5 (July 1919).

33. *The Promise Fulfilled—Outstanding Facts concerning the Work of the Committee on Special War Activities of the National Catholic Welfare Council* (Washington, DC, January 1920); *Civics Catechism on the Rights and Duties of American Citizens*, Committee on Special War Activities, National Catholic Welfare Council, no. 13 (Washington, DC, August 1920).

34. *National Catholic Welfare Council, Reports of Administrative Committee and Departments Made at the Conference of the Hierarchy of the United States* (Washington, DC, September 22–23, 1920). For the history of the NCWC, not always a harmonious one but sometimes marked by internal dissension in which Dougherty played a major part, see Fogarty, *The Vatican and the American Hierarchy from 1870 to 1965*, 214–36.

35. *Address by the Reverend John J. Burke, C.S.P., General Secretary of the National Catholic Welfare Council, at the First Annual Convention of the National Council of Catholic Men*, Washington, DC (September 29, 1920), PAHRC Pamphlets.

36. Ibid.

37. Zazzara, "Pastoral Care of Italian Emigrants."

38. Dunne, "The Church and the Immigrant."

39. Nicola Fusco, "The Italian Racial Strain," in C. E. McGuire, ed., *Catholic Builders of the Nation* (Boston: Continental Press, 1923), 111–26; Palmieri, "The Contribution of the Italian Catholic Clergy to the United States." For this quotation in particular, see Palmieri, 145. Although once stationed at Our Lady of Good Counsel, Palmieri stated that efforts to minister to Italians began after 1870, and he identified St. Anthony's in New York City as their first church, thus inexplicably ignoring St. Mary Magdalen dePazzi.

40. Romanus, "The Future of Our Immigrant Parishes." Although he described procedures that he followed as pastor of an immigrant church, "P. C. Romanus" was a pseudonym. No one was listed under this name in national directories of the clergy.

41. Ibid.

42. Lyng, "Catholic Missionary Society of Philadelphia," 236.

43. Ibid.

44. "New Madonna House for Italian Colony," *Catholic Standard and Times* (August 4, 1923), PAHRC SB-12:2.

45. "New Activities Planned by Missionary Society," *Catholic Standard and Times* (November 2, 1923), PAHRC SB-12:31.

46. Ibid.

47. Pascucci, "No Greater Love than This." Pascucci's unpublished paper is a concise but detailed account of the brief history of Salesian efforts at the Don Bosco Institute.

48. Ibid., 38–39.

49. Ibid., 40–41.

50. Ibid., 42–43.

51. Ibid., 44–45.

52. Ibid., 45–46.

53. Ibid., 46–47.

54. Ibid., 47–50

55. Ibid., 41, and Appendix C, 57–58.

56. "Madonna House Auxiliary to Hold Annual Meeting," *Catholic Standard and Times* (February 16, 1924), PAHRC SB-12:79; "Plan to Extend Work of Missionary Society," *Catholic Standard and Times* (March 15, 1924), PAHRC SB-12:90.

57. "Catholic Missionary Society Shows Progress in Reports," *Catholic Standard and Times* (March 7, 1925), PAHRC SB-12:211.

58. "Catholic Missionary Society Makes its 25th Annual Report," *Catholic Standard and Times,* (March 3, 1928), PAHRC SB-13:290.

59. "Banquet to Mark 25th Anniversary of Madonna House," *Catholic Standard and Times* (January 21, 1928), PAHRC SB-13:274–75; "Silver Jubilee Observance is Held by Madonna House," *Catholic Standard and Times* (January 28, 1928), PAHRC SB-13:278.

60. "Full Text of Address Delivered by His Eminence at Silver Jubilee of Madonna House," *Catholic Standard and Times* (January 28, 1928), PAHRC SB-13:279.

61. Ibid.

62. "Silver Jubilee Observance is Held by Madonna House," *Catholic Standard and Times* (January 28, 1928), PAHRC SB-13:278.

63. "Says Church Fills Need of Italians," *Catholic Standard and Times* (January 14, 1928), PAHRC SB-13:270.

64. Isoleri Papers, "Per la benedizione delle lampade elettriche nella Chiesa di S.MMdePazzi" (January 9, 1922). Isoleri gave the date as January 9, 1920, on this document, but correspondence and other notes indicate a private dedication on January 1 before the public event on January 9, 1922.

65. Isoleri Papers, "Sul matrimonio" (January 15, 1922); "Per la morte di S.S. Benedetto XV" (January 22, 1922).

66. Isoleri Papers, "Benedizione della Bandiere" (November 4, 1923).

67. Ibid.

68. Ibid.

69. "Clerical Appointments and Transfers," *Catholic Standard and Times* (June 5, 1926), 5; "Italian Parish Pastor Announces Schedule," *Catholic Standard and Times* (June 26, 1926), 5; "Young Italians Join Societies of Parish," *Catholic Standard and Times* (July 3, 1926), 5; "Rev. Anthony Garritano 22 Years in Priesthood," *Catholic Standard and Times* (July 24, 1926), 1; "Clerical Appointments and Transfers," *Catholic Standard and Times* (August 7, 1926), 5; "Clerical Appointments and Transfers," *Catholic Standard and Times* (September 18, 1926), 5; "Clerical Appointments and Transfers," *Catholic Standard and Times* (October 2, 1926), 5; "Mission in English to be Given in Italian Church," *Catholic Standard and Times* (October 16, 1926), 5.

70. "Diamond Jubilee Observed by Oldest Italian Parish," *Catholic Standard and Times* (October 22, 1927), PAHRC SB-19:13.

71. Ibid.

72. "Italian Parish Opens New Modern School," *Catholic Standard and Times* (December 3, 1927), PAHRC SB-13:263; "Italian School in South Phila. to be Blessed," *Catholic Standard and Times* (October 27, 1928), PAHRC SB-14:72; "Italian School is Solemnly Blessed by His Eminence," *Catholic Standard and Times* (November 3, 1928), PAHRC SB-14:81–82.

73. "Italian School in South Phila. to be Blessed," *Catholic Standard and Times* (October 27, 1928), PAHRC SB-14:72; "Italian School is Solemnly Blessed by His Eminence," *Catholic Standard and Times* (November 3, 1928), PAHRC SB-14:81–82.

74. "Cardinal to Open Newly Renovated Italian Church," *Catholic Standard and Times* (March 24, 1928), PAHRC SB-13:295.

75. "Newly Renovated Church Formally Opened by Cardinal," *Catholic Standard and Times* (March 31, 1928), PAHRC SB-13:300; "Cardinal's Address at Reopening of Old St. Mary's (Italian) Church," *Catholic Standard and Times* (March 31, 1928), PAHRC SB-13:298.

76. "Cardinal's Address at Reopening of Old St. Mary's (Italian) Church," *Catholic Standard and Times* (March 31, 1928), PAHRC SB-13:298.

77. "Cardinal to Open Newly Renovated Italian Church," *Catholic Standard and Times* (March 24, 1928), PAHRC SB-13:295.

78. "Cardinal is Decorated by King of Italy," *Catholic Standard and Times* (April 28, 1927), PAHRC SB-13:192; "Agreement Found on Roman Question, N.C.W.C. States," *Catholic Standard and Times* (February 9, 1929), PAHRC SB-26:63; "Treaty and Concordat of Holy See and Italian Government is Signed by Cardinal Gasparri and Mussolini," *Catholic Standard and Times* (February 16, 1929), PAHRC SB-26:63; "Signing of Treaty Marked by Italians Living in this City," *Catholic Standard and Times* (March 4, 1929), PAHRC SB-26:64, also under the previous title in SB-19:143; "Sermon delivered by Rev. Dr. Gerald P. O'Hara at St. Mary Magdalen's Church, Phila.," *L'Opinione* (March 4, 1929), PAHRC SB-19:143; "La Solenne funzione di Ringrazione nella Chiesa Italiana di S. Maria Maddalena de Pazzi," *L'Opinione* (March 4, 1929), PAHRC SB-26:64; "St. Donato's Parish Marks Ratification of Treaty Sunday," *Catholic Standard and Times* (June 1, 1929), PAHRC SB-14:160. For a general study of these events and issues, see Rhodes, *The Vatican in the Age of the Dictators*.

79. "Methodist Church is Purchased by Italians," *Catholic Standard and Times* (May 12, 1928), PAHRC SB-14:8; "Edifice Occupied by Italian Parish," *Catholic Standard and Times* (May 19, 1928), PAHRC SB-14:12; "Rev. A. Garritano to Observe Silver Jubilee on Sunday," *Catholic Standard and Times* (October 5, 1929), PAHRC SB-14:206; "Hundreds Receive Holy Communion at Jubilee Mass," *Catholic Standard and Times* (October 12, 1929), PAHRC SB-14:207.

80. "Dual Celebration to be Held Sunday in Italian Parish," *Catholic Standard and Times* (November 2, 1929), PAHRC SB-14:211; "Uptown Italians Assist at Laying of School Stones," *Catholic Standard and Times* (November 9, 1929), PAHRC SB-14:212.

81. Anthony Garritano, Priests' File, PAHRC.

82. "Monsignor Isoleri Dies of Influenza," *Public Ledger* (April 12, 1932), 9; "Weather," *Public Ledger* (April 12, 1932), 2; "Msgr. A. G. Isoleri Dies in 87th Year at Parish Rectory," *Catholic Standard and Times* (April 15, 1932), PAHRC SB-15:284.

83. "Monsignor Isoleri Dies of Influenza," *Public Ledger* (April 12, 1932), 9.

84. Ibid,

85. "Notables Attend Rites for Monsignor Isoleri," *Public Ledger* (April 17, 1932), 12.

86. "Monsignor Isoleri Interred in Crypt of Church He Built," *Catholic Standard and Times* (April 22, 1932), PAHRC SB-14:287.

87. "Priest Bequeaths $34,000 to Charity," *Public Ledger* (April 22, 1932), 2. For an assessment of Isoleri's life, see "Ambassador of Christ," *Catholic Standard and Times* (April 15, 1932), 6.

CHAPTER FOURTEEN.   *The Dismemberment of Our Lady of Good Counsel*

1. Many works describe the "Italian problem." For basic and related issues, see Shaughnessy, *Has the Immigrant Kept the Faith?*; Canevin, *An Examination Historical and Statistical into Losses and Gains*; Emmet Larkin, "The Devotional Revolution in Ireland, 1850–75," *American Historical Review* 77:3 (June 1972): 625–52; Browne, "The 'Italian Problem'"; Vecoli, "Prelates and Peasants"; and Linkh, *American Catholicism and European Immigrants*. For the spiritual status of nineteenth-century immigrants, see Roger Finke and Rodney Stark, *The Churching of America, 1776–1990: Winners and Losers in Our Religious Economy* (New Brunswick, NJ: Rutgers University Press, 1992).

2. *Consultors' Minutes* (June 1, 1931, September 8, 1931), PAHRC; Hugh Lamb to Gerald O'Hara (n.d.), Italian Parish Study File, PAHRC.

3. John P. Thompson to Hugh Lamb (May 4, 1933), Anthony Garritano to Hugh Lamb (February 20, 1933), Francis Aiden Brady to Gerald O'Hara (February 7, 1932), Italian Parish Study File, PAHRC.

4. *Consultors' Minutes* (October 3, 1932), PAHRC.

5. Italian Parish Study File, PAHRC.

6. Ibid.

7. Ibid.

8. Lorenzo Andolfi to Hugh Lamb (August 3, 1931), Joseph A. Hickey to Hugh Lamb (n.d.), Italian Parish Study File, PAHRC.

9. Annunciation Rectory, Proposed Italian Boundaries of Annunciation Parish (n.d.), Italian Parish Study File, PAHRC.

10. Augustinian General Archives (Rome), Aa., Vice Province, Philadelphia (hereafter AGA), 1911–1912. For the contribution by the Augustinian order to making up the financial deficits at Our Lady of Good Counsel and other parishes, see the *Questiones,* the annual reports by pastors at this time.

11. AGA, 1911–1912.

12. AGA, 1917–1918. In particular, see the parish census of 1917; Prendergast's letter to the Holy See (November 6, 1917); Terlizzi's detailed report (February 27, 1918); and the agreement between Archbishop Ryan and Father Thomas Rodriguez Genlis, O.S.A. (February 16, 1899).

13. AGA, 1926.

14. Ibid.

15. AGA, n.d.

16. Dougherty Papers, PAHRC, 80.89.

17. Ibid.

18. Dougherty Papers, PAHRC, 80.7745.

19. "Parishioners Refuse to Let Priest Leave His Old Church," *Record* (May 4, 1933); "Funeral Halted in Protest over Church Merger," *Evening Bulletin* (May 4, 1933); "Crowd Attacks Police Detail in Church Dispute," *Evening Bulletin* (May 4, 1933). These events were extensively reported in front-page articles by local newspapers with additional coverage throughout later editions of each day.

20. "Parishioners Refuse to Let Priest Leave His Old Church," *Record* (May 4, 1933).

21. "Funeral Halted in Protest over Church Merger," *Evening Bulletin* (May 4, 1933); "Crowd Attacks Police Detail in Church Dispute," *Evening Bulletin* (May 4, 1933).

22. "Crowd Attacks Police Detail in Church Dispute," *Evening Bulletin* (May 4, 1933).

23. Ibid.

24. Ibid.

25. "Parishioners Refuse to Let Priest Leave His Old Church," *Record* (May 4, 1933).

26. "Church Opening Urged," *Public Ledger* (July 8, 1933).

27. "Parish Releases Captive Priest," *Evening Bulletin* (October 26, 1933); "Priest Given Freedom," *Inquirer* (October 26, 1933).

28. Dennis J. Dougherty to John M. DiSilvestro (June 10, 1931), PAHRC; see also the Associated Press item facetiously referring to "the progress of Christianity in Philadelphia" in the *American Mercury* (August 1933).

29. "To the People of South Philadelphia," Italian Parish Study File, 1998/37, PAHRC.

30. "To the People of South Philadelphia," Italian Parish Study File, 1998/38, PAHRC.

31. "To the People of South Philadelphia," Italian Parish Study File, 1998/39, PAHRC; AGA, n.d.

32. "The Faithful of Good Counsel should have been consulted, states an Augustinian Father," *L'Opinione* (October 28, 1933).

33. Ibid.

34. Richard A. Varbero, "Philadelphia's South Italians in the 1920s," 255–75, in Allen F. Davis and Mark H. Haller, eds., *The Peoples of Philadelphia: A History of Ethnic Groups and Lower Class Life, 1790–1940* (Philadelphia: Temple University Press, 1973). Varbero's brief but useful account places this long-ignored episode in the broader context of local and ethnic history.

35. *In the Supreme Court of Pennsylvania, Eastern District, No. 289, January Term, 1936, Placido Canovaro et al., Appellants, vs. Brothers of the Order of Hermits of St. Augustine* (Filed March 22, 1937).

36. Peter R. D'Agostino, "Italian Ethnicity and Religious Priests in the American Church: The Servites, 1870–1849," *Catholic Historical Review* 80:4 (October 1994): 714–40.

EPILOGUE. *Parish, Priest, and People*

1. Jay P. Dolan, *The American Catholic Experience: A History from Colonial Times to the Present* (Garden City, NY: Doubleday, 1985); Carey, *The Roman Catholics.*

2. Gavigan, "The Rise and Fall of Parish Cohesiveness in Philadelphia."

3. See Dolan, "A Critical Period in American Catholicism"; Gerald P. Fogarty, S.J., "The Parish and Community in American Catholic History," *U.S. Catholic Historian* 4:3 (Fall 1985): 233–57; Dolan, *The Immigrant Church*; Jay P. Dolan, ed., *The American Catholic Parish: A History from 1850 to the Present*, vols. 1 and 2 (New York: Paulist Press, 1987).

4. Foerster, *The Italian Emigration of Our Times*, 330.

5. "Protestors reach out to Rome," *Boston Globe* (December 11, 2004).

6. Orsi, *The Madonna of 115th Street*. The quotations are found on pages 51 and 224.

7. Peter Brown, *The Cult of Saints* (Chicago: University of Chicago Press, 1981), 21–22.

8. Memorandum, Re: King of Peace Parish (n.d.), Italian Parish Study File, PAHRC.

9. Interview with author (August 1982); interview with author (November 1998).

10. Brown, *The Cult of Saints*, 21–22.

11. For the "devotional revolution" in American Catholicism, see Ann Taves, *The Household of Faith: Catholic Devotions in Mid-Nineteenth Century America* (Notre Dame, IN: University of Notre Dame Press, 1986); and Jay P. Dolan, *Catholic Revivalism: The American Experience, 1830–1900* (Notre Dame, IN: University of Notre Dame Press, 1978).

12. Orsi, *The Madonna of 115th Street*, xvii.

13. See Dolan, *The Immigrant Church.*

14. See Tolino, "Solving the Italian Problem"; idem, "The Church in America and the Italian Problem"; idem, "The Future of the Italian Problem."

15. U.S. Census Bureau, *American Fact Finder, QT-P13, Ancestry 2000. Data Set: Census 2000 Summary File 3 (SF3).*

INDEX

Abbreviations

OLGC   Our Lady of Good Counsel
StMMdeP   St. Mary Magdalen dePazzi

Note: Places in Italy are given with the province to which they presently belong in parentheses; where place names have two forms, both versions are given.

RICHARD N. JULIANI

is professor of sociology at Villanova University.
He is the author of *Building Little Italy:
Philadelphia's Italians before Mass Migration.*